The Science and Art of Renaissance Music

JAMES HAAR

The Science and Art of Renaissance Music

· EDITED BY PAUL CORNEILSON ·

PRINCETON UNIVERSITY PRESS

PRINCETON, NEW JERSEY

Library of Congress Cataloging-in-Publication Data

Haar, James.
The science and art of Renaissance music / James Haar ; edited by Paul Corneilson.
p.   cm.
Collection of previously published essays.
Includes bibliographical references and index.
ISBN 0-691-02874-5 (cloth : alk. paper)
1. Music—16th century—History and criticism.   2. Music—16th century—Theory.
I. Corneilson, Paul E. (Paul Edward)   II. Title.
ML172.H3   1997
780'.9'031—dc21   97-13032
CIP
MN

· FOR ALL MY STUDENTS ·

· CONTENTS ·

SOME YEARS AGO I received a letter from a graduate student who had been "assigned" me in a bibliography class. She enclosed a list of my publications, wrote in a disappointed tone that this was all she could find, and ended by asking me if I could add any titles to the list. At the time I was embarrassed to reply that there was nothing more. Now I am perhaps equally embarrassed to say that there is quite a lot more, enough so that I had to make a choice as to what should be included in this volume. The basic selection was made by my friend and former student, Paul Corneilson, the guiding spirit behind this enterprise. Criteria for exclusion were relatively easy to come by: articles on the origins and character of the early cinquecento madrigal and on traces in the written literature of the activities of *improvvisatori* would be omitted since they had already led to publication in book form, in one case with an energetic and gifted collaborator, Iain Fenlon. Articles reprinted, alone or in anthologies (in English and Italian) were excluded; guests who reappear too often may wear out their welcome.[1]

What to include was a little harder to decide upon. Since the volume should have some coherence, articles on subjects belonging more or less to identifiable themes could be included. After a bit of juggling on the part of both Paul and myself, an appropriate total of subjects and articles was reached. The five categories under which the articles are grouped are among the subjects that have preoccupied me for some years. They are interrelated in a number of ways; my interest in theory, in the madrigal, and in individual figures such as Antonfrancesco Doni and Giovanthomaso Cimello are part of a general concern for music in the cultural life of the Renaissance. A long interest in the multifarious but strangely unified character of Romantic musical thought led me to the last of the topics, Romantic views of early music; this is a subject on which I still hope to write at some length.

A collection of essays originally published over a period of some years, favorably viewed, offers convenience of access and provides the reader opportunity to engage an author in extended mental conversation. Less optimistically looked at, such a collection may resemble an album of fading photographs, what my grandmother used to dismiss as "those old chromos" (i.e., chromolithographs; she was actually referring, in a kind of metonymy, to old people trying to mask the disappearance of youthful charms). I hope of course for a favorable reception to these essays. It is not my intention to apologize for the contents of the book; I have added a few notes at the ends of the articles to correct errors, suggest further reading, or modify details of the argument, but on the whole I stand by what I have written and have not changed the content or style of anything here.

I trust that what the articles say about their subjects is clear enough. I have always tried for clarity of expression and can only hope that the result will not be mistaken for jejuneness of thought. What they say about their author is up to the reader to conclude. A certain preciosity of style in the earlier articles, which caused me to wince a bit as I encountered it, is I hope pruned out of later work; I think there are no other autobiographical hints. Self-revelation has never been my aim, and deliberate suppression of personality has never seemed to me anything but false modesty.

People writing about the past shape it to accord with their own proclivities as well as with the interests and preferences of their own generation. But that we write essentially about ourselves under the guise of writing history I find not so much untrue as uninteresting. Of course we find ourselves interesting; that others should find us so is not a matter of course. In the same way that I find much reductional musical analysis boring, I am wearied by obtrusive self-revelation, by excessive personalizing of the scholarly act. There are not many St. Augustines, past or present, around, and for me even a little Augustine goes a long way.

Cultural history has been a lifelong interest of mine. I smile a bit wanly as I recall that in my graduate-student days I championed it against fellow students "only interested in the notes." The rush toward "contextualizing" music of recent years has nonetheless seemed to me a bit headlong; sometimes brilliant, sometimes flamboyant, occasionally wildly off the mark, it has all too often betrayed a kind of cultural envy of the fabled richness and breadth of thought and method available in other disciplines, but considered lamentably lacking in our own. I remain committed to thinking about music as cultural expression. However, I am more than ever convinced that the act of creating music is one of sublimation of extramusical life and one profoundly *sui generis*. What has been created can, and perhaps should, be continually interpreted and reinterpreted, but it is the musical work itself that interests and moves me. This is only the surface, some would say, but I am an unrepentant admirer of surfaces, steadily suspicious of too drastic a probing for concealed and inadvertent meaning. If the cultural context gets too thick it becomes difficult to find the work at all.

In my student years I held myself a bit aloof from my fellow students. I learned something from their company but I could and should have profited a good deal more from it. Independence of thought and approach was my goal. Fortunately I did pay a lot of attention to my teachers, among whom two made an especially lasting impact: John Ward for his impeccable control and thoroughness, always to be admired if never equalled; and Nino Pirrotta for an inimitable fineness of perception and an unfailing humaneness which gives life and warmth to everything he writes. So I had some good models. Gradually I realized that independence, while never complete, is learned, not proclaimed, and I developed an approach of my own. Roughly described, this consists of finding a subject, often a rather small one, that has something about it that I think intriguingly in need of explanation; doing the best I can by way of explaining it; showing the ramifications into wider areas that I think it has; and suggesting that investigations of the kind I have just made might be useful for others to do. A fairly simple formula but it has worked for me. I do not think I am a miniaturist, but I would rather try to get much from little than gamble with the reverse.

Through the course of my academic career I have learned much from colleagues and students—at Harvard, the University of Pennsylvania, New York University, the University of North Carolina, and in brief stints at the University of Washington, Seattle, Berkeley, and Princeton—as well as from scholars elsewhere who have been active in the fields in which I work. I am grateful to many people and proud to stand in their company as a member of a profession for which I continue to have the greatest respect and affection.

Chapel Hill, North Carolina
January 1996

NOTE

1. A list (complete to 1994) of my published writings, compiled by Stephanie Schlagel, may be found in *The Journal of Musicology* 12 (1994): 398–404.

JAMES HAAR is a true Renaissance man, one of the few scholars who probes the depths as well as the entire breadth of Renaissance music, literature, and culture. Perhaps more than any other, he is a successor to the European tradition of Gustave Reese and Alfred Einstein. His essays are models of detailed but concise writing, often exploring the nooks and crannies of the period, forgotten figures, and lesser known treatises that illuminate more fully the celebrated music of the great composers—such as Josquin and Lasso—who dominate music history textbooks. Jim reminds us that we should leave no stone unturned in practicing musicology; and in article after article, he demonstates that a seemingly insignificant fact or tidbit has implications not only for the way Renaissance musicians and writers thought about the art and craft of music, but also for how we think about Renaissance music today and what significance that has for humanistic study and understanding.

My role has been to deal with cosmetic differences in style, especially bibliographical, between the various articles reprinted here. Typographical errors have been tacitly emended and differences in spelling have been standardized. All of the musical examples have been redone handsomely by Mr. Ward Hammond. Only one of the chapters required substantive alteration: the original version of "Josquin as Interpreted by a Mid-Sixteenth-Century German Musician" suffered some mutilation during the period between the reading of proofs and publication. Half (nos. 1–8) of the contents of Regensburg, Proske-Bibl. Ms C 100 were omitted, and five lines of text and one sizeable footnote were printed twice. As we all know, publishing is not a perfect craft, but in reprinting these essays it is hoped that we have come a little closer to the author's ideal.

Grateful acknowledgment is made to those who have extended permission to reproduce previously published material:

Chapter 1 ("A Sixteenth-Century Attempt at Music Criticism"), originally published in *The Journal of the American Musicological Society* 36 (1983): 191–209.

Chapter 2 ("The Courtier as Musician: Castiglione's View of the Science and Art of Music"), first published in *Castiglione: The Ideal and the Real in Renaissance Culture,* eds. Robert W. Hanning and David Rosand (New Haven: Yale University Press, 1983), 165–89.

Chapter 3 ("Cosimo Bartoli on Music"), originally published in *Early Music History: Studies in Medieval and Early Modern Music* 8 (1988): 37–79.

Chapter 4 ("The Frontispiece of Gafori's *Practica Musicae* (1496)"), originally published in *Renaissance Quarterly* 27 (1974): 7–22.

Chapter 5 ("False Relations and Chromaticism in Sixteenth-Century Music"), originally published in *The Journal of the American Musicological Society* 30 (1977): 391–418.

Chapter 6 ("Zarlino's Definition of Fugue and Imitation"), originally published in *The Journal of the American Musicological Society* 24 (1971): 226–54.

Chapter 7 ("Lessons in Theory from a Sixteenth-Century Composer"), first published in *Altro Polo: Essays on Italian Music in the Cinquecento,* ed. Richard Charteris (Sydney, Australia: Frederick May Foundation for Italian Studies, 1990), 51–81.

Chapter 8 ("Josquin as Interpreted by a Mid-Sixteenth-Century German Musician"), first published in *Festschrift für Horst Leuchtmann zum 65. Geburtstag,* eds. Stephan Horner and Bernhold Schmid (Tutzing: Hans Schneider, 1993), 179–205.

Chapter 9 ("The *Note Nere* Madrigal"), originally published in *The Journal of the American Musicological Society* 18 (1965): 22–41.

Chapter 10 ("The 'Madrigale Arioso': A Mid-Century Development in the Cinquecento Madrigal"), originally published in *Studi Musicali* 12 (1983): 203–19.

Chapter 11 ("Giovanthomaso Cimello as Madrigalist"), originally published in *Studi Musicali* 22 (1993): 23–59.

Chapter 12 ("Notes on the *Dialogo dell Musica* of Antonfrancesco Doni"), originally published in *Music and Letters* 47 (1966): 198–224.

Chapter 13 ("A Gift of Madrigals to Cosimo I: The Ms Florence, Bibl. Naz. Centrale, Magl. XIX, 130"), originally published in *Rivista italiana di musicologia* 1 (1966): 168–89.

Chapter 14 ("The *Libraria* of Antonfrancesco Doni"), originally published in *Musica Disciplina* 24 (1970): 101–23.

Chapter 15 ("Berlioz and the 'First Opera' "), originally published in *19th Century Music* 3 (1979): 32–41.

Chapter 16 ("Music of the Renaissance as Viewed by the Romantics"), originally published in *Music and Context: Essays for John M. Ward,* ed. Anne Dhu Shapiro (Cambridge: Harvard University Press, 1985), 108–25.

Brown   Howard Mayer Brown. *Instrumental Music Printed before 1600: A Bibliography,* 2d ed. (Cambridge, Mass., 1967)

CMM   Corpus Mensurabilis Musicae

Einstein, *Italian Madrigal*   Alfred Einstein. *The Italian Madrigal,* 3 vols. (Princeton, 1949)

Eitner, *Quellen-Lexikon*   Robert Eitner. *Biographisch-bibliographisches Quellen-Lexikon der Musiker und Musikgelehrten der christlichen Zeitrechnung bis zur Mitte des 19. Jahrhunderts* (Leipzig, 1898–1904); 2d ed., 11 vols. (Graz, 1959–60)

EMH   *Early Music History: Studies in Medieval and Early Modern Music*

Fenlon & Haar   Iain Fenlon and James Haar. *The Italian Madrigal in the Early Sixteenth Century: Sources and Interpretation* (Cambridge, 1988)

JAMS   *The Journal of the American Musicological Society*

MD   *Musica Disciplina* [formerly *Journal of Renaissance and Baroque Music*]

MGG   *Die Musik in Geschichte und Gegenwart,* 17 vols. Ed. Friedrich Blume (Kassel and Basel, 1949–68; suppl. 1973–79)

ML   *Music and Letters*

MQ   *The Musical Quarterly*

MRM   Monuments of Renaissance Music

New Grove   *The New Grove Dictionary of Music and Musicians,* 20 vols. Ed. Stanley Sadie (London, 1980)

RIM   *Rivista italiana di musicologia*

RISM   Repértoire International des Sources Musicales

RRMBE   Recent Researches in the Music of the Baroque Era

RRMR   Recent Researches in the Music of the Renaissance

SM   *Studi musicali*

Vogel   Emil Vogel. *Bibliothek der gedruckten weltlichen Vocalmusik Italiens, aus den Jahren 1500 bis 1700* (Berlin, 1892); rev., with additions by Alfred Einstein (Hildesheim, 1962)

MUSIC IN
SIXTEENTH-CENTURY
SOCIETY

A Sixteenth-Century Attempt at Music Criticism

A COMPLAINT SOMETIMES MADE about theorists, at least about those active before the middle of the nineteenth century, is that their concerns are too exclusively
prescriptive, that they rarely describe music, much less evaluate it. As musicians
we can enjoy what we take to be timeless aspects of the music of the past, and we
feel to a certain extent confident in our ability to distinguish level of quality and degree of attractiveness in it—in short to make it live as part of our own musical culture. As scholars we can learn a good deal about the musical life of a period such as
the Renaissance. As analysts we can take almost any music apart and reassemble it,
using theoretical writings of the appropriate period as manuals wherever they are
helpful. But as historians concerned not only with cultural artifacts but also with
the intellectual and artistic outlook of the past we want to know not just how music
was made but why it took the shapes it did, and especially how it was heard and criticized by those who first performed and listened to it. Not how everyone heard it, of
course; if we look at the general reception of art music in our own time we can see
that random sampling of opinion would not get us far, and there is no reason to sen-
timentalize about a past when everyone understood and loved contemporary culture. We do want to know what those critics have to say who are equipped by training and temperament to give sympathetic judgment on modern music; and it is a
group of this sort, comparatively large in some periods and very small in others,
that we would like to have speak to us from the past.

Very few of them do so. For the Renaissance we have, besides a large number of
theorists, various descriptions of music and musicians, seen and heard on state occasions and even in social gatherings. But, as we know, we hear the praise of musicians—usually in vague terms—much more than that of the music itself, and we
usually count ourselves lucky to find a piece so much as mentioned by name. In the
whole of Antonfrancesco Doni's *Dialogo della musica,* in which the music sung by
the assembled company is printed along with their conversation, we get little more
than a passing remark that the piece just sung was beautiful or was the work of a de-
pendably good composer.[1] A more informative source is Vincenzo Giustiniani's
Discorso sopra la musica, with its references to the compositional novelties of
Marenzio and Giovannelli in Rome, of Gesualdo and Fontanelli in Ferrara, of a
group of Neapolitans, and finally of Monteverdi.[2] But Giustiniani was clearly more
interested in singers and instrumentalists, about whom he speaks in some detail,
than in the music itself; and indeed his remarks, such as that on the contrapuntal
rigor of Gesualdo's music, would indicate that he was not much of a connoisseur of
compositional technique.[3]

If we turn to the theorists, we find that from Tinctoris through Zarlino and his
disciples we get fairly frequent mention of composers and even of individual

works, but pieces are usually named because of a single feature such as choice of mode or canonic artifice, and composers are cited only to receive general praise for their skill or, on occasion, blame for what the theorist defines as a *Satzfehler.* Coclico praises Josquin but does not go into detail about his music; Glareanus is concerned largely with mode; Zarlino finds that everything the complete musician should possess in the way of art is contained in the work of Willaert, but he does not really show us how to study that work. We know that theorists were aware of stylistic change, which they praised or damned by turns, and sometimes they give us specific information about it; an example is Finck's contrasting of the dense counterpoint of Gombert to the more open polyphony of Josquin.[4] Instances of this kind of direct dealing with music itself are unfortunately all too rare.

It is clear that music was a favorite topic of conversation in sixteenth-century Europe. And when people spoke of the subject it could not always have been in such superficial terms as those of Doni. On the other hand dialogues such as Bottrigari's *Desiderio,* concerned largely with the tuning of instruments,[5] or Zarlino's *Dimostrationi harmoniche,* in which the assembled interlocutors, including Willaert and Francesco Viola, listen to long, abstruse, and lamentably dull arguments in support of Zarlino's *senario,* could not be thought to resemble the real conversation of real people. Such conversations, it would seem, were never recorded.

There are a few exceptions, and I want to concentrate here on one passage that I find of special interest. It occurs, apropos of nothing in particular, in the second part of Lodovico Zacconi's *Prattica di musica,* a volume written and published in the theorist's last years but reflecting the concerns, tastes, and views expressed thirty years earlier in the first part of his treatise:

> It is both clear and certain that the gifts of the Lord, however manifold (not to say infinite), are divided and distributed by His Divine Majesty in such a way that very often one who possesses one gift does not have another. And work at it as he may, if [the Lord] has not granted it to him by way of nature, or through special grace, he fails in it and ends, as the saying has it, by pounding water in his mortar. We see examples of this in every faculty, every profession, and in music we see and touch upon it as well.
>
> And since I wish to treat of the various styles, modes, and manners of different compositions I say that *musica armoniale* is distinguished by seven particular aspects: that is, by *arte, modulatione, diletto, tessitura, contraponto, inventione,* and *buona dispositione.* Each of these things is necessary to the composer; and to however small or great degree one finds them in one composer, a single quality will stand out more than another, and from this a composer will make his name and become famous. In this regard, and without offense to anyone, I remember that in the year 1584 there was a conversation on music one day held in the presence of many musicians gathered before Don Gioseffo Zarlino; and as the talk turned to the style of this and that composer, he made the above distinctions and then came down to particulars, saying, "What would you have me say? He who has one of these lacks another, and even he who is distinguished in two or three cannot have them all. My own genius (he said, speaking of himself) is given over to regular *tessitura* and *arte,* as is that of Costanzo Porta, who is here present. Striggio had a talent and gift for charming *modulatione;* Messer Adriano

was distinguished by great *arte* and judicious *dispositione*. Morales had *arte, contra-ponto,* and *buona modulatione*. Orlando Lasso possessed *modulatione, arte,* and *bonissima inventione;* and Palestrina had *arte, contraponto, ottima dispositione,* and a flowing *modulatione*. From this it follows that once one has heard the works of these composers, when their music is sung on another occasion one can immediately say, 'This is the work of such-and-such'; and indeed so it turns out to be, for when one has heard the works of one author several times, one can distinguish them at once when hearing them with other works and say that it is the work of such-and-such an author."[6]

This passage, along with a number of, but by no means all, the other anecdotes that are sprinkled through Zacconi's work, and especially the *seconda parte*—making a reading of it full of pleasant surprise and relief—was cited by Friedrich Chrysander some ninety years ago. Chrysander called Zarlino's little speech as reported by Zacconi extremely valuable, and praised it as a "sure guide to the aesthetic currents of his century"; but he did not attempt to explicate it.[7] Zacconi's anecdote has been familiar to students of Renaissance music ever since, but I am not aware of any effort to define his seven categories, which appear on the surface to be vague and overlapping to the point of repetitiveness. Although I cannot claim that I know precisely what Zacconi meant or even that he intended each category to have precise and separate meaning, I think the passage deserves a closer look and will presently proceed with an attempt at clarifying it.

    Zacconi's second treatise is chiefly concerned with rules, copiously illustrated, for counterpoint on a cantus firmus "in cartella & alla mente" ("written [on barred staves] or improvised"), as its title page says. His pace is leisurely and there are many asides, including references to musicians he had known in Mantua, Venice, Munich, and the Habsburg court at Graz. There are familiar admonitions to students about proper attitudes, proper study habits, proper modes of performance. It is tempting to follow Chrysander's lead by giving examples of all this, and I shall in the spirit of Zacconi's work succumb briefly to this temptation before getting to the passage that is our central concern.

    There are many references to older music in both of Zacconi's treatises—more, for instance, than one finds in the writings of Zarlino. Zacconi admired the craft of both the *antichi,* by which term he meant Josquin and his contemporaries, and the *vecchi,* who included not only Willaert and Rore but also Zarlino and Palestrina.[8] He cites older compositions by name, and even says he leafed through a copy of the *Odhecaton* with pleasure and profit.[9] Although he was too young to have known Willaert, Zacconi got information about him from Zarlino, including an account of Willaert improvising a third voice to a written duo, then doing it again in order to improve it.[10] This is of more than anecdotal interest since it gives evidence that performing *contraponto alla mente* was a real feature of musical life, even that of great composers, in the sixteenth century.[11]

    Palestrina was probably known to Zacconi only by reputation; he was admired for the appropriate style of his sacred music, in Zacconi's view as fitting as the style of Marenzio and Monte was for the madrigal.[12] Zacconi also says of Palestrina that his music and that of Victoria can be studied in error-free copies since they, unlike many of their contemporaries, carefully supervised the publication of their work.[13] One word of criticism is ventured; had Palestrina sought his advice Zacconi would have cautioned him about setting the *Cantica* as he did, for "Dio sà con qual animo & intentione" these works are performed by singers.[14]

A number of composers, including Rore, Ippolito Baccusi, Francesco Rovigo, Monte, Porta, Striggio, and one among the moderns, Monteverdi, are mentioned admiringly but only in passing.[15] Zacconi says that he was a student of Andrea Gabrieli, but unfortunately he has nothing to say about his master's personality or teaching method.[16] Lasso was, to judge from the tone of Zacconi's remarks about him, not only his senior colleague at Munich (in the years 1591–94) but also a friend. One reference to Lasso deserves mention here although it is well known. This passage, in which the aging Lasso speaks humbly of his daily compositional exercise, of his holding himself in readiness in case a new commission from his master should come, is instructive about a composer's attitude toward his craft; and it is touching when one remembers that it must originate from Lasso's final period of activity, the time when the magnificent *Lagrime di San Pietro* was written.[17]

Among the many bits of advice to young musicians given by Zacconi several are worth mentioning here. A person wishing to succeed in music, or indeed any worthwhile pursuit, must have certain qualities, namely, *voglia, studio, perseveranza, deliberatione,* and *emulatione* (desire, study, perseverance, resolve, and a sense of rivalry).[18] For composers a healthy spirit of *emulatione* is particularly important, and we are told that Costanzo Porta set out to rival his great master Willaert; that Baccusi during his years at Mantua did all he could to perfect himself in emulation of his colleague Wert; and that Tiburtio Massaino, having met Baccusi in Venice, modeled his compositional activities on the latter's work.[19]

Musicians need to study music if they wish to excel in its practice; in his first book Zacconi warns that a person could study Boethius and Augustine for ten years and "never learn to compose."[20] What aspiring musicians should do, first of all, is acquire and study thoroughly all the good music they can get hold of; next they should score it, a tiresome but necessary task if the secrets of the music are to be thoroughly revealed.[21] In doing this students not only learn a lot, but they also acquire a stock of passages useful in their own work, just as "gioveni innamorati" copy poems into notebooks for ready use in their own impromptu verse-making. No less a composer than Francesco Rovigo solemnly assured Zacconi that he copied and scored passages of other composers' work so as to have a ready stock of ideas and techniques.[22] The young composer should arrange his commonplace book so that under each scored passage there are empty staves; thus he can add thoughts of his own, or can vary those of the compositions before him by exchanging entries, lengthening or shortening rests, adding another point of imitation.[23] In this passage the technique of parody composition, so dear to sixteenth-century musicians but so little referred to by theorists, is described in a thoroughly believable way.

Zacconi, whose instructions on the art of vocal improvisation in the *Primo libro* are well known,[24] has many hints for singers in his second book. Among them are instructions to set the pitch of any piece at a comfortable level for all voices; to change the pitch level when a piece in another mode than the one just sung is chosen; to choose a tempo neither too slow nor too fast, being especially careful about the latter since performers tend to fall behind the beat if it is too fast (elsewhere Zacconi says, however, that one can place the beat slightly late in an artistic manner to give special emphasis); to accommodate one's voice to those of the other singers; and to ornament only where appropriate.[25]

The composers whom Zacconi admired presumably did all the things he thought necessary to achieve proficiency; their inborn talent, nurtured by careful study and practice and sharpened by emulation of their peers, gave them excellence. Yet their music is not identical in nature, perhaps not even equal in value. If we examine the passage with which we are centrally concerned we see first the sententious observation that nature's gifts are not evenly distributed, and that some musicians when compared with others show greater talent in one aspect of composition, less in another. There are in *musica armoniale,* Zacconi's general term for polyphonic mensural music, seven aspects in which excellence can be sought: *arte, modulatione, diletto, tessitura, contraponto, inventione,* and *buona dispositione.* Zacconi apparently thought that the meaning of these terms was self-evident and that they were distinct one from another; otherwise he would have been breaking his own rule, stated only a few pages before the passage here under consideration, that one should never propose terms to students without defining them thoroughly.[26] To a modern reader the meaning and, especially, the distinctive nature of each of the seven qualities are not so clear. Close reading of both of Zacconi's treatises brings partial enlightenment, as we shall see; but the theorist could have helped us more than he did here.

Except for *contraponto,* the words Zacconi chose are not exclusively musical terms, so he may have thought definition unnecessary; this was the kind of language any educated person could use, perhaps about any of the arts. Still, Zacconi employs all these words, if not always in their substantive form, throughout his treatise, and they acquire a musical meaning—in a few instances several allied ones—through use. What is their origin?

The little speech is put into the mouth of Zarlino, and it is clear from the whole of Zacconi's work that he was an admirer of Zarlino. But the language of this passage is not taken from Zarlino, or at least not from any of his published treatises. Of course words such as *arte* and *inventione,* not to mention *contraponto,* were used by Zarlino as by everybody else; *modulatione* was also a word in general currency, as was *diletto.* Zarlino did not use, so far as I know, either *tessitura* or *buona dispositione;* nor did he apply any of these terms as measurements for the quality of music. I have not yet seen these seven terms used by another theorist in any way close to that of the passage under consideration.

This is not to say that Zacconi was entirely original. *Inventione* and *dispositione* are rhetorical terms in common use in the sixteenth century and with the authority of Quintilian behind them. The *Institutio oratoria* of Quintilian was well known and easily available in print throughout the century; Zacconi must have had at least a superficial acquaintance with it.[27] One passage that may have caught his attention is Quintilian's exposition of the standard classical division of oratory: "The art of oratory, as taught by most authorities and those the best, consists of five parts: invention, arrangement, expression, memory, and delivery or action."[28] The five aspects of the orator's art are indeed so suggestive of Zacconi's classification that we may assume Quintilian as at least an indirect source of inspiration. As we shall see, the terms *arte, diletto,* and *modulatione* are also to be found in Quintilian's work. On the other hand, Zacconi, while he gives passing attention to text declamation in other places in his treatise,[29] is not here concerned with it at all (except possibly as a part of *modulatione*). Although he occasionally compares poets and musicians, he goes out of his way to stress the separateness of the two arts, at least in modern times.[30] If he knew the work of Burmeister he does not mention it or appear in any way to have been influenced by it. Zacconi was not, in other words, writing on music as a branch of rhetoric. Nonetheless the debt to Quintilian would appear to be great.

At this point we might examine Zacconi's terms one by one, taking them in the order he gives them.

(1) *Arte* would appear to be so general a word as to make useless any attempt at definition; and since six of the seven composers mentioned by Zacconi are said to possess it we get little help from him here. For Zarlino, following Quintilian and, doubtless, many other classical sources, art is the skillful manipulation of the materials of music.[31] Art is dependent upon nature but can surpass it, and can even correct its flaws: as painters correct flaws in the human form, so musicians can correct the natural sound of the voice through use of instruments designed with artifice.[32] Zarlino in distinguishing art from nature says that art is the "true reasoning behind the task one sets upon, and is as well the necessary skill in working at the task."[33] Elsewhere he defines the art of counterpoint as "a faculty which teaches us to invent [*ritrovare*] various parts of a piece of music and to order [*disporre*] its sounds by means of rational proportion and measured tempo into melodies [*modulationi*]."[34] Here we have not too few but too many terms for comfort.

Zacconi also contrasts nature and art; in one passage he describes the singing of the ancient Greeks as the "operation of nature, not of art," implying that the term *arte* is to be reserved for mensural polyphony.[35] For him, as for Zarlino, art includes both rational study of problems and skill in carrying out planned work.[36] He often combines *artificio* with *arte* as synonymous terms; thus *artificio* consists of the use of imitations, fugues, and canonic requirements (*obligationi*), sometimes used at close intervals, as in the motets of Gombert; at other times the use of contrary motion or other refinements.[37] Through command of art one can display *grand'arte* by using two fugues or imitations at once;[38] here we might note that among the composers singled out by Zacconi, only Willaert is said to possess *grand'arte*. In sum, Zacconi would appear to consider *arte* as the skill of planning and using schemes requiring contrapuntal artifice. Here he resembles all other theorists of his time and indeed of many others in admiring ingenuity of contrapuntal design; but while he praises older composers back to the time of Ockeghem and

Josquin for possession of *arte,* he thinks it still valuable in the music of his own time, lamenting its absence in the work of lesser, unnamed contemporaries.

(2) *Modulatione.* In the sixteenth century *modulatio* was one of the polite Latin words for a musical composition, particularly a motet.[39] This would appear to derive from its definition as melody in a broad sense, or melodic writing within which individual melodic phrases are contained. This broad meaning, applied to ancient music, is at one point given the term by Zarlino.[40] Elsewhere Zarlino simply equates *modulatione* with *aria* or even with the act of singing;[41] and Zacconi also uses the term to mean melody pure and simple.[42]

There was of course plenty of classical precedent for this. Vitruvius calls the three genera of the Greeks *modulationes;* Quintilian gives *modulatio* as the equivalent of the Aristoxenian ῥυθμός, one of the two divisions of music (the other being μέλος).[43] These passages, not to mention Augustine's definition of music as *bene modulandi scientia,*[44] include the notion of measured sound—measured pitch for Vitruvius, measured rhythm for Quintilian and Augustine. It is not then surprising to find that Zarlino refers to the "misura di tempi nelle modulationi" and even defines *modulatione* as *movimento* through various intervals, with slow and fast motion "secondo il tempo mostrato nelle sue figure cantabili."[45] Thus *modulatio* to sixteenth-century theorists means measured, or mensurally organized, melody. And it would seem that a melodic line, whether considered alone or within a polyphonic complex, could be an aesthetic object to be judged and admired; see Zacconi's praise of Alessandro Striggio for his "gift of charming *modulatione*" in the passage above. This is hardly surprising in itself, but it somehow seems more "modern" than anything in Glareanus or Zarlino, more akin to our modes of appreciation.

(3) *Diletto.* For rhetoricians oratory was supposed to give pleasure (*delectatio*) as well as to persuade; again Vitruvius and Quintilian will serve here as classical references.[46] A standard sixteenth-century view among musicians is that of Glareanus, who holds that "musica est delectationis mater," a sentiment echoed by Zarlino.[47] In general music that is well constructed gives pleasure, and for Zacconi it is important that *diletto* be there; composers, he says, should take care to cultivate "una certa maniera facile & dilettevole" so that they can give pleasure both to singers and to listeners. Those who make their music "faticoso & difficile" may find to their chagrin that singers ignore it.[48] That none of the composers cited in the passage above is singled out for this quality must simply mean to Zacconi that they all possessed it.

To Zarlino, conscious of the correct classical position, *diletto* was of secondary importance. Melody alone can give pleasure, but only when there is a text does the music amount to anything.[49] Mindful of sixteenth-century academic strictures about literary genre, Zarlino also says that the "canzonette, dette Madrigali" of the present time can give pleasure but do not truly have power to move the soul.[50] Zacconi characteristically takes a much less lofty position; for him any careful union of words and music gives maximum delight to singers, and in addition ravishes the hearts of listeners.[51]

The simple materials of music give pleasure; in discussing modes Zacconi says that successions of whole tones give delight, placement of semitones distinguishes and defines music.[52] But a principal ingredient in musical pleasure for him is variety of usage, preferably coupled with an element of surprise. Thus a delayed entrance of an imitative voice delights a listener all the more for having foiled his original expectation.[53] Ornament when properly used gives much pleasure; hence it is only fitting that the soprano, to which voice ornament is most readily and fittingly applied, gives more delight than the other voices.[54] Music that lacks proper rhythmic impetus is languid and deficient in *diletto*.[55] The word would then seem to indicate both the natural pleasure in attractive sounds and a connoisseur's reaction to finely executed detail, with the element of surprise adding relish.

(4) *Tessitura*. This word is not in common use among sixteenth-century theorists; Zacconi uses it rarely and Zarlino not at all. Various forms of the verb *tessere* do occur in Zacconi and are nearly always expressive of some kind of interweaving of materials, either of melodic and rhythmic elements within a single voice or of the contrapuntal relationships of melodic lines. Thus syncopations are "contessiture" of figures in a line, or between lines;[56] imitations and fugues are things that "si contessino" alone or over a cantus firmus;[57] at cadences the voices should be well interwoven;[58] rests can be part of the interwoven design of a fugue;[59] in four-voice counterpoint the soprano and tenor have the same "contessuta modulatione."[60] Occasionally the use of proportions is given the participle *contessuta* or the noun *tessitura*.[61] Even the artful mix of consonance and dissonance is achieved by interweaving.[62] On a more general level modern compositions are said to be "con alcuni stili piu vaghi hora tessute."[63] Only once does Zacconi hint at the meaning we would expect for *tessitura,* that of vocal range; and even then he seems to think of it as referring to the ordering of pitches within a mode rather than to range in general.[64]

If *arte* is for Zacconi the planning of contrapuntal designs, *tessitura* is their execution, or what we would call the practical art of counterpoint. That this is an important aspect of sixteenth-century music we can certainly accept; but what meaning is then left for the next term in Zacconi's list?

(5) *Contraponto* has for Zacconi a quite specific meaning, namely, the writing of counterpoint over a cantus firmus. His teaching method is based on use of cantus firmus to a degree unusual even for theorists of his time; he goes so far as to recommend that one learn to write madrigals with the help of a cantus firmus, and as an example gives a quodlibet of incipits of some of the most famous madrigals of the sixteenth century, all *tessute* over a "Salve regina."[65] Zacconi is careful to distinguish *contraponto* from what he calls *mera compositione* or free composition in the various sacred and secular genres of the day.[66] There would seem to be here an implication that *contraponto* as such is not to be found in actual music, but this is not so; a varied if not strictly "true" counterpoint is one of the things Zacconi admires most whenever he sees it, as in the Magnificats of Morales, where the *vero contraponto* of an even-note cantus firmus is mixed with freer treatment of the chant melody without sacrificing the principle of writing against a given part.[67]

Earlier composers wrote sets of *contraponti,* says Zacconi, and he speaks in particular of Costanzo Festa, who over his own melody called "Bascia" was said to have created 120 separate counterpoints.[68] Among the good composers of the next generation all presumably had command of the contrapuntal technique Zacconi called *tessitura;* but only a few right-thinking ones continued to distinguish themselves in the use of *contraponto.*

(6) *Inventione.* A concept to which rhetoricians devoted a great deal of attention,[69] invention was of course important to Zacconi, Zarlino, and other theorists. Zacconi does not, however, use the term very often; when he does, it means either the product of imaginative creation in general or some single idea—a *fuga,* for example.[70] Since a single idea could at the very least dominate the opening section of a piece and determine its mode, its invention was a matter of importance; and if one could not always come up with a completely new melody or point of imitation—Zarlino after all had said that all the easily thought-of ones had been used hundreds of times—one could by some artful arrangement give it an appearance of novelty. This manipulation of material belongs partly to *inventione* and partly to Zacconi's last category, that of *dispositione.*

(7) *Buona dispositione.* Invention and disposition are closely linked in classical rhetoric, and it is surely no accident that Zacconi has them follow one another. But if *inventione* is to him simple and self-explanatory as the act of creation, *dispositione* (which he nearly always prefaces with the adjective *buona* or the combination *ottima & buona*) has a number of related meanings touching on rhythm, mode, singing style, cadential formation, contrapuntal details, and texture. Thus one should strive for well-ordered proportions, mensurations, and rhythmic values.[71] A composer should order (*disporre*) his melodic materials according to the "andamenti e consonanze" of the mode;[72] if like some modern composers he ignores the modes, his works will be "composti à capriccio, e senza veruna buona dispositione,"[73] but composers who know the modes and work within them will be "dominatori di tutte le buone dispositioni harmoniche."[74] Not every voice produces genuine music, but only those "ordinate con debito ordine, e buona dispositione."[75] One may use a variety of cadences, provided they are "fatte con buona & ottima dispositione."[76] Melodic leaps are permitted if used with "debita dispositione"; dissonances should be hidden in the musical texture "con ottima e buona dispositione"; melodies using B♭ should not be introduced into a piece basically using B♮ if not with "ottime dispositioni."[77] A piece may show "buona & perfetta dispositione" in its use of consonances, or "vera & reale dispositione" in its well-ordered succession of note values and rests.[78] Indeed the best "effetti musicali" proceed from excellent voices singing according to "ottima & buona dispositione" in intervals ordered by "distanze sonore" and "gradi consonanti" in accordance with harmonic rule.[79]

At first it would seem that this last category is a grab bag, simply referring to harmonious disposition of all the elements of music. To some extent this is true, but the most telling and most often referred to aspects of *buona dispositione* would seem to be twofold: melodies should be constructed within the modes and should display a graceful arrangement of pitches and rhythmic values; and counterpoint should be ordered so as to achieve the best and most correct harmonic values—for Zacconi surely the order of Zarlino's *senario,* with full triads spaced in narrowing order from bass to soprano.

In brief review, Zacconi held that good music should be artfully planned; it should have fine melodies and give pleasure to singers and listeners; it ought to have well-meshed counterpoint and where appropriate base itself on a cantus firmus; its materials should be fresh and imaginative and these materials should be melodically and contrapuntally ordered so as to achieve the most satisfying sonorities. This is a sound if somewhat conservative set of criteria. All good music in Zacconi's view displayed these qualities to some degree, but not every composer had equal distinction in all seven categories. If we turn to the composers whom Zacconi says Zarlino was speaking of, we see that the great theorist describes his own music as having "regolar tessitura & arte"; in other words, it is conventional in plan and contrapuntal execution. This is an accurate if not flattering estimate of Zarlino's music as we know it, and it speaks well for his self-knowledge if Zarlino really said it; at any rate Zacconi must have concurred in this opinion if he did not invent it and what follows (Zarlino was safely dead when the treatise was written). It seems a bit hard on Costanzo Porta to have his music labeled with tags identical to those given Zarlino; Porta's Masses and motets are rigorous in their use of imitative polyphony, but he used cantus-firmus technique quite a lot and so might have been credited here at least with mastery of *contraponto.*[80] Striggio is said to have had a "talent and gift for charming melody." This sounds like rather faint praise, but it need not mean that Striggio was lacking in everything else, only that he excelled as a melodist.[81] Whether close study of Striggio's madrigals in comparison with those of his contemporaries would bear out this judgment I do not know; my own rather limited knowledge of his music suggests that there is a current of freshness of melodic idea in it, but I cannot claim to know the basis for what is said of him here.

That Willaert's music was thought to show *grand'arte* is no surprise, for both the motets and madrigals from Willaert's mature years are full of contrapuntal artifice—canons, double points of imitation, inversions, double counterpoint. "Giuditiosa dispositione" I would take to mean careful ordering of melodic and contrapuntal materials; Willaert's music, admirable in design and effective if somewhat thick in sound, the whole to be respected if not loved, is to me rather well described here. Morales combines *arte* with *contraponto* in his layout of chant cantus firmi; in the opinion of Zarlino/Zacconi he also writes good tunes. The great popularity of Morales's Magnificats, of which a dozen editions appeared between 1542 and 1614, is sufficient evidence of their attractiveness and perhaps of the effectiveness with which the composer handled the chant as *cantus prius factus.*[82]

Finally come Lasso and Palestrina, saved for last as if a comparison between the two greatest masters of the age was intended.[83] Lasso has art, the gift of melody, and "bonissima inventione," this last superlative evidently referring to what was and is most striking to the educated singer or listener, namely, Lasso's inexhaustible fund of musical ideas. Palestrina also has art, but stands out for *contraponto—*

he does use chant and cantus-firmus technique more than Lasso; for "ottima dispositione," which I take to mean Palestrina's preference for brightly voiced full triads wherever possible;[84] and for "una sequente modulatione," the famous smoothly sculpted melodic lines that have been studied for centuries as if they were characteristic of all sixteenth-century music but which Zacconi tells us were a clearly audible trademark of Palestrina's personal style. In these last two characterizations Zacconi offers us, I think, something really perceptive about the music of the two figures we recognize as the greatest exponents of late Renaissance style.

Zacconi ends by saying that musicians of his time could tell from experience one composer's work from that of another. It would not be fair to say that his categories taken by themselves could hardly afford the basis for such judgments; he and his contemporaries must have had a real "feel" for this music, something we have trouble recapturing—especially if we cling to notions of an angelically faceless "golden age of polyphony." I submit that Zacconi's criteria were meant to be real if not comprehensive, and that they represent a genuine effort at combining technical analysis with aesthetic judgment, the visible remains of what must have been a more mature and thoughtful critical sense than we have hitherto thought to have been in the grasp of Renaissance musicians.

POSTSCRIPT

In this article I should have pointed out that descriptive terms distinguishing the character of the work of visual artists and writers were employed by a number of fifteenth- and sixteenth-century theorists and critics. For a survey of these see Peter Burke, *The Italian Renaissance: Culture and Society in Italy,* rev. ed. (Princeton, 1987), chapter 6: "Taste." Burke mentions music but does not cite Zacconi's work.

The *basse* of Costanzo Festa, long considered to be lost, are convincingly identified and discussed in Richard Agee, "Costanzo Festa's 'Gradus ad Parnassum'," *EMH* 15 (1996): 1–58; see also Agee's edition, Costanzo Festa, *Counterpoints on a Cantus Firmus,* RRMR, 107 (Madison, Wisc., 1997).

A new general study of compositional practice in the Renaissance is Jessie Ann Owens, *The Craft of Musical Composition 1450–1600* (New York, 1997).

NOTES

1. See chapter 12, esp. 283–93.

2. Giustiniani's treatise, dated 1628, is printed in Angelo Solerti, *Le origini del melodramma* (Turin, 1903; reprint, Hildesheim, 1969), 98–128. An English translation, by Carol MacClintock, has been published (in a volume containing Ercole Bottrigari's *Il desiderio* as well) in Musicological Studies and Documents 9 (American Institute of Musicology, 1962).

3. Among works of more or less the same genre as that of Giustiniani is Luigi Dentice's *Duo dialoghi* (Naples, 1552). What the normal educated person in the sixteenth century might be expected to know about music is summarized in those passages referring to the art in Castiglione's *Cortegiano* (Venice, 1528); see especially 1.28, 1.37, 1.47, 2.13. For comment on these passages see chapter 2.

A mid-century view of music and musicians, with an occasional attempt at characterization of musical style, may be seen in Cosimo Bartoli, *Ragionamenti Accademici* (Venice, 1567), fols. 34v–39r. Verdelot's compositions, for example, are characterized thus: "hanno del facile, del grave, del gentile, del compassionevole, del presto, del tardo, del benigno, dello adirato, del fugato, secondo la proprieta delle parole sopra delle quali egli si metteva a comporre." Bartoli also says that the music of Willaert, somewhat vaguely described as having "molto del leggiadro & del gentile," and that of Giachetto da Mantova resemble each other.

4. See George Nugent, "Gombert," *New Grove,* 7:512, for a citation of this passage from Finck's *Practica musicae* of 1556.

5. Bottrigari apparently had a low opinion of the critical abilities of performers, who he says laugh and chatter while the music is going on and "whether the music is sung or played . . . have only one kind of expression, so to speak, whether it's a good Madrigal or a Motet; and they are not interested in anything else." See Bottrigari, *Il desiderio,* ed. MacClintock, 61–62.

6. Lodovico Zacconi, *Prattica di Musica Seconda Parte. Divisa, e distinta in Quattro Libri. Ne quali primieramente si tratta de gl'Elementi Musicali; cioè de primi principij come necessarij alla tessitura e formatione delle Compositioni armoniali . . .* (Venice, 1622; reprint, Bologna, 1967; henceforth *Prattica,* 1622), 49–50 ("De i riti e maniere c'hanno havuto molti Musici, in haver composto le loro Musiche armoniale"):

"E cosa piu che chiara e certa, che li doni del Signore essendo molti (per non dir infiniti,) dalla maesta sua divina sono distribuiti e compartiti in modo, che bene spesso chi ha l'uno, non ha l'altro; e fatichisi pur uno quanto si voglia, che quando per via di natura, ò per particolar gratia, non gli lo concede, non fa nulla, e fa come si dice per proverbio, pista l'acqua nel mortale. Di questo noi n'habbiamo gl'essempij in ogni facultà, e professione; e nella Musica ancora ne lo vediamo e tocchiamo con mano. E però volendo io ragionar de i varij stile, modi, e maniere di diverse compositioni dico; che la Musica armoniale si distingue in sette particolar distintioni: cioè, in arte, modulatione, diletto, tessitura, contraponto, inventione, e buona dispositione. Ciascuna di queste cose è necessaria al compositore; e quantumque ò poco ò assai si trovino in ogn'uno, una però ritrovandosi piu singolarmente che un altra, da quella quel tale ne piglia nome e vien celebrato. Onde in proposito tale senza offensione di niuno io mi ricordo, che l'anno 1584, discorrendosi un giorno di Musica alla presenza de molti di detta professione, innanzi al Signor Don Ioseffo Zerlino, e dicendosi dello stilo di questo, e di quello, e di quello, diede la sudetta distintione, e poi venne à questo particolar dicendo. Che volete mò voi dire? chi hà uno non hà l'altro, e chi n'hà dua o tre non gli può haver tutti. Eccò (dicendo lui di se stesso) che il genio mio, è dedito alla regolar tessitura & arte, come anco è quella del presente Costanzo Porta. Lo Strigio hebbe talento e dono di vaga modulatione, M. Adriano di grand'arte e giuditiosa dispositione. Morales hebbe arte, contraponto e buona modulatione. Orlando lasso, modulatione, arte, e bonissima inventione, & il Palestina, arte, contraponto, ottima dispositione, & una sequente modulatione, dal che ne nasce, che chi ha sentito le cose di detti auttori una volta, cantandosi altre volte altre loro compositioni, subito si sà dire, quest' opera è del tale: e veramente cosi è, poi che; quando l'huomo d'un autore piu volte hà sentito le sue cose, subito frà l'altre sentendole, le sà discernere, e dice è opera del tal autore." Zacconi's use of the past tense for all the composers he mentions reflects the time his treatise was written; at the time he says the conversation took place most of these men were still alive.

7. Friedrich Chrysander, "Ludovico Zacconi als Lehrer des Kunstgesanges," *Vierteljahrsschrift für Musikwissenschaft* 7 (1891): 337–96; 9 (1893): 249–310; 10 (1894): 531–67. The passage is cited in 10:542–43.

8. *Prattica di Musica* [*Prima parte*] (Venice, 1592; reprint, Bologna, 1970; henceforth *Prattica*, 1592), fol. 7r.

9. Ibid., fol. 84r.

10. *Prattica*, 1622, 127. Later (on 153–54) Zacconi acknowledges Zarlino as the source of this anecdote.

11. Zacconi says that he learned how to sing *contraponto alla mente* from Ippolito Baccusi in Mantua (ibid., 84).

12. Ibid., 278.

13. *Prattica*, 1592, fol. 168v.

14. *Prattica*, 1622, 53–54. The *Cantica* referred to by Zacconi are presumably Palestrina's *Motettorum liber quartus ex Canticis canticorum* (Rome, 1584).

15. The reference to Monteverdi, who is coupled by Zacconi with Rore for using dissonance "per trasportarsi à più grate melodie" (*Prattica*, 1622, 63), is perhaps surprising to find in a theorist of conserative bent; Zacconi cites Artusi from time to time, and he certainly did not get this view of Monteverdi from his fellow theorist. But Zacconi seems to have been a fair-minded man who could see in the work of modern composers extension rather than transgression of established practice.

16. Ibid., 83. For accounts of Zacconi's life, derived from his manuscript autobiography, see Francesco Vatielli, "Un musicista pesarese del secolo XVI," *Cronaca musicale* 8 (1904):65–74; idem, "Di Ludovico Zacconi: Ulteriori notizie su la vita e le opere," *Cronaca musicale* 16 (1912): 51–60, 83–92, 103–11 (both reprinted, Bologna, 1968); Hermann Kretzschmar, "Ludovico Zacconis Leben auf Grund seiner Autobiographie," *Jahrbuch der Musikbibliothek Peters* 17 (Leipzig, 1911): 45–59; Hellmut Federhofer, *Musikpflege und Musiker am Grazer Habsburgerhof der Erzherzöge Karl und Ferdinand von Innerösterreich (1564–1619)* (Mainz, 1967), 140–41.

17. *Prattica*, 1622, 161: "Raconterò questo fatto dicendo; che il Sig. Orlando Lasso Maestro di Capella del Serenissimo Duca di Baviera mio Patrone, mi dicea, che per questo nella Musica egli era riuscito tale; perche, ogni dì infallibilmente egli componea qualche cosa; e quando non sapea che si far altro, si mettea à componere una fantasia; e dicendoli io ch'essendo vecchio hormai potea lasciar stare, mi disse. Nò; perche quando il Padrone mi desse da far qualche cosa, havendo io lasciato l'uso di comporre; ò che vi durarei gran fatica, ò ch'io non vi farei cosa degna del mio buon acquistato nome."

18. Ibid., 129–30.

19. Ibid., 49–50.

20. *Prattica*, 1592, fol. 13r.

21. *Prattica*, 1622, 161–62.

22. Ibid., 162: "Ho detto nel Capitolo precedente che lo Scolare provistosi de libre atti à simil professione, partischi quegl'essempij, e gl'essamini ben bene. E perche partitoli in cartella non facesse come fanno alcuni, che vedutone gl'andamenti e le maniere, li cancellano, e non ne fanno più conto; questo tale che bramarà d'imparare, fattone in cartella tutte le sudette prove poco fa accennate, e dimostrate di sopra, ne li noterà tutti in un libro appartato, e lasciandovi spatij sufficienti, d'aggiongervi qualch'altra cosa. . . . E per questo

dico, & essorto à lasciarvi sempre qualche spatio sufficiente à potervi rimettervi altro quando bisognasse; perche, dopò quello ch'uno hà fatto sopra un soggetto, rivedendolo dopò qualche tempo, l'ingegno li suministra sempre di rifarlo meglio.

"Li servirà anco detto appartato libro in notarvi dentro essempij d'altri Auttori che non sono in stampa, non quei treviali, e communi; ma quelli che sono fatti con qualche particolar secreto & arte. . . ."

23. Ibid., 162: "Inoltre, molte volte i Compositori componendo un canto con un disegno, ed à un fine, quell'istesso anco si può lo studio del buon Scolare, sarà anco in questo altro tanto più che sottile e diligente, essaminando, se quella tale compositione col cambio delle parti, isminuitione, ed accrescimento delle pause, si può variare: lasciando da parte di dire, che si provi di cavarne un'altra parte dalle parti originali che li sia somigliante e conforme più che sia possibile."

This passage seems to me more clearly descriptive of sixteenth-century parody technique than any of those (in the work of Frosch, Vicentino, Zarlino, Ponzio, and Cerone) cited by Lewis Lockwood, "On 'Parody' as Term and Concept in Sixteenth-Century Music," in *Aspects of Medieval and Renaissance Music: A Birthday Offering to Gustave Reese,* ed. Jan LaRue et al. (New York, 1966), 569–71.

For a new summary of Renaissance attitudes toward various compositional uses of preexistent musical material, see Howard Mayer Brown, "Emulation, Competition, and Homage: Imitation and Theories of Imitation in the Renaissance," *JAMS* 35 (1982): 1–48.

24. The first part of Chrysander's study of Zacconi (see above, n. 7) is concerned with the art of *gorgia* as taught and illustrated by Zacconi in his first treatise.

25. On these various topics see *Prattica,* 1622, 49 and 55–56; and *Prattica,* 1592, fol. 21v.

26. *Prattica,* 1622, 42: "L'ordine delle scienze richiede, che mai si proponga à Scolari termine senza la sua espositione, dechiaratione, e significatione."

27. Zarlino, who certainly knew Quintilian, draws heavily on the *Institutio oratoria* and may even have chosen the title of his own major work in imitation of it. See Warren Kirkendale, "Ciceronians versus Aristotelians on the Ricercar as Exordium from Bembo to Bach," *JAMS* 32 (1979): 30, n. 153.

28. Quintilian, *Institutio oratoria,* ed. and trans. H. E. Butler (Cambridge, Mass., 1922), 1:382–83 (3.3.1): "Omnis autem orandi ratio, ut plurimi maximeque auctores tradiderunt, quinque partibus constat, inventione, dispositione, elocutione, memoria, pronuntiatione sive actione."

29. In one passage the quality of *diletto* is said to be achieved through good texting (*Prattica,* 1592, fol. 197r).

30. In ancient times, says Zacconi, "i Poeti . . . eran tenuti per [Musica] per la buona, & optima dispositione delle lor Rime" (ibid., fol. 7r); the ancients even derived melody from verse: "Et è da credere che da gl'aeri Poetici, ne sieno venuti gl'aeri Musicali, non estendendosi anticamente la Musica in altro che in dolce maniere di cantar versi & Rime" (ibid., fol. 199r). But in modern times things are different: "Ma io non intendo che Musico sia Poeta, ne che Poeta Musico sia; se non fossero l'uno & l'altro insieme: cioè che à caso si ritrovasse (come facilmente si potria trovare,) che un Poeta fosse Musico; ò che un Musico foss'anco Poeta: perche gli atti & l'operationi loro sono tutte diverse & contrarie dalle operationi & attioni Poetiche & Musicali" (ibid., fol. 12v).

31. *Institutio oratoria,* 1:344–45 (2.17.41): "Ars est potestas via, id est ordine, efficiens, esse certe viam atque ordinem in bene dicendo nemo dubitaverit." Zarlino paraphrases this sentiment in many places.

32. Zarlino, *Sopplimenti musicali* (Venice, 1588; reprint, Ridgewood, N.J., 1966), 23.

33. Ibid., 19: Art is the "principio dell'operare in un'altra cosa, overo è habito certo di fare una cosa con ragione" and is "la vera ragione della cosa, che si hà da fare, & anco l'habito dell'operare."

34. *Istitutioni harmoniche,* 3d ed. (Venice, 1573; reprint, Ridgewood, N.J., 1966), 171.

35. *Prattica,* 1592, fol. 13r.

36. Ibid., fol. 8v. The passage deals with the intrinsic qualities of music, which must be in the minds of composers, and the extrinsic qualities revealed in the music as actually written.

37. Ibid., fol. 7v; *Prattica,* 1622, 154 and 260.

38. *Prattica,* 1622, 259.

39. See RISM 1538[7], *Modulationes aliquot quatuor vocum selectissimae, quas vulgo modetas vocant . . .* , one of the earliest of many examples of this use of the term.

40. *Sopplimenti,* 75: "i Colori ò Arie di esse Cantilene . . . contenuti nelle Modulationi delle loro parti."

41. *Istitutione harmoniche,* 14: "la Modulatione, overo il Cantare"; cf. *Sopplimenti,* 9, 14 ("una Modulatione, over'Aria"), and 279.

42. *Prattica,* 1622, 57: counterpoint is based on "un soggetto di qualche modulatione."

43. Vitruvius, *On Architecture,* ed. and trans. Frank Granger (Cambridge, Mass., 1931), 1:270–71 (5.4.3); Quintilian, *Institutio oratoria,* 1:170–71 (2.10.22).

44. *De musica,* 1.2.

45. *Istitutioni harmoniche,* 171, 96.

46. Vitruvius, *On Architecture,* 1:280–81 (5.5.6); Quintilian, *Institutio oratoria,* 4:92–93 (10.2.27), in which there is mention of those portions of a speech "quae delectationi videantur data."

47. Heinrich Glareanus, *Dodecachordon* (Basel, 1547; reprint, Hildesheim, 1969), 175; Zarlino, *Istitutioni harmoniche,* 13: "essendo l'ufficio propio della Musica il dilettare."

48. *Prattica,* 1592, fols. 81v–82r.

49. *Sopplimenti,* 81: "Essendoche se bene il Canto da se stesso porge diletto; tuttavia congiunto all'Armonia delle parole, non solamente diletta; ma giova anco, secondo la qualità del Soggetto, che si tratta in esse."

50. *Istitutioni harmoniche,* 89.

51. *Prattica,* 1622, 199.

52. Ibid., 45: "i Tuoni . . . danno l'aere, & il diletto melodiale [alle Cantilene], & i semitoni la specificata differenza, e vera distinstione [*sic*]."

53. Ibid., 73. On *diletto* as the consequence of variety in general see also 46–47 and 77.

54. Ibid., 54–55. Here Zacconi describes the qualities of various combinations from two to twelve voices. Four-voice texture is, in the traditional manner, thought to be ideal, but there is a special delight felt "quando ch'una bella voce, e bel cantante sonandosi l'altre parti canta solo; perche in essa si hanno tutte le cose, che si possino bramare; cioè melodia, diletto, compiacimento, & intera soddisfattione." On *diletto* resulting from elegance of ornament cf. Zarlino, *Istitutioni harmoniche,* 239.

55. *Prattica,* 1622, 81–82. Here Zacconi points out that in counterpoint against a semibreve one should not use another semibreve or a dotted minim-plus-semiminim; the result is lacking in motion and hence is not sufficiently *dilettevole.* He adds somewhat complacently that Lasso, Monte, "& altri singolari di questa professione, caddero tutti nel mio pensiero."

56. Ibid., 78.

57. *Prattica,* 1622, 260.

58. Ibid., 88: "ben contessuta parte."

59. Ibid., 134: "quando una fuga di seguito è contessuta di molte pause."

60. Ibid., 267.

61. Ibid., 54: the "Gloria Patri" of a Morales Magnificat is said to be "contessuto di buona e singolar Proportione"; *Prattica,* 1592, fol. 181v: "nelle tessiture di Proportione."

62. *Prattica,* 1592, fol. 175r: "si vede quanto i Musici vanno con le consonanze cattive temperando le buone, & quante durezze tessano dentro alle loro Musiche."

63. Ibid., fol. 8r.

64. *Prattica,* 1622, 47: Willaert in disposing his materials "secondo l'ordine, e tessitura dell'ottavo aere da salmeggiare, ne li rende ottavi per via de loro andamenti e finali."

65. Ibid., 113: the example includes incipits of "Vestiva i colli," "Ancor che col partire," "Io son ferito," "Nasce la pena mia," "Il bianco e dolce cigno," and "Liquidi perl' Amor"—a history of the madrigal from Arcadelt to Marenzio.

66. Ibid., 58.

67. Ibid., 60.

68. Ibid., 198. Among the categories of composition for which Festa, in 1538, received a Venetian privilege allowing him to print all his works was one termed "contraponti." See James Haar, "The *Libro Primo* of Costanzo Festa," *Acta musicologica* 52 (1980): 153, n. 2.

69. It was one of the traditional *partes artis rhetoricae.* An early treatise of Cicero, *De inventione,* is devoted entirely to this subject.

70. *Prattica,* 1622, 79, 154, 260.

71. "Dispositione" appears in the titles of chapters 23 and 24, both of which are concerned with mensurations and proportions, in book 1 of *Prattica,* 1622.

72. *Prattica,* 1622, 47.

73. Ibid., 37.

74. *Prattica,* 1592, fol. 212r.

75. *Prattica,* 1622, 60.

76. Ibid., 74.

77. Ibid., 87, 76, 255.

78. *Prattica,* 1592, fol. 87r.

79. Ibid., fol. 8r.

80. See Lilian P. Pruett, "Porta, Costanzo," *New Grove,* 15:131.

81. Vincenzo Galilei praised Striggio as a "gran contrapuntista, et facile," and described his compositions as "ben tessute." See Frieder Rempp, ed., *Die Kontrapunkttraktate Vincenzo Galileis* (Cologne, 1980), 145. I am grateful to Claude Palisca for calling this passage to my attention.

82. For a highly favorable estimate of Morales's Magnificats by a theorist whom Zacconi admired and respected see Adriano Banchieri, *L'organo suonarino* (Venice, 1605; reprint, Bologna, n.d.), 88: "Tra l'infinita schiera di Musici, c'hanno tessuto ghirlanda di soavissimi concenti al Cantico di Maria Vergine Santissima, sopra gli otto Tuoni di Canto fermo, gratissimi sono quelli di Morales a quattro, et di Vincenzo Ruffo a cinque, gl'uni alla Capella per l'osservanza del Canto fermo, gl'altri all'organo per la vaghezza del concerto, che realmente (vaglia la verità) sono degni di perpetua memoria."

On the use of chant as cantus firmus in Morales's Magnificats see Samuel Rubio, *Cristobal de Morales: Estudio critico de su polifonia* (Madrid, 1969), 260–65.

83. Zacconi does not say that the two are being compared, but the sense of the passage is that such a comparison is implied. For a striking and perhaps influential classical comparison, using the categories of invention and disposition as well as notions of general style, see the contrasting of Demosthenes and Cicero in Quintilian, *Institutio oratoria,* 4:60–61 (10.1.106).

84. The texture of Palestrina's music speaks for itself; but there is some evidence that the composer viewed this aspect of music as something deserving conscious calculation. In a letter to Duke Guglielmo Gonzaga (1570), in which he criticizes some compositions sent him by the Duke, Palestrina says that he has scored the ducal music in order to study it more closely, and that he has found too many unisons in the texture. See Knud Jeppesen, "Ueber einen Brief Palestrinas," in *Festschrift Peter Wagner zum 60. Geburtstag,* ed. Karl Weinmann (Leipzig, 1926), 100–107.

CHAPTER TWO

The Courtier as Musician: Castiglione's View
of the Science and Art of Music

FOR "SCIENCE AND ART" in the title of this paper one could almost substitute the words "theory and practice." Almost, but not quite. Baldassare Castiglione gives no evidence that he knew more than the rudiments of musical theory—either the classical science of harmonics or the subjects of *musica theorica* and *musica practica,* its twofold Renaissance descendants—and his remarks on the actual musical practice of his time are concerned as much with the performer's attitude as with the act of singing or playing.

Passages in the *Cortegiano* dealing with classical anecdote about the power of music will here be grouped with what little Castiglione has to say about the theoretical foundations of sixteenth-century music, the two topics combining to give us an idea of his grasp of music as received knowledge. In this field, loosely defined as musical science, Castiglione has nothing new to say and is not concerned to make his presentation in any way complete or systematic. Nonetheless, it seems important that in the *Cortegiano,* as rarely or perhaps never before in the educational treatises of the Renaissance, there is a genuine mixture of ancient and modern ideas on the nature of music.

Musical performance, as Castiglione understood it from his own experience and his observation of contemporary Italy, had no body of descriptive literature—ancient or modern—on which he could draw.[1] It is not then surprising that he should be more original here, and one wishes he had said much more, so illuminating are his remarks on the music and musicians of his time. Just as ancient and modern doctrine about music are found in mingled bits and pieces in the *Cortegiano,* so theory and practice mix easily in its pages. The result is a sparely drawn but convincingly real picture of how music, and talk about music, figured in the lives of Castiglione's peers. There are other sixteenth-century accounts of music in social context, such as Antonfrancesco Doni's *Dialogo della musica* or even Luis Milán's *El Cortesano,* a work written in emulation of Castiglione's; and there are plenty of humanistic treatises that repeat classical injunctions about the ideal cultivation of music.[2] In modernizing this ideal and making it comprehensible in terms of contemporary musical sound, Castiglione performed a notable service, helping to bring into modern life the dead language of ancient musical thought. That this was no mean feat may be seen if one compares his work to the lumbering classicistic jargon on the subject of music in the work of his older contemporary Paolo Cortese.[3]

In the first book of the *Cortegiano* Count Ludovico da Canossa, here Castiglione's spokesman, turns from literature to music, saying that his courtier should be able to read music (and thus to sing) and to play various instruments since there is nothing better than music for filling moments of leisure and for pleasing women—who in both ancient and modern times have been strongly inclined toward this art. Stung by Gaspare's rejoinder that music is an art suitable only to women and to effeminate men,[4] Ludovico turns from the present to the past and launches into a *gran pelago* of praises of music (1.47; see the appendix, no. 1). This is a sea the waters of which were much traveled in antiquity and in humanistic writings of the fifteenth and sixteenth centuries. The *laus musicae* is found, among classical writings, with particular frequency in treatises on rhetoric, a prime example being Quintilian's *Institutio oratoria;* it also occurs in works dealing with education in a general sense, an example being the closing section of Aristotle's *Politics.*

No subjects were dearer to, or more closely related for, humanistic writers than rhetoric and education, and they repeated whatever they could find in classical literature on these subjects. Greek anecdotes on the power of music had been retold in the Middle Ages in encyclopedic treatises and in the writings of musical theorists. Musical pedagogues of the fifteenth and sixteenth centuries continued to cite them, sometimes as in the case of Gafori profiting from humanistic scholarship to increase their stock of such references.[5] The encyclopedic tradition was carried on by scholars such as Giorgio Valla, who compiled an enormous jumble of examples.[6] Humanistic rhetoricians used the topic of laus musicae as had Quintilian, in service of their subject, and writers on education did the same.

It is not clear whether Castiglione drew the material for the passage in question directly from classical sources or from fifteenth-century writings on education and rhetoric. He had doubtless read Quintilian;[7] but although more than half the material in his musical encomium may be found in the *Institutio,*[8] by no means all of it comes from Quintilian. For example, the closing section, on music in divine worship and as a solace to all classes and all ages of man, is drawn, directly or from some intermediary source, from St. John Chrysostom's commentary on Psalm 41.[9] Single anecdotes might have stuck in Castiglione's mind from passages in Plato, Aristotle, and Plutarch. Or he may have remembered these things through their citation elsewhere. One possibility is the laus musicae in Beroaldo's *Oratio . . . in enarrationem Quaestionum Tusculanarum et Horatio flacii,* which has half a dozen of the instances cited by Castiglione.[10] Other possible sources are fifteenth-century treatises on education. The relationship of the *Cortegiano* to these treatises is a subject I do not feel competent to discuss; I do not even know if Castiglione read any of them.[11] If he had looked at Aeneas Silvius Piccolomini's *De liberorum educatione* he would have seen some of the same anecdotes he used.[12] Others are given in Pietro Paolo Vergerio's *De ingenuis moribus* in a passage that would have struck Castiglione if he had read it because it appears to cite, uncharacteristically for the humanists, examples (admittedly so vague that one cannot be sure of their meaning) from modern music.[13]

Castiglione's laus musicae may be his own compilation but all its contents are very well known and had been widely cited. His list of these anecdotes is one of the duller pages of the *Cortegiano* (though it is more interesting than such listings are in most other writers). Why is it included? Count Ludovico did not mean to show off his erudition, surely; that would have been graceless affectation on his part. I suggest that the laus musicae, a topic emphasizing the extraordinary power of music over human emotions, is included because it represents, in the aggregate, idealized music, an archetypal force that stands behind the practical art. Thus the courtier should be a musician not merely in order to entertain ladies but also to help him reach toward the balance and harmony of spirit that is his highest aim. Renaissance musicians could not find classical models for their art, but they could try, helped by Platonic and Pythagorean doctrine, for audible representation of ideal form, less tangible than as depicted in the visual arts but with a mysterious power all its own. Castiglione is not, as far as music is concerned, an ardent Neoplatonist, but in this passage he alludes, in his own way, to the ideal in music. What sets him apart from doctrinaire humanists on the subject is that he does not stop here as they did.

Castiglione's one reference to the practical musical theory current in his own time is his citation of the rule forbidding successive perfect consonances (1.28; see appendix, no. 2). Anyone trained in the rudiments of composition knew this prohibition by heart, and no one theorist need be cited as Castiglione's source. He might indeed have done well to read up on this negative rule in a theorist such as Gafori before writing the passage. Here are rules 2 and 3 of Gafori's celebrated eight rules of counterpoint, from the *Practica musicae* of 1496:

> The second rule states that two perfect consonances of the same size cannot immediately follow each other in parallel motion, as two unisons, octaves, fifteenths, or also two fifths and two twelfths. . . .
>
> The third rule states that between two perfect consonances of the same size, ascending or descending in parallel or contrary motion, at least one imperfect consonance, as a third, sixth, or the like, should intervene. . . .
>
> A counterpoint containing a single dissonance, as a second, fourth, or seventh, between two perfect consonances of the same size in ascending or descending parallel motion is not allowed . . . for if a clearly heard dissonance is unsuitable in counterpoint, it cannot take the place of and substitute for an imperfect consonance.[14]

The layman's version of these rules, as given in the *Cortegiano* by Giuliano de' Medici, omits two important points: the forbidden perfect consonances are only those in parallel motion, and they must be punctuated by imperfect consonances rather than solely by dissonances.

There is of course no reason to tax Castiglione for imprecise language; he was after all using this detail of music theory merely as illustration of a larger point, the achievement of grace through avoidance of affectation in every courtly activity. Nonetheless the passage is, as Cian has remarked, not very clear,[15] or rather, the illustration seems not a very apt one. Correctly used, imperfect consonances and dissonances are an integral part of the musical fabric; a piece made up entirely of perfect consonances is not so much "affected" as it is unthinkable. The easy grace that is opposed to affected pedantry in music is much better illustrated by Count Ludovico's remark, in the discussion following the passage in question, that a musician who ends a phrase with an easily tossed-off vocal ornament shows that he knows the art and could do more if he chose.[16]

If Giuliano's little excursus into music theory refers less to rules of composition—musical science—than to a manner of performance—musical art—in which dissonance is freely introduced and resolution artfully delayed, the passage makes better sense. More than that, it is historically important. Music making of this kind would then be an example, given along with others in speaking, dancing, riding, and bearing arms, of the courtier's important and, alas, untranslatable quality of *sprezzatura*.[17] This word is familiar to historians of music in its use by Giulio Caccini at the turn of the seventeenth century. Caccini mentions the word in his preface to *L'Euridice* (1600), in his *Nuove musiche* of 1602, and most tellingly in the preface to *Nuove musiche e nuova maniera di scriverle* (1614), where he defines it thus:

> *Sprezzatura* is that charm lent to a song by a few dissonant short notes over various bass notes that they are paired with; these relieve the song of a certain restricted narrowness and dryness and make it pleasant, free, and tuneful [*arioso*], just as in everyday speech eloquence and facility make pleasant and sweet the matters being spoken of. And to the figures of speech and the rhetorical flourishes in such eloquence correspond the *passaggi,* tremolos, and other such [musical] ornaments, which may occasionally be introduced with discretion in music of any mood.[18]

One can see that Caccini took more than the word *sprezzatura* from Castiglione; different as was the music the two men had in mind, Caccini borrowed two specifically musical meanings of the term, one implied and one clearly stated, from the *Cortegiano* to justify his own practice—a practice aimed, as he says, at achieving an effect of "total grace" (*intera grazia*) in music.[19]

Turning in the second book to the practice of music, Castiglione has his spokesman Federico Fregoso begin by emphasizing that the courtier must perform only when urged; if he is too quick to sing or play he will seem like a professional musician instead of one who makes music *per passar tempo*. Because professional musicians were pretty low in the social order of Castiglione's world, this warning was to be taken seriously. But we must not blame Castiglione for the lowly stature of musicians; also we should not think of the *Cortegiano* as a work unfriendly to the practice of music. On the contrary its influence could only have been in the direction of elevating the place of music in the life of the educated classes all over Europe. For example, we tend to think of the English upper classes in the past as having been traditionally philistine about music, made so by their education if not their temperament. This generalization is least applicable, however, for the couple of generations of Englishmen who first read Castiglione in Sir Thomas Hoby's translation, published in 1561. We should also consider that whereas humanistic treatises on education tended to appropriate Plato's distaste for the music of his own time—thus Sassuolo da Prato, a pupil of Vittorino da Feltre, dismissed the (secular) music of the mid-fifteenth century as "inquinata, impudens, corrupta atque corruptrix"[20]—Castiglione on the contrary implies in his work that music such as that performed in Urbino in the early sixteenth century or Rome fifteen years later was worth an educated person's notice, and we know from his letters that he was fond of performing it himself.

The insistence that professionalism in music be avoided was as old as Aristotle's *Politics,* if not older.[21] Aeneas Silvius, among other fifteenth-century humanists, echoed this sentiment;[22] Maffeo Vegio said of an educated young woman that she should not "sing and dance more elegantly than necessary";[23] and it may be recalled that Leon Battista Alberti excelled in music without any training and, it appears, without much practice.[24] Here of course Castiglione's courtier would apply sprezzatura; feigning a slight acquaintance with the art, he would nonetheless take care to give a pretty good account of himself whenever he did perform.

On being asked what kinds of music were best suited to cultivated tastes, Federico gives an interesting and surprisingly systematic list (2.13; appendix, no. 3). First comes the ability to sing well from notated music (*cantar bene a libro*), securely and *con bella maniera,* in other words, to read well and with a good sense of style at sight.[25] The music that Castiglione refers to could include motets and other sacred polyphony and French chansons, but above all he was thinking of the North Italian *frottola,* in vogue when he began his book, and the Florentine-Roman madrigal coming into fashion when he completed it. Much of this music was still circulating in manuscript copies, collections, or single pieces; an example of the latter is the *barzelletta Essi Diva Diana,* which Castiglione asked to have sent to him, *el canto e le parole,* in a letter of 1504.[26] But during the first decade of the sixteenth century the bulk of the repertory of the frottola as we know it was coming out in the beautifully printed volumes published by Ottaviano de' Petrucci in Venice. Petrucci was a native of Fossombrone, a town in the duchy of Urbino and at times a retreat for the ducal family, and there is reason to think that his early career was supported by the duke and even that he may have been educated at Urbino.[27] In 1511 he returned from Venice to Fossombrone, and in the years 1518–20 he visited Rome to intercede for his city at the papal court; whether at any of these times he came in contact with Castiglione is not known.[28] At any rate we can be sure that Petrucci's elegant little books of *frottole* and other part music were well known to Castiglione and his friends.

In saying that the courtier should be able to sing at sight not only securely but "con bella maniera" Castiglione introduces his favorite notion of stylish grace as part of musical performance. How much he meant to imply here by use of the word *maniera* I do not know, although in other contexts he meant a good deal by it.[29] But it is worth noting that recognizably individual style in musical performance was a sought-after and talked-about thing in late fifteenth-century Italy (only in the mid-sixteenth century did the concept of individual maniera begin to be spoken of with regard to music itself). *Improvvisatori* such as Chariteo and, above all, Serafino Aquilano were famous not only for their facility but also for their stylish manner of performance.[30] In the circle of the *Cortegiano* one would expect that l'Unico Aretino, Cristoforo Romano, Giacomo di San Secundo, and especially Terpandro might have been possessed of such skill, although it would have been demonstrated primarily in improvised singing, what Castiglione calls "cantare alla viola per recitare."[31]

During the fifteenth century skill in reading the mensural notation of polyphonic music, once the exclusive property of ecclesiastical singers, came to be taught to laymen as well although it was probably not part of any severely humanistic program of studies.[32] Thus Isabella d'Este studied music with the Franco-Flemish polyphonist Johannes Martini, and the children of Lorenzo de' Medici are said to have been instructed in music by the great Heinrich Isaac. If textbooks on polyphonic music, such as those prepared by Tinctoris for his royal pupil in Naples,[33] are any indication, correctness rather than *bella maniera* was the primary aim of such teaching. Improvised singing (what Ficino and other humanists called "cantare ad lyram") must have required more attention to style, but the professionalism of the *improvvisatori,* dangerously close perhaps to the popular street art of the *cantimbanchi* of Florence and the North Italian cities, was surely a thing to be avoided.

At the turn of the century things seem to have changed somewhat. The art of the *improvvisatori,* much admired in Ferrara and in the Mantua and Milan of Castiglione's youth, was so popular in courtly circles that the poets, some of them aristocrats, and the musicians, some of them professional polyphonists, came to share in it. Thus Marchetto Cara, one of Isabella d'Este's favorite composers, was sent to Venice in 1503, along with a Ferrarese gentlewoman whom he later married, to entertain the exiled Elisabetta of Urbino; their style of singing was reported to be better than anything the Venetians were accustomed to.[34]

All the frottolists must have been good at improvising; the formulaic nature of their written music suggests this, and in spite of their careful printing Petrucci's collections of *barzellette, strambotti,* and the like are better guides for free, semi-improvisatory performance than for literal rendition of the contents of the written page.[35] Castiglione in associating bella maniera with the art of reading music is, I think, recognizing just this state of affairs; the blending of improvisatory skills with the learned science of mensural polyphony, the products of which were now becoming widely available in print; and the leveling of social distinctions in musical performance, with the aristocratic courtier doing very much the same thing, albeit with more sprezzatura and less professionalism, as the scholastically trained singer or the self-taught *improvvisatore.*[36] The appearance of the cultivated amateur on the musical scene in the early cinquecento is an important landmark in the history of music, and Castiglione seems to have been its first chronicler.[37]

In *cantar a libro* as Castiglione defines it, all parts of a polyphonic piece are sung. "Bella musica," but more beautiful still is "il cantar alla viola," or solo singing to instrumental accompaniment, for two reasons. First, one can attend more closely to the "bel modo e l'aria," and second, small errors are easy to detect since the aid and comfort given by singers to each other are lacking here. To those who believe that under differences of circumstance and detail people remain fundamentally the same, it will come as pleasant confirmation to hear that sixteenth-century choral singers fudged through pieces by covering each others' mistakes much as they still do today. Yet Castiglione's second reason for preferring solo song seems odd in the ambience of sprezzatura; perhaps the latter quality did not extend to the making of audible mistakes. In the first reason there are two interesting words, *modo* and *aria.* The latter may be taken to mean melody, or more specifically the fusion of text and music; implied here is the necessity for correct and effective fitting together of words and melody, a union that surely existed in Castiglione's time but one that could not yet be taken for granted. *Aria* may also mean "air" in the sense of an individual manner of singing melodies. *Modo* does not mean "mode" in the technical musical sense but must here be used approximately in the way Petrucci was using it for paradigmatic pieces in his frottola collections (*modo di dir sonetti,* a piece designed to serve any sonnet of orthodox design, for example). One could, in other words, hear the formal or poetic structure more clearly in solo singing. Or, *modo* could be taken to mean the result of *maniera,* the kind of music produced by the individual style of the performer; thus it would be a synonym for *aria.*[38]

Whether Castiglione meant by *viola* a single instrument or an instrumental family (perhaps including the *lira de braccio*) or instead used the word to indicate any instrument suitable for accompaniment (the phrase *cantare alla viola* thus being a kind of synecdoche) I am not sure. If he meant *viola,* the newly fashionable gamba or a *viola da braccio,* literally, this was one term that his translators changed.[39] Both the early French and German versions of the *Cortegiano* substitute lute for viol, and so does Hoby;[40] the lute, already an instrument in prominent use when Castiglione began his work, was by mid-century regarded as the aristocratic accompanying instrument par excellence (and thus again perhaps serving as a generic term).[41] Castiglione himself owned viols and was fond of playing them; he wrote twice to his mother from Rome, at just the time he was completing the second redaction of the *Cortegiano,* asking for his "beloved" instrument to be sent to him.[42] Isabella d'Este, that paragon of musical as well as of all other courtly virtues, learned to play the viol, remarking in a letter of 1499 that she was practicing in order to the be able to accompany her brother Alfonso when she next visited Ferrara.[43] If, by the way, the future Alfonso I d'Este could take time off from his artillery to sing *alla viola,* it seems that one has sufficient proof of the realism of Castiglione's remarks about aristocratic practice of music.

Federico, in ranking modes of performance, gives highest praise to what he calls "il cantare alla viola per recitare." By this Castiglione means improvised song or declamatory speech-song over instrumental accompaniment. This was the art for which Serafino Aquilano and his peers were famous; by means of it the sonnets and *canzoni* of Petrarch and of late fifteenth- and early sixteenth-century *petrarchisti* were performed before courtly audiences. At a lower literary level the same improvisers, and humbler poet-musicians as well, declaimed *strambotti* by this method. Chains of *ottava rima* stanzas, such as those written by Bembo for the carnival at Urbino in 1506, must also have been occasionally performed in this way, and Castiglione's stanzas for *Tirsi* might at some point, if not on the occasion for which they were written, have been sung. The frontispiece to an early edition of Pulci's

Morgante shows an *improvvisatore* declaiming, *lira da braccio* in hand, to an attentive audience.[44] It would have been easy to do the same thing with other epic poetry of the time, including part of Boiardo's *Orlando innamorato,* and it is known that Ariosto's *Orlando furioso* later enjoyed great popularity, both in the poet's own stanzas and in numerous popularized arrangements, performed in this way.[45] What is surprising in this context is that the art of improvised song-and-accompaniment, which appears to have been the domain of professionals—not always of very exalted status even within their class—is grouped with the other musical accomplishments suitable to the courtier. On the other hand, we hear of aristocratic men of genius who are said to have excelled in just this pursuit; Lorenzo de' Medici, despite his bad voice, was said to be one.[46] Here, then, Castiglione might be referring to the kind of performance a humanistically trained person of talent would give. Still, one suspects that in his mind this performance was not so distant from the art of the *strambottisto* as pure humanists could have wished.

In mentioning other instruments Gaspare singles out the keyboard family (perhaps including by implication the lute), useful for the full chords ("le consonanzie molto perfette") they can produce and the ease with which they can produce a variety of effects. A consort of four bowed viols is praised for its sweetness and artifice; this ensemble was perhaps not so common in the early sixteenth century as it later became, but there is contemporary evidence of its use (Castiglione's specification of "da arco" may support the notion that his earlier talk about *viola* referred mainly to a plucked instrument).[47] Only the wind instruments, outlawed to men of good standing since they had been scorned in antiquity by Alcibiades and by the goddess Athena,[48] are excluded, presumably because in playing them one gave up the use of one's voice; also, they distorted one's face, preventing one from making a *bella figura.*

In all this singing and playing, we are reminded, it is enough to be acquainted with the art; but after this dutifully humanistic phrase Castiglione adds, "But the better skilled you are, the better for you." The discreet courtier will choose the right time to perform, at the bidding of a company of friends and equals and especially in the presence of women. He will attend not only to the time of day but also to his time of life; music making, so often the accompaniment of amorous poetry, is suitable only to the young.

On Giuliano de' Medici (hardly a graybeard in 1506) protesting that the *poveri vecchi* should not be deprived of the pleasure of music, Federico replies that he agrees; old men should indeed continue to *cantare alla viola* if they wish but in private and as solace for the unhappiness and troubles that fill their lives. This seems, if one remembers Castiglione's lifelong love for the viola and the melancholy of his later years, a touchingly personal remark.[49]

The long passage on music (not all of it is given here) ends with the acute observation that those who have performed music with some skill, even if in mature years they no longer do so, will enjoy it more than nonmusicians, who hear music as passing sounds that do not really enter their souls and who are affected by it in much the same way dumb beasts are.[50] By blending the Ficinian notion of music's effect on the *spiritus*[51] with that of the usefulness of technical and intellectual grasp of the art, Castiglione comes as close as anyone in his century to presenting a rounded aesthetic ideal for music.

In book three (8) music is briefly mentioned among the accomplishments suitable for women. The passage is chiefly negative in tone: Women should approach musical performance, or dancing, with "una certa timidità," should thus avoid brazen professionalism even more than men. They should shun instruments such as drums, pipes, and trumpets (but, we remember, so should male courtiers). In playing instruments suitable to them women should not make use of elaborate ornaments and fast repeated notes ("quelli diminuzioni forti e replicate") that would draw attention to their skill rather than their sweetness of execution. All Castiglione seems to be saying here is that things he advises against in the musical performance of the courtier are really forbidden in that of the lady of the court. In all other respects, it seems, women are free to take part in music as much as men— allowing for the limitation that much of the *poesia per musica* of the time was addressed to women and so meant primarily for them to listen to. The role of women in aristocratic and indeed in semiprofessional music making at this time is of course well documented.

In addition to the set speeches on music in the *Cortegiano* there are a few scattered allusions, interesting in themselves and valuable in showing the role of music in some approximation of the everyday life of the cultivated society it depicts. The most important of these may be described briefly in their order of occurrence in the work.

1. In the midst of the long discussion of the use of language in book one, Count Ludovico speaks (37) of the differing types of musical usage he has observed, contrasting the brilliant style of singing exemplified by Bidon with the softer, sweeter style of Marchetto Cara (appendix, no. 4). Bidon, a French-born singer from Ferrara who joined the court of Leo X in the latter years of his reign, was mentioned for his stylish singing by Folengo and others.[52] Cara, the well-known composer of frottole at the Mantuan court, has already been cited for his skill as a performer.[53] Castiglione had certainly heard Cara sing at some point near the beginning of his work on the *Cortegiano,* and he must have known Cara's setting of his sonnet "Cantai mentre nel cor lieto fioria," published in 1513.[54] Bidon's singing he came to know at a later point; in the second redaction of the *Cortegiano* the very words used to describe this musician were used, in the same spot, for Alexander Agricola, a Flemish musician who had been at Milan in the 1470s, had later spent some time in Naples and Florence, but who had left Italy in 1493 and had died, in the service of the Habsburg court in Spain, in 1506.[55] The change of name is an interesting example of Castiglione's effort to update his work even if it bespeaks a certain insensitivity about the personal *maniera* of musicians.[56]

2. At the end of book one there is music and dancing, occurring in a way reminiscent of the *Decameron,* performed at the order of the duchess. Two ladies dance, to the music of the accomplished musician-dancer Barletta, a *bassa* and a *roegarze.* Barletta, who is also mentioned in the first book as a professional dancer, was apparently a favorite at the court of Urbino; he is the subject of a letter of 1507 from

Castiglione to Ippolito d'Este.[57] The *bassa danza* was a well-known Italian court dance, under changing guises, from the mid-fifteenth century;[58] about the *roegarze* we know only that it was one of the dances performed at a wedding banquet for Ercole II of Ferrara in 1529, mentioned in the celebrated description of Cristoforo di Messisbugo.[59]

3. Early in the second book Federico, when speaking of the gentleman's need to choose carefully the time and place for display of his accomplishments, criticizes the music lover who fills every conversational pause with singing sotto voce. In the second redaction Castiglione had written "sotto voce a cantare ut re mi fa sol la" to emphasize the inanity of such musical interpolations.[60]

4. In emphasizing that the courtier should select and cleave to one friend, Federico cites as proverbial wisdom the fact that it is more difficult to tune together three instruments than two (2.30), a metaphor for human conduct prophetic of Elizabethan usage.

5. Federico, in a conversation on the force of opinion and prejudice (2.35; appendix, no. 5), illustrates with two anecdotes: in the first some verses thought to be by Sannazaro were acclaimed as excellent but when found to be by another poet were sunk in popular judgment to mediocrity;[61] in the second a motet sung in the presence of the duchess was not judged either good or pleasing until it was revealed to be by Josquin des Prez, whereupon it rose immediately in stature. As the only debunking statement about the great composer known to me, this remark has a certain perverse appeal.[62]

6. In illustration of the notion that the cobbler should stick to his last, Federico speaks of a certain musician who gave up his art to write verses that he thought excellent but that everyone else laughed at (2.39); now he has lost even his musical skills. As Cian remarks, we will never know who this was, much as we would like to.[63]

7. Among the *facezie* in book two is an account (52) by Cesare Gonzaga of a Brescian bumpkin who watched the festivities in Venice on Assumption Day. Asked what part of the ceremonial music he most admired, he replied that the marvel of a strange trumpet that the player half swallowed, then regurgitated, pleased him most. The courtier, though he disdained playing it, was clearly expected to know about an instrument like the slide trumpet or trombone (and we now know that these were used, in addition to the famous long trumpets, in Venetian festival music).

8. In the fourth book the irrepressible Gaspare remarks (48) that the courtier must be something special if Plato and Aristotle are his constant companions; still, he ventures to say that he finds it hard to believe that either of these ancient worthies ever danced or made music.

9. As part of Bembo's description of ideal love (4.62) there occurs what I would call a prose madrigal, surely written during the first flush of enthusiasm for this new poetic-musical genre.

Therefore let him keep aloof from the blind judgment of sense, and with his eyes enjoy the radiance of his Lady, her grace, her amorous sparkle, the smiles, the manners and all the other pleasant ornaments of her beauty. Likewise, with his hearing let him enjoy the sweetness of her voice, the modulation of her words, the harmony of her music (if his lady love be a musician). Thus, he will feed his soul on the sweetest food by means of these two senses—which partake little of the corporeal, and are reason's ministers—without passing to any unchaste appetite through desire for the body.[64]

On this note, with Castiglione characteristically recognizing the real even while emphasizing the ideal, these remarks may end.

APPENDIX

Passages Dealing with Music in the Cortegiano

1. 1.47: Non dite,—rispose il Conte;—perch'io v'entrarò in un gran pelago di laude della musica; e ricordarò quanto sempre appresso gli antichi sia stata celebrata e tenuta per cosa sacra, e sia stato opinione di sapientissimi filosofi il mondo esser composto di musica e i cieli nel moversi far armonia, e l'anima nostra pur con la medesima ragion esser formata, e però destarsi e quasi vivificar le sue virtù per la musica. Per il che se scrive Alessandro alcuna volta esser stato da quella così ardentemente incitato, che quasi contra sua voglia gli bisognava levarsi dai convivii e correre all'arme; poi, mutando il musico la sorte del suono, mitigarsi e tornar dall'arme ai convivii. E dirovvi il severo Socrate, gia vecchissimo, aver imparato a sonare la citara. E ricordomi aver già inteso che Platone ed Aristotele vogliono che l'om bene instituito sia ancor musico, e con infinite ragioni mostrano la forza della musica in noi essere grandissima, e per molte cause, che or saria lungo a dir, doversi necessariamente imparar da puerizia; non tanto per quella superficial melodia che si sente, ma per esser sufficiente ad indur in noi un novo abito bono ed un costume tendente alla virtù, il qual fa l'animo più capace di felicità, secondo che lo esercizio corporale fa il corpo più gagliardo; e non solamente non nocere alle cose civili e della guerra, ma loro giovar sommamente. Licurgo ancora nelle severe sue leggi la musica approvò. E leggesi i Lacedemonii bellicosissimi ed i Cretensi aver usato nelle battaglie citare ed altri instrumenti molli; e molti eccellentissimi capitani antichi, come Epaminonda, aver dato opera alla musica; e quelli che non ne sapeano, come Temistocle, esser stati molto meno apprezzati. Non avete voi letto che delle prime discipline che insegnò il bon vecchio Chirone nella tenera età ad Achille, il quale egli nutrì dallo latte e dalla culla, fu la musica; e volse il savio maestro che le mani, che aveano a sparger tanto sangue troiano, fossero spesso occupate nel suono del citara? Qual soldato adunque sarà che si vergogni d'imitar Achille, lasciando molti altri famosi capitani ch'io potrei addurre? Però non vogliate voi privar il nostro cortegiano della musica, la qual non solamente gli animi umani indolcisce, ma spesso le fiere fa diventar mansuete; e chi non la gusta si po tener per certo ch'abbia i spiriti discordanti l'un dall'altro. Eccovi quanto essa po, che già trasse un pesce a lassarsi cavalcar da un omo per mezzo il procelloso mare. Questa veggiamo operarsi ne' sacri tempii nello rendere laude e grazie a Dio; e credibil cosa è che ella grata a lui sia ed egli a noi data l'abbia per dolcissimo alleviamento delle fatiche e fastidi nostri. Onde spesso i duri lavoratori de' campi sotto l'ardente sole ingannano la lor noia col rozzo ed agreste cantare. Con questo la inculta contadinella, che inanzi al giorno a filare o a tessere si lieva, dal sonno si diffende e la sua fatica fa piacevole; questo è iocundissimo trastullo dopo le piogge, i venti e le tempeste ai miseri marinari; con questo consolansi i stanchi peregrini dei noiosi e lunghi viaggi e spesso gli afflitti prigionieri delle catene e ceppi. Così, per maggiore argumento che d'ogni fatica e molestia umana la modulazione, benchè inculta, sia grandissimo refrigerio, para che la natura alle nutrici insegnata l'abbia per rimedio precipuo del pianto continuo de' teneri fanculli; i quali al suon di tal voce s'inducono a riposato e placido sonno, scordandosi le lacrime così proprie, ed a noi per presagio del rimanente della nostra vita in quella etá da natura date.

2. 1.28: Allora il signor Magnifico,—Questo ancor,—disse,—si verifica nella musica, nella quale è vicio grandissimo far due consonanzie perfette l'una dopo l'altra; tal che il medesimo sentimento dell'audito nostro l'aborrisce e spesso ama una seconda o settima, che in sè è dissonanzia aspera ed intollerabile; e ciò procede che quel continuare nelle perfette genera sazietà e dimostra una troppo affettata armonia; il che mescolando le imperfette si fugge, col far quasi un paragone, donde più le orecchie nostre stanno suspese e più avidamente attendono e gustano le perfette, e dilettansi talor di quella dissonanzia della seconda o settima, come di cosa sprezzata. . . . Un musico, se nel cantar pronunzia una sola voce terminata con suave accento in un groppetto duplicato, con tal facilità che paia che così gli venga fatto a caso con quel punto solo fa conoscere che sa molto più di quello che fa.

3. 2.13: Bella musica,—rispose messer Federico,—parmi il cantar bene a libro sicuramente e con bella maniera; ma ancor molto più il cantare alla viola perchè tutta la dolcezza consiste quasi in un solo, e con molto maggior attenzion si nota ed intende il bel modo e l'aria non essendo occupate le orecchie in più che in una sol voce, e meglio ancor vi si discerne ogni piccolo errore; il che non accade cantando in compagnia perchè l'uno aiuta l'altro. Ma sopra tutto parmi gratissimo il cantare alla viola per recitare; il che tanto di venustà ed efficacia aggiunge alle parole, che è gran maraviglia. Sono ancor armoniosi tutti gli instrumenti da tasti, perchè hanno le consonanzie molto perfette e con facilità vi si possono far molte cose che empiono l'animo di musicale dolcezza. E non meno diletta la musica delle quattro viole da arco, la quale è soavissima ed artificiosa. Dà ornamento e grazia assai la voce umana a tutti questi instrumenti, de' quali voglio che al nostro cortegian basti aver notizia; e quanto più però in essi sarà eccellente, tanto sarà meglio, senza impacciarsi molto di quelli che Minerva refiutò ed Alcibiade, perchè pare che abbiano del schifo.

4. 1.37: Vedete la musica, le armonie della quale or son gravi e tarde, or velocissime e di novi modi e vie; nientedimeno tutte dilettano, ma per diverse cause, come si comprende nella maniera del cantare di Bidon, la qual è tanto artificiosa, pronta, veemente, concitata e de così varie melodie, che i spirti di chi ode tutti si commoveno e s'infiammano e cosí sospesi par che si levino insino al cielo. Nè men commove nel suo cantar il nostro Marchetto Cara, ma con più molle armonia; ché per

una via placida e piena di flebile dolcezza intenerisce e penetra le anime, impri-
mendo in esse soavemente una dilettevole passione.

5. 2.35: E cantandosi pur in presenzia della signora Duchessa un mottetto, non
piacque mai né fu estimato per bono, fin che non si seppe che quella era composi-
zion di Josquin de Pris.

[Italian text: *Il libro del Cortegiano,* ed. Bruno Maier, 2d ed. (Turin, 1964).]

POSTSCRIPT

Much has been written on Castiglione; mine was not the first article to deal with
music in the *Cortigiano* and will surely not be the last. Some details in my study are
clarified in recent work by other scholars. Here are a few suggestions for further
reading:

On Gafori's acquisition of humanist lore see Claude V. Palisca, *Humanism in
Italian Renaissance Musical Thought* (New Haven, 1985), chapter 9;

For a view differing from that of Pirrotta on humanist attitudes toward polyphony see Reinhard Strohm, *The Rise of European Music, 1380–1500* (Cambridge,
1993), 547–50;

On Tinctoris in Naples see Ronald Woodley, "Johannes Tinctoris: A Review of
the Documentary Biographical Evidence," *JAMS* 34 (1981): 217–48; see also the
same author's "Tinctoris's Italian Translation of the Golden Fleece Statutes: A
Text and a (Possible) Context," *EMH* 8 (1988): 173–244;

For information on the *viola* at the beginning of the sixteenth century see Ian
Woodfield, *The Early History of the Viol* (Cambridge, 1984);

On the *studiolo* of Federico da Montefeltro in Urbino (n. 41) see my "Music as
Visual Language," in *Meaning in the Visual Arts: Views from the Outside. A Cen-
tennial Commemoration of Erwin Panofsky (1882–1968),* ed. Irving Lavin
(Princeton, 1995), 265–84, and the references cited there. A new study by Nico-
letta Guidobaldi, *La musica di Federico. Immagini e suoni alla corte di Urbino*
(Florence, 1995), takes up the subject in detail.

NOTES

1. The *Deipnosophists* of Athenaeus, although it could hardly be described as a model for
Castiglione, does give a good deal of space to accounts of musical performance, Greek and
Roman. For a view of the *Cortegiano* as a symposium (the category to which Athenaeus'
work belongs), see Wayne A. Rebhorn, *Courtly Performances: Masking and Festivity in
Castiglione's "Book of the Courtier"* (Detroit, 1978), chapter 5.

2. On Doni's work, see chapter 12 and the literature cited there. For Milán's work, see n.
40.

3. The remarks on music in Cortese's *De Cardinalatu* (1510) are discussed in Nino Pirrotta, "Music and Cultural Tendencies in Fifteenth-Century Italy," *JAMS* 19 (1966): 142–
61.

4. This rejoinder is given to Ottaviano Fregoso in the second redaction of the *Cortegiano,* Castiglione having not yet settled the roles his interlocutors were to play. See *La seconda redazione del "Cortegiano" di Baldassare Castiglione,* ed. Ghino Ghinassi (Florence, 1968), 64.

5. See *Franchini Gafuri Theorica Musicae* [Milan, 1492], facsimile, ed. Gaetano Cesari (Rome, 1934). The first chapter of this treatise, "De effectibus et comendatione musice," was, in the first edition of 1480, comparatively short (it is given in Cesari's volume, 41–43). By 1492 Gafori had learned so much about the subject that he could rewrite this chapter, now called "De Musicis et effectibus atque comendatione musice discipline," at more than five times its original length and with a vastly increased number of references. Gafori was so eager to gain knowledge of classical sources on music that he commissioned translations of Ptolemy and other Greek authors. See F. Alberto Gallo, "Le traduzioni dal greco per Franchino Gaffurio," *Acta musicologica* 35 (1963): 172–74. It is conceivable that Castiglione could have known Gafori in Milan. However, Gafori's writings seem not to be a direct source for what Castiglione has to say about music.

6. Giorgio Valla, *De Musica libri V,* in *De expetendis et fugiendis rebus opus* (Venice, 1501). Valla was also an active translator of Greek treatises on music. For another, earlier example of humanistic literature in which the *laus musicae* figures, see Conrad H. Rawski, "Petrarch's Dialogue on Music," *Speculum* 46 (1971): 302–17.

7. Apart from the general safety of the assumption that every educated sixteenth-century man read Quintilian, one might cite Castiglione's expressed desire that his son be taught Greek before Latin since the latter was closer to the vernacular and would be learned in the normal course of an educated man's life; see Julia Cartwright, *The Perfect Courtier: Baldassare Castiglione,* 2 vols. (London, 1927; first pubd. 1908), 2:171; and compare Quintilian, *Institutio oratoria,* trans. H. E. Butler, 4 vols. (London, 1921), 1.1.12: "A sermone Graeco puerum incipere malo, quia Latinum, qui pluribus in usu est, vel nobis nolentibus perbibit."

8. Quintilian, *Institutio oratoria,* 1.10.9–34.

9. For an English translation of the passage in question, see Oliver Strunk, *Source Readings in Music History* (New York, 1950), 67–68. I am grateful to John Wendland for calling this passage to my attention.

10. See *Varia Philippi Beroaldi opuscula* (Basel, 1513), fols. 12v–14v. The "Oratio habita in enarrationem Quaestionum Tusculanarum et Horatii flacii continens laudem musices" was first published in 1491. Castiglione may have studied briefly with Beroaldo; see C. Martinati, *Notizie storico-biografiche intorno al Conte Baldassare Castiglione con documenti inediti* (Florence, 1890), 9.

11. Some connection between the court of Urbino and the mainstream of Italian humanist educators is provided by the fact that Federico da Montefeltro had studied as a boy with Vittorino da Feltre at Mantua; see William H. Woodward, *Vittorino da Feltre and Other Humanist Educators* (Cambridge, 1897; reprint, New York, 1963), 30. What kind of instruction in the humanist approach to music Castiglione received is unknown to me.

12. For the text, accompanied by an English translation, of Aeneas Silvius' treatise, see *Aeneae Silvii De liberorum educatione,* trans. J. S. Nelson, Catholic University Studies in Medieval and Renaissance Latin Language and Literature, 12 (Washington, D.C., 1940).

13. See Woodward, *Vittorino da Feltre,* 93–118, esp. 107, 108, 117.

14. Franchinus Gaffurius, *Practica musicae,* trans. Clement A. Miller (American Institute of Musicology, 1968), 125–26.

15. *Il Cortegiano del Conte Baldesar Castiglione,* ed. Vittorio Cian, 3d ed. (Florence, 1929), 67n.

16. *Cortegiano,* 1:28. This passage is not in the second redaction of the *Cortegiano;* it might have been prompted by Castiglione's hearing of expert singing, such as that of the Roman singer Bidon, whom he praises in another passage of the final version (see below and n. 52), at some point after 1520. *Groppetto,* a word in this passage that has caused Castiglione's translators some trouble, probably refers to a short trill; see the discussion in Walter H. Kemp, "Some Notes on Music in Castiglione's *Il Libro del Cortegiano,*" in *Cultural Aspects of the Italian Renaissance: Essays in Honour of Paul Oskar Kristeller,* ed. Cecil H. Clough (New York, 1976), 355.

17. English translations of this word range from the literal but most unsatisfactory "disgracing" of Hoby to the sympathetic but rather free "nonchalance" of Singleton. In the *seconda redazione* of his work Castiglione says that the term had been in current usage "da noi," but its origin is unknown and it is not to be found in the first edition of the *Vocabolario della Crusca.* For a recent discussion of the term see Rebhorn, *Courtly Performances,* 33–39.

18. For the Italian text, see Giulio Caccini, *Le nuove musiche,* ed. H. Wiley Hitchcock, RRMBE, 9 (Madison, Wisc., 1970), 45n. My translation differs in detail from that given by Hitchcock.

19. Caccini's borrowing thus seems to be directly from Castiglione, not through an intermediary such as Lodovico Dolce. The closeness of the borrowing is pointed out, although only for one of the two passages in question, by Hitchcock, 44n. Jacopo Peri also made use of the term; see Nino Pirrotta, "Early Opera and Aria," in *New Looks at Italian Opera: Essays in Honor of Donald J. Grout,* ed. William W. Austin (Ithaca, N.Y., 1968), 53.

20. Cesare Cuasti, *Intorno alla vita e all' insegnamento di Vittorino da Feltre. Lettere di Sassolo Pratesi volgarizzate* (Florence, 1869), 69.

21. *Politics,* 8.5.1339b. Plato's opposition to virtuosic professionalism in music (expressed in book 3 of the *Republic,* among other places) was of course well known to humanists.

22. See Woodward, *Vittorino da Feltre,* 240.

23. Ibid., 240.

24. Nanie Bridgman, *La vie musicale au quattrocento* (Paris, 1964), 80, 105.

25. Cf. 1.47, where Count Ludovico says he is not content with the courtier as a musician unless the latter can "intendere ed esser sicuro a libro." This phrase is not to be confused with the technique of improvising counterpoint from the "sight" of a notated voice, called by fifteenth-century theorists "cantare supra librum."

26. See Cartwright, *The Perfect Courtier,* 46–47, and Cian, *Il Cortegiano,* 116n. This piece is unfortunately not to be found in Knud Jeppesen's catalogue of the frottola repertory (*La Frottola,* 3 vols. [Copenhagen, 1968–70]).

27. Claudio Sartori, *Bibliografia delle opere musicali stampate da Ottaviano Petrucci* (Florence, 1948), 13. In 1504 Guidobaldo appointed Petrucci to the town council of Fossombrone, and in succeeding years the printer held a number of civic offices (see ibid., 17, 20–21).

28. In 1513 Petrucci printed, in Fossombrone, the letter of Castiglione to Henry VII of England (*Baldhasaris Castilionei ad Henricum Angliae Regem Epistola de vita et gestis Guidobaldi Urbini Ducis*) as an act of homage to the late Duke Guidobaldo. See Augusto Vernarecci, *Ottaviano de' Petrucci da Fossombrone* (Fossombrone, 1881), 111–12.

29. Cf. the letter of Castiglione and Raphael on Roman architecture, cited among other places in John Shearman, *Mannerism* (Harmondsworth, 1967), 17. Other early uses of the term *maniera,* with meanings allied to social deportment, are given by Shearman.

30. See E. Percopo, *Le rime di Benedetto Gareth* (Naples, 1892); "Vita del facondo poeta

vulgare Seraphino Aquilano per Vincentio Calmeta composta" (1504), in Mario Menghini, ed., *Le rime di Serafino de' Ciminelli dell' Aquila* (Bologna, 1894).

31. These are men spoken of in the *Cortegiano* for their skill as musicians. All but San Secondo are introduced in the first book (5); l'Unico Aretino (Bernardo Accolti) takes some part in the dialogues. Terpandro was a friend of Castiglione (see Cian, *Cortegiano,* 532–33). San Secondo was also a personal friend, and Castiglione made efforts on his behalf at the end of the singer's career (see ibid., 205–6n). San Secondo was apparently a virtuoso performer (see 2.45): "come soglio maravigliarmi dell'audacia di color che osano cantar alla viola in presenza del nostro Jacomo Sansecondo." He is mentioned as a "cantore al liuto" in Pietro Aaron, *Lucidario in musica* (Venice, 1545), 4. fol. 31v.

32. See Pirrotta, "Music and Cultural Tendencies," 137–38, on the aversion of some humanists toward, and the ignorance of others about, the polyphonic art they associated with scholasticism.

33. Tinctoris dedicated several of his treatises to Beatrice of Aragon, daughter of Ferdinand I; see Heinrich Hüschen, "Tinctoris," *MGG,* 13:419. Further information on the relation of Tinctoris to the Neapolitan court may be found in Leeman L. Perkins and Howard Garey, eds., *The Mellon Chansonnier,* 2 vols. (New Haven, 1979), 1:17–22.

34. See Einstein, *Italian Madrigal,* 52. The letter recording this is transcribed in William F. Prizer, "Marchetto Cara and the North Italian Frottola," 2 vols. (Ph.D. diss., University of North Carolina, 1974), 2:282, document 13.

35. From literal reading of what Petrucci gives, many pieces cannot in fact be performed correctly, their musical and poetic form jibing.

36. It is an interesting sign of the changed cultural climate of the end of the sixteenth century that Caccini associates the quality of *sprezzatura* with the art of the professional singer.

37. The importance of the musically literate amateur in sixteenth-century culture is stressed by Manfred F. Bukofzer, "The Book of the Courtier on Music," *Volume of Proceedings of the Music Teachers National Association* 38 (1944): 232–35.

38. On early uses and meanings of the word *aria* see Pirrotta, "Early Opera and Aria," 57–60.

39. Kemp, "Some Notes on Music," 358, thinks the passage refers to the plucked *viola da mano,* a guitar-like instrument much used in informal music making in the early sixteenth century. A bowed *lira da braccio* would be a possible alternative.

40. See *Les quatres livres du Courtisan du Conte Baltazar de Castillon. Reduyct de langue Ytalicque en Francoys* (Paris, [1637]), fols. 41v–42r: "Chanter sur le livre semble ugne belle musicque pourveu que ce soit personne quil le sache bien faire & en bonne mode mais encores plus chanter sur le luc . . ."; cf. Hoby: "Me thinke then answered Sir Fredericke, pricksong is a faire musicke, so it be done upon the booke surely and after a good sorte. But to sing to the lute is much better." Hoby translates *cantare alla viola per recitare* as "singing to the lute with the dittie," this being one of the idiosyncrasies (to use the kind view taken by Bukofzer, "The Book of the Courtier on Music," 230, 234) of his version.

The Spanish version by Juan Boscan (1534) uses *vihuela,* which could refer, like Castiglione's *viola,* either to that instrument or to string instruments in general; see *El Cortesano, traducción de Juan Boscan* (Madrid, 1942), 123. The great Spanish vihuelist Luis Milán wrote a work called *El Cortesano* in emulation of Castiglione but closer in spirit to dialogues of Doni, Aretino, Dolce, and others; in this work music is often mentioned in passing but the musical topics treated by Castiglione are not taken up. See Luis Milán, *Libro intitulado El Cortesano* [Valencia, 1561], Coleccion de libros españoles raros ó curiosos, tomo séptimo (Madrid, 1874).

For the use of lute in place of viol in the German translation of 1565, see Robert Haas, *Aufführungspraxis der Musik* (Wildpark-Potsdam, 1931), 131.

41. Both *lira da braccio* and lute are among the instruments depicted in the *studiolo* of Federico da Montefeltro. See Edmund A. Bowles, *Musikleben im 15. Jahrhundert,* Musikgeschichte in Bildern, III, 8 (Leipzig, 1977), illus. 79. On the studiolo see F. Remington, "The Private Study of Federigo da Montefeltro," *Metropolitan Museum of Art Bulletin* 36 (1941): 3–13.

42. See *Baldassar Castiglione. Lettere inedite e rare,* ed. Guglielmo Corni (Milan, 1969), 26, 38, letters dated 24 August 1521 and 18 March 1522.

43. See Prizer, "Marchetto Cara," 28.

44. See Walter Salmen, *Musikleben im 16. Jahrhundert,* Musikgeschichte in Bildern, III, 9 (Leipzig, 1976), illus. 83. L'Unico Aretino was referred to by Paolo Cortese as a great improviser on the "lyre" (see Pirrotta, "Music and Cultural Tendencies," 161). It is said that when he sang in Rome the shops closed and large crowds gathered; see Bianca Becherini, "Il 'Cortegiano' e la musica," *La Bibliofilia* 45 (1943): 86.

45. See Vittorio Rossi, "Di un cantastorie ferrarese del secolo XVI," *Rassegna emiliana di storia, letteratura ed arte* 2 (1889–90): 435–46, and Giuseppina Fumagalli, "La fortuna dell' Orlando furioso in Italia nel secolo xvi," *Atti e memorie della deputazione ferrarese di storia patria* 20 (1912): 397.

46. Luigi Parigi, *Laurentiana: Lorenzo dei Medici cultore della musica* (Florence, 1954), 12–15. For reference to other aristocratic performers see Bridgman, *La vie musicale,* 73–76

47. Five viols were heard in consort at the Ferrarese banquet of 20 May 1529 described by Messisbugo. See Howard Mayer Brown, "A Cook's Tour of Ferrara in 1529," *RIM* 10 (1975): 234, 238 (see also Brown's remarks about the common Ferrarese practice of doubling voices with viols). For other references to viol consorts in the first half of the sixteenth century, see Haas, *Aufführungspraxis,* 133–34.

48. For Alcibiades and the "flute," see Plutarch's *Life of Alcibiades,* trans. Bernadotte Perrin (Cambridge, Mass., 1916), 2.4–5.7–9, where it is said that Alcibiades not only disliked contorting his handsome face but hated the *aulos* because he could not talk or sing while playing it. Minerva's hatred for the aulos is described, among other places, in Athenaeus, *The Deipnosophists,* 14.616 (6.321ff, in the translation of C. G. Gulick [Cambridge, Mass., 1937]); see also Rawski, "Petrarch's Dialogue," 314n.

49. Cf., however, Aristotle, *Politics,* 8.6.1340b, where it is said that older people may drop musical practice but remain judges of the art.

50. See n. 49.

51. On Ficino's view of music and the *spiritus,* see D. P. Walker, *Spiritual and Demonic Music from Ficino to Campanella* (London, 1958), 3–11.

52. Bidon [Antonio Collebaudi] was at the court of Alfonso I of Ferrara in 1506. In 1511 he visited Mantua, and by 1519 he was a member of the papal chapel, described as such in a letter from Leo X to Alfonso I. See Hermann-Walther Frey, "Regesten zur päpstlichen Kapelle unter Leo X, und zu seiner Privatkapelle," *Die Musikforschung* 8 (1955), 62; Anne-Marie Bautier-Regnier, "Jachet de Mantoue (Jacobus Collebaudi), v.1500–1559: Contribution à l'étude du problème des Jachet au xvie siècle," *Revue belge de musicologie* 6 (1952): 101–2; and William F. Prizer, "La cappella di Francesco II Gonzaga e la musica sacra a Mantova nel primo ventennio del cinquecento," *Mantova e i Gonzaga nella civiltà del Rinascimento* (Segrate, 1978), 269–70. Folengo's mention of Bidon is in *Opus Merlin Cocaii macaronicorum . . .* (1521), fol. 196. Bidon is also mentioned by Cosimo Bartoli; see Bautier-Regnier, "Jachet de Mantoue," 102. His singing was held by the Ferrarese to be syn-

onymous with a standard of excellence against which other musicians could be judged; see Lewis Lockwood, "Jean Mouton and Jean Michel: French Music and Musicians in Italy, 1505–1520," *JAMS* 32 (1979): 218–19.

53. See above and n. 34. The fullest account of Cara's career is to be seen in Prizer, "Marchetto Cara."

54. It appeared in the *Canzoni Sonetti Strambotti et Frottole Liber Tertio* of Andrea Antico. A letter from Cesare Gonzaga to Isabella d'Este, dated 2 December 1510, asked for Cara's musical setting of an unnamed *madrigaletto* and also for "quella aria del sonetto Cantai" (see Prizer, "Marchetto Cara," 2:300, document 28). Cara's setting of this text is a schematic one with much repetition; it is really a "modo di dir sonetti" and as such would suit Castiglione's category of *cantar alla viola* very well. The work was popular enough to have been intabulated for keyboard performance; see Dragan Plamenac, "The Recently Discovered Complete Copy of A. Antico's *Frottole Intabulate* (1517)," in *Aspects of Medieval and Renaissance Music: A Birthday Offering to Gustave Reese,* ed. Jan LaRue (New York, 1966), 683–92, with a facsimile and a transcription of "Cantai mentre nel core." "Cantai" appears in modern edition in Alfred Einstein, ed., *Canzoni . . . Libro Tertio,* Smith College Music Archives, 4 (Northampton, 1941).

The only other poem by Castiglione known to have been set to music during his lifetime is "Queste lacrime mie questi suspiri," a text written for the 1506 carnival at Urbino. The piece, by Bartolomeo Tromboncino, appears in book 11 of Petrucci's *Frottole* (1514). If this setting was written for the 1506 festivities Castiglione may have had some personal contact with Tromboncino; but he does not mention the latter in the *Cortegiano.*

55. On Agricola, see Allan W. Atlas, "Alexander Agricola and Ferrante I of Naples," *JAMS* 30 (1977): 313–19, and the articles by Martin Picker and Edward R. Lerner cited there (313n).

56. Bidon and Cara were together in Mantua in 1511, and Bidon was allowed to prolong his visit, partly because the Ferrarese chapel had been temporarily disbanded; see Bautier-Regnier, "Jachet de Mantoue," 101. Castiglione could possibly have heard both of them, or heard about this visit, at this time. Bidon appears to have stayed about four months in Mantua; see Prizer, "La cappella di Francesco II," 269–70.

57. See Cian, *Cortegiano,* 134, 506.

58. On the *basse danse* see Frederick Crane, *Materials for the Study of the Fifteenth Century Basse Danse* (Brooklyn, 1968); cf. Daniel Heartz, "The Basse Danse, Its Evolution circa 1450–1500," *Annales musicologiques* 6 (1958–63): 287–340. In the second redaction of the *Cortegiano* the ladies performed two *basses danses.*

59. See Cian, *Cortegiano,* 134; Brown, "Cook's Tour," 227n (where the French translator's version of this dance, *rovergoise,* is given).

60. *Seconda redazione,* 92.

61. In the second redaction the poet was Pontano rather than Sannazaro.

62. It is not cited among the sixteenth-century anecdotes about Josquin in Helmut Osthoff, *Josquin des Prez* (Tutzing, 1962).

63. *Cortegiano,* 197.

64. A madrigal text of similar nature is "Quando col dolce suono / s'accordon le dolcissime parole" (speaking of the Florentine-Venetian musician Polissena Pecorina), set by Jacques Arcadelt ca. 1530 and printed in his *Primo libro* (1538? earliest surviving edition Venice, 1539). See *Jacobi Arcadelt. Opera Omnia,* ed. Albert Seay (American Institute of Musicology, 1970), 2.99.

Cosimo Bartoli on Music

To STUDENTS of sixteenth-century music the Florentine man of letters Cosimo Bartoli (1503–72) is known chiefly for two statements made in the third dialogue of his *Ragionamenti Accademici.* One is a comparison of sculptors and musicians, with Donatello and Ockeghem seen as precursors of Michelangelo and Josquin.[1] The other is an encomium of Verdelot, called the greatest composer after Josquin, to which is added the same of Arcadelt who "faithfully trod in the footsteps of Verdelot."[2] A number of musicologists have noticed that Bartoli had quite a lot more than this to say about music, and have cited other remarks from his work;[3] but no one has to my knowledge dealt with the whole of the musical section of the *Ragionamenti,* and only Bartoli's recent and very excellent biographer Judith Bryce has spoken of the subject in the context of its author's career and personality.[4]

By his own account Bartoli was a great lover of music, though to judge *ex silentio* he was neither composer nor particularly skilled as performer.[5] Before we review the contents of his *ragionamento* on music we should have formed an opinion about the extent of his knowledge of the field, and also a sense of how impartial a witness he might be said to be.

Cosimo Bartoli was born into a well-established Florentine family active as wool merchants in the Arte della Lana. He seems to have been destined from an early age for an ecclesiastical career (it was perhaps the greatest disappointment in his life that he never became a bishop), and received education adequate for this calling but not more than that; he never took a university degree. Along with his father and brother he was an early and lifelong supporter of the Medici; as a young man he seems to have been fairly close to Alessandro and Ippolito, and not long after their departures from Florence in 1527 Bartoli too went to Rome, where he frequented the court of Clement VII, newly reconstituted after the pope's return to his sadly ravaged city.[6] Some time soon after the establishment of the Medici dukedom Bartoli returned to Florence; he received benefices providing him some income, and in April 1540 he was named provost of San Giovanni, a short time after Corteccia's appointment as *maestro* at the Baptistry and Duomo.[7]

It seems that Bartoli left Florence as a young man only to follow the Medici or, later, at their behest; he spent the years 1562–72 as a Florentine resident in Venice, an appointment from Cosimo I and his son Francesco, but was homesick the entire time, always eager to be allowed to return (he managed at last to be relieved of his Venetian duties but died shortly after arriving in Florence). Not only were his family and his closest friends in Florence, his intellectual and cultural interests were almost entirely Florentine. He is thus a dedicated if sometimes partial observer of the progress of literature and the arts, especially music, in Florence; but less interested and far less informative about their state elsewhere. This is particularly disappointing in the discourse on music, in which hardly a word is said about Venetian composers and performers, though Bartoli, professedly so interested in music, must have watched along with all of Venice the situation at San Marco after the death in 1562 of Adrian Willaert. The *Ragionamenti* were doubtless written before Bartoli's departure from Florence in that year; but his letters from Venice to his ducal employers mention artists (including Palladio, referred to as "amico mio" in 1568) far more often than they do musicians, and there are no famous names among the latter.[8]

An early member of the Accademia Fiorentina, Bartoli took an active role in the literary activities of that group. During the early and mid-1540s he gave the lectures on Dante which form the core of the *Ragionamenti Accademici;* at this time he wrote at least one comedy, doubtless similar in style to those of friends and fellow academicians such as Giovanni Battista Gelli and Francesco d'Ambra.[9] Everyone wrote occasional verse, and Bartoli can have been no exception, though only one securely attributed poem survives, a "Canzone da cantarsi nel Triomfo" placed at the end of the third *Ragionamento.*

Bartoli was a "modern" and a Tuscan in his literary views, championing not only the *tre corone* of the fourteenth century but fifteenth- and sixteenth-century writers as well, and insisting in pedantic detail on correct Florentine word usage, spelling, and pronunciation.[10] As an interlocutor in dialogues written by his friends Gelli and Carlo Lenzoni he is given expression of views which he doubtless did hold and which are nothing very out of the ordinary for the time.[11] His real contribution to the field of letters lay in editing and translation, especially of the work of two revered fifteenth-century Florentines, Marsilio Ficino and Leonbattista Alberti. Bartoli's edition (1544) of the Italian version of Ficino's commentary on the *Symposium* made an important text available in a period of renewed interest in quattrocento Neoplatonism. His translation of the *De re aedificatoria* (1550) and of Alberti's minor writings is perhaps his most important achievement in this field.[12] It too was a work of Florentine piety, although Bartoli was seriously interested in architecture.

The other literary and scientific works of Bartoli are not of special relevance here; it might simply be noted that his most successful and widely circulated book, *Del Modo di Misurare le distantie . . . e tutte le altre cose terrene, che possono occorrere agli huomini* (1564), a volume that represents him in a surprising number of libraries, is not an original work but a compilation drawn from a number of sources but mainly the *Protomathesis* of Oronce Fine.[13] Bartoli's output does not, of course, approach that of men whose livelihood depended on their writing, the cinquecento *poligrafi* such as his contemporary and sometime competitor (as translator) Lodovico Domenichi. He nonetheless kept active as a writer, and when he left Florence for Venice in 1562 he seems to have taken with him manuscripts that he entrusted to the printer Francesco de' Franceschi; the latter brought out several books by Bartoli up to and even after his death.[14]

Among these works is the volume called *Ragionamenti Accademici . . . sopra alcuni luoghi difficili di Dante* (1567). The five dialogues in this book are indeed concerned with ruminations, wandering hither and yon, on Dante texts. The book's subtitle, "Con alcune inventioni & significati," refers to a bonus for the reader; four of the dialogues are introduced by means of conversation on other subjects, and *ragionamenti* one and two conclude with similar digressions. Taken together these form a *cornice* or framework for the dialogue, following a tradition going back at least as far as the *Decameron.*

Since the lectures on Dante had actually been given, and one of them indeed printed, in the 1540s, the bulk of the book was not new. Events mentioned in the conversational sections are of varying dates, some earlier than the lectures, others as late as the mid-1550s. As in most dialogues of this kind Bartoli was unconcerned about exact temporal placement, though glaring internal inconsistencies seem to be avoided. The approximate dating of the conversation on music will concern us later.

The opening conversation, made in the course of a walk from the Via Larga to the edge of the city on the Via San Gallo, deals with architecture and sculpture.[15] In speaking of the latter Bartoli shows himself a true "modern," praising the work of a young Florentine sculptor named Francesco Camilliani, and pointing to fragmentary antique torsos that, far from being regarded with adoring respect, were waiting to be fitted with new heads and arms to make them serviceable. In the later discussion rounding off the first dialogue one of Bartoli's interlocutors remarks of a statue by Camilliani that had it been found buried, and unearthed as a classical work, it would have received extravagant praise.[16] From here Bartoli proceeds to extol present-day sculptors: Ammanati, Bandinelli, Cellini, and, above all, Michelangelo, who is clearly seen to surpass the ancients in every way.[17]

The walk to the Via San Gallo had a purpose; Bartoli wanted to show his friends a small palace which he had himself designed for Giovanni Battista Ricasoli, at this time (ca. 1538–9) Bishop of Cortona. This is a real building; it had fallen into an unrecognizable state of disrepair but has recently been restored, using Bartoli's detailed description as a guide; it is now in fact called the Palazzo Ricasoli Residence.[18] This work appears to have begun and ended Bartoli's career as an architect; still, there it is, evidence of the author's admiration for Michelangelo and his more than superficial acquaintance with at least one of the arts.

In his discussion of sculpture Bartoli says nothing about technique but is concerned with invention, or sculptural iconography; and he certainly shared the Albertian view of architecture as a profession of ideas, leaving execution up to workmen.[19] This preference for *invenzione* is also characteristic of his discussion of painting, contained in the second, third, and fourth dialogues. If Michelangelo was his ideal in architecture and sculpture, Vasari, a lifelong friend, was his most admired painter. This might seem a relaxing of standards or inconsistency of taste; but it should be remembered that Vasari was generally much admired at the time, that he was more approachable than the austere Michelangelo, that he remained in Medici service throughout his life whereas Michelangelo scorned the new Medici principate, and that he not only painted but like a good academician wrote a history of the subject. Bartoli was among the group of Vasari's friends who got the first edition of the *Vite* to the press and helped to proofread it; and he remained not only a loyal but in his view an intimate friend. In the dedication to Vasari of his translation of Alberti's *De Pictura* (1568), Bartoli refers to the painter as "Messer Giorgio mio," almost reminding us of E. F. Benson's Lucia and her beloved "Giorgino."

Figure 1. Vasari, *Cosimo I with his Artists and Engineers;*
Florence, Palazzo Vecchio, Sala di Cosimo I.

This dedication speaks of Vasari's decoration, "fatta con tanta arte e con sì mirabil giudizio," of the Palazzo della Signoria, commissioned in 1555 by Cosimo I. A group of extant letters from Bartoli to Vasari tells us that it was Bartoli who suggested many of the ideas—*invenzioni*—for the paintings in the Quartiere degli Elementi and the Quartiere di Leone X. Figure 1 shows one painting of Vasari's from the Quartiere di Leone X: a *tondo* showing Cosimo I surrounded by architects, sculptors, and engineers in his service, a theme suggested by Bartoli. The figures have been identified, not with complete unanimity, by several scholars;[20] notably absent is the greatest of all the Florentines, Michelangelo, who even in an allegory could not be depicted as in the service of Duke Cosimo.

The conversations on painting deal with what were presumably actual paintings, looked at and commented upon in detail by the interlocutors, among whom Bartoli is not present.[21] Aside from one or two remarks about color or gesture all the talk is of iconographic intent, of *invenzione,* the "soul" of painting extolled as superior to its bodily execution. In the first of these art-appreciation talks a painting said to have been commissioned—hence ideated—by Bartoli, and to be in a house on the Via del Cocomero, is talked about. The painting, if there really was one, is not known to survive, but this is not pure fiction; a comparison of figure 2 with the very detailed iconographic discussion at the opening of the *Ragionamento secondo,* given in the appendix, will show that Bartoli's plan was carried out in at least a graphic medium.[22]

Entering a house to view a picture commissioned by Bartoli (no. 1 in the appendix), the interlocutors first praise the picture for its size (showing the generosity of the patron), its disposition of materials, its coloring; but above all, the Cavaliere reminds the others, they should note the *invenzione* on which the unnamed painter has acted (no. 2). Then a detailed, very detailed, account of the picture's iconographic program is entered upon, beginning (no. 3) with the reclining nude male at bottom center, identified as the river Arno with all the requisite appurtenances belonging to the Florentine river-god (the Arno as thus represented was the official emblem of the Florentine Academy, something that is not mentioned here). Identification of the female figures is next, with Flora (no. 4) on the left, Minerva on the right; above them are figures of Fortuna and Virtù (left and right, respectively), with Immortality in the center, triumphing over Time (nos. 5, 6). Finally, a résumé of the whole picture is given, along with added information about the various crowns, mitres, and scepters of secular and ecclesiastical power accumulated by deserving citizens (the Medici are not mentioned by name; this would be out of character in the context of the picture, I suppose) (no. 7).

There is never any discussion of the middle of the picture; this suggests that it may have been a title frame all along, perhaps a colored drawing differing in a few details from the woodcut made for Bartoli's translation of Alberti. But there is no reason to doubt Bartoli's authorship of the *invenzione;* thus his credentials as a connoisseur of artistic iconography seem established as well.

And what of music, the subject of ten pages of discussion at the beginning of the third *Ragionamento?* Within this passage Bartoli is said to have gone off with some musicians, prompting his friend Pierfrancesco Giambullari's comment that for some time Bartoli had been noticeably, perhaps excessively, concerned with music. This is not much by way of credentials for him as a critic of music. More to the point is mention, a little later, that Bartoli has given some concerts at his house, featuring musicians in the ducal employ playing (on the viols) music by Gombert.[23] Outside the framework of the *Ragionamenti* but nonetheless relevant in a consideration of Bartoli's musical sensibilities is a passage from Lenzoni's

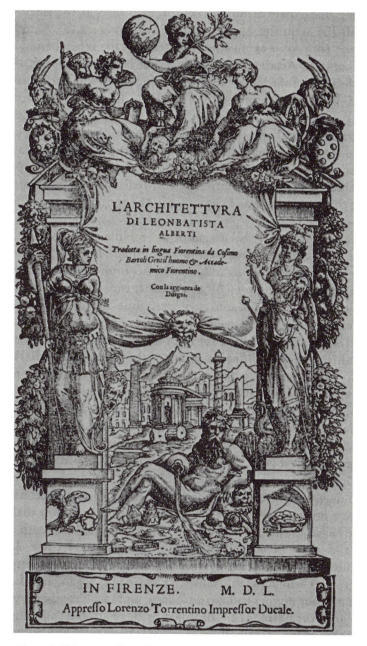

Figure 2. Title page of Bartoli's translation of Alberti's *De Architectura*.
Courtesy of the Rare Books Department, Perkins Library,
Duke University.

dialogue on the *lingua fiorentina,* which Bartoli published after the death of the author, a close friend, and in which he is an interlocutor. In the introduction to the second *ragionamento* of this work the company is at dinner, after which there is music: "The singing began, and the lute playing of our divine Antonio da Lucca, and of il Trombone, with a sweet and true harmony . . . Beguiled by this harmony, all went ever so lightly to sleep, if sleep it can be called, this sweetly narcotic trance in which one hears and understands everything that takes place."[24] Here we have not a picture of a somnolent, overfed, and underattentive audience, but rather an honest attempt to describe the hypnotic power of music, for once one not couched in pretentious Neoplatonic language.

Then there is Bartoli's job as provost of San Giovanni. He lived across the street from the Baptistry and was closely involved with its daily routine, including supervision of the school for clerics. He was apparently involved with appointments, including that of the organist Giovanpiero Manenti, whom he describes to Francesco de' Medici in a letter of 1569 as "mio creato."[25]

Finally, there is the nature of the Bartoli's commentary on music. It begins with an academic discourse on the discipline but soon gets to discussion of *musica prattica,* first of composers and then, at greater length, of performers. There is no question of academicism here, not even of the old saw about the *musicus* who understands versus the performer who merely sings or plays, something one might have expected from Bartoli's attitude towards the visual arts. He speaks here in more direct fashion, as a true if heavily pro-Florentine amateur of the art of music, and his remarks are worth considering in some detail.

The interlocutors in this dialogue were fellow academicians and friends of Bartoli; from what is said about them their comments on music could be directly attributable to them in so far as speakers in this kind of literary dialogue can ever be thought to be quoted by the author rather than serving as mouthpieces. Giambullari as a canon at San Giovanni was certainly in contact with Florentine musical circles, even if not himself an active musician; Piero da Ricasoli, the brother of Bartoli's architectural patron, is said to have observed musical activities in Venice and Rome;[26] and Lorenzo Antinori, who while in Florence took part in the performance (with music by Corteccia) of Francesco d'Ambra's *Il furto,* is known to have been as he says north of the Alps, in France and perhaps in imperial circles—places Bartoli himself apparently never went—on family business.[27]

As for the date of this discussion, a subject on which musicological commentators have differed a good deal, the best thing one can say is that it was probably written in the mid-1550s, albeit in a retrospective vein; the reference to Corteccia as having been *maestro* at San Giovanni for fifteen years suggests 1555 as a good terminus.[28] Mention of Alessandro Striggio as a distinguished virtuoso on the viol, also known for the excellence of his compositions, suggests that Bartoli kept his account to some extent up to date; Striggio could hardly have acquired this reputation or at any rate made Bartoli aware of it before his arrival in Florence in 1559.[29] It must be said, on the other hand, that Bartoli mixes people of two if not three separate generations quite casually, only occasionally mentioning that someone is "now old"; and at least one of his musical anecdotes has been plausibly dated as having taken place in 1530.[30] His fervent praise of Verdelot is surely the result of

personal acquaintance of even earlier date, since there is nothing to suggest that
Verdelot was in Florence, or perhaps even alive, after about 1530.[31] The discussion
of music is in other words a kind of mosaic depicting aspects of Italian musical culture during the three and a half decades from 1525 to 1560.

Given Bartoli's interest in the subject one need not perhaps look for antecedents
to his chatty discussion of music. Yet originality of thought and imaginative freedom are hardly his most salient characteristics;[32] he may have drawn courage to
proceed if not direct inspiration from seeing similar treatments of music already
in print. For the discussion of musical ethos, cosmic harmony, and the proper use
of music in human life, the general topics with which the conversation on music
begins, there was plenty of precedent not only in Ficino, whom Bartoli certainly
read, but in the work of humanistic encyclopedists such as Giorgio Valla, or of musical theorists who in humanistic vein cultivated the *laus musicae* tradition.[33] Bartoli seems to have been only mildly interested in this side of the subject; his classical allusions, apart from quite general use of Apollonian and Orphic themes, are
very few in number. And they are at first negative ones, advising against the study
of music. Of course, these are soon challenged as a defense of music begins. This
form of argument, common to the dialogue in general,[34] is found with regard to music in a work Bartoli must have known, the *Cortegiano*. Castiglione was read by
members of Bartoli's circle, was even awarded by one of them the faint praise of
being one of the best writers of Italian prose among "huomini non toscani."[35] Fur-
thermore, Castiglione was a "modern" whose discussion of the music of his own
time is couched in highly favorable terms, not as a falling-off from antique
standards.

Among other contemporary works dealing with music in a conversational
framework there is Antonfrancesco Doni's *Dialogo della musica* of 1544.[36] Bartoli
may not altogether have approved of Doni—few people did—but he must have
known him; Doni published one of the Dante lectures, later to be incorporated into
the *Ragionamenti Accademici,* in 1547.[37] Then there is the Neapolitan Luigi Den-
tici's *Duo dialoghi della musica* (Naples, 1552), a work in which a few comments
on contemporary music and musicians are interspersed in tracts on *musica theorica* and *practica.*[38] If Bartoli saw this rather feeble effort he may indeed have been
encouraged to write his own version of the subject to show what a cultivated Florentine could do with it.

What he did do with it is the subject of the remainder of this paper. The whole
of the *ragionamento* on music is given here, divided into sections each of which is
followed by brief commentary.[39]

LO ANTINORO / O VERO RAGIONAMENTO / TERZO. / LORENZO ANTINORI PIERO DARICA[-] / SOLI M. PIERFRANCESCO / GIAMBULLARI.

Molto vi vegho turbato Messer Piero mio. *P.* Non vi maravigliate che io stia
cosi sospeso, percio che questo inserviene a tutti coloro, che havendo lo
animo indiritto ò applicato a voler fare alcuna cosa, sono da qualche acci-
dente impediti, di maniera, che non la possono mettere ad effetto. *L.* Io non

vorrei parervi prosontuoso in ricercare la cagione che cosi hoggi vi perturba; dall'altra parte se io sapessi o potessi alleggierirvi il dispiacere, nel quale io vi vegho, desidererei grandemente di farlo. *P.* Dispiacere non certo, ma si bene sospensione di animo; come quello che essondomi hoggi presupposto di volere il trattenimento di M. Cosimo Bartoli, menandolo in qualche giardino a spasso, non lo havendo trovato in casa non lo hò potuto havere. *L.* Ecco forse di quà chi cene sapra dare nuove. *P.* Ben ne venga il nostro M. Piero Francesco, io mi persuado che ancor voi andiate cercando di quel che cercavamo noi. *G.* Io non sò certo lo animo vostro, ma io so bene che venivo io qua per trovare M. Cosimo, per menarlo hogi che e si bel giorno a spasso. *P.* Non vi dissi io che tutti cercavamo una medesima cosa. *G.* Dunque voi siete risoluti che egli non è in casa. *P.* Non secondo che ne ha detto il Garzone, essendo egli uscito fuori con certi Musici. *G.* Io vi sò dire che da un tempo in quà egli si è dato tanto a questa sua Musica, che è pur un poco troppo. *P.* O perche? *G.* Perche la Musica fa troppo gli huomini effeminati & molli. *P.* Ah M. Pier Francesco non biasimate tanto arditamente la Musica, che da tanti & si grandi huomini è stata non solamente tenuta come cosa cara, ma quasi come divina honorata, & grandemente reverita. *L.* Troppo ha ragione M. Pier Francesco, con cio sia che gli huomini doverrebbono andar dietro a quelle cose che gli potessino far conoscere, per constanti & forti; & non per molli, ò effeminati, & a questo proposito mi ricordo di haver letto che Antistene biasimava Ismeno eccellentissimo Musico, riprendendolo, & allegandogli che la Musica non era altro, che una esca da accendere il fuoco de piaceri; Oltre a che voi sapete che Philippo disse al figluolo, come non ti vergogni a sapere sonare tanto bene? *P.* Adagio M. Lorenzo voi che biasimate tanto la Musica giudicate voi che Apollo che fu si eccellente Musico, & Orfeo che se correr le selve & stare i fiumi, & tanti altri huomini eccellenti in questo genere, siano pero da essere biasimati? *L.* A questo lascero io rispondere a M. Piero Francesco. *G.* Non si possono certo biasimare; perche l'uno & l'altro di loro, insegnarono con quel loro sonare & cantare, a quel Secolo rozo, aspro, & duro, come havesse a diventare piacevole, civile, & benigno. Onde gli Antichi finsono che Orfeo fermasse le piu selvaggie fiere, cioè facesse deporre a gli huomini selvaggi & fieri; la fierezza, & la salvatichezza loro: faccendoli divenire mansueti, & humili. Et con la medesima ragione fingevano che egli fermasse i fiumi; alludendo che egli fermava lo strabocchevole corso delli animi che senza regola alcuna, correvano precipitosamente dietro alle loro voglie, & a loro appetiti; & in questa medesima maniera dicono che egli moveva le piante, cio è rimoveva le ostinationi delle indurate menti degli huomini, & le riduceva ad udire la sua Armonia. *P.* A questo modo adunque la Musica era lodevole in costoro? *G.* Lodevole certo per le ragioni allegate. *L.* Come adunque può essere una medesima cosa lodevole & biasimevole? *G.* Tutte le cose che dilettano i sensi nostri, si come pare che facciaia Musica, usate non modestamente nuocono; ma moderatamente giovano, non solo a chi le esercita, ma a chi le ascolta ancora. *L.* Dunque lo error nasce dalla

Antistene
Ismeno. Musica
esca de piaceri.
Filippo riprese il
figluolo de la
musica. Apollo.
Orfeo.

Orfeo che
significhi in
fermar le fiere
& i fiumi.

Orfeo fermare
le piante che
significhi.
Musica è
lodevole.

ignorantia degli huomini, nel non sapere usare le cose. *G.* Certo che chi havesse tanta fortezza di animo, che attendendo alla Musica, non si lasciasse   Musica come si
vincere dalla non so come me la dire snervata dolceza talmente che fussi si-   debbe usare.
curo di non cadere in quella sorte di vitio, che fa come poco di sopra dicemmo gli huomini effeminati; ma se ne servisse solamente per ricreatione
dello animo, con quella modestia, & con quella creanza, che si aspetta, indu-
bitatamente a nobili & a ben nati, credo anzi tengo per certo che non solo sia
lodevole, ma utile: & ardirò di dire ancora necessaria. Percioche oltre a che
ella giova grandemente a ricreare gli animi nostri, occupati per lo piu da una
infinita moltitudine di dispiaceri, che continovamente come frutte di questo
giardino del mondo, pascendoci piu di tosco & di assentio, che di mele o di
ambrosia, ci afflighano & ci tormentano: elle raffrena i giovani da una moltitudine di inconvenienti tanto grande, che è difficile ad annoverarla: & fa che   Musica come
quegli che sono piu oltre di età, considerando diligentemente le molto belle   giovi.
proporzioni & dispensationi de numeri che sono in lei; imparano a dispen-
sare non solo il tempo, ma tutte le operazioni loro, & le sustanzie ancora con
tale proporzione, che ne habbia a risultare il concento & la armonia delle azzioni loro, buono & perfetto: non altrimenti che dalle proportioni, & dispensationi delle misure della Musica ne risulta il concento et la Armonia della
voci, buono & perfetto. Si che molte sono le cose che bene usate sono lode-   Molte cose ben
voli, & male usate, biasimevoli. *P.* A questo modo non la Musica, ma il modo   usate son
dello usarla è quello che voi biasimate. *G.* Troppo havete ragione, che io non   lodevoli, & male
  usate sono
so come io me la possa biasimare, sapendo chiaro, che mediante lei si man-   biasimevoli.
tiene & regge questa Machina del Mondo percioche se non fusse la Armonia
de sette pianetti, & delle altre Sfere de Cieli mediante la quale si mantiene
questo ordine del Mondo, sappiamo certo che questa machina dello universo   La musica regge
si risolverebbe in mente & si rovinerebbe. [fols. 34v–35v].   il mondo.

Bartoli's opening remarks on music are a curious mix of well-worn topics and unusual references. That music should be avoided because certain kinds of it make
men *effeminati* and *molli* is a common Platonic theme echoed by many Renaissance writers;[40] that Apollo was the perfect prototype of a musician is equally so
(*Rep.* 399e). Linkage of Apollo with Orpheus goes back to Pindar (*Pyth.* 4.176)
and is so frequent that it needs no special comment. Some of what Bartoli says
about the civilizing and soothing effects of the art of Orpheus is reminiscent of Castiglione's treatment of the subject and may come from sources common to the two
men.[41] As for the Orphic power to make "correr le selve & stare i fiumi," one might
compare this image with that of Shakespeare:

> Orpheus with his lute made trees
>   And the mountain tops that freeze,
> Bow themselves when he did sing . . .
>   Everything that heard him play,
> Even the billows of the sea
>   Hung their heads, and then lay by.[42]

Less commonplace are the negative classical references to Antisthenes and Philip. The latter refers to Philip of Macedon and his son Alexander the Great; here is the anecdote as given by a Hellenistic writer: "Alexander also loved music and gave serious attention to it, until he was asked by his father if he was not ashamed to sing so well, whereupon he began to neglect singing as an art unbecoming his dignity."[43] The reproof given by the Cynic philosopher Antisthenes is cited by Plutarch: "Antisthenes rightly said, when told that Ismenias was an excellent flute player, that he was a worthless man, otherwise he would not be such a good musician."[44]

Bartoli's views on the proper use of music and on the musical character of cosmic harmony are very much in keeping with those of Ficino, expressed in a number of places including the commentary on Plato's *Symposium* which Bartoli had published in 1544.[45] As a loyal Florentine admirer of the great fifteenth-century Neoplatonist, Bartoli was in conscience bound to treat music in a Ficinian manner; but in the *Ragionamenti Accademici,* at any rate, this approach to the subject was not of prime interest to him. In the next section he gets to a topic he really wanted to talk about, composers of the present and the recent past.

L. Coloro adunque che in questa maniera (che poco di sopra havete racconta) si dilettano della Musica, sono degni di lode, tanto, quanto chi non la sa usare è degno di biasimo. *G.* Cosi certo la intendo. *P.* Ecco adunque che per questa vostra ragione, sono non solamente degni di lode coloro che della Musica in quella maniera si dilettano, ma quelli che in quella sono eccellentissimi: perche senza questi la Musica o si smarrirebbe o perderebbe della sua bonta, o si andrebbe spegnendo del tutto, & di cosi fatti huomini ne ho io conosciuti in questa nostra età pur assai che sono stati lodatissimi. *L.* Deh ditemi per vostra fede chi sono stati quegli, che voi havete conosciuti per tanto eccellenti quanto voi mi dite, & potete lasciar da parte quelli che sono stati avanti a tempi vostri, perche sarebbe un numero infinito, che io so bene che Ocghem

Ocghem musico.
Donatello scultore.
Iosquino Michelangnolo buonarroti.

fu quasi il primo che in questi tempi, ritrovasse la Musica quasi che spenta del tutto: non altrimenti che Donatello ne suoi ritrovò la Scultura; & che Iosquino discepolo di Ocghem si puo dire che quello alla Musica fusse un monstro della natura, si come è stato nella Architettura Pittura & Scultura il nostro Michelagnolo Buonarroti; perche si come Iosquino non hà però ancora havuto alcuno che lo arrivi nelle composizioni, cosi Michelagnolo ancora infratutti coloro che in queste sue arti si sono esercitati, è solo & senza compagno; Et l'uno & l'altro di loro ha aperti gli occhi a tutti coloro che di queste arti si dilettano, o si diletteranno per lo avvenire. Ne crediate che io non sappia che doppo Iosquino ci sono stati molti valenti huomini in questo eserci-

Giovan Monton musico Brumel musicho Isach musico Gio. Agricola musico Marchetto da Mantova musico.

tio, come fu un Giovan Monton, Brumel, Isac, Andrea de Silva, Giovanni Agricola, Marchetto da Mantova, & molti altri, che seguendo dietro alle pedate di Iosquino, hanno insegnato al Mondo come si hà a comporre di Musica. *P.* Poi che ei vi piace il ragionar di coloro che io hò conosciuti, & ne volete il parere mio, ancor che io non sia molto esercitato nella Musica, & non ne sappia dare cosi saldo & vero giudicio come molti altri, per haverne nondimeno io sempre preso grandissimo piacere: & per essermi ogni volta che mi se ne è porta occasione, trovato volentieri dove sono stati i piu eccellenti Musici de quali io habbia havuto notitia, ne ve racconterò quelli che a me pare che meritino di essere ricordati infra gli eccellenti. *L.* Dite per vostra fede. *P.* Io hò conosciuto Adriano in Venetia maestro di cappella in San Marco, le compositioni del quale sono & in Italia & fuori di Italia grandemente lodate, & si tiene che habbino molto del leggiadro & del gentile. In Roma per valente compositore, conobbi a tempi della felice memoria di Papa Leone, Costanzio Festa; le composizione del quale sono in non piccola riputazione; & gia sapete che qui in Firenze Verdelotto era mio amicissimo del quale io ardirei di dire, se io non havessi rispetto alla amicitia, che havevamo insieme; che ci fussino, come invero ci sono, infinite composizioni di Musica, che ancor hoggi fanno maravigliare i piu giudiziosi compositori che ci sieno. Perche elle hanno del facile, del grave, del gentile, del compassionevole, del presto, del tardo, del benigno, dello adirato, del fugato, seconda la proprieta della parole sopra delle quali egli si metteva a comporre. Et hò sentito dire a molti che si intendono di queste cose, che da Iosquino in qua non ci è stato alcuno, che meglio di lui habbia inteso il vero modo del comporre. Dietro alle pedate del quale caminando poi Archadel, si andava in quei tempi che egli stette in Firenze assai bene accomendando. *L.* Amenduoi costoro hò conosciuti ancor io, pero di loro sia detto a bastanza, ma ditemi un poco havete voi conosciuto un certo Giachetto da Mantova. *P.* Conobbilo & quanto a me la Musica sua mi diletta grandemente, & mi pare ch'ella habbia di quello andare delle composizioni di Adriano. Hor ditemi se havete conosciuti nella Magna Gombert, & Crechiglione? amenduoi maestri di Capella della Maiestà Cesarea? *L.* Voi sapete che io sono stato poco alla corte, che se bene sono stato piu mesi, nella Magna, sono stato forzato per le molte faccende a ir dietro a quelle, per espedirle & non, alla corte, pero l'uno & l'altro vidi pure non so che volte, ma non hebbi con quelli molta dimestichezza. *P.* Costoro hanno usato dipoi una altra maniera diversa dalle altre nelle loro composizioni, le quali certamente hanno molto del dilettevole, perche Gomberto ò a 4, o a 5, o a 6, o a 7, o a 8, che egli habbia composto, si come voi sapete che ci sono una infinità di Motetti, ha tenuto uno ordine, che tutte le parti continovamente cantino, con pochissime pose, anzi fugate, strette serratte, inchiodate l'una nella altra, che vi si sente dentro un certo che di grandezza, congiunta con una armonia che ti dà un diletto maraviglioso: & mi ricordo havere uditi questi Musicia di sua eccellentia sonar di viola in casa il Bartolo le cose di questo compositore, con tanto piacere & satisfazzion mia, che io non me la saprei inmaginare maggiore; & quasi simile a queste sono le cose di Crechiglione *L.* Havete voi sentite cantare o sonare le Musiche di un Christiano Olanda, il quale in Anversa è molto riputato. *P.* Poche, ma quelle poche mi sono piaciute assai. *G.* Dove lasciate voi adietro Clemens non Papa, Scobeto, & Morales, che sono tanto nominati fra i musici di hoggi. *P.* O Messer Pier Francesco voi havete ragione che tutti a tre son valenti, & in Ferrara è un certo Cipriano Rore il quale ha composto molto valentemente, & compone

Adriano villart musico.

Constanzio Festa musico.
Verdelotto musico.

Arcadelt musico.

Giachetto da Mantova.

Gombert Crechiglione.

Christian Olanda.

Clemens non Papa

Cipriano Rore.

ancora tutta via. *L.* Et de nostri qua di Firenze? voi non dite cosa alcuna? *P.* Di M. Francesco Corteccia lascierò io parlare qui a M. Pier Francesco, perche per essere Canonici in una medesima chiesa, & conversando virtuosamente del continovo insieme, ne saprà meglio parlare di me. *G.* Di lui accio che ei non paia che io lo faccia per adulazione, dirò questo solo che ci sono horamai tante delle sue composizioni, che da per loro stesse lo fanno conoscere, & oltra questo i tanti virtuosi & valenti scolari che egli ha fatti dapoi in quà che egli è maestro di Capella di sua eccellenzia che gia sono 15: anni, dimostrano quanto in questa sua professione egli sia valente; ma vi diro ben di lui una cosa che voi forse per non praticare tanto continovamente seco quanto ho fatto io, non la sapete. *L.* Dite di grazia. *G.* Sappiate che io credo certo che hoggi egli sia forse cosi gran Theorico, quanto qual si voglia altro che si eserciti in questa professione. *P.* Ditemi un poco non ci habbian noi ancora M. Mattio rampollini, le composizioni del quale vi dò mia fede che gli hanno acquistata una riputazione maravigliosa, & massimo appresso a forestieri. *G.* Certamente è che egli non si puo dire se non che egli sia valente. *L.* Io mi ricordo la ultima volta che io fui in Roma, ritrovandomi un giorno in casa di M. Bindo altoviti, dove erano assai Musici de primi che fussino in Roma in quei tempi, che è si venne a ragionare delle sue composizioni, che elle furono grandemente lodate. *P.* Ei non si può negare la sufficienzia sua, che certo, & nel comporre & nel rimettere ancora è valoroso, presto, & accorto. *L.* Habbiamoci noi altri in Firenze? *P.* Habbiamoci molti di questi giovanni che ci danno continovamente opera, ma per essere giovani non se ne puo dire per ancora altro, se non che si vede che di loro si puo sperare assai con il tempo. [fols. 35v–37]

In this section of his discourse Bartoli gives a surprisingly full treatment of composers, perhaps the most detailed such account to be seen in the work of sixteenth-century writers.[46] The list looks as if it was drawn up at some time in the 1540s, with Cipriano de Rore's stated residence in Ferrara (Rore arrived at the Estense court in 1545–6) its most up-to-date feature. Although not exhaustive, even for Florentine composers (there is, for example, no mention either of Bernardo Pisano or of Francesco Layolle), Bartoli's list is quite a thorough one for composers active in Italy in the period 1510–40, with expectedly scanty (though unexpectedly interesting) mention of *oltremontani* who did not spend time in Italian centers.

It would be simplest to go through the names of composers in the order they are mentioned. First come Johannes Ockeghem and Josquin des Prez, with Bartoli's oft-cited comparison of sculptors and musicians. Parallels between artists in different fields were frequently drawn in this period, most often perhaps between the visual arts and literature (that between Michelangelo and Dante, for which there were strong iconographic grounds, was a very common one). Thus Bartoli's friend Carlo Lenzoni said that Raphael learned from Michelangelo in the way Petrarch learned from Dante.[47] Use of musicians for such parallels is less common but does occur; at the end of the century Alessandro Guarini compares Marenzio to Petrarch, Luzzaschi to Dante.[48] Comparisons of this kind were easily made, and seldom have very much to tell us. In an earlier study I cited Bartoli's passage with the comment that "such comparisons are as nearly devoid of significance as can be," an opinion I now think a bit severe and was hence only moderately pleased to see cited in Bryce's book on Bartoli.[49] Two things about it now seem of genuine interest: the inclusion of music in a "modern," evolutionary view of art, and the choice of composers.

Bartoli saw the arts as steadily rising from the abyss of the old *maniera tedesca;* in this he was, of course, influenced by Vasari for painting, and by his fellow academicians for literature. Earlier in the *Ragionamenti*[50] he speaks of Michelangelo having "aperti gli occhi a questa età," language very similar to what he says Josquin has done for musicians. As an interlocutor in a dialogue by G. B. Gelli, Bartoli is made to say that Florentines have not only equalled but sometimes surpassed the ancients in every field of artistic endeavour.[51] And in the dedicatory letter to his translation of Alberti's *De Statua,* addressed to Bartolomeo Ammanati, Bartoli defends Alberti as having begun to work in a period when the art had been all but extinguished by the barbarian invasions. From Alberti onward progress was steadily made: "For in our century one need not be envious of the finest statues of the most highly praised ancient Roman sculptors, as our own Donatello had already shown, and as not so many years ago our divine Michel Angelo Buonaroti demonstrated."[52] In this letter Bartoli goes on to mention Bandinelli, Cellini, and Ammanati himself, just as in the *Ragionamenti* he cites musicians who are honorable successors to Josquin.

Musicologists know that an evolutionary view of composition as rising from barbarous beginnings to a state of perfection was taken by a number of theorists beginning with Johannes Tinctoris in the 1470s.[53] In the absence of any contemporary history of music corresponding to the work of Vasari, there has been little reason to think that laymen had much historical consciousness about the art. Bartoli's view thus has some importance simply because it is that of an amateur, an observer of musical culture as he was of the visual and verbal arts.

Why did Bartoli choose Ockeghem and Josquin to illustrate his idea of musical evolution? Given his strong Florentine bias one might expect him to have chosen, say, Isaac and Verdelot instead. The posthumous reputation of Josquin was so enormous that Bartoli could not but have known of it; but Ockeghem? The music of the great Franco-Flemish composer might still have been known in Bartoli's youth, but by the time he wrote the *Ragionamenti* the name of Ockeghem (d. 1497) could not have suggested much to anyone other than a historically minded theorist. In the first half of the sixteenth century, music theorists were probably not read widely outside professional musical circles (the *Practica musicae* [1496] of Franchinus Gaffurius might be an exception); but Bartoli may have picked up some acquaintance with writings on music through his friendship with Francesco Corteccia. His most likely source would appear to be the *Dodecachordon* (1547) of Glarean, published in Basel but certainly known in Italy; it is, for example, an important if unacknowledged source for the work of Gioseffo Zarlino.[54] Glarean, whose admiration for Josquin was little short of idolatrous, compared the composer to Virgil, and saw in his music the *ars perfecta* toward which earlier composers had been striving.

Among the greatest of Josquin's predecessors was, in the view of Glarean, Johannes Ockeghem.[55] Here Bartoli seems to have stepped outside his customary intellectual milieu and to have accepted the authority of a non-Florentine, indeed non-Italian expert witness.

Lorenzo Antinori, into whose mouth the comparison of Ockeghem and Josquin is placed, continues with a list of worthy successors of Josquin: Giovan Monton (= Mouton), Brumel, Isaac, Andrea de Silva, Giovanni (= Alexander) Agricola, Marchetto (Cara) da Mantova, "et molti altri." These are indeed well-known names, composers active in the period 1500–25, some but not all with Florentine associations. Bartoli's inaccuracy in two of the names betrays his casual knowledge of some of these men.[56]

Next Giambullari, a figure all respected despite his protestation of not being "molto esercitato nella Musica," continues with discussion of musicians he has known.[57] He does not begin well; surely he could have found something better to say about the *divino Adriano* (Willaert), *maestro* at San Marco and one of the most authoritative musical figures of the whole century, than that his music is *leggiadro* and *gentile*. Costanzo Festa, the extent of whose connections with Florentine musical culture may not have been known to Bartoli,[58] gets even shorter shrift. Jacquet of Mantua, a leading figure in the field of sacred polyphony in the second quarter of the century, is mentioned briefly but not unintelligently as a composer whose work has something of the *andare* of Willaert's music.[59] Before this, however, is a passage of what by Bartoli's standards is purple prose, an encomium of Verdelot. He was a close friend, says Giambullari; but all marvel at the quality of his music. It is Verdelot as madrigalist who is being praised, and the series of adjectives describing the music are all concerned with the composer's ability to match verbal *affetti* with appropriate music.[60]

This is admittedly by a partial judgement; here was a Florentine, or at least a *français toscanisant,* whom one could point to with pride. Yet I think it has real substance: the madrigal as cultivated by Verdelot and then Arcadelt was found, by the men of letters who were its first patrons and in some cases its first poets, a vehicle of supple and expressive rhetorical power, the right musical setting for the neo-Petrarchism of the Florentine intellectual circles of the late republic and the early days of Medici rule. Bembo expressed things a bit differently, he was in fact an outsider to these men; it was *their* taste, *their* language, that is here being praised, not the Bembist doctrines that found musical expression in the madrigals of Rore and Willaert.[61]

The very brief mention of Arcadelt as following in Verdelot's footsteps while he was in Florence is valuable, certainly; for a long time it was the only known documentation for Arcadelt's having lived in Florence.[62] It is also tantalizing, for one feels that Bartoli could have told us more about the composer now thought to be the greatest master of the early madrigal. Evidently the personal connection that he had with Verdelot was lacking here.

Next there is mention of "German" compositions, those of Gombert and Crecquillon. Giambullari has an opinion of this music: in it all the parts are continuously in sounding motion, linked and tied together in *fugato* fashion with few points of rest to produce a style marked by *grandezza* and harmony that gives a marvellous effect—in clear contrast to the style of Verdelot. This review, similar to that of the theorist Hermann Finck contrasting Gombert's style with that of Josquin,[63] is an aesthetic judgement of some pertinacity, again of considerable interest coming from the mouth of one who professes scant knowledge of music. The development of Italian music in two directions, that of the Florentine-Roman circles around Verdelot, Festa and Arcadelt, and that of Gombert and the Venetians Willaert and Rore (who is mentioned a few sentences later) is one we recognize as perhaps the most important trend in the post-Josquin generation. Here we find it stated simply, but with surprising cogency, by a contemporary observer.

This detour to the north leads to mention of "Christiano Olanda" (Hollander) of Antwerp and to Clemens non Papa, known to Bartoli by reputation more than by their music. Mention of these Netherlands-based composers appears to have suggested to Bartoli the names of two Spanish musicians, Scobeto (Escobedo) and Morales, both members of the papal chapel. Next comes "un certo Cipriano Rore" at Ferrara, who has worked and continues to work "valentemente"; faint praise for Rore, already famous throughout Italy by the mid-1540s. Perhaps a tinge of Bartoli's antipathy toward things Ferrarese is in evidence here.[64]

To the question about whether anything could be said about Florentine composers comes an answer devoted chiefly to praise of Francesco Corteccia, said to be a fine composer and teacher, exemplary chapel master and a "gran Theorico" to boot.[65] Matteo Rampollini is also mentioned as a composer whose reputation is especially great among "forestieri." His skill is said to be great at composition and in "rimettere," the latter suggesting that he may have acted in some sort of editorial capacity, perhaps in the refining of his own work, perhaps in aiding younger musicians. The madrigal volume of Rampollini was indeed published outside Italy, in an undated print issued by Jacques Moderne in Lyons. Rampollini's music is said to have been the subject of discussion in Rome, at the house of the Florentine expatriate banker Bindo Altoviti. One would like to know when this discussion, reported by Lorenzo Antinori in these pages, took place.[56] Finally, there is a suggestion that many young Florentine composers may be found, musicians from whom great things may be expected in time. In fact Florence was not in the 1540s an important center of composition; had he chosen to do so Bartoli could have repeated here his plaint about the exodus of talented artists, unable to find patronage in ducal circles, from Florence.[67]

L. Ditemi un poco di grazia M. Piero che vi diletta piu o lo udir cantare, o lo udire sonare? P. Secondo chi io udissi. L. A me piace piu il sonare, perche nello udir Cantare io sento tal volta certe voci stonate, sgarbate, & il piu delle volte disunite che mi danno un fastidio maraviglioso. P. Se voi havesse a tempi della buona memoria di Papa Leone sentito cantare Carpentras, Con-   Carpentras, siglion, Bidon, & Biaseron, & altri de quali al presente non mi sovviene, voi   consiglion Bidon non diresti cosi; che vi dò mia fede, che voi sareste stato uno anno per modo   Biaseron. di dire, attento ad udirli, tanta graziosamente maneggiavano le loro voci, & qui in Firenze fu gia un M. Nicolo di lore ... che cantava con una grazia   Nicolo di lore. maravigliosa. Et il nostro Baccio Moschini non è possibile che habbia can-   Baccio tato con piu grazia. L. Garbatamente certo, che io lo hò sentito pure assai   Moschini.

volte, & fuor di lui non hò sentito in Firenze alcuno, che piu mi piaccia nel suo cantare che Ser Piero & Batista ancora del Corteccia, ben che si potrebbe lodare assai Ser Giampiero se havessi avuto buona voce. *P.* Certo voi havete ragione, che ciascuno di loro canta garbatamente: Ma voi che havete detto che vi diletta piu la Musica delli instrumenti, che quella delle voci, ditemi un poco havete voi mai sentito sonare il Siciliano di Viola? O Francesco da Milano di liuto o di Viola ancora? *L.* L'uno & l'altro ho udito piu volte, & ne loro generi, mi son parsi eccellentissimi. *P.* Voi havete sentiti duoi i piu rari & divini Sonatori della età nostra? i quali amenduoi sono stati miei amicissimi, perche quando la buona memoria del Cardinale Hippolito de Medici era viva, erano amenduoi al servitio di quel Signore il quale come sapete fu sempre amatore, & rimuneratore, & sollevatore di tutti i virtuosi. *L.* O che fama lasciò di se cotesto Signore nella Magna? *P.* Ei non sta bene a dirlo a me, perche mio fratello gli fu servitore, ma per mia fe io conobbi in quel Signore tanta bontà, tanta virtù, tanta magnanimità & tanta liberalità, che io credo che il Mondo sia stato, & sia per stare ancora molte centinaia di anni inanzi che egli habbia un Prencipe di cosi elevato & grande ingegno, & di uno animo dotato di tante eccellenti parti, quanto era il suo. Salvo pero sempre la reverenzia di quei Signori che ancora vivono, de quali non si può fare retto giudicio, perche la vita il fine il di loda la sera. *G.* Voi siete entrato o M. Piero mio in uno ragionamento che harebbe bisogno di piu tempo che forse voi credete, perche voi hareste forse apena incominciato a raccontare le gran qualitati, & le belle doti dell' animo di cotesto Signore, che la notte ci harebbe sopraggiunta. *L.* Troppo dice il vero M. Pierfrancesco, però torniamo di gratia al ragionamento nostro, che io desidero grandemente intendere in quel che il Siciliano & Francesco sono stati l'uno piu dell' altro eccellente, perche amenduoi gli ho sentiti lodare sommamente. *P.* Io non vorrei che voi vi persuadessi che costoro fussino stati amenduoi eccellenti in un medesimo genere di instrumenti, che se bene Francesco da Milano è stato nel sonare la viola eccellente, nel sonare il liuto non di meno è stato non solo eccellente, ma eccellentissimo; & credo che si come insino ad hoggi non ci è nessuno che a lui si sia potuto aguagliare si durerà ancor fatica che per lo avenire se ne truovi alcuno. Il Siciliano poi per maneggiare una viola, la hà maneggiata tanto bene, tanto presto, tanto maravigliosamente, & massime in compagnia di uno instrumento di tasti, che non fu mai sentito, ne credo si possa sentire

alcuno che gli possi inanzi; Ancor che Alfonso della viola sia in questo genere veramente molto eccellente; & raro nel sonare solo, & accompagnato, oltre alla altre virtù che egli hà di comporre & di altro, che sono tali che lo fanno certo sopranaturale. *L.* Io havevo in vero sentito molto lodare uno Alessandro strigia da Mantova, non solo eccellente, ma eccellentissimo nel sonar la viola: & far sentir in essa quattro parti a un tratto con tanta leggiadria & con tanta musica, che fa stupire gli ascoltanti, & oltre ho sentito lodare Alfonso, & lo anno passato quando io passai per la Francia sentij quanto

però al liuto, lodare grandemente uno Alberto da Mantova. *P.* Io non lo hò conosciuto, ma gia da molti Fiorentini venuti di Franzia a Roma, ne senti dire

cose maravigliose, ma ditemi un poco, poi che noi siamo in su questi ragionamenti dove lasciamo noi il nostro M. Antonio da Lucca. *L.* O quanto dite   Antonio da
voi bene, io credo certo che la Natura habbia voluto mostrare nel caso suo   Lucca.
quanto di bene ella sà et può operare, quando ella vuole; perche se bene ella
ci ha dati molti di quelli che noi habbiamo racconti eccellentissimi in una di
queste facultà sole; elle ha voluto mostrare di poi in M. Antonio, la ultima
sua possanza in questa etate; peroche ella lo ha fatto non solo ecellente, in
una di queste facultati sola, ma in molte, a un tratto: perche egli nel sonare il
liuto non cede hoggi a persona, nella viola è miraceloso, & nel sonare il cornetto, credo anzi tengo per certo che avanzi di gran lunga non solo tutti i sonatori dal tempo di hoggi, ma tutti i passati ancora, & credo si starà per lo
avenire gran tempo inanzi se ne truovi alcuno che lo arrivi. *L.* Io udij in Roma
ultimamente Pierino di Baccio nostro Fiorentino che mi piacque grande-   Pierino di
mente nel sonare il liuto. *P.* Valentissimo certo, & se egli vive mostrerrà un dì   Baccio.
che è vero scolare di Francesco da Milano, ancor che e' ci è qualcuno che
hoggi odè cosi volentier lui, & forse piu che non udirebbe Francesco suo
maestro; & veramente fa non piccolo honore alla buona memoria di Baccio
suo padre che sapete quanto era virtuosa. *L.* Voi havete messo M. Antonio
per il primo sonatore di cornetto da tempi nostri; ditemi un poco non ci è
stato un' Moscatello a Milano valente? *P.* Valentissimo certo, & a tempi di   Moscatello da
Leone ci fu un Giovan maestro del cornetto molto maraviglioso, ma a me   Milano.
piace sommamente il sonare di M. Antonio, ne udij mai i piu bei capricci, ne   Giovan maria del
le piu belle fantasie delle sue, ne piu nettamente quei gruppi, quegli andari di   cornetto.
diminuizione, che son tali che mi fanno stupire. *L.* Chi ti habbian noi infra
questi Sonatori di sua Eccellenzia che sieno rari? altri che M. Antonio? *P.*
Tutti sono valenti, ma per sonare uno Trombone Bartolomeo è stato, & è an-   Bartolomeo
cora cosi vecchio veramente raro. Et se bene in Bologna si trova un certo   Trombone.
Zaccheria & il suo figliuolo, & in Venetia Gironimo cugino del detto Bartolo-   Zacharia da
meo che suonano miracolosamente; Bartolomeo non di meno è stato tanto   Bologna.
raro ne tempi suoi, che hà acquistato il Casato & il cognome ancora dalla   Girolamo
virtù di quello instrumento; oltre a che di viola suona ancora benissimo, &   Trombone.
per maneggiare un ribecchino non ha pari; ne solamente hà queste parti, ma
e tanto buono, tanto piacevole, & tanto benigno, che chi havessi a dipignere
la bontà, la piacevoleza, & la benignità del mondo, non potria far meglio
certo che ritrarre lui, con un monte di instrumenti et di amici atorno; & oltre
a questo essendo gia vecchio ha duoi figliuoli che diventano rari. Haveteci
ancora M. Lorenzo da Lucca, non punto inferiore a nessuno di questi che si   Lorenzo da
sono racconti, anzi ha nel suo sonare una certa grazia, & una leggiadria, con   Lucca.
un modo tanto piacevole, che mi fa restare stupido, oltre a che maneggia ancora, & una viola & un liuto con una grazia maravigliosa; & non bisogna di-
sputare de gli altri Musici di questo genere di sua Eccellenzia risolvetevi
pure che tutti sono tanto valenti che ei non e Principe in Italia ne forse fuori
di Italia ancora, che la habbia migliore di lui. *G.* Voi havete ragionato di tanti
Musici & di tanti instrumenti che io credo che noi diventeremo tutti et tre,
essa Musica, o essi instrumenti; ei sarebbe pur bene horamai ragionare di

altro. *L*. Deh M. Pierfrancesco habbiatemi per escusato che io non hò cerco questo ragionamento a caso, & desidero ancora con buona gratia vostra che Messer Piero mi racconti chi egli hà conosciuti per valenti nel sonare di tastami se non gli pare fatica; o almanco se non tutti dirmene parecchi. *P*. Voi havete da sapere che a tempi nostri a me è parso gran sonatore in cotesto genere il Cavaliere, altrimenti il Zoppino da Lucca. Lorenzo da Gaeta ancora quando io me ne ricordo mi fa stupire, perche io non sentij mai nessuno che nel sonare fusse piu capriccioso di lui; ne che piu variasse, che vi dò mia fede che se voi lo havesse sentito sonare, piu di una volta, & non lo havesse veduto, hareste creduto che ei fussino stati duoi, sonatori diversi, tanto differentemente, & diversamente sonava l'una volta dalla altra; & credo quanto a lo organo che a tempi nostri si durerà fatica ad equipararlo. *L*. che vi pare del sonare di Iulio da Modona, non vi piace egli come quel di Lorenzo? *P*. Raro certo & vago è il sonare di Iulio; ma egli vale molto piu in su gli instrumenti di penna che in su gli organi; & io gli sentij gia dire che gli dava il cuore trovandosi in una stanza ove fussino i piu bravi soldati, Capitani, o Principi de tempi nostri, & che ragionassino di qual si voglia cosa piu fiera o piu cruda, o di qual piu si voglia importante negozio, non solo a tutta la Christianità, ma a tutto il Mondo; di sonare di maniera, che quei tali, deposta ogni loro bravura, fierezza crudeza, o quale si voglino importantissimi discorsi, si partirebbono da tali ragionamenti, & andarebbono vicini allo instrumento ad udirlo sonare; & mi ricordo che il Bartholo gia mi disse che una sera essendo il Marchese del Vasto arrivato in poste in Roma, & subito con gli sproni ancora in piede andato da Papa Clemente; & trovatolo a tavola, & entrato dopo la cena in discorso con il Papa & con il Sanga di cose importantissime, il detto Iulio essendo comparso in una parte della Sala con uno instrumento, cominciò di lontano a sonare di maniera, che quei duoi Principi, insieme con il Cardinale de Medici, & con il Sanga, che havevano a risolvere cose importantissime, pretermessono per alquanto tali ragionamenti; & andarono ad udirlo sonare con una attentione maravigliosa; cosa certo che per quella Iera confermò quello che gia mi haveva detto esso Iulio, si che non rimase punto ingannato della openione sua. *L*. Voi mi lodate tanto costui, che io non sò se lo amore ve ne inganna, o che potreste voi dire di Iaches da Ferrara che è hoggi tenuto si raro, & si eccellente? *P*. Io non lo hò conosciuto, Ma io hò ben sentito dire al Moschino, che a tempi suoi non ha sentito sonatore alcuno che gli piaccia piu di lui, parendoli che gli suoni con piu leggiadria, con piu arte, & piu musicalmente che alcuno altro, & sia qual si voglia. *L*. Se il Moschino havesse sentito un Ruggier Francese che hoggi sta al servizio della Regina di Ungheria; come gia lo senti io in Francia; forse non lo loderebbe manco che Iaches, perche costui veramente è tanto maraviglioso, che non si può dir piu. Ma che dite voi del sonare del Moschino? *P*. Il Moschino suona di maniera, o volete Organi, o volete instrumenti, & con una gratia, & con una leggiadria, & con una grandezza, congiunta con una tanta ragione di Musica; che io credo anzi tengo per cosa certa, che egli habbia pochi pari; & se io dicessi forse nes-

Zoppino da Lucca. Lorenzo da Gaeta.

Iulio da Modona.

Marchese del Vasto
Papa Clement

Cardinale de Medici. sanga.

Iaches de Ferrara.

Ruggier Francese

Moschino.

suno, non so se io mi errassi, ma credo di no; oltre alle altre parti sue, che sono dote date dal Cielo a pochi, perche come si disse egli ha cantato, & canta ancor graziosissimamente, & ha composte molte cose garbatissima- mente. Ma quel che mi hà fatto restare maravigliato nel suo sonare, & che io lo ho sentito talvolta sonare per suo piacere senza molti uditori, solamente per suo studio, & durato una hora a pigliare un vaga di sonare in contrabat- tuta, che mi hà fatto deporre ogni fastidio, ogni dispiacere, & ogni amaritu- dine che io havessi qual si voglia maggiore nello animo: & tengo per certo che in questo genere egli habbia pochi che lo arrivino. *L.* Io credo che se noi volessimo raccontare tutti i Musici eccellenti i quali sono a tempi nostri, che questo ragionamento non finirebbe cosi presto; & io vegho Messer Pierfran- cescho che harebbe caro che horamai si ragionasse di altro. *G.* Et che so io se voi volete, che questi ragionamenti durino sempre? Io son pure stato un gran pezzo senza parlare, per vedere se ei vi venivano ancora a noia, e' mi par- rebbe pure che e' si potesse ragionare di qualche altra cosa ancora, piglian- doci qualche gita piacevole. *L.* Di grazia, dove andremo, o di che ragione- remo dite su voi M. Piero che state cosi cheto. *P.* Ei mi sa male, che noi non habbian trovato il Bartholo, che noi celo saremo messo in mezo, & haremolo fatto entrare in su uno ragionamento, che io havevo pensato, che non vi sa- rebbe punto dispiaciuto. [fols. 37–39]

Sixteenth-century performers were, of course, often very famous in their day, bet- ter known than most if not all composers. For the most part their fame died with them; it is surprisingly difficult to find much information about even the most cele- brated *virtuosi* of the day. Only if they composed music formally (by which I mean committing it to writing; nearly all Renaissance performers of distinction were makers of music as well known for their creative style as for their technical prow- ess) did they leave many clues about their careers and their artistic personalities. Thus not all the names mentioned in Bartoli's work can be easily identified. What follows is a list of performers in the order they are mentioned in the text, with what- ever information I am able to give about them.

The discussion of performers begins with an argument over whether singing or instrumental playing is more pleasing; in this context a few derogatory remarks about the ordinary run of singers are offered by Antinori.[68] Giambullari replies that Antinori would not have spoken thus if he had heard some of the great singers of the time of Leo X. He names the following papal singers:

Carpentras [Elzéar Genet]: *maestro di cappella* in Leo's Sistine chapel choir, 1514–21, Carpentras was a well-known composer, chiefly of sacred music but also of the nascent madrigal, as well as a singer.[69]

Consiglion [Jean Conseil]: in the papal chapel from 1514, Conseil visited Flor- ence in 1527 and 1532; *maestro* at the Sistine chapel from 1526 to 1535, he was re- sponsible for recruiting singers to rebuild the chapel after the Sack of Rome. He was also a respected composer.[70]

Bidon [Antoine Colebault (Collebaudi)]: a famous singer, apparently one of the great virtuosi of the early sixteenth century, Bidon served the Estense in Ferrara before joining the papal service. He is mentioned by nearly everyone who discusses music during this period.[71]

Biaseron [Basiron, Beausseron; = Jean Bonnevin]: another composer-singer, he was in the papal chapel from 1514 to 1542.[72]

There follow some Florentine names:

Nicolo di lore . . .: whom Bartoli refers to by this incomplete name is unclear; one possibility is Nicolaus de pictis, *clerico Fiorentino,* in the papal chapel from 1507 to 1529.[73]

Baccio Moschini: the composer of two pieces for the 1539 wedding music in honor of Cosimo I and Eleanora of Toledo, Moschini was an organist (he is later referred to as such by Bartoli; see below), serving at the Duomo in Florence from 1539 until his death in 1552.[74] He is not the same person as Baccio Fiorentino (= Bartolomeo degli Organi), father of the Pierino di Baccio to be mentioned under lutenists. This latter Baccio was confusingly known as both singer and organist;[75] he in fact was succeeded at the Duomo by Baccio Moschini.

Piero and Batista Corteccia: nephews of Francesco Corteccia, both were singers at the Duomo and San Giovanni.[76]

Ser Giampiero [= Giovanpiero Masacone]: a boy singer at the Baptistry, Gianpiero was later a chaplain at San Lorenzo, and a well-known copyist of music for the Duomo and for circles of amateur musicians in Florence, for whom he did several madrigal manuscripts.[77] Bartoli's comment that he would have been a fine singer if he had had "buona voce" is a remark similar to one made about Lorenzo de' Medici's musical gifts.[78]

This completes the list of singers, which could have been longer and more representative had Bartoli included *cantori al liuto* or *improvvisatori* as examples of distinguished vocal artists.[79] It seems clear from the much longer conversation devoted to instrumentalists that his interests as an amateur of musical performance were in their skills, especially those of keyboard players.

Discussion of instrumental virtuosi begins, however, with celebrated players of the viol and lute, including the following names:

Il Siciliano [Battista, Giovanbattista Siciliano]: little is known about this musician, but he must have been exceptional since he is singled out for praise in Ganassi's treatise on the viol.[80]

Francesco da Milano: the most famous lutenist of the period, Francesco was a prolific composer as well. A description of his playing, couched in the sort of language used in Lenzoni's account of the magical performance of Antonio da Lucca and "il Trombone" (see above, and n. 24), is given in Pontus de Tyard, *Solitaire second* (Lyons, 1555), 113–15.[81]

Both these musicians are said by Bartoli to have been in the service of Cardinal Ippolito de' Medici, to whom an effusive tribute as patron of the arts is here paid. Then the two musicians are compared; Francesco is a fine violist but a superb lutenist; il Siciliano is a wonderful viol player, excelling in particular at playing with a keyboard accompaniment.[82]

The list of viol and lute virtuosi continues:

Alfonso della Viola: a Ferrarese composer and performer active at the Estense court for many years, Alfonso was so well known as madrigalist and violist that Bartoli had to include him in this list.[83]

Alberto da Mantova [= Alberto da Ripa, Albert de Rippe]: an Italian lutenist-composer who spent most of his life in the service of the French court, Alberto was nearly as famous as Francesco da Milano. Lorenzo Antinori's remark that he had heard much praise of Alberto when he was in France "lo anno passato" adds another element of chronology to Bartoli's account; Alberto died in 1551.[84] This is especially confusing since it follows a mention of a much younger musician,

Alessandro Striggio: a Mantuan of noble family who settled into Medici service in 1559 and became the chief court composer during the next several decades, Striggio was also noted as a viol player.[85]

"Our Florentines" have to get into this list, and several of them do so:

Antonio da Lucca [= Antonio dal Cornetto]: a sort of universal genius as performer, Antonio is described as unrivalled on the lute, the viol, and the cornetto; this would seem to establish that Antonio da Lucca and Antonio dal Cornetto, referred to often in contemporary anecdotes, are one and the same person. Antonio da Lucca died in 1554; this, along with the earlier reference to Alberto da Mantova and that to Pierino (see below), seems to show that this section of Bartoli's *ragionamento* was written by 1550, then updated to include Striggio.[86]

Pierino di Baccio nostro Fiorentino [= Perino degli Organi]: the son of Baccio Fiorentino [Bartolomeo degli Organi], Perino, who died in Rome in 1552, was a celebrated lutenist and composer, whose career was cut short by an early death.[87]

Another reference to Antonio as "sonatore di cornetto"[88] brings the subject around to wind players, of whom the following are named:

Moscatello da Milano: little is known of Moscatello except that he distinguished himself as a cornettist at the Milanese court around mid-century.[89]

Giovan [in margin: *Maria*] *del Cornetto:* the most famous holder of the name Giovanni Maria is G. M. da Crema, a well-known lutenist and composer active at mid-century or earlier; but a cornettist active at the time of Leo X, as Bartoli says, may be someone else, perhaps a certain Giovanni Padovano del Cornetto or a *trombone* mentioned by Vasari as being in Florence.[90]

Bartolomeo Trombone: the question here is whether this can be the same person as the frottolist Bartolomeo Tromboncino, active as composer and performer in Mantua and Ferrara in the period 1490–1510.[91] It would seem improbable on grounds of age alone, even though Bartoli, here writing perhaps as early as 1540, says Trombone is "gia vecchio," with two sons who are distinguishing themselves as musicians (as well as a cousin, Gironimo, resident in Venice). Little is known about the whereabouts or activities of the frottolist Tromboncino after 1521; in that year he applied to the Venetian Senate for a privilege to print his music, presumably referring to compositions that had not already been printed by Petrucci and Antico.[92] He may indeed have settled in Florence; a Trombone is mentioned by Vasari as a musician serving the Compagnia delle Cazzuola, a Florentine group active in literary and dramatic entertainments in the 1510s and 1520s.[93] According to Bartoli this Trombone of his is a master of stringed instruments as well as winds, is indeed so versatile as well as so beloved personally that he deserves to be painted surrounded by his friends and by a "monte di instrumenti."[94] Bartoli's depiction of this musician as kindly and pleasant to all does not accord with the youthful reputation of the Mantuan frottolist;[95] and it is strange that if Tromboncino is meant here his activity as a composer goes unmentioned. The identity of the two men is thus far from assured, but it cannot at this point be quite ruled out.

Zaccheria da Bologna: this musician, cited along with an unnamed son, is unknown to me.[96]

Lorenzo da Lucca: according to Bartoli a lutenist and violist of rare gift (also, being named in this section, a wind player?), this musician by his placement in the dialogue would seem to have been active in Florence.[97]

The last category is that of keyboard performers, apparently of special appeal to Bartoli. They include the following names:

Zoppino da Lucca (il Cavaliere):[98] a musician of this name is mentioned in Oriolo's *Monte Parnaso;*[99] a Zoppino is named in a letter of 1523;[100] there is reference to Zoppino as composer of music for a play performed in Naples in 1545.[101] Finally, an organist named Zoppino is referred to by Antonfrancesco Doni.[102] Whether even any two of these are the same figure would be hard to say.

Lorenzo da Gaeta: a player of the "chlavisimbolo" by this name is mentioned as a member of Clement VII's private musical establishment in 1526.[103] Bartoli clearly heard him play, in Rome or elsewhere, for he talks in detail about the inventiveness and stylistic variety of Lorenzo's technique, especially at the organ.

Iulio da Modena [= Julio (Giulio) Segni]: judged by Bartoli a better player of stringed keyboard instruments than of the organ, Julio is the subject of two anecdotes about the power of music, new versions of classical myth about musical ethos. Julio Segni was a well-known keyboard performer and composer; his career has been studied in detail by H. Colin Slim.[104]

Iaches de Ferrara [= Jaches Brumel, Jacques Brunel]: a noted composer-performer at the Ferrarese court,[105] Jacques is known to Bartoli only through the good opinion of him expressed by the Florentine organist Baccio Moschini.

Ruggier Francese: said by Bartoli to be in the service of the Queen of Hungary, this musician is so far as I can determine otherwise unknown.

Moschino [Baccio Moschini]: already mentioned by Bartoli as a singer of distinction (see above and n. 74), Moschini is now given a long testimony to his versatility, to his sincere interest in music (Bartoli heard him play without an audience, "solamente per studio"), and to the powerful charm exerted by his playing, particularly that in a manner called "in contrabattuta," presumably in a notably syncopated fashion, a charm sufficient to drive away all the troubles of a listener's spirit.

The conversation on music concluded, Bartoli's interlocutors turn to the business of the third *Ragionamento,* discussion of Dante's *Purgatorio* 18.133–35. For his purposes the musical digression was quite long enough; but music historians could wish Bartoli had said more, particularly about the Florence of his adult years and about the musical situation in Venice during his years of residence there. The conversation on music is uneven in quality as well as spotty in coverage; all the same, it is one of the most informative accounts of cinquecento music that any of its contemporary observers has given us. Particularly valuable is Bartoli's attitude towards composers, whom he treats as artists, creators equal in stature to painters; even performers who compose are separated from this first group. Professional music theorists had, of course, regarded composers in this light for some time; but from amateurs one gets the impression that music was on the whole regarded as a minor art, entertainment but not much more. Humanistic scholars gave music a much higher place, deriving their stance from readings in classical sources; but they seldom saw modern music as equivalent to that of antiquity in stature. Bartoli is one of the first to bridge this gap, and this gives his work distinction and importance as testimony to a changing view of "modern" music in the aesthetic posture of the late Renaissance.

APPENDIX

Regionamenti Accademici 2, fols. 22v–26

Ca. Havete voi veduto un quadro che egli fa dipingere qui presso nella via del Cocomero di certa sua inventione? *M. L.* Non certo. *Ca.* De di gratia andiamo a vederlo, che cosi passeremo il tempo lietamente. *M. L.* Andiamo, ma ecco di quà il Vescovo di Troia che viene inverso noi, aspettiamolo, che' non paia che noi lo fuggiamo. *Ves.* Buona vita M. Lionardo et la compagnia. *M. L.* Buona vita, et buon sempre Monsignor mio. *Ca.* Ben venga Mons. mio Padrone. *Ves.* Buon fratello M. Lodovico dove n'andavi voi che io vi vedeno

(1) quasi ch' mossi per partirvi. *M. L.* à dirvi il vero M. Lodovico mi voleva menar qua presso a vedere certa Pittura che fa fare il Bartoli. *Ves.* Io vo venire ancor' io. *Ca.* Di gratia Monsignor, che ci sara favore, et credo, che vedrete certe sue invenzioni che non vi dispiaceranno. *M. L.* Si ma meglio sarebbe haverci lui, che ce le dichiarebbe. *Ves.* Se noi lo facciamo chiamare egli verra piu che volentieri. *M. L.* Troppo lo havevo fatto chiamare, me egli è cavalcato. *Ves.* Andiamo dunchi da noi, che si io mi ricordo bene e mi pare che gia mi dicesse certi suoi capricci, circha alla Pittura, che questo potrebbe forse essere un di quelli, & sarebbe facil cosa, che vedendolo io me ne ricordassi. *Ca.* Andiamo ch'io per uno harò doppio piacere a sentirvegli raccontare, perche gia un pezzo fa quando questa pittura si cominciò, egli mi ci meno un giorno a vederla, & incominciò a dirmi il significato; ma per essere interrotti non potette finire di dirmelo; ma eccoci gia in su la porta, & è aperta. *M. L.* Et non ci si vede persona, cosa da far qualche burla a questo maestro. *Ca.* Eglie cola il fattore, che scherza con quei putti, et mi conosce, & non gli dara noia che noi entriamo qua da per noi, si che entrate Monsignore, & voi M. Lionardo. *Ves.* Questo e un gran Quadro. *Ca.* Grande certo. *M. L.* Poco maggiore sarebbe una tavola, il Bartoli hebbe sempre lo animo grande. *Ca.* Horsu M. Lionardo. *M. L.* Io dico certo da vero. *Ca.* Lassiamo andare questi ragionamenti et ditemi se la pittura vi piace. *M. L.* Mi piace certo questo scomparti-

mento, & i colori, che mi paiono molti lieti. *Ca.* Queste son cose da lodarne il Pittore, ma io credo che si voi sapessi il significato, loderesti molto la inventione; la quale ricordandosene forse ci dira Monsignore che molto at- (2) tentamente s'e fermò a guardarlo fiso. *Ves.* Io lo guardo attentamente certo, perche oltre a che e mi piace, io voleva ridurmi alla memoria questa inventione, per potervi dare, oltre al diletto che prendono al presente gli occhi chi à guardare questi colori, il diletto ancora della mente in considerare i capricci d'altri. *M. L.* Questo ignudo, che e qui adiacere, e molto bello. *Ca.* Et queste femmine non hanno tutte buona gratia, bella aria, et aspetti differenti, et diverse attitudini? *Ves.* Veramente e' non si puo se non lodare ogni cosa, ma la inventione, vi dellettera forse non meno, che la Pittura. *M. L.* Di questa ci siete debitore voi, che ce l'havete promesso. *Ves.* Io son contento, ma e' non mi par gia che e' sia da fermarsi qui a questo ragionamento, che e' ci potrebbono comparire delle persone, et saremo interrotti. *M. L.* Voi dite troppo bene, et se per aventura voi vene andate inverso casa, noi havermo piacere di farvi compagnia, et per la strada, non vi parendo fatica, ci potrete contentare. *Ves.* Andiamocene adunque et io mi ingegnero di consolarvi. *Ca.* Andate di sopra M. Lionardo. *M. L.* Contentianvi, Hor dite su Monsignore, ma perdonateci se voi vi diamo hoggi questa brigha. *Ves.* Io mi maraviglio di voi, questo mi e sommo piacere hora ascoltate. Quella Figura ignuda che voi vedeste (3)

Fiume di Arno come fatto.

adiacere, laqual pareva, che con il braccio destro si riposasse sopra quella testa del Leone, et che nella mano destra havesse un Giglio, et con la sinistra tenesse il vaso, onde usciva quell' acqua, et il corno della dovitia, come voi potete da voi stessi facilmente giudicare, e inteso dal Bartoli per il fiume di Arno. *Ca.* Deh, diteci Monsignore perche cagione fanno sempre costoro i Fiumi vecchi, et con la barba lunga, et allucignolata? *Ves.* I fiumi si fanno vecchi, perche essi nacquono immediate doppo il Diluvio; et con la Barba lunga, et allucignolate per significare non solo la antichità loro, ma le varie, et diverse acque, che di diversi luoghi con giri tori, et avolti in loro stesse si racolgono. *Ca.* Et quel Corno di dovitia? *Ves.* Voi sapete, che mediante le inondationi de fiumi, portando essi a basso la Grassezza del terreno; le Campagne, ch' essi hanno allo intorno si ingrassano; onde ne nasce di poi la dovitia, et la abbondantia di tutte le cose. *M. L.* Et quella Ghirlanda di quercia, ch'a me parve, che egli havesse in testa, che vuol dire? *Ves.* Io credo, che per la testa si pigli il principio, & il Nascimento de' fiumi, & che il Bartoli habbia voluto, mostrare per questo, che Arno hà il suo nascimento ne Boschi alti della Falterona pieni di Quercie. *Ca.* Et quel ramo di albero, che nel mezzo lo cingneva quasi a guisa di cintura? *Ves.* Voi sapete, ch'intorno ad Arno sono infiniti Alberi. *Ca.* Et quel poco del Manto sbiadato ch' egli si vedeva atorno? *Ves.* Quello significava il Colore della Acque, & quei calzaretti, che che voi vedeste di giunchi, mostrano, che le ripe di esso Fiume, giu basso dove egli quasi mette nel Mare, son piene di Giunchi; ne vi dirò altrimenti il significato della Testa del Leone, perche voi sapete, che ella e la Insegna antica della Città nostra. *M. L.* Diteci per vostra fede quel che egli intese per (4) quella Donna, che io veddi de una delle Bande molto della; laquale posandosi sopra del pie destro, pareva, che riguardasse verso il cielo; & haveva

Fiumi perche con le barbe lunghe & allucignolate.

Corno di dovitia perche a fiumi.

Ghirlanda di quercia perche ad Arno.

Alberi perche ad Arno

Manto sbiadato.

Giunchi perche ad Arno.

Leon perche ad Arno

quei fiori nella destra, & quello Scettro nella sinistra? *Ves.* Quella intese egli
per Flora. *Ca.* Et perche ha ella le Braccia armate? *Ves.* Flora come voi sapete
si intende qui per la Città di Firenze, & le harà fatto le braccia armate per dimostrare la Fortezza di questa città, & di questo fatto; percioche per il braccio destro, si intende la fortezza del Corpo: & per il braccio sinistro la forza
dello animo; volendo mostrare, che gli huomini di questo stato, sono valo-
rosi di Corpo, & intrepidi di animo. *Ca.* E' quei Fiori, che ella pare che con la
destra porgha verso il Cielo perche? *Ves.* Io credo che egli habbia finto che
ella guardi inverso il Cielo, quasi pregando Dio, che imprima nel cuore di chi
la governa, virtu & Animo tale, che ella possa lietamente mostrare i fiori
delle opere sue, circha la giustitia inverso i populi; la quale si denote per lo
Scettro, che ella tiene nella sinistra piu bassa che la destra; alludendo che le
azzioni & le opere di chi ben governa in terra, sono quasi come fiori pieni di
suavissimi odori, in Cielo nel conspetto di Dio. *M. L.* Non mi dispiace questa
espositione, ma ditemi per vostra fede, credete voi che il posare sopra del pie
destro di questa figura, piu che sopra il sinistro, habbia significato alcuno?
Ves. Il posare il pie destro credo che significhi la constantia che ella potrà havere in Dio, ogni volta, che gli porterà la debita Reverenzia si come pare, che
ne dimostri, il pie sinistro, facendo quasi segno di reverire non toccando si
come voi vedesti terra, se non con le punta delle dita: & questo ad amaestra-
mento nostro, perche, se noi reveriremo, come doviamo Dio, poseremo sicuramente & constantemente con il pie destro, sopra una stabile Pietra quadrata; come voi vedeste, che posava essa Flora; la quale pietra cosi fatta si
piglia per la stabilità. *Ca.* O quanto mi diletta questo ragionamento, però diteci di grazia Monsignore, se e' non vi pare faticha, che cintura è quella che
ella hà intorno? *Ves.* A me parvono quegli Instrumenti che gl'Antichi appro-
priarono alle sette arti liberali, i quali non è nessuno di voi che non sappia
meglio di me; & il significato, credo che sia per dimostrare, che noi altri ci
doviamo cingere di esse arti liberali, per diventare mediante quelle piu prudenti, & piu grati a Dio. *Ca.* Et quel velo argentato che usciva di sotto a quelle
due teste del Leone sopra delle spalle? *Ves.* Il bianco è sempre inteso per la
fede. *Ca.* Mi piace, ma quello drappo del quale io la veddi si riccamente vestita, che sembrava quasi che un broccato d'oro, che vuole inferire? *Ves.*
Parlando esteriormente, io credo, che egli habbia inteso, che Flore, cio e Fiorenza sia delle Terre di Toschana la piu ricca, & il Capo qusi di essa Provin-
cia, & parlando interiormente direi forse, che questa Ricchezza significasse
la vivacita, & la grandezza de gli animi nostri. *M. L.* Piacevoli son certo questi significati, & molto utili, & dilettevoli, pero non vi parra fatica di dirci il
significato, & che cosa era quella, che noi le vedemo in Testa? *Ves.* A me
parve un Berrettone alla antica Ducale col Mazzocchio a torno. *Ca.* Si ma e
vi era pure ancora sopra non sò se una Aquila ò altra cosa simile. *Ves.* Una
Aquila è certo. *M. L.* Questa sarà per favor dello Imperadore. *Ves.* Non è mal
significato questo vostro, ma io mi ricordo d'havere letto ch' gli Egizij
quando dipignevano, una Aquila il piu delle volte la intendevano per Dio.
Ca. Si ma che harebbe voluto dire per questo il Bartoli? *Ves.* O che noi
ci ricordassimo di havere sempre Dio sopra del capo nostro, ò che noi lo

Flora per
Firenze.
Braccio destro
armato perche a
Flora.
Braccio sinistro
per lo animo.

Fiori perche a
Flora.

Scettro.

Posar di Flora
sopra il pie
destro.

Pietra quadrata
per la stabilità.

Cinto di Flora

Velo argentato.
Teste di Leone

Berretone ducale
alla antica con il
Mazzochio
Ducale. Aquila
significa Dio.

preggasimo, che venisse à posare sopra di noi. *Ca.* Se io non credessi parere
ò M. Lionardo a Monsignore troppo discortese, io lo pregherrei, che ei fusse
contento, di dichiararci ancora i significati di quell' altra Donna, che armata,
le era al dirimpetto; la quale ancor che comunemente si intenda per una Minerva; a me non dimeno sarebbe molto caro, non havendo molto notizia di
queste; cose di saper la cagione per la quale gli Antichi la dipignessino in
questa maniera. *M. L.* Non crediate che à Monsignore sia mai per parere fatica il contentarci di cosi dolci ragionamenti. *Ves.* Non certo, anzi vi diro
tutto quello, che sopra di cio mi sovverrà, Gli antichi finsono che Minerva
nascesse puramente dal cervello di Giove, senza essersi egli congiunto, ò con
Iunone ò con altro: & la intesono per la virtu intelletiva volendo mostrare,
che dal Profundo segreto della sapienzia di Dio, nascesse ogni sapienza, &
ogni Intelletto puro, & separato da ogni terrena feccia, ò spurcizia, dentro a
gli animi de gli huomini: & oltre à questo la finsono Vergine. *Ca.* Et perche
questo? *Ves.* Perche e' volsono mostrare, che la sapienza non si lascia mai
maculare da alcuna contagione di cose Mortali: Conciosia che ella è sempre
lucida, sempre pura, sempre interra, & perfetta; & per essere i frutti della sapienza eterni, la finsono vergine, cioe sterile quanto alle cose temporali.
M. L. De diteci di gratia Monsignore ch'intesono gli antichi per quella Testa
di Medusa; che tanto da ognuno è celebrata, & che sempre si vede ò nel petto,
ò nello scudo di pallade o di Minerva. *Ves.* Io non mi staro qui à raccontare la
Favola di questa invenzione. *Ca.* Anzi io sono un di quelgli che vi pregho, che
non vi paia fatica, di racontarcela, & di esplicarci di poi il suo significato, che
à questo modo, & M. Lionardo & io ne resteremo molto piu capaci & sati-
sfatti. [There follows an account of the Medusa, with her attributes explained and given 'significance'.] . . . *Ca.* Che vuol dire che sempre nelle statue, ò nelle pitture antiche ella [Minerva] guarda cosi con gli occhi
accigliati, & feroci, inverso una delle Bande? *Ves.* Io credo, che e' facessino
questo per mostrare, che le persone prudenti rare volte possono essere ingan-
nate, percioche sguardando il più delle volte in questa maniera inverso delle
altre, considerando piu con la mente, che con gli occhi delle azzioni di
quelle, le spaventano; come che elle habbino sempre l'animo molto diverso
da quello, che esse mostrano ne gli occhi. *M. L.* Poi che e si vede che gli Antichi non lasciavano cosa alcuna in dietro che non havesse qualche bella, et
utile inventione, io mi persuado, che con qualche bello significato la finges-
sino con la Celata in testa et con una Coraza in dosso alla Anticha, et con una
lancia in mano, le quali cose io harei molto care di intendere. *Ves.* voi sapete,
come poco fa dicemmo ch'essi la tenevano per la Dea della sapienza, et la ar-
marono, volendo mostrare per questo che gli huomini savij, et prudenti, son
sempre armati di consiglio, et di Prudentia, da potersi difendere dalle
Guerre, et da combattimenti; da quali sono o possono essere, continova- (5)
mente oppressati et per la lantita [*sic*] di verde, con un Libro in una della
mani, et con una Girlanda di fiori in testa alzava l'altra mano in verso del
Cielo, et che haveva l'Alie dietro alle spalle, credo io che il Bartoli habbia inteso per la virtù, la quale per essere sempre verde, et per uscir di lei suavis-

Minerva

Minerva
dichinata

Sapienza
vergine.

Testa di Medusa.

Sguardo di
Minerva che
significhi

Celata &
Corazza di
Minerva. Lancia
di Minerva.

Virtù come fatta.

simi odori, sollevandosi con l'Alie sormontando sempre verso il Cielo fu cosi da gli Antichi dipinta, volendo dimostrare, che gli huomini poi che sono mediante lo ingegno, diventati virtuosi, si innalzano, et si sollevano a grado superiore agli altri, et possono mediante le Alie dello intelletto, volando, discorere tutte le cose, che sono in Cielo, et in terra. *Ca.* Non mi dispiace questo significato, ma procedendo all' altra, che stando a sedere si riposava con il Braccio destro sopra di una Ruota, et che haveva i Capelli, che dal vento pareva; che fussino stati spinti dallo Lato dinanzi, et vestita di un cangiante, che appariva di tanti colori che non si discerneva cosi facilmente, sapendo ch'ella è la Fortuna non voglio che vi affatichiate inesplicarla, che io so pur troppo quel che ella sa fare in tutte le cose, vedendosi ogni giorno quanto ella distribuisca male la sua Potentia, et i suoi Beni. *Ves.* Circa che cose? *Ca.* In distribuirgli à chi non gli merita, come, si vede che ella fa il piu delle volte dandone piu che abbondantemente à certi Barbiocchi, che meglio starebbono, a guardare le pecore et i porci, che a vestirsi ò ad addobbarsi dentro alle citta di seta, ò di drappi, non havendo in loro non vo dire virtu alcuna ma ne civilta ne costumi ne qualita di Huomini, anzi il piu delle volte da porci voltandosi a piaceri, o da lupi indrizzandosi alla avaritia. *Ves.* Deh signor Cavaliere ancor voi ven' andate con la Piena e? *Ca.* Perche Monsignore non vi pare che io habbia ragione? *Ves.* Non gia a me anzi mi pare che voi caschiate in quello errore, nel quale comunemente casca la maggior parte de gli huomini. *Ca.* Et che errore è questo? *Ves.* Che voi vi persuadete, che' la Fortuna habbia a tenere la Bilantia del pari, non altrimenti, che se ella fusse la giustizia, o la equita, Non sapete voi che gli antichi la figurarono che ella girasse sempre una ruota, per mostrare la sua instabilita? volendo inferire, ch'ella non sta mai ferma in un proposito, & va sempre variando, hor donando, et hor togliendo queste facultà delle ricchezze, de gli honori, et delle potenzie, che sono veramente beni, & cose sue proprie, & non d'altri, a chi piu le piace . . . [there follows a good deal more moralizing on the vagaries of fortune, not relevant here] . . . *M. L.* Deh passiamo hora mai questo ragionamento et diteci il significato di quella altra donna, che sedendo sopra quel cumolo delle armi, et di libri aperti, piu elevata che le altre, haveva nella destra mano, una palla descrittovi dentro il mondo, et nella sinistra un ramo di Lauro, et in dosso una vesta di un colore cangiante simile a quel' rosato splendore che alcuna volta mostra di se la Aurora quando piu belta che mai si dimostra a mortali. *Ves.* Questa è intesa per la immortalità, e che cio sia il vero, voi vi ricordate, che sedendo sopra le armi, et i libri ella premeva con il destro piede le spalle, et il collo ad un antico vecchione, il quale pareva, che dimostrasse di stare mal volentierei sotto a' detti libri, et alle dette armi, calcato massimo dal piede, et dal peso della immortalità, che altro non è che il Tempo, volendo dimostrare che due solamente sono i mezzi principali, che conducono le cose de mortali alla Immortalita, cio è le armi, et gli scritti. *M. L.* Adunque in quel quadro era lo Arno Flora, Minerva la Virtù, la Immortalità, et il tempo. *Ves.* Eranovi. *M. L.* Deh per vostra fede diteci che ha voluto dir, per questo il Bartoli, o che accozzamento è stato questo suo? *Ves.* Egli ha voluto

(6)

Fortuna come fatta.

Fortuna non tien la bilancia del pari

Immortalità

Tempo, Armi, & li scriti conducono alla immortalità.

per questo mostrare le Azzioni che si fanno adesso in Firenze, et dice che in (7)
su lo Arno, in Firenze, mediante lo ingegno la virtù, et la fortuna si conduce
il mondo alla immortalità a mal grado, et a dispetto del Tempo, onde se ne
acquistano honori, ricchezze, dignità, stati, riputazioni, sapienzia, et felicità
humane, le quali cose voi vedeste, se ben vi ricordate, notate giu da basso intorno ell' Arno, essendovi Mitrie da Papi, corone da Re, capelli da Cardinali,
da Vescovi, scettri, mazzocchi Ducali, insegne, armi, libri, et molte altre
cose simili, che si puo dire, che dimostrino oltre a questo le dignità, et gl' honori, et le qualità, ch' hanno havuto cosi gli huomini come le donne prudenti,
virtuosi, et fortunati nati in su lo Arno in Firenze. *Ca.* Hor questo mi pare
Monsignore mio che in non molto quadro sia un composto, et una invenzione, che habbia et del honorevole, et del utile. *M. L.* Io non aspettavo certo
tanto dal Bartoli, ancor che io sappia che gia molti anni sono, egli si sia sempre dilettato di cose simili: ma eccoci horamai vicini alla casa della Signoria vostra.

POSTSCRIPT

For a good summary of Renaissance musicians' attitudes toward their predecessors, see Jessie Ann Owens, "Music Historiography and the Definition of 'Renaissance'," *Notes* 47 (1990): 305–30.

In two instances my identification of sixteenth-century performers, which I
knew to be tentative, proved to be mistaken. My assumption that Antonio da Lucca
and Antonio dal Cornetto are the same person was too easily made; for argument
that they are different persons and that Antonio da Lucca is the one Bartoli had in
mind, see Anthony M. Cummings, *The Politicized Muse: Music for Medici Festi-
vals, 1512–1527* (Princeton, 1992), 248. The rather unlikely identification of Bartolomeo Trombone with the Mantuan frottolist Bartolomeo Tromboncino is incorrect; a much more probable candidate is Bartolomeo di Luigi Trombone, who
served Cosimo I de' Medici in the 1540s and 1550s (he died in 1564). See Frank
A. D'Accone, "The Florentine Fra Mauros: A Dynasty of Musical Friars," *MD* 33
(1979): 77–137, documents 81, 83, 87–88. Antonio da Lucca and Lorenzo da Lucca
are also mentioned in these documents relating to musicians at the Medici court.

Anthony Newcomb has edited *The Ricercars of the Bourdeney Codex,* in
RRMR, 89 (Madison, Wisc., 1991).

NOTES

1. *Ragionamenti Accademici di Cosimo Bartoli Gentil'huomo et Accademico Fiorentino, sopra alcuni luoghi difficili di Dante. Con alcuni inventioni & significati, & la Tavola
di piu cose notabili* (Venice, 1567), 3. fols. 35v–36r. The passage has been cited often in the
modern literature; see, for example, Einstein, *Italian Madrigal,* 21–22.

2. *Rag. Accad.,* 3. fol. 36. For comment (with regard to Verdelot) on this passage, see H. Colin Slim, *A Gift of Madrigals and Motets,* 2 vols. (Chicago, 1972), 1:61–62.

3. See, for example, Benvenuto Disertori, *Andrea e Giovanni Gabrieli e la musica strumentale in San Marco* (Milan, 1931), liv–lv, Mario Fabbri, "La vita e l'ignota opera-prima di Francesco Corteccia, musicista italiano del Rinascimento (Firenze-1502–Firenze-1571)," *Chigiani* 22 (ser. 2) (1965): 185–217, esp. 199ff.; Andrew C. Minor and Bonner Mitchell, *A Renaissance Entertainment: Festivities for the Marriage of Cosimo I, Duke of Florence, in 1539* (Columbia, Mo., 1968), 50–53; Nino Pirrotta, "Istituzioni musicali nella Firenze dei Medici," *Firenze e la Toscana dei Medici nell' Europa del '500,* 3 vols. (Florence, 1983), 1:37–54, esp. 49–51.

4. Judith Bryce, *Cosimo Bartoli (1503–1572): The Career of a Florentine Polymath* (Geneva, 1983).

5. See *Rag. Accad.,* 3. fol. 34v, where Bartoli is said to be "uscito fuori con certi Musici," prompting his interlocutor-friend Pierfrancesco Giambullari to remark, "Io vi sò dire che da un tempo in quà egli si è dato tanto a questa sua Musica, che è pur un poco troppo"; fol. 36v, where Bartoli is said to have held concerts in his house, employing "musici di sua eccellentia" (Cosimo I, presumably; or, if an earlier date is meant, possibly Ippolito de' Medici).

6. On the aftermath of the Sack of Rome, see Judith Hook, *The Sack of Rome, 1527* (London, 1972), chapter 12; André Chastel, *The Sack of Rome* (Princeton, 1977), chapter 6; Eric R. Chamberlin, *The Sack of Rome* (London, 1979), 205–8.

As for music, the papal chapel was reconstituted in 1528–29, with newly recruited musicians to bolster its ranks; see F. X. Haberl, *Die römische "Schola Cantorum" und die päpstlichen Kapellsänger bis zur Mitte des 16. Jahrhunderts* (Leipzig, 1888), 72–74. And Clement VII had *musici segreti* once more in his employ, musicians such as the keyboardist-composer Giulio Segni [Giulio da Modena] about whom and the pope Bartoli tells an anecdote (*Rag. Accad.,* 3. fol. 38v). See H. Colin Slim, "Segni, Julio," *New Grove,* 17:105.

7. Bryce, *Cosimo Bartoli,* 35. On Corteccia's appointment, see Frank D'Accone, *Music of the Florentine Renaissance,* vol. 8, *Francesco Corteccia, Collected Secular Works: The First Book of Madrigals for Four Voices,* CMM, 32/8 (1981), xi.

8. Bryce, *Cosimo Bartoli,* 140, 278. On Bartoli's Venetian period, see Lionello Puppi, "Cosimo Bartoli, un intellettuale mediceo nella serenissima," *Firenze e la Toscana dei Medici,* 2:739–50.

9. The *Annali* of the Accademia Fiorentina record that a comedy by Bartoli was approved in September 1542. In a letter of 7 February 1565 addressed to Vasari, Bartoli refers to three *comedie* of his, none as yet performed. See Bryce, *Cosimo Bartoli,* 312.

10. Prefaced to Bartoli's edition of Ficino (*Marsilio Ficino, sopra lo amore over' Convito di Platone* [Florence, 1544]) is a treatise, "Osservazioni per la Pronúnzia Fiorentína di Neri Dorteláta da Firénze"; the latter is also said to be publisher of the edition. Whether or not Bartoli himself wrote this tract under a pseudonym, as some have thought (but see the doubts expressed by Bryce, *Cosimo Bartoli,* 215–16), his edition of Ficino's Italian text demonstrates use of idiosyncratic Florentine spellings and employs written accents for every word of more than one syllable.

11. Of particular relevance here are Carlo Lenzoni's *In Difesa della lingua Fiorentina* (Florence, 1556), a work edited by Bartoli and one in which he is an interlocutor, and G. B. Gelli's *Ragionamento sopra le difficoltà di mettere in regole la nostra lingua* (1551), in which Bartoli is again an interlocutor; see Gelli, *Opere,* ed. I. Sanesini (Turin, 1952), esp. 487ff. Giambullari's *Della lingua che si parla e scrive in Firenze* (Florence, 1551) calls Gelli's work *Ragionamenti in fra Cosimo Bartoli e G. G. Belli. . . .*

12. On Bartoli as translator and editor of Alberti's work, see Bryce, *Cosimo Bartoli,* chapter 10. It was Bartoli's translation that was republished and used as the text for the influential English translation published by Leoni in 1726.

13. Judith Bryce, "Cosimo Bartoli's *Del modo di misurare le distantie* (1564): A Reappraisal of His Sources," *Annali dell' Istituto e Museo di Storia della Scienzia di Firenze,* anno 5, fasc. 2 (1980): 19–34.

14. For works of Bartoli published by Franceschi, see the first section of the bibliography in Bryce, *Cosimo Bartoli,* 313–16.

15. *Rag. Accad.,* 1. fols. 1–6v. The interlocutors in the first dialogue, subtitled "il Martello," are Vincenzo Martelli, Angelo della Stufa, and Bartoli himself.

16. *Rag. Accad.,* 1. fol. 19.

17. On this section of Bartoli's text, see Charles Davis, "Benvenuto Cellini and the Scuola Fiorentina: Notes on Florentine Sculpture around 1550 for the 500th Anniversary of Michelangelo's Birth," *North Carolina Museum of Art Bulletin* 13/4 (1976): 1–70, esp. 26ff.

18. On this building, see O. Poli, A. Piccini, and M. Brunetti, *Il recupero di un monumento a Firenze* (Florence, 1973), esp. 22–30, "Cosimo Bartoli Progettista del Palazzo Ricasoli." A photograph of the restored building may be seen in this volume.

19. In the proemio to his *De Architectura,* on page 5 in the 1565 edition of Bartoli's translation, Alberti says of the architect that he is not a laborer but rather "colui, ilquale saprà con certa, & maravigliosa ragione & regola, sì con la mente e con lo animo divisare."

20. See W. Chandler Kirwin, "Vasari's Tondo of Cosimo I with his Architects, Engineers, and Sculptors in the Palazzo Vecchio," *Mitteilungen des Kunsthistorischen Instituts in Florenz* 15 (1971): 105–22; cf. Davis, "Benvenuto Cellini," 21, 65. Vasari himself identifies (without placing them very precisely in the picture) the figures in his *Ragionamenti . . . sopra le invenzioni da lui dipinte in Firenze nel Palazzo Vecchio* (1568) (Pisa, 1823), 221. The foreground figures in classical attire were dead by the time the painting was designed; the background figures in modern dress were still alive. The building held by the figure on the left is of course easily recognizable as the Mercato Nuovo; on the right is a model of the fountains of the villa of Castello, held by Tribolo.

21. The second dialogue, called "il Cavaliere," has as interlocutors Cavaliere Lodovico de' Masi, Lionardo Doffi, and Ferrante Pandolfini, Bishop of Troia. The conversation under consideration here is on folios 22–26 (see appendix). A second painting is discussed at the end of *Rag. Accad.,* 3. fols. 48–53v.

22. This is noted by Bryce, *Cosimo Bartoli,* 274; she also points out other uses of the title-page design by Franceschi and by Torrentino in Florence. Bryce thinks that a painting may actually have existed; and there are some details in the description (mention of colors, and of a *cintura* worn by the river-god Arno, not visible in the woodcut) that support this view; but I am inclined to doubt it, preferring to think of the "painting" as a drawing on which the woodcut title page was modelled. Figure 2 shows Torrentino's title page in the first edition of Bartoli's translation; the Venetian edition of 1565 has an altered version, with the figures on each side reversed and with other differences in detail.

23. For these passages, see above, n. 5.

24. Lenzoni, *In Difesa della lingua Fiorentina,* 2. 38–39: "Così stando si cominciò a cantare, & a sonare il Liutto dal nostro divino Antonio da Lucca, & il Trombone; con una dolce & vera Armonia . . . allettatti dalla Armonia, leggiermente si addormentarono; se dormir si chiama però quel soave sonneferare, che ode e'ntende ciò che si fà."

25. Bryce, *Cosimo Bartoli,* 278.

26. Bryce, *Cosimo Bartoli,* 277, refers to mention of Piero da Ricasoli (whose name has been misread by several scholars as Piero Darica, owing to the appearance of the name in

Franceschi's typeface) in L. Passerini, *Genealogia e storia della famiglia Ricasoli* (Florence, 1861), 80; I have unfortunately been unable to find a copy of this work to consult.

27. Lorenzo was the son of Alessandro Antinori, whose business interests took him abroad, especially to Lyons; Lorenzo there married, ca. 1549, a member of the Florentine Guadagni family. See Gemma Miani's article on the elder Antinori in *Dizionario biografico degli italiani* 3 (Rome, 1961), 456; Emile Picot, *Les Italiens en France au xvie siècle* (Bordeaux, 1901), 99.

28. *Rag. Accad.,* 3. fol. 36v. Pierfrancesco Giambullari's death in August 1555 might be another date to keep in mind in this regard. But see nn. 84 and 86 for the suggestions that at least part of this discussion may have been written a good deal earlier.

29. *Rag. Accad.,* 3. fol. 37v. On Striggio's early life in Mantua and his move to the Medici court, see David S. Butchart, "The First Published Compositions of Alessandro Striggio," *SM* 12 (1983): 17–51, esp. 25ff.

30. The story of Giulio da Modena catching the attention of Pope Clement VII and of Alfonso d'Avalos, Marchese del Vasto, then banishing for a time their cares of state (*Rag. Accad.,* 3. fol. 38v), has been dated at 1530 by Slim, "Segni," 105.

31. There are no documented references to Verdelot as being in Florence after the fall of the republic; see Slim, *A Gift of Madrigals,* 55–65. Only the inclusion of Verdelot as an interlocutor in Doni's *I Marmi* (1552) suggests that if Doni, born in 1513, actually knew the composer in Florence, he may have been referring, despite his allusions to discussions in the Rucellai gardens which would suggest an earlier date, to a period in the 1530s, when both Verdelot and Arcadelt could have been in Florence, as Bartoli's text (fol. 36) seems to suggest.

32. Cf. the opinion of Bryce (*Cosimo Bartoli,* 206), on the whole a sympathetic biographer: "Bartoli had none of Alberti's outstanding originality, the quality of his intellect is far inferior, and the contradictions and paradoxes of his views on life are more likely to be the result of intellectual muddle than of any profound insight into the nature of existence."

33. For a general survey of humanistic aspects of musical thought in the period, see Claude V. Palisca, *Humanism in Italian Renaissance Musical Thought* (New Haven, 1985). A good account of the *laus musicae* as a topic is that of James Hutton, "Some English Poems in Praise of Music," *English Miscellany* 2 (1951): 1–63.

34. See David Marsh, *The Quattrocento Dialogue: Classical Tradition and Humanist Innovation* (Cambridge, Mass., 1980), particularly the chapter on Alberti and the vernacular dialogue.

35. Lenzoni, *In Difesa della lingua Fiorentina,* 25. On Castiglione and music, see Walter H. Kemp, "Some Notes on Music in Castiglione's *Il libro del Cortegiano,*" *Cultural Aspects of the Italian Renaissance: Essays in Honour of Paul Oskar Kristeller,* ed. Cecil H. Clough (New York, 1976), 354–69; see also chapter 2.

36. Doni's work is available in two modern editions: *Dialogo della musica di Antonfrancesco Doni,* ed. Gian Francesco Malipiero (Vienna, 1965), and *L'opera musicale di Antonfrancesco Doni,* ed. Anna Maria Monterosso Vacchelli (Cremona, 1969). For commentary on the work, see Alfred Einstein, "The 'Dialogo della Musica' of Messer Antonio Francesco Doni," *ML* 15 (1934): 244–53; see also chapter 12.

37. Bartoli's second lecture was published by Doni in *Lettioni d'accademici fiorentini sopra Dante. Libro primo* (Florence, 1547).

38. In Dentice's work there are a few citations of musicians (fols. 28f, 32v, 36v) mentioned by Bartoli as well; and there is some similarity of attitude towards singers. The book is composed chiefly of elementary and very dully presented material on music theory, not a good subject for amateur music lovers and one that Bartoli wisely refrained from dealing with.

39. In transcribing passages from Bartoli's work I have corrected obvious typographical errors of spelling and punctuation but have otherwise left the text as is stands, not altering vagaries of orthography or use of accents.

40. For Plato's views on this subject (*Laws* 700–701), see Werner Jaeger, *Paideia: The Ideals of Greek Culture,* trans. Gilbert Highet, 3 vols. (Oxford, 1939–44), 3:237–38. Cf. Zarlino, *Le istitutioni harmoniche,* 1.4.9–10: "Et a far ciò si mossero con ragione, che chiaramente si può vedere, che colori i quali nella gioventù, lassati li studij delle cose di maggiore importanza, si sono dati solamente a conversare co gl'Istrioni, & co parasiti, stando sempre nelle schuole di giuochi, di balli, & di salti, sonando la Lira & il Leuto, & cantando canzoni meno che honeste, sono molli, effeminati, & senza alcuno buon costume. Impero che la Musica in tal modo usata, rende gli animi de giovani mal composti, come bene lo dimostrò Ovidio dicendo; Enervant animos citharae, cantusque lyraeque, /Et vox, & numeris brachia mota suis."

41. Castiglione's version of the *laus musicae* theme (*Cortegiano,* 1.47) is prefaced by a remark, to be refuted just as Bartoli does it, that music is an art suitable only to women and effeminate men. See chapter 2, p. 21. It might be noted that Castiglione says of music, in the passage referred to above, that it makes "l'animo più capace di felicità"; the study of happiness is the theme of the body of Bartoli's third *ragionamento,* to which his discourse on music is an introduction.

42. *Henry VIII,* 3.1. Cf. Zarlino, *Istitutioni harmoniche,* 1.2: "Lino & Orfeo . . . col loro soave canto . . . moveano le pietre da i proprij luoghi, & a i fiumi ritenevano il corso." Ovid's *Metamorphoses,* book 10, was a widely used source for the Orpheus myth.

43. See Quintus Curtius, *Historiae Alexandri Magni Macedonis,* ed. J. C. Rolfe, 2 vols. (Cambridge, Mass., 1946), 1:10, where this story is cited in a summary of the lost first books of Curtius. A reference to Aelian is on the same page; but this is to another musical anecdote about Alexander. Aelian is said to be the source for the tale of Philip and Alexander by Mary Renault, *The Nature of Alexander* (New York, 1975), 39; but I do not find the anecdote in the *Varia Istoria.*

44. *Life of Pericles,* 1.5. This seems concordant with the anecdotes about Antisthenes reported by Diogenes Laertius, *Vitae philosophorum,* 6. For instance, there is a remark addressed by Diogenes the philosopher (*Vitae philos.* 6.104) to a performer showing his skills in a musical spectacle, that human intelligence governs cities and households, not contests of lyre and aulos; and this is reported as in the spirit of Antisthenes. The Ismenias of this tale may be the same musician mentioned by Boethius, *De institutione musica,* 1.1.

45. Marsilio Ficino, *Sopra lo Amore over' Convito di Platone* (Florence, 1544); see esp. Orazione 3.3; Orazione 6.13.

46. The longest list of composers drawn up in the sixteenth century is probably that of Rabelais, in the *Nouveau prologue* to *Le Quart livre des faicts et dicts héroiques du noble Pantagruel* (1552); see Nan C. Carpenter, *Rabelais and Music* (Chapel Hill, 1954), 39–40; but apart from one chronological division (and the mention of a piece of music) it is simply a string of names. Most sixteenth-century lists of musicians do not distinguish composers from performers; an exception is that of Pietro Gaetano, "Oratorio de origine e dignitate musices" (ca. 1565–74; see Slim, *A Gift of Madrigals,* 42–43). Among the more notable lists are those of Philippo Oriolo da Bassano, *Monte Parnaso* (ca. 1519–25; see H. Colin Slim, "Musicians on Parnassus," *Renaissance Studies* 12 [1965]: 134–63); Pietro Aaron, *Lucidario in musica* (Venice, 1545), fols. 31v–32; Luigi Dentice, *Duo dialoghi della musica* (Naples, 1552), fols. 28ff.

47. *In Difesa della lingua Fiorentina* 10. In the dedication of this work Giambullari makes use of the Michelangelo-Dante comparison.

48. The parallel is made in the dialogue *Il farnetico savio overo il Tasso* (1610); see Lorenzo Bianconi, "Il Cinquecento e il Seicento," *Lettera italiana, 6: Teatro, musica, tradizione dei classici* (Turin, 1986), 324.

49. Bryce, *Cosimo Bartoli,* 279n.

50. *Rag. Accad.,* 1. fol. 20.

51. *Ragionamento sopra la difficoltà,* 488–89, in the Sanesi edition of Gelli's *Opere.*

52. *Della Pittura e della Statua di Leonbatista Alberti,* trans. Cosimo Bartoli [1568] (Milan, 1804), 103–5. The whole of the relevant passage is as follows: "Ma io ho guidicato che non vi abbi a dispiacere, che tali ammaestramenti vengono indiritti a voi, come a ottimo giudice del bello ingegno del detto Leonbatista, il quale in quei tempi, ne' quali si aveva nulla o poca notizia della scultura, per essersi in Italia annichilate, anzi affatto spente, mediante le inondazioni de' Barbari, quasi tutte le buone arti e discipline, si ingegnò con il purgatissimo suo giudizio, di aprire una strada facile e sicura a' giovani che inesperti si dilettavano di questa nobilissima arte, e di svegliarli a bene operare in essa con regole ferme e stabili. Forse buona cagione, che in processo di tempo si avesse in detta arte a fare progressi tali, quali si veggono essersi fatti. Poichè in questo nostro secolo non si ha ad avere invidia alle bellissime statue de' lodatissimi scultori antichi Romani, come già dimostrò il nostro Donato, e non molti anni sono ha dimostrato il sempre divino Michel Angelo Buonaroti, e dopo lui Baccio Bandinelli, Benvenuto Cellini, ed ultimamente voi."

53. On this general topic see Edward E. Lowinsky, "Music of the Renaissance as Viewed by Renaissance Musicians," *The Renaissance Image of Man and the World,* ed. Bernard O'Kelly (Columbus, Ohio, 1966), 129–77.

54. For a balanced view of the relationship of Zarlino to Glareanus, see Palisca, *Humanism in Italian Renaissance Musical Thought,* 298ff. Bartoli may, of course, also have read Zarlino's *Istitutioni harmoniche,* which appeared in Venice in 1558. But for Zarlino Willaert, not Josquin, was the touchstone of musical achievement.

The Giorgio Bartoli mentioned by Palisca (pp. 155, 160, 271, 319, 419) as a translator of Boethius and copyist of humanist letters on music is not, as has sometimes been stated, the brother of our Cosimo, but rather a Cosimo di Zanobi Bartoli, a distant cousin; for this error, which originated with the eighteenth-century Florentine scholar Salvino Salvini, see Bryce, *Cosimo Bartoli,* 216.

55. Heinrich Glarean, *Dodecachordon* (Basel, 1547; facsimile, ed. Clement Miller, Musicological Studies and Documents 6 (American Institute of Musicology, 1965), 3. It might be worth noting here that the first two names in Rabelais's list of composers (see above n. 46) are "Josquin des Prez, Olkegan."

56. Agricola, Brumel, and Mouton (whose name was often misread for the more Italian-sounding Monton[e]) are mentioned by Rabelais; "Marchetto Montaono" is among the *cantori al liuto* in Aaron's list (*Lucidario,* fol. 31v); for his "third age" of composers Pietro Gaetano chose "Ochegan, Josquin de pres, Brumel, Fevin, Mouton, Petrus de larue, Andrea de sylva et multi alij nobiles et illustres Musici" (Slim, *A Gift of Madrigals,* 43n).

57. In using this apologetic stance Bartoli may have been thinking of the Platonic view that a well-judging citizen was entitled to pronouncements about the arts even in the absence of expert technical knowledge (*Laws* 658–59).

58. On this, see Richard Agee, "Filippo Strozzi and the Early Madrigal," *JAMS* 38 (1985): 230–36.

59. Bartoli's language is vague, but he probably meant that Jacquet's music has something of the contrapuntal solidity and subtlety of Willaert, which in a general way is true enough.

60. If one compares Bartoli's language with the list of the "excellencies" of counterpoint given by Pietro Aaron, *Compendiolo di molti dubbi segreti et sentenze intorno al canto*

fermo, et figurato . . . (Milan, n.d. [after 1545]), Dii: "Allegro, soave, fugato, harmonioso, commodo, sincopato," it is apparent that Aaron is speaking of music in absolute terms, Bartoli about text–music relationships.

61. On Florentine reluctance to accept Bembo's theories in their entirety, see Bryce, *Cosimo Bartoli,* chapter 11, esp. 232–33; James Haar, "The Early Madrigal: A Re-appraisal of its Sources and its Character," *Music in Medieval and Early Modern Europe,* ed. Iain Fenlon (Cambridge, 1981), 177.

62. For new information (discovered by Richard Agee and John Walter Hill) on Arcadelt in Florence, see Warren Kirkendale, *The Court Musicians in Florence during the Principate of the Medici* (Florence, 1993), 57n and Haar, "Towards a Chronology of the Madrigals of Arcadelt," *The Journal of Musicology* 5 (1987): 34–35.

63. See George Nugent, "Gombert, Nicholas," *New Grove,* 7:512. Finck refers to Gombert, followed by Crecquillon, as among the most distinguished composers of his day; see K[arl] P[hilipp] Bernet Kempers, "Bibliography of the Sacred Works of Jacobus Clemens non Papa," *MD* 18 (1964): 90.

64. See Bryce, *Cosimo Bartoli,* 100, 121, on Medici–Estense hostility and Bartoli's share in it.

65. *Rag. Accad.,* 3. fol. 36v. These remarks are given to Pierfrancesco Giambullari, who as a canon of San Giovanni must have been in frequent and close contact with Corteccia. The latter, who became a member of the Accademia Fiorentina, may indeed have had intellectual interests; if he did lecture or write on musical theory nothing appears to have survived.

66. On Altoviti, see Aldo Stella in the *Dizionario biografico degli italiani* 3 (Rome, 1961), 574–75. A madrigal print published in Rome in the early 1540s, the *Exercitium Seraphicum* of Hubert Naich, is dedicated to Bindo Altoviti, who held *ridotti* devoted to music at this home (perhaps the "accademia degli amici" referred to in Naich's volume); see José Quitin, "Naich, Hubert," *New Grove,* 13:15–16.

67. *Rag. Accad.,* 1. fols. 19v–20. Corteccia may have continued to compose on occasion, but there is nothing to suggest that Rampollini had remained active as a composer. Many younger musicians, such as Giovanni Animuccia and his brother(?) Paolo left Florence for Rome (Arcadelt had already done so before 1539).

68. Some similar remarks may be found in Dentice, *Duo dialoghi,* fol. 28v: "un'altro che cantava il soprano che non mi piacque molto . . . perche pochi Musici si trovano che cantano sopra gli stormenti. . . . Perche tutti errano in qualche cosa, o nella intonatione, o nella pronuntiatione, o nel sonare, o nel fare i passaggi, o vero nel rimettere & rinforza la voce quando bisogna." Franchinus Gaffurius, *Practica musicae* (1496), has a chapter (3.xv) devoted to admonition of singers on their technique and comportment, and ending with Guido d'Arezzo's eleventh-century judgement: "Temporibus nostris super omnes homines fatui sunt cantores."

69. Howard Mayer Brown, "Carpentras," *New Grove,* 3:819–21. The works of Carpentras have been edited by Albert Seay: *Elziarii Geneti (Carpentras). Opera Omnia,* 5 vols., CMM 58 (1972–73).

70. Stanley Boorman, "Conseil, Jean," *New Grove,* 4:667–68. Both Carpentras and Conseil (Consillion) appear in Rabelais's list of composers.

71. Bidon was at the court of Ferrara in 1506; his singing is described by Castiglione (*Cortegiano,* 1.37): "Vedete la musica, le armonie della quale or son gravi e tarde, or velocissime e di novi modi e vie; nientedimeno tutte dilettano, ma per diverse cause, come si comprende nella maniera del cantare di Bidon, la qual è tanto artificiosa, pronta, veemente, concitata e de cosi varie melodie, che i spirti di chi ode tutti si commoveno e s'infiammano e cosi sospesi par che si levino insino al cielo." Information on Bidon at Ferrara may be seen

in Lewis Lockwood, "Jean Mouton and Jean Michel: New Evidence on French Music and Musicians in Italy, 1505–1520," *JAMS* 32 (1979): 191–246.

Bidon was a member of the papal chapel by 1519; see Herman-Walther Frey, "Regesten zur päpstlichen Kapelle unter Leo X, und zu seiner Privatkapelle," *Musikforschung* 8 (1955): 58ff., 178ff., 412ff.; 9 (1956): 46ff., 139ff.; information on Bidon is in 8:62; on Conseil in 8:180–81. Folengo's *Opus Merlin Cocaii macaronicorum* (1512), fol. 96, contains the line "O felix Bido, Carpentras, Silvaque, Broyer [= Bruhier]." "Bidone" is among Aaron's *Cantori a libro,* singers who excel in polyphonic music; he is also mentioned in Oriolo's *Monte Parnaso.*

72. Frey, "Regesten," *Musikforschung* 8:179–80.

73. Ibid., 8:190–91. The lacuna in the text is unexplained by the printer. "Lore . . ." could be the beginning of "Lorenzo," but this is no particular help in identifying the singer, unless the instrumentalist Lorenzo da Lucca (see below) was also a noted singer.

74. Emilio Sanesi, "Maestri d'organo in S. Maria del Fiore (1436–1600)," *Note d'Archivio per la Storia Musicale* 14 (1937): 175. For Moschini's rather undistinguished music, see Minor and Mitchell, *A Renaissance Entertainment,* 203ff., 218ff. He was evidently a fine performer; see below for Bartoli's enthusiastic account of his organ playing. Moschini is mentioned among Florentine musicians whose opinion was worth having in Doni's *Dialogo della musica,* 265 (Malipiero's edition): "Questa a otto gli voglio tutti copiare e mandargli a Fiorenza a Maestro Mauro, al Moschini, a Bartolomeo trombone et a Tianicco."

75. On Bartolomeo degli Organi, see Frank A. D'Accone, ed., *Music of the Florentine Renaissance,* 2: *Collected Works of Alessandro Coppini, Bartolomeo degli Organi, Giovanni Serragli, and Three Anonymous Works,* CMM 32/2 (1967), ix–x.

76. See Fabbri, "La vita . . . di Corteccia," 202, 205–6. Battista was well enough thought of to have a sonnet by Varchi commemorating his death in 1555.

77. See Slim, *A Gift of Madrigals,* 26–27. For evidence of Masacone's copying activities, see Fenlon and Haar, 123–26. A piece by Masacone is also in the 1539 wedding music volume. See Minor and Mitchell, *A Renaissance Entertainment,* 88ff.

78. See Luigi Parigi, *Laurentiana: Lorenzo dei Medici cultore della musica* (Florence, 1954), 14.

79. For Castiglione the art of "cantare alla viola per recitare," solo song of the sort at which *improvvisatori* excelled, was perhaps the best of all musical skills; see *Cortegiano,* 2.13.

80. Silvestro Ganassi, *Lettione secondo pur della prattica di sonare il violone d'arco da tasti* (Venice, 1543), chapter 20, where Joanbattista Cicilian and Alfonso della Viola are said to be the best viol players of the day. Siciliano is also mentioned by Dentice, *Duo dialoghi,* folio 28, in a group "ognun di loro nel suo stormento (à mio giudicio) ottiene il primo luogo."

81. For contemporary references to Francesco, as well as a concise account of his career and compositional output, see H. Colin Slim, "Francesco da Milano, 1497–1543/44: A Biobibliographical Study," *MD* 18 (1964): 163–80; 19 (1965): 109–28. The work of Francesco may be seen in modern edition: *Francesco Canova da Milano: Lute Music,* ed. Arthur J. Ness, Harvard Publications in Music, 3–4. (Cambridge, Mass., 1970).

82. On sixteenth-century viol-and-keyboard music, see Diego Ortiz, *Tratado de glosas* (Rome, 1553); Howard Mayer Brown, *Embellishing Sixteenth-Century Music* (Oxford, 1976), esp. chapter 4.

83. For an account of his career, a long one lasting from the 1520s to the late 1560s, see James Haar, "Alfonso dalla Viola," *New Grove,* 5:164.

84. See Lyle Nordstrom, "Albert de Rippe, Joueur de luth du Roy," *Early Music* 7 (1979):

378–85, an article devoted chiefly to discussion of a modern edition of the composer's works: Jean-Michel Vaccaro, ed., *Oeuvres d'Albert de Rippe,* Le Chœur des Muses: Corpus des Luthistes Français (Paris, 1972).

85. See Iain Fenlon, "Striggio, Alessandro," *New Grove* 18:271–74. The viol on which Bartoli says Striggio plays four voice parts at one time is probably the *lira da gamba* or *lirone.*

86. On Antonio, see the (anonymous) entry "Antonio dal Cornetto," in *Dizionario biografico degli italiani* (Rome, 1961), 3:546–47. He was in Ferrarese service in 1535, then became for a time a favored musician in the service of Cardinal Madruzzo of Trent. For details of this part of his career, see Renato Lunelli, "Contributi trentini alle relazioni musicali fra l'Italia e la Germania nel Rinascimento," *Acta Musicologica* 21 (1949): 41–70, esp. 57–63; cf. Romane Vettori, "Note storiche sul patronato musicale di Cristoforo Madruzzo Cardinale di Trento," *RIM* 20 (1985): 1–43, esp. 27ff.

87. Elwyn A. Wienandt, "Perino Fiorentino and his Lute Pieces," *JAMS* 8 (1953): 2–13; cf. Slim, "Francesco da Milano," 72.

88. Note that Bartoli praises Antonio for his inventiveness of improvisation or composition (his *capricci* and *fantasie*) as well as for his digital technique (*gruppi, andare in diminuizione*).

89. Moscatello was in the service of Ferrante Gonzago in Milan; see Lunelli, "Contributi," 73. He is noted among prominent musicians of Milan in Gaspare Brugatii, *Historia universale dal principio del mondo fino all' anno MDLXIX* (Venice, 1571), 1024.

90. For the Vasari citation, see Slim, *A Gift of Madrigals,* 99n. A "Ioanni Maria dal cornetto" is listed in payment records of the private chapel of Leo X in 1520–21; see Frey, "Regesten," *Musikforschung* 9:140–41. This last Giovanni Maria is probably the same person as Giovanni Padovano del Cornetto, a Venetian musician who returned to the service of the Doge after the death of Leo X; see H. Colin Slim, "Gian and Gian Maria: Some Fifteenth- and Sixteenth-century Namesakes," *MQ* 57 (1971): 570–71; he would seem to be the best candidate for the cornettist named by Bartoli.

91. See William F. Prizer, "Tromboncino, Bartolomeo," *New Grove,* 19:161–63. Tromboncino is last recorded by Prizer as writing a letter from Vicenza in 1535. He was in fact a trombone player; he is cited as such in Mantuan documents. See Prizer, "Bernardino Piffaro e i pifferi e tromboni di Mantova: Strumenti a fiato in una corte italiana," *RIM* 16 (1981): 159.

92. See Richard J. Agee, "The Venetian Privilege and Music Printing in the Sixteenth Century," *EMH* 3 (1983): 27.

93. Slim, *A Gift of Madrigals,* 99n. Antonio Bertolotti, *Musici alla corte dei Gonzaga in Mantova dal secolo XV al XVIII* (1890; reprint, Bologna, 1969), 20, says of Tromboncino that he was in Ferrara in 1513 "e forse dopo passò alla Medicea", but he cites no documentation.

94. Aaron, *Lucidario,* fol. 31v, includes "Messer Bartholomeo Tromboncino" among his *cantori a liuto;* this is, of course, appropriate for a frottolist, and Tromboncino's contemporary at Mantua, Marchetto Cara, is also on the list. Whether Aaron's treatise, published in 1545, should be used as evidence that Tromboncino was still alive then is uncertain at best: Cara had been dead for some time by this date. A "Bartolomeo Trombone" is referred to as very much alive and in Florence by Doni, *Dialogo della musica* (1544); see n. 74 above.

95. See the account of Tromboncino's turbulent personal life in Mantua given by Prizer, "Tromboncino," 161.

96. He might be the "Zaccaria Trombone" who appears in payment records of the private chapel of Leo X for 1519–21; see Frey, "Regesten," *Musikforschung* 9:140–41.

97. A "Lorenzo trombone" is described by Gabriella Biagi-Ravenni, "I Dorati, musicisti lucchesi, alla luce di nuovi documenti d'archivio," *RIM* 7 (1972): 68, as a "fuoruscito lucchese, condannato a morte in contumacia per aver partecipato nel 1531 nel moto degli Straccioni, ed aveva trovato rifugio e lavoro presso il Duca Alessandro de' Medici." A manuscript, *Vita di Vincenzo di Poggio,* survives with a dedication "al magnifico e Virtuoso messer Lorenzo da Lucca musico eccellentissimo dell' Illustrissimo et eccellentissimo Duca di Fiorenza e di Siena" (see Biagi-Ravenni). Cf. Luigi Nerici, *Storia della musica in Lucca* (Lucca, 1880), 194.

98. A "Cavalier dell' Organo di Annoni" is listed among prominent musicians by Brugatii, *Historia universale,* 1024, but he is not identified by name.

99. Slim, "Musicians on Parnassus," 146.

100. See Bertolotti, *Musici alla corte dei Gonzaga,* 26. The letter is from Isabella d'Este to Marchetto Cara, bidding him come to her country retreat along with "Pozzino [a singer of the court], Zoppino et M. Augustino de la Viola con suoi figlioli," and to have these musicians bring their instruments with them.

101. Renato di Benedetto, "Naples," *New Grove,* 14:24.

102. Doni, *Seconda Libreria* (Venice, 1551), 12.

103. Frey, "Regesten," *Musikforschung* 9:145.

104. See Slim's article on Segni in *New Grove,* 17:105, and also his edition of Segni's keyboard music in *Musica Nova,* MRM, 1 (Chicago, 1964).

105. Barton Hudson, "Brunel, Jacques," *New Grove,* 3:384. In a paper read at the annual meeting of the American Musicological Society in Cleveland in 1986, Anthony Newcomb presented evidence of Giaches Brumel as an important and influential composer of instrumental *ricercari.*

ASPECTS OF RENAISSANCE MUSIC THEORY

The Frontispiece of Gafori's *Practica Musicae* (1496)

THE DEPICTION OF CELESTIAL HARMONY (fig. 3) used as title page for the first edition of the *Practica Musicae* has been a great favorite among art historians of iconographic bent; Warburg, Panofsky, Seznec, and Wind have all reproduced and commented on this woodcut at some length.[1] The frontispiece has nothing really to do with the contents of the *Practica*—no more, say, than the Boethian frontispiece of the thirteenth-century Pluteus manuscript has to do with Notre Dame polyphony.[2] But the illustration was surely Gafori's idea rather than that of his printer, Le Signerre.[3] Gafori as a devout Boethian was enamored of myths about cosmic harmony; he expounded Boethius' doctrine of *musica mundana* in the first edition of the *Theorica Musicae* in 1480, expanded upon this treatment in the second edition of that work (1492), and returned to the subject armed with much newly acquired humanistic lore in the *De Harmonia Musicorum Instrumentorum Opus,* published in 1518 though certainly written some years earlier.[4] In the fourth book of this last treatise the cosmic diagram of figure 3 reappears (fol. 74v), this time accompanied by Gafori's own explication of its meaning.

Although the *De Harmonia* is a theoretical work, dealing not with musical instruments but with the arithmetical laws of harmonics, it is quite different from Gafori's *Theorica*. The abstract study of proportions comprising a large part of that treatise is not found in the *De Harmonia,* which is always concerned with string measurements or pipe lengths. The role of the *De Harmonia* in Gafori's trilogy may have been clear to its author at an early date;[5] but the contents of this third treatise could not for the most part have been determined until Gafori had read and absorbed Latin translations of some Greek musical treatises, translations he had had made for his own use in the late 1490s.[6] The *De Harmonia* is closely modeled on the *Harmonics* of Ptolemy, and its fourth book is greatly indebted to the Περὶ μουσικῆς of Aristides Quintilianus. Perhaps Gafori's widened humanistic knowledge led him to commission the woodcut first used for his *Practica;* but as we shall see one of the chief features of this illustration was drawn not from an ancient source, which Gafori would have acknowledged, but from a contemporary one that he would never have credited.

The fourth book of *De Harmonia,* a discussion of the modes, is what concerns us here. It is unlike the first three, which deal soberly with Pythagorean string measurements, in that Gafori does not expound modal theory; he is intent on parading his erudition, of which he had assembled a whole new stock since writing the *Theorica*. Concentrating on the four modes whose names (Dorian, Phrygian, Lydian, Mixolydian) were given to the ecclesiastical tones, he asserts, following Plato, the superiority of the Dorian (chap. 2). These four modes are linked with octave species in the traditional medieval order (chap. 4). Gafori concludes his remarks on the "authentic" modes thus:

LIBER

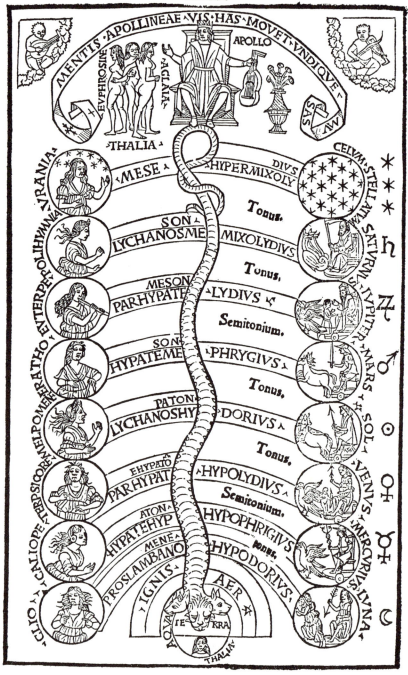

Figure 3. Gafori, *Practica Musicae* (1496), frontispiece.

And there are those who think the modes themselves to be participants of celestial harmony; for they believe that the star of the sun rules Dorian; that of Mars, however, is ascribed to Phrygian. To Jupiter, Lydian; and to Saturn, Mixolydian.[7]

Three of the plagal modes are next described and allotted to the lower planets (chaps. 5–8). To this analogy is joined a planetary scale derived from Cicero's *Somnium Scipionis* and cited by Boethius;[8] thus *proslambanomenos,* the lowest note of the Greek musical system, is equated with the moon, and the rest go in ascending order. The correlation of mode to planets is further developed:

> Therefore Mixolydian (which we have said before is higher than those other modes and is thought more worthy to hold power) is ascribed to Saturn. Hence to the sun may Dorian rightly be compared—Dorian, which, placed in the middle among those seven first modes,[9] is the link between the tetrachords; for the star of the sun, holding a middle place among the seven planets, confers on the others through its rays either light or heat. Hence the poet sang "Stationed in the midst, Phoebus embraces all things."[10] Hypermixolydian, moreover, is attributed to the highest firmament of all, as if a participant of that sublime and divine harmony, and free from corruptible properties.[11]

So far we have Gafori's account of the correlation between planets, modes, and an octave of the Greek *systema teleion*. The modes, despite their Greek names, are those of medieval and Renaissance plainchant theory, the octave *proslambanomenos-mese* being the second or Hypodorian, with a range from *A* to *a*. Gafori was thus adding cosmic analogies to musical concepts he thought to be the same for his contemporaries as they were in antiquity; not for another half century was this easy view of the relationship between ancient and modern music to be questioned.[12] As for the analogies themselves, that between planet and individual notes, or lyre-strings, was derived from a classical source (see above); Gafori's parallels between planets and modes, however, are not to be found in any ancient writer known to me.[13] From figure 3 it would appear that *proslambanomenos* = the Hypodorian mode, which makes no sense. What Gafori meant (explained more clearly by another Renaissance theorist, as we shall presently see) is this: the Hypodorian mode, as understood in his time, started on the bottom note of the Greater Perfect System, *proslambanomenos* or *A*. The others go in ascending order, but there is a difficulty. *Lychanos hypaton,* or *D,* is the starting point not only for Dorian but also for Hypomixolydian, the mode a tone above Hypolydian in chant theory.[14] Gafori avoids this problem by using Boethius' order of modes with Hypermixolydian added at the top.[15] His highest mode is thus one known to his contemporaries by name but not part of the ecclesiastical modal system.

To his explanation of cosmic music Gafori next adds an illustrative poem, a Sapphic ode by his Milanese colleague Lancinus Curtius (Curti),[16] apparently written to order for this purpose. Most of the fifteen stanzas of this poem are about the characteristics of the modes, especially those which accord with the planets they are here associated with; thus the "fiery Phrygian" goes well with Mars, the "bilious Mixolydian" with Saturn. In Gafori's opinion the ancient lyric poets sang odes of this kind. He therefore sets a stanza from Curti's poem, carefully observing the lengths of syllables by using only breves and semibreves so that the music is as quantitative as the verse. His setting is a two-voice one, using Dorian and Hypodorian modes for upper and lower voice.[17] The result has of course nothing classical about it at all; the little song is a *bicinium* in the style of the 1490s, but awkwardly constrained by its quantitative meter. Here again one sees Gafori using classical terminology but thinking in terms of the music of his own time.

A chapter (chap. 12) is devoted to coordinating the Muses with the planetary spheres, the modes, and the octave scale. Gafori refers to a variety of classical sources treating of the Muses: Ovid, Diodorus Siculus, Varro, Hesiod, Fulgentius Planciades, Callimachus, Herodotus, and Aristides Quintilianus.[18] It is odd that after showing all this erudition he does not name Martianus Capella, source of the planet-Muse analogies he uses here. Martianus provides the correspondence of Muses with the eight spheres and the motionless earth; he suggests the musical scale, with Urania sounding a high note, Melpomene a medium one, Clio a low one. And finally, the presence of Phoebus Apollo is mentioned in Martianus' description.[19] Gafori's woodcut is in its musical aspects simply a filling in of detail, most of which we have now examined.

There is a very long tradition connecting the Muses with music; even in Homer the nine Muses chant a dirge, and in the *Theogony* of Hesiod the Muses dwelling on Mount Helicon sang and performed choral dances.[20] Occasionally the Muses were depicted as three in number; these were compared by Greek writers to the lyre strings *hypate, mese,* and *nete,* and by Varro to vocal, wind, and string music.[21] Whether anyone in antiquity made the precise connection of the nine Muses to degrees of a musical scale Gafori does not tell us; he says vaguely that "some persons" (*nonnulli*) have made the comparison, and quotes a series of verses on the subject, but gives no source for them. Warburg suggests[22] that the verses could be by Gafori himself or by his friend Curti; this latter guess is supported both by the style of the poetry and by the fact that it echoes Gafori's thoughts here just as do the lines of the Sapphic ode referred to earlier. Gafori is not, however, the inventor of the complete scale-mode-planet-Muse analogy. He takes it, without acknowledgement (hence the use of *nonnulli*) from his contemporary, in some senses his archrival theorist, Ramis de Pareia, in whose *Musica Practica* of 1482 a diagram (see fig. 4) accompanied by a long explanatory text gives the main elements of Gafori's illustration. Ramis' version of cosmic harmony will be returned to; first the remaining details of Gafori's woodcut ought to be accounted for.

The nonmusical aspects of Gafori's illustration have been treated in some detail elsewhere (see above, and n. 1); here a brief recapitulation, with a bit of added detail not previously described, will suffice. Much of the picture was apparently suggested by passages in the *Saturnalia* of Macrobius;[23] this includes the three Graces dancing at Apollo's right,[24] and the three-headed serpent extending from Apollo to the earth.[25] This serpent might be seen musically as a bow—not a very well made one—drawn across the celestial lyre strings; or it might represent the single string of a cosmic monochord, like that depicted in Robert Fludd's *Utriusque Cosmi . . . Historia.*[26]

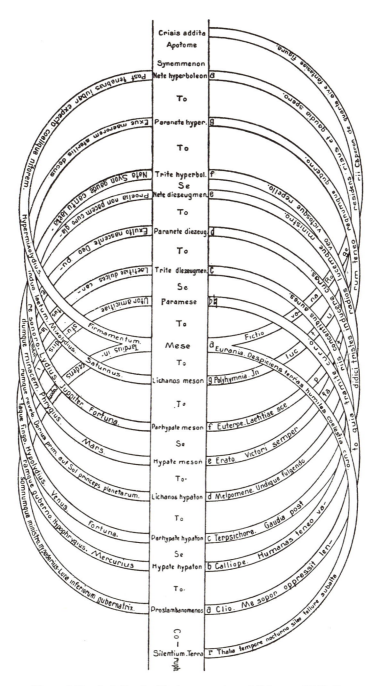

Figure 4. Ramis de Pareia, *Musicae practica,* ed. Johannes Wolf, 61.

We have seen that the inscription above Apollo is from a poem on the Muses ascribed to the late-Roman poet Ausonius (see n. 10 above); the activities of the
Muses inside their sphere-medallions may also be taken from Ausonius.[27] The
planets are shown as *trionfi* within their spheres, following a tradition that was well
established by the end of the fifteenth century.[28] One detail about the planets, mentioned in Gafori's text but not depicted in the woodcut, is the zodiacal houses they
occupy in this cosmic *harmonia*.[29] The cupids playing lute and *lira* in the upper
corners of figure 3 may have been suggested by Hesiod's statement that Cupid
abides with the Graces and the Muses.[30] As for Apollo's instrument, it would seem
to be a *lira da braccio* even though no bow can be seen (unless one reads the serpent
as a World-Bow).[31]

Although the fame of the Spanish theorist Ramis de Pareia rests upon his innovations, suggesting modification of Pythagorean tuning and of the Guidonian hexachordal system,[32] he professed himself a follower of Boethius, and the pages of his
Musica Practica are filled with quotations, exact or modified to suit the circumstance, from the *De Institutione Musica*.[33]

Opening with a definition of music and a statement of its triple division as given
by Boethius (*musica mundana, musica humana, musica instrumentalis*), Ramis
says he will treat *musica mundana* and *humana* in detail in his second and third
books. The promise was unfulfilled, but fortunately a discussion of the topics, described by Ramis as "superficial," is given in the *Practica*.[34] Because he is a good
deal concerned with the importance of the octave in musical theory, Ramis approaches the topic of world harmony through Cicero, twice (1.1.8; 1.3.3) quoting
the Ciceronian planetary scale as given by Boethius and used by Gafori. Cicero's
version of cosmic music, with the earth silent and motionless, gives Ramis another
image: in his revision of the Guidonian hand (1.2.7) he equates the concave palm
of the hand with the place "where there is silence" since there is no motion proper
to this part of the hand just as there is none proper to the earth. The first note is given
to the place where the hand joins the wrist; here there is movement, hence sound.
Succeeding notes are given the joints of thumb and fingers, not "sine ratione" as
Guido had done, but "cum maxima rei similitudine," at each point where there is
separate motion, until the entire three-octave range recommended by Ramis is
completed.[35]

The chapter dealing with *musica humana* and *mundana* approaches the subject
from the standpoint of differences in *ethos* among the modes. It is not surprising
that the Spaniard Ramis, who must often have heard of Arabic musico-medical
theories during his youth, should begin by comparing the modes with bodily humors: protus, or Dorian, dominates the phlegmatic; deuterus or Phrygian the cho-
leric; tritus or Lydian the sanguine; tetardus or Mixolydian the melancholic humor. The authentic modes each have an *ethos* connected with these humors, Dorian
being moderate and suitable for all music, Phrygian exciting, Lydian cheerful and
pleasant, Mixolydian both resistant to and subject to melancholy. The plagal
(hypo-) modes act each in opposition to the authentic ones.[36] A good deal of this
material on modal *ethos* is taken from the opening chapter of Boethius' *De Mu-*

sica. Where Boethius is not detailed or specific enough, Ramis does not hesitate to fill in what he considers the appropriate details, giving to specific modes effects which are mentioned in a general way by Boethius; this is done under the guise of quoting Boethius, and probably gives us an idea of how Ramis must have expounded Boethian theory in the university lectures he is said to have given at Bologna.[37]

Having shown, through modal *ethos,* the connection between earthly music and *musica humana,* Ramis proceeds to *musica mundana.* The Ciceronian world-scale is given after Boethius (1.27), then expanded upon:

> If therefore the moon is *proslambanomenos,* the sun *lichanos hypaton,* it is evident that those planets arrange melody at the interval of a fourth and therefore that the moon is Hypodorian, the sun Dorian. From this it is clear that the moon increases phlegmatic and humid [elements] in man; the sun indeed dries up these elements. Whence these planets, because they are leaders and light-givers, govern the first mode and the second. . . . Dorian, first of the authentic modes, may rightly be compared with the sun, since it holds chief place among the modes as does the sun among planets. For all terrestrial exhalations and sea vapors are raised up by solarian rays, from which meteoric impressions are created. Therefore the harmony between sun and moon is clear. The latter shines by night, the former flees the night; Hypodorian induces sleep, Dorian expels it. Therefore they harmonize both in situation and in conformity with the consonance of the diatessaron.
>
> Mercury indeed rules Hypophyrgian. For this is the mode of flatterers, wherewith the vicious, the wise, and the upright are alike praised . . .; such is the nature of Mercury. . . . Mars indeed controls Phrygian; it is wholly choleric and irascible, for with its wrath it attempts to destroy all the good things of the world. Therefore Mercury, either joined with it or in any aspect is just as evil as Mars itself. For the latter wounds with the sword, the former with the tongue.
>
> Hypolydian indeed is attributed to Venus, who is good fortune; nonetheless feminine in that she sometimes calls forth pious tears. Lydian, since it always denotes joy, may rightly be compared with Jupiter (greater good fortune), who creates men sanguine, benevolent, mild, and jocund. The harmony with Venus [is that] they agree in the diatessaron and in the good fortune of benevolence; nor do they differ except in the range of voices. For the lower voice is not so sweet or so smooth as the higher.
>
> Mixolydian may be attributed to Saturn, since it revolves about melancholy. Hypermixolydian may truthfully be termed *castalian*[38] because it is attributed to the starry sphere or firmament. For this mode above all others has a certain ingrafted sweetness and gracefulness.[39]

Here is the immediate source of the mode-planet correspondence found in Gafori and in the verses of Curti. But this is not all: Ramis, in order to give authority to his words by referring to "that from which music takes its origin," compares the Muses to planets, modes, and scale degrees, following, he says, Macrobius and Martianus Capella.[40] The comparison is of course the same as that used by Gafori. Ramis illustrates his idea with the diagram reproduced here as figure 4.[41] He explains the diagram:

When therefore we draw a circle from the first, that is, silence, to the last, and return, running over the whole harmony as far as the second, we create the Hypodorian. In the way that we have done this, we judge the others should be done, so that we should not cease making circles until we arrive at the last Muse—from which further stretching would be superfluous since it would be a replica of an earlier one; this stretching Roger Caperon asserted to be *crisis,* that above *nete hyperbolaeon,* and the other *coruph,* under *proslambanomenos. . . .* We indeed fear contradicting anything from antiquity; and therefore the first tone will be *proslambanomenos,* the last *nete hyperbolaeon.*[42]

There is evidence that Gafori borrowed the *Practica* of Ramis, probably in 1489. The critical marginalia made by Gafori in a copy belonging to a student of Ramis set off the well-known dispute between the two men and their adherents.[43] Now it becomes clear why Gafori, usually inclined to give his sources as proof of his wide reading, says vaguely that "some people" have made the sphere-Muse-mode comparison; not above using Ramis' idea, he was nevertheless unwilling to recognize its source publicly.

Thus treatises by the two men who headed opposing camps of musical thought at the turn of the sixteenth century both contain detailed accounts of modal *ethos* derived from *musica mundana.* A certain amount of this modal *ethos* found its way into the writings of later theorists, such as Gioseffo Zarlino, who were not much given to talking about musical cosmology;[44] whether the actual composition of Renaissance music was affected by these theories is a question too wide-ranging to be answered here.

Edward Lowinsky, in a paper assembling interesting details in support of his thesis that much Renaissance thinking about music was done in spatial terms,[45] refers to Ramis' use of the Ciceronian world scale. The illustration reproduced in figure 4 is certainly a spatial conception, as is that of Gafori. Both contain the familiar celestial monochord or lyre-string image, implicit in Plato and Boethius and realized graphically in medieval glosses on Boethius.[46] In Gafori this is joined to a literal illustration of the hierarchical Aristotelian universe, reaching vertically from the central earth to the abode of divinity. Ramis' diagram, with its circles both returning on themselves and spiraling upward, suggests at least two other things: one is the image of the serpent devouring its tail, an emblem familiar to Renaissance writers and a figure which could be used to signify the orbital movement of the heavens.[47] The other is the circular motion of sound, a theory accepted by many Renaissance scholars; in the diagram of Ramis one can almost see the spreading sound-circles of the Vitruvian image.[48] Much has been made of Renaissance *Augenmusik,* the use of note patterns that suggest visually the meaning they illustrate. Here one can see the obverse of the coin, which might be termed *Ohrlicht:* space organized in musical terms, a phenomenon at once visible and audible. Only by attempting to understand this blend of sense perception and Platonic vision can we approach the real meaning of *musica mundana* as a philosophical concept rising from evidence presented by the two "highest" senses, sight and hearing.

Postscript

For Gafori as humanist see Palisca, *Humanism in Italian Renaissance Musical Thought,* referred to above in chapter 2. On pages 170–71 of his book Palisca discusses the woodcut that is the subject of this article, emphasizing that it aims at revising Ramis' work as it copies it.

Gafori borrowed a copy of Ramis' treatise from the Bolognese musician and theorist Giovanni Spataro. On Spataro's resentment of Gafori's critical attitude toward Ramis, see Bonnie J. Blackburn, Edward E. Lowinsky, and Clement A. Miller, eds., *A Correspondence of Renaissance Musicians* (Oxford, 1991), 363–64, 453, 455.

An English version of Ramis' *Musica Practica* has recently been published: Clement A. Miller, *Ramis de Pareia, Musica Practica: Commentary and Translation* (American Institute of Musicology, 1993).

The seminal article by D. P. Walker on humanism in Renaissance musical thought has been reprinted; see Walker, *Music, Spirit, and Language in the Renaissance,* ed. Penelope Gouk (London, 1985), section 1.

Notes

1. Aby Warburg, "I Costumi teatrali per gli intermezzi del 1589," *Gesammelte Schriften* (Leipzig, 1932), 1:271, 412–14; Erwin Panofsky, "Titian's Allegory of Prudence: A Postscript," *Meaning in the Visual Arts* (Garden City, N.Y., 1957), 151–58; Jean Seznec, *La Survivance des dieux antiques* (London, 1940), English trans. by Barbara F. Sessions (New York, 1953), 140–42; Edgar Wind, *Pagan Mysteries in the Renaissance* (New Haven, 1958), 46–47, 50, 112–13. The woodcut is reproduced in two English translations of the *Practica,* that of Clement A. Miller (American Institute of Musicology, 1968) and that of Irwin Young (Madison, Wisc., 1969); it is briefly described on page xxix of the latter. The *Practica Musicae,* first printed in Milan in 1496, has been reprinted in facsimile (Farnborough, 1967).

2. On the illuminations of the MS. Florence, Bibl. Mediceo-Laurenziana, Pluteus 29, 1, see Rebecca A. Baltzer, "Thirteenth-Century Illuminated Miniatures and the Date of the Florence Manuscript," *JAMS* 25 (1972): 1–18.

3. For Guilielmus Signer or Le Signerre, see Claudio Sartori, *Dizionario degli editori musicali italiani* (Florence, 1958), 144; Mariangela Donà, *La stampa musicale a Milano fino all'anno 1700* (Florence, 1961), 72–73; Robert Proctor, *An Index to the Early Printed Books in the British Museum* (London, 1898), 1:403. For an assessment of Le Signerre's woodcuts see Friedrich Lippmann, *The Art of Wood-Engraving in Italy in the Fifteenth Century* (London, 1888; reprint, Amsterdam, 1969), 142ff.

4. There is a discussion of the relevant passages, and their sources, in the two editions of the *Theorica Musicae* in my "*Musica Mundana:* Variations on a Pythagorean Theme" (Ph.D. diss., Harvard University, 1960), 362–72. Gafori had a trilogy of theoretical works in mind at an early date, and probably wrote versions of all three of his major treatises well before publishing them. On this see Clement A. Miller, "Gaffurius's *Practica Musicae:* Origin and Contents," *MD* 22 (1968): 105–9. A manuscript copy of the *De Harmonia* dated 1500

is in the Bibl. Laudense in Lodi (cod. min. xxviii.a.9); see Claudio Sartori, "Gaffurius," *MGG,* 4:1240.

For information on another manuscript copy of the *De Harmonia,* one intended for the dedicatee of the printed volume, Jean Grolier, see Franz Unterkirchner, "Eine Handschrift aus dem Besitze Jean Groliers in der österreichischen Nationalbibliothek," *Libri. International Library Review* 1 (1950–51): 51–57. A colored drawing made after the woodcut under discussion here was included in this manuscript; it is reproduced by Unterkirchner, 55. Claude Palisca very kindly called the existence of this manuscript copy to my attention.

5. Even in the 1480 edition of his *Theorica* Gafori speaks of projected "alia volumina" (5.8). The idea of a trilogy may have been suggested to him by the three *Dialoghi* (1434) of Giorgio Anselmi of Parma, which he cites abundantly in the second edition of the *Theorica* as well as in his later works. See Jacques Handschin, "Anselmi's Treatise on Music Annotated by Gafori," *MD* 2 (1948): 123–40; Georgii Anselmi Parmensis, *De Musica,* ed. Giuseppe Massera (Florence, 1961), 29ff. The frontispiece of the *De Harmonia,* with its inscription "Fran. Gafuri. Laudensis. Tria de Musicis Volumina. Theoricam. ac Practicam. et Harmoniam Instrumentorum. Accuratissime conscripsit.," had already been used in the *Angelicum ac divinum opus musicae,* an Italian condensation of the *Practica* published in 1508 (printed, like the *De Harmonia,* by Gottardo da Ponte in Milan).

6. See Gafori's statement to this effect in the dedicatory letter of the *De Harmonia,* fol. 1. On the translations commissioned by Gafori, and the scholars who did them, see Alberto Gallo, "Le traduzioni dal Greco per Franchino Gaffurio," *Acta Musicologica* 35 (1963): 172–74.

7. *De Harmonia,* 4.5. fol. 86: "Sunt et qui coelestis harmoniae modos ipsos participes sentiunt: namque solis astrum dorium regere credunt, Marti vero Phrygium ascripsere. Iovi lydium, ac Mixolydium Saturno."

8. Cicero's order is an undefined tonal descent from the firmament to the moon, the stationary earth being silent though its inhabitants imitate celestial music with voice and instruments; see *Somnium Scipionis,* 5.1. Among all the ancient commentators on this passage Boethius was the most explicit, spelling out a planetary scale identical with that used by Gafori (*De Institutione Musica Libri Quinque,* 1.xxvii; p. 219 in the edition of G. Friedlein [Leipzig, 1867]).

9. Excluding Hypermixolydian, the added eighth mode taken by Boethius (4.xvii) from the *Harmonics* of Ptolemy, and discussed by Gafori in the *Theorica* (1492 ed., 5.8).

10. "In medio residens complectitur omnia phoebus." This line is taken from a poem attributed to the fourth-century Roman poet Ausonius, a little piece in which the Muses and their functions are named. The line preceding that just quoted is "Mentis Apollineae vis has movet undique Musas," used as the motto for Gafori's woodcut. For the poem of pseudo-Ausonius see R. Peiper, ed., *Ausonii Opuscula* (Leipzig, 1886), 412.

11. *De Harmonia,* 4.9, fol. 88v: "Mixolydius igitur (quis & caeteris quos praediximus acutior sit; & meroris imperium tenere existimetur) Saturno ascriptus est. Atque iccirco Dorius soli comparatur quis inter septem ipsos priores modos medius positus singulis proprium saltem tetrachordum communicet, namque & solis astrum medium inter septem planetas continens locum; caeteris vel lucem vel calorem propriis radiis conferre asseverant. Hinc Poeta cecinit In medio residens complectitur omnia phoebus. Hypermixolydium autem omnium acutissimum firmamento attribuunt: quasi illius sublimis ac divinae harmoniae participem: & a corruptibilibus (quas caeteris modulis convenire putant) proprietatibus solutum."

12. Glareanus was probably the first to criticize Gafori's understanding of modal theory;

see the *Dodecachordon* (Basel, 1547), 1.xxi. Girolamo Mei, the first Renaissance scholar who properly understood the difference between ancient and ecclesiastical modes, also criticized Gafori for not studying thoroughly the ancient sources at his disposal. See Claude V. Palisca, *Girolamo Mei (1519–1584). Letters on Ancient and Modern Music* (American Institute of Musicology, 1960), 55–56.

In fairness to Gafori it should be pointed out that in the *Practica Musicae* (1.7; 48–49 in Miller's translation) he speaks of the octave species, next of the classical modes, then only of the ecclesiastical modes, which are arranged "so as not to displease the order of ancient authority."

13. Pliny (*Naturalis Historia,* 2.20.84) and Martianus Capella (*De Nuptiis Philologiae et Mercurii,* 2: 199) link Saturn with Dorian, Jupiter with Phrygian; Johannes Lydus adds Lydian-Mars (*De Mensibus,* p. 20 in the edition of R. Wuensch [Leipzig, 1898]).

14. Greek names were not consistently applied to the ecclesiastical modes until the Renaissance. Their use caused a number of problems then; for an account of some of these difficulties see D. P. Walker, "Musical Humanism in the Sixteenth and Early Seventeenth Centuries," *Music Review* 2 and 3 (1941–42).

15. See *Practica,* 1.7 (p. 47 in Miller), where Hypermixolydian is described as identical in structure to the mode an octave below (Hypodorian). As for the church mode Hypomixolydian, it is said to be named in imitation of the ancient *hypo*-modes, since there was none by that name in antiquity.

16. For information on Curti, a rather bizarre figure who imitated the ancients in dress as well as in literary genres, see M. Pesenti Villa, "I letterati e i poeti," in F. Malaguzzi Valeri, *La corte di Lodovico il Moro* (Milan, 1923), 4:154–56. Curti is the author of a long poem, full of praise for Gafori, printed at the end of the 1492 edition of the *Theorica,* and may also be responsible for the verses quoted in *De Harmonia,* 4.12.

17. This composition was noticed by the greatest student of the modes in the sixteenth century, Glareanus, who mentions it in the *Dodecachordon,* 2.29.

18. See Ovid, *Metamorphoses,* 5; *Diodorus,* ed. C. H. Oldfather et al. (Cambridge, Mass., 1946–), 2:360–65; Varro, *De lingua latina,* 7.20 and 26; Hesiod, opening of the *Theogony;* Fulgentius, *Mitologiarum,* 1.xv; Callimachus, fragments of *Aetia;* the titles (each a Muse) of the nine books of Herodotus' *History;* Aristides, Περὶ μουσικῆς 2; p. 304 in the edition of R. Schäfke (Berlin, 1937).

19. *De Nuptiis Philologiae et Mercurii,* 1.27–29; pp. 19–20 in the edition of A. Dick (Leipzig, 1925): "Superi autem globi orbesque septemplices suavius cuiusdam melodiae harmonicis tinnitibus concinebant ac sono ultra solitum dulciore, quippe Musas adventare praesenserant, quae quidem singillatim circulis quibusque metatis, ubi suae pulsum modulationis agnoverant, constituerunt, nam Uranie stellantis mundi sphaeram extimam concinit, quae acuto raptabatur sonora tinnitu. Polymnia Saturniam circulum tenuit, Euterpe Iovialem, Erato ingressa Martium modulatur. Melpomene mediam, ubi Sol flammanti mundum lumine convenustat. Terpsichore Venerio sociatur auro, Calliope orbem complexa Cyllenium, Clio citimum circulum, hoc est in Luna collocavit hospitium, quae quidem gravis pulsus modis raucioribus personabat. Sola vero, quod vector eius cycnus impatiens oneris atque subvolandi alumna stagna petierat. Thalia derelicta in ipso florentis campi ubere residebat. Interea tractus aerios iam Phoebus exierat, cum subito ei vitta crinalis immutatur in radios, laurusque, quam dextera retinebat, in lampadam mundani splendoris accenditur, fiuntque volucres, qui currum Delium subvehebant, anheli flammantis [lucis] alipedes."

20. Homer, *Odyssey,* 24.60; Hesiod, see the opening of the *Theogony.*

21. See Plutarch, *Symposiacs,* 9.14, a quite full account of the Muses. For Varro see the

citation in Augustine, *De Doctrina Christiana,* 2.17 (Migne, *Pat. Lat.,* 34, col. 49). Varro's description is of three statues of Muses in a temple of Apollo (at Delphi?).

22. *Gesammelte Schriften,* 1:413. Warburg assembles the verses, which are scattered over chapter 12 of the fourth book of *De Harmonia.* He points out that they may be found, doubtless taken from Gafori, in Cornelius Agrippa's *Occulta Philosophia* of 1531 (2.26).

23. Ibid., 1.17.20.

24. Ibid., 1.17; p. 89 in the edition of F. Eyssenhardt (Leipzig, 1868): "Apollinis simulacra manu dextera Gratias gestant, arcum cum sagittis sinistra. . . ." The bow and arrow are not at Apollo's left in the illustration; however, in the medallion of the sun in figure 3 is another Apollo with an arrow.

Wind, *Pagan Mysteries,* chapters 2–3, has a good deal of material on the ways in which the Graces were depicted. His figure 18, from the "Mantegna" *Tarocchi* (ca. 1460) is quite close to the appearance of the Graces in Gafori's woodcut. Wind's explanation (p. 46n) of the vase of flowers in the illustration as representing Macrobius' *crater* through which the divine spirit descends to earth seems overelaborate. The flowers might simply represent the laurel which is one of Apollo's regular appurtenances.

25. *Saturnalia,* 1.20 (p. 115 in Eyssenhardt). For a discussion of how the Serapian monster described by Macrobius was changed into a serpent identified with Apollo (this version made famous in Petrarch's *Africa*), see Panofsky, *Meaning in the Visual Arts,* 153–58; Seznec, *The Survival of Pagan Gods,* 170–79. On the presence of the four elements clustered about the heads of the serpent, see Kathi Meyer-Baer, *Music of the Spheres and the Dance of Death* (Princeton, 1970), 191.

26. Fludd's illustration is reproduced in W. Pauli, "The Influence of Archetypal Ideas on the Scientific Theories of Kepler," in Jung and Pauli, *The Interpretation of Nature and the Psyche* (London, 1955), plate 5 and page 193. Despite Pauli's remark that Fludd's work is "in agreement with old Pythagorean ideas" the monochord is full of musical and cosmological oddities; see Haar, "*Musica mundana,*" 489–95. Mersenne, who strongly disapproved of Fludd, nevertheless borrowed this illustration—without acknowledgment—for his *Harmonie universelle* (Paris, 1636), 8.49. Several of Fludd's diagrams are reproduced and commented on in Meyer-Baer, *Music of the Spheres,* 193–202.

27. For a quite different set of Muse medallions see Wind, *Pagan Mysteries,* fig. 70, taken from the *Melopoiae* of Tritonius (1507).

28. Cf. Seznec, *The Survival of Pagan Gods,* 70.

29. This connection of planets and lyre-strings with the zodiac was probably adapted by Gafori from Ptolemy (*Harmonics,* 3.8).

30. Hesiod, *Theogony,* 1.66.

31. See the contemporary *Parnassus* of Raphael, in which Apollo, surrounded by the nine Muses, is shown bowing a *lira da braccio.* The *lira* could be plucked as well as bowed, however.

32. Gustave Reese, *Music in the Renaissance* (New York, 1954), 586ff.

33. The prologue of the *Musica Practica* (Bologna, 1482; facsimile, ed. Giuseppe Vecchi [Bologna, 1969]; modern edition by Johannes Wolf in *Publikationen der internationalen Musikgesellschaft,* Beihefte 2 [Leipzig, 1901]) begins with a compliment to Boethius. Ramis at one point (1.2.6; pp. 42–43 in Wolf) remarks that during his student days at Salamanca he wrote a treatise in the vernacular to confound one "magister Osmensis" who confused the three Greek *genera* with the three hexachords. Osmensis on seeing the treatise admitted, "Non sum ego adeo Boetio familiaris sicut iste." To this Gafori adds the marginal comment (for Gafori and the treatise of Ramis see below) "Here the author is boasting" (Hic se multum iactat auctor).

34. Ibid., 1.3.3 (pp. 56–60 in Wolf).

35. Ibid., 1.2.7 (pp. 45–46 in Wolf). An illustration of this revised Guidonian hand is given on page 47 in Wolf.

36. Ibid., 1.3.2 (pp. 56–57 in Wolf).

37. Compare the following passage as written by Boethius and as quoted by Ramis:

Boethius, 1.1 (pp. 185–86 in Friedlein):	Ramis, 1.3.3 (p. 56 in Wolf):
". . . ut Pythagorici, cum diuturnas in somno resolverent curas, quibusdam cantilenis uterentur, ut eis lenis et quietus sopor inreperet. Itaque experrecti aliis quibusdam modis stuporem somni confusionemque purgabant, id nimirum scientes quod tota nostrae animae corporisque compago musica coaptatione coniuncta sit."	"Erant autem pythagoricis in morem, ut cum diuturnas in somno curas resolverent, *hypodorio* uterentur, ut eis lenis et quietus somnus irreperet. Experrecti vero *dorio* stuporem somni confusionemque purgabant scientes nimirum, ut ait Boetius, quod tota nostrae animae corporisque compago musica coaptatione coniuncta est."

38. From Κασταλία, a fountain on Parnassus sacred to Apollo and the Muses. Reading this may have given Gafori the idea for his woodcut.

39. Ibid., 1.3.3 (pp. 58–59 in Wolf): "Si igitur Luna proslambanomenos, Sol vero lichanos hypaton, liquet istos duos planetas in diatessaron specie cantus collocandos atque ideo Lunam hypodorium, Solem vero dorium modum tenere. Ex eo liquido constat Lunam flegmatica et humida homini adaugere, Solem vero ipsa humida et flegmatica desiccare. Inde ergo isti duo planetae, quia principalia et luminaria sunt, primum modum regunt cum secundo. . . . Nam dorius primus autenticorum recte Soli comparatur, quia principatum tenet inter omnes modus sicut Sol inter omnes planetas. Nam omnes exhalationes terrestres et vapores marini solaribus radiis elevantur, ex quibus impressiones meteoricae creantur. Convenientia igitur inter Solem et Lunam clara est. Ista lucet nocte, ille noctem fuget; hypodorius somnum ducit, dorius vero expellit. Concordant ergo et loco et conformitate in diatessaron consonantia.

"Mercurius vero hypophrygium reget. Nam iste modus adulatorum est, qui viciosos et sapientes probosque aequo modo collautum . . . qualis est natura Mercurii. . . . Mars vero phrygium tenet, qui totus colericus est et iracundus; nam omnia mundi bona iracundia sua conatur destruere. Iunctus ergo Mercurius cum eo aut in aspectu quodam ita malus est sicut ipse Mars. Nam ille ense vulnerat, iste vero linqua.

"Hypolydius vero ipsi Veneri est attributus, quae fortuna est, feminea tamen, quia provocat ad lacrimas pias quandoque. Lydius vero Iovi, fortunae majori, quo homines sanguineos et benevolos creat mitesque atque iocundos, recte comparatur, cum semper gaudium notet. Convenentia cum Venere in diatessaron atque in bonitatis fortuna concordant nec differunt nisi vocum differentia. Inferior enim vox non ita dulcis est sicut acuta neque suavis.

"Mixolydius vero attribuitur Saturno, quoniam circa melancholiam versatur. Hypermixolydius vero totaliter ponitur castalinus, quoniam coelo attribuitur stellato sive firmamento. Nam hic modus super omnes alios habet quandam insitam dulcedinem cum venustate."

The portion of the passage dealing with Hypolydian and Lydian is cited by Edward Lowinsky, "The Goddess Fortuna in Music," *MQ* 29 (1943): 72.

40. Ramis does not follow Macrobius (*Comm. in Somn. Scip.*, 2.3; [pp. 581–82 in Eyssenhardt]), who makes Calliope the leader of all the Muses. His ordering is taken from Martianus, the passage cited in n. 19 above.

41. Figure 4 is reproduced from Wolf's edition of the *Musica Practica*. In the Bolognese

print of 1482, the diagram was printed without text; the copy reprinted in the facsimile (see n. 33 above) shows, without editorial comment, this textless form. Another copy, in Bologna, Museo Civico Bibliografico Musicale, A 80, has the diagram filled in by hand, with an explanatory rubric describing the lunar-Hypodorian octave on the model of which the other interlocking octave circles are made. The notes of the scale are in the center column, with intervals of tone or semitone marked. The lines describing Muses and planets and modes are not in Ramis' text, though their contents are paraphrased there (1.3.3).

On the question as to whether there were one or two editions of Ramis' work printed in Bologna in 1482, see the introduction to the facsimile edition (pp. iv–v) cited in n. 33 above.

42. Ibid., 1.3.3 (pp. 59–60 in Wolf): "Cum igitur a prima idest a silentio ad ultimam circulum facimus et ad secundam totum concentum remittentes recurrimus, hypodorium procreamus. Quemadmodum igitur de istis fecimus, de reliquis faciendum esse arbitramur, ita quod spiras facere non cessemus, donec ad ultimam musam perveniamus, a qua superflua, si fiat, erit intentio, quoniam replicatio prioris est, ut Rogerius Caperon asserebat esse crisim vocem illam supra neten hyperboleon additam et coruph, quae sub proslambanomeno. . . . Nos vero caveamus ab antiquitate auctore aliquid transvertere. Erit igitur prior vox proslambanomenos, ultima vero nete hyperboleon."

On Roger Caperon and his terminology, which Ramis uses in his illustration but strongly disapproves of, see my "Roger Caperon and Ramis de Pareia," *Acta Musicologica* 41 (1969): 26–36.

43. For Gafori's having borrowed a copy of Ramis' works, see Wolf's edition of the *Musica Practica,* x; cf. Massera, *Georgii Anselmi Parmensis. De Musica,* page 28, and the plate following page 32, a page from the *Musica Practica* with annotations in Gafori's hand. The controversy is briefly summarized in Reese, *Music in the Renaissance,* 586–87; some interesting details are given in Albano Sorbelli, "Le due edizione della *Musica practica* di Bartolome Ramis de Pareia," *Gutenberg Jahrbuch* 5 (1930): 105–14.

44. See book 4 of Zarlino's *Le istitutioni harmoniche* (Venice, 1558).

45. "The Concept of Physical and Musical Space in the Renaissance," *Papers of the American Musicological Society,* 1941 (1946): 57–84.

46. An example may be found in Paris, Bibliothèque Nationale, MS.lat.7203, an early twelfth-century Boethian gloss. See Jacques Handschin, "Ein mittelalterlichen Beitrag zur Lehre von der Sphärenharmonie," *Zeitschrift für Musikwissenschaft* 9 (1927): 193–208. In this representation a two-octave scale like that in Ramis' diagram is equated with the planets by seven of the angelic hierarchies.

47. The emblem is contained in the *Hieroglyphica* of Horus Apollo, known in Florence as early as 1419, first printed in 1505. See George Boas, *The Hieroglyphics of Horapollo* (New York, 1950), 29.

Guy le Fèvre de la Boderie's *La Galliade* (Paris, 1578) opens with an image in which the firmament is explicitly likened to a serpent devouring its own tail. On this poem see D. P. Walker, *Spiritual and Demonic Magic from Ficino to Campanello* (London, 1958), 122–24.

48. Cf. Vitruvius, *De Architectura,* 5.3.6–7. A passage in Ficino's commentary on the *Timaeus* of Plato (*Opera* [Basel, 1576], 1456) describes sound as a series of spiralling ovals, very suggestive of Ramis' diagram.

False Relations and Chromaticism
in Sixteenth-Century Music

THE RISE OF CHROMATICISM in the music—and particularly in the Italian madrigal—of the sixteenth century has long interested scholars. In the search for evidence of developing major-minor tonality, conducted in Burckhardtian hopes for signs of the modern musical world in Renaissance culture, tonally strengthening sharps and flats seemed important evidence. Tonally disruptive chromaticism could at the same time be used as demonstration of a Spenglerian decay in the contrapuntal fabric, or seen as analogous to the breakdown of tonality under the burden of nineteenth-century chromaticism. Heroes and villains in the saga could be identified (with Rore and Marenzio seen consistently as heroes, Gesualdo formerly a villain but now perhaps an anti-hero), and this not only by modern scholars. Zarlino disliked the "cromatici," and Artusi's opposition to the "moderni" who broke contrapuntal laws is described in every survey of music history; the suggestive parallel with the nineteenth century has led one scholar to compare Artusi with Hanslick[1] (elsewhere, for all I know, he may be directly likened to Beckmesser).

Many of these concerns and attitudes now seem dated. Modality and tonality are no longer often seen as opposingly self-contained systems; the rise of the *seconda prattica* no longer seems—it was never so intended—aimed at the destruction or total replacement of the classical polyphonic system. Our own tolerant acceptance of disparate trends, our preference for theories of circular change over those of evolutionary progress, may of course also come to look very dated; but that is a subject for a different sort of argument than is proposed here. In these pages, I would like to discuss aspects of sixteenth-century chromaticism apparent on the surface of the music, without attempting generalizations on the larger tonal significance of the phenomena described.[2] The one general conclusion I shall attempt to support is that a good deal of chromaticism in this music is the result of what appears to have been a genuine liking for the cross relation—the *mi-fa* clash—not only among avowed chromaticists but also in the work of composers who wrote basically diatonic music, or who were at most, to use Kroyer's classification, "intermediate" chromaticists.[3]

What is chromatic music in the sixteenth century? Remembering the fate of Nicola Vicentino, who attempted to convince his unbelieving contemporaries that the chromatic genus existed in what they regarded as unimpeachably diatonic polyphony, one should respond to this question with some care.[4] The closest one might come to an answer that would have been generally accepted in the sixteenth century is that intentionally chromatic music contains melodies using the small or chromatic semitone (c–$c\sharp$ or $b\flat$–$b\natural$) in addition to the large or diatonic semitone (a–$b\flat$ or, with musica ficta, $c\sharp$–d).[5] Even Vicentino, for whom the mere presence of the skip of a minor third indicated an admixture of the chromatic genus,[6] was careful to put directly chromatic melodic movement into the music he wished to be known as belonging to that genus; in this way he made use of the chromatic tetrachords of antiquity.

Chromaticism for the sixteenth century thus meant a kind of melodic writing. Only as a consequence (and with a good deal of attendant difficulty over intonation)[7] did the polyphonic texture, or the whole piece, become chromatic. There appears to have been no regularly used term for music full of sharps and flats, but without direct melodic chromaticism.[8] Pieces to which this description applies may nonetheless sound quite chromatic, at least in the sense of being harmonically colorful, to our ears. Without attempting to say precisely how they sounded to sixteenth-century ears, we may assume that they created an effect different from music that remained within the untransposed confines of its chosen modal species.

In late sixteenth-century music, unexpected accidentals sometimes give the impression of having dropped from the sky, with no preparation and no consequences. Nearly all sixteenth-century chromaticism is, however, encountered in movement from one sonority to another, orderly in plan if sometimes daring in the motion of individual voices. There are several distinct harmonic progressions by means of which sixteenth-century composers achieved a coloristic result without recourse to melodic chromaticism.[9] One was the use of a chain of progressions with the bass moving by fifths or fourths, following what we are accustomed to call the circle of fifths (ex. 5.1).[10] From the time of Josquin's celebrated use of this device in *Absalom fili mi*,[11] it was an occasional resource; by the middle of the sixteenth century it had become a commonly used one, remaining in vogue through the century. Despite the apparent tonal "strength" of each pair of chords, this seems primarily a coloristic device, sometimes almost waywardly so, allowing the composer quick departure from (and, if he chose, easy return to) the main tonal center. In later sixteenth-century music, one sometimes finds real if fleeting establishment of new pitch levels reached by this process (sometimes with the help of harmonic sequence). Use of the circle of fifths, without other progressions and without ellipsis, does not, of course, call for melodic chromaticism, nor does it create false relations.

Example 5.1 Rore, *Rex Asiae et Ponti*, mm. 1–3

A second progression often involving musica ficta, or sharps and flats outside the mode,[12] is one in which the bass moves by tone or semitone (thus often in a *mi*-

fa relationship) up or down (ex. 5.2). The higher bass note in this progression is often beneath what we would term a chordal inversion, a phenomenon covered by discant theory, in which behavior of all the chord parts, wherever they may lie, is discussed even though no special recognition of a chordal entity surviving the accident of rearrangement of its members was a part of that theory. Although melodic chromaticism of the sixteenth-century sort (using the small semitone) is not called for in this progression, it can be chromatic enough in our sense and can create plenty of what Zarlino, as we shall see, calls "nonharmonic relations," particularly in what for want of a better term is called the V–IV progression (ex. 5.3). Or chromaticism can result from coloristic decoration applied to a diatonic stepwise progression (ex. 5.4).

Example 5.2 Lasso, *Sibylla Libyca*, mm. 42–46

Example 5.3 Lasso, *Sibylla Europaea*, mm. 3–5

Example 5.4

a. Willaert, *Sacro fonte regenerate*, mm. 71–73

b. Rore, "Pommi ov' il sol occide," mm. 10–11

Alteration of the third degree over a static bass is another common way in which harmonic color is introduced. This often occurs between the end of one phrase and the beginning of the next (ex. 5.5), a point at which many of the rules for correct counterpoint seem to have been suspended.[13] This change of color can also occur in mid-phrase, sometimes, but not always, as a result of a large leap in one of the voices (ex. 5.6). The alteration of degree may even take place in the same voice without giving rise to suspicions that the chromatic genus is lurking in the wings (ex. 5.7). There is an audible cross relation in all these examples, but the steadying influence of the stationary bass seems to lessen its effect.

The fourth type of progression by which accidentals foreign to the mode may be brought in is that in which the bass moves by a third, major or minor, up or down (exx. 5.8–11). In all of these progressions, the use of accidentals creates strongly heard cross relations, however fine the tuning of the (presumably just) thirds may be in performance.

Example 5.5

a. Willaert, "O dolce vita mia," mm. 1–5

b. Pigna, "Deh torn' a me mio sol," mm. 1–4

Example 5.6

a. Barré, "Era il bel viso," mm. 12–14

b. Willaert, "Io mi rivolgo,"
   m. 22

c. Rore, "Se ben il duol," mm. 1–2

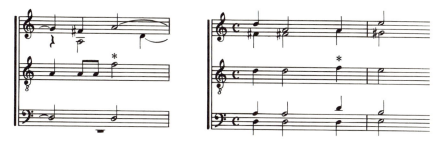

Example 5.7

a. Fogliano, "Tua volsi esser mai," mm. 19–22

b. Schiavetti, "Era il bel viso," mm. 5–7

Example 5.8 Major third up

a. Perissone Cambio, "Scarpello sì vedrà," mm. 9–11

b. Barré, "Corro la fresca," mm. 26–27

c. Lasso, *Carmina chromatico*, mm. 1–5

Example 5.9 Major third down

a. Ghibel, "La verginella," mm. 18–21

b. Alessandrino, "Sia vile agl' altri," mm. 15–16

c. Lasso, *Sibylla Phrygia*, mm. 8–10

Example 5.10 Minor third up

a. Mouton, *Benedicam Dominum in omni tempore*, mm. 10–11

b. Willaert, *O invidia nemica*, mm. 23–24

c. Ruffo, "Non rumor di tamburi," mm. 10–11

Example 5.11 Minor third down

a. Rore, "Come la notte ogni fiammella," mm. 19–22

b. Tudino, "Altro che lagrimar," mm. 3–4

c. Scipione della Palla (?) "Che non può far donna," mm. 1–3

d. Gero, "Dolcemente s'adirà," mm. 42–44

Instances of progressions with the bass moving by a major third are common in the late sixteenth century, indeed are associated with the style of Marenzio and his contemporaries (see ex. 5.12). When used earlier in the century they are self-consciously chromatic in intent, as the opening of Lasso's *Prophetiae Sibyllarum* (ex. 5.8c) shows. It is difficult to use accidentals in this progression without melodic chromaticism in a single voice. The coloristic minor-third progression, on the other hand, can easily be written with diatonic voice leading in all parts (this perhaps making the false relation all the more striking); its frequent use can be seen much earlier, and in the mid-century madrigal it becomes a noticeable stylistic accessory.

Example 5.12 Marenzio, "Quell' augellin che canta," mm. 16–20

Bass movement in thirds is a characteristic feature of much Renaissance polyphony, so much so that it should be considered a "strong" progression in the language of harmony textbooks (ex. 5.13). If all the thirds between outer voices in example 5.13 were made major through chromatic alteration ($g\sharp, f\sharp$ in the cantus; $e\flat$ in the bass), Josquin could be converted into a Sibylline prophet in no time. Without going to this extreme, one can see that chains of falling thirds may create problems of musica ficta even in the style of Josquin (ex. 5.14);[14] but in general, the use of a bass line with many skips of a third need not produce cross relations.

Example 5.13 Josquin, *Missa Pange lingua*, Kyrie II, mm. 58–61

Example 5.14 Josquin, *Benedicite omnia opera Domini*, mm. 1–7

Deliberate use of a false relation in this progression begins to show up in the frottola repertory, where it can serve as an effective way to separate phrases (ex. 5.15). Occasionally in this music, the cross relation turns up in mid-phrase, as in example 5.16, from a *strambotto* of which both text and music have been attributed to the celebrated improviser Serafino Aquilano.[15] The generally rough texture of this piece leads one to think that the cross relation was the result of chance, carelessness, or even faulty technique. What might be termed "correct" usage can be seen in a piece by an expert technician, Arcadelt (ex. 5.17), where the cross relation is mitigated by the presence of an intervening chord. Even in Arcadelt, the intervening chord can be merely hinted at (ex. 5.18), or left out altogether (ex. 5.19).[16] In example 5.19, the cantus *e* in the fourth measure could be given an editorial flat, eliminating the cross relation. No singer with cantus partbook in hand would have flatted the note, however; and it is my contention that clashes of this sort were not only tolerated but liked by sixteenth-century musicians. Certainly they occur often enough in the work of the best composers to preclude our simply labeling them *gaucheries.*

Example 5.15 Anonymous, "Per sonetti": "Ben che la facia," second phrase

Example 5.16 Serafino Aquilano (?), "Se'l zapator il giorno," mm. 1–6

Example 5.17 Arcadelt, "Occhi miei lassi," mm. 58–60

Example 5.18 Arcadelt, "Madonna mia gentile," mm. 22–24

Example 5.19 Arcadelt/Berchem, "Pungente dardo," mm. 12–16

As the expressive possibilities of the tonal vocabulary were developed in the course of the century, use of chromaticism to underscore word meaning became a regular feature in the madrigal. Heliseo Ghibel was surely proud of his chromatic setting of Ariosto's "Ben furo aventurosi i cavallieri," beginning with the tonally adventurous point of imitation seen in example 5.20. Cipriano de Rore's celebrated use of expressive chromaticism[17] would lead one to believe that he chose false relations to emphasize verbal meaning. So he did, sometimes; but Bernhard Meier, after conscientiously trying to see meaning in every one of Rore's cross relations, admitted that "false relations may not always be considered as being textually determined."[18] An instance of a textually neutral false relation in Rore's work may be seen in example 5.21, viewed by Meier as resulting from an explicitly marked observance of *fa super la*.[19] This is a point that seems generally true of sixteenth-century composers: a turn of melody or harmony that could effectively underscore the meaning of a word or phrase could elsewhere be used for purely musical reasons. Music as the servant of the text, in other words, had its days off.

Example 5.20 Ghibel, "Ben furo aventurosi i cavalieri," mm. 1–5

Example 5.21 Rore, "La vita fugge," mm. 35–36

Composers did not thus always use chromaticism for expressive purposes. When they did, their vocabulary was not uniform, and it changed as the century wore on. If one compares Arcadelt's setting of the phrase *et io piangendo* in "Il bianco e dolce cigno" with that of Vecchi (in a piece paraphrasing much of Arcadelt's setting), Arcadelt's V–IV progression (ex. 5.22a) seems milder, more old-fashioned than Vecchi's direct chromaticism (ex. 5.22b), yet no less effective.[20] Both are pale by comparison with what Marenzio and Monteverdi, not to say Gesualdo, were to do. The usage of these composers is beyond the scope of this article, though I think it could be studied in a way similar to what is being tried here. One or two points could simply be mentioned as examples. The long-spun resolution of suspensions over a number of measures, a device beloved of Monteverdi, results in numerous cross relations formed by the different rates of speed at which individual voices resolve, a kind of magnification of small-scale clashes in earlier music and often productive of the same kinds of false relation. In Marenzio and his contemporaries, the use of root-position chords so heavily emphasized in mid-century music is modified, with many six-three sonorities introduced, so that a more graceful bass line results—at the same time incorporating many of the chromatic progressions described here.

Example 5.22

a. Arcadelt, "Il bianco e dolce cigno," mm. 5–10

b. Vecchi, "Il bianco e dolce cigno," mm. 9–12

The occasional chromatic false relations seen in Arcadelt and his contemporaries become much more frequent in the music of the next generation of madrigalists. This phenomenon is not restricted to a particular place; it is not, for instance, peculiar to Venetian composers and so is not special evidence of Venetian love of color, as Einstein seems to stress.[21] Antonio Barré in Rome, Pietro Taglia in Milan, Stefano Rossetti in Florence all provide numerous examples. The composer I choose for demonstration here, Hoste da Reggio, was in the service of a member of the Gonzaga family and was active in Mantua and later in Milan.[22] Hoste cultivated the declamatory, rhythmically supple *madrigale arioso* style popular in the 1550s.[23] His music is not at the level of Rore's madrigals, or equal in grace and fluency to that of Ruffo, the other great madrigalist of this generation; but it is competently wrought and is full of tonal surprises.[24] Chromatic false relations of the kind discussed above are to be found in abundance; if one were to include examples in which an audible cross relation can be heard through one or two intermediate chords, they are almost too numerous to count. The following are some instances of direct cross relations: (1) change of third over the same bass (ex. 5.23a–c); (2) bass movement up a tone (ex. 5.23d); (3) bass movement down a tone (ex. 5.23e), here for a final cadence (!), following change of third over the same bass; (4) bass movement up a minor third (ex. 5.23f–h); (5) down a major third (ex. 5.23i); (6) down a minor third (ex. 5.23j–k). The generally fluid, rather restless harmonic language of these madrigals may be illustrated by a typical opening phrase (ex. 5.23l) and a typical ending (ex. 5.23m). Though Hoste knew the value of chromaticism for expressive purposes (he wanders as far afield as $a^\flat$ to set the words *più dura* in one piece),[25] the examples given from his works are not used for effects of word painting; they are part of the composer's tonal language, a restive and experimental idiom in itself.

Example 5.23 Excerpts from madrigals by Hoste da Reggio

a. "O quante volt'," mm. 32–34

b. "Non vi vieto per questo," mm. 5–7

c. "Crudel di che peccato," mm. 22–24

d. "Se'l dolce sguardo di costei," mm. 24–25

e. "Gente a cui nulla fede," mm. 41–43

f. "Così fan questi giovani," mm. 30–31

g. "Si le vive faville," mm. 31–32

h. "Poi che mia ferma stella," mm. 51–53

i. "O beata colei," mm. 20–21

j. "Donna se per mirar," mm. 13–14

k. "Deh qual prova maggior," mm. 29–31

l. "Deh qual prova maggior," mm. 1–4

m. "Madonna per voi ardo," mm. 28–31

In a few cases, the cross relations are not only direct but simultaneous, making one wonder whether they can or should be interpreted literally (ex. 5.24). No theory of "cautionary" accidentals would seem to account for these spots.[26] If they are not mistakes—the left-hand partbook not knowing what the right is doing—they are further evidence of the deliberate indulgence in cross relations characteristic of this music.

Example 5.24

a. "Hoste, "O quante volt'," mm. 4–7

b. Barré, "E nella face," mm. 32–35

One progression I have not found in the work of Hoste da Reggio is bass movement up by a major third, a chord sequence in which direct melodic chromaticism is almost inevitable. For all his venturesome attitude toward false relations, he seems to have avoided use of what in the sixteenth century would have been called the chromatic genus. His contemporaries did not hold back from taking this step; Rore's celebrated chromatic experiments come from this time, and composers influenced by the theories of Nicola Vicentino were producing explicitly marked *madrigali cromatici* in the 1550s. The *Prophetiae Sibyllarum* of Lasso opens with a progression labeled in the text as chromatic (see ex. 5.8c, above), and using bass movement of a major third.[27]

Vicentino, whose defense of the chromatic genus as a legitimate way of writing polyphony is well known, supplied examples of melodic chromaticism both in his treatise and in his later madrigals.[28] This music also contains examples of false relations produced by diatonic melodic movement, often in bass progressions of a minor third.[29] Deliberate use of the chromatic genus by Vicentino could sometimes have been avoided, had he so wished, by rescoring of chordal passages, as a comparison of examples 5.25a and b shows. The music he described favorably as "participata e mista," rather than having the "asprezza" of completely diatonic music,[30] had in the works of other composers already been in existence without need of the self-consciously introduced chromatic genus and its small melodic semitone. This is said not to minimize Vicentino's contribution but to stress that the sound of chromatic false relations was evidently liked by composers, even those apparently little interested in reviving the ancient genera.

Example 5.25

a. Vicentino, *Alleluia*, mm. 1–6

b. A "diatonic" version

Critics of Vicentino's theories spoke disparagingly of the new chromaticism. Ghiselin Danckerts, an opponent of Vicentino in the latter's debate with Lusitano, wrote scornfully of "how one finds in present days that music of the diatonic genus has come into such disorder, under these new-fangled composers' pretexts of writing in a new fashion, that the form and melody of authentic and plagal modes no longer exists."[31] Zarlino devoted a good deal of space to refuting the *cromatici*, with Vicentino not named but surely meant as their leader.[32] First stating that properly tuned counterpoint cannot be written around a tenor in the chromatic or enharmonic genus (at a later point Zarlino says that the reason the ancients were successful in these genera is that they sang melodies over drone basses or accompaniments using only the simplest perfect intervals), Zarlino continues by denying that modern composers who claim to be writing in these genera are actually doing so, since they use only the characteristic pitch intervals (in addition to some other, extraneous ones) without the rhythmic and textual correspondences (*numero* and *parole*) of the ancients. Nor is the appearance of major and minor thirds, undivided in their tetrachords, a sign of enharmonic or chromatic genera. These intervals appear undivided in the diatonic genus as well, else no melody could be written—any more than one could speak or write if always compelled to go through the alphabet in order without skipping letters. What is really happening in the music of his time, Zarlino continues, is that there are pieces full of sharps and flats which should be seen as diatonic with an admixture of the chromatic.[33] Such usage is valuable for expressive purposes and also for transposing music,[34] but insistence on composing whole pieces in the chromatic genus leads only to ugliness and absurdity.

Zarlino apparently approved of at least some of the "diatonic" chromaticism I have been describing. His views on false relations are something else again. In a chapter (3.29) discussing parallel intervals, he points out that parallel major thirds and major sixths lack "harmonic relationship," a term he promises to explain later, and so should be avoided; parallel minor thirds and major sixths are less objectionable. Thus far he has been talking of stepwise motion; when the movement is by skip (the example shows thirds and sixths moving by major and minor thirds), the progression is absolutely forbidden. In the next chapter, the harmonic relation, and its absence, are explained:

> When we say that the parts of a composition do not have a harmonic relation between their voices, we mean that the parts are separated by an augmented or diminished diapason, or by a semidiapente or tritone or similar interval. The harmonic relation does not involve merely two simultaneous notes distant in pitch. It occurs rather among four notes contained in two voices that form two consonances [ex. 5.26].[35]

Example 5.26 Zarlino: The nonharmonic relation

Diagonal connecting of notes shows the false relations, among which the first in example 5.26 is of prime interest for our subject. Zarlino says these are not as bad as if they were in a single voice but are very noticeable in two-voice writing and should be avoided if correctness is the composer's goal. In many-voice composition these intervals may be unavoidable, especially in fugal or imitative writing. Should the "defect" occur, however, it should be in music that remains within its chosen mode, not as the result of accidentals. An example of the latter, in the touchy E mode, is given by the theorist (ex. 5.27); Zarlino's judgment of a passage such as example 5.28 may thus be imagined. In the next chapter, Zarlino repeats his admission that avoidance of the "non-harmonic" relation is less crucial in compositions for many voices; still, he would prefer to see a major third followed by a minor third rather than by another major third.

Example 5.27 Zarlino: Nonharmonic relation caused by an accidental

Example 5.28 Fabrianese, "Miser chi mal' oprando," mm. 1–4

The teaching of counterpoint traditionally began with two-voice writing, and there is a sizable literature of duos in sixteenth-century music. But much Renaissance polyphony of three and more voices is made out of varyingly combined duos. The false relations in most of the examples I have cited being audible as if only two parts were present, one can only conclude that Zarlino would have regarded these as borderline cases verging on objectionable chromaticism. For this reason, care was taken to include a few citations from the music of Zarlino's revered teacher Willaert, whom he would never have criticized; the more adventurous experiments of a man like Hoste da Reggio would presumably not have met with his approval.

Zarlino's discussion of the nonharmonic relation does not appear in brief compilations of his work such as the *Compendio* of Tigrini (1588). It is faithfully copied, however, in Cerone's *El Melopeo*.[36] Artusi's *L'Arte del contraponto* not only repeats but elaborates on Zarlino's point, adding that one should not go from unison to major sixth by contrary motion or from fifth to sixth by parallel motion if the parts move by semitone and minor third respectively; that major and minor sixths in parallel motion (using the skip of a third) are poor; and that parallel major thirds using this skip are equally bad—all because they create a *mi-fa* or nonharmonic relationship.[37] Thus the examples from mid-century madrigals cited here would not have met with Artusi's approval; his censure of Monteverdi's chromaticisms can hardly be wondered at.

Renaissance theorists from Tinctoris on clucked disapprovingly at infractions of their rules, which of course were meant to instruct beginners in the art of correct composition. There is no reason to think that in any period—let alone the restless mid-sixteenth century, in which the roots of the *seconda prattica* lie—were their precepts followed to the letter by experienced composers. Theorists' views of the chromatic false relations I have cited are thus to me not of damning importance, though Zarlino's close observance of detail is always worth noticing.

What emerges here, I would hope, is the acceptance of, and in some composers even a somewhat exaggerated preference for, false relations created through use of written accidentals. As the examples given here show, there is often no melodic need—*fa super la* or anything else—satisfied by this chromaticism. It seems clear that such accidentals were regarded as salutary condiment to the blandly diatonic modal framework within which sixteenth-century musicians worked. The repertory covered here is limited in genre and in time span. Earlier music, though it has fewer written accidentals, could certainly be looked at more than I have done in this regard.[38] Intabulations and other instrumental music could provide a rich field for investigation.[39] The oft-mentioned delight in false relations taken by English musicians could be added to the corpus of music I have been concerned with; and the few examples from motets cited above show that the madrigal was not the only genre in which this sort of thing occurred. As a general observation, I would say that the introduction of melodic chromaticism in theory and practice at the middle of the sixteenth century was not so much a revolutionary movement as a symptom of general tonal change proceeding quietly under the surface of the contrapuntal fabric. And as advice (offered a bit diffidently but nonetheless sincerely), I would encourage editors of this music not to suppress all false relations they come upon, at least not through introduction of "correct" editorial accidentals, lest they rob the music of some of its piquant "non-harmonic" charm.

APPENDIX

The Musical Examples

Sources

5.1   Cipriano de Rore, *Rex Asiae et Ponti* (1565), mm. 1–3.
        Source: *Opera Omnia,* ed. Bernhard Meier, CMM 14 (American Institute of Musicology, 1971), 5.88.
5.2   Orlando di Lasso, *Sibylla Libyca* (*Prophetiae Sibyllarum,* no. 2, written ca. 1560), mm. 42–46.
        Source: *Das Chorwerk,* vol. 48, ed. Joachim Therstappen (Wolfenbüttel, 1937), 9.
5.3   Lasso, *Sibylla Europaea* (*Prophetiae Sibyllarum,* no. 9), mm. 3–5.
        Source: *Das Chorwerk,* vol. 48, 20.
5.4   (a) Adrian Willaert, *Sacro fonte regenerata* (1544), mm. 71–73.
        Source: *Das Chorwerk,* vol. 59, ed. Walter Gerstenberg (Wolfenbüttel, 1956), 6.
        (b) Rore, "Pommi ov' il sol occide" (1548), mm. 10–11.
        Source: *Opera Omnia,* vol. 3 (American Institute of Musicology, 1961), 68.
5.5   (a) Willaert, "O dolce vita mia" (1544), mm. 1–5.
        Source: Einstein, *Italian Madrigal,* vol. 3, no. 28.
        (b) Francesco Pigna, "Deh torn' a me mio sol" (1569), mm. 1–4.
        Source: RISM 1569[32], 25.
5.6   (a) Antonio Barré, "Era il bel viso" (1558), mm. 12–14.
        Source: RISM 1558[13], page 11 in reprint of 1560[10].
        (b) Willaert, "Io mi rivolgo" (1559), m. 22.

Source: *Opera Omnia,* ed. Hermann Zenck and Walter Gerstenberg, CMM 3, vol. 13 (American Institute of Musicology, 1966), 49.

(c) Rore, "Se ben il duol" (1557), mm. 1–2.

Source: *Opera Omnia,* vol. 4 (American Institute of Musicology, 1969), 107.

5.7   (a) Giacomo Fogliano, "Tua volsi esser mai" (1515), mm. 19–22.

Source: Einstein, *Italian Madrigal,* vol. 3, no. 28.

Reduction: semibreve = quarter note.

(b) Giulio Schiavetti, "Era il bel viso" (1562), mm. 5–7.

Source: RISM 1562[6], 11.

5.8   (a) Perissone Cambio, "Scarpello sì vedrà" (1550), mm. 9–11.

Source: *Di Perissone Cambio il segondo libro di madregali a cinque voci* (Venice, 1550), 29.

(b) Barré, "Corro la fresca" (1558), mm. 26–27.

Source: RISM 1558[13], no. 21.

(c) Lasso, *Carmina chromatico* (*Prophetiae Sibyllabrum,* prologue), mm. 1–5.

Source: *Das Chorwerk,* vol. 48, 5.

5.9   (a) Heliseo Ghibel, "La verginella" (1554), mm. 18–21.

Source: *Il primo libro di madrigali a quattro voci di Heliseo Ghibel* (Venice, 1554), no. 17.

(b) Alessandrino, "Sia vile agl' altri" (1555), mm. 15–16.

Source: RISM 1555[27], 9.

(c) Lasso, *Sibylla Phrygia* (*Prophetiae Sibyllabrum,* no. 8), mm. 8–10.

Source: *Das Chorwerk,* vol. 48, 18.

5.10   (a) Jean Mouton, *Benedicam Dominum in omni tempore,* mm. 10–11.

Source: *Das Chorwerk,* vol. 76, ed. Peter Kast (Wolfenbüttel, 1959), 9.

(b) Willaert, *O invidia nemica* (1559), mm. 23–24.

Source: *Opera Omnia,* vol. 13, 14.

(c) Vincenzo Ruffo, "Non rumor di tamburi" (1557), mm. 10–11.

Source: RISM 1549[31], 22.

5.11   (a) Rore, "Come la notte ogni fiammella" (1557), mm. 19–22.

Source: *Opera Omnia,* vol. 4, 93.

(b) Cesare Tudino, "Altro che lagrimar" (1554), mm. 3–4.

Source: Theodor Kroyer, *Die Anfänge der Chromatik im italienischen Madrigal des XVI. Jahrhunderts,* Publikationen der Internationalen Musikgesellschaft, 4 (Leipzig, 1902), 151.

(c) Scipione della Palla (?), "Che non può far donna" (written ca. 1558), mm. 1–3.

Source: RISM 1577[8], no. 11 (tenor part missing).

On the composer and date of composition of this *aria per recitar stanze,* see Nino Pirrotta, *Li due Orfei* (Turin, 1969), 247ff.

(d) Jhan Gero, "Dolcemente s'adirà" (1541), mm. 42–44.

Source: RISM 1541[14], 47.

5.12   Luca Marenzio, "Quell' augellin che canta" (1595), mm. 16–20.

Source: *Le opere complete*, ed. John Steele (New York, 1975), vol. 7, 8.
Reduction: none.

5.13   Josquin des Prez, *Missa Pange lingua* (written ca. 1510), Kyrie 2, mm. 58–61.
Source: *Das Chorwerk,* vol. 1, ed. Friedrich Blume (Wolfenbüttel, 1929), 7.

5.14   Josquin, *Benedicite omnia opera Domini,* mm. 1–7.
Source: *Werken,* Motetten, vol. 13 (Amsterdam, 1954), no. 53.

5.15   Anonymous, "Per sonetti" : "Ben che la facia" (1506), second phrase.
Source: RISM 1506^3, fol. 9v.

5.16   Serafino Aquilano (?), "Se'l zapator il giorno" (before 1495), mm. 1–6.
Source: Claudio Gallico, *Un libro di poesia per musica dell'epoca d'Isabella d'Este* (Mantua, 1961), 121.

5.17   Jacques Arcadelt, "Occhi miei lassi" (1538), mm. 58–60.
Source: *Opera Omnia,* ed. Albert Seay, CMM 31, vol. 2 (American Institute of Musicology, 1970), no. 36.

5.18   Arcadelt, "Madonna mia gentile" (1538), mm. 22–24.
Source: *Opera Omnia,* vol. 2, no. 29.

5.19   Arcadelt / Berchem, "Pungente dardo" (1538), mm. 12–16.
Source: *Opera Omnia,* vol. 2, no. 41.
On the composer of this piece, see above, n. 16.

5.20   Ghibel, "Ben furo aventurosi i cavalieri" (1554), mm. 1–5.
Source: Ghibel, *Primo libro a 4,* no. 25.

5.21   Rore, "La vita fugge" (1542), mm. 35–36.
Source: *Opera Omnia,* vol. 2 (American Institute of Musicology, 1963), 34.

5.22   (a) Arcadelt, "Il bianco e dolce cigno" (1538), mm. 5–10.
Source: *Opera Omnia,* vol. 2, no. 18.
(b) Orazio Vecchi, "Il bianco e dolce cigno" (1589), mm. 9–12.
Source: *Madrigali a cinque voci di Horatio Vecchi, Libro primo* (Venice, 1589), no. 1.

5.23   Excerpts from madrigals by Hoste da Reggio
(a) "O quante volt' " (1554), mm. 32–34.
Source: *Il primo libro delli madrigali a cinque voce* (Venice, 1554), no. 4 (quintus part missing).
(b) "Non vi vieto per questo" (1554), mm. 5–7.
Source: *Il secondo libro delli madrigali a quattro voce* (Venice, 1554), no. 1.
(c) "Crudel di che peccato" (1554), mm. 22–24.
Source: *Il primo libro a tre voci* (Milan, 1554), 14.
(d) "Se'l dolce sguardo di costei" (1547), mm. 24–25.
Source: *Primo libro de madrigali a quatro voci* (Venice, 1547), no. 8 in reprint of 1556.
(e) "Gente a cui nulla fede" (1547), mm. 41–43.
Source: *Primo libro a 4,* no. 11.

(f) "Così fan questi giovani" (1554), mm. 30–31.
Source: *Secondo libro a 4,* no. 2.

(g) "Si le vive faville" (1547), mm. 31–32.
Source: *Primo libro a 4,* no. 7.

(h) "Poi che mia ferma stella" (1547), mm. 51–53.
Source: *Primo libro a 4,* no. 15.

(i) "O beata colei" (1547), mm. 20–21.
Source: *Primo libro a 4,* no. 1.

(j) "Donna se per mirar" (1547), mm. 13–14.
Source: *Primo libro a 4,* no. 5.

(k) "Deh qual prova maggior" (1547), mm. 29–31.
Source: *Primo libro a 4,* no. 1.

(l) "Deh qual prova maggior" (1547), mm. 1–4.
Source: *Primo libro a 4,* no. 1.

(m) "Madonna per voi ardo" (1547), mm. 28–31.
Source: *Primo libro a 4,* no. 1.

5.24   (a) Hoste, "O quante volt'," mm. 4–7
Source: See No. 5.23a.

(b) Barré, "E nella face" (1558), mm. 32–35.
Source: RISM 1558[13]; page 12 in reprint of 1560[10].

5.25   (a) Nicola Vicentino, *Alleluia* (1555), mm. 1–6.
Source: Henry Kaufmann, *The Life and Works of Nicola Vicentino (1511–c. 1576)* (N.p., 1956), 138.

(b) The same piece rewritten "diatonically."

5.26   Gioseffo Zarlino: Example from *Le istitutioni harmoniche,* 3.30.
Source: Zarlino, *The Art of Counterpoint,* trans. Guy A. Marco and Claude V. Palisca (New Haven, 1968), 65.

5.27   Zarlino: Example from *Le istitutioni harmoniche,* 3.30.
Source: Zarlino, *Art of Counterpoint,* 67.

5.28   Tiberio Fabrianese, "Miser chi mal' oprando" (1549), mm. 1–4.
Source: RISM 1549[31], 9.

Postscript

Although I still find the general argument in this study to be sound and its conclusions justified, I would now alter its language a bit. Using terms such as "harmonic progressions," borrowed from common-practice harmonic theory, is convenient but not necessary; nearly all the examples cited here can be described in terms of hexachordal melodic movement or in reference to modal scalar patterns. I continue to think that vertical sonorities were deliberately chosen in this music, but they can be talked about without reference to the harmonic syntax of the eighteenth century.

On the Vicentino–Lusitano controversy (p. 93 and n. 4), see Paul Boncella, "Denying Ancient Music's Power: Ghiselin Danckert's Essays in the 'Generi inusitati'," *Tijdschrift van de Vereniging voor nederlandse Muziekgeschiedenis* 38

(1988): 59–80. For Aaron's discussion of notated accidentals (n. 9) see Margaret Bent, "Accidentals, Counterpoint, and Notation in Aaron's *Aggiunta* to the *Toscanello in musica*," *Journal of Musicology* 12 (1994): 306–44.

Absalom fili mi, referred to as the work of Josquin, has been questioned as his and tentatively attributed to Pierre de la Rue. See Joshua Rifkin, "Problems of Authorship in Josquin: Some Impolitic Observations. With a Postscript on *Absalom fili mi*," *Proceedings of the International Josquin Symposium, Utrecht 1986* (Utrecht, 1991): 45–52; Jaap van Benthem, "Lazarus versus Absalon: About Fiction and Fact in the Netherlands Motet," *Tijdschrift van de Vereniging voor nederlandse Muziekgeschiedenis* 39 (1989): 54–82. The articles by Edward Lowinsky cited in n. 11 have been reprinted in Lowinsky, *Music and the Culture of the Renaissance and Other Essays,* ed. Bonnie J. Blackburn, 2 vols. (Chicago, 1989), 1:221–39, 230–61. For a carefully reasoned critical view of Lowinsky's views on *musica ficta* see Jaap van Benthem, "Fortuna in Focus: Concerning 'Conflicting' Progressions in Josquin's *Fortuna dun gran tempo*," *Tijdschrift van de Vereniging voor nederlandse Muziekgeschiedenis* 30 (1980): 1–50.

Vicentino's *L'Antica musica* may now be read in an English translation; see Maria Rika Maniates, ed. and trans., *Ancient Music Adapted to Modern Practice* (New Haven, 1996).

Notes

1. See Hans F. Redlich, "Artusi," *MGG,* 1:749. The emphasis, in the musical examples to be cited in this study, on progressions whose roots lie a third apart may suggest to readers a parallel with nineteenth-century interest in such progressions. No cyclic significance for this parallel is claimed.

2. Since there will be a number of references here to Lasso's youthful experiment in chromaticism, the *Prophetiae Sibyllarum* (ed. Joachim Therstappen, *Das Chorwerk,* vol. 48 [Wolfenbüttel, 1937]), I should mention two scholars who deal with the tonal framework of this cycle. Edward Lowinsky, *Tonality and Atonality in Sixteenth-Century Music* (Berkeley, 1961), 39–41, considers it an example of "triadic atonality"; William Mitchell, "The Prologue to Lasso's Prophetiae Sibyllarum," *The Music Forum* 2 (1970): 264–73, sees tonal order evident after Schenkerian reduction. I would incline to agree that tonal order is present, though I find Mitchell's analysis on the whole inappropriate in method for this music.

3. Theodor Kroyer, *Die Anfänge der Chromatik im italienischen Madrigal des XVI. Jahrhunderts,* Publikationen der Internationalen Musikgesellschaft, 4 (Leipzig, 1902), 15–16. Kroyer's monograph remains the best general treatment of this subject. He distinguishes "mittelbarer Chromatiker" from declared chromaticists writing avowedly new music.

4. On Vicentino's debate with Lusitano, held in 1551, over whether the chromatic and enharmonic genera existed in sixteenth-century polyphony, see Henry W. Kaufmann, *The Life and Works of Nicola Vicentino (1511–c.1576),* Musicological Studies and Documents, 11 (American Institute of Musicology, 1966), 22ff. Vicentino was judged the loser (and was fined), with the music of the day declared to be in the diatonic genus. It would be interesting to try to identify the *Regina coeli,* a performance of which is said to have sparked the debate.

5. The vexatious question of tuning and temperament, which cannot be dealt with here, is a consideration. Equal temperament is out of the question; for Vicentino and others, $c–d^\flat$ was a major semitone (usable in transpositions of diatonic music) $c–c^\sharp$ a minor or fully chro-

matic semitone. I here consider the diatonic semitone as large, the chromatic semitone as small, true for just intonation (see Zarlino, *Le istitutioni harmoniche* [Venice, 1558; facsimile, New York, 1965], 3.xix). In Pythagorean intonation, the two are reversed, with the *leimma* or small semitone a diatonic interval, the *apotome* or large semitone a chromatic one (see Gafori, *Practica musicae* [Milan, 1496; facsimile, Bologna, 1972], book 1, chap. 2).

6. See Kaufmann, *Vicentino,* 25. For Zarlino's reaction to this view, see below.

7. Zarlino (*Le istitutioni harmoniche,* 3. 1xxiii, 1xxviii) maintains that chromatic intervals cannot be kept in tune in a polyphonic texture. Zarlino's own methods of calculating untempered diatonic intervals were, ironically enough, to be criticized later by G. B. Benedetti, and then by Vicenzo Galilei; see Claude V. Palisca, "Scientific Empiricism in Musical Thought," *Seventeenth Century Science and the Arts,* ed. H. H. Rhys (Princeton, 1961), 114ff. Vicentino himself criticized his adversary Lusitano for a passage (in the latter's *Introduttione* of 1553) of four-part writing using chromatic and enharmonic intervals with many vertical mistunings. See Vicentino's *L'Antica musica ridotta alla moderna prattica* (Rome, 1555; facsimile, ed. Edward Lowinsky, Documenta musicologica, ser. 1, vol. 17 [Kassel, 1959]), fol. 98. Elsewhere in his treatise (fol. 65v), Vicentino recommends performance "in the chamber with a low voice" for enharmonic music—presumably because of the difficulties of intonation; cf. Kaufmann, *Vicentino,* 137.

8. Juan Bermudo, *Declaración de instrumentos musicales* (Ossuna, 1555; facsimile, ed. Santiago Kastner [Kassel, 1957]), fol. 22, speaks of the *semichromatico* as a mix of diatonic and chromatic elements, probably referring to the practice of Spanish intabulators.

9. The term "harmonic progression" means here two successive sonorities produced by acceptable melodic movement in several voices (four remained the norm for didactic purposes throughout the century). It has no necessary connection, however implicit, with tonality; in fact the teaching of discant, from which Renaissance composers learned to write chords, seems rarely to have coincided, as a subject, with the teaching of mode.

Of course chromatic inflection within a given voice was governed by principles, and informed practice, of melodic writing. Sixteenth-century theorists were aware of the problems caused by conflicting demands of horizontal and vertical elements in the music of their time; the *aggiunta* of Aaron's *Toscanello in musica* (Venice, 1529; facsimile, Bologna, 1969), added to the work "a complacenza de gli amici," gives ample evidence of this. My emphasis on harmonic considerations is deliberate but carries no implication that melodic factors are of lesser importance.

10. The opening of this piece is a serviceable but unsurprising example of the category named above. As it goes on, *Rex Asiae* becomes exceptional in its obsessive use of the circle of fifths (from *a* on the sharp side to *e*♭); mm. 63–69 (in Meier's edition) present one of the longest uninterrupted series of these progressions in sixteenth-century music.

Complete identification of the musical examples is given at the end of the chapter. All pieces are presented in 2:1 reduction (except as noted); measures are counted by the breve. Texts are included only when of special importance. All accidentals except those written over or under the notes are in the original sources; *each accidental is good only for the note immediately following it.* Original sources are given where there is no modern edition; date of composition or first publication is given where known. Asterisks are used to indicate chromatic progressions not immediately obvious.

11. *Werken van Josquin des Prez,* Supplement, ed. W. Elders (Amsterdam, 1969), 22. For a discussion of this piece, with references to modern literature on it, see Helmuth Osthoff, *Josquin Desprez* (Tutzing, 1965), 2:108ff.

The scholar who has been most interested in the role played by the circle of fifths in sixteenth-century musical practice is, of course, Edward Lowinsky. Since he is concerned to show avoidance of *mi-fa* relations in this progression, and I am here concerned with their use, his work is not directly relevant to this study; but it should be known by all students of the period. See, in particular, two articles: "The Goddess Fortuna in Music," *MQ* 29 (1943): 45–77; and "Matthaeus Greiter's *Fortuna:* An Experiment in Chromaticism and Musical Iconography," *MQ* 42 (1956): 500–519; *MQ* 43 (1957): 68–85.

12. For Zarlino, one of the chief uses of chromatic intervals was for transposition; see *Le istitutioni harmoniche,* 3.lxxvi. Vicentino argued vehemently against this, pointing out that transpositions, however remote, simply duplicated the intervals of the untransposed genus; see *L'Antica musica,* fol. 47. In this case, what Zarlino called chromatic, Vicentino maintained—correctly, I think—was diatonic.

13. Raising the third degree at the end of phrases, often specified in prints from the middle of the sixteenth century on, was seldom indicated earlier in the century, though it may well have been common practice. For editorial recognition of this see, for example, Einstein's edition of Verdelot, "Madonna qual certezza" (*Italian Madrigal,* 3:21–23). An altered degree at the end of a phrase can mean an awkward interval for one voice when the next phrase begins. Approaching the problem another way, Vicentino recommends a rest between the notes involved in a "bad" leap (*salto cattivo*); see *L'Antica musica,* fol. 75v.

14. For a discussion of tonal features in Josquin's *Benedicite omnia opera Domini,* see Lowinsky, *Tonality and Atonality,* 20ff.

15. See Claudio Gallico, *Un libro di poesia per musica dell'epoca d'Isabella d'Este* (Mantua, 1961), 139. On the manuscript, dated 1495/96, from which the piece in example 5.16 is taken, see Knud Jeppesen, *La Frottola,* vol. 2, in Acta Jutlandica, 41/1 (Copenhagen, 1969), 76ff.

16. Example 5.19, "Pungente dardo," was printed in Arcadelt's *Primo libro;* in editions from 1546 on, it is ascribed to Berchem, to whom it is "probably" assigned by Albert Seay, ed., *Jacobi Arcadelt. Opera Omnia,* CMM 31, vol. 2 (American Institute of Musicology, 1965–70), xxiv. Cf. Dale Hall, "The Italian Secular Vocal Works of Jacquet Berchem" (Ph.D. diss., Ohio State University, 1973), 335.

17. On Rore as a chromaticist, see Einstein, *Italian Madrigal,* 410ff.

18. Bernhard Meier, ed., *Cipriano de Rore. Opera Omnia,* CMM 14, vol. 2 (American Institute of Musicology, 1959–75), v.

19. Ibid., v.

20. In example 5.22a, Albert Seay puts an editorial flat over the cantus *e* in measure 8, the third full measure of the example (see *Opera,* 2.38). I would not, since there seems no expressive or technical reason requiring it. Whether one would want to be so daring as to use an *e♮* for the last cantus note in the preceding bar I am not sure.

21. *Italian Madrigal,* 318–19, 440, 533. To be fair to Einstein, he does ascribe the mid-century interest in harmonic innovation to "a whole set of North Italian musicians, in Venice, Verona, and Milan" (*Italian Madrigal,* 411).

22. In several of his publications, Hoste is described as "maestro della musica" of Don Ferrante Gonzaga, a son of Isabella d'Este and captain general of Charles V's armies. See Vogel, 1:321–22. Nothing is known about Hoste other than what is in the dedicatory letters of his prints. Kroyer, *Die Anfänge der Chromatik,* 98, lists Hoste's *Primo libro a tre voci* (1544) as a collection with "mittelbarer Chromatik."

23. A major source for the *madrigale arioso* is the series of *Libri delle Muse . . . a quattro voci* (RISM 1555[27] and its numerous reprints, including 1558[13] and 1562[7]) published in Rome by Antonio Barré, himself a composer in this style. Among musicians heavily influenced by the syncopated declamatory style of these pieces was the young Giaches Wert.

24. My thanks are due to a group of graduate students in a class at New York University who transcribed Hoste's *Primo libro a 4* and struggled valiantly with the problems in musica ficta these madrigals pose.

25. "Questa donna gentil," in *Il primo libro* . . . *a quattro voci* (Venice, 1547, reprint, 1556; p. 28 in the latter edition), m. 34; the piece begins and ends in the second (D) mode.

26. On cautionary accidentals, see Frank D'Accone, "Matteo Rampollini and his Petrarchan Canzoni Cycles," *MD* 27 (1973): 83–86; Don Harrán, "New Evidence for Musica Ficta: The Cautionary Sign," *JAMS* 29 (1976): 77–98. Harrán's view of problematic accidentals in the sixteenth-century madrigal is far enough from mine that I would consider some of the examples in his article—differently interpreted—as instances of the deliberate cross relation I am here speaking of. I would expect Harrán to take, in return, a "cautionary" view of my argument.

27. Among the declared chromaticists of the period are Cesare Tudino, Francesco Orso, and Giulio Fiesco. See Kroyer, *Anfänge der Chromatik,* 79ff; Henry W. Kaufmann, "A 'Diatonic' and a 'Chromatic' Madrigal by Giulio Fiesco," *Aspects of Medieval and Renaissance Music: A Birthday Offering to Gustave Reese,* ed. Jan LaRue (New York, 1966), 474–88.

28. For a concise account of Vicentino's theory, see Kaufmann, *Vicentino,* 135ff; cf. Maria Rika Maniates, "Vicentino's 'Incerta et occulta scientia' Reexamined," *JAMS* 28 (1975): 333–51. Vicentino's fifth book of five-voice madrigals (1572) contains many chromatic passages; the frequent use of progressions with bass movement by a major third is pointed out by Kaufmann in his edition of Vicentino's music (*Opera Omnia,* CMM, 26 [American Institute of Musicology, 1963], vii).

29. Typical examples may be seen in "Donna s'io miro" (book 5, no. 1), and in book 5, nos. 2, 4, 6, and 7 (*Opera,* 77, 79, 84, 92, and 96).

30. *L'Antica musica,* fol. 52; cf. Kaufmann, *Vicentino,* 134.

31. This excerpt from Danckerts's unprinted *Trattato* . . . *con una dichiaratione facilissima sopra i tre generi di essa musica (ca. 1555)* is cited in Lewis Lockwood, "A Dispute on Accidentals in Sixteenth-Century Rome," *Analecta musicologica* 2 (1965): 27 (the translation is mine).

32. *Le istitutioni harmoniche,* 3.lxxiii–lxxx. For an English translation, see *The Art of Counterpoint,* trans. Guy A. Marco and Claude V. Palisca (New Haven, 1968), 270–90.

33. *Le istitutioni harmoniche,* 3.lxxvii: "ma quando ritrovaremo alcuna [cantilena], che habbia in se simili caratteri ♭ & ♯; allora diremo, che procede per le chorde Chromatiche, mescolate con le Diatoniche."

34. On whether transposition should be regarded as a species of chromaticism, see n. 12 above.

35. *Le istitutioni harmoniche,* 3.xxx. I cite the passage from *The Art of Counterpoint,* 65.

36. Pedro Cerone, *El melopeo y maestro* (Naples, 1613), 13.xxxi: "De las Relaciones dissonantes y falsas."

37. G. M. Artusi, *L'Arte del contraponto* (Venice, 1586–89, reprint 1598; facsimile of 1598 edition, Hildesheim, 1969), 33–35.

38. Partial signatures in fifteenth-century music provide numerous instances in which cross relations occur if no editorial accidentals are added. Many of these might well go "uncorrected." It is possible to suppose that clashes of this kind went out of favor in the classical polyphony of the early sixteenth century and were reintroduced by mid-sixteenth-century composers of a restless bent.

39. One aspect of this is studied in Charles Jacobs, "Spanish Renaissance Discussion of Musica Ficta," *Proceedings of the American Philosophical Society* 112 (1968): 277–98. See also Howard M. Brown's remarks on the lutenist Albert de Rippe's liking for simultaneous cross relations and "various freedoms with regard to accidentals" in a review of volume 3 of the collected works of Rippe, edited by Jean-Michel Vaccaro, in *ML* 57 (1976): 442–43. Rippe's intabulations, in fact, contain quite a few examples of *mi-fa* relationships in progressions of the types discussed above.

Zarlino's Definition of Fugue and Imitation

IN THE THIRD BOOK of his *Istitutioni harmoniche* (1558) Zarlino devotes separate chapters to the terms *fughe* and *imitationi,* making in his careful way a distinction ignored or only hinted at by earlier theorists: fugal passages have exact intervallic correspondence between participating voices, whereas imitations may ignore the sequence of tones and semitones in the leading voice. Students of the history of fugue, including Müller-Blattau, Ghislanzoni, Mann, and Horsley,[1] have taken note of Zarlino's terminology and have thought it—not always for precisely the same reasons—important. Alfred Mann discusses it as follows:

> We find in Zarlino's comprehensive treatment of fugue the foundation of a new termi-
> nology. He is the first to distinguish between fugue (*fuga, consequenza, reditta*) and
> imitation (*imitatione*). Entrances at the perfect intervals of unison, fourth, fifth, and
> octave are now the only ones recognized as constituting a fugue; entrances at all other
> intervals are called imitation. . . . In his fundamental distinction between fugue and
> imitation, however, Zarlino appears as a systematic rather than progressive theorist,
> for there is no indication in his text that it is a tendency toward tonal orientation which
> prompts him to single out entrances at the unison, fourth, fifth, and octave as the only
> true fugal entrances.[2]

For Müller-Blattau, Zarlino's distinction is of great importance because it separates fugue from the "kontrapunktischen Manier" of imitation. This is not because one is more thorough-going than the other, for as we shall see both fugue and imitation can, for Zarlino, be either canonically exact (*legata*) or free to break off wherever the composer wishes (*sciolta*); it is rather the theorist's supposed insistence on tonally important intervals like the fourth and fifth—those most nearly allowing exact intervallic correspondence—that has interested students of the fugue.

Here there is a difficulty, noticed by Mann: Zarlino seems in these definitions to be unconcerned with "tonal orientation"; he "ignores the tonal answer, which, by his classification, is no different from any other imitation and has no place in fugues."[3] It is true that Zarlino, unlike his contemporary Vicentino,[4] does not speak of tonal—or better, modal—answers. But of course he knew their importance, and how to use them; the duos written to illustrate the twelve modes in book 4 of the *Istitutioni* have several clear examples of modal answers,[5] and in Zarlino's terms would be defined as mixtures of fugue and imitation. At the end of the seventeenth century Angelo Berardi still speaks of *fuga reale* as that in which all intervals correspond exactly. G. M. Bononcini, on the other hand, after defining *fuga propria* or *regolare* as that in which exact correspondence of tones and semitones is observed, makes an exception for tonal adjustment; in a *fuga regolare* one may answer a fifth with a fourth.[6]

It is characteristic of seventeenth- and even eighteenth-century theorists that they should preserve Zarlino's terminology while altering its meaning. A whole group of writers in the late sixteenth and early seventeenth centuries had repeated or paraphrased the definitions of fugue and imitation given in the *Istitutioni:* Artusi, Tigrini, Pontio, Cerreto, Cerone, and Zacconi all wrote on the subject.[7] Some of what they have to say is useful in clarifying Zarlino's meaning, as will presently be seen; others, by emphasizing that *fuga* is concerned with answers at perfect intervals, *imitatione* with those beginning at imperfect and dissonant intervals, may have helped form the views of modern scholars, which I believe to be rather superficial and in part mistaken. On the whole, theorists up to the middle of the seventeenth century at least *meant* to preserve Zarlino's thought. In writers like Bononcini, however, one sees deliberate change in the meaning of these terms; and by the eighteenth century only the words remain. Thus Rameau, at once admirer and critic of Zarlino, dismisses imitation as free fugato, whereas in fugue one must proceed with "plus de circonspection," following a whole set of rules familiar to us all as defining the tonal fugue.[8]

Rameau was of course not trying to explicate Zarlino but was using old terminology adapted to new purposes. Twentieth-century historians of fugue have been more careful than Rameau, but after all they do not have his excuse; and in looking for prophesy of the future in Zarlino's remarks on fugal procedure they have really failed to see the application of his definitions to the music of his own time. A closer reading of the text is clearly called for. The following passages are given as they occur in the 1573 edition of the *Istitutioni,* slightly altered and expanded from the first edition of 1558.

DELLE FUGHE, O CONSEQUENZE

Et tal modo di far cantare le parti in cotal maniera da i Prattici diversamente è stato nominato; percioche alcuni considerando, che le parti cantando insieme al modo detto, l'una segue l'altra alla guisa di uno, il quale fuggendo sia seguitato da un'altro; l'hanno chiamato Fuga; alcuni Risposta; percioche tra loro cantando par che l'una parte all'altra quella istessa modulatione rispondi con proposito; alcuni l'hanno addimandato Reditta; essendo che l'una parte viene à ridire & à referire quello, che l'altra hà detto, o cantato prima: alcuni altri l'hanno chiamato Consequenza; poi che da quell'ordine di Modulatione, che primieramente è detto dall'uno de Cantori in una parte, con-

ON FUGUES, OR CONSEQUENCES

And such a way of writing the voice parts has been called different things by musicians. For some, considering that when the parts sing together in this way one follows the other, in the manner of the first fleeing, pursued by the second, have named it Fugue. Others style it Response, because in performance it seems that one part aptly answers another with the same melody. Some have named it Repetition, since one part repeats and refers to what the other has said or sung. Yet others have named it Consequence because in this kind of melody what is first sung by a performer on one part may consequently be repeated by another. But still others have termed it Imitation, because he who fol-

sequentemente si può da un'altro repli-
care. Ma alcuni altri l'hanno detto Imitatione: percioche quello che segue il
primo, quanto puote cerca di imitarlo; si
ne gli Intervalli & ne i Tempi, come anco
nelli Movimenti; & si sforza di ridire
tutto quello, che hà detto il primo. Et se
bene tutte queste tendono ad un fine; le ri-
durremo a tre capi soli: cioè alla Fuga,
alla Imitatione & alla Consequenza; &
diremo prima, Fuga esser la Replica, o
Reditta di una particella, overo di tutta la
modulatione fatta da una parte grave,
overo acuta della cantilena; da un'altra
parte, overo dalle altre parti del concento, procedendo l'una dopo l'altra per
alquanto spacio di tempo, per gli istessi
intervalli nello istesso suono, o voce;
overamente per una Diapason, over Diapente, o pure per una Diatessaron più
grave, o più acuta. Dipoi Imitatione no-
minaremo quella Replica, o Reditta, la
quale hò già dichiarato nella Fuga; quella
però, che non procede per gli istessi Intervalli; ma per quelli, che sono in tutto
differenti dalli primi; essendo solamente
li movimenti che fanno le parti cantando
& le figure ancora simili. Ma la Consequenza diciamo essere una certa Replica,
o Reditta di modulatione, la quale nasce
da un'ordine & collocatione di molte Figure cantabili, fatta dal Compositore in
una parte della Cantilena; dalla quale ne
segue un'altra, o più dopo un certo spacio
di tempo.[9]

lows the first part tries to imitate it as best
he can, both in intervals and time values,
and in [melodic] movements; he is thus
constrained to repeat everything the first
performer has sung.

Since all these aim at the same end, we
shall reduce them to three headings:
Fugue, Imitation, and Consequence. Let
us say first that Fugue is the copy or repetition by one or more parts of the voice-
complex of a section or of a whole melody sung [first] by one part, high or low,
of the composition. The parts may proceed one after the other at any distance of
time, using the same intervals, singing at
the unison, the octave, the fifth, or the
fourth below or above. Next, we shall call
Imitation that copy or repetition which is
like what I have already described for the
Fugue, except that it does not proceed by
the same but by quite different intervals,
the rhythmic and melodic figures of the
two parts being nonetheless similar. We
call Consequence a certain copy or repetition of a melody, rising from an ordering of many vocal figures, written by the
composer in a single voice—from which
one or more other voices follow it at a pre-
scribed length of time.

Of the three terms Zarlino would like to see in general use, we may dismiss *Consequenza,* which is simply a strict fugue or imitation written as a single part—what
"Musici poco intelligenti"—usually call *Canon.* Both fugue and imitation may be
either *legata*—strictly carried out through a whole section of a piece—or *sciolta,*
broken off whenever the composer finds it convenient to do so.[10] Either may proceed in parallel motion or in contrary motion (*per Arsin et Thesin*). After giving
examples of *fuga sciolta* (at the octave) and *fuga legata* (one at the octave, in similar motion, another at the third in contrary motion, an interval giving exact intervallic correspondence), Zarlino goes on to speak in detail of imitation.

Delle Imitationi, & quel che elle siano	On Imitations, and what they are

Non di poco utile è la Imitatione alli Compositori: imperoche oltra l'ornamento, che apporta alla cantilena, è cosa di ingegno & molto lodevole; & è di due sorti, si come è la Fuga: cioè Legata & Sciolta. E da i Prattici etiandio chiamata Fuga; ma in vero tra la Fuga & la Imitatione è questa differenza: che la Fuga legata o Sciolta, che ella si sia, si ritrova tra molte parti della cantilena, lequali, o per movimenti simili, o per contrarij, contengono quelli istessi intervalli, che contiene la lor Guida, come hò mostrato: ma la Imitatione sciolta, o legata, come si vuole; quantunque si ritrovi tra molte parti (come mostraremo) & procedi all' istesso modo; nondimeno non camina per quelli istessi intervalli nelle parti consequenti, che si ritrovano nella Guida. La onde; si come la Fuga si può fare all'Unisono, alla Quarta, alla Quinta, alla Ottava, overo ad altri intervalli; *cosi la Imitatione si può accommodare ad ogni intervallo dall'Unisono & dalli nominati in fuori.* [my italics] Per ilche, si potrà porre alla Seconda, alla Terza, alla Sesta, alla Settima & ad altri intervalli simili. Diremo adunque che la Imitatione è quella, la quale si trova tra due, o più parti; delle quali il Consequente imitando li movimenti della Guida, procede solamente per quelli istessi gradi, senza havere altra consideratione de gli intervalli. Et la cognitione tanto delle legate, quanto delle sciolte si potrà havere facilmente, quando si haverà conosciuto quello, che voglia dire Fuga legata & Fuga sciolta.[11]

Imitation is a very useful thing to composers. For besides the ornament it provides music, it is ingenious and praiseworthy in itself. It is of two kinds, just like Fugue: that is, strict and free. Practical musicians indeed call it fugue; but there is this real difference between fugue and imitation. Fugue, whether strict or free, occurs in many voice parts of a piece, and these contain, as I have shown, the same intervals as does the Guide—whether in similar or contrary motion. On the other hand imitation, free or strict as you wish, though it too occurs in many parts (as will be shown), and proceeds as does fugue, nonetheless does not show in its course the identical intervals in the consequent voices as are formed in the Guide. Now, as one can write Fugue at the unison, the fourth, the fifth, the octave, or other intervals, *so one can manage Imitation at every interval from the unison and the above-named intervals on.* Thus one will be able to make use of the second, the third, the sixth, the seventh, and other like intervals. Let us then say that Imitation, found between two or more voices, is that procedure in which the Consequent, while imitating the movements of the Guide, proceeds merely by the same steps, without regard for the precise intervals. If one understands the meaning of strict and free Fugue he will easily recognize strict and free imitation.

The examples for this chapter include one showing *imitationi sciolte,* a duo with a half-dozen points of imitation at various intervals and in a mixture of similar and contrary motion; one illustrating *imitatione legata,* a strict canon at the third, hence inexact intervallically; another canon at the octave but in contrary motion, thus again inexact in correspondence of tones and semitones; and a canon at the fifth below, strictly carried out and intervallically exact except for two not very prominent occurrences of G-F-E in the guide, answered inexactly, hence imitatively, by C-B-A in the consequent.[12] This last example is called by Zarlino a "misto di Fuga & Imitatione." Two things should be noted here: first, an example of canon at a perfect interval, the fifth, is included in the chapter on imitation; and second, Zarlino does not suggest that a B♭ be supplied everywhere in the lower voice to make the imitation exact, or fugal.

First, then, the distinction between fugue and imitation is not based on use of perfect as opposed to imperfect intervals, as is usually said. Use of intervals like the third will almost certainly result in imitation, not fugue; but imitation is possible at the perfect intervals as well (see the italicized text in the passage quoted above). This observation is trivial as regards the example cited above, but it could be of greater importance in other situations; one can easily imagine subjects that stress intervals impossible to imitate exactly at the fourth and fifth without chromatic alteration. There is no need to imagine them, in fact; such subjects occur quite often in music of pervadingly imitative texture, from the time of Josquin through the sixteenth century. If it is true, as Imogene Horsley says, that "in practice composers with their usual skill in circumventing difficulties, often omit the note or notes that would make the answer at the fifth inexact,"[13] still there are plenty of examples of composers including, sometimes even emphasizing, such notes. Each instance of this sort must doubtless be judged individually; in the terms of this discussion one could decide in favor of fugue by means of *musica ficta* applied to make canons or points of imitation intervallically symmetrical, or one could leave the music alone, settling for Zarlino's concept of imitation. Later I shall give some examples in which decisions of this kind must be made. At this point it should be emphasized that for Zarlino imitation is by no means a second-class form of fugue; indeed he goes out of his way to describe it as "molto lodevole."

No theorist before Zarlino seems to have elaborated upon this distinction between fugue and imitation. Nor do his exact contemporaries introduce it; Bermudo, for instance, gives a definition of *fuga* accompanied by a three-voice example of what Zarlino would have called fugue at the octave below and imitation at the third above.[14] And although I think Zarlino's discussion is amply illustrated in the music of his teacher Adrian Willaert and so possibly the result of Willaert's precepts, a fellow pupil, Nicola Vicentino, makes no explicit mention of fugue versus imitation in his *Antica musica ridotta alla moderna prattica* of 1555. Vicentino stresses the modal importance of fugal entries at the fourth and fifth, advising alteration of the answer to fit within the modal octave. About "fuguing" at other intervals he says little except that caution is necessary, since in writing a fugue at, say, the second, one is in danger of going outside the mode;[15] this could be taken to mean that in such cases Vicentino recommends imitation rather than exact fugue, but he does not say so explicitly.

It is among Zarlino's disciples in the theorists of succeeding generations that further mention of fugue and imitation is made. But before we turn to them, one earlier theorist, not heretofore cited in this context, should be called in to testify. Pietro Aaron gives the two terms as synonymous in his earliest treatise, the *De institutione harmonica* of 1516:

Imitatio in Cantilenis sive fugatio de parte in partem fieri solet. Est autem ideo dicta imitatio/sive fugatio: quia subsequens: vel antecedens: praecedentis voces partis/vel subsequentis easdem nomine/sed locis diversas repetit: & vel quasi imitando pronunciat/vel quasi subsequendo fugare videtur.[16]	Imitation or fugue between parts is customarily practiced in musical compositions. It is called imitation or fugue because the consequent (or antecedent) voice repeats the very notes of the preceding part or else repeats notes identical in name though different in location. Thus it sings as it were in imitating; or seems, in following, as it were to give chase.

Here Aaron is defining exact fugal imitation at the octave or another perfect interval, with the imitating voice following (or anticipating) the main statement. All that is important here is the use of *imitatio,* a word not used in earlier works defining *fuga,* such as the *Diffinitorium* of Tinctoris.

In a later work, the *Lucidario* of 1545, Aaron, who appears to have spent some time in Venice in his middle years,[17] approaches Zarlino's view much more closely.

DI ALCUNI PROGRESSI DA MOLTI FALSAMENTE CHIAMATI FUGA, OPPENIONE	A VIEW OF CERTAIN PROGRESSIONS WRONGLY CALLED FUGUE BY MANY
Gia dannoi molte volte fu havuto consideratione alla poca avertenza, & vana oppenione di alcuni, i quali si credono creare nelle loro compositioni quello, che dal musico è chiamato Fuga, la imaginatione de quali non sara in tutto quella, ch'alla fuga si conviene, imperoche essi considerano tal effetto solamente convenirsi alla fuga, conciosa che esso sia appartenente etiando al canon. Il quale appresso de Greci val quanto regola, come seguitando intenderai.	In our circle there has often been discussion of the carelessness and mistaken opinion of those who think they are writing in their music what the musician terms Fugue. Their view is in fact not at all in accordance with what pertains to fugue, since the effect [they strive for] is thought by them to belong solely to fugue, whereas it may also be found in canon (which among the Greeks means rule, as you shall later see).
Se da te sara considerato, come procedano le note, o sillabe del sopra posto essempio, vederai, che di necessita bisognera, che il Tenore pausi i dui tempi del Canto, & procedendo tal principio non sara l'effetto somigliante al Canto, perche esso procede da re, mi, fa, sol, il qual processo è la prima Diatessaron, & il Tenore da ut, re, mi, fa, il quale è processo	If you will consider how the notes or syllables proceed in the above example [see ex. 6.1], you will see that the tenor, having waited the space of two breves in the canto, does not have the same effect in its beginning as does the canto, since the latter proceeds in the first species of fourth—*re mi fa sol*—while the tenor sings the third species of fourth—*ut re mi fa*. This is ignored by many people to

della terza Diatessaron, la onde per essere da molti tal via ignorata, diranno, che sia fuga per Diapason, percioche il principio del Tenore rende ottava al canto. Et cosi in tutte le altre imitationi danno il titolo alla fuga non convenevole al cominciamento di colui che lo segue, onde nascono inconvenienti manifestissimi.[18]

such an extent that they call [ex. 6.1] a fugue at the octave since the beginning of the tenor sounds an octave with the canto. And so in all other examples of imitation they give the unsuitable name of fugue to the beginning of that part which follows—whence arise the most obvious difficulties.

Example 6.1 is the falsely named fugue to which Aaron refers. Zarlino would call this an illustration of *imitatione sciolta;* the fact that the interval is a perfect one, the fifth, makes no difference. In a *resolutione* of the false opinion he has just countered, Aaron cautions the reader that fugues may be written at the unison, the fourth, the fifth, or the octave, but may be so called only if the hexachord syllables are the same—that is, if the imitation is intervallically exact. If not, he advises calling them "Canon per Diatessaron, ò per Diapente, ò come ti piacera, & non fuga."

Example 6.1 Aaron, *Lucidario* (Venice, 1545), 2.10

It is tempting to think that by "dannoi" (see the beginning of the passage given above) Aaron meant a circle of enlightened musicians, with himself and the young Zarlino included, around Willaert in Venice. At any rate his view of fugue and imitation seems quite similar, if not so systematically presented, to that of Zarlino[19]— except that the latter deplored the barbarism of calling strict fugue or imitation by the name of canon, which ought to mean only the rule directing its performance. Aaron, like Zarlino, makes no distinction in quality between fugue and imitation; he simply wants them kept separate. Why should this distinction have been important to the two theorists—and possibly to all of Willaert's circle in Venice? I shall try to give an answer at a later point in this study.

Among the theorists who echo Zarlino's definitions of fugue and imitation, only the Spaniard Cerone seems to have noticed Aaron's discussion as well. In book 14 of his monumental *Melopeo* the passage quoted above from the *Lucidario* appears, along with Aaron's example; Cerone's only comment is that "the moderns call this Fugue even though it does not proceed by means of the same numbers and intervals."[20] Next Zarlino's distinction between fugue and imitation is paraphrased by the Spanish theorist. An example of *fuga sciolta* at the fourth is given, along with the caution that one should keep the subject inside the hexachord if the intervals are to be reproduced exactly by the second voice. Imitation is said to make use of intervals such as the second, third, sixth, and seventh, but also, exceptionally, the fourth and fifth.[21]

A chapter on imitation, again close to Zarlino's text, follows. Then comes a chapter on the two types of imitation, *libre* and *con obligacion*.[22] Cerone's examples, given here as example 6.2, are revealing: both are at the perfect interval of the fifth, and nowhere is it suggested that accidentals be introduced to make the imitation fugally exact—even though a brush with a melodic diminished fifth and a harmonic cross relation may be seen in example 6.2b.

Example 6.2 Cerone, *El Melopeo y Maestro* (Naples, 1613), 14.10

a. *libre*

b. *obligada*

Since melodies that exceed the range of a hexachord are hard to reproduce exactly, Cerone says that composers *casi siempre* write "mixed" canons showing a combination of fugue and imitation. A canon given as illustration (ex. 6.3) is marked by the theorist with a cross to show where imitation stops and fugue begins. At this point Cerone advises the beginner that he may simply call things like this *canon;* the distinctions are made to be of use to professionals, and to "demonstrate the precious artifices of music."[23]

The subject evidently intrigued Cerone, for he has still more to offer. Chapter 13 has a tabular example showing a subject beginning with descending thirds (D-B-G); against this are given fugues starting on G-E-C above and below, imitations starting (at a later point) on A-F-D above and below.

Finally Cerone provides an example of a three-voice canon, described as "Imitation for three voices, which can be sung at the fifth and the ninth below" (ex. 6.4).[24] Though a slightly improbable piece of music, this example seems to me

Example 6.3 Cerone, *El Melopeo*, 14.11

Example 6.4 Cerone, *El Melopeo*, 14.18

particularly important in its resolutely diatonic character; where fugally exact repetition occurs, as between the two lower voices, it is on an equal footing with the inexact imitation both show in relation to the leading voice.

None of the other writers following Zarlino on this point devoted as much space to it as did Cerone, admittedly a loquacious theorist in general. Artusi makes a brief reference to Zarlino's distinction, emphasizing the occurrence of imitation at intervals other than the perfect ones.[25] Tigrini stays very close to Zarlino's text, and thus says that imitation may occur at any interval, perfect or otherwise.[26]

A somewhat more individual treatment of the subject may be found in the *Dialogo* of Pietro Pontio. In distinguishing between fugue and imitation Pontio seems to add little beyond a certain grammatical ambiguity:

> L'imitazione sarà questa, che imitarà un Motetto, Madrigale, ò Canzone con gli istessi movimenti; mà non servarà il valore delle figure del Motetto, ò Madrigale, od altra cosa, che si sia; nè tampoco alle volte gli stessi Tuoni, & Semituoni: Questo modo adunque si dirà imitatione; e questa è la differenza, che si trova tra la fuga, & l'imitazione.[27]

> Imitation is that which imitates a motet, madrigal, or canzone with the same melodic movements. But it does not preserve the figures of the motet, or madrigal, or what have you; nor does it always so much as keep the same [relationship of] tones and semitones. This procedure is then called imitation; and such is the difference between imitation and fugue.

By *figure* Pontio means note values; at an earlier point in his treatise he defines an *Inventione,* by which he means a point of imitation, as *reale* if it preserves *figure, nomi & intervalli* (note values, solmization degrees, and general intervals), *non reale* if any of these are imitated inexactly.[28] Examples of these various situations are given, including one *inventione* (ex. 6.5) that is *reale* (fugal) in the first tone, *non reale* (imitative) in the fourth tone. Pontio's definition is something of an improvement upon Zarlino's, for there are countless points of imitation in sixteenth-century music that are inexact in rhythm as well as in pitch, with the latter being often a matter of different intervals, not just of different hexachordal structure.

Example 6.5 Pontio, *Dialogo del R. M. Don Pietro Pontio* (Parma, 1595), 46–47

a. 1st tone

b. 4th tone

In saying that "imitation is that which imitates a motet, madrigal, or canzone" Pontio is surely referring to a point of imitation, for he is distinguishing it from fugue; but his awkward language can be explained, I think, with the realization that the term *imitatione* meant more than one thing to him. By way of bringing up the subject of *inventione* Pontio remarks that a composer who wrote a piece too closely resembling that of another man would be judged ignorant and of little worth unless this were done "per qualche imitatione di Messe, over Ricercarij"—"through a certain imitative procedure in Masses or Ricercari"; if the composer were so minded he could choose the same points of [fugal] imitation, and even the same harmony.[29]

Like Pontio I am running out of terms and am beginning to stumble over the meanings of "imitation"; but it seems clear that what Pontio means by the term in the passage just cited is the procedure we usually call "parody." This has been convincingly demonstrated, for the case in hand and for sixteenth-century practice in general, by Lewis Lockwood.[30] In the passage distinguishing imitation from fugue Pontio may then be trying to say two things at once, trying without notable success to combine Zarlino's terminology with another, broader meaning of the term *imitatione*. In an earlier work Pontio again uses the word in the general sense; he disapproves of cross relations, but says they are tolerable when done *per imitatione,* as in a passage he himself wrote in his *Missa Ancidetemi,* where he wished to take up the material used in the [Arcadelt] madrigal.[31]

Pontio, a lesser Zarlino, had his followers, among them Scipione Cerreto, whose remarks on "fughe à imitatione" paraphrase Pontio's distinction between fugue and imitation; Cerreto adds that one should take care to "osservare il Tuono" in writing imitations—meaning that tonal answers are frequently necessary.[32]

In the writings of the last theorist we shall consider here, Lodovico Zacconi, one sees Zarlino's distinctions fading, his terminology being edged toward a usage we find recognizably familiar. At one point in his *Prattica in musica* Zacconi repeats Zarlino's definitions of *fuga legata* and *fuga sciolta,* adding that imitation, in contrast, means that the answering voice does not have to repeat the *figure* of the guide but can merely imitate the melody in a general way—following "l'integrità della modulatione."[33] But elsewhere he advances terminology of his own: *fuga naturale* is used for Zarlino's *fuga,* the later seventeenth century's *fuga reale; fuga accidentale* is defined as inexact imitation, but the example shows that Zacconi is thinking of tonal answers.[34] And in mentioning *fuga legata* and *fuga sciolta* as defined by Tigrini, Zacconi says that practicing musicians now call the first canon, the second imitation.[35] In several places the "via delle imitationi" is spoken of as a general contrapuntal procedure: after mastering note-against-note counterpoint, compared to *libri volgari,* the student should try to learn the "Latin of music" by trying *fughe* based on a borrowed melody, and finally by beginning to compose freely in two parts that imitate each other, this method called *fantasia.*[36] Finally, Zacconi extends the meaning of *imitatione* to include sequential repetitions within a single voice.[37]

•

If Pietro Aaron had, at least in his early work, used *imitatio* as a casually chosen synonym for fugue, Zarlino used *imitatione* with deliberate intent. The musical distinction between fugue and imitation, at first sight a rather pedantic one, seems to me of real importance on several counts, not least the application of *musica ficta* in imitative contrapuntal passages. In a moment we shall turn to this problem. But first Zarlino's choice of the term *imitatione* deserves some notice. That the principle of *imitazione della natura* was of central importance to sixteenth-century musicians hardly needs stressing here,[38] but does the word itself when used for contrapuntal procedures have any connection with this principle?

The frequent use by sixteenth-century composers and publishers of the phrase *Missa ad imitationem . . .* for parody Masses is surely relevant here;[39] as Pontio's words show, the procedure we call by the name of parody, a process in which one composer copies features of another man's work almost as if it were an object in Nature, was thought of as closely akin to the technique of contrapuntal imitation in general.

Zarlino's normal word in speaking of modal ethos or of setting words to music is *accommodare;* one "suits" the music to the expressive character of the text by choice of the proper mode and by using just declamatory procedures. Writing of the "accommodation" of music to words, Zarlino describes the power of the text to convey "o per via della narratione, o della imitatione" various sentiments; it is the musician's duty to select melodies and harmonies "simile alla natura" of these sentiments.[40] Thus the composer's melodic subject or invention can be in its way an imitation of nature. At an earlier point in the *Istitutioni* Zarlino reminds composers that melodies used in fugal entries should be properly separated in time and should begin slowly, for

. . . veramente in ciò & in ogn'altra cosa dobbiamo imitar la Natura, il cui procedere si vede esser molto regolato; conciosia che se noi haveremo riguardo alli Movimenti naturali, ritrovaremo, che sono ne i loro principij alquanto più tardi, di quello, che non sono nel mezo & nel fine; come si può vedere in una Pietra, che sia lasciata cadere dall'alto al basso; della quale il Movimento è più veloce, senza dubio, nel fine, che non è nel principio. Imitaremo adunque la Natura & procederemo in tal maniera, che li Movimenti, che faranno le parti delli Contrapunti non siano molto veloci nel principio; ilche osservaremo etiandio nel mezo & nel fine di ciascuna parte, quando dopo le Pause incominciaranno à cantare.[41]

Truly in this and in all things we should imitate Nature, whose workings are most orderly. Thus if we observe motion in Nature, we shall see that it is somewhat slower at its start than in midcourse or at the end—as can be seen in a stone, the motion of which when dropped is surely faster at the end than at the beginning. Let us therefore imitate Nature by proceeding in such a way that the movement of contrapuntal voices is not very fast at the outset. We should also observe this in the middle and end of any voice part, whenever that part begins to sing after some rests.

From the passage above it seems a short step to the notion that fugal entries "imitate the nature" of the subject they follow. Why then did Zarlino not simply call all fugal procedure imitation? He seems rather discontent with the term *fuga;* for exact canons he prefers *consequenza,* and he suggests in place of *fuga* words like *replica* and *reditta. Fuga,* a term without rhetorical meaning or classical associations, may even have struck Zarlino's circle in Venice as something of a barbarism. It was nonetheless in common use, and Zarlino as practical musician doubtless knew it would remain so. But he could at least define it precisely by calling it an exact repetition of something else, hence different from an imitation. Musicians could then choose either to restate a subject in another voice, or to imitate its character more or less closely. The fact that imitation is far more common than fugue in the music of the middle and later sixteenth century should not lead even the most enthusiastic humanist among us to think of this music as therefore more imitative of nature; but Zarlino's choice of language may nevertheless have a strong current of humanistic thinking behind it.

·

Modern scholars when writing about sixteenth-century antecedents of the tonal fugue have tended to prefer Vicentino's discussion of *fuga* to that of Zarlino; Vicentino sets up no rigid categories, appears to speak directly and in chatty fashion about practical matters, and stresses the connection of fugue to tonal thinking more than Zarlino does. In fact the two theorists do not contradict each other but rather give useful complementary information.[42] Zarlino, like most theorists before him and many after his time, does have a certain fondness for setting up categories. But on the whole, and certainly in this instance, his distinctions make eminently good sense. If one looks for examples of *fuga* and *imitatione* in the polyphonic music Zarlino presumably knew best, that of his master Adrian Willaert, they are not at all hard to find. Even the theorist's seemingly pedantic stress on fugue and imitation in contrary motion turns out to be very practical; if lengthy canons *per arsin et thesin* do not abound, there are innumerable examples of points of imitation, strict or free, in melodic inversion.

By way of testing Zarlino's ideas I looked through two collections of Willaert's motets, those in the *Musica nova* of 1559 and the second book of four-voice motets, published in 1539 and reprinted in 1545.[43] Examples of *fuga sciolta,* exactly carried out points of imitation at the unison, fourth, fifth, and octave, are so numerous that there is no point in discussing single instances; but a few examples of Zarlino's other categories might be instructive.

Fuga legata, the strict canon at a perfect interval allowing for exact intervallic correspondence, is plentifully represented in the motets of the *Musica nova.* Willaert chooses for the most part the interval of the fifth above or below; the fugal exactness of the canon is indicated in several motets by the use of partial signatures. In *Sustinuimus pacem—Peccavimus* (no. 9), for instance, a motet with the inscription "Canon. Fuga quatuor temporum in diapente remissum," the upper voice has a signature of one sharp. Any written ♮ in this voice is carefully answered by a written ♭ in the lower voice, and nowhere is use of *musica ficta* likely in one voice but difficult to apply in the other.[44] This motet is typical of the canonic pieces in the *Musica nova;* intervallic exactness was obviously one of Willaert's aims. A slightly more evident bow toward imitation may be seen in one or two of the motets in *Musica nova,*[45] but troublesome spots are rare, and would be rarer still except for the editor's somewhat inconsistent use of *musica ficta,* evidently placed without very much regard for preservation of fugal exactness.[46]

Imitatione legata, canon without perfect equivalence of intervals, seems uncommon in Willaert, but there are instances. One is the "Canon duorum temporum fuga in subdiapente" in the four-voice *Ave regina coelorum.*[47] Here the canon is a Phrygian melody on E, answered on A below; the obvious problem is how the F's in the upper voice, approached in a variety of ways, are to be answered in the lower: B♮ or B♭. The editor has inserted a few flats here and there, and a few more could conceivably be added; but there is no way to make the imitation exact enough for it to be called fugue (despite its superscription). Example 6.6 shows the opening of the piece, followed by passages in which fugal exactness is not feasible (as marked by asterisks). Notes over which I have placed a "♭?" are places in which *musica ficta* could be introduced in an effort to make the imitation more nearly exact. I do not, however, think these flats necessary or even especially desirable.

This piece is a clear example of imitation; and Zarlino nowhere says that one should try to get imitation as close to fugue as possible. One consequence of his distinction between the two is that there is no need to try to keep the solmization of canonic melodies exactly alike; a defective fugal canon simply becomes a perfectly acceptable imitative one.

More complicated, since the examples are so much more numerous, is the phenomenon of *imitatione sciolta.* The opening of Willaert's four-voice *Beatus Joannes—Ipse est,*[48] given in example 6.7, is a good illustration. How long should the written E♭'s in alto and bass obtain? In all probability for just one note, in the alto at any rate; thus what looks like a strictly fugal opening becomes an example of *imitatione sciolta.*

Imitations of this kind may be found at many points within these pieces, not just in opening figures. Use of intervals such as the third, guaranteeing imitation rather than fugue, is more common within pieces than at their openings,[49] but the perfect intervals remain the most frequently used ones. The kind of small problem that attention to Zarlino's distinctions can pose is illustrated in example 6.8, a passage from the middle of the first part of Willaert's *Usquequo Domine—Illumina.* In this example of three-part imitation the alto could possibly be "fugally" inflected by flatting the E's in its version of the figure, but the result would be curious in sound; it seems better to consider this another example of *imitatione sciolta.*

Sometimes the composer decides everything himself. In example 6.9 Willaert provides an example of mixed imitation and fugue (between superius and alto) so clear that Zarlino could have used it for an example. But more often the decision is left to the performer or to the modern editor. Zarlino's definitions do not provide certain solutions, but they may be of real help if we can simply decide whether the case at hand is one of fugal or of imitative procedure.

Example 6.6 Willaert, *Ave regina coelorum*, mm. 1–12, 20–31, 63–70

*The rests as given in this part are clearly in error. The facsimile from a MS source for this piece, reproduced on p. ii of the volume from which this example is drawn, gives them correctly.

Example 6.6, cont.

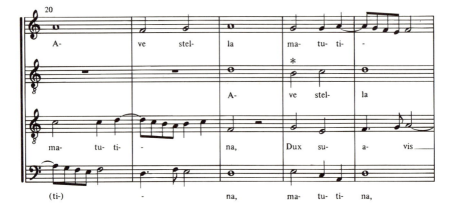

Example 6.6, cont.

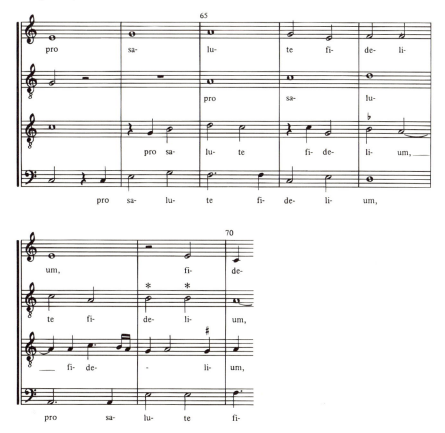

Example 6.7 Willaert, *Beatus Joannes—Ipse est*, mm. 1–13

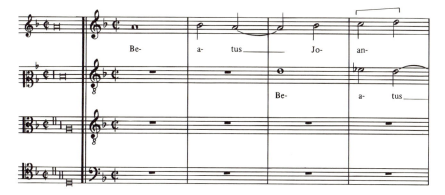

Example 6.7, cont.

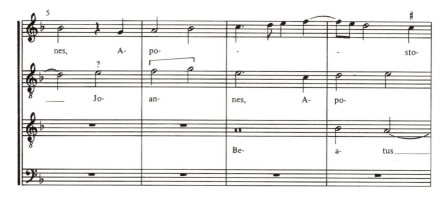

Example 6.8 Willaert, *Usquequo Domine—Illumina,* mm. 23–29

Example 6.8, cont.

Example 6.9 Willaert, *Congratulamini—Beatam*, mm. 31–39

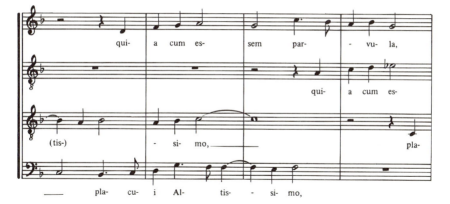

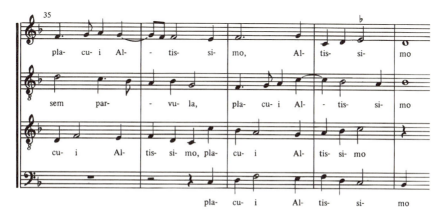

·

Writing about music of the turn of the sixteenth century, Putnam Aldrich describes problematic imitative entries in this way:

> If the imitation is to be strict the modal octave, or at least the portion of it used in the subject, will be transposed a fifth or a fourth. An accidental inserted in the part by the composer will insure that such a transposition was intended. In the absence of any accidental it is sometimes difficult to determine whether or not strict imitation (and therefore transposition) was intended to be arrived at through musica ficta.[50]

Edward Lowinsky, describing a group of ricercari by Willaert, takes a different tack:

> Each time the question is whether a motive introduced by Willaert in an unambiguous solmization should preserve its character in transposition one or two fifths lower through the addition of accidentals necessary to observe the original solmization. Each time the editors agreed that this must have been Willaert's intent.[51]

These statements introduce two topics not expressly treated by Zarlino in connection with fugue and imitation. Vicentino warns against fugal entries that go outside the mode, but limits himself to favoring entries at perfect intervals and to recommending adjustment of fifths to fourths so as to keep answering voices within the octave. On the matter of modal transposition in imitative entries he, like, Zarlino, is silent.[52] As for solmization patterns, they are of course implicit in any talk of the relationship of tones and semitones in a melody; in defining imitation Zarlino is in effect saying that hexachord relationships need not always be kept intact in successive entries. What he does not say is what Lowinsky asks, whether one should employ fugue in order to keep exact a very distinctive thematic outline.

Solmization patterns, when transposed literally from one voice to another at any interval other than the octave, can result in modal ambiguity or even modulation. This causes problems in contrapuntally imitative music from the middle of the fifteenth century on.[53] Of course a composer might have wanted to work out a highly chromatic series of modulatory phrases by means of exactly transposed entrances at the interval of a fourth or fifth; Lowinsky has discussed some intriguing instances of this and similar procedures in the music of Josquin and his successors.[54] If not deliberately made chromatic for experimental or expressive purposes, however, Renaissance polyphony remains within the limits of a diatonic modal system. Just what these limits are, and how modal theory may be said to govern polyphonic practice over a wide span of time, are subjects beyond the scope of this study. But if we are to believe the theorists at all, the individual voices of a polyphonic piece all subscribe to either the plagal or authentic compass of a single mode—exceptionally, perhaps, to pairs of closely related modes. Solmization patterns are mentioned in this regard only as they characterize the species of fourth and fifth which go to make up the various modal octaves.

If, then, the solmization of a subject changes when transposed to another interval, an entry at this second interval may not be an exact answer to the subject but instead an imitation of that subject, copying the intervallic makeup of its guide as closely as is possible within the portion of the modal octave corresponding to its range. The music of Josquin contains many examples illustrating such modally governed imitation. The openings of three Masses—*Allez regretz, Ave maris stella,* and *Pange lingua*—are instances (ex. 6.10). In example 6.10a the symmetrical spacing of answers at the fourth below and above the subject would at first suggest identical solmization on *ut . . .*, the starred note then a *fa*. But an E♭ in the alto at the end of measure 6 would take that voice outside the mode, for no good reason; it seems much more sensible to consider the alto answer as being on *fa . . .*, hence ending on a *mi* at the starred note.[55] The bass entry in example 6.10b, its B♭ strikingly different in sound from the E in the subject's corresponding spot, cannot here or in other movements of the Mass be raised a semitone. Nor should the E's in the other three voices be lowered; context in the final entry, as well as in other sections of the work (cf. Agnus Dei III, m. 64), makes this alteration impossible.[56] Thus the bass part remains in G-Dorian like the others, using a different segment of the octave and sung to a hexachord pattern beginning on *re* against the *ut . . .* (or *re,* followed by a mutation) of the subject.

Example 6.10

a. Josquin, *Missa Allez regretz,* Kyrie, mm. 1–10

b. Josquin, *Missa Ave maris stella*, Kyrie, mm. 1–7

c. Josquin, *Missa Pange lingua*, Kyrie, mm. 1–8

In example 6.10c a flat could be added to the third note of the bass and alto entries (this is actually done in the Credo, where a persistent *mi-fa* undulation marks the subject). But such an alteration causes problems two measures later, and results in modal transposition in the answering voices, which otherwise fit well within a segment of the normal Phrygian octave. A subject opening on *mi* answered by an imitation on *re* (cf. ex. 6.5b above) seems, at least in the terms of this study, Josquin's intention. A special problem arises in the *Qui tollis* of the Gloria in this Mass, where successive entries of the subject on B, E, A, and D give B-C-B, E-F-E, A-B♭ (written in)-A, D-*E*-D. Lowinsky argues that the E in the final entry should be flatted to preserve thematic symmetry.[57] This is indeed possible, but if B♭ can be regarded as a normal occurrence in untransposed Phrygian (lying as it does above the basic *mi-la* tetrachord inside the mode's species of fifth), E♭ involves a real transposition, and a double one at that, of the mode. Zarlino's concept of imitation here again supports a diatonic rendering of this final entry.[58]

Further examples from music of the early and middle sixteenth century could be added,[59] but I think those already given suffice to demonstrate my point (interested readers are encouraged to hunt up examples of their own). Naturally counter-examples could also be found without difficulty; there are pieces in which hexa-chordal symmetry seems intended, often playfully so, even in strongly diatonic pieces.[60] Here *musica ficta* resulting in fugally exact entries could be applied even at the cost of temporary dislocation of the mode.

•

In summary I think it can be said that Zarlino's definition of fugue and imitation, at first reading a distinction of interest only to other theorists, was made for very prac-tical reasons. As two equally valid aspects of contrapuntal technique, imitation and fugue serve to unify compositions and to further the concept of *imitazione della natura*—all the while remaining subservient to an unstated but strongly im-plied idea of diatonic modal unity. The emerging *seconda prattica* of the later six-teenth century gave rise to music that the essentially conservative Zarlino could not have, would not have wished to account for. Yet in a sense his theory was not behind the times. If, as Alfred Mann says, Zarlino's theory "ignores the tonal an-swer, which, by his classification, is not different from any other imitation," this is because his concept of *fuga* and *imitatione* is a broader and more thoughtful theory of tonal fugue than that of his contemporaries. Taking note of these distinctions will not give us final answers for application of *musica ficta* to imitative entries; it may indeed only support timid diatonicists and give pause to hardy chromaticists among us. Perhaps, though it is not final answers about *musica ficta* that we want, only more refined criteria for making individual decisions.[61] This it seems is what Zarlino is offering us.

POSTSCRIPT

In this study I deliberately emphasized *imitazione della natura* in the Aristotelian sense; in doing so I left out the equally important rhetorical meaning of imitation, the adroit and creative copying, à la Cicero or Quintilian, of a model. The reader is referred to the first study in this book and the references given there, in order to get a more balanced view of the subject.

A similar tilt in favor of modal "purity" at the expense of hexachordal corre-spondence can be seen in my treatment of the musical examples. This was also de-liberate but it now strikes me as a little extreme, especially in instances such as ex-ample 6.10a, where cadential figures would seem to call for adjustment in favor of fugal exactness (the *Missa Allez regretz* is, by the way, no longer attributed to Jos-quin). I had a point to make; but on a subject as slippery as application of ficta acci-dentals it is hard to stay perched firmly on any point. The work of scholars such as Margaret Bent and Karol Berger on this subject should now be taken into account. See Bent, "Musica Recta and Musica Ficta," *MD* 26 (1972): 73–100; Bent, "Dia-tonic Ficta," *EMH* 4 (1984): 1–48; Berger, *Musica ficta: Theories of Accidental In-flections in Vocal Polyphony from Marchetto da Padova to Gioseffo Zarlino* (Cam-bridge, 1987).

NOTES

1. Joseph M. Müller-Blattau, *Grundzüge einer Geschichte der Fuge* (Kassel, 1931), 51; Alberto Ghislanzoni, "La genesi storica della Fuga," *Rivista musicale italiana* 52 (1951): 1; Alfred Mann, *The Study of Fugue* (New Brunswick, 1958), 19; Imogene Horsley, *Fugue: History and Practice* (Glencoe, 1966), 11, 54.

2. Mann, *The Study of Fugue,* 19, 23.

3. Ibid., 23.

4. See Nicolo Vicentino, *L'Antica Musica ridotta alla moderna prattica* (Rome, 1555; facsimile, ed. Edward Lowinsky [Basel, 1959]), 4.32, fols. 88v–89.

5. Examples illustrating modes 1, 5, and 10 (renumbered 3, 7, and 12 in the 1573 edition of the *Istitutioni*) show use of modal answers. Edward Lowinsky calls attention to these duos in *Tonality and Atonality in Sixteenth-Century Music* (Berkeley, 1961), 31–32.

6. See Ghislanzoni, "La genesi storica," 3–5; Mann, *The Study of Fugue,* 43–45.

7. Each of these theorists will be considered separately below.

8. Jean-Philippe Rameau, *Traité de l'harmonie* (Paris, 1722), 3.44.332. Johann Joseph Fux, on the other hand, repeats Zarlino's definitions with surprising faithfulness, allowing for his altered concept of mode. See Fux, *Gradus ad Parnassum* (Venice, 1725; facsimile, New York, 1966), 140, *De imitatione:* "Imitatio fit, quando pars sequens antecedentem sequitur post aliquam pausam servatis iisdem intervallis, quibus antecedens incessit, nullô Modi, Toni, Semitonique habitâ ratione; id quod fieri potest in Unisone, Secondâ, Tertiâ, Quartâ, Sextâ, Septimâ, & Octavâ."; 143, *De Fugis in genere:* "Quapropter alio definitio, quâ Fuga ab imitatione distinguatur, statuenda est. Dico ergo: Fuga est quarundam Notarum in parte praecedenti positarum ab sequente repetitio, habitâ modi, ac plerumque toni, semitonique ratione."

9. *Le istitutioni harmoniche* (Venice, 1573), 3.54.257. In the 1558 edition this is chapter 51. For a translation of the 1558 text, see *The Art of Counterpoint,* trans. Guy A. Marco and Claude V. Palisca (New Haven, 1968), 126–27.

10. The use of *fuga* to mean a point of imitation that may be broken off at any time may be found as early as Ramos. See *Musica Practica Bartolomei Rami de Pareia,* ed. Johannes Wolf (Leipzig, 1901), 2.1.1.68: "... quod voces, quae sequentur in tenore, non discordent cum illis, quia, cum fuga incipit discordare, in similitudine fiat immediate dissimilitudo, ita ut non faciat contra regulas, supra dictas."

11. *Le istitutioni harmoniche,* 3.55.262–63 (chap. 52 in the 1558 edition); cf. *The Art of Counterpoint,* 135.

12. See *The Art of Counterpoint,* 136–41, for transcriptions of these examples.

13. Imogene Horsley, "Fugue and Mode in Sixteenth-Century Vocal Polyphony," *Aspects of Medieval and Renaissance Music: A Birthday Offering to Gustave Reese,* ed. Jan LaRue (New York, 1966), 414–15.

14. Juan Bermudo, *Declaración de Instrumentos musicales* (Ossuna, 1555; facsimile, ed. Macario S. Kastner [Kassel, 1957]), fol. 137: "Es la fuga una sucessiva distribucion de una mesma clausula en principio, o en qualquiera o tro lugar de la cantilena: o es repeticion de clausula."

15. *L'Antica Musica,* 4.32, fols. 88v–89.

16. Pietro Aaron, *Libri tres de institutione harmonica* (Bologna, 1516), 3.lii.

17. See D. P. Walker, "Aron," *MGG,* 1:665.

18. Pietro Aaron, *Lucidario in musica* (Venice, 1545), 2.x. This passage is briefly discussed by Peter Bergquist, "Mode and Polyphony around 1500," *Music Forum* 1 (1967): 119.

19. Cf. Aaron's description of fugue in his *Compendiolo di molti dubbi . . .* (Milan, s.d. [1550?]), chapter 70: "Fuga over consequenza, non è altro che una somiglianza di intervalli, Musici, gli quali è mestiere che siano simili di forma & di nome. Et tal fuggire si fa in quattro modi cioè per unisono, per Diatessaron, per Diapente & per Diapason, & per le loro composte, o replicate."

20. Pedro Cerone, *El Melopeo y Maestro* (Naples, 1613), 14.2.763.

21. Ibid., 14.4.765–66.

22. Ibid., 14.10.770–71.

23. Ibid., 14.11.772.

24. Ibid., 14.18.777.

25. Giovanni Maria Artusi, *L'Arte del Contrapunto ridotto in tavole* (Venice, 1586), 31.

26. Orazio Tigrini, *Il Compendio della musica* (Venice, 1588; facsimile, New York, 1966), 4.2–5., esp. 107.

27. *Dialogo del R. M. Don Pietro Pontio* (Parma, 1595), 106.

28. Ibid., 46–50.

29. Ibid., 45.

30. "On 'Parody' as Term and Concept in Sixteenth-Century Music," *Aspects of Medieval and Renaissance Music,* 560–75. On page 570 Lockwood quotes the two passages from Pontio's *Dialogo* given above (n. 27 and n. 29), and says of them "the point of interest in both is again the use of *imitatione* as a term referring to two interrelated compositions, in contradistinction to *fuga,* the familiar alternative sixteenth-century term for contrapuntal 'imitation,' as later understood." In view of Pontio's use of terminology borrowed from Zarlino, I believe the meaning of the passages in question should be taken as I have tried to do above; for Pontio *imitatione* has both a specific and a general definition.

31. *Ragionamento di Musica del Reverendo M. Don Pietro Pontio* (Parma, 1588), 68–69. The passage quoted by Pontio from his Mass is derived from Arcadelt's *Ancidetemi pur,* mm. 15–16 and 28–29 in the edition of Albert Seay, *Jacobi Arcadelt. Opera Omnia,* vol. 2 (American Institute of Musicology, 1970), 10.

32. Scipione Cerreto, *Della Prattica Musicale Vocale et Strumentale* (Naples, 1601), 3.15.212. Cerreto's admonishment about observing the mode, already seen in Vicentino's chapters on fugue, appears in many seventeenth-century theorists. Christoph Bernhard in his *Tractatus compositionis augmentatus* (ca. 1650) calls the tonal answer, for which he gives examples from the works of Palestrina, *consociato modorum.* See Joseph Müller-Blattau, ed., *Die Kompositionslehre Heinrich Schützens in der Fassung seines Schülers Christoph Bernhard* (Leipzig, 1926), 53.98.

33. Lodovico Zacconi, *Prattica in musica. Seconda parte* (Venice, 1622), 4.15.265.

34. Ibid., 2.65.113–14. Zacconi's terms, it should be noted, have no connection with diatonic or chromatic practice.

35. Ibid., 3.35.166–67.

36. Ibid., 2.28.79; 3.55.220. Use of the term *fantasia* in this sense may be seen in Zarlino also; cf. *Le istitutioni harmoniche,* 3.26.200 (1573 edition).

37. Zacconi, *Prattica,* 3.46. 129; cf. Pontio, *Ragionamento,* 90–91.

38. On this subject see Armen Carapetyan, "The Concept of *Imitazione della natura* in the Sixteenth Century," *MD* 1 (1948): 47–67; Leo Schrade, "Von der 'Maniera' der Komposition in der Musik des 16. Jahrhunderts," *Zeitschrift für Musikwissenschaft* 16 (1934): 3–20; 98–117; 152–70.

39. See Lockwood, "On 'Parody'," 563. In a chapter called "Von der Imitation," Christoph Bernhard gives lists of the composers who "mehr wert sind [ge]imitiret zu werden." See Müller-Blattau, *Die Kompositionslehre,* 43.90.

40. *Le istitutioni harmoniche,* 4.32.319 (1573 edition).

41. Ibid., 3.45.238.

42. At one point Vicentino seems to approach Zarlino's concept of imitation as it chiefly concerns us here. In a chapter on composing canons (*L'Antica Musica,* 4.33. fols. 89v–90) he says: "Et si de avvertire che quando il Tenore farà il Canon con il Contr'alto in quinta, che s'il Tenore sarà per b. molle, il Contr'alto verrà per ♮ incitato; & si fugerà di far quarto, per non fare che in quello venghi il tritono." (One should take note that when the tenor is in canon with the alto at the fifth, if the tenor is on a B♭, the alto will be on an [E]♮ and one should avoid the interval of the fourth, lest the tritone should occur in the second voice). This passage begins with a recommendation that the non-canonic voices begin "con l'imitatione del Canon."

In one detail Vicentino's terminology does differ slightly from that of Zarlino. By *arsin et thesin* in imitative counterpoint Zarlino means contrary melodic motion (*Le istitutioni harmoniche,* 3.60.260). Vicentino uses this term to mean imitation in syncopated rhythm (*L'Antica Musica,* 4.32, fol. 88v); then in the next chapter (fol. 90) he employs the term with the meaning Zarlino gives it.

43. See *Adriani Willaert. Opera Omnia,* ed. Hermann Zenck and Walter Gerstenberg (American Institute of Musicology, 1950–), vols. 2, 5.

44. The F's in the upper part are flatted at almost all important points, and the resulting B♭'s in the canonic voice do not disrupt the modal *concentus.* Thus the question of whether an exact canon such as this involves modal transposition—a problem considered in a general way later in this study—seems academic; Willaert takes care to keep his canonic voices within the general mode of the motet.

45. See *Veni Sancte Spiritus* (no. 11), mm. 46–51, 52–57, for instance. Possibly Zarlino would allow at moments like this a small admixture of imitation (cf. his example of mixed fugue and imitation on p. 264 of the *Istitutioni*) in what otherwise meets his definition of fugue.

46. For examples of this see *Salve sancta parens* (no. 15), mm. 31ff., and *Aspice Domine* (no. 17), mm. 84 and 87.

47. Willaert, *Opera,* 2.35. The canon is praised as a skillful one in Gustave Reese, *Music in the Renaissance* (New York, 1954), 372. A curious example of a four-part canon with entries at successive fifths (G-D-A-E), may be seen in Verdelot's *Dignare me laudare te,* printed in Albert Smijers, ed., *Treize livres de Motets parus chez Pierre Attaingnant en 1534 et 1535,* (Paris, 1936), 3.39. The very diatonic character of this piece makes it a particularly good instance of *imitatione legata.* I am grateful to Benjamin Peck of New York University for calling this piece to my attention.

48. Willaert, *Opera,* 2.71. The *secunda pars* of this motet begins with a motive imitated at the third below, then at the fifth above (both of these inexact intervallically), and finally at the octave in exact *fuga sciolta.*

49. Vicentino, *L'Antica Musica,* 4.13–14, fols. 78r–79, advises sticking to the perfect intervals at the opening points of imitation in a piece, saving the other intervals, which he here terms "cattive prese di voci," for later points, where *inganni* such as syncopated entries may also be used to good effect.

50. Putnam Aldrich, "An Approach to the Analysis of Renaissance Music," *Music Review* 30 (1969): 10.

51. Edward Lowinsky, foreword to *Musica Nova,* ed. H. Colin Slim, MRM 1 (Chicago, 1964), xi.

52. On this point see Horsley, "Fugue and Mode," 416. Glareanus does speak of canons at the interval of the second above and below, pieces in which the two voices sing in separate, normally unrelated modes. His examples, canonic duos from Josquin's *Missa Mater Patris* and *Missa Malheur me bat,* show mixtures of Ionian and Dorian, and of Phrygian and

Dorian. See *Dodekachordon,* 3.xxiv (2.276, and examples 105–10 in the translation of Clement A. Miller [American Institute of Musicology, 1965]).

53. Somewhat similar problems are caused by sequential ostinato patterns within a single voice in the music of Obrecht, Isaac, and their contemporaries. See Marcus van Crevel, "Verwante Sequensmodulaties bij Obrecht, Josquin en Coclico," *Tijdschrift der Vereeniging voor Nederlandse Muziekgeschiedenis* 16/2 (1941): 107–24.

54. See especially his "The Goddess Fortuna in Music," *MQ* 29 (1943): 45–77, and "Matthaeus Greiter's *Fortuna:* An Experiment in Chromaticism and in Musical Iconography," *MQ* 42 (1956): 500–519; 43 (1957): 68–85.

55. Raising the corresponding B♭ in the tenor and F in the bass would produce a stylistically improbable result, more like an Elizabethan dance-song than like Josquin. And comparison with the opening of Agnus I in this Mass, where the context prohibits an F♯, shows that the notes in question should be sung as written.

56. See also the major sixth degree in the plainchant hymn on which the Mass is based (*Liber Usualis,* 1259).

57. "The Goddess Fortuna," 60–61. It should be noted that Lowinsky is in general opposed to the notion, at least as it applies to music of the fifteenth century, that one voice part should be regarded as occupying a transposed form of the basic mode. See his "Conflicting Signatures in Early Polyphonic Music," *MQ* 31 (1945): 227–60, and "Conflicting Views on Conflicting Signatures," *JAMS* 7 (1954): 181–204.

58. Lowinsky's statement ("The Goddess Fortuna," 61) that a D-E♮-D entry in the bass involves a "shift from Phrygian to Dorian, breaking up the tonal unity of this marvellously organized section of the Mass" does not strike me as convincing; the bass entry revolves about E and F, ending on an E-A fifth. To flat the first E's is, I think, to confuse the modal clarity of this entry and of the whole *concentus.* The *phrasis* of Glareanus's modal theory, by which mode is established in a single voice, has to do with the range and intervallic quality of a whole phrase, and is thus not determined by an opening point of imitation.

59. Entries on successive fifths, involving inexact imitation, may be seen in the *tertia pars* of Josquin's *O admirabile commercium* and in Festa's *Deduc me domine;* see Edward Lowinsky, ed., *The Medici Codex of 1518,* MRM 4 (Chicago, 1968), 38, 56. A particularly troublesome instance of this kind may be seen in Francesco de Layolle's *Occhi miei lassi,* mm. 55ff.; see Frank A. D'Accone, ed., *Music of the Florentine Renaissance* (American Institute of Musicology, 1969), 4.60. Here a subject beginning on F is imitated by three voices beginning on E, A, and D respectively; no amount of musica ficta can make these points of imitation fugally exact.

60. See, for example, Compère's *Chanter ne puis* in Helen Hewitt, ed., *Ottaviano Petrucci. Canti B,* MRM 2 (Chicago, 1967), 220. Here a double series of entries on successive fifths seems (though the editor apparently did not think so) to call for *la-re* solmization throughout the first series, *sol-ut* throughout the second.

61. On this see the very sensible remarks of Lewis Lockwood in "A Sample Problem of Musica Ficta: Willaert's *Pater Noster,*" *Studies in Music History: Essays for Oliver Strunk,* ed. Harold Powers (Princeton, 1968), 169.

Lessons in Theory from a
Sixteenth-Century Composer

WE HAVE BEEN ACCUSTOMED to looking at the course of Renaissance music as a series of great names arranged in chronological order, with direct or indirect teacher-pupil relationships connecting many of the composers: Dufay-Ockeghem-Busnoys-Obrecht-Josquin-Mouton-Willaert-Rore-Lassus (*or* Mouton-Arcadelt-Palestrina), etc. Such lists became all but canonical in nineteenth-century musicological writings from the time of Kiesewetter and Fétis; their origin goes back, however, to the Renaissance itself, when writers on music liked to cite groups of *antichi* and *moderni,* sometimes linked like beads on a musical rosary by teacher-student connections.[1] Aside from its unfairness to composers who cannot easily be fit into such lists, this brand of historiography has mixed fact and fiction, true and false chronology, convincing and improbable lines of influence. In so doing it has created additional work for twentieth-century writers trying to order the factual data we now have about the music of the fifteenth and sixteenth centuries. There seems nonetheless to be an enduring appeal about the making of these lists; even as we smile at the naiveté of earlier linear groupings we are busy making new ones: a current example is the fuss over who started the "L'homme armé" tradition and how the links in this chain, at least up to Josquin, should be arranged.[2]

Theorists as well as composers can be arranged in linear descent. This was done only sporadically and indirectly in the Renaissance. But ever since the appearance in the late eighteenth century of Martin Gerbert's pathbreaking editions of medieval theorists,[3] there has been a tendency to think of writers on musical theory in a series parallel to that of composers. For the Renaissance, we might have something like the following: Ugolino-Tinctoris-Gafori (or, in a second column: Ramos-Aaron-Spataro)-Fogliano-Glareanus-Zarlino-Zacconi-Cerone-Banchieri.[4]

Several of the names on this list are also known as composers, either primarily so (Banchieri), in about equal measure of theoretical and practical work (Gafori), or in secondary relationship of practice to theory (Ugolino, Tinctoris, Zarlino)— known in this way to us, it should be added. That a theorist should be a composer as well seems natural enough; a list of such figures, from Philippe de Vitry through Rameau to Hindemith and Messiaen, would be easy enough to compile. And only if one is imbued with Romantic notions about creativity and pedagogy as opposite poles is it surprising that a composer should also be a sometime theorist. Many have been; in the Renaissance more composers may have set down on paper their ideas, or at any rate prescriptions, about compositional rules than we know. The lost "Musica" of Dufay, cited by Gafori, is a tantalizing example.[5]

Did Renaissance musicians learn the art of composition from studying formal treatises? Scholarly opinion has tended to answer this question with a negative.[6] In the choir schools where young musicians got their start, instruction must surely have been oral; if textbooks were used they were for teachers, not students. Composers' methods of teaching polyphony were probably directed toward singing first, improvised counterpoint next, and writing last, a practical method quite unlike the organization of most treatises.[7] For whom then were these treatises designed? In some instances, such as the work of Tinctoris, they were directed first toward noble patrons, or their children, who may or may not have read them.[8] Some, especially the more learned writings, may have been intended for students in the universities, where the reading of works on musical theory is a well-documented tradition.[9] An audience wider than a small group of "other theorists" must have existed in the sixteenth century, for publishers surely expected to sell the treatises issued in fairly large numbers—if doubtless in small impressions—by Renaissance presses.[10]

Composers and other teachers of music doubtless owned, or had access to, copies of formal treatises. There is no evidence that they used these works as textbooks, in the modern sense of that term. What they may well have done is to formulate pedagogical methods of their own, citing or paraphrasing theorists whose authority they respected. Most of this instruction must have been oral, but one can always hope to find evidence on paper that will show something of how musical composition was taught at a practical level.[11]

Such evidence is provided by the Neapolitan composer Giovan Tomaso Cimello (ca. 1510–80). Cimello published a book of madrigals and one of *villanelle,* and a few other compositions, including a motet, survive.[12] He may have given instruction in music to noble pupils while in the service of the Colonna family in Rome and Naples; and near the end of his life (1571–73) he had a post as teacher of grammar and music at the seminary in Benevento.[13] Scattered testimony from musicians, including the well-known Giulio Belli, exists in praise of his musicianship, and as late as 1623 he is referred to as a "learned and excellent musician."[14]

In an autograph letter dated December 1579, Cimello speaks not only of his poetic and musical compositions but also of his views on chant, which he says "should follow the art of metrics so as to preserve its proper accents"; he further refers to the thirty-four possible *fughe* based on species of fifth, fourth, third, and tone, useful for composers who wish to write motets on Offertories, Graduals, or other chant.[15] One passage in the letter is an attack on Boethius, whom Cimello judges to be "totally wrong" as a theorist because of his adherence to Pythagorean intonation and his consequent lack of distinction between major and minor tones; by this time it would seem that Cimello was familiar with the work of Zarlino and perhaps of Fogliano on just intonation. In several passages of this epistle Cimello refers to his *regole nove* on music, taken from him in an unfinished state but later recovered and readied for publication. He boasts that his rules were known in Spain and France, that "Orlando" [Lassus?] came to visit him and to profit from his instruction, and that "many composers in Italy" had written to him about points of theory. His *libretto* on theory contains, he says, the whole art of proportions, of counterpoint, of improvisation, and so forth.[16]

This could of course be empty boasting, a self-glorification meant to impress the exalted recipient of Cimello's letter. Certainly no printed treatise by Cimello is known to survive. But there are two extant manuscripts of theoretical content that may with some confidence be associated with him. Neither is explicitly signed, but both mention the musician's name often enough to make it clear that at least some of what Cimello talks about in his letter of 1579 does in fact survive.

In Bologna, Civico Museo Bibliografico Musicale, MS B 57, there is a short notational treatise attributed to Cimello by Gaetano Gaspari on the basis of strong internal evidence.[17] It consists of eight folios, in quarto, of text and examples, plus three additional folios of music which clearly belong with the treatise.[18] The manuscript is neatly written (Gaspari calls the writing "beautiful"), in a mid-to-late sixteenth-century hand; text and examples are enclosed on each page in an inked frame. Since a good deal of the text is cast in first person, one might think the manuscript to be an autograph, but this cannot be so; in two places whoever was copying the text remarked "qui manca alcune parole"; there are some errors in the musical examples; and the two-voice counterpoint around which the whole treatise is organized does not appear under its rubric on folio 3v but at the end of the text. The work could have been copied by a pupil or correspondent of Cimello. If the treatise was sent in a letter, which is what its use of first person suggests, it would have had no title; and if the letter was signed the copyist may simply have omitted both the signature and some sort of closing section preceding it (the treatise ends abruptly, without a closing flourish). The recipient might even have been the person who sent Cimello the two-voice counterpoint in the first place.

Evidence that this little treatise was the work of Cimello is easily gathered from its contents. It begins thus:

> Before I come to correcting the above piece, sent to me by my [friend], I think it necessary to write something about the perfection of the four largest note values: *maxima, longa, brevis* and *semibrevis*.[19]

Midway through the text comes the rubric referred to above:

> Soprano sent to Cimello, and corrected and scored by him in *numero senario* of the cut circle [₵] and *numero ternario* of the uncut circle [O].[20]

Cimello's manuscript is not completely unknown to modern scholars. The astute Gaspari cited two of its more memorable passages, one containing an anecdote about Josquin and the other mentioning Tinctoris and Gafori, in his catalogue of the Bologna library.[21] Donna G. Cardamone and Keith Larson, two leading scholars in the field of the Neapolitan madrigal, both comment on it (as well as on the second Cimello manuscript, to be discussed below).[22] In an important article on differing interpretations of the mensural system in the fifteenth and sixteenth centuries, Anna Maria Busse Berger quotes from the Bologna manuscript to show Cimello's stand on the principle of minim equivalence.[23] Part of Cimello's anecdotal account of the origins of the "L'homme armé" Mass tradition is cited by Leeman L. Perkins, who has also noted Cimello's mention of the composer Lhéritier.[24]

No one has to my knowledge looked very closely at Cimello's work as a whole; a brief account of its contents therefore seems in order here.

The author's main purpose is to demonstrate the workings of the mensural system through comment on and correction of a melody sent to him by an unnamed correspondent (the melody, as will be seen, has an accompanying tenor but this voice is free of comment or correction). This method was not originated by Cimello. Though not characteristic of Tinctoris, who except for the *Liber de arte contrapuncti* uses short examples (as does Cimello before he gets to the melody in question), use of whole little pieces in two-part counterpoint is common in Gafori's *Practica musicae,* a work Cimello gives ample evidence of knowing well. Like Cimello, Gafori comments on only one voice, for him the tenor. Cimello's test piece is, however, far longer than any of Gafori's examples, and can be seen as a more practical exercise in that it purports to be a real piece, the work of a student submitted for the teacher's correction.

Since the author speaks (fol. 6v) of his admiration for Tinctoris, "whom I would rather believe than any other author writing on music," and of Gafori, the former's "most intimate friend,"[25] I have tried to see whether Cimello draws directly on the work of these theorists. He seldom if ever quotes directly, but in a number of places he does I think show reliance on these, for him, Neapolitan authorities—more on Gafori than on Tinctoris, suggesting that he may have had access to some of the unpublished treatises of Tinctoris but probably owned a copy of Gafori's *Practica musicae,* which after its publication in 1496 went through a number of editions and was doubtless in wide circulation.[26]

Cimello begins with the definition of perfect note values. This is of course commonplace material, but his derivation of the breve and long from poetic syllables already suggests a reading of Gafori (cf. *Practica,* 2.1). Next comes a discussion of the signatures O and ₵. In referring to the circle as made up of beginning, middle, and end, Cimello again seems to paraphrase Gafori (*Practica,* 2.8); his use of the term *numero senario,* "più perfetto che altro numero," which at first I thought might indicate knowledge of the work of Zarlino and hence a relatively late date of composition, probably comes from Gafori as well.[27] But Cimello makes his own use of the term: six is the number of semibreves, with two semibreves sung to the beat (*battuta*), in a measure (*casella*) of ₵ while three semibreves fit in a bar or scoring (*ispartimento*) of O. This is a good instance of Cimello's practical pedagogical approach; music is to be laid out, indeed composed, within metric units demarcated by barlines. Except for tablatures, theory preceded practice in the use of barlines; but Cimello's treatise, which dates in some form if not in this redaction from the 1540s, is surely an early example of their use.[28]

Appended to his discussion of perfect signatures is a reference to proportions, necessary since the piece to be discussed is signed ₵ 3/2. A Latin definition of proportion (Cimello regularly switches from colloquial Italian to Latin when he wants to make an important point or display his erudition), "proportio in musica est duorum numerorum inequalium comparatio,"[29] is given in order to emphasize that two numbers must be present if the proportion is to be considered rational. A mensural sign with a single number is, he says irrational, like comparing three cows to two horses ("dicendo tre bovi contro due cavalli"; this homely image is in the same sentence that began with the ponderous Latin definition). By insisting on the use of two numbers, Cimello follows both Tinctoris and Gafori.[30] Like all theorists who, up to the time of Rameau, demanded this, Cimello was fighting a losing battle; in his own madrigal volume of 1548 his publisher Gardano uses a "3" to indicate 3/2 proportion.

Next comes a series of examples of perfection in the breve, said to be applicable to other note values according to the mensural signatures used. Two points are of interest here. One is the caution that when two semibreve rests on the same line ("in un medesima riga") follow a breve, the breve will be perfect and the rests part of the next mensural unit.[31] The second is that a two-note ligature *cum opposita proprietate* (that is, consisting of two semibreves) should not be separable but should be considered a breve; thus a breve preceding this ligature should not be imperfected by the ligature's first semibreve. This is not to my knowledge a point made by many theorists, and Cimello may have derived it from practical experience.[32] Tinctoris does refer to it in his *Tractatus de regulari valore notarum,* where ligated notes along with coloration and dots of division are exceptions to the general rule that the first of an "imperfect" number of smaller notes always imperfects the preceding larger one.[33] Cimello may have read this; but his phrasing, that a pair of ligated semibreves always represents a breve, is a typically practical rule-of-thumb bit of advice.

Dots preventing imperfection are briefly mentioned; the dot of perfection and a double point of 'transportatione' indicating syncopation. The latter is certainly taken from Gafori; Tinctoris seems not to have used this term.[34]

Cimello warns his reader that in all note values (of O) one beats by the minim and that minims are always—except when a proportional sign is in effect—equal. The signatures ⊙ and ₵ do not call for enlarged minims but only three instead of two to the semibreve. To solve the difficulty that a measure (a breve in ⊙ or a semibreve in ₵) will have an awkward uneven number of minim beats, he recommends that one compose by the double breve to a measure in ⊙ (eighteen minims or nine beats), a single or double breve in ₵ (six or twelve minims, three or six beats).[35]

This discussion of perfect prolation is preliminary to a story of which Cimello was fond; he refers to it twice (fol. 2v–3r, 6r) in the Bologna treatise, and it is a recurrent motif in the jumble of topics making up the Naples treatise. Here is the Bologna version:

These things are attested to by Ockeghem and Josquin, who in their time were composers of great authority and who did not err in use of perfect prolation. I have heard from disciples of Josquin that Ockeghem, having written a chanson called "L'homme armé" added to it these words as canon: *crescat in duplum.* One might say that "L'homme armé" could be called a double man, of living flesh and of steel; and thus the notes and rests of this chanson and of the *Missa "L'homme armé"* [tenor] were doubled. Nor did these composers ever resolve the canon into *tempus perfectum* since they could sing such a *tenor* [from the canon]. A pupil of Josquin whose name I remember—he was called Giovan Lhéritier—told me that he gave this *tenor* to a *mastro* to sing, and the latter sang it well according to the sign [of prolation]; Josquin laughed because the singer did not observe the words "L'homme armé," that it was a canon, *crescat in duplum*. Lhéritier told me that after laughing a good deal Josquin told the singer how this Mass was written and how it should be sung. If the solution of the *tenor* in this Mass were not doubled, then *tempus* and prolation—breve and semibreve—would be equal, which would be something superfluous, and superfluous things are to be cut out; what can be done with economy should not be done with superfluity.

A resolution of this Mass *tenor* in *tempus perfectum* was made by Ottaviano Petrucci of Fossombrone, the famous printer, whom I have known and spoken with, I cannot say when or on what occasion, but it was in Sora, famous city of the *Equicoli*. [fols. 2v–3r]

For proof that this is true see the Osanna of this Mass [*"L'homme armé" super voces musicales*] where three parts sing in the semicircle with *sesquialtera* proportion and the fourth, which has the sign of perfect prolation, lacks the figures for *sesquialtera* (3/2), yet one sings three minims to the beat since the *tenor* says "Osanna. Gaudet cum gaudentibus." Certain composers have thought that one should execute all passages in this prolation, without the figure 3/2, in *sesquialtera,* and have thus written in their works. It saddens me that some have taken bad example, thus lessening the credit of the composer [Josquin] who wrote so skillfully, sweetly, and melodically.[36] [fol. 6r]

There are a number of things of interest here. Cimello's claim to have known both Lhéritier and Petrucci is chronologically just possible, and with no evidence to confirm or deny it his assertion can be taken at face value. What Petrucci was doing in Sora is not known, and Cimello frustratingly avoids giving even an approximate date; it must have been in the 1530s.[37] Lhéritier is not known to have been in Naples but he did reside in Rome in the 1520s, after which his whereabouts are unknown. Cimello is most likely to have met him in Rome, which suggests that Lhéritier may have been in that city as late as the 1530s or even 1540s.[38] A connection between Lhéritier and Josquin—a sample of the teacher-student chain referred to at the beginning of this study—is possible but is otherwise undocumented. The anecdote about Josquin and the tenor of his *Missa "L'homme armé" super voces musicales* is intriguing but loses some verisimilitude when one considers that the tenor, though indeed written in minim notation which is to be performed in augmentation (it is as Cimello says resolved in Petrucci's print of the Mass), has in none of its extant sources the canon *crescat in duplum* (a number of sources do, however, use "Gaudet cum gaudentibus" in the Osanna).

This is not the place to go into detail about the history of "L'homme armé." One or two points are nonetheless worth mentioning here. First, the chanson which has the best claim to be the source for the Mass tradition is without convincing attribution, though it has generally been ascribed to Robert Morton.[39] Pietro Aaron gives priority to Busnoys for the composition of a "L'homme armé" chanson written in perfect prolation;[40] and Richard Taruskin has argued that this piece could well be the one attributed to Morton.[41] The twentieth-century scholars are all, in varying degrees, cautious on this point. Aaron on the other hand makes his statement with assurance—though without letting us know for certain that Busnoy's chanson is the one we now have. Cimello is equally positive in giving Ockeghem the priority in the minim-notation "L'homme armé" tradition—also without identifying or citing the piece. Perhaps he knew a "L'homme armé" chanson now lost; or his anecdote may be secondhand, unsupported by knowledge of actual music. Aaron is probably a more dependable witness than Cimello to the "L'homme armé" tradition, but there seems no reason to discount Cimello, who seems proud of his knowledge here, completely.

The image of "L'homme armé" as a double man, of flesh and of steel, is reminiscent of the canon for the sixth of the Naples "L'homme armé" Masses.[42] But if these Masses, which apparently originated at the Burgundian court, were already in Naples by Cimello's time he gives no sign of knowing them. Nor does he refer to Tinctoris' *Missa "L'homme armé,"* which not only uses minim notation for the *tenor* but actually includes the canon *crescit in duplum* which Cimello attributes to Ockeghem and Josquin.[43] And there is at least one treatise by Tinctoris that Cimello did not know, or at any rate did not cite here, the *Proportionale musices,* for in this work Tinctoris deals (3.2–3) disapprovingly with minim notation as a sign of augmentation; he even mentions the canon *crescit in duplo* used by Dufay in the *Missa "Se la face ay pale."*[44]

After a brief, somewhat tangled discussion of how to beat a *sesquialtera* proportion in major prolation (a point returned to later in the treatise), and some friendly talk about the possibility of human error in realizing such things, the rubric for the test piece follows, with some blank space after it; the piece itself is given later, on folios 8r–10r. Since, says Cimello, this piece has many examples of imperfection and alteration, he will now go on to give some rules on these subjects; most of the remaining text is devoted to these prescriptions. Cimello's advice on these matters is more interesting when one looks at his commentary on the piece sent to him; this will be considered with the piece below.

Near the end of his text, but before the citation of the test piece, comes the second passage singled out by Gaspari (fol. 6v).

And the Most Reverend Johannes Tinctoris, chaplain and chapelmaster to Ferrante, king of Naples and Sicily, in whom I have more trust than in any other author on music, wrote enumerating the four perfect notes: the maxima is worth eighty-one minims, which make forty-and-one-half beats; the *longa* is worth twenty-seven minims, which make thirteen-and-one-half beats; the breve is worth nine minims, which make four-and-one-half beats; the semibreve is worth three minims, which make one-and-one-half beats. And though it is tiring and difficult to compose in perfect prolation, it will not be so if in the dotted circle ⊙ one writes two breves per bar, and in the dotted semi-circle ℂ one writes two semibreves per bar, since the two half-beats make one whole.

This was also the practice of Franchino Graffurio *[sic],* who was then in Naples *maestro di cappella* of the Nuntiata and a dear friend of Tinctoris. Thus I shall say the response "Emendemus in melius que ignorantes peccavimus" and "recedant vetera nova sint omnia."[45]

From the language of this passage it would appear that Cimello drew the whole of his notational treatise from the writings of Tinctoris. As we have seen, this is not really the case; there are few if any passages that come directly from a Tinctoris text.[46] It is interesting to see that on the one hand Tinctoris remained for Neapolitans a revered figure whose authority was undiminished, and that on the other hand his actual writings, only two of which had been printed, may by the mid-sixteenth century no longer have been available in Naples.[47] What probably did survive were compilations, more or less closely derived from the work of Tinctoris, made by teachers like Cimello.

As for Gafori, Cimello's claim that he was *maestro di cappella* at the church of the Nunziata is not corroborated elsewhere, and has been dismissed as groundless.[48] Perhaps Cimello's information was inaccurate here; but an association between Tinctoris and Gafori in the years 1477–80 is attested to in the latter's "official" biography appended to his *De harmonia musicorum instrumentorum* of 1518.[49] It is possible that Gafori if not *maestro* at the Nunziata might nevertheless have had some connection with this important church during his Neapolitan period, years which saw the completion and publication of his *Theorica musicae.* In any event Cimello clearly did draw upon Gafori's *Practica musicae;* he may have considered this work to be a faithful representation of the doctrines of Tinctoris, which on the whole it is. Neither of the older theorists discussed the writing of mensural music by the measure or *casella,* as Cimello would have it. How early this practical pedagogical application of mensural theory may have been in use would be hard to say, but from Cimello's language it would seem to have been widely accepted in his time.

In addition to the test piece, Cimello included some other music at the end of the Bologna treatise (following the passage cited above). One is a two-part counterpoint dating from a period "when the ancients had not yet invented the sign of the circle for perfect time." The beginning of this example, not identified by Cimello, is given here (see ex. 7.1); I have been unable to find a source for it, but perhaps a reader will have greater knowledge or better luck than I.

Example 7.1 Tenore quando da gl'antichi non era trovato il segno dal circolo perfetto per il numero ternario

Two other bits of music elude identification. One is a single-voice example which follows directly on the Tinctoris-Gafori passage cited above. Its use of *sesquialtera* following a beginning without marked mensuration makes no sense here, and the example must be corrupt (if the opening were in perfect prolation it could be a final reference to the problem of *sesquialtera* following that mensuration, which Cimello refers to twice in the treatise) (see ex. 7.2).

Example 7.2

[sic]

After the two-part example from the time of the "antichi" there is a statement by Cimello about his having collected, when he was young, compositions showing special artifice. Among these was a canon, showing use of perfect prolation and blackened notes. What follows (see ex. 7.3), a piece called "Canon. Qui autem sunt in carne deo placere non possunt," seems totally unrelated to the text, and if it is a canon at all I do not see what the resolution might be. Again I appeal to puzzle-loving readers for elucidation.

Example 7.3 Canon "Qui autem sunt in carne deo placere non possunt"

Finally, after the test piece, there is a page of music that is apparently meant as further examples of artifice in the work of older composers. None is identified, but each has Latin tags to accompany it. They are for the most part biblical citations. The first example has "unusquisque manebit in sua vocatione" (cf. 1 Corinthians 7:20: "unusquisque in qua vocatione vocatus est in ea permaneat") at the beginning, "nulla dies sine linea maximum in punctis" (source unknown) at the end. The second is prefaced by "semper pace habebunt" with "o vos felices qui tot et tanta perfruimini in pace" at the end (I have not found sources for these). For the third example Cimello chose "redde unicuique secundum opera sua" (cf. Matthew 11:27: "reddet uniquique secundum opus eius"). The last example, an incipit for four voices, has "nemo me condemnat" over the superius, "nec te condemno" above the bassus (cf. John 8:10–11: "nemo te condemnavit" and "nec ego te condemnabo"). The impulse to apply these biblical scraps to music may have come to Cimello from his citation of Josquin's "Osanna. Gaudet cum gaudentibus" (cf. Romans 11:15: "gaudere cum gaudentibus, flere cum flentibus").[50]

The four musical incipits, all puzzle pieces of various sorts, come from Pierre de La Rue (Agnus III of the *Missa "L'homme armé,"* Kyrie of the *Missa "O salutaris hostia"*), Josquin (*Missa "L'homme armé" super voces musicales,* Agnus II), and Ockeghem (Kyrie I of *Missa cuiusvis toni*). From his earlier remark about his collecting activities as a young man, Cimello would have us believe that he found these pieces himself. So he might have, but it seems too great a coincidence that all four are cited, in different order but in close conjunction, by Glareanus.[51] It would then appear that by the time this treatise was sent off Cimello had seen the *Dodecachordon* even though he never mentions Glareanus.

The cantus part of the piece sent for comment to Cimello is copied twice in the Bologna manuscript; once as sent, with marginal comment added, then in corrected form and barred (by the two-breve unit except where notational figurations make this impractical); after this comes the uncorrected tenor. Cimello or his copyist should have looked at the latter, for it seems to be missing seven breves' worth of music, perhaps a line of the original skipped in copying. To save space I will give the piece in transcribed form along with the corrected form of notation in the cantus, using notes for Cimello's commentary (see ex. 7.4 and table 1). It might be observed that the melody makes repeated use of a motif suggestive of the opening of the "L'homme armé" tune.

A manuscript in Naples, Biblioteca Nazionale Vittorio Emanuele III, shelfmark VH 210, contains a miscellany of material in which Cimello's "regole nove" are included, in a somewhat garbled and probably abridged form. The manuscript, 190 paper pages (195mm. × 135mm. in size) bound in vellum, is unsigned and without a general title, though some of its varied contents have individual headings. The only clue to its sixteenth-century ownership is the following inscription, a baptismal record written upside-down on the last page (otherwise blank except for a tiny musical scribble):

Salvatore Sansone figlio di Sebastiano Sansone e di Marsilia Vinciguerra. battezato per D. Giov. [?] Domenico Riccardo sacrestano la mammana Tomasina de Marino [?] a 6 di agosto 1589 [1569?]. Porta nova p[ate]r [?] figlio omnes angeli.[52]

I have been unable to trace any of the people mentioned here; all that is sure is that the place is Naples, "Porta nova" being one of the six *seggi* or quarters of the city, and that the date is late sixteenth century. Whether Sebastiano Sansone could have been a friend or pupil of Cimello is unknown, and the only thing that might link this inscription with the manuscript's contents is that the last section of the volume (fols. 174r–190r) is chiefly devoted to liturgical rubrics, one of them concerning the mother of a newborn child. But such is the state of this manuscript that even here there is an interruption (fols. 186v–188r) for an illustration and explanation, not the first in the volume, of the Guidonian hand.

Cimello's connection with this manuscript is demonstrated, as in the Bologna treatise, through frequent mention of his name as author of *regole*. Unlike the Bologna manuscript, the Naples volume is not a single work but a collection, indeed a jumble of various subjects, some pursued to a degree of completeness and others clearly fragmentary. It is written in several textual and musical hands, of which two alternate and predominate; the one that opens the volume might possibly be that of

Example 7.4 Two-voice counterpoint sent to Cimello

Example 7.4, cont.

Example 7.4, cont.

Example 7.4, cont.

Example 7.4, cont.

TABLE I
Notes for Example 7.4

(a) "Punctus divisionis qui non cantatur" (dot of division, not sung).
(b) "Secunda alteratur" (second [semibreve] is altered). The two semibreve B's are curiously missing in the uncorrected melody.
(c) "Punctus divisionis" (dot of division).
(d) "Punctus translationis et alterationis" (dot of transposition and alteration). The comment is given four notes too late in the uncorrected melody. What Cimello means by "transposition" here is that the dot prevents one from reading the last semibreve of the preceding bar as one of a group of three.
(e) The bracketed bars in the *tenor* are missing in the manuscript.

TABLE 1—Continued
Notes for Example 7.4

(f) "Secunda alteratur" (the second [semibreve in the ligature] is altered). This is an example of Cimello's tenet that a pair of ligated semibreves should be considered a breve.

(g) "Ultima semibrevis alteratur" (the final semibreve is altered). Tinctoris might have disagreed, reading the semibreve in the next measure as the last of six, a "sufficient" number providing the reading:

(h) "Punctus divisionis et translationis et semibrevis alteratur" (dot of division and transposition, and the semibreve [preceding the breve in the same bar] is altered). The uncorrected melody had the two semibreve rests on the same line, indicating that they should be read as a unit (see above, and n. 31). Cimello's interpretation of the dot is that it marks the end of a unit beginning with these rests, making four semibreves plus a breve; he reads the semibreve succession not as 3 + 1 but as 1 + 3, of which the last belongs with the preceding breve. This leaves 1 + 2, meaning that the rests must be divided and the semibreve preceding the breve altered.

(i) "Due note v'e [se?] ligate efficiunt brevem et secunda alteratur" (two notes [semibreves] when ligated form a breve, and the second is altered). This macaronic note expands upon (f) by referring to two pairs of semibreves in ligature.

(j) "Ligatura non debet dividi punctatur [quia] una brevis et debent esse semibreves" (a ligature should not be divided by a dot since it is a breve; semibreves should be used instead). In the uncorrected melody the notes d″–c″ are written as a ligated pair of semibreves with a dot in the middle, something Cimello disapproves of and therefore rewrites as two separate semibreves.

(k) "Hec notule non debent colorari ante maiorem" (these notes should not be blackened before a longer note). The semibreve-breve d″–e″ are colored in the uncorrected melody, unnecessarily since the semibreve would imperfect the breve through a simple method of counting.

(l) "Brevis perfecta propter numeralem perfectionem" (the breve is perfect because of numerical perfection); that is, because it is followed by three semibreves.

(m) "Brevis perfecta similiter" (the breve is perfect for the same [above] reason).

(n) "Brevis perfecta quia vacua et plena non possunt coniungi" (the breve is perfect because void and full [white and black] cannot be joined); this follows the Aristotelian principle enunciated by Tinctoris and many other theorists that opposites cannot coexist.

(o) "Secunda semibrevis alteratur inter duas pausas breves" (the second of two semibreves between two breve rests is altered).

(p) "In signo temporis perfecti non cadet alteratio in minimis et sic ultima brevis ante longam imperficitur a duobus anterioribus minimis" (in *tempus perfectum* [with minor prolation] alteration of the minim does not occur, and so the last breve before the long is imperfected by the two preceding minims).

(q) "Pausa nunquam alteratur" (the rest is never altered); hence the semibreve and semibreve rest in this bar do not produce alteration but rather imperfection on each side.

(r) "Brevis notula est imperfici ante longam" (the breve is imperfected before the long), as it would not be before another breve.

TABLE I—Continued
Notes for Example 7.4

(s) "Punctus hic dicitur punctus perfectionis" (the dot here is called a dot of perfection), preventing imperfection by the first of the four following semibreves.

(t) "Secunda semibrevis alteratur" (the second [of a pair of] semibreves is altered).

(u) "Secunda semibrevis nunc non alteratur quia senarius numerus est completus et non habet defectum propij cum fit alteratio" (in this case the second semibreve is not altered because the six-fold number is complete and has no lack of proper number as [there is] when alteration is made). The six semibreve values in question are the four in measure 46 and the two in measure 47.

(v) "Queste potranno esser bianchi che la longa è imperfetta quantum ad partes propinquas" (these notes could as well be white since the long is imperfected by secondary parts [semibreves]).

(w) "Punctus translationis" (dot of transposition). This does not appear in the corrected melody, which is in any event corrupt here, with measure 55 copied a third too low.

(x) "Secunda semibrevis alteratur" (the second semibreve is altered).

(y) "Punctus divisionis pausarum" (a dot of division between the rests). In the uncorrected melody the rests in measures 57–58 are on the same line and are separated by a dot. Cimello improves this notation by placing the rests on different lines and removing the dot.

(z) "Semibrevis ante ligaturam alteratur quia talis ligatura putatur brevis notula" (the semibreve before the ligature is altered because such a ligature is considered a breve).

(aa) "Falsitas quia similis ante similem non potest imperfeci et debet colorari" (wrong because in the case of like before like one cannot imperfect but should use black notes). In the original the notes in measure 63 are white; Cimello corrected this.

(bb) "Ligatura ultima alteratur" (the last note of the ligature is altered).

(cc) "Punctus divisionis" (a dot of division).

(dd) "Falsitas quia similis ante similem non potest imperfici quia brevis similis est pars sue brevis similis sed est pars longe" (wrong because like before like cannot be imperfected, for the breve is [not?] part of its like breve but is part of the long). Cimello solved this, as in (aa) above, by blackening the notes of measure 70.

Cimello himself, though this cannot be proved; in general the scripts look as if they come from fairly late in the century.[53]

A list of the manuscript's contents is given in table 2. Much of this material, however interesting it might be as documentation of Cimello's career and varied interests, is not to the purpose here; space permits only brief comment on those passages that show Cimello as teacher of the basic art of composition.

Section 2 contains elementary information on notes, clefs, the Guidonian hand, and the church modes. Rules for mutation are included (fols. 38v–39r, 41r, 53r–58r), with many examples; evidence of Cimello's informality is his use of "do," already evidently in vernacular use by Italians in place of "ut." There are some singing exercises (fols. 37v, 47v–48v) for beginners (*principianti*), consisting of various intervals in abstract patterns.

TABLE 2

Contents of Naples, Biblioteca Nazionale Vittorio Emanuele III, MS VH 210*

Folios	
1r–33v	1. *Avvertimenti* on various points of Latin grammar
34r–51r	2. "Practica delle Regole et avertimenti dati per lo canto fermo"; "Regole del canto fermo et figurato"; "Regole per il canto figurato" [miscellaneous plainchant on fols. 49r–51r]
51v	blank
52r–65r	3. "De intonationibus psalmorum"; "Regole per conoscere et sapere fare le mutationi"; "Regola per intonare li toni regolari con lorgano"; "Alcuni osservationi del contrapunto necessarie, et utili"; "Modo di comporre Salmi et Magnificat"; "Vari moti di note per imparare li principianti el sonare sopra la parte. Regola di Marancia"
65v	blank
66r–85v	4. "Regole per il contrapunto seu compositione"
86r–115r	5. "Regole nuove del Cimello"; "Del Cimello. Per sapere formare le fughe in musica bisogna conoscere tutte le variationi del diapente del diatessaron del ditono del tono et del semitono"; "Cimellus de musica et Poeta et de dominis huius etatis" [this appears to be some sort of title, but nothing relevant follows]
115v–20v	blank
121r–76r	6. Chant examples: Magnificat antiphons; chants for Mass Ordinary and Proper, some liturgical rubrics
176v–82v	blank
183r–90r	7. Liturgical rubrics; explanation of gamut and Guidonian hand

*This table gives only a rough idea of the manuscript's subject matter, which sometimes changes by the page.

Section 3 begins again with chant, giving more information on mutations. Then comes a set of examples (fols. 59r–60v) "for playing the [psalm] tones on the organ when one sings in counterpoint" (*in musica*). This evidently refers to *alternatim* practice, which Cimello clearly thought common enough and important enough to be included in basic instruction. Example 7.5 shows the intonation for the first tone.[54]

Example 7.5 Primo tono. Per intonare nell' organo

"Some necessary and useful observations on counterpoint" (fols. 61r–62r) show consonances and their prohibited use in parallel motion. Above a warning about *mi contra fa* (fol. 62v) is the word "Toscanellus"; and indeed this passage and one on psalms and Magnificats that follows are taken from Pietro Aaron's *To-scanello in musica;* the passages in Cimello are cited from book 2, chapters 14 and 18. On folio 64r there is material said to be from the rules of "Marancia."[55] This material consists of ascending and descending scales in various note values and rhythms, designed for beginners to play and perhaps to harmonize; the student is informed that use of sharps and flats and of numbers (3 and 6) can be an aid in play-ing counterpoint over a bass. It is surprising, and perhaps not altogether credible, to see figured bass symbols in a treatise that originated before the middle of the six-teenth century. The mention of Marancio makes it clear that this is a later addition and that we have nothing like Cimello's undiluted thought in the Naples manu-script (it should be kept in mind that in his letter of 1579 Cimello does refer to hav-ing revised his thoughts about theory at least once); still it is, even if from the 1580s, an early example of the use of such symbols.[56]

Section 5 is a set of rules for "counterpoint or composition." First come (fol. 66r) some simple accompaniments to a *canto fermo:* thirds in note-against-note counterpoint; 3–5 and 3–6 successions in minims against a semibreve tenor, pas-sages of semiminims against semibreves; and cadences with suspensions. Note that the essentials of Fuxian species counterpoint are already crystallized here. On folio 66v we hear what I assume is Cimello's confidential voice:

> In order to shorten and simplify the art of counterpoint so that the student will not de-spair of learning it after having seen so many books on plainchant, he [the student] ought to know and to reflect that everything can be found in these few but varied forms of motion over [the *canto fermo*]. Having learned these, he can go on to many graceful and masterful passages, varied and skillful; soon these will be committed to memory, and from memory pass to his lips, becoming his own interpretation.[57]

This could apply both to what has preceded and to what follows (up to fol. 83v): use of syncopations; dealing with various steps and skips in the *canto fermo;* how to interrupt (*fuggir* or *rompere*) the cadence; use of *sesquialtera,* avoidance of rhythmic sequence (a device used with "languid" effect in works of the *antichi*). *Tenor* parts and counterpoints are given in all [eight] modes (fols. 78vff.), with "del Cimello" at the end of one of them. This section, which really is a very practi-cal demonstration of free counterpoint against a tenor, ends surprisingly, but in a way characteristic of the Naples volume, with a discussion of O and ⊕, C, ₵, Ɔ, and Ɔ 2 mensurations, a topic covered in the Bologna treatise. Except for this closing bit Cimello has given much of what his confidential statement to students promised.

On folio 86r a new section, promisingly entitled "Regole nove del Cimello," the rubric later repeated with "private" added to it, begins. First there are some simple rules about what one can and cannot do in moving from one interval to another; each interval is treated separately, rather in the manner of Zarlino's counterpoint treatise (book 3 of *Le istitutioni harmoniche* [Venice, 1558]). Now and then comes a bit of "inside" information, one of Cimello's "private" rules. An example (fol. 91v) is use of the tritone in a suspension figure, normally forbidden but allowed "to show the harshness and cruelty of some word" (see ex. 7.6). Another is the direc-

tion (fols. 92v–93r) to avoid repeating a suspended note in order to change syllables on it (see ex. 7.7).[58] Still another is the requirement that the last note of every
passage in a diminution or rapid passage, if it is followed by a change of direction,
be consonant; thus example 7.8 is a specimen of something to be avoided. Like-
against-like or note-against-note counterpoint should be completely consonant
even when in very short note values (fol. 98v); but in *canzoni franzesi* the author
has seen exceptions to this rule. These details, given as useful tips for the young
composer, are interesting evidence of an increasing preoccupation with control,
down to Jeppesen-like attention to detail, of every element, including text setting,
in the contrapuntal fabric. Sixteenth-century music as perceived by musicians of
pedagogical bent was already hardening into a *stile antico,* even before a real *seconda prattica* had developed.

Example 7.6

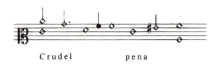

Crudel   pena

Example 7.7

Tu   non voi ben a   me   Tu   non voi ben   a   me

Example 7.8

[bad]

   Folios 94r–96r in this section are concerned with the *battuta* and questions of
tempo. Here Cimello is not repeating the doctrines and anecdotes of the Bologna
treatise (this repetition does occur elsewhere; the "L'homme armé" tale is, for example, told twice more, on fols. 99v and 103v). He begins by commending passages of rapid motion which "imitate birds like the nightingale." These are to be
found in the mensurations O and C, where one beats two minims to the *battuta.* Cimello is chagrined to note that not only in "concenti sacri" but in "fast and difficult madrigals where minims and occasionally seminimims are used in syncopation," musicians use the cut signature ₵ and then sing by beating a single
semibreve, sometimes a single minim, to a very slow *battuta.* Even in the most famous Roman musical establishments this practice, lamentable since it disregards
the meaning of the mensural signs, can be observed. Here Cimello is commenting on a phenomenon of his time, the merging of the *note nere* and *note bianche*
notations which had been distinct in the 1540s.[59] The beat itself, Cimello goes on

to say, should normally be neither fast nor slow but moderate; but in some motets, madrigals, and *villanelle* one should quicken the beat because this variety of speed gives greater pleasure.[60]

Two last items of interest in this section can be noticed. On folios 100r–101v all the melodic variants, using upward and downward steps and skips, of fifths, fourths, thirds, tones, and semitones—thirty-two in all—are illustrated "so that one can know how to construct imitative points in music."[61] Folios 106r–114v contain examples, for "principianti," of more singing exercises, which here are mainly patterns of diminution or ornamentation of every interval. These pages with their beamed groupings of semiminims and fusas look like cursive notation of the seventeenth century; it would be nice to know the date of their copying here.

Cimello's *regole nove* are nothing like a complete counterpoint treatise, although they do cover a good deal of material in their own way. The lack of a plan and an orderly sequence may of course not be the author's fault, but the result of the fragmentary and disjointed transmission, possibly through the notes of several students, of his thought. What both the Bologna and Naples treatises show is the personal mark of a teacher, presenting and commenting on the material in a very idiosyncratic way, and occasionally adding "tips" drawn from his own experience. This I think offers a valuable glimpse of how music may actually have been taught in the sixteenth century.

Postscript

Interest in the *"L'homme armé"* tune and its use as a cantus firmus seems to find a late revival in Cimello; but in fact it continued, becoming more and more tinged with antiquarian sentiments, through the whole of the sixteenth century. See my "Palestrina as Historicist: The Two L'homme armé Masses," *Journal of the Royal Musical Association* 121 (1996): 191–205, and references to post-Josquin "L'homme armé" compositions found there.

For a good survey of historicism in Renaissance musical thought, see Jessie Ann Owens, "Music Historiography and the Definition of Renaissance," referred to in the comments on chapter 3. And for more on Cimello, this time as composer-pedagogue, see chapter 11.

In choosing Tinctoris and Gafori together as his point of reference for details of notational theory, Cimello may have recognized their didactic urge toward making the mensural system more regular and coherent, an idea stressed in Anna Maria Busse Berger, *Mensuration and Proportion Signs: Origins and Evolution* (Oxford, 1993). Tinctoris may have been in contact with the Burgundian court in the 1470s and may have encountered the six "L'homme armé" masses now in Naples (Biblioteca Nazionale, MS vi.E.40); on this see Ronald Woodley, "Tinctoris's Italian Transcription of the Golden Fleece Statutes: A Text and a (Possible) Context," *EMH* 8 (1988): 173–205.

Cimello is not the only sixteenth-century theorist to remain interested in notational questions and to regret modern neglect of and ignorance about details of the mensural system. Giovanni Spataro, Pietro Aaron, and others in their epistolary circle often wrote about these matters during a twenty-five year period beginning in 1517. See *A Correspondence of Renaissance Musicians,* referred to in the comments on chapter 3. Cimello's letter to Cardinal Sirleto (see above and n. 15) is reprinted in chapter 11 below.

NOTES

1. Among the most famous lists of composers made during the Renaissance are those of Tinctoris (in the prologue to his manuscript treatise *Proportionale musices* [ca. 1473], given again in slightly different form in the prologue to another manuscript treatise of his, *Liber de arte contrapuncti* [1477]), which mark the beginning of a new era in music with Dunstable, followed by Dufay and Binchois. Adrianus Petit Coclico's *Compendium musices* (Nuremberg, 1552) gives a very confused list of musicians who were "inventors" (Ockeghem is one), "mathematicians" (Dufay, Tinctoris, and Gafori are among these), "distinguished musicians" who united theory and practice (Josquin above all but younger composers as well, down to Willaert), and "poeti," young and unnamed figures. The list in Hermann Finck's *Practica musicae* (Wittenberg, 1556) contains very similar names though the categories are different; the canon of great names in Renaissance music was already becoming fixed. The distinction between older and younger generations so clearly drawn in the unpublished *De musica verbalis* of Stoquerus (ca. 1570) is found in a number of other theorists, among them Zacconi (*Prattica di musica* [Venice, 1592], 1.ix), who speaks of *antichi* like Josquin, *vecchi* such as Willaert and Palestrina, and unnamed *moderni.* Precise identification of teacher-pupil relationships is often implied by Renaissance writers, but is usually made explicit only for single pairs of composers.

2. On this see Leeman L. Perkins, "The L'Homme Armé Masses of Busnoys and Ockeghem: A Comparison," *The Journal of Musicology* 3 (1984): 363–96; Richard Taruskin, "Antoine Busnoys and the *L'homme armé* Tradition," *JAMS* 39 (1986): 255–93; and the communications from Don Giller, David Fallows, and Richard Taruskin in the latter journal, 40 (1987): 149–53. See also Lewis Lockwood, "Aspects of the 'L'homme armé' Tradition," *Proceedings of the Royal Musical Association* 100 (1973–74): 97–122.

3. *Scriptores ecclesiastici de musica sacra potissimum* (St. Blasien, 1784). Most Renaissance theorists do mention earlier writers, but ordered lists of them are rare. One exception is the list, admittedly highly selective, given by Scipione Cerreto, *Della prattica musica vocale et strumentale* (Naples, 1601), 4.

4. The reader might like to compare this list with the Renaissance section (a longer list in that it includes Spanish and German theorists as well as writers on instrumental practice) in Gustave Reese, *Fourscore Classics of Music Literature* (New York, 1957).

5. See Franz Xaver Haberl, *Wilhelm Du Fay* (Leipzig, 1885), 21; David Fallows, *Dufay* (London, 1982), 242; F. Alberto Gallo, "Citazioni da un trattato di Dufay," *Collectanea historiae musicae* 4 (1966): 149–52. Gafori's citation of a Dufay treatise is in an autograph treatise in Parma, Biblioteca Palatina, parm. MS 1158.

6. A typical judgment is that of Charles Hamm, "Dufay [du Fay], Guillaume," *New Grove,* 5:674: "Dufay learnt to write music not from any formal study but from performing under these men [Nicolas Malin and Richard Loqueville in Cambrai], probably from copying music, and from varied associations with those older musicians who were composers themselves and in those ways were his teachers."

7. Coclico, however much one may doubt his credentials, gives a convincing account of how a Renaissance composer [Josquin] taught pupils he judged apt: first of all, correct sing-

ing, with good vocal technique, pronunciation, text adjustment, the art of improvised ornament; then a brief study of consonances and a start on singing counterpoint against a given
line; finally, the art of counterpoint for three, four, five, and six voices, taught through example. See Coclico, *Compendium musices,* 2, fol. Fiiv. On the resemblances between Coclico's
own music and that of Josquin, see the sympathetic account in Bernhard Meier, "The Musica Reservata of Adrianus Petit Coclico and its Relationship to Josquin," *MD* 10 (1956):
67–105. It is only fair to theorists of the late Renaissance to say that a more practical teacher-
to-student approach is evident in a number of treatises of the sixteenth and early seventeenth
centuries; but though their language loosened up, the organization of formal treatises remained conventional.

8. Tinctoris addressed some of his work to Ferrante, King of Naples; and he seems to have
acted as tutor to Beatrice, Ferrante's daughter; two of his treatises are dedicated to her. See
Ronald Woodley, "Johannes Tinctoris: A Review of the Documentary Biographical Evidence," *JAMS* 34 (1981): 217–48, esp. 233.

9. A standard work on this subject is Nan Cooke Carpenter, *Music in the Medieval and
Renaissance Universities* (Norman, Okla., 1958).

10. See Åke Davidsson, *Bibliographie der musiktheoretischen Drucke des 16. Jahrhunderts* (Baden-Baden, 1962), a work which has some gaps but nonetheless gives a clear picture of the subject.

11. An example of an informal treatise, slightly later than the work of Cimello, is the
sketchbook of Costanzo Porta: Bologna, Civico Museo Bibliografico Musicale, MS B 140.
See Edward E. Lowinsky, "Early Scores in Manuscript," *JAMS* 13 (1960): 126–73, esp.
148–50.

12. See Donna G. Cardamone, "Cimello, Tomaso," *New Grove,* 4:404. Cardamone gives
Cimello's birthdate as ca. 1500, but this would make him almost 80 when he wrote to
Cardinal Sirleto in 1579, offering his active service as composer.

13. Raffaele Casimiri, "Musica e musicisti a Benevento sulla fine del secolo XVI," *Note
d'archivio per la storia musicale* 13 (1936): 77–85.

14. Belli says, in the dedication of his *Missarum sacrarumque cantionum . . . liber primus* (Venice, 1595), that he learned "musicam hunc cognitionem at usum Neapoli . . . à
D[on] Cimello." Cimello's student Francesco Sorrentino spoke in praise of him, and so did
the latter's student Orazio di Caposele, writing in 1623. See Keith Larson, "The Unaccompanied Madrigal in Naples from 1536 to 1654" (Ph.D. diss., Harvard University, 1985):
240–41.

15. The latter is printed (from a manuscript, presumably Cimello's autograph, in the Vatican library) in Carlo Respighi, *Nuovo studio su G. P. da Palestrina e l'emendazione del Graduale Romano* (Rome, 1899), 135–38; and in Raffaele Casimiri, "Lettere di musicisti
(1579–1585) al Cardinal Sirleto," *Note d'archivio per la storia musicale* 9 (1932): 102–5.
No *fughe* such as Cimello refers to are known to survive; but in the Naples manuscript of his
writings (see below) there is a rubric "per sapere formare le fughe in musica" followed by
examples of the thirty-two musical motifs possible if every ascending and descending use
of intervals between the semitone and the fifth is utilized.

16. "Io c'ho fatto un libretto e poi di tutta l'arte de segni di proportioni de Contraponti di
componere d'infinite habilitadi d'improviso ec. è non ho a cui grande dedicarle che m'aiutasse" (Casimiri, "Lettere di musicisti," 104). The last sentence may explain why Cimello's
theoretical work was never published.

17. Gaetano Gaspari et al., *Catalogo della Biblioteca Musicale G. B. Martini di Bologna*
(Bologna, 1890–1943), 1:204–5: "Discorso sulle prolazioni e sui tempi dagli antichi di Tomaso Cimello," a title given to the treatise by Gaspari, who also added folio numbers and
occasional marginal comments (chiefly names of musicians cited by Cimello).

18. Gaspari's annotation on the first of these pages says "Questi esempi vanno uniti al precedente MS del Cimello." Since I have studied both the Bologna treatise and that in Naples, Biblioteca Nazionale, MS VH 210, from microfilm, I cannot give as complete a physical description of these manuscripts as I would like.

19. "Prima ch'io venga alla correttione del precedente canto a me mandato del mio M—mi pare necessario ch'io scrivo alquanto della perfettione delle 4ro note maggiori massima longa breve semibreve." On the "letter-tract," an epistolary genre that served as a means of scholarly communication in the 1470s and 1480s, see Ronald Woodley, "The Printing and Scope of Tinctoris's Fragmentary Treatise *De inventione et usu musice,*" *EMH* 5 (1985): 239–68, esp. 255–56. Woodley speculates that Tinctoris sent the printed extracts of *De inventione* to various scholars accompanied by letters, "rather in the way that modern scholars, more informally, distribute offprints." This practice surely survived into Cimello's time.

20. "Soprano mandato al Cimello e da lui corretto e spartito a numero senario del circolo tagliato, e numero ternario del circolo intiero." On Cimello's use of the term *numero senario* see below and n. 27.

21. See above n. 17.

22. Donna G. Cardamone, *The "Canzone Villanesca alla Napolitana" and Related Forms* (Ann Arbor, 1981), 1:163n, 220–21; Larson, "The Unaccompanied Madrigal," 185–86.

23. Anna Maria Busse Berger, "The Relationship of Perfect and Imperfect Time in Italian Theory of the Renaissance," *EMH* 5 (1981): 1–28, esp. 22.

24. Perkins, "The L'Homme Armé Masses," 381n; Perkins, "Lhéritier, Jean," *New Grove,* 10:710.

25. "Suo carissimo amico." For the passage in which this phrase occurs, see below and n. 45.

26. See Gafori, *Practica musicae* (Milan, 1496), trans. Clement A. Miller, Musicological Studies and Documents 20 (American Institute of Musicology, 1968), ix, for a list of editions of the work.

27. Cf. Gafori, *Practica musicae,* 2.viii: ". . . senario numero, qui perfectus est spherica & circularis illa circumferentia . . . naturaliter noscitur esse producta."

28. Lampadius's *Compendium musices* (Berne, 1537) may contain the earliest extant examples of barring. See Edward E. Lowinsky, "On the Use of Scores by Sixteenth-Century Musicians," *JAMS* 1 (1948): 17–23; and Lowinsky, "Early Scores in Manuscript," 128ff. Otto Kinkeldey, *Orgel und Klavier in der Musik des 16. Jahrhunderts* (Leipzig, 1910), 193, points out that *partire* and *spartire* at first referred to the barring of individual voices, which is what Cimello means by it. He cites a passage from Nicola Vicentino, *L'Antica musica ridotta alla moderna prattica* (Rome, 1555), in which barring by the breve or long is recommended as "a sure way of correcting errors" in many-voice compositions.

29. Cf. Gafori, *Practica musicae,* 4.i: "Proportio rationalis est duarum comensurabilium quantitatum in discreto vel in continuo ad se invicem comparatio." Tinctoris's definition in the *Proportionale musices* and the *Terminorum musicae diffinitorium* (Treviso, 1495) uses quite different wording.

30. Gafori, *Practica musicae,* 4.i, Tinctoris, *Proportionale,* 3.ii. Tinctoris makes much more of a point of the necessity for two numbers than does Gafori.

31. Willi Apel, *The Notation of Polyphonic Music, 900–1600,* rev. 5th ed. (Cambridge, Mass., 1953), 111, makes this point without giving theoretical evidence for it. Tinctoris, *Tractatus alternationum* (manuscript treatise without date), opens with an example of two

semibreves, on the same line, preceding a breve (which in the context is to be imperfected by two succeeding minims); for a modern edition of this treatise see n. 33. Gafori, *Practica musicae,* 2.6, says merely that "duas contiguas semibreves pausas rectius duas tertias ipsius perfecte brevis continere: quod & recentiores frequentant."

32. Apel, *Notation,* 114, says that a ligated pair of semibreves is always in practice treated as a breve, calling for alteration rather than imperfection. Again no sources are cited.

33. *Tractatus,* 1.3, see Johannis Tinctoris, *Opera theoretica,* ed. Albert Seay, Corpus scriptorum de musica, 22 (American Institute of Musicology, 1975–78), 1:151–52; see n. 46 below.

34. *Practica musicae,* 2.ii. On Gafori's derivation of this term from a lost treatise by Dufay, see Gallo, "Citazioni da un trattato di Dufay," 151.

35. The beat or *battuta* thus comprises a *tactus,* a downbeat and an upbeat. For a clear diagram of how the *tactus* was beat in various mensurations see Adriano Bachieri, *Cartella musicale nel canto figurato, fermo, & contrapunto* (Venice, 1614), 35.

36. "Quelli che attestano Occheghen, et Giosquino che a loro tempi erano Compositori di gran autoritade, quali non errano in tal prolatione perfetta ch'io l'ho inteso da discepoli di Giosquino c'havendo Occheghen composta una Canzone detta l'Homme Arme cipilose queste parole come canone crescat in duplum che l'Homme Arme si puo dir homo doppio di carne viva e di ferro, et cosi fecero addoppiare le note e le pause di tal canzone, e messa cosi titulare l'Homme Arme ne essi autori vi fecero risolutione mai, nel tempo perfetto, che tal tenore lo cantavano essi Mastri e mi dissero anco tali discepoli di Giosquino che me recordo il nome d'uno chiamato Giovan l'heriter che dava a cantare quel tenore a qualche mastro, e colui il cantava bene secondo il segno e Giosquino rideva ch'egli non notava le parole l'Homme Arme, ch'era Canone, come crescat in duplum e si disse, che all'hora rideva alquanto, e poi gli diceva il come fu composta tal messa e come dovea cantarsi. Se la risolutione di tal tenore in tal messa non fosse per tale addoppiamento come saria una medesima cosa il tempo cioe la breve, et una medesima cosa la prolatione, cioe la semibreve, questa cosa saria soverchia, et superflua sunt resecanda, et quod fieri potest per pauciora non debet fieri per plura.

"E la risolutione di tal tenore di tal messa in tempo perfetta la fece fare Ottaviano Petrucci da forosempronio famoso stampatore, ch'io l'ho conosciuto, e gl'ho parlato non posso qui dire il quando e'l come, ma in Sora Città famosa degli Equicoli.

". . . e che sia vero vedi l'osanna di tal messa dove tre cantano nel semicircolo in proportione sesquialtera: a la quarta che ha il segno della prolatione perfetta non vi son le cifre della sesquialtera 3/2, e si canta per essa proportione a tre minime a battuta che c'e il tenore Osanna. Gaudet cum Gaudentibus, a certi Compositori han pensato, che senza cifra di numero 3/2 si debbano passare tutti li canti di tal prolatione perfetto cantar in sesquialtera, e cosi l'han posta nelle loro Compositioni, che mi e dispiaciuto che alcuni ne piglino mali essempi per lo credito bono del Compositore che compone bene leggiadramente, e dolcemente, et ariosamente."

37. Sora ("degli Equicoli" refers to an ancient Italic tribe) is about equidistant from Rome and Naples; it is close to Cimello's birthplace of Montesangiovanni. In Cimello's time Sora was a fief of the Della Rovere family.

38. On Lhéritier see Leeman L. Perkins's article in *New Grove,* 10:710. William F. Prizer informs me that he has discovered documentation of Lhéritier's presence in Mantua in the 1520s.

39. See Perkins, "The L'Homme Armé Masses," 370–72. The only attribution for this chanson is "Borton" [= Morton?] in Rome, Biblioteca Casanatense, MS 2856; in its other source, the Mellon Chansonnier, it is anonymous.

40. *Thoscanello de la musica* [better known by the title of its 1529 reprint, *Toscanello in musica*] (Venice, 1523), 1.xxxviii.

41. Taruskin, "Antoine Busnoys and the *L'Homme armé* Tradition," 289–92. For David Fallows's objections to this view see his communication in *JAMS* 40 (1987): 147–48.

42. See Judith Cohen, *The Six Anonymous L'Homme Armé Masses in Naples, Biblioteca Nazionale, MS VI E 40,* CMM, 85 (American Institute of Musicology, 1968), 30; cf. Barbara Haggh's communication in *JAMS* 40 (1987): 139–43.

43. Tinctoris may have written his "L'homme armé" Mass (which survives in Vatican City, Biblioteca Apostolica Vaticana, Cappella Sistina, Cod. 35) ca. 1492. The canon *crescit in duplum* appears in the tenor of several movements; minim notation as *integer valor* is found in the Sanctus. Martini's *Missa "La martinella,"* also in Cappella Sistina, Cod. 35, uses the canon *crescit in duplo;* but the *Missa "L'homme armé"* of Compère in the same source does not. The *Missa "L'homme armé"* of Vaqueras uses minim notation with the canon *ad longum.* See *Monumenta polyphonica liturgica Sanctae Ecclesiae Romanae,* ed. Laurence K. J. Feininger, 1.1.8 (Rome, 1948). A modern edition of Tinctoris's Mass is in the same series, 1.1.9; see also *Johannis Tinctoris. Opera Omnia,* ed. William Melin, CMM, 18 (American Institute of Musicology, 1976).

44. *Proportionale musices,* 3.2–3.50 in the 1978 edition of Albert Seay (see n. 33).

45. "E quel molto Rev^{do} Giovanni Tinctoris Cappellano e Maestro di Cappella del Re Ferrante d'Aragona Re di Napoli e di Sicilia a cui ho piu credito ch'a tutti altri autori di Musica scrisse numerando le note quattro perfette, la Massima vale ottant'una minime che fan quaranta battute e mezza, la longa vale vintisette minime che fan tredici battuta e mezza, la breve vale nove minime che fan quattro battute e mezza, la semibreve vale tre minime che fan una battua e mezza, e però gl'e faticoso e difficile il componere nella prolatione perfetta, ma non sara se non nel circolo col ponto ⊙ si compone due brevi per casella, e nel semicircolo col ponto 𝇋 si compone a due semibreve per casella, che le duo mezze battute si fan per una battuta, e cosi faceva franchino Graffurio, che stava all'hora in Napoli Maestro di Cappella della Nuntiata suo carissimo amico, si che diro R/Emendemus in melius que ignorantes peccavimus, et recandant vetera nova sint omnia." The phrase "recandant . . . omnia," following upon the beginning of an Ash Wednesday responsory, is apparently a biblical phrase; cf. 1 Samuel 2:3: "recedant vetera de ore vostro" and 2 Corinthians 5:17: "vetera transierunt ecce facta sunt nova omnia."

46. Chapter 16 of the *Tractatus de regulari valore notarum* (manuscript treatise written ca. 1474–75; Seay, 1:131–32), gives the note values in minims as does Cimello; but Tinctoris says nothing about *battute*.

47. The most important surviving source for Tinctoris's theoretical work, Valencia, Biblioteca Universitaria, MS 835, a manuscript copied in Naples and perhaps done under the author's supervision, was part of the library of Ferdinando d'Aragona, duke of Calabria, who spent his adult life in Spain and who left this manuscript and much else to the library of the convent of San Miguel de los Reyes in Valencia. See Tammaro de Marinis, *La biblioteca napoletana dei re d'Aragona* (Milan, 1947–52), 2:164–65, 207. The chief other fifteenth-century source, also probably Neapolitan, of Tinctoris's work is now in Bologna, Biblioteca Universitaria, MS 2573.

48. See Alessandro Caretta, Luigi Cremasoli, and Luigi Salamina, *Franchino Gaffurio* (Lodi, 1951), 61n.

49. Clement A. Miller, "Early Gaffuriana: New Answers to Old Questions," *MQ* 46 (1970): 367–88, esp. 372.

50. The title of the canon referred to above (see ex. 7.3), is also biblical, drawn from Romans 8:8.

51. Henricus Glareanus, *Dodecachordon* (Basel, 1547), 3:445, 442, 455.

52. Larson, "The Unaccompanied Madrigal," 186n, reads the date as 1589, which is probably correct, though at first glance (at a microfilm copy) the "8" looks very much like a "6."

53. The paper appears to be all of the same size. Whether the volume is made up of separate fascicles, which seems probable, could not be determined from the film.

54. Full information on organ versets as played in Italy at the turn of the century may be seen in Adriano Banchieri, *L'organo suonarino* (Venice, 1605), fol. 59r.

55. Larson, "The Unaccompanied Madrigal," 186n, identifies this figure as Giuseppe Marancio (d. 1621), organist at the Neapolitan church of the Nunziata from 1594.

56. The earliest example known to Kinkeldey of printed music containing sharps and flats (though not figures) in the bass is Giovanni Croce's *Motetti a otto voci . . . comodi per le voci, e per cantar con ogni stromenti* (Venice, 1594) [=RISM C4428]. See Kinkeldey, *Orgel und Klavier,* 196.

57. "Per accortar et abbreviare l'arte del contraponto et che il discepolo non si sconfida d'impararlo vedendo tanti et tanti libri di canto piano deve sapere et considerare, che tutte consisteno sempre in questi pochi e varij moti sopra li quali imparsi devono molti leggiadri et maestrali passaggi varij et arteficiosi accio che poi improvisamente vengono a memoria e dalla memoria alla lingua interprete sua."

58. Another reference to text setting is found on fol. 100r, where we learn that dissonant notes should not bear text syllables but may do so if the text refers to rise and fall—the example is "Eccolo sopra il ciel e giaccio a terra" and scale passages are used to illustrate it.

59. For a survey of this subject see chapter 9.

60. ". . . cantando un mottetto un madriali ò canzone villanesche si debbe stringere la battuta che con tale varie di estrettezza più piaccion e più dilettino" (fol. 96r).

61. "Del Cimello. Per sapere formare le fughe in musica bisogna conoscere tutte le variationi del diapente del diatessaron del ditono del tono et del semitono" (fol. 100r).

Josquin as Interpreted by a Mid-Sixteenth-Century German Musician

HOW MUCH OF JOSQUIN'S MUSIC was known to Orlando di Lasso is hard to gauge.[1] Both sacred and secular music by Josquin (along with pieces over-generously attributed to him) continued to circulate in manuscript and print during Lasso's youth; but to one who was exerting himself to compose "in the new fashion of the Italians" the work of the older musician would have seemed very out of date.[2] How it struck a more provincial, and less gifted, contemporary musician active in Regensburg during Lasso's first years at Munich is the subject to be discussed here.

The motets and Masses of Josquin enjoyed continuing favor, especially in Spain and Germany, apparently appealing to both Catholic and Protestant tastes. Whether there was a "Josquin Renaissance" in Germany in the middle third of the sixteenth century,[3] or whether his sacred music, admired by Luther and other prominent figures, simply remained in the repertory longer than it did elsewhere, German printers issued and reissued Josquin's music, especially the motets, over a twenty-five-year period.[4] Of special interest here are two Nuremberg prints of 1539, the *Liber quindecim missarum* of Johannes Petreius and the *Missae tredecim quatuor vocum* of Hieronymus Grapheus [= Formschneider], anthologies containing nine Masses by Josquin.[5]

These volumes were doubtless known to Johannes Buechmaier, a young musician active at the time in Nuremberg. In 1556 Buechmaier moved to Regensburg, where he taught for a time at the Protestant gymnasium.[6] In 1559–60 Buechmaier copied and dedicated to the Regensburg town council a choirbook containing ten of his own compositions along with works by Clemens non Papa and, representing an older generation, Josquin, Isaac, and Pierre Moulu.[7]

An elaborate and beautifully copied dedicatory letter, addressed to the "melissimis et prudentissimis dominis, consuli et Senatui Ratisponensi, dominis et patronis suis," opens the volume. The letter consists largely of a traditional *laus musicae,* citing Greek and Biblical names as guarantors. Near the end of his letter (dated at Regensburg, 24 December 'anno lx^{mo}') Buechmaier says that he intends to show his whole cantor's store of learning ("omnem meam mentem et Studium"):

> And that I might seem not unpleasing to your greatness, I have copied out for your Church some twenty Masses and Introits assembled and written in an accurately accomplished book. Some of these are composed by me, some taken from the works of others and resolved, as can be seen in the index of Masses drawn up on the next folio. I offer and dedicate these works to your judgment.[8]

The *Index Cantionum* is as follows:

1. Missa duarum facierum Petri de Molu resoluta per Joannem Buechmayerum. 4 Vocum. fol. 1.
2. Missa sancti spiritus Vogelhucheri. 4 Vocum. fol. 21.
3. Introitus Benedicta sit sancta Trinitas Isaac. 4. Vocum. fol. 35.
4. Introitus Viri Gallilei Isaac. 4 Vocum. fol. 38.
5. Missa Bewar mich herr. Joannis Buechmayri. 4 Vocum. fol. 40.
6. Missa Caro mea Clementis non Papae. 5 Vocum. fol. 63.
7. Missa La sol fa re mi Josquini. 4 Vocum. resoluta per Joannem Buech-mayerum. fol. 95.
8. Missa O praeclara Isaac. Resoluta per Joannem Buechmayerum. 4 Vocum. fol. 118.
9. Missa Pange lingua Josquini. resoluta per Joannem Buechmayerum . 4 Vo-cum. fol. 147.
10. Missa lome arme Josquini. resoluta per Joannem Buechmayerum. 4 Vocum. fol. 173.
11. Missa Dum transisset sabbatum Joannis Buechmayeri. 5 Vocum. fol. 202.
12. Missa Maria Magda[lena] Joannis Buechmayeri. 5 Vocum. fol. 228.
13. Introitus Viri Gallilei Joannis Buechmayeri. 4 Vocum. fol. 263.
14. Introitus Puer natus Joannis Buechmayeri. 4 Vocum. fol. 266.
15. Introitus Benedicta sit sancta Trinitas Joannis Buechmayeri. 4 Vocum. fol. 270.
16. Introitus Resurrexi Joannis Buechmayeri. 4 Vocum. fol. 273.
17. Introitus Benedicta Isaac. 4 Vocum. fol. 277.
18. Introitus Puer natus Joannis Buechmayeri. 4 Vocum. fol. 281.
19. Missa Virtute magna Joannis Buechmayeri. 4 Vocum. fol. 284.
20. Missa Angelus Domini Joannis Buechmayeri. 5 Vocum. fol. 305.

Of these works nos. 1, 7, and 8 are taken from Petreius's *Liber quindecim missarum;* no. 9 is from the *Missae tredecim* of Formschneider; no. 10 is found in both collections. The Isaac Introits (nos. 3, 4, and 17) are drawn from the *Choralis Constantinus,* published by Formschneider in Nuremberg in 1550 and 1555. The source for no. 6 would appear to be a 1557 print by Phalèse in Louvain.[9] Buechmaier's own works, some of them identified as parodies of works by Clemens non Papa (no. 19), Stephen Zirler (no. 5), and Isaac (the Introits),[10] appear as *unica,* along with no. 2, by a German contemporary who may have been a friend of Buechmaier.[11] The other Masses by Buechmaier are probably parodies as well. The *Missa Maria Magdalena* (no. 12), for example, is based on a motet by Clemens, first published in 1546 but probably known to Buechmaier from a Nuremberg print of 1554.[12] Whether Ludwig Daser's Mass of the same name, also said to be based on Clemens's motet, is related to Buechmaier's work I have not yet been able to determine; the tempting possibility of a Munich connection remains to be investigated.[13]

In both his dedicatory letter and in the index Buechmaier describes the Masses of Isaac and Josquin contained in the choirbook as "resoluta" by him. What did he mean by this, and where did he get the term? Examination of the music shows that Buechmaier tinkered with it, changing the mensuration and altering and adding to the music itself. The term *resoluta* would appear to have come to him from the Nuremberg teacher and theorist Sebald Heyden.

Heyden, who in his *De Arte Canendi* of 1540 professed himself to be an admirer of Josquin and his contemporaries, as much for the quality of the music as for its pedagogical usefulness[14] (could he have transmitted this admiration to Buechmaier, some twenty years his junior?), postulates an equal tactus operable in all music, the more readily observable if the various mensurations are subjected to *resolutio*. He defines the term thus: "What is Resolutio? Resolutio is the transcription of the more abstruse values of notes into a certain more familiar form."[15] This transcription is basically twofold, consisting of reduction or augmentation of values according to a general maxim (*Regula Catholica*) stipulating that all diminution and augmentation is to be understood and judged on the basis of the essential integral tactus, that of the semibreve.[16] Heyden provides a table of augmentations and diminutions of "essential" values, followed by twelve rules for resolution by augmentation or diminution to and from various tempora and prolations. Apparently only the most expert singers could resolve augmented, diminished, or proportional notation at sight; at least some of these resolutions were thus meant to be of practical value.

Heyden retains the original duple or triple mensuration in all of the *resolutiones.* Buechmaier would appear to go Heyden one better; every one of the resolutions in his choirbook is to ₵, regardless of whether the original tempus is perfect or imperfect. There is some precedent for this in Heyden's book; citing the Kyrie of Agricola's *Missa Malheur me bat,* the theorist remarks that the notation of the piece with its use of *fusae* presents a complex appearance intimidating to young singers. He therefore "resolves" the piece, changing the mensuration from O to ₵ and doubling the notes values according to his own first rule of *resolutio* (from "essential" values to simple diminution).[17] Here the perfect tempus would of course become modus, still presumably audible in performance since breves would be sung at a tempo corresponding to Agricola's "essential" semibreves. It is interesting to see Heyden adopting a *horror fusae* position at a time when Italian musicians were writing pieces *a note nere* under the signature C.[18]

Buechmaier's "resolutions" do not on the whole follow Heyden's rules; his near-universal choice of ₵ shows his understanding of this signature to be that of practical musicians of his time, an "essential" mensuration rather than a diminution.[19] He therefore does not double note values when resolving O (or C) to ₵.[20] Much of the music changes rather little in resolution, since most breves in O are imperfected. Perfect breves must be dotted or have an added repeated-note semibreve; rests must be counted with care, then rewritten;[21] and prominent melodic ideas emphasizing perfect tempus are, when this can be easily done, adjusted. The opening of the *Missa Pange lingua,* as found in the *Missae Tredecim* of 1539 and as resolved by Buechmaier, may be compared in transcription (ex. 8.1); they look more different in modern score than in their sixteenth-century partbook or choirbook format.

Short passages of triplets in all three of the Josquin Masses are resolved, with ♩ ♩ ♩ typically becoming ♩ ♩ ♩.[22] Sections in *tripla* proportion, such as the "Et vitam venturi" of the *Patrem* in the *Missa Pange lingua,* are on the other hand retained, with the "resolved" mensuration ₵3 indicated; triple or sesquialtera proportion seems to have been the only ternary mensuration still usable for Buechmaier.

The tenor of the *Missa L'homme armé super voces musicales* posed a particular problem for Buechmaier since it is notated in perfect prolation calling for augmentation in performance. Petrucci leaves this unresolved, as does the scribe in the mid-sixteenth-century manuscript Cappella Sistina 154.[23] Petreius and Formschneider give both the original notation and a resolution. Heyden considers this notation in his fifth rule, where ₵ and ☉ in relation to essential values call for tri-

Example 8.1 Missa Pange lingua, Kyrie I

a. *Missae Tredecim, 1539[2]*

b. D-Rp, Ms C 100

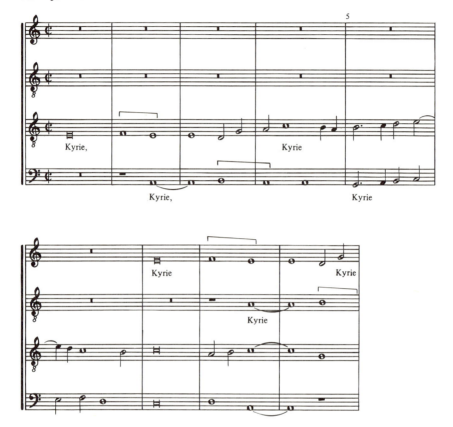

pling perfect values, doubling imperfect ones, and quadrupling altered ones unless the alteration is to be performed by the singer, in which case the notes to be altered are first doubled.[24] This rule is followed by the Nuremberg printers but is ignored by Buechmaier, who plows ahead with his usual signature. Example 8.2 shows Josquin's tenor in Kyrie I, first as given by Petrucci and most manuscript sources, next as resolved by Heyden (and the Nuremberg printers), and finally as transcribed by Buechmaier. Here "resolution" is pushed to the point of falsifying the character of the melody; only the slow speed of the tenor in relation to the other voices saves it from absurdity.

These resolutions probably helped the leader of a group of singers—perhaps Buechmaier himself—as much as they aided the singers. Buechmaier did not stop here. Various passages in the Masses where he evidently judged the music difficult melodically or contrapuntally, or perhaps simply archaic by the standards of 1560, were rewritten. One such passage occurs in the Et in terra of the *Missa La sol fa re mi,* where Buechmaier replaces Josquin's elegant but rhythmically tricky superius (ex. 8.3a) with a typically bland counterpoint of his own (ex. 8.3b). This passage

Example 8.2 Missa L'homme armé super voces musicales, Kyrie I, tenor

a. Petrucci et al.

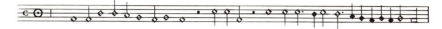

b. Heyden, 1539[1], 1539[2] et al.

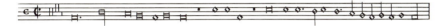

c. Buechmaier

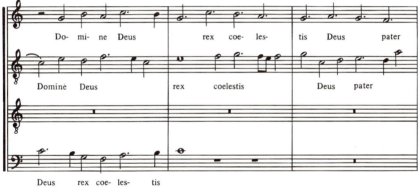

Example 8.3 Missa La sol fa re mi, Et in terra, mm. 20–25

a. *Liber Quindecim Missarum*, 1539[1]

b. Buechmaier (superius)

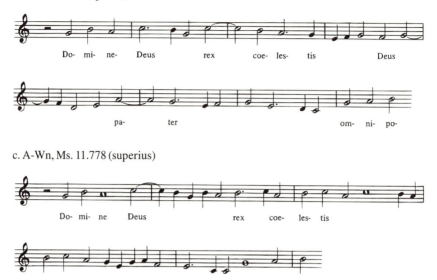

c. A-Wn, Ms. 11.778 (superius)

bothered other musicians as well; another version may be found in a Habsburg court manuscript of the third decade of the sixteenth century (ex. 8.3c).[25]

In the Et in terra of the *Missa L'homme armé super voces musicales* a passage featuring a repetitive circling figure characteristic of Josquin and some of his contemporaries (ex. 8.4a) is replaced by what Buechmaier evidently considered a more up-to-date *redicta* (ex. 8.4b); in this instance he rewrote both superius and altus.

To modernize Josquin's music in a thoroughgoing way was beyond Buechmaier's abilities and perhaps beyond his intentions. But where he saw opportunities he took them. Final cadences were enriched with thirds;[26] here Buechmaier may have followed a precedent offered in Agnus Dei I of the *Missa Pange lingua,* where the tenor in the source he knew (*Missae tredecim*) climbs to a third above the final; other sources give the tenor's figure a third lower (see ex. 8.5a and 8.5b). In the third Agnus Dei (Buechmaier like his source does not know the second Agnus Dei) the altus in the 1539 print concludes with a G falling to the final E; some other sources have only the E; Buechmaier uses only the G (see ex. 8.5c–e).[27] In the *Missa L'homme armé* a third is provided in the final sonority of all movements save the Agnus Dei, even though this means adding notes outside the *cantus prius factus* to the tenor, and making hash of the text (ex. 8.6). In some places Buechmaier seems to feel that Josquin's melodic lines are inconclusive; he therefore adds final notes, risking stylistic and contrapuntal impropriety as he proceeds (ex. 8.7).[28] This is allied with some more substantial additions made to the music in an effort to fill in some of the "bare" spots in the texture of Josquin's music.

Hermann Finck, writing in praise of the music of Gombert, whom he describes as a pupil of Josquin, says that although Josquin was a great contrapuntist his music

Example 8.4 Missa L'homme armé super voces musicales, Et in terra, mm. 4–6

a. 1539[1]

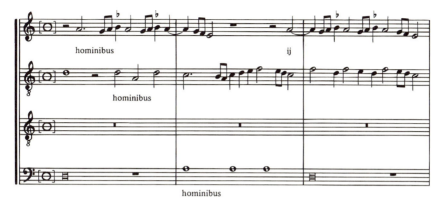

b. Buechmaier

Example 8.5 Missa Pange lingua

a. Agnus I, 1539[1]

b. Agnus I (tenor, ed. Smijers, from various sources)

c. Agnus III, 1539[2]

d. Agnus III (altus, ed. Smijers)

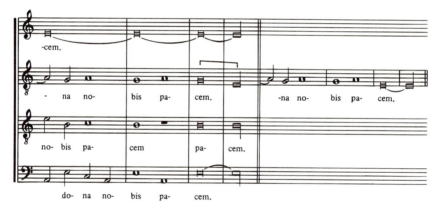

e. Agnus III (Buechmaier)

Example 8.6 Missa L'homme armé super voces musicales, Et in terra, mm. 56–58

a. 1539[1]

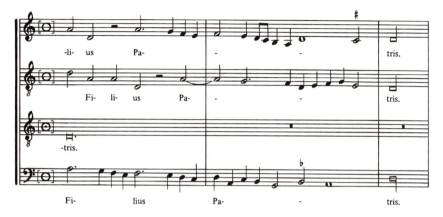

b. Buechmaier

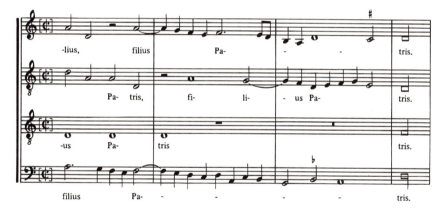

was thinner (*nudior*) than modern taste approved and that "he [Gombert] composes music altogether different from what went before. For he avoids pauses, and his work is rich with full harmonies and imitative counterpoint."[29] Buechmaier was evidently of the opinion that Josquin's music had too many pauses and harmony that was not always full enough for modern tastes. He set about to remedy this by adding music in some of the pauses. The opening of the *Missa La sol fa re mi* in his transcription (ex. 8.8) shows him at work.

Aside from fragmentary imitation of Josquin's altus in measure 4, Buechmaier's bass shows preoccupation with full triadic sound and harmonic definition. That this comes at a price, that of melodic and modal incongruity with Josquin's music, did not concern him. The Christe of this Mass shows (ex. 8.9) even heavier interference; Josquin's opening duo, based entirely on the solmization motive of the Mass, is "harmonized" with neutral melodic material, and the upper-voice extensions

Example 8.7 Missa L'homme armé super voces musicales, Christe (Buechmaier),
mm. 40–44

* = notes added by Buechmaier

include the downward-fifth cadence beloved of Lasso and his contemporaries
(mm. 22–23).[30] Oddly—but typically—Buechmaier leaves most of the lower duo
alone; perhaps it was harder for him to find notes, or to adapt to the upper voices
what he had just written for the lower ones.

His next attempt at filling in the blanks in this Mass comes in the "Crucifixus"
of the Patrem (ex. 8.10), where he adds four breves' worth of music in the bassus
under a superius-altus duo. The sudden stop at measure 104 is very odd indeed; it is
as if Buechmaier were making his changes as he copied the Mass, and found nowhere to go after the G in measure 103 (if that note, which in any event creates parallel fifths with the superius, is discarded the bassus could well continue, and the
reader might wish to experiment with carrying on the line for another four
measures).

Example 8.8 Missa La sol fa mi re, Kyrie I

a. 1539[1]

b. Buechmaier

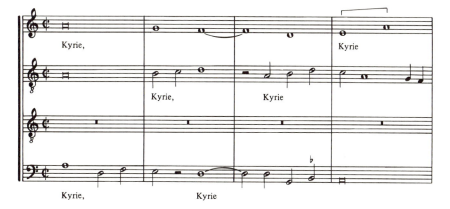

Example 8.9 Missa La sol fa mi re, Christe, mm. 1–9

a. 1539[1]

b. Buechmaier

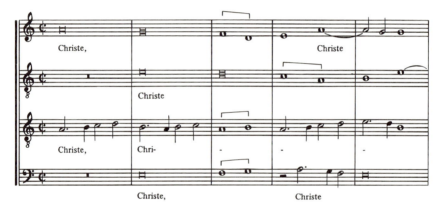

Example 8.10 Missa La sol fa mi re, Crucifixus, mm. 100–107

a. 1539[1]

b. Bassus added by Buechmaier, mm. 100–104

The most thoroughgoing series of additions in this Mass occurs in the "Pleni sunt coeli" of the Sanctus. Of the twenty-five measures comprising this movement only the last four are free from Buechmaier's additions. Here Josquin concentrates almost exclusively on the solmization theme, in various permutations and *inganni*.[31] Buechmaier is unable to find anywhere to introduce another entry of the subject, missing an easy chance in the superius (at mm. 35–36 of the Smijers edition); he seems to have had no interest in the motivic character of the music, aiming only at providing as many thirds and full triads as he can.

Buechmaier's final tampering with the *Missa La sol fa re mi* comes in the three-voice "In nomine" of the Benedictus, where he adds a bassus to the ten-measure opening duo and alters a few bars of the top voice. That he was doing this as he went along becomes clear when the music breaks off (at m. 110 of the Smijers edition) and a note says "In nomine quere in fine Missae proxime sequentis"; indeed the whole of the "In nomine," with some errors in Buechmaierian counterpoint in his first try corrected, is found at the end of Isaac's *Missa O praeclara.*[32]

Similar additions are made in the other two Josquin Masses copied by Buechmaier. In the *Missa Pange lingua* the Christe has an altus, proceeding in parallel thirds with the tenor, in measures 31–34, the sort of addition that could have been improvised by singers who knew the piece. A second interpolation in this movement, in the tenor in measures 42–44, adds a few chord tones leading up to the tenor's entry (ex. 8.11). This, though it spoils the imitative symmetry of the counterpoint, may show Buechmaier in a practical vein, preparing the tenor for what might have seemed a difficult entry.

Example 8.11 Missa Pange lingua, Christe, mm. 42–45

a. 1539[1]

b. Tenor added by Buechmaier, mm. 42–45

In the Et in terra of this Mass Buechmaier tried for once to add something in the style of Josquin; he wrote an altus in measures 24–26 in imitation of the tenor and bass entries on "Gratias agimus." The passage, published by Brusniak,[33] is clumsy, with the imitation beginning on a downbeat instead of Josquin's upbeat, and forced into inexactness after four notes; perhaps Buechmaier was well advised not to try in general to compete with the Master. As if admitting defeat, he left most of the rest of the Mass alone—until the Benedictus, where, regaining courage, he rewrote the opening ten bars in a triumph of pedestrian sonority over Josquin's "pauses" (ex. 8.12).

Example 8.12 Missa Pange lingua, Benedictus, mm. 1–11

a. 1539[1]

b. Buechmaier

a. 1539[1]

b. Buechmaier

In the *Missa L'homme armé super voces musicales* Buechmaier not only resolves the tenor's ⊙ to ₵, he often breaks up long notes (and occasionally puts together repeated ones) for purposes of texting. This procedure can be found in other manuscript and printed sources of Josquin's Masses, and is indeed evident in the two Nuremberg editions of 1539; but Buechmaier often does it differently from what is found in those two sources. Here he was following what may have been a common practice, solving the problem of tenor texting by treating the cantus firmus as a sort of archetype to be individualized in performance.[34]

A number of small alterations, single notes added here and there, are found in the *L'homme armé* transcription. The celebrated mensuration canon of the second Agnus Dei is resolved, as one might expect, in all voices (ex. 8.13). This version, similar to one found in another sixteenth-century source,[35] works reasonably well if one forgives the parallel octaves in the second measure. As in the *Missa La sol fa re mi,* Buechmaier reserves his heaviest "corrections" for the Pleni sunt coeli. After following Josquin for the first ten measures he extends measures 46–49 by doubling some note values and making slight alterations to fit. Measures 50–56 correspond to Josquin's 49–55. Another doubling of values, with a bassus part added, alters and lengthens measures 56–57 (= Buechmaier, measures 57–59). From here to the end of the section Buechmaier not only extends the music by doubling note values but actually recomposes the music (ex. 8.14).[36]

What are we to make of Buechmaier's "resolutions"? It is easy to judge them harshly, and difficult to resist a sense of shock at this tampering with the work of the Prince of Renaissance musicians. On the other hand we should remember that there was a tradition, going back nearly a century behind Buechmaier, of adding *si placet* parts to polyphonic compositions. There is in fact a fifth, *si placet* voice added to the final Agnus Dei of the *Missa L'homme armé super voces musicales* in a Roman source of the 1550s; its composer, "Jo. Abbat.," a member of the Papal Chapel, may also have composed the "Et in Spiritum" section of the Patrem, which occurs only in this source.[37]

Buechmaier's additions and changes are possible proof that at mid-century Josquin was not simply revered by theorists such as Heyden and Finck, or included in anthologies by printers for the glory of his name, but still performed, albeit from a text we would not consider authentic.[38] If the works were sung from Buechmaier's "resolutions" what was the effect of his uniform use of the signature ₵? The larger ternary groupings of the *Grosstakt* could still emerge from a sensitive performance, but the singers would have had no visual clues for this and may simply have plodded on a semibreve at a time. Whether the tempi for Josquin sung in 1560 were

Example 8.13 Missa L'homme armé super voces musicales, Agnus Dei II (Buechmaier), mm. 1–6

Example 8.14 Missa L'homme armé super voces musicales, Pleni sunt coeli, mm. 58–68

a. 1539[1]

b. Buechmaier

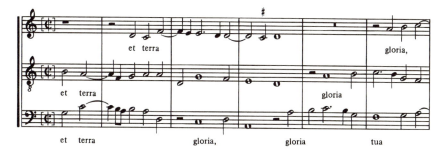

a. 1539[1]

b. Buechmaier

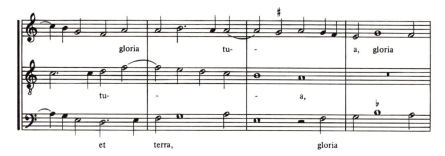

a. 1539[1]

b. Buechmaier

the same as those of 1500 we do not really know; we are in other words faced here with problems of authenticity in performance, almost as if Buechmaier's transcriptions should be compared with those of Franz Commer rather than with earlier sixteenth-century sources.

Certainly the added music shows Buechmaier to have been concerned with fullness of sonority, a concern typical of his generation.[39] The sound of newer music was thought to be superior to that of Josquin's time by theorists as well as by workaday musicians.[40] It may have been naive of Buechmaier to "improve" Josquin, but not out of character for a musician of his time. Still, this activity suggests a kind of provincial mentality, a desire for the new inhibited by notions of what one was told was to be revered. If many German musicians of this period were like Buechmaier, it is no great wonder that Albrecht V wanted not another German as court composer but a cosmopolitan musician versed in the new Netherlandish and Italian styles. Buechmaier at Regensburg and Lasso at Munich in 1560 show us something of the wide range of skill and taste existing in the musical culture of this period.[41]

POSTSCRIPT

I am sure there must be more examples of mid- and late-sixteenth-century "improvement" of Josquin and other earlier composers, and would love to hear about them. For a study of the sixteenth-century fortunes of Josquin motets see Stephanie Schlagel, "Josquin des Prez and His Motets: A Case Study in Sixteenth-Century Reception History" (Ph.D. diss., University of North Carolina, 1996).

NOTES

1. Lasso based two Magnificats (*Benedicta es caelorum* and *Praeter rerum seriem*) on Josquin motets. Several manuscripts from the Munich Hofkapelle at mid-century contain works by Josquin; one, Mus. Ms. 41, has six-voice reworkings of two four-voice Josquin motets. See Bayerische Staatsbibliothek, *Katalog der Musikhandschriften,* 1. *Chorbücher und Handschriften* (Munich, 1989), 161 (and consult Register 2).

2. Lasso's "opus 1" print of 1555 is described on its title page as "faictz (a la nouvelle composition d'aucuns d'Italie) par Rolando de Lassus."

3. The term is that of Helmuth Osthoff. See his *Josquin Desprez,* 2 vols. (Tutzing, 1962–65), 1:90. Sebald Heyden, in the preface to book 2 of his *De Arte Canendi, ac vero signorum in cantibus usu* (Nuremberg, 1540) says "Nos vero quicquid de ea re hic tradiderimus, si ipsum ex probatissimis Musicis, Josquino, Brymelo, Oberto, Isaaco, & similibus, ita esse convincamus, quidni fide digni videbimur?" See Clement A. Miller, "Seybald Heyden's *De Arte Canendi:* Background and Contents," *MD* 24 (1970): 80–81, 84; see also Clement A. Miller, ed. and trans., *Seybald Heyden. De Arte Canendi* (American Institute of Musicology, 1972).

4. Josquin's music appears in eighteen German prints from 1536 to 1559. See François Lesure, ed., *Recueils imprimés, xvie–xviie siècles,* RISM B I, 1 (Munich, 1960).

5. RISM 1539[1] and 1539[2]. Petreius's volume contains six Masses by Josquin; that of Formschneider reprints two of these, adding another, the *Missa Pange lingua* in its first printing (the RISM entry for 1539[2] lists five Masses by Josquin but the attributions for two of these are incorrect).

6. The best account of Buechmaier's life is that of Wilfried Brennecke, *Die Handschrift A. R. 940/41 der Proske-Bibliothek zu Regensburg* (Kassel, 1953), 104–14.

7. Regensburg, Proske-Bibliothek, Ms. C 100. I came upon this manuscript in the course of studying concordances for Josquin Masses; but I am not the first to examine Buechmaier's work. Friedhelm Brusniak, "Der Kodex A. R. 773 (C 100) von Johann Buchmayer in der Proske-Bibliothek zu Regensburg: Ein Beitrag zur Geschichte der Vokalpolyphonie in Deutschland um 1560," in Christoph-Hellmut Mahling and Sigrid Wiesmann, eds., *Gesellschaft für Musikforschung. Bericht über den internationalen musikwissenschaftlichen Kongress Bayreuth 1981* (Kassel, 1984), 288–93, has examined the manuscript and has noted some of the same things I have. Brusniak states (p. 288n) that a full study of the manuscript is planned by him; to my knowledge this has not yet appeared.

8. "Et quis videor vostra amplitudine non displicere, in certo libro congestas ac conscriptas esse aliquot missas et introitus pro vostro templo viginti ego conscripsi, partim a me compositas, partim resolutas et ab alijs assumptas, ut videre est in indice Missarum quem versum ostendet folium eas vostra prudentia offero et dedico."

9. See Karlheinz Schlager, ed., *Einzeldrucke vor 1800,* RISM A I/2, 150: C2677. *Missa cum quinque vocibus, ad imitationem moduli Caro mea, condita.*

10. See Brusniak, "Der Kodex A. R. 773 (C 100)," 290–91.

11. For Vogelhucher (or Vogelhuber) see Eitner, *Quellen-Lexikon,* 2d ed., 9:119–20.

12. The motet appears in RISM 1554[10], *Evangelia dominicorum et festorum dierum mu-*

sicis numeris pulcherrime comprehensa & ornata. Tomi primi . . . (Nuremberg, 1554); for a modern edition see *Clemens non Papa. Opera Omnia,* ed. K[arl] P[hilipp] Bernet Kempers, 21 vols. (American Institute of Musicology, 1951–76), 4.16. Also in the collection is a five-voice setting of *Dum transisset sabbatum* (see no. 11) by Sebastian [= Christian?] Hollander, a work I have not been able to see, and one of *Angelus Domini* (see no. 20) by Clemens; this latter work has some resemblances to Buechmaier's Mass, but not enough to prove it as his model.

13. The Daser Mass is in Munich, Bayerische Staatsbibliothek, Mus. Ms. 9; see *Katalog der Musikhandschriften,* 70.

14. See above, n. 3.

15. *De Arte Canendi,* 2.7.188: "Quid est Resolutio? Resolutio, est abstrusioris Notularum valoris, in vulgatiorem aliquam formam, transcriptio."

16. *De Arte Canendi,* 2.7.119: "Regula Catholica. Ut omnia Augmentatio ac Diminutio quantitatis Notularum ad essentialem Semibrevis Notulae integrum tactum relative intelligi, & aestimari debet. . . ."

17. *De Arte Canendi,* 2.375–79.

18. On this topic see chapter 9.

19. Cf. Hermann Finck, *Practica musica* (Wittenberg, 1556), Fii^v: "ista nota ◇, quae apud recentiores uno tactu valet."

20. In one passage, the "Pleni sunt coeli" of the *Missa L'homme armé super voces musicales,* Buechmaier does double note values, but not consistently; he is not "resolving" the mensuration but rewriting the music. See below, and example 8.14.

21. I found only one error in the rests, in the tenor of the "Et incarnatus" of the *Missa L'homme armé,* where twenty rather than eighteen imperfect rests are given.

22. Cf. Finck, *Practica musica,* Fiii: "ibi tres syllabas habes, quae simili celeritate, qua unum expressisti ad horologii tactum pronunciandae sunt, quamvis prior syllaba duplici quantitate superat reliquas, sic etiam sentiendum est, quando tres notae ad unum tactum inciderint, ex quibus prima dimidio tactu, reliquae duae etiam dimidio tactu mensurantur, hoc pacto ♩♪♪."

23. On this manuscript, copied in Rome between 1550 and 1555, see Mitchell P. Brauner, "The Parvus Manuscripts: A Study of Vatican Polyphony, ca. 1535 to 1580" (Ph.D. diss., Brandeis University, 1982), 51, 163, 310.

24. *De Arte Canendi,* 124–25. The sixth rule, dealing with perfect prolation in relation to diminution, doubles these figures. Heyden uses the Christe of the *L'homme armé* Mass as an example. Buechmaier joins all the repeated notes and resolves the altered notes from breves to longs; otherwise his resolution corresponds with that of Heyden.

25. Vienna, Österreichische Nationalbibliothek, Ms. 11.778. See *Census-Catalogue of Manuscript Sources of Polyphonic Music, 1400–1550,* 5 vols. (American Institute of Musicology, 1979–88), 4:92.

26. This is especially true of the *Missa L'homme armé;* see below, and example 8.6.

27. Other sources also have a G ending; see *Werken van Josquin des Prez,* ed. Albert Smijers, 55 vols. (Amsterdam, 1922–69), Missen, Deel 4: ix–xiv, 27.

28. Cf. the Christe of the *Missa Pange lingua,* measure 28, where a dotted breve A is added; and the "Qui tollis" of the Et in terra pax of the same Mass, measures 61–62, where the last note of the superius is extended by another long, and a dotted-breve C is added to the altus line.

29. *Practica musica,* Aij: "Florit tunc etiam, Josquinius de Pratis, qui vere pater Musicorum dici potest, cui multum est attribuendum: antecellit enim multis in subtilitate & suavitate, sed in compositione nudior, hoc est, quamvis in inveniendis fugis est acutissimus, utitur tamen multis pausis. . . . Nostro verò tempore novi sunt inventores, in quibus est Nicolaus

Gombert, Iosquini piae memoriae discipulus, qui omnibus Musicis ostendit viam, imò semi-tam ad quaerendas fugas ac subtilitatem, ac est author Musices plane diversae à superiori. Is enim vitat pausas, & illius compositio est plena cùm concordantiarum tùm fugarum."

30. See Siegfried Hermelink, "Die Gegenquintsprungkadenz, ein Ausdrucksmittel der Satzkunst Lassos," in Carl Dahlhaus et al., eds., *Gesellschaft für Musikforschung. Bericht über den internationalen musikwissenschaftlichen Kongress Bonn 1970* (Kassel, 1971), 435–38.

31. On this see James Haar, "Some Remarks on the *Missa La sol fa re mi,*" in Edward E. Lowinsky, ed., *Josquin des Prez: Proceedings of the International Josquin Festival-Conference* (London, 1976), 564–88, esp. 577–79.

32. Isaac's Mass, not to be considered here, is "resolved" in a way similar to those of Jos-quin. See Martin Staehelin, *Die Messen Heinrich Isaacs,* 2 vols. (Bern, 1977), 2:28: in the Regensburg manuscript the Isaac Mass shows that "Vielfach sind die Ligaturen aufgelöst, die Mensuren vereinfacht und Pausen mit Zusätzen Buchmayers ausgefüllt." As for the Moulu Mass, which is an ingenious piece performable with or without rests, Buechmaier's resolution adopts the version without rests.

33. Brusniak, "Der Kodex A.R. 773 (C 100)," 293.

34. There are a number of examples of this practice. One of the most interesting is Gio-vanni Spataro's "resolution" of the tenor in the *Patrem* of the *Missa La sol fa re mi,* found in Bologna, Arch. mus. di San Petronio, Ms. A. XXXI.

35. Staatsbibliothek zu Berlin—Preußischer Kulturbesitz, Ms. Mus. theor. 1175, fols. 86v–87. See *Werken van Josquin des Prez,* Missen, 1: vii, 33.

36. For Brusniak, "Der Kodex A.R. 773 (C 100)," 291, this passage marks "die Grenze zur Geschmacklosigkeit." It might be possible to side with Buechmaier in feeling that Jos-quin's movement concludes in a somewhat breathless manner.

37. See Brauner, "The Parvus Manuscripts," 310–11. Johannes Abbate, described as "De S. Germano, Italus, Altus," entered the Cappella Sistina on 6 July 1535 and was still there in 1552. See F. X. Haberl, "Die römische *Schola cantorum* und die päpstlichen Kapell-sänger bis zur Mitte der 16. Jahrhunderts," *Vierteljahrsschrift für Musikwissenschaft* 3 (1887); reprinted as *Bausteine für Musikgeschichte* 3 (Leipzig, 1888): 75, 78, 91.

38. I say "possible proof" because there is no evidence that Ms. C 100 was ever used.

39. One indication of this is Buechmaier's choice of a choirbook format in which the bas-sus is under the superius on the verso, the altus and tenor on the facing recto; he evidently considered the music "from the bass up."

40. Tinctoris extolled the generation of Ockeghem; for Glareanus, Josquin was the finest of composers; Finck thought Gombert the best; to Zarlino, Willaert was the new Pythagoras and the touchstone of taste. Each generation of writers on music, at least until the end of the sixteenth century, preferred the newest music.

41. The difference in compositional level between the work of Buechmaier and that of Lasso may be seen from a comparison between the examples given above and the parodies of Josquin's *Benedicta es* and *Praeter rerum seriem* in Lasso's Magnificats nos. 69–70. See Orlando di Lasso, *Sämtliche Werke,* Neue Reihe, vol. 15, ed. James Erb (Kassel, 1986), 228–74. Since both works are for six voices, Lasso also did a certain amount of "filling in" blank spaces in Josquin's motets to create his own six-voice textures. The sensitivity with which the older composer's ideas are coaxed by Lasso into the service of a newer style is remark-able; but in some places, particularly in Magnificat no. 69, the procedure is not fundamen-tally different from that of Buechmaier. For a study of Lasso's parody Magnificats, see Da-vid Crook, *Orlando di Lasso's Imitation Magnificats for Counter-Reformation Munich* (Princeton, 1994).

ON THE ITALIAN
MADRIGAL

The *Note Nere* Madrigal

LIKE WHITEHEAD'S PHILOSOPHERS after Plato, students of the madrigal who read Alfred Einstein find that they can but add footnotes to his great work. This paper is submitted as respectful comment on one topic treated by Einstein, the curious appearance of "black-note" madrigals in Venetian music prints of the 1540s. That such pieces are more than a mere notational trick, that they reflect in part the stylistic change which overtook the madrigal about 1540, is a view convincingly stated by Einstein and by a few other scholars, notably Erich Hertzmann.[1] But the line between notational fad and stylistic advance is doubtless a thin one; where to draw it, and how best to characterize music written in this "chromatic" notation, are the subject of this study.

If one may judge from prints advertising their contents as *madrigali a note nere,* pieces written in this notation have the mensuration sign C, in contrast to the more typical ₵ of the period. The note values are on the whole shorter, with much of the text declaimed on minims and semiminims; and although the blackness of the page is not always striking, a *note nere* madrigal is visibly darker than, say, a typical Verdelot madrigal. To illustrate this contrast two facing pages from the cantus part of Cipriano de Rore's first book of five-voice madrigals, the *Madregali Cromatici* of 1544, are shown in figure 5; a piece in *note nere* is followed by one in the standard notation of the period, the *misura commune* or *note bianche.* One's first reaction is that these pieces are simply written in halved note values. With the sign of diminution now removed, these values become equivalent to those of the ordinary madrigal, and the music is thus unchanged; the notation has simply been altered, perhaps "modernized." For some pieces this indeed seems to be true; and from one point of view this halving of note values and elimination of the *diminutum* sign could even be thought of as a more honest notation, the replacing of a mock proportional sign originally used in order to avoid short note values in appearance while getting them in practice—what Curt Sachs amusingly calls a *horror fusae* notation.[2] The *diminutum* sign, by far the most common mensuration symbol in early sixteenth-century music, including the madrigal of the 1530s, is of course no longer a true proportional sign since it usually has no relation to any undiminished values, but something of its original meaning of diminution doubtless survived. Therefore pieces in ₵, with note values mainly white, and those written in C, with many short black notes, would seem to be simply graphic variants of the same musical style. Not only do some madrigals of ca. 1540 appear to bear this out, but some contemporary remarks on the new notation deal with it in this way. In his *Lucidario* of 1545, Pietro Aaron says of the change that it is only apparent; if people observed the meaning of the proportional signs they would realize that a breve in ₵ and a semibreve in C are the same thing. And Ghiselin Danckerts in his

Figure 5. Cipriano de Rore, *Madregali cromatici* (1544), xiii–xiv. Courtesy of
Wolfenbüttel, Herzog August Bibliothek

Trattato of the late 1550s speaks in strongly disapproving language of *note nere* pieces, which he sees not as notational reform but as mere novelties.[3]

Aaron's tone, when he speaks of the *note nere,* is also uncomplimentary; perhaps not all musicians looked at the new style of writing from the standpoint of proportional theory, as he thought should be done. If they had, it is hard to see why the new notation neither replaced the old completely, nor did it die out after being in vogue for a short period. Instead the two notational styles continued to exist side by side for the rest of the century.[4] Although there are exceptions, sacred music on the whole tended to remain in ₵ and to look "white," *note nere* writing being confined to the madrigal and especially to its lighter forms. Praetorius, as he looked back on the music of the generations preceding him, noticed this, and observed also that the length of the notes in recent music, while it varied from piece to piece, seemed to have little to do with the mensuration sign used, that one could not tell from the notes whether a piece was written in ₵ or C.[5] At the end of the sixteenth century, then, *note nere* pieces are not necessarily much blacker than any other music. In the early years of the sixteenth century it is also hard to see the difference between pieces bearing a ₵ signature and those without the slash—almost none of them has many black notes. But the short note values, having once been introduced by means of the *note nere* technique of the mid-century, remained available for use, and after the 1550s were often taken over into pieces with the *diminutum* signature. In other words, that side of *note nere* writing which was simply graphic change had its effect, the establishment of the short time values. But the very fact that the ₵ signature—which I hesitate to call *alla breve* for reasons that will presently appear—did not vanish is proof that no very exact proportional relationship existed between C and ₵ when these signatures were used for whole pieces. Praetorius remarks that ₵ indicates a somewhat faster tempo;[6] his testimony comes perhaps a bit late, but writers as magisterial as Glareanus, or as practical-minded as Sylvestro di Ganassi, these men contemporaries of the *note nere* madrigalists, tend to deny fixed proportional meaning to C versus ₵ when these signs are used for entire pieces. Glareanus in fact says that signatures such as C and ₵ are among those a composer may affix to various movements of a long work, to prevent monotony; and ₵ is one of those signs that can be used if one wants to speed up the *tactus* a bit.[7]

A piece written in *note nere* is not then, simply an exercise in halved note values. In trying to find out what it is one can puzzle over the various names given this notation during its period of greatest vogue, the decade of the 1540s. The earliest print to mention the new device (though not the first in which it appears) is Girolamo Scotto's publication in 1540 of the madrigals of Claudio Veggio, "Con la gionta di sei altri di Arcadelth della misura a breve."[8] *Misura a breve;* or *misura di breve,* used for a number of prints;[9] *alla misura breve* occurs as well.[10] What does this mean? Einstein interprets it as "short measure,"[11] meaning that the tactus is applied to a shorter value. For *misura breve* this is possible, although no theorist seems to use the term. But *misura di breve* is more difficult to translate as "short measure," particularly since that short measure would be a measure, or better a tactus, on the semibreve; in Curt Sachs's terminology music in which the motor rhythm is on the minim, with the up- and downbeats which comprise the tactus taking place within a semibreve.[12] This indeed fits the music of *note nere* madrigals quite well, for it would be difficult to imagine these pieces conducted in any large unit, and for some of them the minim might be the unit of measure.[13] And theorists of course admitted that the tactus could, indeed usually did, fall on the semibreve; Zarlino, for instance, says that "È ben vero che i Moderni applicarono primieramente alla Battuta hora la Breve, & hora la Semibreve imperfette."[14] In fact the semibreve was the ordinary unit of time-beating, and what we call *alla breve* has as time-units what appear to be breves but, the sign of diminution now being taken literally, what are really semibreves. The German theorist Listenius points this out when he says that the whole or major tactus is that applied to the breve when this value is not diminished; and he contrasts this with the common or minor tactus, applied to the imperfect semibreve.[15] Here it might be noted that black-note madrigals when referred to as *misura di breve* were contrasted with *misura commune,* the ordinary ₵.[16]

Now, whether or not the tactus fell on the written breve in pieces signed with ₵ (in many pieces it seems more likely that the unit of time-beating was in fact the written semibreve[17]), the notation still indicated a diminution. In the C signature, however, a written breve was a *real* breve, regardless of its actual speed. There is no reason to believe that *misura* necessarily or always refers to *tactus;* at least one theorist, although unfortunately not an Italian, distinguished between measure and tactus.[18] It is possible that *misura di breve* refers to music written in the old *integer valor;* not necessarily or even probably music performed in a proportionally accurate way, of course. At least one early student or performer of the *note nere* madrigal indeed tried to measure a piece by its breves; a Jhan Gero madrigal in Gardane's *Il vero terzo libro . . . a note negre* has been completely measured off in breves in the copy in Bologna, Biblioteca Musicale G. B. Martini. It is hard to say whether this measurement was meant to aid in performance, although it was carried out for all four voices. If a performance with the tactus on the breve was attempted, the piece must have been rather difficult to sing; and theorists of the time warn against the folly of trying to beat in breves music that moves in semibreves.[19] One should perhaps not use the "human frailty" argument in historical study, but it is tempting to think that the term *misura di breve* caused some confusion even in 1540, and that this is why it was abandoned for the self-evident *note nere.*[20]

Before leaving the term *misura di breve* we might take note of one contemporary theorist who mentions it. Nicola Vicentino's *L'Antica musica ridotta alla moderna Prattica* of 1555 has a chapter describing various types of coloration and ending with this statement:[21]

> & altri segnano i canti tutti neri con il segno imperfetto non tagliato; & quella compositione da Cantanti è detta cantare à misura di breve
>
> Cantar alla breve detto da Prattici

This of course explains nothing, except that the new notation was the work of practical musicians rather than theorists and so, by implication, a bit suspect. But Vicentino does say that *crome colorite* (♪) come eight to the *battuta,* and *semicrome*

(♪) sixteen, which means a tactus on the semibreve. And elsewhere he adds, this a remark which could be useful in interpreting the madrigal of the period, that singers may change tempo when the music calls for it, and that those who say that in beating time *alla breve* one ought not to change tempo, do it nonetheless in practice, just as orators pace their speeches.[22]

There is a third term used for *note nere* pieces; beginning with the second edition in 1544 of Cipriano de Rore's *Primo Libro a 5,* the term *cromatico* was occasionally employed.[23] This seems to be a bit of humanistic dressing up for the *note nere,* a borrowing from Greek although not from ancient musical terminology since it has, as was crossly noticed by Ghiselin Danckerts in the 1550s, no apparent connection with the chromatic genus.[24] *Croma* as a term for the flagged semiminim existed side by side with *fusa* during the sixteenth century. Where it was first used I am not sure, but it appears in as early a treatise as the *De Cantu Figurato* of Johannes Hothby, that is, in the late fifteenth century.[25] In its most literal sense *cromatico* must mean music full of *crome,* which does in fact describe the *note nere* pieces rather well. But by extension it also means of course a piece full of black (or literally, colored) notes, though not those blackened by the rules of *hemiolia.* Classical writers on music ordinarily used chromatic in quite another sense, but I have found a passage that might have been seized upon for the purpose at hand by some humanistic wit: in the ninth book of Martianus Capella's *De nuptiis Mercurii et Philologiae* the chromatic genus, that made up of semitones, is said to be thus called because it lies between the diatonic and the enharmonic as colored or chromatic objects are between white and black.[26] Since *note nere* pieces are not all black but only more black than white, the analogy fits quite well. The highly "colored" rhetorical style of Martianus[27] suggests another meaning for the term chromatic, to be explored a bit later. After 1550 "chromatic" cannot be counted on to indicate *note nere;* in a print such as the first book of Giulio Fiesco of 1554,[28] *cromatico* refers to the newly resuscitated chromatic genus. Only the term *note nere* finds lasting acceptance.[29] Antonfrancesco Doni's label of *canti turchi* is one of his dreadful puns, nothing more.[30]

At this point one may well wonder what's in a name. *Note nere* pieces are not merely ordinary madrigals in halved note values. What then are they? Einstein has given one answer by showing that many *villanella* collections are written in black notes with a signature of C.[31] The patter of these pieces looks lively on the page in its quarter- and eighth-note dress, and surely it is so; that is, the semiminims of *villanelle* are faster than the minims of cut-time madrigals, though perhaps not twice so fast. This rapid patter may indeed have been transferred to the madrigal from the *villanella* or *villanesca.* Just before the appearance of *note nere* pieces in serious madrigal collections comes the *Canzone villanesche alla napolitana* of 1538, a print in which no mensuration signs are used but which has pieces full of semiminims (♩) though no smaller values. And many villanella prints in following years show not only declamation on quarters and eighths, but a playful syncopation that is also to be seen in the *note nere* madrigal. Yet Einstein hesitates, as he says, to connect the frivolous villanella with the imposingly serious madrigal of Cipriano de Rore and other members of Willaert's circle.[32] And it would seem that the connection is actually rather slight. The villanella is never described as being written in *note nere,* for instance; and a distinguishing feature of the black-note madrigal, the contrast between quite fast and quite slow motion, is not especially characteristic of the villanella. Besides, the kind of syncopation employed in the madrigal is more artful than the rather simple homophonic syncopation typical of the villanella. The two genres use the same time signature and the same scale of note values, but this does not yet explain the *note nere* pieces.[33]

Contrast between fast and slow motion seems an essential feature of this music, a feature which can be found here and there in pieces a good deal older than the real *note nere* madrigals. In the frottola prints of Petrucci one occasionally sees a piece that, style apart, is close in its notational practice to the madrigals of the 1540s. ₵ is Petrucci's normal mensuration sign, with the swing of the typical frottola rhythm going in ♩ ♪ ♩ ♪ ♩ ♪ ♩ or, also in ₵, ♩♩♩♪♩♪♩♩. And the use of C does not necessarily have anything to do with shorter note values. But a piece such as "Si si si tarvo [t'avrò]" from the seventh book (ex. 9.1) is a black-note frottola moving in a lively pattern of semiminims, its third phrase offering an amusing *allargando* in

Example 9.1 Petrucci, "Si si si tarvo tarvo"

minims. This sort of piece is surely an ancestor of the *villanella* in notation as well as in style.

A more typical use of the C signature in this period is seen in example 9.2, from a frottola of Tromboncino moving in semibreves and minims with some ornamental semiminims. At the end of this piece is a postlude marked by running semiminims under the signature ₵. Here a proportional relationship between the two signs must still hold, so that in performance one would halve the note values of the last section, and runs of *crome* or *fusae* would result in fact though not written—Sach's *horror fusae* theory in application.[34]

Neither Petrucci nor Antico shows real *note nere* procedure, and I have not found much evidence of it in the rather scant printed sources of the 1520s and early 1530s. As late as 1537–38, in the madrigal prints of Ottaviano Scotto devoted to Verdelot, little difference between pieces in ₵ and those in C can be observed. For Verdelot the serene "white" style is only very occasionally modified by the more nervous declamation and the playful turn of eighth notes (*crome*) seen in his "Per alti monti" (ex. 9.3). Though Arcadelt and Willaert have a good deal to do with the *note nere* movement, Verdelot seems to stand rather apart from it.

Example 9.2 Tromboncino, "Per mio ben ti vederei"

Example 9.2, cont.

Example 9.3 Verdelot, "Per alti monti" (cantus)

Per alti monti . . .   Che sovente   ij   in gioco

Before we turn to the first real *note nere* collections a word should be said about Italian prints of instrumental music during the early decades of the century. The keyboard tablatures of Antico and then of the Cavazzoni are certainly full of black notes, with many runs of quarters and eighths and even some sixteenths. Antico uses both ₵ and C; the Cavazzoni prints have only ₵. Both publishers bar the music by the breve. If one compares an intabulated frottola from Antico's book with its vocal model (see, for example, "Si è debile il filo" of Tromboncino, fols. 4v–5r in Petrucci's seventh book of frottolas, no. 14 in Antico's *Frottole intabulate* of 1517), one sees that the newly introduced small note values are diminutions which ornament but do not replace the originals; that is, the note values have not been halved, only complemented by the ornamental use of small values apparently more acceptable to an instrumental performer than to a singer of the period.

In 1538 Antonio Gardane began to publish in his adopted city of Venice.[35] And in the next year at least two of his prints show recognition of the *note nere* principle, though neither is yet advertised in this way. One, the music from the wedding festivities of Cosimo de' Medici and Eleonora of Toledo, has seven *canzone* by Francesco Corteccia, described as having been sung during the performance of a play. The pieces are arranged so that every other one, including the first, is in C with note values noticeably smaller than the even-numbered pieces in ₵. This may have been done partly for appearance's sake, but there is a real suggestion that the pieces were meant to sound different as well as look different from each other. The *note nere* pieces are certainly fussier in texture than their companions, and one is tempted to posit a degree of fast-slow alternation of tempo. But at any rate the *note nere* style is here used consciously.

The other 1539 print is Arcadelt's fourth book of four-voice madrigals. Here the quiet classicism of Arcadelt prevails for all but two pieces, a noticeably syncopated *note nere* piece by Arcadelt himself, and, at the end of the book, an anonymous setting of Petrarch's "Pace non trovo et non ho da far guerra," identified in other sources as the work of Yvo.[36] Einstein called attention to this piece as one of the most striking of the early *note nere* madrigals,[37] and it is an especially good realization of the possibilities for the kind of pictorialism the *note nere* style could provide—the stretching and contracting of temporal values to match the constant oxymora of the text (see ex. 9.4 for samples from the cantus part of this piece). Not every contrast in madrigalian poetry can be expressed by fast notes versus slow ones, but where these will do the *note nere* style supplied them with a new sharpness. One cannot here change the time signature and double note values, for the gamut of temporal values, breve, even a rare long, to *semicroma,* is larger than that of the older madrigal. Many of the "chromatic" madrigals of Cipriano de Rore (see ex. 9.5) show this kind of contrast, and the *canti turchi* printed in Doni's *Dialogo* of 1544 are similarly full of florid runs opposed to long holds.

Example 9.4 Yvo, "Pace non trovo" (cantus)

Example 9.5 Rore, "Altiero sasso" (cantus)

Yvo's piece shows not only temporal contrasts but the use of a good deal of syncopation, sometimes easy but often the slightly more involved kind recommended by theorists as a way of ornamenting simple counterpoint (see ex. 9.6, from the *Compendium* of Coclico, a modest example of this kind of ornamental syncopation). The combination of extreme contrasts of note values plus a good deal of syncopation may have made the *note nere* pieces seem a bit difficult. Doni, writing in 1544, says that not everyone who can compose music is able to sing the *canti turchi*,[38] this though he himself wrote one or two pieces in the new notation for his *Dialogo.*

Example 9.6 Adrian Petit Coclico, *Compendium musices* (1552)

During the years following the first *note nere* print, Claudio Veggio's madrigals of 1540, a number of publications advertising the new *misura* appeared; one of the most important was Gardane's *Primo libro . . . a misura di breve* of 1542, which was reprinted no fewer than eleven times.[39] Prints labelled *misura commune* or *a note bianche* advertised the old ₵ notation at the same time. After about 1555 no new prints proclaim the blackness or whiteness of their contents, but the two notations go on existing side by side. If the readers consult the list of *note nere* prints given at the end of this study they will notice that all of them, at least all those published during the 1540s, are produced by the printers Antonio Gardane and Girolamo Scotto in Venice. Given the preeminence of Venice as a publishing center and the great amount of printing done by these two men, this is not very surprising. But Einstein conjectures that Scotto may have been at least in part behind the innovation in notation.[40] It is true that Claudio Veggio's dedicatory letter in the 1540 print of his madrigals says that Scotto, in order to make the madrigal book a more desirable offering to the patron, Count Anguissola, has added the six pieces in *misura a breve*.[41] Besides this, there are prints of 1541 and 1542 called *Madrigali di Geronimo Scoto con alcuni a la misura breve*,[42] indicating that Scotto himself wrote pieces in this style. But music written in *note nere* antedates Scotto's entry into publishing (though not, perhaps, the activity of older members of his family). And Gardane is even more active than Scotto as a printer of these works. The relationship between Scotto and Gardane is a complicated one, and this is not the place to enter into the question of who stole what from whom. However, one aspect of their relationship that I have not seen comment on deserves mention here. In the dedicatory letter accompanying the *Primo libro . . . a due voci* of Jhan Gero, printed by Gardane in 1541, the signature is that of Scotto, who writes to Cesare Visconte on behalf of "casa nostra," suggesting that Scotto and Gardane were for a time partners.[43]

It does not seem likely, then, that *note nere* were the invention of a printer, although their novelty was doubtless used for advertising purposes by both Gardane and Scotto. Nor does it seem that any one composer can be credited with being the first to use the new style of writing. Einstein inclines toward the villanellists, especially Nola;[44] but as we have seen, the villanella is not quite the same thing as the "chromatic" madrigal. The importance of Cipriano de Rore's first book of madrigals *a 5* for the stylistic development of the madrigal is so great that use of *note nere* technique in these pieces is certainly significant. But again, *note nere* writing antedates Rore's first publications, though not by much. The list of composers writing "chromatically" is a long one; it includes the Venetian circle around Willaert, a Roman group including Yvo and Hubert Naich, and the Florentine Corteccia. The man who may be really important here is, curiously enough, the classicist Arcadelt, whose connections with both Florence and Rome and whose general fame make him a central figure. Arcadelt's *note nere* pieces are not many, but they are markedly more syncopated, more uneven rhythmically, in general more "nervous" than the rest of his madrigals. And it should be noted that Antonfrancesco Doni, after complaining in his *Dialogo* about having to sing the old-fashioned "Il bianco et dolce cigno" of Arcadelt, goes on to say that he doesn't much care for *note nere* pieces either, the juxtaposition suggesting that he might be thinking of Arcadelt in connection with the newer style. Yet I doubt that any single composer can be connected with the origins of *note nere* use; its quite general popularity in the 1540s is the important thing. One rather unlikely name in the roster of black-note composers ought to be mentioned at this point. Palestrina, on the whole not a great innovator as a madrigalist, wrote a few pieces in *note nere* style, one being the fourteen-stanza canzone "Da fuoco così bel nasc'il mio ardore,"[45] appearing in Cipriano's *Secondo Libro a 4* of 1557. Einstein describes this work as a highly typical example of the temporal contrasts of the *note nere* style.[46] And he also mentions the fact that each stanza of the canzone ends with a line from Petrarch's sonnet "Pace non trovo et non ho da far guerra." Here two of the many shining strands in Einstein's great book may be woven together; Palestrina's piece turns out to be a kind of *hommage* to the "Pace non trovo" of Yvo discussed above, first published almost twenty years earlier. At the end of each of the fourteen sections, when the Petrarchan line is quoted, Palestrina quotes, rather freely to be sure, from Yvo's setting, creating an interesting parody the details of which deserve separate treatment.

·

To this point we have discussed aspects of the *note nere* madrigal without fully characterizing it. This is deliberate, for the "chromatic" technique can be seen as not an end in itself but rather as one of the means used by madrigal composers while a new style, characterized by conscious, even rather extreme straining after effective and expressive declamation of the text, was getting under way. This is a period that might indeed be termed manneristic, and for once music here was not awfully far behind the other arts. But *kulturgeschichtliche* comparisons can be dispensed with here, and this discussion can end with another footnote, a final theory about the meaning of the term *cromatico.* As we have seen, there is here no direct connection with the musical meaning of the Greek χρωματιχὸς. But χρῶμα and its Latin translation *color* were also used as rhetorical terms. A famous passage in Plato's *Republic* credits the effectiveness of poetry to its "musical coloring" (τῆς μουσιχῆς χρωμάτων).[47] A number of other references could be cited, but one from Quintilian, in which the performance of an orator was said to lack only "color" for real distinction, will do.[48] Color in a rhetorical sense means ornament, stylistic flourish. The predilection of Renaissance humanists for classical rhetoric is well known; but does this have a connection with music? Possibly it does. Sixteenth-century theorists peak of ornamenting simple lines through diminutions and syncopations; Coclico even uses *coloratus* as a term for such ornamented lines (see ex. 9.6). Syncopations are common enough in vocal polyphony, but diminutions, at least written ones, are for the early sixteenth century at any rate mostly confined to instrumental tablatures. The instrumental diminutions of course make use of small, black note values. Their *note nere* are ornaments. It seems quite likely that the *note nere* of madrigals are at least in part ornaments of the same kind, written out *passaggi.* If one compares short-note passages in these madrigals (see ex. 9.3–5) with the instrumental diminutions given by such a writer as Sylvestro di Ganassi in 1535, one finds them similar in kind though not so extensively used. And here a theorist for once speaks to the point: in a discussion of cadences Vicentino gives some highly ornamented examples using ♪ and ♬ values, and says "avenga che alcuni nelle loro dispositioni di voci diminuiscono quelle in varij modi à imitationi delli stromenti."[49]

Cromatico may then refer to the musical rhetoric of these madrigals: a colorful style moving now quite fast, now with exaggerated slowness; making use of syncopations, of pictorial devices, and of ornamental *passaggi,* all written out with the care a polished humanistic rhetorician would expend on speech whose color was as important as its substance. It seems no accident that a composer as great as Cipriano de Rore is closely connected with the *note nere* technique, for its appearance signalizes the coming of age of the madrigal.

Appendix

A Chronological List of Note Nere Prints

A brief list of prints advertising their contents as *note nere, cromatico,* or *misura a breve* was given by Theodore Kroyer, *Die Anfänge der Chromatik im italienischem Madrigal des XVI. Jahrhunderts* (Leipzig, 1902), 45–47; a fuller one was made by Erich Hertzmann, *Adrian Willaert in der weltlichen Vokalmusik seiner Zeit* (Leipzig, 1931), 43. The list given below, while longer and more detailed than either

Kroyer's or Hertzmann's, is by no means complete since it includes only prints that mention *note nere* or its equivalent in their titles. Many other sixteenth-century collections use the black notation without designating it as such; these could not be included here, but some of the more important ones are referred to in the body of the paper.

1. 1540.   *Madrigali a quatro voci di messer Claudio Veggio, con la gionta di sei altri di Archadelth della misura a breve. Novamente con ogni diligentia stampati. Venetiis, apud Hieronymus Scotum, 1540* [Vogel 2:287–88]

   In Veggio's dedicatory letter, to Count Federico Anguissola, one reads that ". . . li quali [Veggio's madrigals] perche piu vi sian cari, vengono accompagnati di sei altri del la misura a breve, donativi dal cortesissimo Messer Hieronimo Scotto, che con quelli desidera habbiate memoria di lui." In addition to the six madrigals of Arcadelt, four of Veggio's pieces are written in *note nere*. And Veggio, along with Perissone Cambio, Ruffo, Riccio, Palazzo, Nolet, and Doni himself, belongs to the group of composers who contributed *canti turchi* to Doni's *Dialogo della musica* of 1544.

2. 1541.   *Di Girolamo Scotto i madrigali a tre voci con alcuni alla misura breve novamente posti in luce. Venetijs apud ipsum authorem. 1541.* [Vogel 2:204–5] Reprinted in 1549. Only three of the fifty-six pieces in this collection are written in the *misura breve.*

3. 1542.   *Madrigali a quatro voce di Geronimo Scotto con alcuni a la misura breve, et altri a voce pari. Novamente posti in luce. Libro primo. Venetijs, apud ipsum authorem, 1542.* [Vogel 2:204] Scattered through this print are eight pieces in *note nere,* including two by Willaert.

4. 1542.   *D. autori il primo libro di madrigali de diversi eccellentissimi autori a misura di breve novamente con grande artificio composti et con ogni diligentia stampati et posti in luce. Venetijs apud Antonium Gardane, 1542.* [Vogel 2:384] Reprinted in 1543, 1546, 1547, 1548, 1550, 1552, 1557, 1560, 1563, 1567; some of the reprints are by Scotto and one (1563) is by Francesco Rampazetto. The latter reprints (from 1548 on) substitute *note ne[g]re for misura di breve.*

5. 1543.   *Il secondo libro de li madrigali de diversi eccellentissimi autori a misura di breve novamente stampato a quatro voci. Venetijs apud Antonium Gardane. 1543.* [Vogel 2:385] Reprinted in 1552 by Scotto. The Scotto edition of 1567 is, as Vogel points out, drawn mainly from the *Primo libro* (No. 4 above).

6. 1544.   *Di Cipriano*[50] *il primo libro de madregali cromatici a cinque voci con una nova gionta del medesimo autore. Novamente Ristampato & da infiniti errori emendato. Venetijs apud Antonium Gardane. 1544.* [Vogel 2:142]

This print, of which the first edition of 1542 lacked the designation *cromatici,* was reissued in 1552, 1554, 1559, 1562 (these three by Scotto), 1563, 1576, 1593. All but three of the thirty-eight pieces in this collection have the signature C. For fast-slow contrasts, ornamental *passaggi,* and pictorialisms using fast motion and quick-syncopations this set of pieces is a sort of textbook of examples.

7. 1545. *Agostino Licino. Primo libro di duo cromatici de Agostino Licino Cremonese da cantare et sonare composti una parte sopra l'altra con la sua resolutione da parte novamente posti in luce. A due voci. Venetijs apud Antonium Gardanum. 1545.* [Claudio Sartori, *Bibliografia della musica strumentale italiana stampata in Italia fino al 1700* (Florence, 1952), 12]

For a brief discussion of Licino's duos see Alfred Einstein, "Vincenzo Galilei and the Instructive Duo," *Music and Letters* 18 (1937), 363–64.

8. 1546. *Agostino Licino. Il secondo libro di duo cromatici. . . . Venetijs apud Antonium Gardanum. 1546*

In his dedicatory letter Licino mentions but does not elaborate on "mio libretto secondo, che noi chiamiamo duo cromatici." But *cromatico* here does refer to black notes.

9. 1545. *Di Vincentio Ruffo musico eccellentissimo li madrigali a quatro voce a notte negre novamente da lui composti et posti in luce con ogni diligentia corretti et stampati. Libro primo. Venetiis. 1545* [Gardane] [Vogel 2:175–76]

Reprinted in 1546, 1552 (now called *madrigali cromatici*), 1556, 1560 (*a notte negre;* published by Scotto). Ruffo, a contributor in *note nere* style to the *Dialogo* of Doni, was evidently considered by the latter to be a good representative of the style despite his youth; on fol. 6v of the *Diaglogo* Doni has an interlocutor say "da buoni musici, come è Vincenzo Ruffo, non possono uscire se non cose rare."

10. 1549. *Di Jehan Gero musico eccellent. Libro primo delli madrigali a quatro voce, a notte negre. Da lui novamente composti. Et con somma diligentia stampati. Et da gli suoi propij exemplari estratti. Opera nova artificiosa et dilettevole, come à Cantanti sarà manifesto. Venetijs. Apud Hieronymum Scottum. 1549.* [Vogel 1:283–84]

11. 1549. *Di Jehan Gero musico eccellent. Libro secondo delli madrigali a quatro voce, a notte negre. Da lui novamente composti . . . come à Cantanti sarà manifesto. Venetijs. Apud Hieronymum Scottum. 1549.*

Gero occasionally uses the signature ₵ although C predominates. The first book is written in rather long note values, but the second contains the long runs of *crome* typical of *note nere* style.

12. 1549. *Libro terzo de d. autori eccellentissimi li madrigali a quatro voce a notte negre novamente posti in luce con somma diligentia corretti et stampati. In Vinegia appresso Girolamo Scotto. 1549* [Vogel 2:390]

This print contains a few pieces with the signature ₵ and a number in which the C looks as if the line had been removed by the printer.

13. 1549.   *Il vero terzo libro*[51] *di madrigali de diversi autori a note negre, composti da eccellentissimi musici con la canzon di cald'arrost, novamente dato in luce. In Venetia appresso Antonio Gardane. 1549.* [Vogel 2:390]

As can be seen from Vogel's list of contents, these two prints have no pieces in common. The relationship between Scotto and Gardane, once that of colleagues (see above, and n. 43), had evidently deteriorated. For the *Canzon di cald'arrost* see Alberto Cametti, "Jacques du Pont e la sua 'Canzon di cald'arost' (1549)," *Rivista musicale italiana* 23 (1916), 273–88, including a transcription of the piece.

14. 1549.   *Libro primo delli madrigali cromati di Messer Pauolo Aretino. Venetiis, apud Hieronymum Scottum. 1549.* [Vogel 1:41] *Cromati* may be, despite Vogel's (!), a legitimate adjective, from the late Latin *chromata;* see "cromate" in Carlo Battisti and Giovanni Alessio, *Dizionario etimologico italiana* (Florence, 1950–57) 2:1172. But *chromata* was really a substantive; see Aegidius Forcellinus, *Totius Latinitatis Lexicon,* ed. James Bailey (London, 1828), 1:356: "A nostris Musices *chromata* dicuntur nigree notulae minutiores, vel a colore . . . vel quod in chromatico modulationis genere praecipue locum habent." For bibliographical data on Aretino see Francesco Coradini, "Paolo Aretino (1508–1584)," *Note d'archivio per la storia musicale* (1924): 1:143–48, 275–78; (1926), 3:192–203.

15. 1549.   *Henricus Schaffen nobil francese. Li suoi madrigali a quatro voce a notte negre, da lui nuovamente composti, & da le sue proprie coppie fidelissime & corettissime con diligentia stampati. Opera nova et bellissima quanto alcuna altra che sino a hora sia stata posta in luce. In Vineggia Appresso Girolamo Scotto. 1549.* [Vogel 2:201]

Schaffen's madrigals, which in his dedicatory letter he describes as "il primo frutto che gia nella mia prima etade con gran faticha ho aquistado," do not seem as remarkable as their publisher would have us believe; but they are good examples of *note nere* writing in a somewhat light vein (no. 5, "Lasso che deggio far," is an especially lively "chromatic" piece).

16. 1552.   *Del Martoretta il secondo libro di madrigali cromatici a quatro voci novamente da lui composti & dati in luce. In Venetia apresso di Antonio Gardane. 1552* [Vogel 1:426]

Martoretta's first book (1548), although for the most part in C and in *note nere* style, is not described as such.

17. 1552.   *Di Heliseo Ghibeli il primo libro de madrigali a tre voci a note negre novamente per Antonio Gardane ristampato & da molti errori emendato. In Venetia appresso di Antonio Gardane. 1552.* [Vogel 1:289]

The first edition of this print seems to be lost. Unlike other three-voice collections written in C (but not described as *note nere*), which are mostly *villanelle* or *napolitane,* this print contains serious madrigals; it may have been didactic in intent.

18. 1554.　*Cesare Tudino de Atri, li madrigali a note bianche, et negre cromati-cho, et napolitane a quatro. Con la gionta de dui madrigali a otto voci. Da lui novamente composti, et da li suoi proprii exemplari corretti et posti in luce. Venetijs apud Hieronymum Scotum, 1554.* [Vogel 2:259] *Cromaticho* should probably read *cromatiche* in this title. It is not a synonym for *note nere* but rather another kind of piece, one in the chromatic genus. Two pieces in this print, "Altro che lagrimar" and "Piango cantand'ogn'hora," are labelled *cromatico* because they are chromatic in Vicentino's sense. For a discussion, with examples, of these pieces see Theodor Kroyer, *Die Anfänge der Chromatik,* 79–82.

19. 1565.　*Il primo libro a note negre a due voci composto per Bernadin Lupac-chino dal Vasto con alcuni di Gian Maria Tasso nuovamente stamp-ato. Con la gionta di alcuni Canti di nuovo ristampati. In Venetia appresso Girolomo Scotto. 1565.* [Vogel 1:371–72]

On the popularity of these duos, reprinted numerous times (as late as 1701), see Oscar Mischiati, "Lupacchino," *MGG* 8:1315. The 1565 print is not the earliest for this collection. In Sartori, *Bibliografia,* 23, there is listed an edition of 1559, itself "con ogni diligentia ristampato"; the first edition seems to be lost. But of all the numerous reprints (differing slightly in content from one to another, at least for the earlier ones) only the 1565 print is called *a note negre.* In the print I have consulted, dated 1560, twenty-four of the thirty-six pieces are in C, twelve in ₵; and a real difference in the scale of note values used may be seen between the two.

Additional note. Since writing this paper I have had brought to my attention two additional references to "chromatic," sufficiently interesting to deserve mention here. One is the use of "El Cromato" (cf. Appendix, no. 14) as the title of a three-voice instrumental piece in Vincenzo Ruffo's *Capricci in Musica* (Milan, 1564), fol. 15v. The piece is actually quite "white" in appearance, even *semicrome* being written as flagged white notes (as in Attaingnant's keyboard tablatures). Nor is it chromatic in the tonal sense. But it does employ mensural coloration; being written in the archaic C signature, it has frequent groups of blackened semibreves and minims. Here is an added, surely capricious, meaning for "chromatic."

The other use of the term, called to my attention by Nino Pirrotta, is in a description of music for the tragedy *Alidoro,* performed in Reggio on 2 November 1568, and printed in Giovanni Crocioni, *L'Alidoro o dei primordi del melodramma* (Bologna, 1938), 87: of the choruses it is said that "perch' essendo di musica cromatica et con poche alterationi, se n'andavano a un corso consueto nel parlare ordinario senza mai replicar cosa alcuna." Although this statement is not entirely clear, it would seem to refer to *cromatica* as music in short, fast-declaimed values, suitable for musical speech moving at the speed of conversational speech.

POSTSCRIPT

A large section of the *note nere* repertory, including nos. 1, 4, 5, 12, and 13 of the Appendix to this study, has appeared in modern edition. See Don Harrán, ed., *The Anthologies of Black-Note Madrigals,* 5 vols. (American Institute of Musicology, 1978–81). See also Harrán, "Some Early Examples of the *Madrigale Cromatico,*" *Acta Musicologica* 41 (1969):240–46.

A major study of the *tactus* problem is J. A. Bank, *Tactus, Tempo, and Notation in Mensural Music from the Thirteenth to the Seventeenth Centuries* (Amsterdam, 1972).

For a study of Danckert's treatise, concentrating on the chromatic genus, see Paul Boncella, "Denying Ancient Music's Power: Ghiselin Danckert's Essays in the 'Generi Inusitati'," *Tijdschrift van de Vereniging voor nederlandse Muziekgeschiedenis* 38 (1988):59–80.

On Gardane's beginnings as a music printer see Mary S. Lewis, *Antonio Gardano, Venetian Music Printer, 1538–1569,* vol. 1: *1538–1549* (New York, 1988), 17–34.

The separate treatment of Yvo's "Pace non trovo" and the Palestrina madrigal cycle modeled on it is found in my *"Pace non trovo:* A Study in Literary and Musical Parody," *MD* 20 (1966): 95–149. For the duos of Gero, see Lawrence Bernstein and James Haar, eds., *Ihan Gero: Il Primo Libro de' Madrigali Italiani et Canzoni Francese a due voci* (New York, 1980).

NOTES

1. See Einstein, *Italian Madrigal,* 368, 398–400; and Erich Hertzmann, *Adrian Willaert in der weltlichen Vokalmusik seiner Zeit* (Leipzig, 1931), 42.

2. *Rhythm and Tempo* (New York, 1953), 214. Use of the sign of diminution to obtain short note values without their fussy appearance is demonstrated by Loys Bourgeois in his *Le droict chemin de musique* of 1550 (facsimile, ed. P. André Gaillard, Documenta Musicologica, ser. 1, vol. 6, Kassel, 1954), chapter 9.

3. *Lucidario* (Venice, 1545), 3.15, quoted in Hertzmann, *Adrian Willaert,* 43–44: "tali Mandriali a note nere, non saranno cantati a brevi, ma a semibrevi, perche in un tempo, over battuta, non passa altro, che una semibreve, o tanto suo valore, laqual' semibreve, o quantita sua, in detto segno C, indugia tanto, quanto la breve di questo segno ₡, passa, Et per tal modo da te è compreso, et creduto, che tali Mandriali si cantino a breve, e non secondo il proprio, et natura del segno, Conchiudendo che tal misura, o tempo non è a breve, ma a semibreve, Perche come habbiamo detto, non altro passa, che una semibreve per tempo, Et questo per la velocita delle note apparenti, et dimostranti."

Danckerts has this to say in his *Trattato di Ghiselin Danckerts . . . sopra una differentia musicale sententiata . . . contro il perdente venerabile D. Nicolò Vicentino . . .,* book 3, chapter 5, *Dell'Error di coloro che fuora d'ogni Raggione Intitolano le loro Compositioni alla Misura di Breve:* "Oltra i sopradetti errori sono anchora alcuni d'essi compositori novelli i quali incorreno in questo altro errore cioè Che per parere di dire qualche cosa grande e nuova, e volendo per questo esser tenuti apresso gli ignoranti, da piu che gli altri nella musica, Intitolano le opere loro per madrigali delle note negre composte alla misura di Breve, ponendo per la semibreve la minima, & per la minima la semiminima, e per la semiminima la croma e per la croma la semicroma, e cosi ponendo tutte le altre figure nel valore della sub-dupla proportione, dando a loro per guida e duce il segno del tempo perfetto cosi O, over del tempo imperfetto cosi C. Il qual segno fa contrario effetto al titolo sopradette, perche sotto questi sudetti segni si dee cantare in una misura il valore d'una semibreve e non d'una Breve come dicono i sudetti titolanti, la qual breve e la valuta d'essa, si canta in una misura sotto la guida di questo segno $\mathₑ{C}$ over di questo C2 intendendon però il minor numero, sottoposto il magiore di sorte che queste opere sono anchora esse con ignorantia grande e manifesto er-rore impropramente intitolate da i loro Authori, poi che la natura del segno fa effetto con-trario al titolo."

For the date of this treatise see P. J. de Bruyn, "Ghisilinus Danckerts, Kapelaanzanger van de Pauselijke Kapel van 1538 tot 1565—Zijn leven, werken en onuitgegeven tractaat," *Tijdschrift van de Vereniging voor nederlandse Muziekgeschiedenis* 17 (1949), 145–47. I am indebted to Claude Palisca for calling my attention to Danckerts' attitude toward *note nere.*

4. For the persistence of *note nere* writing during the later sixteenth century see Einstein, *Italian Madrigal,* 400, 511.

5. Praetorius, *Syntagma musicum* (Wolfenbüttel, 1619), 3.51: "quia Madrigalia et aliae cantiones, quae sub signo C semiminimis et Fusis abundant, celeriori progrediuntur motu, Motectae autem, quae sub signo ₵ Brevibus et Semibrevibus abundant, tardiori." See the passage quoted in Heinrich Bellermann, *Die Mensuralnoten und Taktzeichen des XV. und XVI. Jahrhunderts,* 2d ed. (Berlin, 1906), 76: "*Claudius de Monte Verde praeponiret* das ₵ in denen, so er uff Mottettenart gesetzet und *ad tactum alla breve* musicirt werden können: in den andern allen aber, darinnen mehr schwartze als weisse Noten *praeponirt* er das C . . . . Etliche vermengen es durcheinander, bald in diesem ₵, in andern das C und kann man gleichwohl an den Noten oder gantzem Gesange keinen Unterscheid erkennen."

6. *Syntagma musicum,* 3.vii, summarized in Sachs, *Rhythm and Tempo,* 223: C is "etwas langsamer und gravitetischer" than ₵. The reason, says Praetorius (*Syntagma musium,* 51), is this: "Ideo hic celeriori, illic tardiori opus est tactu, quo medium inter dua extrema servetur, ne tardior progressus auditorum auribus pariat fastidium, aut celerior in praecipi-tium ducat." Cf., however, Hans Otto Hiekel, "Der Madrigal-und Mottetentypus in der Mensurallehre des Michael Praetorius," *Archiv für Musikwissenschaft* 19–20 (1962–63), 40–55; Hiekel believes that Praetorius maintained a proportional relationship of 2:1 be-tween ₵ and C. The basic tactus of early sixteenth-century music, the breve in ₵, became the semibreve in ₵ by the end of the century, in Hiekel's view (p. 53n).

7. Glareanus, *Dodecachordon* (Basel, 1547), 3.viii, quoted in Sachs, *Rhythm and Tempo,* 223: one can cross the circle or semicircle "quod tactus fiat velocior." Cf. Sylvestro di Ga-nassi, *Opera intitulata Fontegara* (Venice, 1535), facsimile edition (Milan, 1934), chap. 13: "& advertisse che l'ordine de questo signo ⊖ richiede la batuda sopra la breve & in questi la semibreve O ⏀ dato che il piu de li cantori & sonatori non considerano altro che lo acomo-darsi de la lor differentia." Ganassi's signs are not so clear, but he recognizes that the old meaning of the proportional signs is now weakened. And even Pietro Aaron, in another con-text (*Toscanello in musica,* Venice, 1539, 1.xxxviii) says, "Ma piu dubbiosi restano ne gli seguenti, cioe che in questo segno C sia ogni semibreve dupplichera comparato a questo ₵. . . ."

As for the absolute duration of the tactus, and the question of whether this duration was a fixed one, it would seem that by the mid-sixteenth century at any rate the tactus could be speeded up or slowed down. See the remark of Johannes Oridryus, *Practicae musicae utri-*

usque praecepta brevia (1557) on "celeriorem aut tardiorem tactum," quoted in Carl Dahlhaus, "Zur Theorie des Tactus im 16. Jahrhundert," *Archiv für Musikwissenschaft* 17 (1960), 26; and cf. Vicentino's remark about changes of tempo, quoted in this chapter (see below and n. 22). Dahlhaus' study presents convincing evidence against the concept of fixed tactus.

8. See Appendix, no. 1. It should be noted that Aaron, writing before 1545 (*Lucidario;* see n. 3 above) says ". . . Diremo adunque, essere poco tempo, che da molti Compositori, è usato un certo modo di comporre, dalloro chiamato, A note nere. . . ."

9. See Appendix, nos. 4, 5.

10. See Appendix, nos. 2, 3.

11. *Italian Madrigal,* 399. Unfortunately Einstein often refers elsewhere to *misura di breve* as meaning ₵ or *alla breve.*

12. *Rhythm and Tempo,* 219. Danckerts in his *Trattato* pointed out the discrepancy between the term *misura di breve* and the tactus of the music it described; cf. n. 3 above.

13. See Einstein's description, *Italian Madrigal,* 405, of a print of Cimello madrigals in which a piece is said by its author to contain a whole *botta* within a minim; on this see now chapter 11, below.

14. *Istitutioni harmoniche,* 2.49.257, in the collected edition of 1589. For other references to the various kinds of *tactus* see Sachs, *Rhythm and Tempo,* 219–223, and Dahlhaus, "Zur Theorie des Tactus im 16. Jahrhundert," 22–39, superseding Georg Schünemann, "Zur Frage des Taktschlagens und der Textbehandlung in der Mensuralmusik," *Sammelbände der Internationalen Musikgesellschaft* 10 (1908), 73–114.

15. Nicolaus Listenius, *Musica* (1549), facsimile edition, ed. Georg Schünemann (Berlin, 1927), 2.x: "Totalis [tactus], seu Integralis, quem alias Maiorem vocant, est, cum brevis tactu non diminuto mensuratur pro modo ac temporis ratione. Generalis seu vulgaris, quem alias Minorem vocant, est cum Semibrevis aut duae minimae sub tactum cadunt integrum."

16. Cipriano de Rore's *Secondo libro de Madrigali a cinque voci . . . a misura comune* (Venice, 1544) was meant by the composer, or more probably the publisher Gardane, to be a contrast to the first book of "chromatic" madrigals published in the same year.

17. See the remark of Agostino Pisa, *Battuta della musica* (Rome, 1611), 128, on the *L'homme armé* Mass of Palestrina: "Et perche la detta Messa si canta ancora alla semibreve, se bene e sotto questo segno ₵. . . ." This remark is quoted in the interesting article of Michael B. Collins, "The Performance of Sesquialtera and Hemiola in the Sixteenth Century," *JAMS* 17 (1964), 11n. Cf. Adrian Petit Coclico, *Compendium Musices* (1552; facsimile, ed. Manfred Bukofzer, Documenta Musicologica, ser. 1, vol. 9, Kassel, 1954), "De Tactu et Mensura": for the tactus on the semibreve Coclico says "qui nunc est communis tactus in omnibus signis."

18. Loys Bourgeois, *Le droict chemin de musique,* chap. 6: "Tacte donques est en chantant comprendre les notes, leurs pauses & poinctz d'augmentation soubz un abesser ou frapper . . . egal à un lever. . . . Mesure est nombrer (sans chanter qui voudra) les notes. Leurs pauses & poinctz d'augmentation comme les signes le requirent. . . . C'est pourquoy (improprement touteffois) on prend mesure pour tacte es signes diminués."

19. Gregor Faber, *Musices practicae erotematum libri duo* (1552), 1.9: "Minor [tactus] quidem usitatissimus est, atque semibrevem notam complectitur. Sunt autem qui hunc tanquam vulgatum contemnentes, egregios se, si Diis placet, cantores praestare arbitrantur, dum ad maiorem qui duabus semibrevibus perficitur, se conferunt"; quoted by Dahlhaus, "Zur Theorie des Tactus im 16. Jahrhundert," 31.

20. Several of Gardane and Scotto's *misura di breve* prints were renamed *a note nere* in later reprints. Compare Vogel, 2:632 and 641; 634 and 642.

21. Nicola Vicentino, *L'Antica musica ridotta alla moderna prattica* (1555; facsimile edition, ed. Edward Lowinsky, Documenta Musicologica, 1.17, Kassel, 1959), 4.10. fol. 77r. It should be noted that Vicentino seems to use *misura* and *battuta* interchangeably.

22. Ibid., 4.42., fols. 94r–94v.

23. For uses of the term see below, Appendix nos. 7, 8, 9, 14, 16, 18. As late as 1620 "chromaticos" was used by Francesco Rognoni to characterize the rapid black notes of his *Passagi*. See Hans Engel, "Diatonik—Chromatik—Enharmonik," *MGG*, 3:413–14.

24. *Trattato*, 3.iv: *De gli Errori che fanno quelli che intitolano i lor canti Chromatici:* "Oltra ciò tra quelli compositori novelli sono alcuni che aggiungendo error sopra errore e volendo parere apresso gli ignoranti di questa scientia piu dotti et eccelenti: et ancho[ra] piu copiosi de gli altri. Non studiano in altro che in dare alla stampa gran quantita di opere Musicali/ piene delli disordini et ignorantie predette. Intitolandole per Chromatice come pare per lo libro primo de Madrigali Chromatici a quattro voci stampato in Venetia da Hieronimo Scoto nel 1543 [a lost print?], & ancho[ra] per lo libro primo di Madrigali Chromatici a cinque voci stampato similmente in Venetia/ ma da Antonio Gardane nel 1544 [the Cipriano madrigals]. i quali libri ho veduti e considerati diligentemente tutti/ parte per parte; e non solo non truovo in luogho alcuno de i lor canti un progresso intiero di tre intervalli appropriati al tetrachordo Chromatico, ma non vi trovo ne ancho[ra] un solo intervallo a grado qualsia del detto genere Chromatico. . . ." Danckerts concludes that these composers and publishers do not know what the chromatic genus is, and he compares them to heretics trying to upset sound doctrine. Having been involved in the controversy between Vicentino and Lusitano over the chromatic genus, Danckerts was of course very preoccupied with the term and so naturally was annoyed at seeing it used in an unusual way.

25. C. E. H. de Coussemaker, *Scriptorum de Musica medii aevii nova series,* 3. 330. Hothby's "eight figures" of notes go from *maxima* to *semicroma;* Coussemaker's illustration has only seven note values, ending with the *croma*. Sixteenth-century writers using *croma* rather than *fusa* include, besides Vicentino, Vanneo (*Recanetum de musica aurea,* 1533), Ganassi (*La Fontegara,* 1535), and Lusitano (*Introduttione facilissimo,* 1553).

26. *De nuptiis Mercurii et Philologiae,* 9.955f.: "chroma, quod hemitonis componitur: sicut enim quod inter album nigrumque est, color dicitur, ita hoc chroma, quia inter utrumque [enharmonic and diatonic] est, nominatur." Cf. Pierre Gassendi, *Manuductio ad Theoriam, seu partem Speculativam Musicae* (1654), 3: *De Generibus Musicae:* ". . . Forte autem chromaticum, seu coloratum dictum est a speciali notarum chordas experimentium colore" (5.586 in the collected edition of Gassendi published in Florence, 1728). Gassendi's treatise, a rehash of classical music theory, here takes something from sixteenth-century practice.

27. The style of Martianus is described by its author as "paginam venustans multo illitam colore." See *The Oxford Classical Dictionary* (1949), 543.

28. *Di Giulio Fiesco il primo libro di madrigali a quatro voci . . .* (Venice: Gardane, 1554). This print has at least one piece in characteristic *note nere* style, "Amor là vaga luce," on pp. 8–9. But "Baccio soave," p. 25, called "chromatico," uses a ¢ signature and slower time values. It is chromatic in Vicentino's sense of genus.

29. The term *note nere* rang a bell near the end of the century. See Vecchi's amusing "Far una canzone senza note nere," a white-note piece in which one verse adds "Ne vi far cifra ò segno contra segno," published by Einstein, *Italian Madrigal,* vol. 3, no. 87, from Vecchi's *Libro secondo* of *canzonette* of 1580.

30. Doni, *Dialogo della musica* (Venice, 1544), fol. 9v: ". . . et a dirvi il vero questi canti turchi, se non son begli, non me quadrano. *M.* Come canti turchi? *B.* Sì questi a note nere si domandano canti turchi se tu non lo sapessi. *M.* Chi gli ha battezzati? *B.* Il Doni. *M.* Adunque non son turchi, se son battezzati, ò voi gli dite turchi battezzati."

31. *Italian Madrigal,* 364, 399, et passim. Erich Hertzmann and Gustave Reese also speak of the influence of the *villanella;* see Reese, *Music in the Renaissance* (New York, 1954), 320.

32. *Italian Madrigal,* 399.

33. Although some *note nere* madrigal prints contain pieces in a light patter style, this is not the rule, and madrigals seem to have been held apart from lighter forms by publishers. The *Primo libro de villotte a quatro voci* of Antonio Barges (Venice: Gardane, 1550) has eighteen pieces, all in C and with short note values, but these are not advertised as *note nere;* and the last four pieces, called "madrigali" in the *tavola,* are in ₵.

34. The opposite procedure, ₵ changing to C with the implication of slowing down, though here probably not in a strict proportional sense, is occasionally seen in Petrucci, an example being Pisano's "Che deggio far che mi consigli Amore" in the *Musica de meser Bernardo pisano sopra le Canzone del petrarcha* of 1520, no. 16.

35. 1539 is Gardane's first year according to Fernanda Ascarelli, *La tipografia cinquecentina italiana* (Florence, 1953), 192. But several prints, of motets and of chansons, were issued by Gardane in 1538; see Claudio Sartori, "Gardane," *MGG,* 4:1376–78.

36. The Arcadelt madrigal is "Viddi fra l'herbe verde." The Yvo piece is credited to him in the 1541 reprint of Arcadelt's fourth book, and also in Gardane's *Il vero terzo libro . . . a note nere* of 1549, no. 5. For Yvo [Barry?] see the first chapter of Kurt Huber, *Ivo de Vento* (Munich, 1918).

37. *Italian Madrigal,* 399.

38. *Dialogo della musica,* fol. 15r: "trovato hò molti che san comporre, che non cantano quei canti turchi."

39. See Vogel, 2:384.

40. *Italian Madrigal,* 399.

41. See Appendix, no. 1.

42. See Appendix, nos. 2, 3.

43. Jhan Gero, *Il primo libro de madrigali italiani, et canzoni francese a due voci* (Venice: Gardane, 1541). In this dedicatory letter Scotto says of two-voice madrigals that "a i Prencipi, & a Signori si conviene: questa e da essi adoperata, quando ritratti dal tumulto de la moltitudine, con alcuni dimestici familiari, gustano la melodia, che nasce da l'intelletto de gli ottimi Compositori."

44. *Italian Madrigal,* 366–67.

45. Raffaele Casimiri, ed., *Le Opere complete di Giovanni Pierluigi da Palestrina* (Rome, 1939–), 2.67. The work was first printed in *Di Cipriano de Rore il secondo libro de' madrigali a quatro voci con una canzon di Gianneto sopra di Pace non trovo con quatordeci stanza . . .* (Venice: Gardane, 1557).

46. *Italian Madrigal,* 436.

47. *Republic* 601B.

48. Quintilian, *Institutio oratoria,* 4.2.89.

49. *L'Antica musica,* 3.23. fol. 51v.

50. In Munich, Bayerisches Staatsbibliothek, Mus. MS 45, there is a *Missa a note negre* by Cipriano de Rore, a parody mass said to be based on a chanson by Rore himself. For a discussion of this piece see Alvin Johnson, "The Masses of Cipriano de Rore," *JAMS* 6 (1953): 236–37, and Johnson, "Rore," *MGG,* 11:899.

51. In 1554 Gardane published a fourth book in this series, but containing madrigals described as *a note bianche,* all in ₵. See Vogel, 2:392; RISM 1554[28].

The "Madrigale Arioso": A Mid-Century Development in the Cinquecento Madrigal

IN 1555 THE SINGER AND COMPOSER Antonio Barrè, who had been living in Rome for several years and who was at this time a member of the Cappella Giulia,[1] began a career as music printer in Rome with the first of a series of volumes called *Libri delle Muse*.[2] A device showing Apollo and the nine Muses in beneficent posture accompanies these books, which include anthologies of madrigals and *villanelle* for three, four, and five voices as well as a *Liber . . . Musarum* containing four-voice motets. The Muses did not restrict their protection to Barrè; his volumes were quickly reprinted by Scotto, Gardano, and Rampazzetto in Venice, and in fact the set is something of a bibliographical tangle, with some first editions evidently lost, some books with the same title having entirely different contents, and perhaps with the Muses themselves transferred from Rome to Venice as the series was continued.[3] The last of the anthologies was printed in 1563, after which Barrè's career as music publisher seems to have come to an end.[4]

Of concern here are Barrè's three anthologies of four-voice madrigals, volumes bearing the subtitle "madrigali ariosi." The adjective *arioso* had not to my knowledge been hitherto used to qualify the madrigal; it appears in a few other madrigal prints of this period, crops up once or twice in the next generation, and then disappears.[5] Whether it has real meaning, and what that meaning may be, is the subject of this paper; at this point I shall only say that Barrè himself does not give us any help in the way of a definition. The much later use of the term, first as an adjective with *recitativo* and later as a freestanding term, is outside the bounds of this investigation.[6]

Barrè's four-voice anthologies are chiefly though not exclusively the work of composers resident in Rome at this period or earlier: Arcadelt, Palestrina, Lasso, de Monte, Rossello, Paolo Animuccia, Barrè himself, Ghiselin Danckerts, Lupacchino, Matelart, Zoilo, Ferro.[7] There is some indication of a connection with Neapolitan musical circles, represented by Nola, Stefano Lando, perhaps youthful works by Lasso, de Monte, and Wert.[8] A few names, such as those of Rore, Ruffo, and Berchem, fit less easily into this picture;[9] there are some composers whose place of activity is unknown to me, and Messer "Incerto" appears more often than one could wish. Nonetheless it appears that Barrè was drawing on a local repertory for much of the music he printed, and these anthologies give a good picture of the madrigal in Rome at mid-century.

The adjective *arioso* seems to have been used chiefly if not exclusively for four-voice madrigals. These pieces are more often than not in the *misura breve* (C) but this is not universal; even after allowing for some carelessness in designating signature on the part of the printer, one sees a mix in the mensural signs and perhaps a mix of *note nere* elements in pieces written in *alla breve* ($\mathvarphi$) mensuration. In many respects the Roman madrigal of the 1550s is an outgrowth of the *note nere* anthologies of the 1540s, with elements of syncopation, use of durational extremes, and declamation on short note values; some of the pieces in Barrè's anthologies would fit comfortably in the Venetian collections of the preceding decade.[10] This is by no means always the case, however, and I think the *madrigale arioso* is not merely the *madrigale cromatico* under a new name. I began work on this repertory expecting to find that the poetry, apart from some canzone cycles given places of honor in the prints, would consist mainly of *ottava* stanzas, on the face of it the most likely form for madrigals which claim to be "aria-like." There are indeed a large number of such stanzas; but one also finds sonnets, canzone stanzas, and madrigals pure and simple. As Einstein has pointed out, these anthologies contain a lot of declamatory writing, much of it in homophonic texture.[11] His remarks are, as is so often the case with anyone studying the madrigal, what stimulated my interest in the first place: a *madrigale arioso* might, I concluded from reading what Einstein says about it, be a piece simulating the declamatory style of the *aria* (as that term was used in the sixteenth century, to mean a more or less stereotyped melodic pattern used as the basis for improvisatory singing of narrative or lyric verse). This might seem to imply monodic performance, with the superius voice accompanied by instruments on the lower parts. For some *madrigali ariosi* such a mode of performance might be suitable, and I suppose it would nearly always be possible; but quite a few of these madrigals suggest instead that in accordance with a common sixteenth-century convention the madrigal is here a polyphonic imitation of, or substitute for, a solo *aria* rather than a monody in polyphonic dress.

Einstein saw something distinctive in this repertory; but I think he may have seen both more and less than is actually there—more in the sense that the anthologies are not as uniform in style as his description would suggest, and less in that he did not go much further than saying that the pieces are declamatory and often homophonic, a thing that could be said about a great many madrigals of the middle of the century. Before I attempt to describe more closely the idiosyncratic elements of the *arioso* madrigal a brief excursus on the word itself is in order.

In the dedicatory letter of the *Primo libro delle Muse a 4* of 1555 Barrè says he has collected some "*madrigaletti*" by various authors, pieces he calls "ariosi e piacevoli."[12] The dedication of the *Libro secondo* of 1558 refers to its contents as "questi Madrigali ariosi, e belli";[13] and this is all Barrè has to say on the term. Either of two sixteenth-century meanings for *arioso*, one being "serene, or limpid," and the other synonomous with an easy, fluent, slightly capricious quality, might do here.[14] Neither of these suggests that Barrè meant anything in particular by the adjective. Petrucci's use of the term *aer* for pieces designed as models, on which any poem of form equivalent to that of the *aer* could be sung, gives possible context for a remark by the frottolist Marchetto Cara that calls a certain kind of music "aierose"; but it is likely that he meant no more than a punning reference to music made out-of-doors as more "airy" than that written indoors.[15] Giovanni Battista Doni's description of enharmonic melodies as lacking qualities he calls "belle ed ariose" implies that *arioso* indicates a natural kind of tunefulness, allied to if not identical with the concept of *aria*.[16] If Barrè used the term in this sense, as

Einstein seems to think he did, he may have been trying to call attention to a particular manner of composition, or he may have simply been claiming that the madrigals in his anthologies were pretty pieces.

Evidence that Barrè meant something more than "novi," "dilettevoli," "bellissimi" by his use of "ariosi" will be looked for in the music itself. But first it might be noted that he used the term not for all his publications but only for the four-voice collections in the *Libri delle Muse* series. A few other musicians of the period seem to have known the term as a special one; the *Canzone* of Rinaldo da Montagnana, published in 1558, contain "alcuni madrigali aierosi"; Stefano Rossetti's *Primo libro* of 1560 is said on its title page to include "Madrigali a quattro voci Insieme alquanti Madregali ariosi."[17] In both prints the *arioso* pieces are specifically designated; and in both volumes these pieces bear close enough resemblance to those in Barrè's anthologies to make one believe that the term may have enjoyed some currency as a description of a recognizable *maniera* in madrigal composition.

To judge from Petrucci's use of the term, *aria* in the first half of the sixteenth century meant melody—a line of such a simple and easily memorizable melodic and rhythmic shape as to make it useful for anyone wanting to sing a poem of his choice, or his composition, and yet one provided with a certain stylishness of detail as well as a solid harmonic foundation in the accompanying parts. If *arioso* means "aria-like" one might look for tunes in Barrè's anthologies. That they are to be found there, either on the surface or tantalizingly veiled, may be demonstrated with a few examples. In the *Primo libro* of 1555 there is a setting by Ghiselin Danckerts of two stanzas from *Orlando furioso,* beginning with the famous line "Ruggier qual sempre fui tal esser voglio" ("Ruggier" is here replaced by "Fedel"; Ariosto's heroic names were often removed in order to give the poetry wider application). Imbedded in Danckerts' somewhat rigid polyphonic structure is an, or perhaps *the,* heroic melody associated with Ariosto's verse, an *aria* from which the *Ruggiero* bass pattern may have evolved (ex. 10.1). Here it acts as a migrant *cantus prius factus* appearing by turns in all the voices. I have written elsewhere about this melody; here I will only say that it is as clear an *aria* as one could wish for.[18] Pieces using this tune appear in the madrigals of Berchem, Corteccia, and a number of other composers, but they are not to be found in Barrè's volumes; Danckerts' piece, surely a *madrigale arioso* in one sense of the term, is unique here.[19] No other madrigal in this repertory shows so clear-cut a use of a preexistent tune.

Example 10.1 Danckerts, "Fedel qual sempre fui tal esser voglio" (Libro 1° [1557[11]], no. 3)

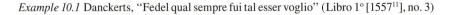

There are, however, abundant hints in Barrè's collections that other *arie* existed and were made use of. In the *Primo libro delle Muse a 5* the place of honor at the beginning of the books is given to Arcadelt's cyclic setting of the Petrarchan canzone "Chiare fresche e dolci acque." This piece was not new in 1555; one of its stanzas had been printed as early as 1542,[20] and it is possible that the whole cycle had been composed by that time. Through the five stanzas of the piece runs a tune, clearly visible (chiefly but not exclusively in the superius) though, unlike Ishtar, never completely unveiled. Example 10.2 shows this melody as it appears in each of the five stanzas. Two phrases of the melody are clearly evident here, separated in

Example 10.2 Arcadelt, "Chiare fresch'e dolci acque" (Libro 1° a 5 [1555²⁶], no. 1)

a. 1ᵃ parte, tenor, mm. 3–9

b. 2ᵃ parte, tenor, mm. 19–27

c. 3ᵃ parte, superius, mm. 1–6

d. 4ᵃ parte, superius, mm. 1–3, 35–40

e. 5ᵃ parte, superius, mm. 1–13

the examples by aspiration signs. The whole of the tune may have been somewhat longer, with intermediate phrases dipping down to G or lower; but these are less clear in Arcadelt's music. In example 10.3 a hypothetical "basic" version of the melody, suitable for singing two heptasyllabic verses or one endecasyllabic line, is offered; it represents what seems basic in the melody not only as Arcadelt uses it but in the work of other composers as well.

Example 10.3 Hypothetical melody

Use of this melodic type may be found in several pieces in Barrè's collections, including a cyclic canzone by the young Palestrina;[21] it shows up in madrigals published during the preceding decade,[22] and it is one of the *arie* used by Berchem (along with the melody given in ex. 10.1) in his *Capricci,* a large collection of settings of stanzas from *Orlando furioso.*[23] In some cases this melody, as well as other melodic formulas for which I am here using the term *aria,* may be found in all voices, but it is most frequently encountered in the superius; this is especially true of Barrè's examples. Although I repeat that this does not necessarily indicate any intention of monodic performance on the composer's part, the *madrigale arioso* does seem to be conceived with the superius in a dominant role (Danckerts' *aria,* cited in ex. 10.1, is a clear exception to this), with occasional passages in near-equal imitative counterpoint providing the exception rather than the norm.

The music in Barrè's *arioso* volumes is grouped rather loosely by mode.[24] Within these groupings one can see use of melodic types which suggests that there might have been *arie* for some of the most often used modes; in other words, composers may have associated certain types of melodic writing with individual modes. This procedure could in part have been instinctive, but there is too much melodic resemblance between works in the same mode by different composers for it to have been an unselfconscious procedure. The connection between mode and melodic formula offered by psalmody was of course in the minds and ears of all these composers, and could have been equally familiar to the *cantastorie* and *improvvisatori* who declaimed verses to music that must have consisted of variations on a small number of basic tunes. What I am suggesting here is that there may have been at this time some well-known melodies (the word used here in the sense of melodic type, subject to much variation in content and even order of phrases) associated with the most popular modes; these were familiar to improvisers as well as to more learned musicians, and indeed the latter may have borrowed these *arie* for their own use, in *madrigali ariosi* among other places.

The term "mode" as used here should not be taken too literally. The melody of example 10.1 as I have encountered it is most often used in, or on, G; but it is occasionally seen in C and in F as well. Example 10.2, though it appears most often in C, turns up fairly often in F, and occasionally in G. Perhaps these melodies are as much hexachord tunes as they are modal *arie,* and examples 10.1 and 10.2 might be

Example 10.4 Barrè, "Dunque fia ver dicea che mi convegna" (first stanza) (Libro 1°
[1557¹¹], no. 1)

called *ut-sol arie;* melodic types using the minor-third modes would then form a
class of *re-la* tunes. But I do not mean to suggest that all these melodies are simply
major or minor in character. In Barrè's volumes there are groups of pieces unified
by mode but not very much else (the pieces ending on A, which I shall call third-
fourth mode, are an example).[25] Pieces on G with one flat, nearly all identifiable as
transposed second mode, on the other hand, show so strong a degree of melodic resemblance that they clearly point to the use of, or derivation from, a common par-
ent melody. Example 10.4, the superius line of the first piece in Barrè's four-part
cycle of contiguous stanzas from *Orlando furioso,* which opens the *Primo libro a 4*
of 1555, shows this *re-la* melodic type. The other three stanzas show considerable
melodic variety; but they share a good deal of material, including a restricted melodic range suggestive of recitation formulas; descending patterns outlining the
pentachord and tetrachord characteristic of the mode; and lines rising from F♯ or G
to B♭ returning to cadence first on F♯, then on G. These materials are freely varied
and freely ordered from piece to piece within Barrè's cycle, but within a single

piece they often show a consistent pattern. In example 10.5 a selection of second-mode melodies drawn from nearly two dozen such pieces in all three books of Barrè's *arioso* anthologies is presented for purposes of comparison with the melodies given in example 10.4.

Example 10.5

a. Tostolo, "Miser in van mi dogl'e mi lamento" (1557[11], no. 10)

b. Ferro, "Quanto più mirar fiso" (1557[11], no. 11)

c. Paolo da Fuligno, "Pensier dicea che'l cor m'agghiacc' et ardi" (1558[13], no. 20)

d. d'Incerto, "Moro sol per amarvi, ah crudel sorte" (1558[13], no. 10)

e. Palestrina, "Perch' al viso d'amor porteva insegna" (1562[7], no. 24)

f. Lasso, "Ben veggio di lontan'il dolce lume" (1562[7], no. 27)

The melodies cited in examples 10.1 and 10.2 had, I am convinced, a real preexistence outside the madrigal. For the melodic lines quoted in examples 10.4 and 10.5 I am less certain that there was any single prototype, although use of recitative-like lines alternating cadences on dominant and final must have been common property among improvisers. The descending tetrachord, the melodic pattern under which the Romanesca bass developed, was certainly in common use, and its pathetic connotations would seem to have been well established, by the middle of the sixteenth century.[26] Whether or not a second-mode *aria* existed as such is not really the point; what is clear is that in these madrigals there is intentional use of aria-like, hence *arioso,* melodic elements.

It is difficult to know how far to go in looking for melodic similarities of this kind. I am aware of the dangers involved, particularly that of mistaking coincidence of resultant detail for coincidence of intent or inspiration. But for this repertory as for much sixteenth-century music there has been little study of melody as such, little effort to establish typologies of melodic design for any genre or period. I submit that analysis done in purely melodic terms would be a useful additional tool for anyone wanting to get a closer understanding of the madrigal; but here I merely suggest one kind of thing to look for, in one subdivision of the madrigal at mid-century—and only for those pieces in which the importance of a single melodic line appears to outweigh that of point-of-imitation contrapuntal procedure.

The most immediately evident trait of the *madrigal arioso* is not melodic but rhythmic. These pieces are full of syncopation, often of the staggered *arsis-thesis* type so evident in the *note nere* madrigal of the 1540s, but even more often carried out in block chords.[27] Use of syncopation to a degree more pronounced than in any other genre was viewed by sixteenth-century writers as a trademark of the madrigal, although this cannot be said to have been true for the genre in every period.[28] Rhythmic displacements can here be seen most characteristically at the minim-semiminim level in pieces signed C, at the semibreve-minim level in those with the signature ₵ (these are not, as I have emphasized elsewhere, the same thing written in two different ways but rather an indication of tempo, somewhat slower for the first category than for the second).[29]

Sometimes this syncopation is used as a means of setting off the beginnings of poetic lines, as if the singers were emphasizing the poetic divisions by taking audible breaths (ex. 10.6), a technique surely reminiscent of improvisatory performance.[30] Often an entire line, especially an eleven-syllable line, is set in strongly declamatory syncopated style. This is particularly noticeable at the beginnings of pieces, but in some madrigals it can be seen in almost every line.

Example 10.7 shows one of the most common of these patterns, repeated with little change in a surprising number of the *arioso* madrigals.[31] Patterns like this are not found for the first time in Barrè's anthologies. Cipriano de Rore made use of them, as example 10.8 shows, although Rore's use of such declamatory rhythms is not in my judgment as frequent or pronounced as Einstein would have it.[32] They may also be found in the madrigals of Gero and other contributors to the *note nere* anthologies,[33] as well as in prints of the 1540s devoted to the works of single composers. In the repertory assembled by Barrè this kind of

Example 10.6 Paolo Animuccia, "La fiamm' ove tutt' ardo" (1558[13], no. 13)

Example 10.7 Nola, "Tosto ch'il sol si scopr' in oriente" (1557[11], no. 16)

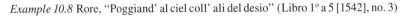

Example 10.8 Rore, "Poggiand' al ciel coll' ali del desio" (Libro 1° a 5 [1542], no. 3)

declamatory pattern becomes a pronounced mannerism, surely meant to call attention to itself. It is mannered not only in its frequency but also because the declamatory rhythms, while they give support to the scansion of the poetic lines, do not always or necessarily emphasize the most important words, but rather sound like one way, out of several, of reading the lines aloud. Even when all voices move in these rhythms their syncopated pull against the tactus can be felt, and the resolution of tension at the end of the line is clearly audible. The use of rhythmic groupings such as 3 + 3 + 2 inside a 4 + 4 framework is of course common throughout the whole two-century period we call the Renaissance, but its aim and effect are in this repertory not the achieving of rhythmic counterpoint but a declamatory ebb and flow of length and stress.

Other uses of syncopation may be noticed in these pieces. One that is of special interest is a calculated anticipation of the beat, a kind of ragtime effect often but not always part of a cadential progression, sometimes but not inevitably part of the [♩] ♩ ♪ ♪ | ♩ ♪ ♪ 3 + 3 + 2 series (ex. 10.9).[34] When all the voices do this at once the effect is one of suspension of the beat, though I would maintain that the tactus is still meant to be felt; when, as sometimes happens, the lowest voice or pair of voices moves on the beat, a kind of rubato is created.

What have these syncopations to do with the *arioso* quality of this music? I suggest that their intention is deliberate, an attempt to get into written form a freely declamatory improvisatory quality; in other words, the composers are trying to capture something of the manner of performance an *improvvisatore* might have used in declaiming narrative or lyric verse over a simple accompaniment. Nino Pirrotta has written that the early composers of the *villanella* "set out to recapture in its upper line the manner and mannerisms of popular singers";[35] here something of the same quality has been transferred to the "serious"

Example 10.9 Maresio, "Hor ved' Amor che giovanetta donna" (1562[7], no. 31)

madrigal. Whether this means that the *arioso* style is of Southern origin I am not sure. As we have seen, a number of the composers represented by Barrè's anthologies were active in Naples in the 1540s and 1550s; and at least one text, set by Nola in Barrè's *Primo libro* of 1555, is mentioned by a Neapolitan chronicler as having been a popular song in Naples.[36] The idea of a Naples-Rome current in the madrigal, running counter to the Venetian manner represented by Willaert and his pupils, gives an added dimension to the picture of the mid-century madrigal.

In their use of stock melodic patterns and their choice of freely declamatory rhythmic patterns, these pieces would seem to have a special, popularesque character that justifies Barrè's use of the term *arioso*. Not every piece in the anthologies shows these characteristics to an equal degree, and some madrigals are in this respect "fillers" (or, as in the case of Rore's "Ben quì si mostr' il ciel," the opening piece in the *Terzo libro* of 1562, included because of the composer's fame). The fact that major composers such as Lasso, Wert, and Palestrina are not only represented in these collections but contribute pieces in recognizable if not extreme *arioso* style gives the repertory more than passing significance, and in the case of Palestrina alters somewhat our view of this composer as a docile follower of Arcadelt's manner whenever he wrote madrigals.[37] The mannerisms of the *arioso* style subsided in the music of the next generation but did not altogether disappear. What was gained in the experiments of this group of composers was above all rhythmic flexibility, freeing the madrigal from the regular chansonesque declamatory patterns imposed on it by Verdelot, Festa, and the earlier work of Arcadelt—without recourse to the heavily contrapuntal style of Willaert. New patterns of rhythmic regularity could be, and in fact were to be, imposed as the century went on;[38] but the possibility of freer, quasi-improvisatory declamation remained as a technical and expressive resource in the later development of the madrigal.

POSTSCRIPT

If I were writing this study now I would try to draw some broader conclusions about connections, or lack of them, between the arioso style and other homophonic or near-homophonic textures in the later sixteenth-century madrigal. The early work of Giaches de Wert is heavily marked by text-driven arioso writing; on this see now Howard Mayer Brown, "Petrarch in Naples: Notes on the Formation of Giaches de Wert's Style," *Altro Polo: Essays on Italian Music in the Cinquecento,* ed. Richard Charteris (Sydney, 1990), 16–50, and his "Verso una definizione dell'armonia nel sedicesimo secolo: sui 'Madrigali ariosi' di Antonio Barrè," *RIM* 25 (1990): 18–60. Wert never completely abandoned this style, and his younger contemporaries and successors used it from time to time as well. For Monteverdi's debt to Wert in this regard see Gary Tomlinson, *Monteverdi and the End of the Renaissance* (Berkeley and Los Angeles, 1987), especially chapters 2–3. A stunning example of arioso writing after 1600 is "Vi ricordi o boschi ombrosi" in Monteverdi's *Orfeo,* which evokes the tradition of the *improvvisatori* shared by the frottolists of ca. 1500, the arioso madrigalists of ca. 1550, and the *balletto* of the end of the sixteenth century.

But what has been described as arioso writing in the later works of Wert and the Ferrarese madrigalists of the turn of the century (and Marenzio as well) is in my judgment something rather different, namely, use of dance-driven canzonetta rhythms, based on subdivisions of a steady beat rather than on additive textual flow. The result may be deceptively similar but the impetus is not the same. *Musique mesurée* on the other hand may owe a real if unacknowledged debt to arioso writing; here the art of the *improvvisatori* is formalized into pseudo-classical posture.

On Antonio Barrè see John Steele, "Antonio Barrè: Madrigalist, Anthologist and Publisher. Some Preliminary Findings," *Altro Polo,* 82–112. The printing history of Barrè's madrigal books is clarified in Maureen Buja, "Antonio Barrè and Music Printing in Mid-Sixteenth Century Rome" (Ph.D. diss., University of North Carolina, Chapel Hill, 1996). For a discussion of *ut-re-mi* tonalities in theory and practice see Cristle Collins Judd, "Modal Types and *Ut-Re-Mi* Tonalities: Tonal Coherence in Sacred Vocal Polyphony from about 1500," *JAMS* 45 (1992): 418–67.

NOTES

1. See Thomas Bridges, "Barrè, Antonio," *New Grove,* 2:180–81. Barrè signed as one of the witnesses to the exactness of the sentence of judgment in the debate between Vicentino and Lusitano (7 June 1551), as this sentence was printed in Vicentino's *L'Antica Musica.* See Nicola Vicentino, *L'Antica Musica ridotta alla moderna prattica* (Rome, 1555; facsimile, ed. Edward E. Lowinsky, Kassel, 1959), fol. 98v; cf. Henry W. Kaufmann, *The Life and Works of Nicola Vicentino (1511–c. 1576)* (American Institute of Musicology, 1966), 22–23.

In 1552 Barrè's *Madrigali a quattro voci libro primo* was published in Rome by Valerio and Luigi Dorico. This volume contains settings of a good deal of little-known poetry, probably of local origin (including the opening madrigal, a piece serving as dedicatory poem and addressed to the Roman jurist Honofrio Vigili). Only now and then do the madrigals of this collection suggest the style of the *madrigale arioso.* RISM 1555[27], the first edition of the *Primo libro delle Muse a 4vv,* contains two other occasional poems set by Barrè (omitted from the subsequent editions of the print); see Vogel, 2:644–45. I have been unable to obtain a microfilm copy of this first edition; musical examples in this paper are cited from the edition of 1557 made by Gardano in Venice.

2. Barrè was apparently both printer and publisher for a time, although at the beginning and end of his commercial career he may have been merely a printer. He had his own type for the *Libri delle Muse* and some other music prints; but he borrowed type from Antonio Blado in 1560 and 1563; from Dorico in 1564; and his edition of Vicentino's *L'Antica Musica* of 1555 has a colophon reading "Stampato in Roma appresso Antonio Barre, a instantia di don Nicola Vicentino," indicating that Vicentino paid for the work and that Barrè was only its printer. The date of this volume is 22 May 1555; if the *Primo libro delle Muse a 5vv* was re-

ally, as Barrè says in his dedication (again to Honofrio Vigili), "Le primitie della mia stampa," it must have been printed before 22 May of that year.

3. The series of *Libri delle Muse* is as follows:

A. For four voices
1. RISM 1555[27]: *Primo libro delle Muse a 4 vv / Madrigali ariosi di Ant. Barre et altri diversi autori . . .*, Rome: Barrè, 1555. This volume was reprinted by Gardano and other Venetian printers over a thirty-year span; see RISM 1557[17], 1558[12], 1559[18], Vogel, 1562[3], RISM 1565[10], 1569[21], 1578[20], 1582[7], 1584[6].
2. RISM 1558[13]: *Secondo libro delle Muse a 4vv / Madrigali ariosi, de diversi eccell[mi] autori, con doe canzoni di Giannetto . . .*, Rome, Barrè, 1558. Reprints: RISM 1559[17] (Scotto), 1560[10] (Gardano).
3. RISM 1562[7]: *Il terzo libro delle Muse a 4vv / Madrigali ariosi, da diversi eccell. musici raccolti . . .*, Rome, Barrè, 1562. Reprint: RISM 1563[9] (Rampazzetto).

B. For five voices
1. RISM 1555[26]: *Primo libro delle Muse a 5vv / Madrigali de diversi authori,* Rome, Barrè, 1555. Reprints: RISM 1555[25] (Gardano), 1561[8] (Scotto).
2. RISM 1557[22]: *Secondo libro delle Muse a 5vv / Madrig. d'Orlandus di Lassus con una Canzone del Petrarca,* Rome, Barrè, 1557. Reprints: RISM 1559[16] (Gardano), 1561[9] (Scotto). These differ in contents from Barrè's print.
3. RISM 1561[10]: *Il terzo libro delle Muse a 5vv . . .*, Venice, Gardano, 1561. Reprints: RISM 1569[18] (Gardano), 1580[9] (Gardano).
4. RISM 1574[4]: *Il quarto libro delle Muse a 5vv,* Venice, li figl. di Antonio Gardano, 1574. Reprints: RISM 1582[6] (Gardano).
5. RISM 1575[12]: *Il quinto libro delle Muse a 5vv,* Venice, Gardano, 1575.

C. For three voices
1. RISM 1562[8]: *Il primo libro delle Muse a 3vv . . .*, Venice, Scotto, 1562. Presumably there was an earlier edition, now lost, from the press of Barrè.
2. Vogel, 1555[5]: *Secondo libro delle Muse a 3vv / Canzoni Moresche di diversi Aut. . . .*, Rome, Barrè, 1555 [not listed in RISM].
3. RISM 1557[20]: *Secondo libro delle Muse a 3vv / Canzon Villanesche alla Napolitana . . .*, Rome, Barrè, 1557.
4. RISM [S 2624. *Il secondo libro delle Muse a 3vv / Madrigali di Girolamo Scotto . . .*, Venice, Scotto, 1562.
   There are thus three different volumes all called *Secondo libro delle Muse.*
5. RISM 1562[9]: *Il terzo libro delle Muse a 3vv / Canzon francese di Adrian Willaert . . .*, Venice, Scotto, 1562.

D. Motets
1. RISM 1563[3]: *Liber primus Musarum cum 4vv . . . ab Antonio Barrè collectarum . . .*, Venice, Rampazzetto, 1563. It would appear that Barrè edited this collection for Rampazzetto.

4. The only volumes printed by Barrè himself at or after this time are Lasso's *Terzo libro a 5vv* (1563), for which type borrowed from Blado was used, and Olivier Brassart's *Primo libro a 4vv* (1564), printed with type borrowed from Dorico. See Suzanne Cusick, "Valerio Dorico, Music Printer in Sixteenth-Century Rome" (Ph.D. diss., University of North Carolina, Chapel Hill, 1975), 39.

5. The word *arioso* appears in the following prints: Rinaldo da Montagnana, *Della Canzone . . . con alcuni Madrigali aierosi a 4vv* (Scotto, 1558); Stephano Rossetti, *Il Primo Li-*

bro de Madrigali a 4vv Insieme alquanti Madregali ariosi (Gardano, 1560); Lancilotto Fidelis, *Il Primo Libro di Madrigali aerosi a 4vv* (Gardano, 1570); *Il Turturino. Il Primo Libro delle napolitane ariose da cantare et sonare nel leuto . . . per . . . Cornelio Antonelli da Rimino detto il Turturino* (Scotto, 1570); Giovan Piero Manenti, *Madrigali Ariosi a Quattro* (Gardano, 1586); Spirito Pratoneri, *Madrigali ariosi . . . a 4vv* (Venice: Vincenzi, 1587). Of these only the first two are closely related in style to the contents of Barrè's *arioso* volumes.

In Andrea Gabrieli's *Canzoni alla francese et ricercari ariosi, Libro quinto* (Venice, 1605) the last four pieces are called "ricercar arioso"; they would appear to be based on chansons rather than madrigals. I am grateful to Giulio Ongaro for calling these pieces to my attention.

6. For some uses of the term in the early eighteenth century see Jack Westrup, "Arioso," *New Grove,* 1:582.

7. Biographical information on these composers may be found in the relevant articles in *New Grove.* Arcadelt was no longer in Rome by the mid-1550s; the length of time spent there by Lasso and de Monte is not known precisely, though both were in Rome between 1552 and 1554. Many though not all of these composers were associated with the Sistine or Julian Chapels or served at San Giovanni in Laterano. Some, like Matelart and Zoilo, were young men just beginning their careers when these anthologies were published. Vincenzo Ferro may have been a friend of Barrè; he was one of those who signed in testimony of the exactness of the *sententia* against Vicentino as it appeared in the latter's *L'Antica Musica;* see above n. 1.

8. Other Neapolitan composers represented in these volumes include Luigi Dentice and, judging from his name, possibly Lerma.

9. The "Giaches de Ferrara" mentioned in Luigi Dentice, *Due Dialoghi della Musica* (Naples, 1552) is presumably Wert but could possibly be Berchem. See Carol MacClintock, *Giaches de Wert (1535–1596): Life and Works* (American Institute of Musicology, 1966), 23n.

10. On the "black-note" madrigal see chapter 9. The Venetian anthologies of Gardano and Scotto have been edited by Don Harrán, *The Anthologies of Black-Note Madrigals,* 5 vols. (American Institute of Musicology, 1978–81). Harrán's informative introduction to the first of these volumes contains references to his other writings on the subject.

11. Einstein, *Italian Madrigal,* 208, 645.

12. The letter is given in full by Luigi Werner, "Una rarità musicale della Biblioteca Vescovile di Szombathely," *Note d'archivio per la storia musicale* 8 (1931): 95.

13. In the dedication of RISM 1558[13] Barrè says to Monsignor Monaldo Monaldeschi de la Cervara, the dedicatee, "ho voluto sotto l'honorato nome di V. S. questi Madrigali ariosi, e belli . . . dare in luce."

14. For the first definition see Salvatore Battaglia, "arioso, 2," in *Grande Dizionario della lingua italiana* (Turin, 1961), 1:658; for the second see Carlo Battisti and Giovanni Alessio, "arioso, 3," in *Dizionario etimologico italiano* (Florence, 1950–57), 1:289.

15. Mantua, Archivio di Stato, Autografi Busta 6 contains a letter of Cara to Federico Gonzaga, dated 15 September 1514, in which Cara regrets being unable to come to the country and set some poetry discovered by Federico at a *mercato* in Gonzago, material as yet unprinted; Cara acknowledges that "le cose composte in su la val de la marzetta sono molto più aierose de quelle composte in camera." The letter is given in full in William F. Prizer, *Courtly Pastimes: The Frottole of Marchetto Cara* (Ann Arbor, 1980), appendix 1, document 101, page 294.

16. Giovanni Battista Doni, "Due Trattati," in *Lyra Barberina,* vol. 1 (1763 [written in the 1630s]), 4:292: "Consistono [le melodie enarmoniche] in intervalli estremi, cioè molto

piccoli e molto grandi, e però tanto è più difficile con essi comporre melodie belle ed ariose."

17. Rossetti's volume has been edited by Allen B. Skei, in RRMR, vol. 26. Five pieces in the volume are designated "arioso"; they have, in varying degrees, the melodic and rhythmic qualities described in the present study as typical of this subgenre of the madrigal. Particularly striking in its resemblance to works in Barrè's collection is Rossetti's no. 22, "Dolce foco d'Amor," a second-mode *aria* (see below on pieces of this kind).

18. James Haar, "Arie per cantar stanze ariostesche," in *L'Ariosto: La Musica, I Musicisti* (Florence, 1981), 41–43. The melodic character of Danckert's piece is noted in a general way by Einstein, *Italian Madrigal,* 645.

19. Danckerts wrote a four-stanza cycle on another famous section of *Orlando furioso* (32.40–43). Only the superius of this composition survives; in the first stanza the melody cited above in example 10.1 is used as a two-line *aria,* to be repeated four times. See James Haar, "Madrigals from Three Generations: The Ms. Brussels, Bibl. du Conservatoire royal 27.731," *RIM* 10 (1975): 248–50.

Barrè and Danckerts evidently knew each other personally; Barrè's testimony as witness to the Lusitano-Vicentino debate (see n. 1) was given to Danckerts and included in his *Trattato . . . sopra una differentia musicale.* It is curious all the same to see Danckerts, who disapproved of the *note nere* innovations, and also of the new vogue for note-against-note writing, contributing a piece in C mensuration to a volume full of homophonic pieces. See chapter 9 above; cf. Claude Palisca, "A Clarification of 'Musica Reservata' in Jean Taisnier's 'Astrologiae'," *Acta Musicologica* 31 (1959): 138. On Danckert's treatise see Lewis Lockwood, "A Dispute on Accidentals in Sixteenth-Century Rome," *Analecta Musicologica* 2 (1965): 24–40.

20. Stanza three, for three voices, appeared in RISM 1551[10], an anthology of three-voice madrigals; stanza four, for four voices, was printed by Gardane in 1542[17], the first of the *note nere* anthologies. The cycle is printed in Einstein, *Italian Madrigal,* 3:52, and in Albert Seay, ed., *Jacobi Arcadelt. Opera Omnia,* vol. 7 (American Institute of Musicology, 1969), nos. 30, 54.

21. Bembo's "Voi mi ponest' in foco," a four-stanza cycle, no. 1 in the *Libro secondo a 4vv* (1558[13]). Curiously, but perhaps understandably, Palestrina's setting of "Chiare fresch' e dolc'acque," number 25 in the same volume, does not use this melody. Other madrigals in the *Libro secondo* which show use of this *aria* include no. 2, Lerma's "Fra bei Ginepr' e mirti," and no. 15, Matelart's setting of "S'Amor crudel irato à darmi morte."

22. In the *Primo libro a misura di breve* (1542[17]) use of this melody can be seen in nos. 4 (Berchem, "Chi vuol veder") and 13 (Naich, "Benchè la donna mia," mm. 44ff); in 1543[17], a reprint of the *Primo libro,* no. 18 (attributed to Naich but actually by Nola), "Proverbio ama chi t'ama," is another example. Arcadelt's "Tra freddi monti," no. 17 in Gardano's *Vero terzo libro a note negre* (1549[31]), uses the *aria* at the end to declaim a line of quoted direct speech.

Many examples of the use of this melody can be found in prints of the works of individual composers at this time. As one example, there are three (nos. 2, 9, 11) in the *Secondo libro di li madrigali a 4vv* (Venice, 1548) of Gabriello Martinengo.

23. It is very prominent at the opening of Berchem's huge cycle. See Dale Hall, "The Italian Secular Vocal Works of Jacquet Berchem" (Ph.D. diss., Ohio State University, 1973), appendix, nos. 24–25 (the opening two stanzas of the cycle). One should also note that Berchem uses the second-mode lament *aria* (see below) in his cycle; see numbers 29–33 in Hall's appendix.

24. In the *Primo libro,* for example, the opening four-stanza cycle (the order is given as found in the edition of 1557[17] and its reprints) is in transposed second mode; there follow six

madrigals in G mode, six more in transposed first-second modes, five in modes 3–4 (ending on A; no flat), three in F mode, and a final four in transposed first-second mode.

Groupings of pieces by mode was common in madrigal and motet prints, particularly those issued by Gardano, in this period. For a stimulating discussion of modal groups in sixteenth-century music, see Harold S. Powers, "Tonal Types and Modal Categories in Renaissance Polyphony," *JAMS* 34 (1981): 428–70.

25. Examples are those from the first book listed above, n. 24; nos. 8–9 of book 2, and nos. 3–6 of book 3.

26. On the long-observed custom of singing the verses of Petrarch and Ariosto to *arie* or *modi* of determined pattern see Gioseffo Zarlino, *Le istitutioni harmoniche*, 3.lxxix; on the differing expressive character of *modi* in mid-sixteenth-century Lombardy and Naples see Alessandro Piccolomini, *De la institutione di tutta la vita de l'homo nato nobile e in città libera* (Venice: Scotto, 1542), fol. 50v, cited in Donna Cardamone, "The 'Canzoni Villanesca alla Napolitana' and Related Italian Vocal Part-Music: 1537 to 1570" (Ph.D. diss., Harvard University, 1972), 348.

27. What Vicentino calls the *inganno* or trick of having imitative entries in close succession on downbeat and upbeat is mentioned in his *L'Antica Musica*, 4.42. fol. 88v. Syncopation in one or two voices against a steady beat in others is cited by Harrán, *Anthologies of Black-Note Madrigals*, 1.lvii, as a particular feature of the music of Naich, a Roman composer of the 1540s. Syncopation of this kind is quite common in the *note nere* anthologies; that of the block-chord variety is also to be found, if not quite so often.

28. See, for example, the remark of Pietro Pontio at the end of his *Ragionamento di Musica* (Parma, 1588), 160: "Vi fo anco sapere, che il suo proprio [the madrigal's] è di fargli delle Semiminime assai, e anco delle Minime in sincopa. Sappiate ancora, che spesse volte le parti debbono andare ugualmente insieme, con moto però veloce di Minime over de Semiminime."

29. See chapter 9, p. 203.

30. This kind of syncopation at the beginning of a phrase is typical of the *note nere* madrigal as well; the difference in the *madrigali ariosi* is the frequency with which all voices (as they do in ex. 10.6) observe this initial syncopated breath.

31. This pattern is used exactly as in example 10.7 in a number of pieces; with some small variants it occurs in at least two-thirds of the madrigals in Barrè's *arioso* anthologies.

32. Einstein, *Italian Madrigal*, 419ff.

33. Examples by Naich, Arcadelt, Corteccia, Gero, Hoste da Reggio, and Ruffo may be seen in Harrán, *Anthologies of Black-Note Madrigals*, vol. 1, nos. 11, 14, 25, 47; vol. 2, nos. 9, 14, 21, 26; vol. 3, nos. 6, 9, 13, 27.

This kind of syncopation is quite different from the dance-like rhythms of frottola settings, even though the latter show use of some of the same devices.

34. Other pieces showing pronounced use of this technique of anticipating the beat (at the beginning of a phrase or in mid-phrase) include Barrè's "Non è pena maggior cortesi amanti," Vincenzo Ferro's "Quanto più miro fiso," Lupacchino's "Il dolce sonno mi promesse pace," Alexandrino's "Sia vile agli altri e da quel sol amata," and Ruffo's "Come nave ch'in mezzo all'onde sia," all from the *Primo libro*.

35. "Early Opera and Aria," in *New Looks at Italian Opera: Essays in Honor of Donald J. Grout,* ed. William W. Austin (Ithaca, N.Y., 1968), 61.

36. "Tosto che'l sol si scopre in oriente," mentioned among a large number of pieces said to have been popular in late sixteenth-century Naples, in Giovanni Battista del Tuffo, *Ritratto ò modello delle grandezze, delicizie, e maraviglie della nobilissima città di Napoli* (manuscript of 1588), fol. 210; cited in Cardamone, "The 'Canzone Villanesca'," 240, 243.

37. Peter Wagner, "Das Madrigal und Palestrina," *Vierteljahrsschrift für Musikwis-*

senschaft 8 (1892): 442–43, speaks of Palestrina's early madrigals as showing the "Gestalt" of the madrigal in Rome in the second third of the sixteenth century; but he does not analyze or describe this "Gestalt." Einstein stresses the derivative character of Palestrina's early madrigals; see *Italian Madrigal,* 311ff. He is, to be fair, speaking here of Palestrina's *Primo libro* of 1555; but he does not acknowledge the contribution of Palestrina to the *arioso* repertory even though he praises (pp. 437–38) the contribution of the two cycles in Barrè's *Libro secondo.*

Palestrina's three pieces in Barrè's *Terzo libro* (1562[7]), which are highly characteristic of *arioso* style, are not well known to modern scholars since Franz Haberl in his edition of Palestrina's work (Leipzig, 1862–1907) gives them incomplete, with bass and tenor parts only (they survive complete in the reprint of 1563[9], but this was not known to Haberl nor to Einstein when he wrote *The Italian Madrigal*); Raffaele Casimiri's edition (Rome, 1939–) does not contain them at all.

38. Ruth I. DeFord, "The Evolution of Rhythmic Style in Italian Secular Music of the Late Sixteenth-Century," *SM* 10 (1981): 43–74.

Giovanthomaso Cimello as Madrigalist

THE GREAT MADRIGALISTS of the mid and late sixteenth century, composers such as Rore, Lasso, Wert, and Marenzio, must have impressed their contemporaries as much, if not necessarily in the same way, as they do now. They gave musical distinction and stylistic direction to the genre; their settings of cinquecento verse are often readings that are not only rhetorically affective but powerfully interpretive, more satisfying intellectually as well as emotionally than most of the genre-obsessed literary commentary of the day. In its beginnings in the third decade of the century, the madrigal was simpler stylistically and less ambitious in aesthetic aim; the work of the Florentine-Roman composers of the 1520s and 1530s is *musica per poesia per musica,* differing in style but not essentially in level from the art of the frottolists.[1] The early madrigalists were competent musicians, and in the case of Arcadelt at least, something more than that; but they worked within limits imposed by their own backgrounds and by the expectations of their patrons.

As the madrigal spread throughout, even beyond the Italian peninsula, a progress made easy by the successful enterprise of the Venetian publishers Antonio Gardano and Girolamo Scotto, musicians of varying degrees of talent and skill tried their hand at it, responding to the literary tastes of the circles they moved in and imitating the models made available to them in print. Alfred Einstein's great survey of the madrigal groups minor composers around its most important figures, a method inevitable for a scholar of his generation and in essence still a defensible one. The breadth of his knowledge, acuteness of his insight, and generosity of his spirit give his work continuing validity. But Einstein is often less than generous, even less than fair, to composers he judged to be beneath the first rank. And in the great expanse of the cinquecento madrigal there are far more circles, spreading out from local epicenters, than even Einstein could account for. One of these, a mid-century group around Giovanthomaso Cimello, is the subject of this article.

Composers like Cimello, who were not located in cosmopolitan centers or in the service of wealthy and sophisticated patrons, did what they could. They admired and imitated from afar; yet they were free to express individuality of thought and manner. In Italian music there was as yet no one like Michelangelo, a figure to over-awe all sculptors who followed. The work of musicians responding to Rore, or perhaps still to Arcadelt, was rather like that of sixteenth-century poets to Petrarch, Ariosto, or later to Tasso; they could imitate where and how they chose, without undue regard for their own position on the scale of greatness.[2]

Giovanthomaso Cimello (ca. 1510–after 1579) was a Neapolitan musician chiefly known today as a villanellist, only natural since the *villanella* was mid-century Naple's distinctive contribution to musical literature. The contents of his

Canzone villanesche al modo napolitano a tre voci (1545) are discussed by Einstein and, more fully, by Donna Cardamone.[3] They are musically very typical of the genre as practiced by G. T. di Maio, G. D. da Nola, and other contemporary Neapolitans. The texts are also characteristic; if Cimello wrote all or even some of them he understood the *villanella* very well. If he is the author of the *battaglia villanesca* that closes the volume he knew the battle pieces of Jannequin, perhaps of Werrecore, and of their imitators;[4] he also knew how to incorporate the required onomatopoetic nonsense into the texts, for his three peasant soldiers, with money to burn and full of comic-heroic boasts, brag that "in singing they know how to counterfeit trumpets, drums, even artillery":

> Venimo tre soldati / per spender molto in esser allogiate / e siamo tutti tali / che ben montamo sopra selli armati / e con stocchi e pugnali / provati in molte rotte / damo de ponta le migliori botte. / Corremo grosse lancie / et affrontamo presto / e cantando sapemo contrafare / tamburri trombe artiglieria e fischiare / e vi'l faremo qua sentir mo presto. / Pati pati pata / ben haggia chiuca che sta qua / faine fan faine fre le laron / de chi desio fossi'io patron / von von von von fossi io patron / pon pon pon pon / deh che l'havess' io mo / tricque tricque tricque / di ti chiù cruda mai nacque / ta ra rira / beata chi n'allogiarà.[5]

It is however with Cimello as serious madrigalist that we will be concerned here. His single volume of madrigals, issued by Gardano in 1548 and apparently never reprinted, may not have attracted much attention outside local circles, although Gardano thought well enough of one piece, "Non è lasso martire" (no. 9) to reprint it in his *Vero terzo libro . . . a note negre* of 1549.[6] The book has nonetheless a number of features that Cimello meant to be attention-getting, perhaps to serve as a model for composers under his influence to imitate.[7]

Before getting to the contents of this book it might be well to give some evidence that Cimello was indeed regarded as a kind of local authority. A minor cleric, apparently married in earlier life since he mourns the death of a son in his madrigal volume and since in an autograph letter (see below) he speaks openly of the latter's progeny, Cimello seems never to have held a permanent post in Naples, though he was for a short time paid as a teacher of grammar and music in Benevento, in the Neapolitan *regno*. He was attached, or tried to attach himself, to the entourage of Giovanna D'Aragona, the estranged wife of Ascanio Colonna (his madrigal volume is dedicated to two of her sons). It is at Giovanna's court in Naples in the 1540s that we first hear of him, a reference in a preface by the grammarian Domenico Gamucci.[8] Here we learn that Cimello had written a set of *regole* on music and grammar, and was angry over losing them by theft.[9] He seems indeed to have been both poet and musician, in a small way justifying the assertion in a seventeenth-century book on the antiquities of the town of Arpino that he was a "man celebrated for music and for poetry."[10]

In the *Primo libro* of four-voice motets (1547) by the Neapolitan organist Giovanni Giacomo Lucario, possibly Cimello's pupil, there is an *Alma redemptoris mater* by Cimello; there is also a set of Latin hexameters, addressed to Lucario, from Cimello's pen.[11] Two of the texts in his own madrigal volume are by Cimello;

another Latin epigram appeared in a Neapolitan collection of Latin verse published in 1551.[12] In that same year Cimello contributed a poem to Lusitano's *Epigrammatum que vulgo motetta dicuntur.*[13] The autograph letter mentioned above contains references to Cimello's Latin and vernacular poetry and in particular to a book of *sonetti spirituali,* another of *epigrammi per spirituali,* and to a poem in *terza rima* entitled *Le Notte delle streghe,* on which he worked for a long time, doing research on witchcraft in and around Benevento.[14]

More music by Cimello appeared in volumes by Marc' Antonio di Maio (1551) and Francesco Sorrentino (1560), the latter an avowed student of Cimello.[15] Others who claim Cimello as teacher include Giglio Napoletano, G. B. Martinelli, and Giulio Belli.[16] His name survives into the seventeenth century, known to Orazio di Caposelo, who in 1623 refers to him as a "learned and excellent musician."[17] In addition to the *regole* on grammar and music Cimello wrote a short treatise, *Della perfettione delle quattro note maggiori massima, longa, breve, semibreve,* in which he says he follows in the tradition of Tinctoris and Gafori both of whom he associated with Naples, adding that he had met "at some time" a number of musical celebrities, including Ottaviano de' Petrucci.[18]

Finally, in a somewhat rambling letter addressed to Cardinal Guglielmo Sirleto in Rome and dated 13 December 1579, Cimello gives, in defensive and occasionally selfpitying language, a good deal of information about himself. The letter, published by Casimiri and also in an obscure turn-of-the-century book on Palestrina, is interesting enough to cite in full; it is given in an appendix to this article.[19]

From this account we learn that Cimello had spent some time in Rome; the "signori grandi" he says he served must have been members of the Colonna family.[20] There he had been treated as an enemy by a former friend, the composer Annibale Zoilo; he had since written some kind of treatise dealing with plainchant reform (elements of this, along with the *trentaquattro fughe* he mentions in connection with it, are to be found in a Neapolitan manuscript containing a miscellaneous group of Cimello's writings)[21] which he hoped Zoilo, said to be in charge of the task of reforming the chant, would be willing to look at.[22] Having returned to his native town of Montesangiovanni for reasons of health, he found his son determined on a military career, one in which he perished leaving Cimello in charge of five [grand]sons, all by the time of the letter ready and willing to be of service to the Cardinal.

In Naples at some point—the chronology of this letter is impossible to fix, and it seems that Cimello is recounting episodes from various parts of his life—he arranged for the printing of "tante . . . opre nove di Musica." This may or may not refer to the two volumes that survive today. In any event his *regole nove,* which were never printed and which he said at one point (see above, and n. 9) had been stolen from him, he claims to have been of wide use in correcting composers' errors. Even "Orlando" [di Lasso?] came and studied them; this is hard to believe unless it refers to the young Lasso's period of residence in Naples in the late 1540s.[23]

Despite his service to "signori grandi," presumably Marc' Antonio Colonna's establishment, Cimello could not, he says, find any dedicatees to favor, or underwrite, his works, most of which remained unpublished. He was nonetheless ready to place his experience and talent, known to many in Rome, at the service of the Cardinal and even to come to Rome; meanwhile he arranged to send some music with the letter, untested in performance since he was living in a remote place with no trained singers—where "non si conosce l'Antifonario." The pieces were to be tried out, he suggests, by a group of musicians led by "ms. Alessandro," perhaps the singer-instrumentalist-composer Alessandro Romano.[24]

Letters in this mixed vein of boasting and self-pity are not rare; sixteenth-century *poligrafi* like Antonfrancesco Doni and Lodovico Domenichi, men who lived by their wits and their ready pens, wrote them all too often.[25] Many such hangers-on in cinquecento society were dabblers in all the arts, including music as one of their sidelines; Cimello is exceptional in being a trained or at least self-taught musician who cultivated a taste and had some sort of talent for literature. From his case we may learn that composers of the time could and occasionally did write their own verses, a practice for which additional hard evidence is always welcome. We also learn, from his references to Tinctoris as well as from the testimony of local students and colleagues, that there was something of a Neapolitan school, one which looked to Rome as a center but had its own traditions as well, flourishing in the mid-sixteenth century—the period of the young Lasso's residence in Naples and subsequent move to Rome.

Cimello seems to have had a strong pedagogical bent. This is evident from remarks made about him by other musicians (see above), from the rough manuscript treatises by him which survive, and from his madrigal print. Turning to the latter, we might first examine the title, a characteristically idiosyncratic one. Like the Florentine Mattio Rampollini he chooses a "correct" designation, separating texts from musical settings: DI *GIOVANTHOM. CIMELLO / LIBRO PRIMO DE CANTI A QUATRO VOCI / Sopra Madriale & altre Rime Con li Nomi delli loro authori volgari & con le / Più grande necessarie osservanze instromentali, e più convenevoli avvertenze / De toni accio si possono anchora Sonare, / & Cantare insieme.*[26]

In the volume Cimello distinguishes between madrigals and other kinds of verse such as sonnets and ottava stanzas. His choice of spelling is also deliberate. *Madriale* had been in use among trecento writers such as Sacchetti; more important, it is the spelling used by Pietro Bembo in the *Prose della vulgar lingua,* a work the self-consciously literate Cimello must have known.[27] Next, Cimello promises to give the names of the poets, a rare and gratifying departure from practice customary in his time, and again the mark of a *littérateur*.[28] After that comes an odd bit of phraseology, promising "osservanze instromentali" and "avvertenze" useful and necessary for combined vocal and instrumental performance. At first I thought that the single surviving copy of Cimello's print must simply be lacking these rubrics, an opinion shared by Einstein.[29] But nothing seems to be missing in the print; Gardano usually gave what his titles promised; and the madrigal volume of Marc' Antonio di Maio, a work probably influenced by Cimello, is also said on its title page to include "le più necessarie osservanze Instrumentali" but has no explanatory rubrics for users. The *osservanze* may be, I believe, no more than a copious number of written accidentals, present in both Cimello and Maio's books.[30] If this practice were carried out with real consistency the music might have been intended to be ready for instrumental performance, a kind of intabulation in mensural notation (on the other hand *instromentali* might be a general rather than specific term, referring merely to means of performance). The idea, doubtless laudable and certainly of interest to modern editors and performers, is not fully carried out; nevertheless some of Cimello's accidentals are more than routine, are conceivably a guide to the practice of his time, as several passages drawn from the collection will illustrate (ex. 11.1a–c; see page 244).

The volume has no letter of dedication; instead there are poems in Italian and Latin celebrating Giovanna d'Aragona and her sons Fabrizio and Marc' Antonio Colonna. Fabrizio, the chief dedicatee and the elder son, died young; Marc' Antonio, possibly Cimello's employer in later years in Rome, was a boy of thirteen at this time. He was to achieve great fame as the captain-general of the victorious allied forces at Lepanto in 1571. His mother, a member of the Aragonese royal family, was famed both for her great beauty and for her independence in living apart from her husband, Ascanio Colonna.[31] In a sonnet addressed to Fabrizio, Cimello hints that he had received a sort of commission, just as Apelles had been empowered by Alexander the Great to paint portraits; after this rhetorical flourish the poem is merely a versified dedication. A Latin tetrastich comparing Fabrizio to Caius Fabritius follows on the same page.[32] The next opening is given over to a longer Latin poem, hexameters in praise of the two brothers and of their mother, with mention of their exile from Rome and with much reference to the symbol of the *columna,* something the family must have been rather used to. I will not presume to judge the quality of Cimello's Latin verse (the Italian sonnet is frankly not of first quality); but merely to be able to write classicizing Latin poetry instead of the usual adulatory vernacular prose by way of dedication sets him apart, as he no doubt intended.

The music is in general very much in the style of the black-note anthologies printed by Gardano and Scotto throughout the 1540s, an up-to-date idiom practiced by Cimello with perfectly acceptable skill and with results (see ex. 11.2) approaching the *arioso* style of the Roman madrigalists published by Antonio Barrè in the 1550s.[33]

Cimello took more than routine interest in questions of mensuration and *battuta;* he uses the C of *misura breve* (actually *alla semibreve*) for most of the pieces, but subjects it to further diminution in three compositions, and on occasion uses other mensurations as well (see below), putting his avowed expertise in mensural theory to practical use. This is surely done with didactic intent; as a run through the thirty pieces in his volume will show, Cimello evidently meant for this collection to be, from its title page on, a sort of paradigm for the use of musicians who wanted or needed practical illustration of the art of madrigal composition. Not, be it noted, composition in the grand style of Cipriano de Rore, at least that of Rore's five-voice madrigals, except for a few rhetorical details; Cimello was by talent equipped, and perhaps by temperament content, to practice the Arcadeltian madrigal as adapted by contributors to the Venetian anthologies of the 1540s.[34]

Since the composer went to the trouble of identifying the poets he set we should look at the texts with some interest. They are listed in table 1. Of the twenty-nine

Example 11.1

a. "Canzon tra vivi qui fuor di speranza," mm. 1–3

b. "Anchor che la partita," mm. 14–18 (repeated in mm. 18–22)

c. "Figliol mio troppo," mm. 34–36

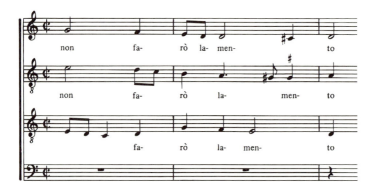

Example 11.2 "Di voi già non mi doglio," mm. 1–4

Italian texts chosen by Cimello, nineteen were, to judge from the index of the *Nuovo Vogel* and a run through anthologies published up to ca. 1550, set by him alone. He evidently knew the work of Bembo, Ariosto, and Petrarch well, for his choice of verses by these poets was both unusual and sensitive. One wonders why the lovely stanza he picked from *Orlando furioso* was not noticed by other composers, or why the bittersweet imagery of "Quest'è colui ch'il mondo chiam' Amore" from Petrarch's *Trionfo d'amore* was not a popular choice among madrigalists. In general the verses of well known poets are given in good versions, with only minor variants from established texts.[35] The art of making a poetic *centone* from scattered verses of Petrarch, not uncommon in the work of mid-century literary amateurs, is demonstrated with some skill (nos. 21 and 26, "Stanze fatte de versi del Petrarca"); equally skillful is the poetic-musical quodlibet (no. 25), its texts and cantus lines drawn from Gardano's *Primo libro di diversi autori.*

Half of the texts in this collection come from provably, or in a few cases conjecturally, local sources. First in poetic importance is the sestina stanza from Sannazaro's *Arcadia* (no. 16). But placed first in the volume is poetry by Vittoria Colonna, not only the most famous poet of her day but a member of the family to whom Cimello dedicated his work (she was the aunt of Fabrizio and Marc' Antonio Colonna). Vittoria Colonna was thus by extension a "Neapolitan"—she did reside in Naples and Ischia at various periods—and she was married to an uncle of the soldier-poet Alfonso d'Avalos, represented by two poems in Cimello's volume.[36] It would be nice to know if Alfonso wrote both "Anchor che la partita," ascribed to him by Cimello, and the longer variant of its theme and language "Anchor che col partire," made famous in Rore's setting.[37] The local princely circle to which Cimello pays homage is a closed one; Alfonso d'Avalos, nephew by marriage of Vittoria Colonna, was himself married to a sister of Giovanna d'Aragona Colonna, the Gratia-like figure whose sons are the dedicatees of the madrigal print.

Other Neapolitan connections may be observed. An Accademia degli Sereni (see table 1, no. 3) did exist in Naples, and was in fact prominent in the cultural life

TABLE I

	Cimello's Title	Capoverso	Remarks
1.	Commiato di Canzone della S. Vittoria Colonna Marchesa di Peschara	Canzon tra vivi fuor di speranza	The text is the close of the canzone *Mentre la nave mia lungi dal porto.*[a] No other setting is known.
2.	Madriale di don Alfonso davalo Marchese del Vasto	Anchor che la partita	A variant, set by a number of composers (see *Nuovo Vogel* 3:96), of the better known *Anchor che col partire* made famous in Rore's setting. Whether it should be considered a "primitive" form of the poem, as Einstein says, I am not sure.[b]
3.	Madriale ancho del cimello per la comedia delli sereni Accademici Napoletani	Veni giocosa e florida Thalia	On the Accademia dei Sereni see n. 38.
4.	Rime di pietro Bembo Cardinale	Di voi gia non mi doglia	The fourth stanza of the canzone *Voi mi poneste in foco.*[c] The only known setting of this stanza.
5.	Versi del Primo triompho del Petrarca	Quest'è colui che 'l mondo chiam' Amore	*Trionfo d'Amore* 2, lines 76–87. The text is as given in standard editions except for line four, where Cimello has "Mansueto fanciul e fiero veglio," Petrarch reads "Giovencel mansueto e fiero veglio."
6.	Stanza di Lodovico Ariosto	Gia in ogni parti gli animanti lassi	*Orlando furioso* 8.79, the only known setting of this stanza. In line five Cimello changes "Orlando" to the more generic "amante."
7.	Commiato di Canzone del Petrarca	Fuggi'l sereno e'l verde	The last stanza of *Canzoniere* 268, *Che debb'io far che mi consigli amore,* cited accurately. Of the many settings of this text only that of Ferabosco (1° *a 4,* 1542) is earlier than this.
8.	Versi di sestina del Petrarca	Prima ch'io torni a voi lucenti stelle	*Canzoniere* 22, *A qualunque animale alberga in terra,* accurately quoted.
9.	Madriale di fortunio spira	Non è lasso martire	A frequently set text; only the version of Antonio Martello (1° *a 5,* 1547) precedes that of Cimello.
10.	Madriale di fabio Ottinello	Oime ardenti sospiri	This and no. 11 are otherwise unknown in the madrigal literature. Both authors were members of the Accademia degli Sereni.

TABLE I—Continued

	Cimello's Title	Capoverso	Remarks
11.	Madriale di mattheo ricoveri	Madonna io mi distrugge	
12.	Rime di Pietro Bembo Cardinale	Lasso ch'io fuggo e per fuggir non scampo	The first six lines, given accurately, of a canzone in *Gli Asolani*.
13.	Versi del primo triompho del Petrarca	Pensier in grembo e vanitade in braccio	*Trionfo d'Amore* 4, lines 115–20, the only setting of these lines. Petrarch's last line, "Sallo il Regno di Roma e quel di Troia," is given by Cimello as "Qual nel regno di Roma o'n quel di troia."
14.	Stanza di Vincenzo bel prato conte d'aversa d'apruzzo	Sa ben ch'io l'amo & tengo per mia Dea	The only known setting of this text. On bel Prato see n. 41.
15.	Madriale di don Alfonso Davolo Marchese del Vasto	Non offende più morte	Also set by M. A. di Maio, *1° a 4* (1551), number 13, a collection including works by Cimello and written under his influence.
16.	Versi di sestina di giacobo sannazaro	Come notturno uccel nemico al sole	*Arcadia,* Eclogue 7, first stanza; accurately cited. Cimello's setting appears to be the earliest known.
17.	Versi di sonetto del Petrarca	Ma voi che mai pietà non discolora	*Canzoniere* 44, *Que'n Tesaglia ebbe la man si pronte,* sestet, a text with no known other settings.[d]
18.	Versi di sonetto del Petrarca	Oime lasso e quando fia quel giorno	*Canzoniere* 122, *Diciasette anni à già rivolto il cielo,* sestet, quoted accurately.
19.	Commiato di canzone di Luca contile	Dal pelago di pianto e di paura	As yet I have found no textual source for this poem, nor for no. 22. On Contile see above and n. 39.
20.	Madriale di Giovan Vincenzo bel prato Conte d'aversa	Piangete occhi dolenti	
21.	Stanza fatta de versi del Petrarca	Quanto veggio m'è noia & quanto ascolto	A *centone,* drawn from Petrarch's *Canzoniere* and *Trionfi;* the resulting stanza makes as much sense as these compilations ever do.[e]
22.	Commiato di canzone di Luca contile	Canzon se dimostrarti in neri panni	
23.	Madriale di Francesco Corfinio	Tu sei Cupido quel che'l tutto vinci	No textual source has been found for this poem.
24.	Stanza ancho del Cimello per Lelio suo figlio	Figliol mio troppo 'nanti'l di tuo spento	

TABLE I—Continued

Cimello's Title	Capoverso	Remarks
25. Madriale fatto delli principij delli canti e madriali del primo libro de diversi autori	Chi volesse saper che cosa è Amore	A quodlibet, with the text a good enough madrigal metrically and formally but only in a very generous view making continuous sense. Cimello's music is drawn from RISM 1543[17], the second edition of Gardano's *Primo libro d'i madrigali . . . a misura di breve.*[f]
26. Stanza fatta de versi del Petrarca	Mirate qual'amor fa di me stratio	Like no. 21 a *centone*, this one entirely from the *Canzoniere*,[g] it makes surprisingly good sense as an ottava stanza. On the performance rubric for this piece see n. 49.
27. Versi di sonetto del Petrarca per lo novo segno del tempo imperfetto raddoppiato, che fa la proportione subdupla, e si canta una minima per botta intera	Hor son qui lasso e voglio esser altrove	*Canzoniere* 118, *Rimansi a dietro il sestodecimo anno,* sestet, quoted accurately. Cimello's *proportione subdupla* is discussed in the text of the article.
28. Madriale di Mattheo colle	Se'l tacer né l'assenza	No textual source is known for this poem.
29. Versi di sonetto del Petrarca per detto segno	Piangea madonna e'l mio signor ch'io fossi	*Canzoniere* 155, *Non fur ma' Giove e Cesare sì mossi,* lines 5–14, cited accurately. The "detto segno" is that of Cimello's *proportione subdupla.*
30. Canzon Francese	Iesu mon dieu en qui ie croy	A *chanson spirituelle* of unknown origin.[h]

[a] See Vittoria Colonna, *Rime,* ed. Alan Bullock, (Rome, 1982), 47–49. The last line here reads "Che m'è nettar il foco, ambrosia il pianto"; Cimello has "Ch'ambrosia il foco e nettar m'el pianto," a transposition not found in any of the textual sources known to Bullock.

[b] Einstein, *Italian Madrigal,* 404. Given Cimello's acquaintance with the circle to which d'Avalos belonged one would think he would have known what the truth was about this text. In any event, the attribution of the version used by Rore depends on Cimello's designation of *Anchor che la partita* as by Alfonso d'Avalos.

[c] Bembo, *Gli Asolani,* Venice, 1505, [28]. The text as given there differs slightly from that used by Cimello:

Bembo	*Cimello*
E di voi non mi doglio,	Di Voi gia non mi doglio
Quanto d'Amore, che questo vi comporte;	Quanto d'amore che tanto vi comporte
Anzi di me, ch'ancor non mi discoglio.	Anzi di me ch'anchor non mi discoglio
Ma che poss'io? con legge inique e torte	Ma che poss'io s'amore regge sua corte
Amor regge sua corte.	Con leggi iniqu' e torte
Chi vide mai tal sorte	Chi vidde mai tal sorte
Tenermi in vita un huom con doppia morte.	Tener in vita un huom con dargli morte.

TABLE I—Continued

^d There are in Cimello's version some minor textual discrepancies from the established Petrarchan text. Line two in Petrarch is "E ch'avete li schermi sempre accorti," in Cimello "E c'havete li schermi molto accorti"; in line three the Petrarchan text is "Contra l'arco d'amor che 'ndarno tira," in Cimello "Contra colpi d'amor che 'ndarno tira"; in line four Petrarch's text begins "Mi vedete," that of Cimello "Vedetemi."

^e The stanza's sources are as follows: 1) *Canzoniere* 283.8; 2) *Trionfo di morte* 2.186 (Petrarch reads "Ma 'l viver senza m'è duro e forte," Cimello "Si l'esser senza voi m'e duro & forte"); 3) *Canz.* 105.69; 4) *Canz.* 217.11; 5) *Canz.* 300.3; 6) *Canz.* 183.2; 7) *Canz.* 153.4; 8) *Canz.* 160.14. Except for line two Cimello's text has only very minor differences from that of Petrarch.

^f For a modern edition of 1543¹⁷ see Harrán, ed., *The Anthologies of Black-note Madrigals,* 1, American Institute of Musicology, 1978. Cimello, anticipating the technique to be used in Lodovico Balbi, *Musicale Esercitio,* Venice, 1589, takes the superius voices of madrigal incipits in Gardano's anthology and composes new counterpoint beneath them, taking care to vary the sonorities and imitative entries used in the originals; he also transposes a number of incipits in order to give coherence to his own piece, which has in a limited way textual coherence as well. Of his choices only the first, Willaert's *Chi volesse saper che cosa e Amore* (no. 4 in Gardano's print) is in o mensuration; but Cimello retains this metric signature throughout his piece. The works chosen, following the piece by Willaert, are as follows: 2) Ubert Naich, *Canti di voi le lodi* (no. 10); 3) Ferabosco, *Io non so dir parole* (no. 33; on this text see Harrán, *The Anthologies* 1.16; 4) Yvo [Barry], *Apri la porta homai* (no. 8); 5) Yvo (or Paolo Aretino; see Harrán, liii), *Deh dolce pastorella* (no. 11); 6) Naich (Rampollini? Berchem? see Harrán, lix, where Berchem is favored as composer), *Che giova saettar un che si more* (no. 23), a well-known text from Bembo's *Asolani;* 7) Verdelot, *Perche piu acerba sei e piu rubella* (no. 22), in which Cimello notates three F♯s not in Gardano's print; 8) Naich, *Proverbio ama chi t'ama e fatto antico* (no. 18), a popular Petrarchan text from *Canzoniere* 105, stanza 3; 9) Naich, *Che dolce piu che piu giocondo stato* (no. 13), a text from *Orlando furioso* 30.1; 10) anon, (but attributed to Vincenzo Ruffo in the latter's 1° a 4 of 1545, p. 6), *M'alcum non puo saper da chi sia amato,* a stanza from *Orlando furioso* 19, 1 (the "Ma" at the beginning of the line is introduced by Cimello to tie the verse in with what has preceded it).

Cimello's musical quodlibet makes surprisingly good sense, and the textual *centone* comes out as an acceptable madrigal with a bit of internal rhyme, balance of seven- and eleven-syllable lines, and a final couplet.

^g The sources for Cimello's stanza are as follows: 1) *Canz.* 71.73; 2) *Canz.* 32.14; 3) *Canz.* 190.10: "Scritti avea di diamanti e di topazi" (Cimello reads "Catena di diamanti e di topatio"); 4) *Canz.* 266.4; 5) *Canz.* 82.12; 6) *Canz.* 32.11; "E'l riso e'l pianto e la paura e l'ira" (Cimello reads "La doglia e'l pianto la paura e l'ira"; 7) *Canz.* 206.22; 8) *Canz.* 255.8. The changes in several lines are fairly extensive; they appear to be the result of Cimello's wishing his own stanza to make better sense.

^h It may be my own unfamiliarity with the literature of the *chanson spirituelle* that prevents me from recognizing this text. It is as follows: "Jesus mon dieu en qui le croy / Fais my obeir a ta loy / Pour vivre ainsi quil appartient / Car ie proteste devant toy / Que mourir vueil en celle foy / Que saincte eglise croit e tient." What is not clear is whether the "saincte eglise" is Catholic or Protestant.

of the city in the years 1546–48. It seems likely that a number of the madrigals in Cimello's volume originated from contact with the "Sereni." Among the Academy's members were Fabio Ottinelli (see no. 10), Matteo Ricoveri (no. 11), and Vincenzo bel Prato (nos. 14, 20).³⁸ Luca Contile, a Tuscan courtier-poet of some note (texts by him are to be seen here in nos. 19 and 22), was acquainted with Vittoria Colonna and was in the service of Alfonso d'Avalos (in Milan) until the latter's death in 1546, after which he accompanied his patron's widow to Ischia and Naples.³⁹ He wrote at least one comedy, *Argea,* around this time; it is tempting to think of him as author of the comedy for the "sereni Academici" of Naples, for which Cimello supplied text and music of a madrigal-intermedio (no. 3).⁴⁰

Vincenzo bel Prato, Conte d'Aversa, was a Neapolitan nobleman of strongly religious bent, at first of Waldensian leanings, later a staunchly Counter-Reformation Catholic.[41] One wonders whether the *chanson spirituelle* which closes Cimello's book, and which might be judged from its severe text to be Reformist in intent, was a response to pre-Tridentine religious stirrings in Naples.[42]

Fortunio Spira, a poet of scholarly inclinations known chiefly through his association with Pietro Aretino, is not recorded as having spent any time in Naples; his "Non è lasso martire" (no. 9) may have been picked up by Cimello from a printed source, Domenichi's first book of *Rime diversi di molti ecc. autori*.[43] As for Mattheo Colle and Francesco Corfinio, I have as yet found no information on them; I assume, subject to welcome substantiation or correction, that they were of local origin, friends or academic acquaintances of Cimello.[44] In sum, the contents of the book show both an educated taste and a response to local literary culture. Cimello's own textual contributions are worth citing here; one is a suitably comic-erudite poem (no. 3) for the "sereni Academici"; the other (no. 24) is a touching personal tribute to the composer's dead son:

> Veni, giocosa & florida Thalia,
> Con l'altre tue sorelle
> Saggie leggiadr' & belle
> A far piu adorn' & lieto il nostro choro
> Et date'l sacro alloro
> A li Sereni che con canti & versi
> Dolci soavi & tersi
> Lodan' insiem' amore,
> D'accortezze diletti & gioie autore.
>
> Figliol mio, troppo 'nanti'l dì spento,
> Ma[l] per me che per te'n ciel vivi meglio,
> S'io dir sapesse il duol che nel cor sento
> Farei pia mort'e'l tumul vetro e speglio.
> Per non sfogarlo non farò lamento
> Né ragion mi torrà, né'l farmi veglio
> S'io non t'ho visto mai vivo ne morto
> Con te sepolto sia ogni conforto.

Twenty-one of the thirty pieces are in *misura comune* (C), with many black notes, with both minims and semiminims regularly, and fusas occasionally, bearing text syllables, and with the tactus presumably on the semibreve, similar to the "chromatic" or *note nere* madrigals seen in the four anthologies of Gardano and Scotto published between 1542 and 1549.[45] Four madrigals use *misura alla breve* (₵) and are written in longer, "whiter" values. Though surely aware of the theoretical differences between these two signs Cimello seems to have used them as did his contemporaries, more as indication of tempo than of exact proportional relationship. Two compositions (nos. 27, 29) are in C with an explanatory rubric, calling it "lo novo segno del tempo imperfetto raddoppiato, che fa la proportione subdupla, e si canta una minima per botta intera." In both these madrigals fusas as well as semiminims regularly carry text syllables, giving the work the look of a page of seventeenth-century music; and the up- and downbeats of the tactus fall on the semiminim. Whether this tactus is the same speed as that of the *misura comune* is not specified, so in practice we may have simply another tempo, a slightly slower beat to accommodate the very short notes. Yet Cimello calls it *proportione subdupla;* if strictly carried out this would suggest that the works in *misura alla breve* (₵) are meant as examples of *proportione dupla,* though not necessarily to be performed as such. This is heady mensural stuff for a mid-century madrigalist, but not for a reader, like Cimello, of Tinctoris and Gafori.[46]

By way of completing his demonstration of mensural theory Cimello includes a piece (no. 25) in *tempus perfectum* (O; see ex. 11.3) and, even more surprising, one in *tempus imperfectum* with major prolation (C), the latter a composition that is hard to read at sight since the composer was obviously forcing material conceived in the ordinary rhythms of the mid-sixteenth century into an artificial mensural framework (ex. 11.4).[47] Certainly Gardano was not used to printing music using

Example 11.3 "Chi volesse saper che cosa è Amore," mm. 1–3

Example 11.4 "Come notturno uccel nemico al sole," mm. 1–3

these mensurations; he had to make a O out of two facing C's, and his Ͼ looks as if it were done partly by hand. Finally, there is a madrigal (no. 15) entirely in blackened notes, including many breves and semibreves (the text is full of images of death); other composers had done this, and it is no surprise that as in similar instances there is no mensural sign given.[48]

Cimello has one more notational surprise to offer, no. 26, a Petrarchan *centone* forming an ottava stanza. It is to be sung "prima con le pause e poi senza pause fuor che li sospiretti"; that is, one can perform the piece as written or in telescoped form with no rests other than semiminims (see ex. 11.5a–b). This is both a bow to the notational canons of previous generations and a hint that devices such as this, used by seventeenth-century experts in canonic technique, were already in vogue in the 1540s.[49]

Is there anything instructive about tonal principles in Cimello's collection?

Example 11.5

a. "Mirate qual'amor fa di me stratio," mm. 1–3

b. "Mirate qual'amor fa di me stratio," mm. 1–5 senza pause

Given the hint on his title page, and his general didactic bent, it would not be surprising to find the pieces identified by mode; unfortunately they are not, but as in many Gardano volumes of the period there does seem to be an arrangement by signature and in part by mode. In this book the first twenty-five pieces are modally grouped in ascending order; this can be seen in table 2. As sometimes happens in these volumes, the order disintegrates near the end; why this should be so is not clear, but it is possible that Cimello originally intended to close the volume with no. 25, a poetic and musical *centone* which he must have considered a tour de force.

A glance at table 2 will show that Cimello did not use the standard high-low clef combinations stressed as fundamental in Harold Powers's studies of what he has called "tonal types."[50] The composer nonetheless seems intent on demonstrating the placement of modes in specific tonal contexts, which is if I understand them correctly what both Powers and Siegfried Hermelink have wished to emphasize as modal theory brought into practical use.[51] The modal labels in table 2 are what I think Cimello intended but am not so confident about as to say they *are* his choice. If he was indeed a loyal follower of Tinctoris, Cimello should have regarded his tenor lines as modally determinant.[52] They are often just that, but not always; they do not inevitably pair up with the cantus lines at the distance of an octave, and where there is a discrepancy I am inclined to think that the cantus part, always most important in the compositional scheme of these madrigals, is what expresses the mode. This is particularly true where the authentic-plagal distinction, not in any event so clear in Cimello as the modal classifier could wish, is not strengthened by congruence of ambitus between cantus and tenor.

The F and G modes are regular as to finals and octave species if not always in focused authentic-plagal discrimination. For the D mode Cimello seems intent on showing that transposition—by a fourth, to G, a fifth to A, or an octave to the higher D—is of great importance. Here, as in cinquecento polyphonic settings in general, the bass should be examined; it is the voice that most needs relocation in order to fit within the Guidonian gamut. This very simple criterion for modal analysis has, I think, been insufficiently stressed. The D and E modes meet on a common ground at the pitch-class A; these two modes interact very comfortably, if confusingly for the cataloguer, at a pitch crucial to both modes (this is true for nos. 7–11 in Cimello's print). Distinction between authentic and plagal in the E mode is for Cimello's music as for that of everyone else especially hard to make.

Most striking of all the madrigals from the standpoint of mode is no. 12, with a final on G and a signature of three flats; two E♭s and one A♭ written, with a B♭ of necessity understood (see ex. 11.6). This, going Tinctoris one better, is a triply-transposed E-mode piece, or so I read it.[53] At this point one might reconsider Cimello's title-page language about the "più convenevoli avvertenze de toni accio si possano anchora Sonare & Cantare insieme." If *toni* here really refers to mode, were arrangements of this kind intended not just for the sake of orderliness but also to make things easier—though in just what way would be hard to say—for concerted performance? No. 12 with its three flats, surrounded by pieces without any, would appear to discourage such a hypothesis; but with the exception of nos. 15

TABLE 2
Modal Arrangement in Cimello's *Libro Primo*

Clefs*	Signature	Final	Mode	Remarks
1. MATB	b	G	2	In nos. 1–4, the cantus ends on D, the tenor on G. Nos. 1–6 employ transposition by a fourth.
2. MTTB	b	G	2	
3. STTB	b	G	2	
4. MATB	b	G	2	
5. SAAB	b	G	1	Cantus ends on G.
6. MATB	b	G	1–2	Cantus ends on D, tenor on G; the tenor includes the ambitus of modes 1 and 2.
7. SSMT	b	A, D	1	Nos. 7–8 appear to illustrate the first mode at the level of the *affinalis,* transposed by a fifth. The flat in number 7 is an anomaly.
8. SMAT		A	1	
9. TrSMT		D	1	
10. SAAB		A	3–4	Nos. 7–11 also illustrate the close connection, when the pitch A is involved, between the D and E modes.
11. SATB		E-A	3–4	
12. TrMMT	bbb	G	3–4	The E mode is here presented in triple transposition.
13. SAAB		A	3–4	The cantus ends on A, the tenor on C♯.
14. SAAB		A	3	
15. SSMBar	b	A	3	Transposition by a fourth.
16. SAAB		E-A	3–4	Cantus ends on E, tenor on A.
17. STTB	b	F	5–6	Cantus seems to be in mode 6, tenor in mode 5, here and in no. 18.
18. STTB	b	F	5–6	
19. SATB	b	F	6	Cantus ends on A, tenor on F.
20. MATB	b	F	6	
21. SATB	b	F	5–6	Again the cantus seems to be in mode 6, the tenor in mode 5.
22. SAAB		G	7–8	
23. SAAB		G	8	Cantus ends on G, tenor on D.
24. SATB		G	8	Here the cantus ends on D, the tenor on G.
25. SAAT		G	8	Cantus ends on D, tenor on G.
26. SAAB	b	A	3–4	
27. SMABar		A	3–4	
28. SAAB	b	G	2	
29. SAAB	b	F	6	
30. SAAB	b	G	2	

* Clefs: Tr = G², S = C¹, M = C², A = C³, T = C⁴, Bar = F³, B = F⁴

Example 11.6 "Lasso ch'io fuggo e per fuggir non scampo," mm. 1–3

and 26, the rest of the volume's ordering would tend to conform it. A fully satisfactory explanation for the tonal ordering so often used in Gardano's prints remains to be made; but I think that practical in addition to theoretical reasons must have been of some importance.

In matters of musical detail these madrigals show good technical control, some variety of pace and mood, and a good deal of harmonic piquance. Much of the latter comes from closely juxtaposed thirds containing the cross-relation called by Zarlino "non-harmonic relation."[54] Example 11.7a–d shows some instances of this (including two brief but undeniable simultaneous cross-relations); it is so common a feature of the composer's style as to approach a stylistic obsession. Cimello is not above clichés; every *sola* and *lasso* gets its appropriate solmization equivalents, every *sospir* has *sospiretti* to set it off. But few madrigalists of the

Example 11.7

a. "Anchor che la partita," mm. 4–7

b. "Quest' è colui ch'el mondo chiam'amore," mm. 1–4

c. "Non è lasso martire," mm. 7–10

d. "Oime ardenti sospiri," mm. 25–28

time, including the young Lasso, could resist these. If there is a general weakness in this music it is that of short-windedness; nearly all of Cimello's melodic ideas lead directly and with surprising speed to a cadential forumla, and he cannot manage the kind of artful overlap and concealment of cadential gesture within the texture that Rore and Willaert were so good at. This is a failure characteristic of the madrigal of the 1540s and 1550s in the hands of minor composers; achieving variety and breadth of phrase structure seems to have been as difficult for them as it was for some mid-eighteenth-century composers.

Once in a while Cimello slows his pace to stretch out a phrase in longer-than-usual notes. He will occasionally use the same melodic material at different speeds; a good example is the text-inspired repetition of the beginning of no. 9 at its close (ex. 11.8). And though most of his cadences are predictable in every way,

Example 11.8

a. "Non è lasso martire," mm. 1–5

b. "Non è lasso martire," mm. 16–20

he can now and then show the kind of imaginative variety of pace and articulation that the work of Cipriano de Rore offered composers of the time so many instances of. An example of Cimello's best use of varied pace and scoring is given in example 11.9.

Example 11.9 "Prima ch'io torni a voi," mm. 14–25

Example 11.9, cont.

Composers of Cimello's generation—at least those living outside Venice—
could not on the whole absorb the full impact of the music of Willaert and Rore,
whose influence was greater on a younger circle, that of Lasso and Wert. They were
nonetheless a restive group, not wholly satisfied with repeating a style molded by
Verdelot, Festa, and Arcadelt. Behaving in a way similar to the practice of composers in many other periods in Western musical history, they fiddled with details,
chiefly rhythmic and harmonic, of a received style. In the *arioso* madrigal they
achieved a new plateau of naturalism in musical diction; but large-scale novelty of
musical thought was harder for them to find. Cimello is of some interest as a provincial contributor to this generation in search of a new style. He is a good deal
more intriguing as what I think his madrigal volume shows him to be, a teacher, no
great theorist, but a workaday musician who sought to instruct by example, at the
same time demonstrating the continuing artistic vitality of his Neapolitan
homeland.

APPENDIX

*Letter, dated 13 December 1579, from Cimello to Cardinal Guglielmo Sirleto in
Rome (Bibl. Ap. Vat. Cod. 6193, 2. 501)*

Mons. Illmo e R^mo e Padrone mio osser^mo.
Ho pur vinto il timor, e preso ardire di scrivere e mandar miei versi latini e volgari
e canti a V.S. Illma e R^ma nati veramente dall'Allegrezza, che m'ha portata il ms.
Gabriele Neofito, col dolce e soave Nome di V.S. Illma e R^ma la qual noti l'animo e
non l'ingegno.
Mi scuso ch'io venni à Roma son d'intorno a diece anni, nè venni à farle rive-
renza e barciarle la Papabil mano, colpa della mia mala sorte, che mi trovato odiato
dal ms. Hannibal Zoilo, tanto caro servitore di V.S. Illma e R^ma per debile cagione,
qual durò, per ch'ella me lo riconciliò. Venne quà con un mio amico, in casa a ve-
dermi chè lo tenni a favore grande per la servitù sua appò V.S. Illma e R^ma e per la

sua virtù, che la stimai piu ch'assai dopo molti ragionamenti e canti mostrati per le
mie regole nove ch'egli le gustava, gli mostrai certa opretta ch'io facevo in terza
rima delle streghe, che due n'eran qui state brugiate, ed io l'havevo essaminate e
confortate, al partir il ms. Alessandro me la tolse, ch'io pensai che fosse stato quel
amico, che se fosse state finita non h'havrei fatto caso, scrissi al Capitano d'Arpino, che passando un Giovine tale lo domandasse di questo e lo pregasse che la
rendesse ch'io l'havrei finita e poi mandatela a Sua S. e così la rihebbi, e l'ho finita
et ampliata, che non sol ci hò visti molti libri e processi in molti lochi quali si con-
frontano, ma sono stato in Benevento per anni, hò visto il loco della Noce et ho
parlato con vecchi e vecchie della Città e delle terre finitime (si c'hora stà al Suo
Commando, e l'hò poi intitolate le Notti delle streghe). Io l'amo come figlio, e mi
duolsi ch'in Roma vedendomi, mi voltava le spalle e mi fu detto che si lamentava di
me non poco, si che V.S. Illma e R^ma si degni mitigarlo, che se siamo amici gli pia-
cerà quel ch'io gli scriverei per la riformatione de Canti piani, della quale l'impresa
si dice essere stata data è lui, che bisogna havere l'arte metrica, e saper bene come
si conservino gli accenti e le sillabe brevi nell'ascendere de Canti, e le longhe nel
descendere e delli ponti delle parole e sentenze per ben ponere le Neume e delle variationi del Diatessaron e del Diapente e ditono e semidittono e tono maggiore e
minore vocale per poi poterne cavare le trenta quattro fughe, c'have ogni tono regolar et irregolare, quando un compositore volesse componer un mottetto sopra
l'Introito over offertorio e graduale et altro canto piano etc. et altre avvertenze che
ci sono necessarie perché sian più brevi e che s'intendano le parole finite di sillabe
vicine e non divise et allontanate, e dove si faccian le aggiuntioni di note per qualch'ornamento di passaggio et altre cose.

S. mio gliè sopra un anno ch'alquanto infermato venni a Casa à ripigliare l'aria
del paese, fui subbito ristorato, trovai mio figlio con gran amicitia de forusciti ch'e-
gli era fiscal, e Capitan à guerra non potei con gridi, contrasti, consigli e ragione-
voli esshortationi, ritrarlo e rimoverlo da si vana e perigliosa impresa talche ci ha
lasciate la vita per troppo ardir e troppo desio di servir à i nostri SS^i Ill^mi m'ha la-
sciati cinque figlioli, tre grandi e duo piccioli, ch'io manderei volentieri a servire
che son atti, l'un di venti anni letterato, l'altro di deciotto armigero, l'altro di quin-
deci, atto a servir in camera et à tavola—.

Io son sforzato di tornar à Napoli, ch'avevo composte le stampe, per tante mie
opre nove di Musica per le regole nove da me trovate, che quanto s'e composto, et
havevo io prima composto è pien de difetti e d'errorj, senza scuse e difensioni, e
son arrivate in Spagna e Francia, et Orlando venne a trovarmi e pigliarle che non
potea negarle, Compositori molti d'Italia me n'han scritto, e l'ho mandate e l'usato
ecc. Nella teorica ho trovato Boetio tutto falso, che non conobbe il tono maggiore
e il tono minore, nè conobbe il semitono maggiore diatonico, nè il minore ch'è sol
nel b molle nè la divisione del tono maggiore in semitono minore di quattro commi
et in semitono maggiore di cinque Commi, nel genere Chromatico, nè la divisione
del tono minore in duo semitoni minori nel b molle solo. Nè conobbe le proportioni
loro d'onde tutti questi intervalli, nascono, et sic bassus est et deceptus, sequendo i
Pitagorici che similmente non conobber altro che il soprettano epogdoo e così ben
si dice qui cadit à puncto cadit à toto. Io c'ho fatto un libretto e poi di tutta l'arte de

segni di proportioni de Contraponti di componere d'infinite habilitadi d'improviso ec. è non hò a cui grande dedicarla che m'aiutasse, hò composto un libro de sonetti spirituali, l'altro d'epigrammi per spirituali, lascio le cose amorose giovinili
et altre cose in prose ec. si chè farò come potrò, in Roma non hebbi mai ventura
colpa dell'astrea che le stà sopra che non vuolse mai favorirmi, e pur ho servito a
SS^{ri} grandi ma indarno, non mi resta altra speranza che'l venir a baciarle il Piede
auguror, eveniet, Carmina numen habent.

S. mio, il ms Gabriele Neofito tutti questi giorni che m'è venuto in Casa, m'ha
stretto, come d'opra pia da non negarsi, ch'io lo facessi portatore d'alcuni miei
componimenti, e l'hò voluto fare non curando che qui non sian cantori, da provare
prima i Canti, nè poeti da veder et essaminare versi. V.S. Illma et R^{ma} sia l'aristarco,
et il mio Apollo mio Achille che tal Coppia sempre mi sta nella memoria, e nel dir
l'officio specialmente. ch'Iddio per sua benignità m'essaudisca, che così potrei venir a Roma et haver pane honorato ec. Invoco ms. Alessandro à far provar il Mottetto da qualch'amico com' è ms. Giovan Maria, ms. Pietro da Picinisco, ms. Luigi
et altri giuditiosi e lor sia lecito, mutare, mancar, aggiunger e rinuovare et hab-
bianmi compassione che stò in questo Morrone dove non si conosce l'Antifonario.

Il Canone che non è novo per le sillabe e vocali, l'hò fatto novo con le quantitadi
mutate, e con la proportione sopraterza di $^4/_3$ che dicon sesquiterza che non si trova:
se—sesqui significat totum aliquid et totius dimidium, e pur questo hò mutato in
Boetio che fu pur si grande in lingua Greca.

Perdonimi V.S. Illma e R^{ma} dello scrivere lungo e troppo libero e famigliare e dia
la colpa à ms Gabriele qual raccomdano à lei come fosse mio figlio, e similmente à
confusione di questi altri hebrei le raccomando i suoi figliuoli che cotesti un giorno
si battezzin, anchora ecc. e fò fine co'l baciarle mille volte la Papabil mano fin ch'io
venga à baciarle degnamente il Piede. Di Montesangiovanni hoggi 13 di x^{bre} 1579.

Di V.S. Illma e R^{ma} ognor più affettionate servitore

Il Cimello.

S'à V.S. Illma e R^{ma} e paresse ch'io componessi alcune cose così in Musica com'
in versi latini e volgari a Sua Santità, io tirerei ben le corde del mio ingegno che non
sarei de gli ultimi e delli minimj e s'io havessi insieme il peso di questi Canti piani,
si guadagneriano centinaja di migliaja, ch'al mio giuditio s'havria credito in tutta
Europa, et liceat mihi hoc dicere, ch'io so quanti son in Roma et essi tutti, levata
l'invidia, san qual che son io, et experientia est rerum magistra, ch'io hò veduto
anco delle cose ch'escon da Roma. Hoc audeo dicere Illmo Sirleto, sed cum exeat
etc.

POSTSCRIPT

When I first submitted this piece for publication a reader remarked that it was "just
another study of a madrigal book." I was a little offended by this, but the fault may
have been partly mine; in describing Cimello's volume in so much detail I may

have obscured the chief point I was trying to make, namely, that the book is unique in the madrigal literature in its openly didactic nature. There is nothing wrong with its contents from a purely musical standpoint; but Cimello seems to have been a teacher first, composer second. In some ways his collection of madrigals may be taken as extended examples illustrating his attitudes toward madrigal poetry and toward mensural polyphony. This study may then best be read as a complement to chapter 7 above, where Cimello's work as theorist and teacher is dealt with.

NOTES

1. For a fuller statement of this view of the early madrigal, which to some extent takes issue with those of scholars such as Alfred Einstein, Walter Rubsamen, and Dean Mace, see James Haar, "The Early Madrigal: A Re-appraisal of its Sources and its Character," in *Music in Medieval and Early Modern Europe,* ed. Iain Fenlon (Cambridge, 1981), 163–92; cf. Fenlon and Haar.

2. Sixteenth-century theorists gave increasing emphasis to a succession of "great" composers, usually beginning with Josquin; and there were some expressions of diffidence on the part of musicians in the face of the work of composers such as Josquin, Willaert, and Rore; see James Haar, "Self-Consciousness about Style, Form and Genre in Sixteenth-Century Music," *SM* 3 (1974): 219–32.

3. Donna Cardamone, *The Canzone Villanesca alla Napolitana and Related Forms, 1537–1570,* 2 vols. (Ann Arbor, 1981), 1.3; Einstein, *Italian Madrigal,* 382–83. Einstein reprints one of Cimello's *villanelle;* two others are included in Erich Hertzmann, ed., *Adrian Willaert und andere Meister: Volkstümliche italienische Lieder zu 3–4 Stimmen,* Das Chorwerk 8 (Wolfenbüttel, 1930).

4. Jannequin's *La guerre,* published in 1528 and reprinted in 1537, was made easily available in Italy through Gardano's printing of it in 1545 (RISM J446); it had appeared in Dorico's *Secondo libro de la Croce* (RISM 1531[4]) as well. The *Bataglia taliana* of Werrecore (Matthias Fiamengo) was not published in Italy until 1549; but it had appeared earlier in Germany (1544[19], Petreius' *Guter . . . teutscher Gesang)* with its Italian text, and may have been known throughout Italy before its printing there. On battle pieces in the sixteenth century see Don Harrán, "The Concept of Battle in Music of the Renaissance," *Journal of Medieval and Renaissance Studies* 17 (1987): 175–94. (Harrán does not mention Cimello's piece.)

5. *Canzone villanesche al modo napolitano a tre voci di Thomaso Cimello da Napoli Con una Bataglia villanescha a tre del medesimo autore novamente poste in luce. Libro primo* (Venice, 1545), 21. Einstein, *Italian Madrigal,* 382, and Cardamone, *The Canzone Villanesca,* 151, both comment briefly on this piece.

6. RISM 1549[31], no. 6; the last line of text and music, given only once in Cimello's book, is repeated in the *Vero terzo libro.* The text, by Fortunio Spira, was a popular one; eleven other settings, the earliest that of Antonio Martorello (1547), are listed in the index of *Il nuovo Vogel: Bibliografia della musica italiana vocale profana pubblicata dal 1500 al 1700,* 3 vols. (Pomezia, 1977). "Non è lasso martire" and "Di voi gia non mi doglio" (no. 4 in Cimello's print) are found in Brussels, Bibliothèque du Conservatoire royal, MS 27.731 (fols. 80v–82) a cantus part book of Florentine provenance begun in the 1530s but containing later additions; see Fenlon and Haar, 149–53.

7. Einstein's account (*Italian Madrigal,* 405) of the volume, placed characteristically in the middle of a discussion of Rore's madrigals, is disappointingly negative in tone as well as inaccurate in detail. A much better account is to be found in Keith Larson, "The Unaccompanied Madrigal in Naples from 1536 to 1654" (Ph.D. diss., Harvard University, 1985), 181–96. I am most grateful to Keith Larson for sharing his thoughts on Cimello with me. Much but by no means all of the material in his sketch of Cimello's life and work I had uncovered independently before I was directed to his excellent dissertation, but there is no doubt that Larson's work on the subject should take precedence over mine.

8. See Cardamone, *The Canzone Villanesca,* 106, citing a preface by Gamucci to Paolo del Rossi, *Regole osservanze et avvertenze sopra lo scrivere corettamente la lingua volgare Toscana in prosa et in versi* (Naples, 1545). At the end of the book, said to have been edited by Cimello, there is a poem by the latter in honor of Vincenzo bel Prato, dedicatee of the volume.

9. They later turned up, apparently, for Cimello refers to them in a general way in the autograph letter cited below. The contents of these *regole,* which have recently been located in the Biblioteca Nazionale in Naples (MS VH 210), are discussed briefly by Larson, "The Unaccompanied Madrigal," 185–86, and more fully in chapter 7 above.

10. Bernardo Clavelli, *L'Antica Arpino* (Naples, 1623), 17: "... appunto mi sovviene dell'Epigramma del Cimelli dal Monte San Giovanni (che fù nell'età nostra huomo di buone lettere, e versatissimo nella Musica, e nella Poesia) di cui per non esser lungo, basterà ne apporti due ultimi versi, che sono i seguenti[:] Nil refert domus haec, quid diruta sic sit, & hortus. Clara Oratoria nomine semper erit." By "età nostra" Clavelli means modern as opposed to ancient times; Cimello's verses have to do with a supposed house of Cicero in Arpino. The village of Monte San Giovanni in Campano from which Cimello hailed is close to Arpino; though in the Neapolitan *regno* they are actually nearer to Rome than to Naples.

11. See Richard Sherr, ed., *Giovanni Giacomo Lucario. Concentuum qui vulgo motetta nuncupantur liber primus (Venice, 1547)* (New York, 1987). In this collection there is another *Alma redemptoris* by Giovanni Andrea Alcalà di Supino, a musician mentioned by Scipione Cerreto, *Della prattica musicale vocale* (Naples, 1601), as among "compositori eccellenti della città di Napoli ch'oggi non vivono"; he may be another student of Cimello.

12. See Cardamone, *The Canzone Villanesca,* 107.

13. Although Cimello does not mention the theorist-composer Lusitano in his own writings, he may have known Lusitano in Rome; the two shared an interest in mensural theory. See Robert Stevenson, "Vicente Lusitano: New Light on His Career," *JAMS* 16 (1962): 72–77.

14. Cimello appears to have taught both grammar and music at the [diocesan] seminary, perhaps also at the Duomo, in Benevento in 1570–73. See Raffaele Casimiri, "Musica e musicisti a Benevento sulla fine del secolo XVI," *Note d'archivio per la storia musicale* 13 (1936): 80–81, for the relevant pay records. Cimello's work on *streghe,* if it was ever finished, has not so far turned up. If he studied old legends and current stories connected with the *noce di Benevento* he anticipated the work of Pietro Piperno, published in the next century, on the subject. See Larson, "The Unaccompanied Madrigal," 185.

15. Maio's *Libro primo di madrigali* (1551), also printed by Gardano, contains two madrigals by Cimello. Sorrentino's *Libro primo a 4, 5 e 6vv* (1560), a volume not known to survive, is mentioned by Giuseppe Pitoni, *Notizie de' contrapuntisti e de' compositori di musica dagli anni dell'era cristiana 1000, fino al 1700* (1744) [Rome, Biblioteca Ap. Vat. Capp. Giulia MS 1–2(2)], 500, who says the work was published by Dorico in Rome. Pitoni

does say explicitly that Sorrentino was a Neapolitan and a student of Cimello; cf. Giuseppe Ottavio Pitoni, *Notitia de' contrapuntisti e compositori di musica,* ed. Cesarino Ruini (Florence, 1988), 81.

16. See Cardamone, *The Canzone Villanesca,* 106–9; cf. Maria Lopriore in *Dizionario bibliografico degli italiani,* 25:560–61. Belli says, in his *Missarum, sacrarumque cantionum . . . liber primus* (Venice, 1595), that he learned (possibly in Rome if not in Naples) "musicam hunc cognitionem at usum Neapoli . . . à D. Cimello."

17. For Caposele see Cardamone, *The Canzone Villanesca,* 107. For another seventeenth-century citation of Cimello see above n. 10.

18. The treatise survives in Bologna, Civico Museo Bibliografico Musicale, MS B 57. For a study of its contents see chapter 7 above. Cimello says he met Petrucci in the city of Sora, which is near Arpino and his native town of Monte San Giovanni; this gives his claim more verisimilitude since Petrucci was in Rome for various period and could have visited Sora, whereas he is not known to have been in Naples.

19. See Raffaele Casimiri, "Lettere di musicisti (1579–1585) al Cardinal Sirleto," *Note d'archivio per la storia musicale* 9 (1932): 97–111. The letter was published, as Casimire remarks "con lieve mende," in Carlo Respighi, *Nuovo studio su Giovanni Pierluigi da Palestrina e l'emendazione del Graduale Romano* (Rome, 1899), 135–38. The original letter is preserved in Rome, Biblioteca Ap. Vat., Cod. 6195, fol. 501; I am grateful to the staff of the Vatican Library for supplying me with a photocopy of it.

20. In the dedication of G. B. Martelli, *La nuova et armonica compositione a 4* (Rome, 1564), the author says that Cimello, acknowledged as his teacher, was in the service of Marc' Antonio Colonna. Larson, "The Unaccompanied Madrigal," 187, suggests that the dedication of Cimello's madrigal book may have been occasioned by the marriage of Fabrizio Colonna to Ippolita Gonzaga, daughter of Ferrante Gonzaga, in 1548. He also points out that Cimello is mentioned in a stanza by Francesco Bellana in praise of Felice Orsini, who married M. A. Colonna in 1552.

21. See chapter 7 above.

22. Annibale Zoilo was among the composers charged with revising chant books according to Tridentine and humanistic precepts; see Harry Lincoln's entry in *New Grove,* 20:704. The commission was given to Zoilo in 1577, not long before the date of Cimello's letter; but Cimello may be referring to a period some years before this.

23. Ferrante Gonzaga, Lasso's first patron, is said to have frequented meetings of the Accademia degli Sereni, which flourished in Naples in 1546–48 and for which Cimello wrote music (see below); perhaps the young Lasso could indeed have met Cimello, but one cannot be sure of this. See nn. 39 and 40 below.

24. On Alessandro Romano see Patricia Myers in *New Grove,* 12:185–86. Alessandro, who may be a different person from the brother of the papal singer G. A. Merlo (a member of the papal chapel from 1551 to 1590), joined the papal chapel himself in 1561; see Richard Sherr, "The Diary of the Papal Singer Giovanni Antonio Merlo," *Analecta Musicologica* 23 (1985): 75–128, esp. 83, 113.

25. For a good account of the careers, interests, and idiosyncrasies of sixteenth-century *poligrafi* see Paul Grendler, *Critics of the Italian World, 1530–1560: Anton Francesco Doni, Nicolò Franco, and Ortensio Lando* (Madison, Wisc., 1969).

26. Rampollini's undated volume, published in Lyons by Moderne, is entitled *Il Primo Libro de la Musica . . . sopra di alcune Canzoni Del Divin Poeta M. Francesco Petrarca;* the word *madrigal* is not even mentioned. An earlier example of this kind of distinction is Petrucci's 1520 print entitled *Musica de messer Bernardo pisano sopra le Canzone del petrarcha.*

27. On the spelling of *madrigale* see *Vocabolario degli Accademici della Crusca,* 11 vols. (Florence, 1863–1914), 9:619, where citations from the work of Bembo and other authors are given. Francesco Corteccia used the spelling *mandriale* for all his publications in the genre; as a member of the Accademia Fiorentina he was doubtless influenced by theories about the origins of the word advanced by fellow academicians such as Benedetto Varchi, who recommended *madriale* and *mandriale* as acceptable spellings; see Varchi, *L'Ercolano* in *Operette istoriche,* ed. Gaetano Milanesi (Florence, 1887), 344.

28. This would seem to be a special preoccupation of Cimello's; in the madrigal volume of Maio mentioned above (n. 15), his pieces are identified by the author whereas those set by Maio are not. The poets are Marchese del Vasto [= Alfonso d'Avalos], "Amanti il vo pur dir," and Luigi Tansillo, "Di quanto soffro il pregio amor sia questo."

29. Einstein, *Italian Madrigal,* 404. Note the similarity of Cimello's language to that in the title of Rossi's *Regole osservanze et avvertenze,* mentioned above in n. 8.

30. Mary S. Lewis tells me that Gardano's prints of this period contain quite a few notated accidentals in general; still, I believe that Cimello and Maio intended something special in this regard. A bibliographical description of Cimello's volume is given by Lewis, *Antonio Gardano, Venetian Music Printer, 1538–1569* (New York, 1988), 1:597–99.

31. See the relevant entries on members of the Colonna family in vol. 27 of the *Dizionario biografico,* as well as that by Giuseppe Alberigo on Giovanni d'Aragona in 3:694–96.

32. This reference is presumably to Gaius Fabricius Luscinus, a Roman military hero of incorruptible virtue, for Cicero the model of the *bonus vir* (Cicero, *De Officiis,* 3.4.xxii).

33. Einstein's verdict on Cimello's music (*Italian Madrigal,* 406) strikes me as unnecessarily harsh; but he is comparing Cimello with Rore.

34. Cimello may have seen Rore's first two books *a 5* in print; but it might be recalled that rather few of Rore's four-voice madrigals had been published by this time; a few pieces appeared in Perissone Cambio's *Primo libro* of 1547, a few more in the *Madrigali de la Fama* (RISM 1548[8]).

35. Variants of any importance are given in the notes on individual pieces in table 1. Lopriore's judgment (*Dizionario biografico,* 25:562) that "i testi letterati sono arbitrariamente manipolati" in Cimello's volume is evidently derived from Einstein's opinion (see above n. 33).

36. A third text attributed by Cimello to Alfonso d'Avalos is found in Maio's *Libro primo* of 1551 (see above n. 28). On Alfonso d'Avalos see, in addition to the entry by Gaspare De Caro (in the *Dizionario biografico,* 4:612–16), Giovanni Battista Tafuri, *Istoria degli scrittori nati nel regno di Napoli,* 3 vols. (Naples, 1744–50), 3:403–4, who cites stanzas from *Orlando furioso* [23: 28–29] referring to him and says that his poems were "dettate con sommo spirito, ed elegante leggiadria; che meritarono d'esser impresse nella Raccolta de' più celebri, et eccellenti Autori, che in quei tempi fiorirono." On the Neapolitan intellectual circle of Vittoria Colonna see Suzanne Thérault, *Un cénacle humaniste de la Renaissance autour de Vittoria Colonna châtelaine d'Ischia* (Florence, 1968).

37. Rore's madrigal was first published in Cambio's *Primo libro a 4vv* of 1547; its very quick rise to popularity suggests that it may have been known in advance of its publication. Evidence that Cimello was indeed acquainted with the Avalos family comes from the dedication of Tomaso Giglio, *Liber primo di motetti a 4vv* (1563); the work is dedicated to Inigo d'Avalos, son of Alfonso, and refers to Cimello as the "commun maestro" of him and of Giglio.

38. Michele Maylender, *Storia delle Accademie d'Italia,* 5 vols. (Bologna, 1926–30), 5:190–92, calls it the Accademia dei Sireni, basing his spelling on a reference to the academy in Luca Contile, *Ragionamenti sopra la proprietà delle imprese* (Pavia, 1574), 47: "Fu

quella di Napoli detta l'Academia de Sireni dalla Sirena, perché a suo nome si edificò Napoli chiamata Partenope, che fu una delle tre Sirene secondo Licofronte." The *impresa* of the academy was, naturally enough, a *sirena*. With several other groups, academies called Eubolei, Ardenti, and Incogniti, the Sireni flourished from ca. 1546 to 1548, when all such groups were banned by the viceroy Don Pietro di Toledo, who suspected them—probably quite groundlessly—of seditious plotting. Cimello's madrigal for what he calls the Sereni must have been written in the period 1546–48. As for the name of the group, Fabio Ottinelli, a founding member (and author of a text, no. 10, in Cimello's volume) wrote, in a prefatory letter to his *Ingeniosa et admodum utilis Repetitio super Celebratissimum lege imperium dig.* (Naples, 1547), that it was called that of the "*Sereni*" for the *serenità* of its members. Cimello's spelling thus receives support. There may have been a word-play on serena-sirena here, recalling the title of an earlier madrigal print, the *Libro primo de la Serena* (Rome, 1530), which carries as device a woodcut Siren.

39. Contile is said to have written fifty sonnets in honor of Giovanna d'Aragona Colonna; see *Dizionario biografico,* 28:494, 502.

40. This possibility is weakened by the fact that the Accademia degli Sereni was suppressed in 1548; see above n. 38.

41. On bel Prato see *Dizionario biografico,* 8:49. Tafuri, *Istoria,* 3:408–9, has words of praise for bel Prato: "Si exercitò anche ben sempre nel comporre poeticamente in Toscano, e le sue rime, che uguaglirano le più culte, e leggiadre de' più accreditati Rimatori di qual tempo, furono inserite nelle Raccolte generali, e precisamente nel Tomo primo delle *Rime Sciolte.*" By this volume Tafuri presumably meant Lodovico Dolce, *Primo volume delle rime scelte di diversi autori* (Venice, 1564), which does contain (pp. 541–46) some verse by bel Prato.

42. In his introduction to the motet volume of Lucario (see above n. 11), Sherr suggests that Lucario, a member of Cimello's circle, set texts suggesting a Reformist tendency, in which the poet bel Prato shared.

43. (Venice, 1545), 200. On Spira see Henry Kaufmann, "Francesco Orso da Celano: A Neapolitan Madrigalist of the Second Half of the Sixteenth Century," *SM* 9 (1980): 228–32.

44. A Giovanni Vincenzo Colle taught philosophy at the University of Naples in the 1560s and published a philosophical tract in 1553; see Pietro Manzi, *La Tipografia napoletana del '500,* 6 vols. (Florence, 1971–75), 2:99–100. In volume 3 of Manzi's work there is mention of Fabio Ottinelli, said there to have written a *favola boscareccia* in verse, called *Trebatio* (published in 1613); to have been a young man in the 1540s; and to have written "componimenti minori che si rinvengono qua e là nelle raccolte del tempo tanto in voga."

45. For the contents of these anthologies (RISM 1542[17], 1543[18], 1549[30], 1549[31] and their reprints), see the modern edition of Don Harrán, *The Anthologies of Black-Note Madrigals,* 5 vols. (American Institute of Musicology, 1978–81).

46. Cimello wrote at some length about the mensural system; see above and n. 18. Controversy over mensural questions including the meaning of C and Ȼ continued through the period; see the references cited in chapter 9. In no. 12 of his madrigal volume Cimello uses C to start, then another C with shorter note values, for the text "A raddoppiar i mei dolori."

47. In his treatise on mensural values Cimello speaks of the difficulty of this mensuration, advising that it is easier to manage if two semibreves are taken to the *battuta*.

48. The piece may have been intended as mourning for the author of its text, Alfonso d'Avalos, who had died in 1546. For some examples of blackened notes with symbolic rather than mensural significance, see *New Grove,* 6:339; 13:375.

49. Walter Blankenburg, in *MGG,* 7:1958–86, gives an informative survey of canonic artifice as practiced in the sixteenth and seventeenth centuries. For a seventeenth-century ex-

ample of a *Cantilena con le pause, e senza pause,* very much less elaborate than that of Cimello, see Angelo Berardi, *Documenti Armonici* (Bologna, 1687), 1.30. 83–84.

A more direct source for Cimello's device is the *Missa Alma redemptoris mater,* also
known as *Missa Duarum Facierum,* by Pierre Moulu, printed in *Missarum decem . . . Liber
Primus* (Rome, 1522; reprinted in *Liber Quindecim Missarum* [Nuremberg, 1539]). In the
table of contents of the latter print (tenor part book only) the work is labeled "Missa duarum
facierum & plus, canitur enim vel cum pausis, vel sine pausis." The Rome volume may well
have been known to Cimello, and the Moulu piece a subject of discussion in his circle. By
what may be sheer coincidence the lone surviving copy of the Rome volume is in Naples,
Biblioteca Nazionale. I am grateful to Alvin H. Johnson for calling Moulu's work to my attention; it is also mentioned by Larson, "The Unaccompanied Madrigal," 191.

50. Harold Powers, "Tonal Types and Modal Categories in Renaissance Polyphony,"
JAMS 34 (1981): 428–70.

51. Ibid.; cf. Siegfried Hermelink, *Dispositiones modorum* (Tutzing, 1960).

52. Johannes Tinctoris, *Liber de natura et proprietate tonorum* (1476), ed. Albert Seay, 2
vols. (American Institute of Musicology, 1975), chap. 24; 1:86, in Seay's edition.

53. Tinctoris, *Liber de natura,* chaps. 46–49, gives examples of melodies in single and
double transposition, the first mode appearing on G (with one flat) and C (with two flats) as
well as on D.

54. For Zarlino two consecutive major thirds produce a *mi-fa* clash. On this subject see
chapter 5 above.

ANTONFRANCESCO DONI:
WRITER, ACADEMICIAN,
AND MUSICIAN

Notes on the *Dialogo della Musica* of Antonfrancesco Doni

THE WELCOME APPEARANCE in a modern edition[1] of Antonfrancesco Doni's *Dialogo della musica,* out of print since the first and only edition of 1544 ceased to be available from the Venetian press of Girolamo Scotto, makes it appropriate to comment on the work at this time, some thirty years after Alfred Einstein, writing in the pages of *Music and Letters,*[2] called the attention of the musical world to Doni. With the full text of the work now available, the madrigals contained in it scored and placed where they occur in the dialogue, one can find Doni's remarks about music, some of which have often been quoted in isolation, in the context he intended, and his ingenious, indeed unique plan can be appreciated: two *serate* or *veglie,* part literary, part musical, part anecdotal fluff, given in full. To compare small things with great, in Doni's work we have a *Decameron,* or a *Courtier,* with all the music its company was said to perform actually laid out before us. And if the text of Doni's work is no masterpiece even by the standard of his other writings, the music in isolation not of great importance as an anthology, still in combination they give a suggestive and perhaps a historically valuable glimpse of the role of music in sixteenth-century society.

I

Doni realized, and was proud, that he had created something new.[3] Judging from the fact that the work was never reprinted and that little reference is made to it in the sixteenth century, one can assume that it was not a great success. From the location of the surviving copies it is hard to say whether it ever had much circulation; but some of the extant copies have corrections and show other signs of use, and two have on the title page sixteenth-century signatures using the formula "di [owner's name] e degli amici," allowing one to hope that the work was handed round to be read and sung by convivial groups.[4] Its author doubtless hoped for more gain and more fame than it brought him; his disappointment is evident in the fact that except for one or two later scattered attempts[5] he abandoned music for belletristic essays and dialogues, or whatever category his bizarre literary output of the 1550s might be said to fall under.

Perhaps because of its very nature—a dialogue professedly about music the contents of which touch on the art only sporadically and in anecdotal fashion,[6] and a collection of madrigals hidden inside the covers of a book (it was published in partbooks, but only the *canto* has the text of the dialogue, and of the surviving copies most are of the *canto* only)—the work received little notice. Doni mentions it, twice for good measure, in his *Libraria,* but I have found no other sixteenth-century references to it.[7] In later times it was occasionally picked up by some antiquarian or scholar of eclectic tastes, such as the Florentine academician Anton Maria Salvini (1653–1729).[8] Apostolo Zeno saw it, indeed owned a copy,[9] and what he says of Doni in general is certainly applicable to the *Dialogo:* "It is so much the practice of Doni, in all his fantastical writings, to blend truth with falsehood, that the reader is unable to discover when he is ludicrous, or when serious." The lively English is the translation of Burney, who also ran across Doni's work in Padre Martini's library at Bologna,

> where I transcribed a considerable part of it. The author, a whimsical and excentric character, tinctured with buffoonery, was not only a practical musician and composer by profession, but connected and in correspondence with the principal writers and artists of his time.[10]

To the more scientific tastes of the nineteenth century Doni's work was of little use, so that men like Kiesewetter saw it only to disapprove of its contents.[11] But it found its way into the pages of bibliographical catalogues,[12] thence to become known to the scholarly world. Alfred Einstein introduced the *Dialogo* to the twentieth century, writing of it with his inimitable combination of learning and sympathetic understanding.[13] For Italian readers Gian Francesco Malipiero provided first an atmospheric introduction to Doni as musician[14] and now a complete edition of the work itself.

Although a full-length study of Doni as man and writer has yet to be written, most of the important biographical material has been assembled,[15] and his early life, leading up to and including the years 1543–44 spent in Piacenza and Venice, when the *Dialogo* was written, has been ably sketched by Einstein. Here I shall try merely to give a notion of what kind of musician Doni was, what circles he moved in, and what his qualifications were for writing a work on music, not to mention music itself. In a number of letters written shortly before the *Dialogo,* he describes himself as a *musico,* one who can sing, play, compose, and copy music. To Cosimo de' Medici, Duke of Florence, Doni writes from Piacenza on 27 March 1543: "Son musico, scrittore, dotto in volgare." He sends to the Duke (to whom he was later to give a copy of the *Dialogo*), along with a motet by Giachet Berchem, "à vostri Cantori una mia Canzone" as well as two sonnets, "scritti di mia mano, & disegnati i canti, i sonetti, & le carte." To Cardinal Alessandro Farnese Doni writes, also in 1543, that he is "scrittore, sonatore, cantore, & dipintore, più che di mezza taglia." At the end of a long letter (his first published work) describing to the sculptor Giovan'Angelo his life in Piacenza, Doni adds that he is "sending "de miei disegni, & de le mie musiche." Applying for a position in the service of Paolo Giovio, he describes himself thus: "Io son Fiorentino, Prete; & mi diletto di scrivere, come voi vedete, e vedrete cantare, sonare, disegnare, et poetizzare: bench' io non ho *cum quibus;* & spesso son *sine quibus.*" Lest he be thought too bohemian from this account, Doni hastens to add that "in somma son galante huomo: ho bel viso; son ben fatto; va diretto sulla persona; mi specchio; me setolo; & mi lavo il volto & le mani di saponetti bolognesi ogni mattina ogni mattina, ch'io non fallo mai."[16]

Doni, who was not particularly modest, seems to have made no great claims for himself as a musician, either composer or performer. Even in the dedicatory letters prefixed to the part-books of the *Dialogo* he speaks more of music he has heard than of what he himself has done, and he claims credit rather for the originality of the dialogue as a whole than for any music of his own. In the last of these letters Doni writes to his friend Ottavio Landi that after hearing the musical wonders of Venice he has kicked aside all the instruments he plays and has decided that he might as well "sew up my mouth, and candy my ears." Alfred Einstein has already pointed out that for Doni the move from provincial Piacenza to the Venice of Willaert and his circle was an exciting and unsettling experience.

Apparently Doni was not in fact an accomplished musician, though he sometimes said he would like to have become a virtuoso had circumstances permitted.[17] Still, he doubtless had had a bit of theoretical training, and he confesses that in his youth he learned to play the flute and the *viola,* though he soon (like his greater contemporary Cellini) discarded the former instrument.[18] But in the *Dialogo* he speaks of himself as playing the *viola* in a group of instrumentalists, either in Piacenza or, to judge from the names of the other players, in Milan, where he had spent some time on the way from his native Florence to Piacenza.[19] We may gather from all this that Doni, if no professionally skilled musician, must have been able to hold his own in a company of virtuosi some of whom were probably much more accomplished than he was; that he was conversant with the musical practices, taste, and gossip of his day; and that he was capable of scribbling down a few musical compositions of his own. As we shall see, the madrigals credited to him in the *Dialogo* have very much the air of a semiskilled amateur at work.

II

Though anything but learned or even serious in tone, the conversations of the *Dialogo* were obviously meant to represent in informal pose the activities of an academy. All his life Doni was enchanted by the idea of academies; the high point of his strange life must have been the early 1550s in Venice, where he ran, or said he ran, the affairs of the Accademia Pellegrina—even though the nature and accomplishments of this group, Doni being its chief spokesman, may be in part fictitious.[20] In Piacenza he was one of the leading figures of the short-lived Accademia Ortolana, and during his Florentine stay of 1545–48 he managed to associate himself with the austere Florentine Academy, where he spoke on Petrarch and for which he even acted as secretary for a year.[21] In his *Seconda Libraria* (Venice, 1551) he devotes pages to the names and activities of Italian academicians, becoming their first if not their most trustworthy bibliographer.

Even if he had thought of the project earlier, he must have drawn much material, musical and otherwise, for the *Dialogo* from his associations with members of the Accademia degli Ortolani in Piacenza. In a long letter to his friend the sculptor Giovan'Angelo, dated June 1543, he writes of his acceptance in the artistic and musical circles of Piacenza, and of the literary activities of the Ortolani, which he makes sound quite serious and intensive; Pegasus, he says, could not carry all the works of the Ortolani even if the divine beast had the capacity of a pack mule. And of course Doni had done his share of literary work. To this he adds: "And besides taking my part in the Muses' work, I have had to compose music," the results of which effort he promises to send on.[22] Apparently he was a leading figure in this group, and in the center of its musical activity. Another picture of the Ortolani is given by Lodovico Domenichi, a Piacentine man of letters close enough to Doni to be the recipient of many letters and an interlocutor in the *Dialogo:*

> Before leaving the subject of academies I must mention another, set up by a few lively wits in Piacenza in 1543, more as a joke than for anything serious; this academy was put under the protection of the *Dio degli Horti . . .* And although organized by carefree young men mostly for fun and games, nonetheless we spent our time honourably and with profit to those who took part.[23]

Doni was secretary of this Academy, alternating with Bartolomeo Gottifredi, a poet given, under the name Bargo, a big role in the *Dialogo.*[24] Its members were apparently welcomed in the best houses of Piacenza; Domenichi, speaking as interlocutor in another dialogue, Giuseppe Betussi's *Il Raverta,* asks:

> What more could one want, than to enjoy the loving favor and the noble generosity of the illustrious Counts Giulio and Agostino Landi, the regal splendor of Count Girolamo Angosciuola or . . . the generosity of Count Teodosio Angosciuola? How could one tear oneself away from the sweet and virtuous company of the Magnifico Cavalier Sig. Luigi Cassola, at whose house poets cluster like mendicants at a church?[25]

Nearly all the names mentioned by Doni in the first part of the *Dialogo,* whether of noble patrons, gentlewomen, men of letters or musicians, can be identified as belonging to the circle described by Domenichi.[26] Of these the most important are Domenichi himself; Luigi Cassola, one of the chief poets of the madrigal literature of the 1530s and 1540s, a man whom Doni mentions several times in the *Dialogo* and to whom he wrote a number of letters; and the musicians Claudio Veggio, Girolamo Parabosco, and Paolo Iacopo Palazzo, whose works appear in the *Dialogo* and the first two of whom act as interlocutors.

It seems, then, that Part 1 of the *Dialogo* may be taken as an imaginative recreation of the activities of the Accademia Ortolana during the year 1543. Of the four speakers Bargo can be identified as Bartolomeo Gottifredi, secretary of the Academy; Michele may be the Michele Novarese of the list of composers, a young man perhaps in the service of the Torniela family in Piacenza, addressed by Doni in a letter of 1544 as "musico diligente" and "molto virtuoso figliuolo" (Einstein's suggestion that Doni uses Michele's name to cover his own ideas, even one of his own compositions, "Di tre rare eccellenze," is a good one, particularly if Michele was just a boy at this time);[27] Hoste and Grullone are obviously pseudonyms, which I have been unable to track down.[28] As for the composers represented in the first part of the work (see table 1), Claudio Veggio (nos. 1 and 13) and Girolamo Parabosco (nos. 8 and 9) were both in Piacenza at this time; Paolo Iacopo Palazzo (no. 10) and Tommaso Bargonio (no. 11) were part of the same local group of musicians;[29] and

TABLE I

Musical Contents of the *Dialogo della musica*

	Poet	Composer	Concordances
1. Donna per ac-quetar vostro desire	Bartolomeo Got-tifredi; see *Rime diversi di molti ecc. autori,* Lib. 1° (Venice, 1549), 250	Claudio Veggio	
2. Ma di chi debbo lamentarmi hai lasso	Ariosto, *Orlando furioso,* 32.21	Vincenzo Ruffo	Ruffo, *I° à 4* (1545, 1546, 1552, 1556), no. 32; Florence, B. N. C., MS. Magl. XIX; 130, no. 3. Reprint in L. Torchi, *L'arte musicale* 1.215.
3. Lassatemi morire		Pre Maria Riccio	
4. S'amante fu gia-mai di sperar privo	Luigi Cassola; see *Madrigali del Mag. Sig. L. Cassola Piacentino* (Venice, 1544), 110	Arcadelt	
5. Il bianco e dolce cigno	Alfonso d'Avalos	Arcadelt (can-tus); *centone* in lower voices by Doni?	Arcadelt, *I° à 4* (cantus) (1539), no. 1.
6. Noi v'abbian donne mille nuov' a dire	Doni	Doni	
7. O conservi d'amor che cosi spesso	Doni	Doni	
8. Pur converra ch'i miei martiri amore		Girolamo Parabosco	Reprint in Fran-cesco Bussi, *G. Pa-rabosco, Composi-zioni* (Piacenza, 1961), 7.
9. Giunto m'ha amor fra belle e crude braccia	Petrarch, *Canzo-niere,* no. 172 (octet only)	Parabosco	

TABLE I—Continued

Musical Contents of the *Dialogo della musica*

	Poet	Composer	Concordances
10. Maledetto sia amore e quel che disse		Paolo Iacopo Palazzo	
11. Alma mia fiamma e donna	Pietro Aretino; see his *Capricciosi & Piacevoli Ragionamenti,* 2.3.385 in ed. of 1660 (Amsterdam, Elzevier)	Tomaso Bargonio	
12. Di tre rare eccellenze	Lodovico Domenichi; *Rime* (Venice, 1544), fol. 62v	Michele Novarese (= Doni?)	
13. Madonna il mio dolor è tant' e tale	Doni; see *Lettere* (1544), fol. 129v	Claudio Veggio	
14. S'io potessi mirar quell'occhi belli		Noleth	
15. Chiaro leggiadro lume che dal cielo	Doni (?)	Doni (?)	
16. Deh perchè com'è il vostro al nome mio		Perissone Cambio	Perissone, *I° à 5* (Venice, 1545), no. 1.
17. Nessun visse giamai più de me lieto	Petrarch, *sestina* "Mia benigna fortuna," stanza 7	Parabosco	Parabosco *I° à 5* (Venice, 1546), no. 17.
Canzone [= sestina] Alla dolc'ombra	Petrarch, no. 142	Giacchetto Berchem	*Primo libro de le Muse à 5* (Venice, 1555).
18. Ingenium ornavit Pallas, ornavit potentem Tenor: Argentum et aurum	Tenor: Acts 3:6		
19. Cantai mentre ch'io arsi del mio foco	Giovanni Brevio	Parabosco	Reprint in Bussi, *Parabosco,* 12. The same text is set by Cipriano de Rore as no. 1 in his *Primo libro à 5* (1542).

TABLE I—Continued

Musical Contents of the *Dialogo della musica*

	Poet	Composer	Concordances
20. Ave virgo gratiosa 2ª pars: Rubicunda plusquam rosa	First two verses of hymn for feast of Immaculate Conception, as given in a sixteenth-century printed source. See G. M. Dreves, *Analecta hymnica,* 19.22.	Perissone?	This text was set à 6 by Berchem (*Motetti de la Simia,* 1539) and Willaert (*Musicorum omnium,* 1542), but neither resembles the setting given here. An "Ave virgo gratiosa" of Verdelot, otherwise unknown, is mentioned by Pietro Aaron, *Toscanello in musica* (ed. of 1562, fol. 25v), but is not described in enough detail to enable one to identify it with Doni's piece.
21. Beatus Bernardus quasi vas auri solidum 2ª pars: Factus est quasi ignis.		Willaert	Wolfenbüttel, Herz. Aug. Bibl., MS. Auct. 4.28; Treviso, Bibl. cap., MS. 4; MS. 29.
22. Giunto m'ha amor fra belle a crude braccia	Petrarch (cf. no. 9)	Perissone Cambio	Verdelot *à 6 voci* (Venice, 1546).
23. Quis tuos presul valeat nitenti pileo 2ª pars: Quin tenes legum Tenor: Felix o vivas princeps presulque		Cipriano de Rore	Wolfenbüttel, Herz. Aug. Bibl., MS. 293, no. 29.
24. Madonna il mio dolor è tant' e tale	Doni (cf. no. 13)	Claudio Veggio	
25. Amorosette fiore		Arcadelt	
26. À tout jamais d'ung vouloir immuable		Jacques Buus	
27. Madonna hor che direte	Doni; see *Lettere,* (1544), fol. 129v	Claudio Veggio	

Pre Maria Riccio (no. 3), though called *padovano,* may have been living in Piacenza, since he and his family are described as personal friends by Bargo, and his brother is the recipient of a letter from Doni.[30] Doni himself seems to have composed nos. 6 and 7, and, under the name of Michele, possibly no. 12. This leaves only a madrigal by Arcadelt (no. 4) and one by Vincenzo Ruffo (no. 2) to account for (the *centone* on Arcadelt's famous "Il bianco e dolce cigno" [no. 5], may have been the work of Doni himself; see below). Doni speaks of Ruffo as if he knew the composer, and it is possible that they had met in Milan, where Ruffo seems to have been in these years, or that the young Ruffo had paid a visit to nearby Piacenza. "Ma di chi debbo lamentarmi" appears in any event to be Ruffo's first published madrigal. But Doni does not claim to know the great Arcadelt, and how he got hold of two pieces by this master (cf. no. 25) I do not know. About no. 4, "S'amante fu giamai," there is some mystery; it will be discussed presently.

Even the madrigal texts have in several instances local connections: no. 1 is by Gottifredi, no. 4 by Cassola, nos. 6, 7, and 13 by Doni, no. 12 by Domenichi. And much of the conversation among the four speakers is about local personages or events. It is quite conceivable that Doni was writing the first part of the *Dialogo,* and collecting from his friends the madrigals to put into it, just when he was actively taking part in the doings of the Ortolani. Certainly he had finished this first section before he left Piacenza for Venice at the beginning of 1544, for in a letter of 19 November 1543, a half-joking, half-truculent epistle addressed "à poeti e musici," he says "Cicero holds that music consists of numbers, tones and measures; but this time in my *Dialogo* I have used neither square nor compass."[31]

The lure of Venice must have been very strong; early in 1543, when Doni was just establishing himself in Piacenza, he wrote to a friend of his desire to go there. When he did leave for Venice the Ortolani were breaking up, perhaps had been forced to disband;[32] Domenichi and Parabosco certainly went to Venice about the same time (Parabosco perhaps earlier), and Claudio Veggio may have gone back and forth between the two cities. In Part 2 of the *Dialogo* only Bargo and Michele remain of the original speakers; Girolamo Parabosco, Claudio Veggio, Lodovico Domenichi, and Count Ottavio Landi come along from Piacenza; the composer Perissone Cambio, probably resident in Venice, is introduced, and a lady called Selvaggia, who as Einstein points out is Isabetta Guasca, herself a poetess and the object of Doni's professed adoration, joins the company. The second part of the work is described as taking place the night after the first, and the absence of Grullone and Hoste is remarked, but the setting has obviously changed to the greater stage of Venice. Doni could hardly have occupied as central a position in Venetian musical life as he had in Piacenza, and in fact he must have felt his amateur status rather keenly; in the last of the four dedicatory letters of the *Dialogo* he writes to his friend Ottavio Landi (who as a speaker in Part 2 was evidently present only in spirit):

> I wish that you could be here, to see the divinity of the women, of the musicians, of the instruments. I have kicked aside my rustic pipes—transverse, curved and straight; and I've thought of sewing up my mouth and candying my ears, so discontented am I at not being able to do anything.

In the dedicatory letter of the tenor part, addressed to the Marchese Malvicino of Piacenza, Doni compares, in a passage that has often been quoted,[33] the modest performances and means of Piacenza to the musical splendors of Venice, in particular the singing of Polissena Peccorina and the direction of the *maestro perfetto* Adrian Willaert, of whom he speaks in awestruck terms.

But even if he was reduced for the time being to the status of an onlooker, Doni must have worked busily at getting himself accepted in the artistic society of Venice. He evidently impressed the printer Girolamo Scotto, who before the year was out had printed the *Dialogo* and also a volume of Doni's letters; by April 1544 he was able to write to Claudio Veggio in Piacenza, begging the composer on behalf of Scotto to send another book of madrigals to be published;[34] and later, when Doni set himself up as a printer in Florence, he may have used type borrowed from Scotto.[35] It is perhaps typical of Doni's personal and professional relationships with others, always tending to deteriorate, that upon his return to Venice in 1549 he worked for Giolito and then Marcolini, but had no more to do with Scotto.

Doni must therefore have gained admittance as a listener if not a performer to exalted musical circles in Venice. The music sung by *la Peccorina* and played by expert instrumentalists under Willaert's direction, as described in the letter cited above, he heard at the house of

> the devotee of this music, and one enamored of all divine composition, a gentleman and excellent wit, a native Florentine, one Neri Capponi. I became his friend through Francesco Corboli, a splendid fellow; and thanks to him I saw, heard, and felt all this divine music. This Messer Neri spends hundreds of ducats a year on such *virtù,* and keeps it all to himself; he wouldn't let a piece of music out of his hands, were it even to his own father. Now, since I can't send you that music, I send you this [the *Dialogo*].

This passage is quoted by Einstein, unfortunately with a mistranslation that rather spoils its sense. Edward Lowinsky gives the passage correctly translated, and suggests that Neri Capponi could in fact have been Willaert's patron and that the long-delayed publication of Willaert's *Musica Nova* of 1559 may have been caused in part by Capponi's restrictive patronage.[36] Anne-Marie Bragard adds the hypothesis that Willaert's arrangement of Verdelot madrigals for solo voice and lute may have been done for Polissena Peccorina and her circle.[37] Neri Capponi does seem to have had a kind of musical academy at his house, with Willaert at its head; Sylvestro Ganassi confirms its existence in the dedicatory letter, addressed to Capponi, of Part 2 of his *Regola Rubertina* of 1543.[38]

Doni does not go so far as to place the second part of the *Dialogo* in an actual Venetian musical academy; the days of the Accademia Pellegrina were yet to come. The conversation in Part 2, dominated by a somewhat tiresome discourse on feminine virtue delivered by Domenichi, goes on much as it did in Part 1, although toward the end the music crowds in more and more. One gets the feeling that Doni wrote up topics of conversation more or less left over from the days in Piacenza, but that in Venice he was busy gathering music together and arranging for the publication of the *Dialogo* and of his letters. It is possible, and very typical of Doni, that printing of the work began before he had finished writing it all;[39] about half-way through the second part he abandons the more or less careful spacing of talk versus music in the original plan, and simply crowds in what music he had in his possession, in quite haphazard order, bringing the work to a somewhat breathless close. Near the end Domenichi remarks that he will arrange for a concert of singers and instrumentalists, naming some of the best-known performers in Venice,[40] to take place the Sunday following; but no third part was actually written.

The sources on which Doni drew for the music of the second part are rather harder to track down than those of Part 1. Since Parabosco seems to have been a personal friend, his further contributions (nos. 17, 19) are understandable. In a few instances the author of the *Dialogo* may simply have asked for contributions and got them; the eight-voice chanson "À tous jamais" (no. 26) must have been one of the *canti à otto* for which Doni thanks Jacques Buus profusely in a letter of April 1544,[41] and to which he responds by giving Buus a copy of the *Dialogo.* The two pieces by Perissone (nos. 16, 22) may have been written partly at Doni's request; Perissone's *Primo libro à 5* (1545), which opens with "Deh perchè" (= *Dialogo,* no. 16), is said on its title page to have been composed "a compiacimento de diversi suoi amici."[42] Claudio Veggio certainly supplied Doni with music (here nos. 24 and 27); of his eight-voice "Madonna il mio dolor" (no. 24), the setting of a text by Doni, he is made to say in the *Dialogo* (p. 265): "This piece no one has seen, because I wrote it at Doni's request."

The longest piece in the *Dialogo* is Giachet Berchem's setting of a complete *sestina* of Petrarch, "Alla dolc'ombra de le belle frondi" (not numbered in Doni's list of the madrigals). Berchem, who had had separate pieces printed as early as 1538 but had not yet had a whole work devoted to him, here figures as a composer of importance. Doni has little to say about the piece, and that little platitudinous ("La mi par pur bella questa sestina, et una musica buona; ma come può altrimenti d'un tal musico eccellente? Ora per non lodar quel che si loda da se stesso" [p. 163]). But he might have known Berchem; in 1543 he sent a motet of the latter's to Cosimo de' Medici.[43] At the time the *Dialogo* was written Berchem may have been living in Venice, since in the dedication of his *Primo libro à 5* of 1546 he is described as a member of a Venetian gentleman's household.[44] Another composer apparently moving in Venetian musical circles is the rather obscure Noleth (or Nolletto), presumably the composer of no. 14, "S'io potessi mirar," followed by the comment: "I am delighted with this perfect little madrigal; I would swear it is the work of Nolet. Let us sing it again." He is represented in some of Verdelot's publications ca. 1540, and appears in Gardane's *misura à breve* anthologies of the 1540s.

Of the remaining pieces no. 15, "Chiaro leggiadro lume," may be by Doni himself (see below), and a hint is thrown out that no. 20, "Ave virgo gratiosa," could be the work of Perissone Cambio (who as an interlocutor presents it to be sung, then asks how everyone likes it). The motet "Ingenium ornavit Pallas" (no. 18), given without comment, is not ascribed to anyone; the fact that it uses in the tenor a cantus firmus on a text, "Argentum et aurum non est mihi. Quod autem habeo hoc tibi do," used in a motet by Adrian Willaert,[45] need not mean that the piece was

written by Willaert, for Doni would not have kept this a secret. He does print a motet of Willaert's, "Beatus Bernardus" (no. 21), a piece that does not appear among
that composer's published motets—although in style it resembles, with its canonic
middle voices, a number of motets by Willaert—with the comment: "One can tell
that this is by Messer Adriano; it is most certainly excellent."[46] How did he get
hold of it? From the composer himself or by stealth, a little greasing of the palm of
some member of Willaert's musical establishment? There is also a motet by the
great Cipriano de Rore, "Quis tuos presul" (no. 23); Einstein, after pointing out
that the text of the piece shows it to be dedicated to Cristoforo Madruzzo, Cardinal
Archbishop of Trent, says that Doni's publication of it "can hardly have met with
Rore's approval," since the composer did not at all like having single pieces fall
"into the hands of any old person who wanted to print them."[47] Finally, there is a
six-voice madrigal by Arcadelt, "Amorosetto fiore" (no. 25), again not known
from other publications, although an unrelated four-voice setting of this text is in
Arcadelt's *Quinto libro à 4* (1544), no. 6. At the time the *Dialogo* was written Arcadelt was in Rome, and before that he had been in Florence; that he may have spent
some time in Venice is indicated by the text of the madrigal (*Libro primo,* no. 16)
addressed to Polissena Peccorina.[48] Again Doni gives no clue as to how he got hold
of the piece.

At the end of the *Dialogo* two pieces promised for performance are left unsung,
hence unprinted.[49] These are described as a "Canto à 6" by Lionardo Barré and
one "à 7" by Verdelot, both of whose names appear in the table of *musici compositori.* Whether Doni really had these pieces in his possession but could not get Girolamo Scotto to print anything more, or whether he was simply faking, is hard to say
for certain although, Doni's character and reputation being what they were, not
hard to guess. In any event pieces answering to this description are not to be found
among the published works of Verdelot and Barré.

III

As a musical anthology Doni's collection is curious in make-up and very uneven in
quality. To begin with, the appearance of four motets and a chanson in Part 2 has
very much the look of the author's having grabbed at anything available. Motets do
appear in printed madrigal collections from time to time, and so do chansons; but
for both to be found, and to be shoved in near the end of the collection where they
are found intermingled with madrigals, there seems no precedent and little reason.
If, on the other hand, Doni was trying to inject a note of realism by suggesting that
groups of singers assembled for an evening sang French and Italian, sacred and
secular pieces all mixed together, his scheme might justify itself. Similarly the
mixture of good and bad, accomplished and ineptly written works might have been
done to show that singers informally gathered performed what music they had,
without bothering much about matters of style or quality (cf. Doni's remark,
quoted below about young singers not stopping to "comb through" the style of the

music they read). It should be noted that in the *Dialogo* the interlocutors are not provided with printed or manuscript partbooks, but are handed individual pieces out of the *carnaiolo* (small repository or pouch) in Grullone's possession in Part 1, in Michele's hands in Part 2. From evidence provided by a number of sixteenth-century paintings we know that music circulated in individual pieces, which we often see rolled up or crumpled in singers' hands; Doni himself often speaks in his letters of single madrigals he is sending a friend, and it is not difficult to imagine many amateurs such as those depicted in the *Dialogo* having a small chest full of individual pieces, of widely differing character, written on scraps of paper (it would be a great find to discover undisturbed such a *carnaiolo*).

One aspect of musical style in the 1540s is shown quite clearly in the *Dialogo,* especially in Part 1: the prevalence of the relatively new madrigal *à note nere,* written in short note values with the time signature C.[50] Nos. 2, 3, and 10 are particularly good examples of this style, with their fussy syncopation, fast-against-slow alternation of time values as the meaning of the text suggests such changes, and occasional bursts of ornamental figures in very short note values. The two four-voice madrigals of Claudio Veggio, nos. 1 and 13, also illustrate the style, no. 13, "Madonna il mio dolor," being an especially striking case: the musical setting of the first two lines of this madrigal is recapitulated in exact diminution in all four voices for the last two, creating an absurd effect of $33^1/_3$-into-78 r.p.m. speeding up. The text of this piece was, according to its author, Doni himself, designed to satirize conventional madrigalistic poetry;[51] here Veggio may have entered into the joke. In the course of remarks on the present state of music Michele says (p. 70) that "many who can compose don't [can't?] sing these *canti turchi,*" the latter term being his name for the Turkish = Moorish = black appearance of such pieces, an indication that for singers used to the rather placid and even movement of most of Arcadelt and Verdelot's madrigals the *note nere* pieces were difficult to read through—which indeed they are. For Doni the *note nere* madrigal was apparently always *à 4,* all the pieces for five or more voices being written in the traditional ₵ signature: this despite the recent appearance of Cipriano de Rore's *Madrigali cromatici,* the most famous examples of the type, *à 5.*

The music contained in Part 1 gives a clue to the level of provincial musical life in the 1540s–quite high, apart from Doni's own contributions and the rather stiff and awkward effort of Bargonio (no. 11). Pre Maria Riccio and Paolo Iacopo Palazzo acquit themselves well here, writing the fussy, syncopated kind of piece described above. Claudio Veggio, represented by two madrigals in each part of the *Dialogo,* was obviously a musician of skill, whose madrigal volume, adorned with six pieces *à note nere* by Arcadelt, had been published by Scotto in 1540. One feature of Veggio's style, seen here in all four pieces, even the eight-voice "Madonna il mio dolor" (no. 24; in reality four voices, each echoed by a canonic follower at the unison, with very little overlap), is his use of full and exact musical recapitulation, the setting of each poem's last two lines reproducing that of the first two—a joke in no. 13, but a serious trademark of style in the others. Girolamo Parabosco, also represented by four compositions, lifts the level of the whole collection by the quality of his contributions, spontaneous and imaginative while at the same time a little reserved and severe. Einstein devotes several pages, as always full of under-standing and sympathy, to Parabosco; and a good study in Italian, by Francesco Bussi, has appeared more recently.[52] Parabosco, who was a good organist and com-poser, a poet, playwright, and author of *novelle,* handsome, successful with women, must have been all that Doni himself wanted to be, as this outburst, given to Claudio Veggio in the *Dialogo* may show:

> The rest of us are worth nothing. Who composes music? Parabosco. Who writes po-etry? Parabosco. Who sings, who has countless accomplishments? Parabosco. It is too much.

But Doni has the grace to make Parabosco, who was about twenty years old at this time, reply simply and modestly to this bit of spleen.

In Part 2 there are the dignified motets of Willaert and Rore (nos. 21 and 23), rather out of place in this context. Arcadelt's six-voice "Amorosette fiore" (no. 25) is not very interesting; he is not well represented in the *Dialogo.* The *sestina* by Berchem, with its effectively planned alternation of voice parts and its thematic unity by means of a kind of head-motive—a favorite device of Berchem's, used also in his *canzone* "A qualunque animale" (*Primo libro à 4,* published before 1550)—is a good piece of work, not exciting in any way. The chief novelty of Part 2 is its inclusion of eight-voice pieces, evidently new to Doni, for he (as Domenichi) proposes sending them to a group of Florentine musicians, perhaps friends of his youth:

> These in eight parts I'd like to copy and send to Florence, to Maestro Mauro, to Mo-schino, to Bartolomeo Trombone and to Gianicco.[53]

As for Doni's own compositions, they deserve separate mention.

> Let us sing four pieces for four worthy fellows:[54] two in which words and music are all twisted about *(mutati i canti e le parole d'ogni suo diritto),* so that, as you will agree, the singers will have something to talk about; and two by Girolamo Parabosco, a youth so talented that one piece alone would be enough to make you marvel. Think, then, how infinitely talented he must be.

With these words Grullone introduces *canti* 6–9, with 6 and 7, "Noi v'habbiam donne" and "O conservi d'amor," presumably by Doni himself. No. 6, a *masche-rata* from its text, is riddled with errors that have to be corrected somehow or other before the piece can be sung through;[55] "O conservi" is in better shape, but both pieces are indescribably clumsy in phrase construction and in contrapuntal han-dling, and of very pedestrian quality in melodic material. Was Doni, who always protested that he was a musician only by avocation,[56] a real bungler who cheekily put his music in the same company as that of his betters (the two madrigals follow-ing, by Parabosco, are among the freshest and most graceful of the whole collec-tion)? Was he deliberately parodying the clumsiness of inexpert amateurs who tried to compose? Or could these madrigals be the result of slight skill combined with satiric intent? It seems impossible that the pieces could have been meant seri-ously. Every cadence is given a pointless little flip in some inner voice (see exx.

12.1 and 12.2). There are exaggerated changes of register for no reason (ex. 12.3). "Expressive" contrasts are made in a flat-footed way (ex. 12.4). There are octaves, fifths, incomplete measures; and everywhere the silly pedestrian air of a sixteenth-century *musikalischer Spass* suggests itself. Alas, the lack of anything really clever or funny also suggests that the joke was partly on the composer.

After the four pieces have been sung Hoste is made to say that he liked no. 6; he then asks that the company take up the matter of musical theory:

> I should like us to turn to these musical proportions, and to dispute about perfect and imperfect accords; on mensurations, on major and minor fifths; on how one can make perfect chord combinations—in what way one can order the seconds and sevenths that are imperfect.

Example 12.1 "O conservi d'amor," mm. 16–17

Example 12.2 "Noi v'habbian donne," mm. 7–10

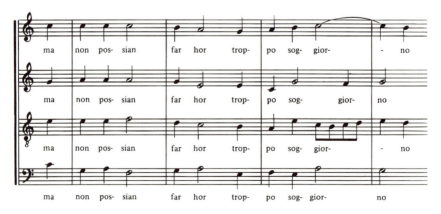

Example 12.3 "Noi v'habbian donne," mm. 28–31

Example 12.4 "O conservi d'amor," mm. 28–32

This sounds like the talk of a rather ill-equipped pedant, with unsure taste (he admired "Noi v'habbiam donne"). Bargo answers patiently enough:

> The discourse of a good musician, as you know, makes concord of all. Of course, the octave and fifth are perfect, the seventh and second imperfect; it is the forcefulness of a composer's style that makes imperfect seem perfect—though if he were to have three or four successive fifths it would make for an ugly composition. You should know that there are some who talk well about music but have bad musical inventiveness and worse practical skill *(buona ragione e cattiv' aere e pessima practica);* others have good practical skill but no knowledge; others still little musical sense for all their practical accomplishments and knowledge.

Short and unpretentious though this musical treatise is, it is too much for the company, and Grullone breaks it off by saying that "our wish here is to entertain each other, not to hold school." But Bargo's reference to disparities of talent, knowledge, and practical skill among musicians is interesting in this context; and his remarks are expanded by Michele, who says he knows of many who cannot sing *canti turchi,* can barely get through the "Passera" of Verdelot,[57] in spite of the great advance in musical standards in recent years:

> In my time one was considered another Josquin if one could sing this madrigal. [Now] how could one call a singer excellent if he were asked to "sing the Passera" and were unable to get through it?

There follows an oft-quoted passage in which Michele says that Josquin would cross himself in wonderment to see how far music has progressed;[58] such are the skills now required that Michele can think of at most four men (he does not name them) who really qualify as masters. He then adds that "if everyone who knew how to arrange sounds could do it well, I should be among the number of masters." Einstein guessed that Michele might be Doni himself; and even though Michele Novarese seems to have been a real person Doni may well have put his own sentiments into this interlocutor's role. If that is so the composition attributed to Michele, a setting of Domenichi's *ottava* "Di tre rare eccellenze" (no. 12), may also be by Doni; it is a very simple and quite undistinguished piece, even if not quite so awkward as nos. 6 and 7. From all this it seems likely that Doni, conscious of possessing only limited skills as a composer but not wanting to stay completely in the background, made a few settings of his own, archly refrained from claiming them outright as his, and in the case of nos. 6 and 7 covered his awkwardness by exaggerating it while he satirized *mascherata* and madrigal texts: "Mutati i canti e le parole d'ogni suo diritto."[59]

Both Vogel and Einstein credit Doni with still another piece, *canto* 15, "Chiaro leggiadro lume." This appears as the musical sequel to a passage in praise of Isabetta Guasca, the "Selvaggia" of the *Dialogo* (see p. 106). In view of Doni's repeated declarations of love and admiration for Isabetta Guasca, it seems likely that he wrote at least the text. As for the music, though it is a bit better made than "Noi v'habbiam donne," it does not really exceed the limits of taste and technique shown in "Di tre rare eccellenze." Doni speaks in a letter, written from Piacenza in March 1543, of having composed a madrigal, words and music, in honor of the Guasca, whom he had met at Alessandria before coming to Piacenza.[60] Unless proof of someone else's authorship should turn up there seems no reason not to credit "Chiaro leggiadro" to Doni; and it is respectable enough to raise him a small notch as a composer.

IV

Read in context, all Doni's remarks about music in the *Dialogo* are of some interest; but only a few need be singled out for mention here: the discussion of the *centone* on "Il bianco e dolce cigno," the problem of the *chiave,* and talk having to do with vocal and instrumental practice.

The Centone

Madrigal nos. 3 and 4, "S'amante fu giamai" and "Il bianco e dolce cigno," are both attributed to Arcadelt in the text of the *Dialogo*. After their performance the words of the first, said to be by Luigi Cassola, are praised;[61] and then comes a discussion of the second, of which only the superius is Arcadelt's, the lower voices being a tissue of verbal and musical quotations from other madrigals:

> *B.* I don't wonder that you don't say who has written this other one, that comes to blows with "Il bianco e dolce cigno."
>
> *H.* I like that sort of whimsey.
>
> *B.* I don't.
>
> *H.* So much the worse for you; it was done for those who would enjoy it. If it isn't to your taste, forget it; I think it is a pretty, a pleasing invention.
>
> *G.* You see that one can do with music whatever one wants; I'll show you that if a person decides against doing things the right way, he can simply produce a hodgepodge. Here you have one piece with the soprano completely at odds with the other words below. Here is another in which the words once belonged to a different piece, and this piece had different words—and you see, the pieces now go better than they did before.
>
> *B.* Who is their author?
>
> *G.* The *maestro* who has wounded them so that they cry out for help.
>
> *B.* Very satisfying; I knew that much before.

From Grullone's coy refusal to say who was responsible for the *centone* we may infer that Doni himself did it, or at least wished to imply that he did. In another place Michele allows that the writing of a *centone* is not so difficult:

> If everyone who knew how to arrange sounds *(fare gli accordi)* could do it well, I should be among the number of masters. In a month one can learn how to make a *zibaldone,* but for invention and imitative counterpoint to be joined with harmony [that is another thing].

Actually the three lower voices of "Il bianco e dolce cigno" work pretty well, even though the resulting piece is horribly clumsy when compared to Arcadelt's graceful original; the arranger even manages a bit of imitation near the end, not easy to do within the framework of a quodlibet. The arrangement seems to have been done with care, for the verbal and musical quotations are reasonably faithful, sometimes indeed transposed or lightly altered, but on the whole recognizable when their source is known, even taken from the corresponding voice part more often than not. Besides, a real effort seems to have been made to suggest Arcadelt's style by the use of a great many quotations from his own madrigals—as far as I can tell by restricting quotations to the work of early madrigalists, chiefly Verdelot and Festa, in addition to Arcadelt.[62]

Grullone speaks as if the first Arcadelt piece, "S'amante fu giamai," had also

TABLE 2
The Centone

Here is a list of the fragments quoted in the *centone* (no. 5), with all the identifications I have been able to make. Perhaps someone more diligent or luckier than I can complete the list. References are to Emil Vogel, *Bibliothek*. The quotations are from the openings of madrigals unless otherwise stated. Small changes and transpositions are not noted. The date given is that of the earliest publication known to me.

Superius:	Complete text of Alfonso d'Avalos's "Il bianco e dolce cigno," with Arcadelt's superius used intact.	
Altus:	Triste amarilli mia	Verdelot (Vogel, *Samml.*, 1533[1] [1530])
	Sol' et pensoso	Arcadelt (Vogel, Veggio 1, 1540)
	Io ard'amor	—
	La dolce vista della donna mia	Verdelot (Vogel, Verdelot 1, 1541)
	Fu fors'un tempo fui	—
	Si grand' è la pietà	Arcadelt (Vogel, Arcadelt 36b, 1539)
	Felic' è il bel desio	—
	Più non sent'il mio duol tanto m'adoglia	Arcadelt (Vogel, Arcadelt 31, 1539): second statement of opening line
	Folle chi sper'o cred'amor	—
	Crudel'acerba	Arcadelt (Vogel, Verdelot 6a, 1538)
	Amor per cui sol vivo	—
	Desio perche mi meni	Arcadelt (Vogel, Arcadelt 31, 1539)
	Si come belle sete	—
	Amor con tal dolcezza mi vi farete	—
	Bella Fioretta	Arcadelt (Vogel, Arcadelt 1, 1539 [1538?])
	Ridendo la mia donna	Festa (Vogel, Verdelot 16, 1537)
	Perche sete si bella	—
	Venut'era madonna	—
	Qual io mi sia per la mia lingua s'ode	—
Tenor:	Se saper donna curi	Anon. (Verdelot?) (Florence, B. N. C., MS. Magl. XIX, 122–5, no. 14)
	Afflitti spirti miei	Verdelot, *I° à 4,* 1533 (Paris, Bibl. G. Thibault) (cf. Vogel, Verdelot 7, 1537)
	Madonn'oime	Arcadelt (Vogel, Arcadelt 4, 1541)
	Io che viver sciolt' havea pensato	Arcadelt (Vogel, Verdelot 6a, 1540)
	Madonna mi consumo	Festa (Vogel, *Samml.* 1537[3])
	Vostra merce madonna	Arcadelt (Vogel, *Samml.* 1542[2])
	Credete sempre haver di lei mercede	—
	Che più foco al mio foco	Arcadelt (Vogel, Arcadelt 1, 1539)
	Madonna mia gentile	Arcadelt (Vogel, Arcadelt 1, 1539)
	Se del mio amor temete	Verdelot (Vogel, *Samml.* 1530[1])
	Alma mia luce pura	Arcadelt (Vogel, Arcadelt 31, 1539)

TABLE 2—Continued
The Centone

	Non son questo non son Donna che sete	—
	Quand'io pens'al martire	Arcadelt (Vogel, Arcadelt 1, 1539)
	Si dolce lume uscia	—
	Voi ve n'andat'al cielo	Arcadelt (Vogel, Arcadelt 1, 1539)
	Doglioso già lungo tempo priva	—
	Felice è la ragion qual senza moto	—
	O lieti amanti	Arcadelt (Vogel, Veggio 1, 1540)
Bass:	Con soave parlar con dolce accento	Verdelot, 2° à 4, 1534 (Paris, Bibl. G. Thibault) (cf. Vogel, Verdelot 8, 1536). In Bologna, Civ. Mus. Bibl. Mus., MS. Q 21 (ca. 1526).
	Si nel mirarvi	—
	Altro non è il mio amor	G. Berchem (Vogel, Arcadelt 36b, 1539)
	Se'l tuo partir mi spiacque	Arcadelt (Vogel, Arcadelt 1, 1539)
	Occhi miei lassi	Arcadelt (Vogel, Arcadelt 1, 1539)
	Mentre gl'ardenti rai cercai fuggir del sole	Arcadelt (Vogel, Veggio 1, 1540)
	Madonna [= Madonna io sol vorrei]	Verdelot (or Festa or A. de Silva), 1° à 4, 1533 (cf. Vogel, Verdelot 7, 1537)
	Deh come pur al fin	Arcadelt (Vogel, Arcadelt 1, 1539)
	Deh dimmi amore	Arcadelt (Vogel, Arcadelt 1, 1539)
	Poss'io morir	Arcadelt (Vogel, Arcadelt 1, 1539)
	Fra più bei fiori	Arcadelt (Vogel, Arcadelt 1, 1539)
	D'amanti*	Festa, "Amanti, amanti" [tenor] (Vogel, Verdelot 16, 1537)
	Così nel mio parlar voglio esser aspro	(not the setting in Flor., B.N.B., MS. Magl. XIX, 164–167)
	Per che l'inferno è sol vedersi privo	Verdelot (Vogel, Verdelot 5, ca. 1537); = 2nd line of "Altro non è il mio amor"
	Quanto che più rimirro	—

*The four fragments ending with this are fused together musically, giving the appearance of a continuous quotation.

been subjected to alteration, the words of a madrigal presumably by Arcadelt removed and another poem put in its place. The *Dialogo* would seem to be the unique source of this Arcadelt title, which is possible but a bit strange; whether the same piece exists under another title I have as yet been unable to ascertain. If it does, this kind of piracy by substitution, without the justification of pious intent that a spiritual *contrafactum* would have, is shocking even by sixteenth-century standards; but from Doni's words it was apparently not uncommon. Here is one more thing to watch for in studying the madrigal literature of the period.

The "Chiave"

Near the end of what seems an unnecessarily long and now not very amusing discourse on the various meanings (and of course double meanings), uses, and praiseworthy attributes of keys *(chiavi),* Bargo breaks in to say: "What would musicians do without the clef *(chiave),* which they use with or without a flat *(che l'adoprano or molle et ora acuta)?"* This passage is straightforward enough. But the dissertation on the *chiave* was adapted by Doni from a letter addressed to Gottifredi, as secretary to the Accademia degli Ortolani, while the latter was away from Piacenza; and in this alternate text, a good deal longer than what is printed in the *Dialogo,* the passage referred to above is given in the following form:

> Come la farebbono i musici senza la chiave, che ora l'adoprano corta, hor lunga, hor molle hor dura, sonando acuta et quando spuntata?[63]

Here *acuta* and *spuntata* would seem to mean sharp and flat; *molle* and *dura* would refer to the two hexachords commonly called by these names (on F and G respectively). But *corta* and *lunga* do not suggest anything having to do with clefs or hexachord systems, unless a short or wide total range of clefs *(a voci pari* as opposed to normally spaced clefs) could be implied; or some reference to high and low transpositions effected by clef could be intended.

These are admittedly not very satisfactory explanations; but that Doni was talking about *chiave* in the sense of clef, in part in the sense of transposition by clef, is clear from another passage, in which Grullone peevishly complains that

> This piece changes clefs, a thing that happens more often than I can tell you. One can search the world over without finding a pair of books all in the same mode *(tuono)* and clef arrangement. A pox upon these clefs and these fantastical brains [that think them up].

This is said just before the performance of *canto* 3, Riccio's "Lassatemi morire," which has a signature of one flat and the "normal" clef arrangement of S.A.T.B. *Canto* 2, Ruffo's "Ma di chi debbo lamentarmi," has no flat; its clefs are treble, mezzo-soprano, alto, and tenor, one of the *chiavette* combinations used for transposition at this time.[64] It is certainly true that few collections of printed music show great care for grouping pieces by clef or mode (unless they are especially designed with reference to modal affinities); that singers may have resented this inconsistency and disliked the *chiavette* system in general is hinted at by Doni.[65]

Performance

In the *Dialogo* we are not told as much as we should like to know about the performance of the madrigals included, to say nothing of music in general. This is disappointing but hardly surprising, for the work has no didactic intent but aims at entertainment; besides, the readers of the *Dialogo* presumably already knew how madrigals ought to be sung. In another place Doni remarks that a company of young musicians does not "comb through" the style of the music they sing, nor dispute points of rhetoric in the text.[66] Now and then a few hints are given, however, and they may be summarized here. First, the madrigals were sung one to a part; for the four interlocutors of the first section there are only four-voice madrigals, and one reason for Doni's running the number of speakers up to eight in Part 2 (the spoken material is very unequally divided among the interlocutors) is the possibility of introducing madrigals for five, six, and eight voices. No women are present in Part 1; Hoste, who is assigned the top voice, presumably sang falsetto; Michele, perhaps still a boy, performs the alto. The majority of the pieces in Part 1 are in the "normal" S.A.T.B. arrangement of clef and range, so that the superius does not go very high. In other pieces the range is quite high, however, and one wonders if the pieces were transposed (none are written so that the top voice can be sung an octave lower, a technique of *voci pari* writing), either arbitrarily or by the use of clefs, which Doni apparently disliked.

The singers were given their first notes as solmization syllables by whoever presumably led the performance: "*Bargo.* Via, questo che è nuovo, *la, re, re,* su Grullone, *la, la.*" "*Michele. Sol, re, sol, ut,* una quinta sotto Grullone" (pp. 24, 83). Occasionally someone bored by the conversation hums to himself: "*Claudio. Ut, ut, mi, re, mi, fa, sol, fa, mi*" (p. 122). Yet more realistic is a false start, for Berchem's *sestina* "Alla dolce ombra":

> M. This bass is wrong, or you are singing it wrong; look: *ut, sol*—two rests are missing. Put six where there are four.

The mistake is actually written into the music (not noted in Malipiero's edition); singers must then have been used to correcting notational errors (if a group were to go through the *Dialogo* they would get plenty of practice) when trying out pieces.[67]

Throughout the work Doni gives the impression that his convivial company was sight-reading all the music. Two madrigals (nos. 10, 11) are described as "new; never yet seen nor sung by anyone" (p. 71), and nos. 22 and 23 are called "nuovi nuovi" (p. 211). That the first time through, then as now, was not usually satisfactory is suggested by the company's being urged to repeat their performance (nos. 3, 12, 13, 14). But there is no reference to any particular difficulties encountered except for the hint (pp. 35, 70) that, as mentioned above, *canti turchi* were hard to sing. In fact there is very little comment about the pieces themselves: one passage in Ruffo's "Ma di chi debbo lamentarmi" is singled out for praise (p. 23); at one point Arcadelt, or rather Arcadelt's simpler, "classical" manner, is described as out of fashion, "troppo vecchio" (p. 35). On the whole talk about the pieces is cut short with the observation that it is useless to praise that which praises itself in performance: not a bad remark, but one would like to know whether Doni, or any amateur of his day, did or could talk about music in detail.

During the course of the *Dialogo* some poems are recited without music; and twice Ottavio Landi takes up an instrument to accompany some kind of improvised musical performance of poetry: once he asks for his *viuola* to accompany his own recitation of verses by Virginia Salvi (p. 209), and once he is asked by Selvaggia to take up his *lira* and play while she sings a group of sonnets given at the very end of the work (p. 315). Reference to this kind of performance suggests the ambiance of the *Decameron* or the *Paradiso degli Alberti,* and is no more specific than they are; but it is interesting to see that the sort of musical company Doni describes may have alternated the singing of polyphonic madrigals with improvisations of *strambotti* or sonnets to a strummed accompaniment.

All this suggests that the words were more important than the music, or at any rate that in performances of madrigals much attention was paid to the texts. So we like to think, and so we like to admonish young madrigalists now; but Doni hints that even in the Golden Age there were singers quite indifferent to the texts they sang:

> B. Why does one not say "these words are of the wondrous Cassola, those of the divine Aretino," as one says "this piece is by so-and-so, that by such-and-such?"
>
> G. You would like a whole Bible with commentary. Perhaps singers who know as little of facts as they do of words (for them *sol mi fa re* would be words enough) are satisfied with just singing. But men of intellect know very well whose words they sing. As for me, I've sung with a good many who know enough to say, "Ragione è ben ch'alcuna volta io canti" is by Giacchetto Berchem, "Lasciare il velo" is by Layolle.[68]

There are a number of references to instrumental music, with names of quite a few musicians given. Some are performers Doni knew in Piacenza; see the dedicatory letter to the alto partbook, or the fuller list, including the "bonissimi sonatori di strumenti Claudio Veggio, il Brambiglia, e Giuseppe Villano," given in a letter describing musical life in Piacenza.[69] Others are musicians Doni met on his travels, such as the poet-musican Giovaniacopo Buzzino, described as part of Count Massimiliano Stampa's household in Milan.[70] Of him Doni tells a tale illustrative of musical practice in these days when manuals of instrumental playing and ornamentation were beginning to appear:

> M. Giovaniacopo Buzzino was playing the soprano *violene,* as he does so marvelously, when some nobody came up to him in the midst of his performance to say: "O signore, move your fingers a bit more slowly; it looks so ugly to see you move your fingers so much on the neck of the instrument." Buzzino, accommodating himself to this bit of insolence, began to play without diminutions, whereupon the poor dolt, hearing the melody so lacking in grace, shamefacedly asked him to start moving his fingers again.

Other musicians named are Venetians in the circle of Polissena Peccorina and thus presumably of Willaert: Antonio da Cornetto, Paolo Vergelli (the *piffero*), M. Iacopo, M. Chechin *(viola),* Domenico Rossetto (lute), Matteo Romano *(violone),* M. Battista dal fondaco *(cornetto),* Francesco Steffani (singer), along with Perissone Cambio as singer and Parabosco at the *strumento.*[71] These are presumably professional musicans; of one of them, the famous Antonio da Lucca (or *da Cornetto*) Doni tells a tale suggesting that he knew the performer.[72]

Anton da Lucca was working out *(ricerca)* fantasies and doing the most divine things when an ignorant layman suddenly jumped up and said: "O Antonio, play a bit of accompaniment for singing *strambottoli . . .*" Antonio replied: "Away with you, go sing *strambotti* to the braying of an ass."

These and similar stories about poets *versus* ignoramuses suggest that artists, whether professionals or amateurs gifted with some *virtù,* considered themselves a race apart from, and well above, the level of ordinary humanity. Many other accounts of sixteenth-century life confirm this; Doni was saying nothing new. But his illustrations are lively and specific; more than that, they have a certain quality that makes the modern reader feel some sympathy with Antonfrancesco Doni, not on the whole a lovable figure: his standing in the artistic world of his times, at least in a great centre like Venice, was never very assured, his gifts as far as poetry and music are concerned pretty limited, and much of his talk in the *Dialogo* seems that of a near-outsider trying to make himself heard. Perhaps just because of this his descriptions of Italian literary and musical activities are of real value to us; he knew just enough to be a shrewd and informative, if unorthodox, reporter of the wonderfully vivid culture flourishing about him.

POSTSCRIPT

Another edition of Doni's *Dialogo* appeared after this article was published: Anna Maria Monterosso Vacchelli, *L'opera musicale di Antonfrancesco Doni* (Cremona, 1969). A good recent discussion of Doni's work is to be found in Martha Feldman, *City Culture and the Madrigal in Venice* (Berkeley and Los Angeles, 1995).

New information amplifying or correcting details in my study may be found as follows. On Luigi Cassola see Giuseppe Gangemi's entry in the *Dizionario biografico degli italiani,* 21 (Rome, 1978), 518–20. Neri Capponi's identity and activities are described well in Richard Agee, "Ruberto Strozzi and the Early Madrigal," *JAMS* 36 (1983): 1–17; in this article Agee argues persuasively that Arcadelt was in Florence when he set the madrigal text referring to Polissena Peccorina; there is in fact no evidence that he was ever in Venice. Definitive information on the manuscript circulation and printing of Willaert's *Musica nova* may be found in Anthony Newcomb, "Editions of Willaert's *Musica Nova:* New Evidence, New Speculations," *JAMS* 26 (1973): 132–45; see also Richard Agee and Jessie Ann Owens, "La stampa della *Musica nova* di Willaert," *RIM* 24 (1989): 219–305.

On "Maestro Mauro" see Frank D'Accone, "The Florentine Fra Mauros: A Dynasty of Musical Friars," *MD* 33 (1979): 77–137.

The remark that "few collections of printed music show great care for grouping pieces by clef or mode" is mistaken; my own subsequent work as well as that of such scholars as Harold Powers has shown that publishers such as Antonio Gardano, if not composers, did indeed group compositions in this way, beginning in the 1540s.

Antonio da Cornetto and Antonio da Lucca are *not* the same person; see the postscript following chapter 3 above.

Several further possible quotations in Doni's *centone* have been suggested by H. Colin Slim, *A Gift of Madrigals and Motets,* 2 vols. (Chicago, 1972), 1:209.

NOTES

1. Antonfrancesco Doni, *Dialogo della musica,* ed. G. Francesco Malipiero [transcriptions by Virginio Fagotto] (Vienna, 1965).

2. "The 'Dialogo della Musica' of Messer Antonio Francesco Doni," *ML* 15 (1934): 244–53. This article was published at the same time in Italian in *La Rassegna Musicale* 7 (1934): 405–14.

3. In the dedication of the alto book (each partbook has a separate dedication) Doni writes to G. B. Asinelli that he hopes the four libretti of the dialogue will please by reason of being "una invenzione non molto usata" (p. 4 in Malipiero's edition). And in more boastful vein, to Giovanni Antonio Volpe when sending the latter a copy of the *Dialogo,* "I have now planted my standard in Venice; have performed a feat of arms with the printer's press; and have as it were outdone (or undone) Josquin in this music that I send you" (et mezzo tagliato a pezzi Iosquino in questa musica, c'hora vi mando); *Lettere d'Antonfrancesco Doni* (Venice, 1544), fol. 112.

4. There are listings of the extant copies of the *Dialogo* in a number of books, the most nearly accurate being those of Cecilia Marsili-Libelli Ricottini, *A. F. Doni, scrittore e stampatore* (Florence, 1960), 20, and Francesco Bussi, *Umanità e arte di Gerolamo Parabosco* (Piacenza, 1961), 185. But since there are several additions and corrections to be made even to these, I shall here give a list of the copies known to me:

> Bologna, Civico Museo, Bibl. Mus. (= Liceo Musicale): a complete copy (inscribed "di Cristoforo beati, e degl'amici"), and a second copy of the canto.
> Bologna, Bibl. Univ.: canto ("di M. Pier Sangiugni e degl'amici").
> Chicago, Newberry Library: canto and bassus.
> Florence, Bibl. del Conserv.: complete.
> Florence, Bibl. Naz. Cent.: canto (a second copy came to this library from the H. Landau collection but was sold; this is the copy erroneously described as being in the Bibl. Laurenziana).
> London, British Library: canto (bound in a large volume of Doni's works, entitled "Opere di A. Fran. Doni, T. 2, Vinegia, 1562," this suggests a redaction of Doni's works spoken of by the author; but the *Dialogo* carries its original date of 1544).
> Padua, Bibl. Univ.: tenor.
> Paris, Bibliothèque du Conservatoire: canto.
> Venice, Bibl. Marciana: canto and tenor (the property of Apostolo Zeno).
> Verona, Accademia Filarmonia: complete, and a second copy of the tenor.
> Vienna, Gesellschaft der Musikfreunde: canto(?); not now listed in the library's catalog.

5. The bishop of Piacenza, to whom the canto of the *Dialogo* is dedicated, did not take Doni into his service; nor did he respond with a gift to the honor done him by the dedication; see Doni's remark in the earlier editions (1551, 1555), suppressed in later editions of the *Libraria Seconda,* p. 13: "Il Trivulzio dee dare al Doni per avergli dedicati i suoi dialoghi sulla

musica." In Doni's *Secondo Libro di Lettere* (Florence, 1547), fols. 9–10, there are two letters dated 1545, half-complaining, half-threatening, addressed to "Rever. Monsignor Vescovo," perhaps this same bishop of Piacenza.

For a probable Florentine musical undertaking of Doni's see chapter 13 below.

As late as 1554 Doni was still occasionally sending music to possible patrons, as is shown by his letter to Guidobaldo II of Urbino, published in his anti-Aretino tract *Il Terremoto* (Venice, 1556), p. [31].

6. More systematically concerned with musical theory, though not devoid of anecdote, is the *Due Dialoghi della musica* of Luigi Dentice (Rome, 1553), which is, however, dully written and contains no music. The only other work with this title known to me is the *Dialogo della musica* of Nicolo da Ponte (Venice, 1579), an extremely tedious verse dialogue of a moralizing nature, hardly touching on music at all.

7. *La Libraria del Doni fiorentino* (Venice, 1550), fol. 11v, 64v. In a letter addressed to Doni by Alessandro Campesano, dated 13 July 1543, the latter writes: "Mi duole altresi che, scrivendo al Domenichi, io fossi cosi parco in ragionare della vostra musica, degna di gran lode per quattro rispetti, come ancho disse esso S. Pietro [Aretino?]." See *Novo libro di lettere* (Venice, 1544), fol. 78v–79. In spite of the early date this might be construed as referring to Part 1 of the *Dialogo*.

8. Salvini's copy of the canto (all that survives), full of pedantic but not very helpful annotations, is in the Biblioteca Riccardiana in Florence. My thanks are due to Berta Maracchi Biagiarelli and Antonietta Morandini of the Riccardiana staff for identifying and helping me to decipher Salvini's remarks.

9. The copy (canto and tenor) in the Biblioteca Marciana in Venice has Zeno's bookplate on it. On the title page is the stamped date of 1625 with the initials of an earlier owner, "F. O."

10. *A General History of Music* (London, 1787), 3:158–59. Burney quotes in the same place from Zeno's notes on the *Bibl. della Eloquenza Italiana* of Fontanini (Venice, 1753), 2:180.

11. Kiesewetter's disparaging remark is quoted by Einstein, *Italian Madrigal,* 193.

12. References by Weckerlin, Vogel, and Gandolfi are listed by Einstein in the article referred to above (n. 2), 244. Einstein corrects and amplifies Vogel's bibliographical entry; see his suppl. to Vogel's *Bibliothek,* in the 1962 reprint of that work, 2:635. But his own description is strangely full of errors; even the table of contents of Malipiero's edition has quite unaccountable mistakes in it. See table 1 of this article for a more nearly correct listing of the contents.

13. See both the article cited above and the section of *Italian Madrigal,* 193–201, called "The Camerata of Antonfrancesco Doni."

14. *Antonfrancesco Doni musico* (Venice, 1946). Malipiero's introduction to his new edition adds little to this monograph's view of Doni.

15. See Salvatore Bongi, *Novelle di M. Antonfrancesco Doni colle notizie sulla vita dell' autore raccolta da Salvatore Bongi* (Lucca, 1852). All subsequent writers on Doni have drawn on Bongi's thorough work.

16. *Lettere* (1544), fols. 24, 30, 36v, 40v, 51.

17. This confession is made in a letter to Pietro Aretino, dated 28 March 1543 (*Lettere,* fol. 25).

18. This is a statement made in Doni's *I Marmi* of 1552, quoted by Malipiero, *Dialogo,* p. xi.

19. *Dialogo,* 23–24.

20. See Michele Maylender, *Storia delle accademie d'Italia,* 5 vols. (Bologna, 1926–30),

4:248: "[Nothing could] riuscì à far svanire in noi la suppozione, che l'ingegno bizzarro del Doni non si sia sfogato in ricamare intorno ad una semplice Accademia Veneziana detta dei Pellegrini un apparato d'origine, di vicende e di aggregazioni che non ebbe reale esistenza." Be this as it may, Doni was able to get the Venetian printer Francesco Marcolini to publish a number of his own works with "Nell'Accademia Peregrina" appearing on their title pages.

21. Salvino Salvini, *Fasti consolari dell'Accademia fiorentina* (Florence, 1717), 63, where Doni's election as the Academy's first secretary is spoken of.

22. *Lettere,* fol. 39.

23. Lodovico Domenichi, "Dialogo delle Imprese," p. 239 in the Lyons edition of 1559.

24. See *Dialogo,* 211, where Bargo is addressed as Gottifredi by another speaker; his pseudonym is simply the first syllable of first and last names jammed together.

25. Giuseppe Betussi, *Il Raverta. Dialogo nel quale si ragiona d'amore e degli effetti suoi* (1544), ed. Giambattista Verci (Milan, 1864), 78.

26. Precise identification of many, though not all, of the people Doni speaks of may be had from Luigi Mensi, *Dizionario biografico piacentino* (Piacenza, 1899). See also Cristoforo Poggiali, *Memorie per la storia letteraria di Piacenza* (Piacenza, 1789); Bussi, "La Musica," in *Panorama di Piacenza,* ed. Emilio Nasalli Rocca (Piacenza, 1955), 227–47. I am grateful to Sig. Conte Emilio Nasalli Rocca, librarian of the Biblioteca Comunale in Piacenza, for allowing me to consult there manuscript additions to Poggiali and Mensi's printed works.

27. *Italian Madrigal,* 196. The letter from Doni to Michele is printed in Doni's *Lettere* (1544), fol. 95v–96. Another letter to Michele, dated at Florence in 1547, is printed in Doni's second volume of letters, published in that year in Florence.

28. Einstein's speculations about the identity of Hoste (*Italian Madrigal,* 196) are interesting, but there is no evidence linking either Hoste da Reggio or Pietro da Hostia, both musicians of the time, with Piacenza. In his *Secondo libro di lettere,* fol. 46v, Doni addresses a letter to one Valerio degl'Osti (Hosti), of whom I know nothing further. The only *hoste* (= innkeeper?) mentioned in the text of the *Dialogo* is one Pier dalle Chiavi of Padova, but his name occurs only casually (p. 33). Grullone is described by Bargo as a musician, not a poet (p. 16: "Se foste rimatore, come siete musico"), so perhaps he was one of the local circle of performers. A Grullone is mentioned in Doni's *I Marmi* of 1552, 54f., in the course of a dialogue describing the performance of comedies and *intermedi* in Florence; but he is not identified in any way.

29. *Dialogo,* 82; Palazzo is described by Michele as "mio amicissimo, il quale oltre che egli è valente maestro, è persona per un virtuosa amorevole"; and Bargonio is called a "giovane di buone lettere, e latine e volgari," one who "sa e comporre canti e parole, latine e volgari." In a letter to Claudio Veggio, dated Venice 10 April 1544, Doni sends his greetings to Bargonio (*Lettere,* fol. 111).

30. *Dialogo,* 32. For Doni's letter to Luigi Riccio see *Lettere,* fol. 23.

31. *Lettere,* fol. 72v.

32. Maylender, *Storia delle accademie,* 4:149. Cf. Leopoldo Cerri, "L'Accademia degli Ortolani, MDXLIII," in *Strenna piacentina* (1896), 76, where it is said that a preacher, "fingendosi scandalizzato," declaimed against the academy and its members.

33. See Armen Carapetyan, "The Musica Nova of Adriano Willaert," *MD* 1 (1946): 203; Gustave Reese, *Music in the Renaissance,* rev. ed. (New York, 1959), 323–24; Einstein, *Italian Madrigal,* 198.

34. *Lettere,* fol. 110v.

35. Bongi, *Novelle di M. Antonfrancesco Doni,* xxxii.

36. Edward E. Lowinsky, "A Treatise on Text Underlay by a German Disciple of Fran-

cesco de Salinas," in *Festschrift Heinrich Besseler* (Leipzig, 1962), 248. Lowinsky brings evidence in support of Carapetyan's thesis that the *Musica Nova* was a reprint of an earlier collection called by Willaert *La Peccorina,* dedicated to Polissena Peccorina, and printed ca. 1546–49, assuming that Neri Capponi had by this time died and so released Willaert's music. In his *Libraria* of 1550 Doni mentions "motetti e madrigali" of Willaert, à 4, à 5, and à 6 (fols. 65–65v), which would include all but the seven-voice pieces in the *Musica Nova;* but he mentions no titles other than the *Villanesche* of 1545.

37. "Etude bio-bibliographique sur Philippe Verdelot," Acad. royale de Belgique, Classe des Beaux-Arts, Mémoires, 11 (Brussels, 1964), 13.

38. See Claudio Sartori, *Bibliografia della musica strumentale italiana stampata in Italia fino al 1700* (Florence, 1952), 8–9. As Lowinsky says, information about this particular Neri Capponi is hard to come by despite the fact that he must have been a member of what was, and is, one of the greatest Florentine families. In the large manuscript volume of Luigi Passerini, "Genealogia e storia della famiglia Capponi" (1852) in the Bibl. Naz. Cent. in Florence, there is a reference (Tavola 20.323) to a "Neri di Gino di Neri di Gino Capponi," born in 1504: "Visse celibe e morì nel 1594." If this is the right man the death date, improbably late in any case, could be mistaken or even turned around, which would then support Lowinsky's theory. Further search in the Capponi archives in the Archivio di Stato of Florence have produced no more information; and the present head of the family, Count Neri Capponi, was unable to tell me anything about his sixteenth-century namesake.

39. Cf. the remarks of the printer Marcolini in *I Mondi* of 1553, about "how Doni's manuscripts went to press while the ink was still wet, and how sometimes the printers had to stop for want of copy." I quote from Gerhard Bing, "Nugae circa veritatem: Notes on Anton Francesco Doni," *Journal of the Warburg Institute* 1 (1937), 305.

40. See below for this list of musicians and identifications of some of them.

41. *Lettere,* fol. 121: "Volendo ringratiar V. S. d'i canti a otto partoriti dal fertile intelletto vostro, et donatimi dalla mano della cortesia vostra, non sarebbe possibile. Pero . . . accettar questa mia musica rozza laqual con l'amor, ch'io porto, doni alla S. V.; il presente è picciolo, & l'affetto è grande."

42. Vogel, 2:67.

43. *Lettere,* fol. 24.

44. Vogel, 1:85. In the dedicatory letter a complaint is lodged against those who steal madrigals, like "crows that often deck themselves out as swans." Since Doni acknowledges Berchem in the *Dialogo* it is to be hoped that he was not this time one of the "crows." Einstein, *Italian Madrigal,* 433, calls attention to a 1555 edition of Berchem's *Primo libro à 4,* a year earlier than the one listed by Vogel. But there must have been a still earlier edition, for Doni mentions a collection of four-voice madrigals by Berchem in his *Libraria* of 1550, fol. 64v.

45. *Venator lepores—At Francisce* (*Motetta à 6vv,* 1542, no. 16), reprinted in Willaert, *Opera Omnia,* ed. Hermann Zenck and Walter Gerstenberg (American Institute of Musicology, 1952), 4:81. The melody is in any event not the same, though its use, a twofold repetition in the tenor, unrelated to other musical material in the piece, is similar to *Ingenium ornavit Pallas.* The text is from Acts 3:6, the words of St. Peter about to perform a miracle. It is possible that the use of *Argentum et aurum* as cantus firmus means that *Ingenium ornavit Pallas* is related by way of occasion to Willaert's motet, if in no other way. Two other motets by Willaert, nos. 15 and 18 of his *Musica quinque vocum* of 1539 (*Opera Omnia,* 3:78, 90), may also be related in subject matter; each has a *cantus firmus cavato dalle vocali* of phrases addressed to Francesco Sforza, son of Lodovico il Moro (the "Francisce" of *Venator lepores* may be Francesco Sforza).

46. Walter Gerstenberg, to whom I wrote about this motet, does not dispute its authenticity. He very kindly supplied me with manuscript concordances for *Beatus Bernardus;* see table 1.

47. *Italian Madrigal,* 385. The second quoted fragment is from a letter of Giulio Bonagionta, a friend of Rore's, this given also by Einstein.

48. Einstein, *Italian Madrigal,* 164. In the course of this piece ("Quando col dolce suono") occur the words "S'udeste Pulissena direste, ben direste, ben d'udir Sirena. Io che veduta l'ho vi giuro ch'ella è più che'l sol assai lucente bella," which sounds personal enough if the words could be Arcadelt's.

49. See *Dialogo,* 212, 292.

50. For an attempt to characterize this madrigal, see above, chapter 9.

51. In a letter to Tiberio Pandola in which the text of this madrigal is enclosed, Doni writes (*Lettere,* fol. 128v): "So che vi riderete M. Tiberio leggendo de i miei madrigali. . . . Tuttavia voi vedrete, com'io ho poetato per burlarmi del mondo; & per farmi beffe d'alcuni scattolini d'amore; i quali non sanno uscire di *Madonna io v'amo et taccio, & S'io havessi pensato;* & simili altri ciabattarie."

52. *Italian Madrigal,* 444–48; Francesco Bussi, *Umanità e arte di Gerolamo Parabosco,* 2 vols. (Piancenza, 1961).

53. Moschino (= Baccio Moschini) is an interlocutor in Doni's *I Marmi* of 1552. He and Bartolomeo Trombone are both praised highly by Cosimo Bartoli in chapter 3 of the latter's *Ragionamenti* (1567); see above, chapter 3.

54. "Di quattro valenti huomini" might suggest that the four pieces are each by a different composer; but Doni immediately says that the last two are by Parabosco, and since the texts of nos. 6 and 7 are probably by him, one assumes that the music is his also.

55. See the notes in Fagotto's transcription of the piece, 49–53. Unfortunately the corrections are arbitrary, and some places are wrongly interpreted, so that the piece as printed is probably rather far from Doni's intentions.

56. See his letter to Paolo Ugone (*Lettere,* fol. 106): "Hora la musica V. S. dee sapere che la mi diletta per capriccio; & mi piace saper fare quando è bisogna qualche cosetta; ma che io sia innamorato di note, d'archetti & di tasti S[ignor] nò. Son più inclinatio alle lettere, & a un certo più grave essercitio."

57. Presumably Verdelot's setting *à 4* of Petrarch's sonnet "Passer mai solitario." Einstein, *Italian Madrigal,* 249, casts some doubt on Verdelot's authorship of this piece ("In the pictorial interpretation of the text [it] goes far beyond Verdelot's style"). But from the time it was first published in 1540 it seems to have been well known and accepted as Verdelot's work. The piece, written in the somewhat unusual mensuration of O, is indeed quite a tricky one, with text declaimed on very short syllables, with protracted syncopations, and with several passages of ornamental character, like written-out divisions.

58. Cf. the later remark of Grullone (p. 82): "Anche Ysach faceva que' suoi canti, et era maestro; ora sarebbe scolare a gran pena."

59. A passage in Doni's letter "A Poeti e Musici" (*Lettere,* fol. 71v), which, as we have seen, contains several references to the *Dialogo* although dated five months before its issue, is pertinent here: "Io ci ho messo certi canti ladri, assassanati, stropiati per farvi dir qualche cosa; & per far conoscere i begli da brutti, & la buona musica dalla cattiva, poi trovarete li quegli scorretti per farvi dir male a vostro dispetto." But in sending the composer Jacques Buus a copy of his *Dialogo* Doni confesses that Buus will find here "qualche imperfettione," attributable in part "al poco saper mio," in part "alla brevita del tempo." This sounds like an honest admission.

60. *Lettere,* fol. 13v–15, to Lodovico Bosso: "Ho composto un canto, & le parole in lode della divina Isabetta Guasca; il quale so che non vi dispiacerà, perche mi sete affettionato: & ve lo mando" (but the text of the madrigal is not included).

61. *Dialogo,* 46. The poem is printed in Cassola's *Madrigali* (Venice, 1544), 110. From the text of the *Dialogo* it is clear that only this piece is by Cassola, not the next as well, a point misunderstood by Einstein (Vogel, 2:635; Einstein, *Italian Madrigal,* 186).

62. A list of the quoted fragments in the three lower voices, with all the identifications I have been able to make, is given in table 2 of this chapter.

63. *Lettere,* fol. 87. The letter is dated 3 December 1543, and so was written at the same time as the *Dialogo* was in process of composition.

64. See Arthur Mendel, "Pitch in the Sixteenth and Early Seventeenth Centuries, part 3," *MQ* 35 (1948): 357; Hans Engel, "Chiavette," *MGG,* 2:1187.

65. In another context I have suggested that Doni, in taking a group of four madrigals from Vincenzo Ruffo's *Primo libro à 4vv* for use in a manuscript collection, transposed one of them in order to bring its clefs and signature into line with the other three. See chapter 13.

66. *Lettere,* fol. 71 (the letter "A Poeti e Musici").

67. Doni acknowledges that errors creep into musical texts, through the inattention or perverseness of copyists (p. 46); and later on (p. 231) Michele says: "Before I forget it, Bargo, those pieces we sang last night (i.e., Part 1) went badly in I don't know how many places." Bargo replies facetiously that this was done so that they would please everyone, even those who had been—like the music—assassinated. Michele then says that all those who have "fallen by a stroke of the pen" will be put to rights in a table of corrections at the end; alas, this is not supplied.

68. These two pieces appear in Arcadelt's *Primo libro* but were only rarely (perhaps not at all when Doni was writing) acknowledged in print as the work of Berchem and Layolle; see Vogel, 1:31.

69. *Lettere,* fol. 38.

70. Ibid., fol. 37.

71. Antonio da Cornetto is Antonio da Lucca, famous both as a lutenist and a cornettist. He is given high praise by Bartoli in the latter's account of famous performers of the time; see Benvenuti, *Andrea e Giovanni Gabrieli,* p. liv. Matteo Romano is perhaps the Matteo della viola mentioned in the list of musicians given by Ortensio Landi in his *Setti libri di cathaloghi* (Venice, 1552) and quoted in Paolo Molmenti, *La storia di Venezia nella vita privata,* 5th ed. (Bergamo, 1911), 4:323n.

72. Perhaps Doni had met Antonio da Lucca; his good friend Francesco Sansovino addressed a letter to the musician at just about this time, when Doni and Sansovino were also in correspondence. See *Lettere di M. Francesco Sansovino sopra le dieci giornale del Decamerone* (Venice, 1544), 61–62.

A Gift of Madrigals to Cosimo I: The Ms. Florence, Bibl. Naz. Centrale, Magl. XIX, 130

WORKING AT A PROBLEM in the history of music can sometimes be like trying to solve a number of jigsaw puzzles that have unaccountably been jumbled together: one finds clues and missing pieces, but rarely do they lead to a solution of the original problem; instead they divert one's attention and start off a new hunt. In studying a group of related madrigals and their composers, among whom the name of Ihan Gero figured, I was led[1] to the manuscript named in the title above; it has for some years been described as a group of madrigals by Ihan Gero.[2] The ten madrigals— the manuscript is surprising for the small number of pieces it contains—are anonymous in Magl. XIX, 130, but one of them is entitled "Pace non trovo," a setting of a famous Petrarch sonnet. Gero's "Pace non trovo" was the very piece that I was most interested in; but here it was that things went awry. The madrigal turned out to be not Gero's setting but one fairly solidly attributed to Yvo [Barry], a singer in the Cappella Sistina under Paul III.[3]

Next came the unsettling discovery that none of the ten madrigals seemed to be by Ihan Gero; or at any rate none of them appear ascribed to him in Venetian music prints of the 1540s and 1550s, in which Gero—although nothing is known of his life or whereabouts—figures with some regularity. Instead five of them turn out to be the work of Vincenzo Ruffo, all of them printed in the latter's first book of four-voice madrigals of 1545. Yvo's "Pace non trovo," first published in 1539, was evidently a fairly popular piece and was reprinted several times. Over "Con lei foss'io," the second madrigal in the manuscript, there is a certain amount of conflict in the printed sources; but the contenders are Arcadelt, Francesco Corteccia, and—supported by the best evidence—Giaches de Ponte. Gero did write a setting of "Con lei foss'io," but one unrelated to that in the manuscript.[4] Still another piece, "Per ché la vit'è breve," turns up, in slightly altered form, in Filippo Azzaiolo's *Secondo libro de Villotte* of 1559, there attributed to Arcadelt.[5] This leaves, curiously enough, only the first and last pieces in the collection unidentified (see the formal listing of the manuscript's contents at the end of this study). But there are a number of things about this manuscript one would like to know: why a manuscript instead of a print, for example; why so small a number of pieces; who compiled and wrote it; when (does it antedate the printed versions of the madrigals for which there are concordances?); where; for what purpose?

It seems best to begin with a description of the manuscript; it is of course included in Bianca Becherini's catalogue[6] of the musical manuscripts in the Biblioteca Nazionale, but I shall here stress some details that she naturally does not stop for, and make some minor corrections. Magl. XIX, 130, is a set of four partbooks, in modern bindings, of surprisingly large size: 335 × 232 mm. Einstein quite rightly remarks that the partbooks "have entirely the character of a presentation copy,"[7] and in the bassus (!) there is evidence of this; the ornamental woodcut, of which more will be said in a moment, contains, inked in by hand, a dedication, "All'Ill.mo et Eccel.mo S. Duca Cosimo."[8] Aside from their size, and the fact that they show no signs of use, the partbooks are distinguished as ornamental in nature by some fairly carefully done pen-and-ink decoration, all four books having ornamental capitals and assorted flora and fauna (different in each book) in the wide margins of the first madrigal (see fig. 6). No coloring is used, and the ink seems to be the same as that used for the musical notation; both music and ornament could be by the same hand. The very wide margins are identical in size for all pages of the four books, which were completely ruled in advance with eight five-line staves. That these large margins were left with the idea of ornamenting all the pages, or at least all those on which pieces begin, is shown by the presence of fragmentary decoration for the last madrigal in the altus book, the ornament drawn in pencil and partially inked (see fig. 7).

Each of the books is further garnished by an elaborate woodcut (fig. 8) with the Medici arms at the top, "Fiorenza" at the bottom. This illustration, in the shape of a frame, is sometimes filled in with a depiction of three laureated poets, with a reclining nude figure below them represented pouring water from a vase and accompanied by a recumbent lion. Or the frame may be left empty and the designation of the voice part (and in the case of the bassus, the dedication to Cosimo de' Medici) filled in by hand; but here the impression of the complete illustration on the rather coarse paper can easily be seen even though the center part of the woodcut has not been inked. This combination of woodcuts and pen-and-ink drawing or lettering is a rather peculiar one, almost suggesting that the manuscript was meant to be a kind of study or sketch for an elaborately printed work. Both the ornament and the musical calligraphy, neat but not especially distinguished in character, have a faintly amateurish quality and would seem not to be the work of a professional copyist.

On the frontispiece of the tenor part is written in a cursive hand, old but obviously later than that of the manuscript, "Madrigali di Joan Gero." Why this should be here, and why the Hispanized form of Gero's first name (he is called Ihan by the printers Gardano and Scotto, and in one dedication is referred to as "Gian") I do not know; but here the ascription of the manuscript's contents to Gero evidently began. Henry Prunières, having examined the manuscript in April 1908, confirmed this ascription, adding that the first madrigal in the manuscript, "Voi ch'ascoltate," is also used to open Gero's *Primo libro à* 4 of 1549.[9] Einstein accepted this attribution, excluding only the second piece "Con lei foss'io," which he gave on the basis of its appearance in a Gardano print to Giaches de Ponte;[10] and others have followed suit.[11] But Gero's piece is not at all like the opening madrigal of the manuscript (to judge from the one surviving voice part, the tenor). It is quite natural that collections, musical or literary, should open with this text—or a paraphrase of it—since it is the first sonnet of Petrarch's *Canzoniere.*[12] But not only is

Figure 6. "Voi ch'ascoltate," Altus partbook, MS. Florence,
Bibl. Naz. Centrale, Magl. XIX, 130

Figure 7. "Che degg'io far," Tenor partbook, MS. Florence,
Bibl. Naz. Centrale, Magl. XIX, 130

the music in Magl. XIX, 130, different from that of Gero, the text is not the same
either. Gero sets Petrarch's sonnet; the "Voi ch'ascoltate" in the manuscript is an
ottava rima stanza.

Einstein describes the madrigals of Magl. XIX, 130, as "very 'literary'."[13] This
is true, though perhaps in a slightly different sense from what Einstein meant. No.
9, "Pace non trovo," is Petrarch's sonnet intact; no. 8, "Per ché la vit'è breve," is a
setting of the first seven lines of a Petrarch canzone. There is more Petrarch: no. 2,
"Con lei foss'io," sets the closing stanza and *commiato* of the sestina *A qualunque*

animale. But nos. 1 and 10, although they bear Petrarchan titles, are actually not the sonnets the first lines suggest but instead are *centoni*, each an ottava rima composed of lines taken from various Petrarchan poems and combined into a new, half-sensible order. Thus no. 1, "Voi ch'ascoltate":

Voi ch'ascoltate in rime spars'il suono	(sonnet 1)
del pensier'amoroso che m'atterra	(sonnet 29)
muover contr'a costei di ch'io ragiono	(*Trionfo della Castità*)
ristrett'in guisa d'huom' ch'aspetta guerra	(sonnet 88)
ov'i raggi d'amor sí caldo sono	(canzone 8, stanza 6)
venit'a me s'el pass'altri non serra	(sonnet 61)
ch'io vi discopprirrò de miei martiri	(sonnet 11)
le mie speranze e i miei dolci sospiri.	(sonnet 131)

And the final piece, "Che deggio far," goes in similar vein.

The literary pastime of centonizing Petrarch was not uncommon and was apparently quite respectable; even Bembo is said to have done it. The two *centoni* in Magl. XIX 130, are the work of the Sienese poet Giulio Bidelli, with "Voi ch'ascoltate" standing appropriately at the head of his *Dugento stanze con due capitoli tutte da versi del Petrarca*.[14] Placed at the beginning and end of the manuscript, "Voi ch'ascoltate" and "Che deggio far" suggest that it was compiled in a somewhat self-consciously "literary" fashion, for the delectation of people who knew their Petrarch pretty well.

No. 3 in the manuscript, "Ma di chi debbo lamentarmi," is a famous stanza of Ariosto (*Orlando furioso*, 32.21). Nos. 4–7, which are obviously related to one another in theme and language, are actually four stanzas from a sestina, this fact obscured by their being given out of order in the manuscript. The correct order, to judge from the rhyme scheme, is (1) "Monti, selve, fontane, piaggi e sassi"; (2) "Fiere silvestre che per lati campi"; (3) "Ben mille notti ho già passato in pianto"; (4) "O fortunato che con altre rime." After some searching on my part these four stanzas revealed themselves to be a part—stanzas four to seven—of a double sestina in Sannazaro's *Arcadia*, *Egloga quarta*. The text used by Ruffo is faithful to Sannazaro except that a reference to Elpino, one of the pastoral interlocutors, is suppressed in "Ben mille notti."[15]

Petrarch—straight and centonized; Ariosto; Sannazaro; the manuscript does have a high literary tone. It seems a bit odd that incomplete poems and, in the case of the Sannazaro verses, stanzas given out of order, should be included. The much-admired Ariosto stanza is all right, of course; only Iachet Berchem seems to have made anything like a real attempt, at that highly selective, to render *Orlando furioso* in music.[16] "Per ché la vit'è breve" and "Con lei foss'io," though fragments, are the beginning and end respectively of long poems, and each makes a certain sense as it stands. It is only the Sannazaro verses that seem carelessly placed (not necessarily carelessly composed, for the four pieces show enough consistency of style and material to suggest that they were written as a set even though Ruffo himself did not publish them in order). Of course composition of entire canzoni or sestine was never too common, and was particularly rare among the first generations of madrigalists. In Antonfrancesco Doni's *Dialogo della musica* of 1544[17] there is a complete setting of Petrarch's "Alla dolce ombra de le belle frondi" by Iachet Berchem; this is both an early and a symptomatic example, for publication of complete cycles was often linked with academic (in the case of Doni, quasi-academic) patronage. Thus Ruffo in his younger days could set fragments of a large poem, as here; but Giovanni Nasco, his contemporary and rival at the Accademia Filarmonica in Verona, published a complete setting of the sestina "A qualunque animale" in 1548,[18] and Ruffo himself after his return to Verona published canzoni, even a complete sestina.[19] In a way the presence of this fragmentary poem, like the ambitiously planned but only partly completed ornamentation of the manuscript, suggests its real character: a gift aimed to please and even to impress, but on the whole a sketch or impression of something that might have been fuller or grander. Whether time was lacking, encouragement absent, or intention simply greater than powers of execution, it is hard to say; but later, when the time comes to speculate on the identity of the manuscript's compiler, these may all perhaps be seen to have played a part.

All ten madrigals are written in the *misura a breve* or *note nere* notation fashionable in the 1540s; and all of them display characteristic features of music using this notation: much contrast between long and short note values, the first often used for declamatory chordal passages on some word such as *doglia*, the second employed in runs or ornamental cadence patterns of a surprisingly fussy nature; and a good deal of syncopation, particularly for "staggered" entrances of imitative figures.[20] This sort of madrigal developed sometime after 1535 and was at the height of its popularity during the decade 1540–1550, when the printers Antonio Gardane and Girolamo Scotto advertised it in the titles of several anthologies.[21] As an example of *note nere* style Yvo's "Pace non trovo" is extreme, almost a caricature; the exaggerated antitheses of the Petrarchan sonnet it sets are doubtless the reason for such mannered writing. "Con lei foss'io" is much tamer, closer to the madrigal of the 1530s in style except for a few imitative entrances using a good deal of staggered-entrance syncopation. As for "Per ché la vit'è breve," written in a kind of post-frottola style, its black notes are suggestive rather of the use of short note values in the *villanesca* of the period. The five madrigals by Ruffo are particularly imaginative in their use of the possibilities opened by increased use of short note values, all but the very shortest able to bear syllables of text. The closing passage of "Ma di chi debbo lamentarmi," with its ingenious use of falling triadic figures in highly syncopated imitative succession for the words "Ond'io non ho mai fine al precipitio mio," was singled out for praise by the rather blasé interlocutors of Doni's *Dialogo*, in which the piece was first printed in 1544.[22]

As for the first and last madrigals in the manuscript, both conform to the general style of the others; more than that, they are quite a lot like the Ruffo madrigals, particularly the four from the incomplete sestina. And they resemble each other closely enough so that it does not seem overbold to claim that they are by the same composer. They are of almost exactly equal length; this is perhaps not surprising since they are the setting of two *ottave* of similar character. Each has a complete repetition of the music for the whole last line; again this could be coincidence, but there is in addition much similarity between the two. In both there is insistent, almost obsessive use of the upbeat pattern ♪♪♪♩ to begin imitative figures; both use to about the same degree the staggered syncopation described above, and both show a slight awkwardness in construction, there being more dead stops at the end of poetic lines than is good for the continuity of the music. In some ways "Voi ch'ascoltate" and "Che deggio far" look like imitations of Ruffo's madrigals, by someone less fluent and less imaginative than he. There are even some individual passages strongly resembling one another. Compare these settings of *sospiri* and *sospirando*:

Example 13.1

a. Ruffo, "Fiere silvestre"

b. Anonymous, "Voi ch'ascoltate"

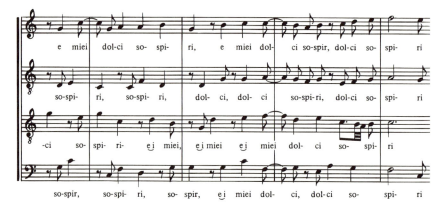

c. Anonymous, "Che degg'io far"

"Sospirando" is admittedly a word that was often treated in the manner above; and yet the resemblances here seem more than superficial. There are other points of resemblance in imitative usage, in phrase design, in the pattern of whole pieces; and everywhere Ruffo comes off better. A comparison of this kind is dangerous since there is a natural tendency to credit the work of a composer known to be competent with more distinction than a poor anonymous piece can show; and if "Voi ch'ascoltate" should turn out, say, to be by Arcadelt or by Ruffo himself, it would be very embarrassing all round. Yet it does seem possible that the composer of "Voi ch'ascoltate" and "Che deggio far," perhaps the same man as the compiler of the manuscript, was imitating the style of Ruffo, whose works account for half the contents of Magl. XIX, 130.

The compiler of the manuscript apparently acted also as editor, for the music is carefully set down and in a few instances shows the presence of a knowledgeable hand. In Ruffo's "Ma di chi debbo lamentarmi" an error in the superius as it is printed in Doni's *Dialogo* (three repeated G's which should be F's) is corrected; since the correction is also made in the piece as it appears in Ruffo's *Primo libro à 4* of 1545, this may only indicate that the manuscript version was taken from the latter print. The musical text of Yvo's "Pace non trovo" is slightly different in the manuscript, including an open fifth final chord in place of a full triad, from its printed version. Two madrigals in Magl. XIX, 130, are given in transposition; "Per ché la vit'è breve" and "Ben mille notti" are both transposed down a fifth. In the case of "Per ché la vit'è breve" there are a number of variants, some quite substantial, in the inner parts of the piece from its text as printed by Azzaiolo in his second *Villotte* book of 1559. Since this print is of late date and is probably not an impeccable source in any event, it is hard to say whether the compiler of Magl. XIX, 130, actually made changes on his own, whether Azzaiolo altered the piece by changing—on the whole simplifying—the inner voices, or whether the manuscript represents an earlier source now lost. But the transposition of "Ben mille notti" seems deliberate, and was evidently done in order to bring the range of the piece and, with one exception, its choice of clefs, into line with the three other Ruffo settings of the

Sannazaro sestina. As the pieces appear in the manuscript, the four together and all in the same tonal ambitus, they are definitely meant to be taken as a set, an arrangement not clear in Ruffo's *Primo libro*.

Sixteenth-century printers were on the whole not very careful about arranging pieces, even those obviously related to each other, into groups with the same ambitus, clef, and key signature, Antonio Gardane being perhaps a bit more conscious of this than other printers. That it was noticed and that performers disliked changes of clef—or perhaps the necessity to transpose—is indicated by a remark of one of the interlocutors in Doni's *Dialogo*, possibly speaking for the author when he says "questo canto muta chiave, che venga poco meno ch'io non vò dire. Può fare il mondo che non si trovi una volta un paio di libri che sien tutti d'un tuono, et d'una chiave medesima; che sia maledetta la chiave, et questi cervelli fantastiche."[23] In the instance of "Ben mille notti" the editor or compiler of the manuscript seems to have taken a deliberate step to remedy such inconsistency.

Although a presentation copy, Magl. XIX, 130, has no dedicatory letter and is undated. From its contents it would seem to have been compiled in the early 1540s, but there is no precise evidence in the music itself; one of the pieces, "Pace non trovo," was printed as early as 1539, but there is no reason to think of the manuscript as antedating printed sources for the music it contains, so that the precise date of appearance of any of the ten pieces in print would not help in dating the manuscript. It is dedicated to "the most illustrious and excellent Duke Cosimo," that is to say, to Cosimo I de' Medici, who became the second duke of Florence in 1537. The arms on the frontispiece are, however, not simply the Medici *palle* but include the *stemma* of the House of Toledo as well. Cosimo de' Medici married Eleonora of Toledo in the summer of 1539, and since the arms of the bride's family were customarily displayed at the time of the wedding, perhaps for a short time afterwards, it seemed to me at first likely that the manuscript was presented to Cosimo at the time of his wedding and could thus be dated 1539–40. The official music for the wedding is known; the madrigals sung and played in G. B. Strozzi's intermedi for a comedy by Antonio Landi, with music by Francesco Corteccia, Mattio Rampollini, and others, were published in the year of the wedding.[24] But the madrigals in Magl. XIX, 130, could have been intended as a kind of wedding present; and indeed the frontispiece looks a bit like some of the decorations for that wedding as described by an eyewitness, the Florentine academician Pierfrancesco Giambullari.[25] At any rate the woodcut may have been designed by someone who saw Florence embellished by numerous triumphal arches and emblematic representations for the entry of the bridal pair.

There are objections to dating the manuscript this early, however. For one thing, the dedication would probably have been to Cosimo and Eleonora, not to the duke alone, if it had been presented at the time of the wedding. Then, it seems unlikely that Ruffo, whose work does not appear in print at all until 1542[26], should have written all these madrigals by 1539, although it must be admitted that nothing is known of his whereabouts and activity during these years. Nor is it sure that Bidelli's *centoni* were in circulation by 1539, since they were not printed until five years later; again one could not be sure of this. But we shall see that there is positive evidence in favor of a later date for the compiling and writing of the manuscript.

The frontispiece (fig. 8) should now be examined a bit more closely. The three poets, given the word "Fiorenza" at the bottom, one would assume to be Dante, Petrarch, and Boccaccio, and the river-god beneath a Tuscan divinity, the Arno, accompanied by a Florentine lion. The fact that the poets represented in the manuscript itself are Petrarch, Ariosto, and Sannazaro does not really matter since the woodcut could not have been made for the manuscript (witness its clumsy use in incomplete form, with the impression showing through on the paper) but must have been taken from some printed work. The whole thing now appears to be a kind of emblem or *impresa* for some literary undertaking; no motto accompanies it, but amid the decorative garlands on the first page of the altus part is a scroll with the legend ΚΑΜΑΤΟΣ ΕΥΚΑΜΑΤΟΣ, suggesting that effort expended on literature and music is a pure labor of love. Both frontispiece and motto have a very academic air.

An academy was in fact founded during the early years of the reign of Cosimo I. In November 1540, a group of prominent Florentines, among them Bartolomeo Panciatichi, Giovanni Strozzi, and Cosimo Bartoli, formed the Accademia degli Umidi, the first manifestation of the formally organized sixteenth-century academy in Florence. After a few months the new academy passed under the patronage of Cosimo, who apparently stipulated that the name be changed; and in March 1541, the proudly austere name of Accademia Fiorentina was adopted.[27] From its inception the Accademia Fiorentina was dedicated to study of Italian, and particularly Tuscan, literature, perhaps somewhat self-consciously departing from the preoccupations of the earlier Accademia Platonica. For a group with this aim the frontispiece reproduced in Magl. XIX, 130, would have made an excellent device. It was not the official *impresa* of the academy; but it does include what was in fact the academy's symbol: the Arno, "as a human figure, with two plants, one a laurel, the other an olive" as the only device of the Florentine Academy.[28] And indeed publications, as late as the eighteenth century, which may be considered officially those of the Academy preserve this emblem.[29]

Domenichi considers it worth mentioning that the Accademia Fiorentina had no motto to go with its representation of the Arno.[30] But what of the Greek inscription appearing in the madrigal manuscript? It has been listed as a motto of the Medici,[31] but I have so far found no reference to its use by a member of the family. Domenichi again provides some useful information. He speaks of a Florentine named Francesco Campana who had made, as an *impresa* for some books in the Biblioteca Laurenziana that he intended to have published, a device consisting of a number of books, some open and some closed, above which rises a kind of classical lamp, and behind this a scroll containing the very motto in question, given in Greek and translated by Domenichi as "labor that does not tire."[32] Whatever books Domenichi may have had in mind, the motto in the form he describes it does appear on the title page of a work published under the auspices of the Accademia Fiorentina: *Lettioni d' Academici fiorentini sopra Dante*, printed by Antonfrancesco Doni in Florence in 1547.

Figure 8. Frontispiece of MS. Florence, Bibl. Naz. Centrale, Magl. XIX, 130

Francesco Campana was a man who, though erudite and particularly learned in
Latin,[33] was principally a man of affairs; serving Florence in the last days of the
Republic, then becoming a confidant of Alessandro de' Medici and acting as the
latter's ambassador to the court of Clement VII, he managed to hold favor under
Cosimo I as well, acting as *primo segretario* to the Duke and being appointed *prov-
veditore* of the Studio Pisano.[34] He was interested in the new Florentine Academy
as well; in 1541 the first consul of the Academy, Lorenzo Benivieni, chose Campana as one of his two *consiglieri*; some general meetings of the group were held in
his house; and after his death a funeral oration preached on 25 March 1548 described him as having contributed not a little to the Studio Pisano, the Studio Fiorentino, and consequently to the Academy.[35] His motto, although it did not become
the permanent one of the Accademia Fiorentina, was obviously in the spirit of the
group and was, in fact, used officially by them in at least one publication, the *Lettioni* mentioned above. This would seem to draw the manuscript we are here studying into the orbit of the Accademia Fiorentina.

In 1547 another work of at least quasi-academic character was printed by Doni
in Florence: *Prose antiche di Dante, Petrarca et Boccaccio et di molti altri nobili et
virtuosi ingegni, nuovamente racolte*. Doni was the collector—if indeed not partly
the inventor—of this work, which he issued while he was Cosimo I's official
printer. Here one might expect to see the woodcut of Magl. XIX, 130, with its three
poets, and in fact it is used, on the page following the title page. The combined
arms of Medici and Toledo appear in several places in this work,[36] and with reason:
it is dedicated to Eleonora of Toledo by Doni, who describes himself in a letter,
dated 31 July 1547, as the "tanto obbligato servitore dell'Illustrissimo & Eccellentissimo suo consorte." So appropriate to this book is the woodcut with its laureated
Tuscan poets and its use of the Medici Toledo arms that it seems reasonable to
think of the book as the occasion for the woodcut's being made, and its use in the
manuscript the result of its simply being available at the time.

As for the bottom half of the woodcut with its river-god symbol of the Florentine
Academy, a connection with Antonfrancesco Doni again suggests itself, for Doni
if not a regular member of the Academy was for a certain time connected with it. In
1545, during the consulate of Bartolomeo Panciatichi, some new rules, including
the creation of the post of secretary, were drawn up. In the next year a secretary, his
term apparently of one year's duration, was chosen for the first time, and Doni,
"pure assai noto per le molte opere sue," was chosen.[37] The two books mentioned
above, the *Lettioni sopra Dante* and the *Prose antiche*, were apparently printed or
at least readied for publication during Doni's year as secretary of the Academy;
since the former contains Campana's Greek motto and the latter has the "poets"
woodcut, both then used in Magl. XIX, 130, it seems likely that Antonfrancesco
Doni had a hand in the manuscript and that its date, if the woodcut was really prepared for the *Prose antiche* volume, might be 1547; not much before this latter volume, at any rate.

All of this might be sheer coincidence and Doni simply the printer involved in
issuing the two books; but curiously enough, both the "poets" woodcut, the woodcut with the Medici-Toledo arms used on the title page of the *Prose antiche*, and the

one containing the Greek inscription are used in later books by Doni, all of them printed by Francesco Marcolini in Venice. These include *La Zucca* and the *Fiori della Zucca* of 1551–52 ("poets" woodcut); the *Trattati diversi di Sendebar indiano* of 1552 (Medici-Toledo woodcut; the work is dedicated to Cosimo I); *Tre libri di lettere*, 1552 (again the Medici-Toledo woodcut); *I Marmi* of 1552–54 (the "poets" woodcut and the one with the Greek inscription); and *I Mondi* of 1552–53 (the Greek inscription). In other words Doni regarded these illustrations as his own, at any rate not the property of the Accademia Fiorentina.

Antonfrancesco Doni (1513–74) was a Florentine by birth. He left the city in 1540, starting a period as travelling a "virtuoso" which included a stay in Piacenza (1543) and one in Venice (1544), the principal result of these being the writing and publication of the *Dialogo della musica* in the spring of 1544. He seems to have returned to Florence in September of 1545 (if the dating of his letters can be believed) and to have remained there until sometime in 1548. By early in 1549 he was again in Venice, starting that phase of his career identified with the Accademia dei Pellegrini. For a brief period, from the beginning of 1546 until sometime early in 1547, he managed to hold the office of *stampatore ducale*, enjoying a monopoly granted by Cosimo I. Perhaps using type from Girolamo Scotto in Venice,[38] he printed a small number of works, including the two titles mentioned above.[39] Among items projected but probably never printed was a *Lamento di Santo Alesso confessore tradotto in canzona, e messo in canto figurato.*[40] He seems not to have issued any music during his short period of activity as a printer, a period that ended early in 1547 when Lorenzo Torrentino was granted the ducal monopoly.[41] But while he was a printer Doni was doubtless able to have woodcuts made; he is known to have commissioned the engraver Enea Vico to make some copperplate portraits, among them one of himself.[42] The woodcuts used in Magl. XIX, 130, would then seem to have been done for Doni during the year 1546–47, whether or not the manuscript was actually written in that year. When Doni left for Venice, he took some of these woodcuts with him, waiting for the opportunity, which he subsequently found with Francesco Marcolini, to use them again.[43]

Doni gives in the *Dialogo* of 1544 ample proof of his interest in music; it is even possible that several of the madrigals in the book were written and composed by him.[44] And from his letters it seems clear that a part of whatever social success he enjoyed during his years of travel after he left Florence for the first time was owing to his musical abilities. On the other hand he took pains to say on several occasions that he was really a man of letters, music being only a subsidiary interest, a lesser side of his career as "virtuoso."[45] What he probably meant by this was that he turned to music when he thought it would bring him some recognition or profit. Apparently not enough of either came his way through music, for after the publication of the *Dialogo* with its twenty-eight madrigals he never again had any music printed, nor is it positively known that he wrote any more. Nevertheless musical topics occur with some frequency in his later writings, and among his letters are several testifying to a continuing interest in music, perhaps to continued activity as a musician. Of special interest is a letter addressed to Cosimo de' Medici, dated at

Piacenza on 27 March 1543. Doni introduces himself to the duke as a native Florentine now "presso à tre anni" absent from his native city. Among his qualifications (for entering Cosimo's service, apparently) he lists ability as a musician, a writer, and a scholar in Italian and Greek. Then he goes on to say

> io mando à vostra eccellentia, un motetto di Giacchetto Berchem; degno certo di venire alle mani di tal signore. & mando à vostri Cantori una mia Canzone, mandovi due Sonetti composti dalla mia sprofondata memoria scritti di mia mano, & disegnati i canti, i sonetti, & le carte.[46]

This letter was written before the publication of the *Dialogo*, it is true, so that Doni could have been referring to material that was to go into that publication.

Four years later Doni addressed a similar letter[47] to Cosimo, writing from Florence to the duke who had gone to Pisa. In this epistle he sends the duke a motet in honor of the Medici family, a piece which after acquiring Doni had decorated with the Medici *palle*. Not being able to finish it in time to give to Cosimo in person, he sends it to the duke "insieme con questo libro di mie compositioni," hoping that the duke will listen to the motet and read the "compositioni" (perhaps Doni's second volume of collected letters, printed in 1547). Printed with this letter is an answer addressed to Doni as "carissimo nostro," in which Cosimo says he expects no less pleasure from hearing and reading the gifts than Doni's works customarily supply him. It is always possible that Doni could have written such an answer himself, particularly since the letters were not printed until 1551, after he had established himself in Venice; nonetheless it is interesting to find confirmation of the fact that in 1547 he was still sending gifts of music to possible patrons such as Cosimo. No such letter exists to confirm authorship of the manuscript here in question; but Doni's remark, in the epistle just cited, that "ch'era di mio grandissimo contento poter presentarlo di mia mano" suggests that he not only sent literary and musical gifts but often gave them to patrons in person.

Still later Doni tried once again to please by means of a musical offering. In 1554 he wrote to Guidobaldo della Rovere, duke of Urbino, in much the same vein, suggesting that he continued to dabble in music: " . . . presento alcuni frutti del mio ingegno . . . et alcune carte di musica le quali ho composte e scritte di mia propria mano et disegnate, ma so ancora piú e so far meglio." Printed with this letter is an answer (presumably) from the duke, thanking Doni for his "mirabil musica."[48] What is pertinent in these letters is Doni's reference to having not only written music but copied it out and ornamented the pages. In other letters he says of himself that he is a "scrittore, sonatore, cantore, & dipintore" (to Cardinal Alessandro Farnese) or that "mi diletto di scrivere, come voi vedete, et vedrete cantare, sonare, disegnare, et poetizzare" (to Paolo Giovio).[49] A great deal of Doni's writing survives, of course, and in the *Dialogo* some of his music may be seen. If the evidence thus far presented is convincing in linking his name and hand with the manuscript Magl. XIX, 130, we may see him here again active as editor, copyist, perhaps composer (nos. 1 and 10?); and even as an illustrator or miniaturist if the ornamented pages of the manuscript may be thought to be in his hand.

Supposing Doni to have been the compiler of the manuscript, we could assume that he got it up during his Florentine stay of 1545–48, and that it was presented to Cosimo I about 1547, when the woodcut frontispiece would have been available for use. The manuscript without the woodcut as yet on it could have been written earlier, but the same paper is used throughout, and the use of the Greek motto discussed above, and drawn in by hand, suggests again the period during which Doni was connected with the Accademia Fiorentina. Could the madrigals actually have been performed by members of this august group? It is not impossible, although the manuscript itself shows no signs of use. On at least one occasion during this period the Accademia commissioned some music: Corteccia set some madrigals performed in the intermedi of Francesco d'Ambra's comedy *Il Furto,* presented by the academicians several times during the year 1544.[50] But on the whole the interests of this Academy were purely literary. Nor was Cosimo I particularly devoted to music; naturally collections of printed madrigals were dedicated to him from time to time,[51] and in accounts of his early life one hears occasionally of his studying or performing music;[52] yet there is no reason to suppose that he ordered musical manuscripts from Doni or anyone else. But Antonfrancesco Doni was hardly the man to wait for an order; as has been suggested above, he often peddled his wares in the hope of attracting support and patronage. This leads one to suppose that if Magl. XIX, 130, was actually his work, it represented a kind of elaborate sample of his abilities as editor, perhaps as composer, as miniaturist. A small number of madrigals, neatly presented, would have sufficed for this (and they need not have been pieces previously unprinted; the ducal recipient of the manuscript would hardly have tracked down the history of these anonymous madrigals);[53] if this offering were favorably received greater things, such as the establishment of a ducal press equipped to publish music, might follow. They did not follow, and Doni soon left Florence. There is little reason to think that the manuscript would have been submitted after 1548, when Doni made a quite final break, possibly under the unpleasant circumstances that so often surrounded his comings and goings, with his native city. The half-mythical Pellegrini of Venice, of whom Doni was spokesman and self-appointed guiding spirit, touched on music often in the years that followed, but Doni was busy with other projects and never reestablished himself as a printer of music.

APPENDIX

FLORENCE, BIBLIOTECA NAZIONALE CENTRALE, MS. MAGL. 19, 130

	Poet	Composer	Concordances
1. Voi ch'ascoltate	G. Bidelli, *Centoni del Petrarca* (1544), no. 1		
2. Con lei foss'io	Petrarch, sestina *A qualunque animale* (*Rime*, 22)	Giaches de Ponte (Arcadelt; Corteccia)	*Primo libro . . . a misura di breve* (1542), no. 36, an oft-reprinted collection; the piece is first attributed to Corteccia, then to Arcadelt, but in the later reprints it is always given to de Ponte. See Vogel, 2:384. Cf. Vogel, *Samml.*, 1575[3], 1583[2] (the latter frequently reprinted), both of which anthologies contain *Con lei* attributed to de Ponte. There are a number of intabulations of this popular piece including RISM (B 1,1) 1546[24], 1566[29], 1574[13], and two keyboard versions, in A. Gabrieli, *Canzoni alla francese*, lib. 6 (Sartori, *Bibliografia*, 1605g, 133).
3. Ma di chi debbo lamentarmi	Ariosto, *Orlando furioso*, 32. 21	Vincenzo Ruffo	Doni, *Dialogo della musica* (1544), no. 2; reprint in Malipiero, ed., *Dialogo* (Vienna, 1965), 17. Ruffo, *Primo libro a 4* (1545, etc.), no. 29; reprint in Torchi, *L'arte musicale*, 1:215.
4. Ben mille notti	Sannazaro, *Arcadia*, *Egloga 4* (nos. 4–7)	Ruffo	*Primo libro a 4*, no. 3; MS version is transposed down a 5th.
5. Fiere silvestre	see no. 4	Ruffo	*Primo libro a 4*, no. 6; reprint in Vogel, *Samml.*, 1585[1].
6. Monti selve fontane	see no. 4	Ruffo	*Primo libro a 4*, no. 7.
7. O fortunato che con altre rime	see no. 4	Ruffo	*Primo libro a 4*, no. 5.
8. Per ché la vit'è breve	Petrarch (*Rime*, 71)	Arcadelt	Filippo Azzaiolo, *Il 2° libro de Villotte del fiore . . . a 4* (1559, 1564), 11; reprint in G. Vecchi, ed. (Azzaiolo, *Il 2° libro*, etc., Bologna, 1953, 41). MS version is transposed down a fifth and a good deal altered in the middle voices.
9. Pace non trovo	Petrarch (*Rime*, 134)	Yvo Barry	Arcadelt, *Quarto libro a 4* (1539, 1541), no. 38; *Il vero terzo libro . . . . a note negre* (1549), no. 4; Vogel, *Samml.*, 1569[a]. Reprint in *MD* 20 (1966), 134ff.
10. Che deggio far che mi consigl'amore	G. Bidelli, *Centoni del Petrarca*, no. 7		

1. Voi ch'ascoltate

2. Con lei foss'io

3. Ma di chi debbo lamentarmi

4. Ben mille notti

5. Fiere silvestre

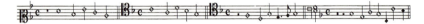

6. Monti selvi fontane

7. O fortunato

8. Per ché' la vit'è breve

9. Pace non trovo

10. Che degg'io far

POSTSCRIPT

In the family of articles gathered in this book this is one of my favorite children, even though—or perhaps because—it has never drawn much notice. Assembling the bits of information that make up this study led to particularly satisfying results, for me at any rate. The sketch given here of that ever-interesting picaresque hero Antonfrancesco Doni shows him engaged in a combination of activities each of which he was known to have pursued singly. The combination of musician, artist-illuminator, writer, perhaps plagiarist/thief seems to me to make a vivid portrait of a man who so well represents the underside of cinquecento culture.

Two books which appeared shortly after this article was published are of special relevance to it. One is a modern edition, with valuable commentary, of the wedding music for Cosimo I and Eleanora of Toledo: Andrew C. Minor and Bonner Mitchell, *A Renaissance Entertainment: Festivities for the Marriage of Cosimo I, Duke of Florence, in 1539* (Columbia, Mo., 1968). The other is Paul Grendler's informative *Critics of the Italian World, 1530–1560: Anton Francesco Doni, Nicolo Franco, and Ortensio Lando* (Madison, Wis., 1969).

"Per ché la vit'è breve" is printed in Albert Seay, ed., *Jacobi Arcadelt. Opera Omnia*, 7 (American Institute of Musicology, 1969), no. 57, after the Azzaiolo print of 1559. On p. xxi of the same volume Seay gives the version of the piece found in Magl. XIX, 130.

The manuscript has now been renumbered as II. III. 437–40.

NOTES

1. My thanks are due to Thomas Bridges for having first called my attention to this manuscript. I am also grateful to Signora Levi and to the staff of the Sala dei manoscritti of the Biblioteca Nazionale Centrale for allowing me to consult the work and to have made the photographs reproduced in this study.

2. All references to the manuscript that I have seen describe it in this way; the reasons for this quite mistaken attribution will be explained presently.

3. For Ivo Barry and his setting of the Petrarch sonnet see James Haar, "*Pace non trovo*: A Study in Literary and Musical Parody," *MD* 20 (1966): 95–149.

4. Gero's "Con lei" appears in his *Secondo libro . . . à 3 voci* (Venice, 1556), no. 9. It is the same as an anonymous setting in *Madrigali à tre et arie napoletane* (RISM [ca. 1537][8]), no. 2. As for Gero's "Pace non trovo," printed also in his *Secondo libro*, no. 4, it *is* related to Ivo's setting; for details see the article cited in n. 3.

5. *Il secondo libro de villotte del fiore alla padoana con alcune Napolitane e madrigali à 4 voci* (Venice, 1559), 11; page 41 in the modern edition of this work by Giuseppe Vecchi (Bologna, 1953). Curiously enough I find no other source for this setting; the title is a frequent one in madrigal prints, but the "Per ché la vit'è breve" attributed to Corteccia in Gardane's *Primo libro à misura di breve* of 1542 is not related musically, nor is that of Perissone Cambio (*Primo libro à 4*, 1547); another contemporary setting *a 4*, unrelated musically, is that of Lupacchino (*Primo libro à 4*, 1543).

6. Bianca Becherini, *Catalogo dei manoscritti musicali della Biblioteca Nazionale di Firenze* (Kassel, 1959), 56–57.

7. Einstein, *Italian Madrigal*, 262.

8. The manuscript came into the Magliabechi collection from the Biblioteca Palatina left by the last of the Medici to the state and joined to the Biblioteca Magliabechiana in 1771, according to an order given six years earlier by the Grand Duke Francesco. See Domenico Fava, ed., *La Biblioteca Nazionale Centrale di Firenze e le sue insigni raccolte* (Milan, 1939), 43–44. There is a partial catalogue (Magl. X, 161) of the Palatine manuscripts that came into the Magliabechi collection at this time, taken from a larger catalogue made by G. Menabuoni of the Biblioteca Palatina; but the Ms. Magl. XIX, 130, is not mentioned in it.

9. Written on a blank page of the cantus part: "Ces madrigaux sont l'oeuvre de Jhan Gero—le premier 'Voi ch'ascolte' se trouve dans le premier livre de Madrigaux à 4 parties imprimé à Venise en 1549. H. Prunières, Avril 1908."

10. *Italian Madrigal*, 262. Einstein is said to have written beneath Prunières's note one, dated 1938, which said only the first madrigal to be by Gero; see Becherini, *Catalogo*, 56. But this note is not now to be found in the manuscript.

11. See for instance Luigi F. Tagliavini, "Gero," *MGG*, 4:182.

12. Cf. Jacquet Berchem's *Primo libro à 5* (1546); Sigismondo d'India, *Terzo libro à 1 & 2* (1618). And various poets of Petrarchistic leanings open their collection with Petrarch's first words; the *Rime* of Gaspara Stampa is one example. "Voi ch'ascolte" is a title appearing with great frequency in madrigal prints, even if not always standing at the beginning. Sometimes the text that follows is Bidelli's *centone* (see below) rather than the Petrarchan sonnet, an example being Hoste da Reggio's setting in his *Terzo libro à 4* (Venice, 1554), 13.

13. *Italian Madrigal*, 262.

14. This is the title of the 1563 (Venice) edition, and is what the work is usually referred to as. "Che deggio far" is no. 7 in this collection. Bidelli apparently added *centoni* as the work was republished, for in an edition of 1548, called simply *Centoni del Petrarcha di M. Giulio Bidelli senese*, there are only 50 *stanze*. A still earlier edition is mentioned by Giovanni Maria Mazzuchelli, *Gli Scrittori d'Italia* (Brescia, 1753–63), 2:1208: *Centoni diversi del Petrarca raccolta di M. Giulio Bidelli ad instantia di Leonardo detto il Furlano*, 1544. According to Mazzuchelli, Bidelli, "di professione Libraio . . . si diede specialmente a comporre Centoni in Ottave e in Capitoli tessuti de' versi del Petrarca, nel qual genere di Poesia si è acquistato molto nome." He was apparently a friend of Aretino. Bidelli also published a volume of *Rime* (Venice, 1551), of a very Petrarchesque cast.

15. The pieces are in correct order neither in the manuscript nor in Ruffo's *Primo libro a 4*, and no more of the sestina is to be found in his *Primo libro*. I have not been able to find other settings of this much of the poem, let alone the complete sestina, although individual stanzas were set (to judge from their titles only) by Maddalena Casulana, *Libro secondo a 4* (1570) ("Monti selvi"); Marenzio, *Libro primo a 4, 5, e 6* (1588) ("Fiere silvestre"); Lucretio Quinziani, *Primo libro a 5* (1588) ("Monti selvi"); Francesco Stivorio, *Primo libro a 5* (1585) ("Ben mille notti"), and *Primo libro a 4* (1583) ("Fiere silvestre").

16. His *Primo secondo et terzo libro del Capriccio . . . sopra le stanze del Furioso* (Venice, 1561) contains 93 stanzas from Ariosto's epic. See Einstein, *Italian Madrigal*, 564–65, for a discussion of Berchem's principles of selection.

17. See the edition by Gian Francesco Malipiero (music scored by Virginio Fagotto), vol. 7 in the *Collana di Musiche Veneziane inedite e rare* published by the Fondazione Giorgio Cini (Vienna, 1965).

18. *Madrigali di Giovan Nasco a 5 voci* (Venice, 1548), a print containing an exceedingly pompous dedication to the "Signori Filarmonici" of Verona. Jachet Berchem also composed "A qualunque animale" in its entirety; see his *Primo libro a 4* (Venice, 1556), nos. 1–

6. He was evidently inspired by the setting of "Con lei foss'io" that appears in Magl. XIX, 130, for he uses the superius of that setting intact in his own "Con lei foss'io," recomposing the lower three voices in very elaborate form but with a good deal of reference, at strategic points, to the lower voices of the earlier setting. And since there is a certain amount of thematic unity, almost amounting to a latter-day "head motive" in the superius of the first five pieces of the sestina, his entire cycle may be said to have sprung from the de Ponte (Arcadelt-Corteccia) "Con lei foss'io."

19. "Chiunque spira in questa breve vita," in Ruffo's *Terzo libro a 4* (Venice, 1560).

20. For a fuller attempt at characterizing this kind of madrigal, see chapter 9.

21. See Vogel, 2:384ff.

22. *Dialogo della musica*, ed. Malipiero; see p. 17 for the madrigal, p. 23 for the comment. This madrigal had previously been reprinted by Luigi Torchi, *L'arte musicale in Italia*, (1897), 1. 215.

23. *Dialogo*, 24.

24. *Musiche fatte nelle nozze dello Ill. Duca di Firenze il S. Cosimo de Medici et dell'Ill. Consorte sua Mad. Leonora da Tolleto* (Venice, 1539). Corteccia reprinted his madrigals in his *Primo libro a 5 e 6* and his *Primo libro a 4*, both of 1547.

25. *Apparato et feste nelle noze dello Illustrissimo Signor Duca di Firenze, & della Duchessa sua Consorte, con le sue Stanze, Madriali, Comedia, & Intermedij, in quelle recitati* (Florence, 1539), especially p. 13: at the city gate "era . . . un altro gran' frontispitio, figuratovi dentro lo Imperatore sedente sopra uno scoglio, Coronato di Lauro & con lo sceptro nella man' destra, sotto la quale & a piei di sua Maesta, Giaceva il gran' fiume Betis appoggiato sopra un vaso di due bocche, spargente gran copie d'acque, & sotto la sinistra di Augusto, il grandissimo Danubio che per entrare con VII bocche nel Mar maggiore, figurato era quivi con un vaso che per tante aperture pareva che spargessi le sue acque."

26. See Lewis Lockwood, "Ruffo," *MGG*, 11:1076–80. "Ma di chi lamentarmi," printed in Doni's *Dialogo* of 1544, seems to be the first madrigal by Ruffo to be printed. Of course the date of printing is no sure guide to the date of composition; but Ruffo went on publishing through the 1550s and 1560s, and did not save up compositions for years before they were printed.

27. For a summary of the early history of the Accademia degli Umidi—Accademia Fiorentina, see Michele Maylender, *Storie delle Accademie d'Italia* (Bologna, 1926–30), 5:363–67; 3:1–9. The works listed by Doni in his *Libraria seconda* (Venice, 1551), fol. 107, as having been written by members of the Accademia degli Umidi are surely pure whimsy, as their titles ("Il Ranocchio, Del trovar le vene abondanti d'acqua & di fondare pozzi mirabilmente") suggest.

28. Paolo Giovio, *Dialogo dell'Imprese militari et amorose, con un Ragionamento di Messer Lodovico Domenichi nel medesimo soggetto* (Lyons, 1559), 165: "Ma dove lasciare i Signori Accademici Fiorentini; non hanno anch'eglino alcuna bella & honorevole Impresa, essendo essi maestri e prencipi della lingua Toscana, e singolari in tutte le scienze? Lo. Io non potrei dir tanto de' meriti loro, ch'essi di molto più non fossero degni. Però quanto all'Impresa loro, dico, ch'ella è il fiume d'Arno in figura humana con due piante, l'una d'alloro, e l'altro d'oliva, senz'altro motto."

29. Salvatore Salvini, *Fasti consolari dell'Accademia fiorentina* (Florence, 1717), has a title page showing a laureated nude figure pouring water from a vase, a lion couchant beneath him; cf. *Notizie letterarie, ed istoriche intorno agli uomini illustri dell'Accademia fiorentina* (Florence, 1700), with the same title page ornament.

30. Giovio, *Dialogo*, 165: " . . . senz'altro motto. Onde di loro direbbe il Giovio, che hanno fatto un Corpo senz'anima."

31. See Carlo Padiglione, *I motti delle famiglie italiane* (Naples, 1910), 66. By some stretching ΚΑΜΑΤΟΣ ΕΥΚΑΜΑΤΟΣ might be made to refer to "iugum meum suave est, et onus meum leve," (Matt. 2:30), from which the *impresa* of a yoke with the motto *Suave* over it was made by Giovanni de' Medici (Leo X). For use of this device in a musical manuscript see Edward E. Lowinsky, "The Medici Codex: A Document of Music, Art, and Politics in the Renaissance," *Annales musicologiques* 5 (1957): 67. There is on one of the ornamented pages (see fig. 7) of Magl. XIX, 130, a suggestion of the pattern of a yoke; its appearance as a Medici device is dealt with in a general way by Jacopo Gelli, *Motti e Imprese di famiglie e personaggi italiani*, 2d ed. (Milan, 1928), no. 1658. Cosimo I used an elaborate *impresa* with a unicorn in the center and a pattern of yokes on the sides; see Girolamo Ruscelli, *Le imprese illustri* (Venice, 1572), 113. In the Museo degli Argenti of the Palazzo Pitti there is a tapestry, said to have been designed by Bronzino, with the Medici-Toledo arms in the center, a pattern of yokes on the sides.

The actual source of the motto would seem to be a passage in Euripides's *Bacchantes*, lines 64–67:

> Ἀσίας ἀπὸ λαίας
> ἱερὸν Τμῶλον ἀμείψασα θοάζω
> Βρομίῳ πόνον ἡδὺν κάματόν τ' εὐ-
> κάματον, Βάκχιον εὐαζομένα.

32. *Ragionamento*, 171–72: "Io conobbi il primo anno, cho io venni à Firenze, un dottissimo huomo di grandissima esperienza delle cose del mondo, che fù Francesco Campana; il quale per essere egli letterato e virtuoso, amava e favoriva grandemente i suoi pari. Costui, dovendosi dar principio à stampare i libri rari & equisiti della libreria de' Medici in S. Lorenzo, fece fare una Impresa per metterla in fronte de' libri; la quale era un Leggio con una Lucerna, e molti libri sopra e d'intorno, parte chiusi e parte aperti, con questo motto Greco ΚΑΜΑΤΟΣ ΕΥΚΑΜΑΤΟΣ. Il quale motto suona in nostra lingua, come sarebbe a dire, fatica senza fatica. Perché, ancorché lo studio delle lettere sia molto laborioso, è però tanto il diletto, che se ne trahe, che ciò non par fatica à chi lo fa volentieri."

33. He published a study on a passage in the Aeneid, called *Quaestio Virgiliana*, printed at Bologna in 1526 (the Greek motto is not, however, used here).

34. For a brief biographical sketch of Campana see P. G. Negri, *Istoria degli scrittori fiorentini* (Ferrara, 1722), 189. In *I Marmi* (1552), 3. 24–26, Doni speaks of Campana as being a great man who now, only a few years dead, is in danger of being forgotten. According to Francesco Dini, "Francesco Campana ed i suoi," *Archivio storico italiano*, ser. 5, vol. 23 (1899), 315, Campana died during the summer of 1546.

35. See Salvini, *Fasti consolari*, 2, 59, 72.

36. For an illustration see Cecilia Ricottini Marsili-Libelli, *Anton Francesco Doni scrittore e stampatore. Bibliografia delle opere e della critica e annali tipografici* (Florence, 1960), 39. On p. 355 of the same work is a reproduction of the title page of the *Lettioni . . . sopra Dante*, with its Greek motto.

37. Salvini, *Fasti consolari*, 59–60, 63. Doni's dedicatory letter in the *Lettioni*, published according to the colophon on 28 June 1547 (but the letter is dated 4 July 1547!), is addressed to Panciatichi, thanking him for all the favors he has accorded Doni since the latter's return to Florence; which if he were to recount would "farsi arrossire molti di quegli che vogliono esser chiamati & nobili & magnifici; non essendo altro l'instituto loro che perseguire i buoni & poveri virtuosi." Doni evidently felt a special debt of gratitude to Panciatichi, whose influence had perhaps got him the secretariat of the Academy; for the rest the theme of the despised virtuoso was a common one with Doni.

38. See Salvatore Bongi, "Vita di M. A. F. Doni," *Novelle di M. Antonfrancesco Doni colle notizie sulla vita dell'autore* (Lucca, 1852), xxxii; this is still the most complete biographical sketch of Doni.

39. Marsili-Libelli, *A. F. Doni*, Appendice: "Annali," 339–56; Fernanda Ascarelli, *La tipografia cinquecentina italiana* (Florence, 1953), 137–38.

40. This is mentioned in a letter from Doni to Francesco Revesla, dated at Florence, 10 March 1547 (see Marsili-Libelli, *A. F. Doni*, 339).

41. See Domenico Moreni, *Annali della tipografia fiorentina di Lorenzo Torrentino impressore ducale*, 2d ed. (Florence, 1819), viff.

42. Giorgio Vasari, *Le vita de' piú eccellenti pittori scultori ed architettori*, ed. G. Milanesi (Florence, 1878–82), 5:428.

43. See Scipione Casali, *Annali della tipografia veneziana di Francesco Marcolini da Forlí* (Forlí, 1861), xiii–xiv: "I legni adoperati dal Doni in Firenze durante il breve tempo ch'ivi tenne una stamperia, si veggono usati da Marcolini promiscuamente coi suoi proprii nelle edizioni dopo il 1550." Luigi Servolini, *Supplemento agli annali della tipografia veneziana di Fr. Marcolini compilato da Scipione Casali* (Bologna, 1958), 14–15, says of Doni's *Prose antiche* of 1547 "ma tipi e legni del Marcolini." But the truth would really seem to be the other way around, and Casali, who repeats in other words (p. 212n.) what is quoted above, appears to have been right. There is no reason to think that Doni met Marcolini, who in any event had been away in Cyprus, until after his return to Venice.

44. In the text of the *Dialogo* Doni is rather coy about authorship of madrigal texts and music, so that it is hard to tell whether he was trying to minimize his role as composer or to suggest that it was actually considerable. But from the hints given in the course of the *Dialogo* it seems likely that three madrigals are by Doni—both text and music—and that he also set to music a text by his then friend Lodovico Domenichi; see Vogel, 2:635.

45. In a letter to Paolo Ugone Doni says "hora la musica . . . dee sapere che la mi diletta per capriccio; & mi piace saper fare quando è bisogna qualche cosetta; ma che io sia innamorato di note, d'archetti, & di tasti S[ignor] no. Son piú inclinati alle lettere, & a un certo piú grave essercitio" (*Lettere*, 1544, fol. 106). And elsewhere he writes in much the same vein.

46. *Lettere d'Antonfrancesco Doni* (Venice, 1544), fols. 24–25.

47. Printed, together with Cosimo's answer, at the end of Doni's *Zucca* (1552), fol. 271.

48. The letters, dated 1554, are printed in Doni's libellous attack on his erstwhile friend Pietro Aretino (*Il Terremoto*, Venice, 1556, p. [31]). In Bongi, *Vita di M. A. F. Doni*, lxvi–lxvii, Doni's gift to the Duke is called "un dialogo sulla musica scritto a mano, e diverso da quella stampata." But it seems doubtful that it was anything this extensive; Doni himself, never one to understate, does not claim anything more than what is quoted above.

49. *Lettere* (1544), fols. 31, 51v.

50. Salvini, *Fasti consolari*, 39–40: " . . . per esser la maggior parte degli Accademici occupati nella Festa, che fu fatta due volte nella Sala del Papa, recitandovi la Commedia di Francesco d'Ambra, intitolato *il Furto*, e per la terza volta, alla presenza del Duca Cosimo, nella Villa di Castello." Corteccia published these madrigals in his *Primo libro a 4* (1547).

51. The music of the 1539 intermedi was of course addressed to Cosimo; then, all four of Corteccia's madrigal prints were dedicated to the Duke. And Mattio Rampolini's *Primo libro . . . sopra di alcune Canzoni del . . . Petrarca* (1560?; Vogel's date is probably too late; cf. Einstein, *Italian Madrigal*, 288) is addressed to Cosimo, the composer saying "So bene che si alte dolce et musical parole meritavano esser composte dal padre de la Musica Lo excellentissimo Iosquino & Adriano, Giacheto et altri piú valenti compositori che non sono io . . . "

52. See Cecily Booth, *Cosimo I, Duke of Florence* (Cambridge, 1921), 44. Baccio Baldini, *Vita di Cosimo de Medici I Granduca di Toscana* (Florence, 1578), 80, says that Cosimo "dilettossi sempre mai piú che d'alcun altro piacere della musica," but gives no concrete instances.

53. Doni might have hoped to pass off all the madrigals as his own compositions. He was certainly not above appropriating material for his own use; he admits in a letter of 1546, to Tomaso Baroncelli (*Secondo libro di lettere*, Florence, 1547, fol. 40) that he stole from the latter a manuscript copy of the *Dialoghi* of Gelli, in order to print this work, which he did in September 1546. And some of the contents of the *Dialogo della musica* suggest that a bit of musical theft may been practiced there.

The *Libraria* of Antonfrancesco Doni

IN THE MEDLEY OF INTERESTS and occupations making up the career of Anton-francesco Doni (1513–74)—Florentine priest, poet, *novellatore*, letter writer, musician, polemicist, traveller, gossip, and, at the end, hermit—there is a stint of activity in what would seem for him an unlikely field, that of bibliography. Doni is in fact generally credited with being the first bibliographer of Italian literature;[1] he would certainly appear to be one of the first to include music in a published book list.

What later became known as Doni's *Prima Libraria* was published in 1550 by the Venetian printer Gabriel Giolito as *La Libraria del Doni Fiorentino. Nella quale sono scritti tutti gl'Autori vulgari con cento Discorsi sopra quelli. Tutte le tradutioni Fatte all' altre lingue, nella nostra & una tavola generalmente come si costuma fra Librari.*[2] As its title indicates, the work is a list of printed books written in, or translated into, Italian; it is divided into six categories, the last devoted to music: "La musica stampata. Madrigali, mottetti, messe, et canzoni. L'ultima parte del Primo Trattato."[3] The last phrase tells us that Doni had more in the offing; and indeed a *Seconda Libraria*, listing works in manuscript, appeared in Venice, printed by Francesco Marcolini, the next year.[4] Then, in 1557 Giolito reissued both works in a single volume as *La Libraria. . . . Divisa in tre trattati* (the latter part of the *Seconda Libraria*, a description of the names, devices, and writings of Italian academicians, was now listed as a separate section).[5]

If Doni was among the first to publish a list of printed music, it is a pity that he did not do a better job of it.[6] Compared with the painstakingly detailed catalogue drawn up by Ferdinand Columbus to record his own purchases of music,[7] Doni's list is casual in the extreme. But Columbus's entries stop about 1535; for the years 1535–50 Doni's catalogue, incomplete and sometimes perfunctorily made though it may be, is an important source of information. And though the *Libraria* is a flimsy piece of work in comparison with the *Abecedaria* and *Supplementa* of the Colombina catalogue, it is no less informative than surviving publishers' lists of the late sixteenth century.[8]

We have ample testimony of his interest in music in Doni's *Dialogo della musica* of 1544:[9] he was a singer, perhaps a composer; an organizer of musical performances in provincial Piacenza, then a listener or hanger-on at some distinguished musical *accademie* in Venice. For a time, when he revisited his native Florence in the mid-1540s, Doni may have toyed with the idea of becoming a music printer himself.[10] And as the madrigals and motets contained in the *Dialogo della musica* show, he was a collector, possibly a somewhat unprincipled one, of the music of others.[11] Whether he actually owned all the music described in the *Prima Libraria*,[12] or simply saw it at the houses of publishers and in the possession of acquaintances—

"friends" is perhaps not the word to use for associates of the cantankerous and fickle Doni—cannot be determined, and is not really important. He was living in Venice at the time the *Libraria* was compiled, and most of the music he lists was printed by the Venetian houses of Girolamo Scotto and Antonio Gardano. The regrettable fact that not all of the music issued by Gardano and Scotto up to the time the *Libraria* was written[13] is included therein suggests that Doni listed music he knew, even if he did not necessarily own it, rather than copying publishers' lists.

It is not surprising that Doni did not get all the Italian, even all the Venetian music prints of ca. 1535–50. Though he may at first have aimed at completeness, he soon wore down; as we shall see, his catalogue gets sloppier as it goes on, and at its end he gives up, saying that to include all the printed music of his time would entail writing a book as large as a whole volume of music—so he quite simply stops where he is, finishing with a small and rather eccentrically chosen list of theoretical works.[14] What does seem strange is that Doni, acquainted with a number of musicians and a frequenter of musical gatherings in the most cosmopolitan city of Italy, did not know the output of German, Flemish, or French printers, even that of Jacques Moderne in Lyons. The section of the *Libraria* devoted to music has as preface a letter to the composer and organist Jaches Buus, whom Doni asks to obtain from some French musician a list of music printed in France.[15] If he ever got such a list, Doni made no use of it.

After the early 1550s Doni's interest in music appears to have waned.[16] The 1557 reprint of the *Libraria* has, as we shall see, very few additions to the catalogue of 1550. It is of course possible that Doni, who was away from Venice in the years 1555–1558,[17] did not supervise the preparation of this reprint, or indeed pay much attention to its contents. As for the posthumous edition of 1580, it does not contain even the additional entries of the 1557 printing; it was apparently taken from the first edition of 1550.[18]

Given below are the contents of the *Prima Libraria*. Doni's entries are given in their original form and order on the left; on the right is my effort—some of it admittedly guesswork—to catalogue Doni's catalogue. All prints are those of Antonio Gardano or Girolamo Scotto in Venice unless otherwise specified.

LA MUSICA STAMPATA. MADRIGALI, MOTTETI, MESSE ET CANZONI.
L'ULTIMA PARTE DEL PRIMO TRATTATO. [FOLS. 63V–67 IN ED. OF 1550]

Madrigali a Quattro, e Motetti

[madrigals]
Archadelt, libri cinque

    1) Arcadelt 1 ff. (1539, 1541, 1543, 1544, 1545 [not listed in Vogel: see Ernst Hilmar in *Analecta Musicologica* 4. 160], 1546): *Il primo libro . . . a 4v.*;

    2) Vogel: Arcadelt 31 ff. (1539, 1541): *Il vero secondo libro*[19] *a 4v.*;

    3) Vogel: Arcadelt 34a ff. (1539, 1541, 1543): *Del tertio libro de i madri . . . a 4v.*;

<table>
<tbody>
<tr><td></td><td>4) Vogel: Arcadelt 36b ff. (1539, 1541, 1545): Il quarto libro . . . a 4v.;</td></tr>
<tr><td></td><td>5) Vogel: Arcadelt 39 f. (1544, 1550): Il quinto libro . . . a 4v.</td></tr>
<tr><td>Adriano, villotte</td><td>Vogel: Willaert 2 (1545):[20] Canzon villanesche . . . di Messer Adriano a 4v.</td></tr>
<tr><td>Animuccia</td><td>Vogel: Animuccia 1 (1547): Primo libro . . . a 4 a 5 & a 6v. de l' Animuccia.</td></tr>
<tr><td>Anselmo Reulx duo libri</td><td>1) Vogel: Reulx 1 ff. (1543): Di Anselmo Reulx Madrigali a 4v.;
2) Vogel: Reulx 4 (1546): Secondo libro . . . a 4v.</td></tr>
<tr><td>Antonio Cimello</td><td>Vogel: Cimello (1548): Di Giovanthom. Cimello[21] libro primo . . . a 4v.</td></tr>
<tr><td>Bernardo Lupachini duo libri</td><td>1) Vogel: Lupacchino 2 f. (1543): Di Bernardino Lupacchini dal Vasto Madrigali a 4v.;
2) Vogel: Lupacchino 4 (1546): Il secondo libro . . . a 4v.</td></tr>
<tr><td>Bertoldo Don</td><td>Vogel: Bertoldi, Don Bertoldo (1544): Il primo libro de Madregali di Don Bertoldo da Castel Vetro a 4v.</td></tr>
<tr><td>Baldassare Donato villanesche</td><td>Vogel: Donato 4 (1550): Le Napollitane . . . a 4v. (Scotto, dated 15 January 1550; Gardano also printed this set of pieces in 1550).</td></tr>
<tr><td>Cipriano Rore</td><td>Vogel: Rore 36 (1550): Il primo libro . . . a 4v. (Ferrara: Buglhat & Hucher; "novamente poste in luce"); Vogel: Rore 37 (1551), a printing by Gardano also said to be "novamente dati in luce," seems to be the earliest Venetian edition.</td></tr>
<tr><td>Claudio Veggio</td><td>Vogel: Veggio 1 (1540): Madrigali a 4v. (Scotto).
Vogel: Veggio 2 (1545), a Gardano print marked "Novamente Ristampato," is a good deal reduced in content; the possibility of an earlier edition by Gardano suggests itself.</td></tr>
<tr><td>Diversi autori tre libri</td><td>1) RISM 1542[17] = Vogel: 1542[2] ff. (1543[1], 1546[1], 1547[1], 1548[3], 1550[1]): Il primo libro . . . de diversi eccell. autori . . . 4v.;
2) RISM 1543[18] = Vogel: 1543[2]: Il secondo libro . . . de diversi ecc. autori . . . a 4v.;
3) RISM 1549[30] = Vogel: 1549[1]: Libro terzo de d. autori . . . a 4v. (Scotto); or RISM</td></tr>
</tbody>
</table>

1549[31] = Vogel: 1549[2]: *Il vero terzo libro
. . . de diversi autori . . . a 4.* (Gardano).
Doni says nothing about the existence of
rival third books in this series, the *madrigali a note negre.* Up to 1550 books 1 and
2 were printed by Gardano; but until more
is known of the relationships between
these two printers, it seems unwise to say
whose series this was.

Dialogo della musica dal Doni RISM 1544[22] = Vogel: 1544[1]: *Dialogo della
musica di M. Antonfrancesco Doni
Fiorentino.*

Enrico Scaffen Vogel: Schaffen[22] (1549): *Henricus Schaffen
. . . li suoi Madrigali a 4v.*

Francesco Corteccia duo libri 1) Vogel: Corteccia 2 f. (1544, 1547): *Libro
primo . . . a 4v.*;
2) Vogel: Corteccia 4 (1547): *Libro secondo
. . . a 4v.*

Francesco Biffetto Vogel: Bifetto 1 (1547): *Madrigali a 4v.*
A *Libro secondo a 4v.*, given in Vogel as
printed by Gardano in 1548, is not listed
by Doni.

Florian Candonio Vogel: Candonio (1546): *Il primo libro de
madrigali di Floriano Candonio For'
Juliano . . . a 4v.*

Ferabosco Vogel: Ferabosco, [Domenico] (1542): *D'il
Ferabosco il primo libro . . . a 4v.*

Fama RISM 1548[8] = Vogel: 1548[1]: *Madrigali de la
Fama a 4v.* (Scotto); *or* RISM 1548[7] =
Vogel: 1548[2], Gardano's slightly altered
version of the same print. Which came
first, and which Doni refers to, I cannot
say.

Francesco Mannara [1557 ed.] Vogel: Manara 2 (1555): *Di Francesco
Manara il primo libro . . . a 4v.*

Giovan Gero, duo libri 1) Vogel: Gero 1 (1549): *Di Jehan Gero . . .
libro primo delli Madrigali a 4v.*
2) Vogel: Gero 2 (1549): *Di Jehan Gero . . .
libro secondo delli Madrigali a 4v.*

Gian de Ferrara Vogel: Ihan (1541): *Il primo libro de i madrigali di Maistre Ihan, Maestro di Capella
dello Ecc. Sig. Hercole Duca di Ferrara.*
Since Doni later refers to "Metre Ian" one
cannot be sure that this identification is

	correct, but it seems the most likely prospect.
Giordan	? For Giordano Passetto see below. A "Fra Jordan" is represented by one piece in RISM 1531[4] = Vogel: 1531[1]
Gabriel Martinengo	Vogel: Martinengo 2 (1544): *De Gabriel Martinengo Madrigali a 4v.* A *secondo libro a 4v.*, published by Scotto in 1548, is not listed by Doni.
Hoste da Reggio	Vogel: Hoste de Reggio 2 (1547): *Primo libro . . . a 4v.*
Hippolito Cera frate di S. Gioanne Polo[23] *[1557 ed.]*	Vogel: Ciera 2 (1554): *Madrigali del Laberinto a 4v. libro primo. Composti da . . . Don Hippolito Ciera.*
Iachet Berchem	? Vogel: Berchem 2 (1556): *Di Iachet Berchem il primo libro di Madrigali a quattro Voci, per lui composti nuovamente . . . dati in luce* (Gardano). Doni's entry suggests that an earlier edition once existed, but the language of the title page seems evidence to the contrary.
Iordan Passet [1557 ed.: frate di S. Gioanne Polo]	Vogel: Passetto (1541): *Madrigal . . . per il Doct. Musico M. Giordano Passetto, Maestro di Capella, del Domo di Padoa. Libro primo.* It is not clear whether Doni's listing of *Giordan* (see above) refers to Passetto.
Lamberto Curtois	Vogel: Courtoys (1580): *Lambert Courtoys . . . Madrigali a 5v.*, is the only surviving print devoted to this composer. Pieces *a* 3 and *a* 5 by him may be found in anthologies such as RISM 1562[3] = Vogel: 1562[4] and RISM 1563[7] = Vogel: 1563[1]; he is mentioned in the title of the latter print. The *Lamberto* of RISM 1543[18] = Vogel: 1543[2] is Pierre Lambert, according to Eitner, *Quellen-Lexikon*, 3:87; 6:24. Doni seems here to be naming an otherwise unknown print.
Lodovico Novello mascharate	Vogel: Novello (1546): *Mascharate di Lodovico Novello . . . Libro primo a 4v.*
Musica fatta nelle nozze del Duca di Firenze	RISM 1539[25] = Vogel: 1539[1]: *Musiche fatte nelle nozze dello ill. Duca di Firenze il sig. Cosimo de Medici.*

Martoretta	Vogel: Martoretta 1 (1548): *De lo ecc. musico La Martoretta li madrigali a 4v. [primo libro]*

Perissone duo libri madrigali & villote

1) Vogel: Perissone 3 (1547): *Primo libro . . . a 4v. di Perissone Cambio.*

2) ? No *2° a 4v.* is listed in Vogel or otherwise known. The print may be lost, or Doni may be confused; he lists only one book *a 5v.*, whereas two survive (see below).

3) Vogel: Perissone 4 (1545): *Canzone villanesche alla napolitane a 4v. di Perissone.*

Paolo Aretino duo libri madrigali & lamentationi

1) Vogel: Aretino 2 (1549): *Libro primo delli madrigali cromati di M. Pauolo Aretino.*

2) ? No *2° a 4v.* is known; there is a *Libro primo a 5v.* (Scotto, 1558), described on the title page as *"novamente dati in luce,"* and not mentioned by Doni among madrigals *a 5v.* It is possible that by "duo libri" Doni meant one of madrigals, one of lamentations.

3) ? Eitner, *Quellen-Lexikon* 7:311, lists under Aretino *Piae, ac devotissimae Lamentationes Hieromiae Prophetae,*[24] published by Scotto in 1563; on the title page the work is described as "Nunc primum a Dom. Paulo Aretino compositae." There seems no reason to prefer Scotto's word to Doni's here; an earlier edition of the *Lamentationes* may well have existed.

Pietro Paolo Ragazzoni	Vogel: Ragazzoni (1544): *Madrigali di Pietro Paolo Ragazzoni di Parma a 4v.*
Simeon Belielau	Vogel: Boyleau 2 (1546): *Madrigali a 4v. de Simon Boyleau nobile francese.*
Stanze del Bembo cinquanta	Vogel: Ponte 1 (1546): *Cinquanta Stanze del Bembo con la musica di sopra composta per . . . Giaches de Ponte . . . a 4v.*
Tutuual [1557 ed.: *Tuduual*]	? No print devoted to secular or sacred works by Tudual[25] survives, to my knowledge. For sources of individual pieces by this composer see W. Kirsch in *MGG*, 13:942–943.
Tromboncino	RISM [c. 1520][7] = Vogel: [1520²]: *Frottole de Misser Bortolomio Tromboncino & de Misser Marcheto Cara con Tenori & Bassi tabulati . . .*

The date of 1520 is confirmed in the catalogues of Ferdinand Columbus; see Chapman (n. 7), no. 55, p. 68, where the print is attributed to Antico. A [later?] reprint of this title was also in Columbus's library, but no copies are known to survive; see ibid., no. 89, p. 73. Whether this collection is what Doni meant by his entry I am not sure, but nothing else seems likely.[26]

Verdeloth	Vogel: Verdelot 8b ff. (1540, 1541, 1544, 1545, 1549): *Di Verdelotto Tutti li Madrigali del Primo, et Secondo Libro a 4v.*
Vincenzo Ruffo	Vogel: Ruffo 13 f. (1545, 1546): *Di Vincentio Ruffo . . . li Madrigali a 4v. [primo libro]*

Questi son quanti madrigali et cose a quattro voci ch'io mi ritrovo in esser. i motetti a quattro son questi.

Adriano due libri	1) *Famosissimi Adriani Willaert . . . Musica 4v., . . . vulgo Motecta . . . Lib. primus,* 1539, Scotto; reprint 1545, Gardano.
	2) *Motetti di A. Willaert, Lib. secondo 4v.,* 1539, B. &. O. Scotto; 1545, Gardano.
Gombert due libri	1) *Gomberti excell . . . Musica 4v. (vulgo Motetta nuncupatur) . . . Lib. 1* [1539], Scotto; 1541, Scotto (= RISM 1541[4]), also Gardano.
	2) *Nicolai Gomberti . . . Motectorum lib. 2, 4v.,* 1541, Scotto; 1542, Gardano.
Iachet	*Jachet chori Sancti Petri urbis Mantuae magistri motecta 4v . . . lib. 1,* 1539, 1544, Scotto; 1545, Gardano.
Morales	RISM 1543[15]: *Morales hispani . . . musica cum vocibus quatuor, vulgo motecta cognominata . . .* 1543, Scotto; 1546, Gardano (= RISM 1546[9]).
Metre Ian	RISM 1543[4]: *Symphonia quatuor modulata vocibus . . . musici Joannis Galli alias chori Ferrariae magistri quae vulgo (Motecta Metre Jehan) nominatur . . . ,* Scotto.
Del Fiore	Probably not Moderne's four books of this title, but RISM 1539[12]: *Primus liber cum quatuor vocibus. Fior de mottetti tratti*

	dalli mottetti del fiore (Gardano) *or:* RISM 1545[4]: *Flos florum primus liber cum quatuor vocibus. Motteti del fior* (Gardano).
Lucarino	RISM 1547[7]: *D. Ionanis Iacobi Lucarii concentuum qui vulgo motetta nuncupantur. Liber primus 4v.*, Gardano.[27]
Verdelotto	RISM 1549[12]: *Electiones diversarum motetorum . . . 4v . . . auctore excell. musico Verdeloto et quorundam musicantium aliorum . . .* (Gardano), *or:* RISM 1549[15]: *Elletione de motetti non piu stampati a 4v. di Verdelotto et di altri . . . autori . . .* (Scotto).
Simon Bolieau	*Simonis Boyleau Genere Galli . . . motetta 4v.*, 1544, Scotto. See Eitner, *Quellen-Lexikon*, 2:164–165.
Io Muton	? The only collection of motets by Mouton known to me is the 1555 print of LeRoy and Ballard in Paris: *Ioannis Mouton . . . selecti alicquot moduli . . . Lib. 1.* Doni may be referring here to RISM [1521][6]: *Motetti e canzone libro primo*, described in Columbus's catalogue as "*Moteti et canzone li⁰. p⁰. Jo. mouton et aliorum autorum*, R[oma]. 1520." See Chapman, (n. 7), p. 50 and no. 67, p. 70; cf. Knud Jeppesen, "An Unknown Pre-Madrigalian Music Print in Relationship to Other Contemporary Italian Sources (1520–1530)," *Studies in Musicology. Essays in the History, Style, and Bibliography of Music in Honor of Glen Haydon*, ed. James Pruett (Chapel Hill, 1969), 3.
Iaches Buus	*Libro de Motetti a 4v. di M. Jacques Buus . . .* 1549, Gardano. See Eitner, *Quellen-Lexikon*, 2:255.
Vincenzo Ruffo et	? No book of motets *a 4v.* is known to survive; see Lewis Lockwood in *MGG*, 11: 1077. For Ruffo's motets *a 5v.*, see below.
Quei del Frutto	RISM 1539[13]: *Primus liber cum quatuor vocibus. Mottetti del frutto . . .* (Gardano), *or* reprints of this volume: RISM 1549[10] (Gardano), RISM 1549[10a] (Scotto).

L'altre cose a cinque non sono in tanto numero ma le son bellissime al giuditio
mio et fra tante che ne son composte, queste poche ho posto in registro.
Motetti e Madrigali a cinque

[madrigals]

Antonio Martorello	Vogel: Martorello (1547): *Il primo libro di madrigali a 5v. di Antonio Martorello Milanese.*
Bernardo Lupacchino	Vogel: Lupacchino 1 (1547): *Il primo libro a 5v . . . per l'ecc. musico Bernardino Lupacchino dal Vasto . . .*
Cipriano Rore tre libri et le Vergini	1) Vogel: Rore 1 f. (1542, 1544): *Di Cipriano il primo libro de madregali cromatici a 5v . . .* [title of 1544 and subsequent eds.];
	2) Vogel: Rore 10 (1544): *Di Cipriano il secondo libro . . . a 5v.*;
	3) Vogel: Rore 17 (1548): *Di Cipriano Rore . . . il terzo libro . . . a 5v.*;
	4) Vogel: Rore 16 (1548): *Musica di Cipriano Rore sopra le stanze del Petrarcha in laude della Madonna . . .*
Don Nicola	Vogel: Vicentino 1 (1546): *Del unico Adrian Willaerth Discipulo Don Nicola Vicentino Madrigali a 5v . . .*
Diversi duo libri	1) RISM 1542[16] = Vogel: 1542[1]: *Il primo libro d'i madrigali de diversi ecc. autori a 5v. . .* No second volume in this series is known to exist.
	2) ? Perhaps RISM[18] = Vogel: Verdelot 6a, 1540): *Le dotte et ecc. compositioni de i madrigali a 5v. da diversi perfettissimi Musici fatte . . .* Vogel: 2. 302, lists this print under Verdelot because its contents are so similar to those of his Verdelot 6 (ca. 1538) and 6b (1541), both of which list Verdelot in the title (see below). Doni may not have examined the prints carefully, or may not have worried about discrepancies of this kind.
Francesco Corteccia	Vogel: Corteccia 1 (1547): *Libro primo de Madriali a 5 & a 6v. di Francesco Corteccia.*
Francesco Portinaio madrigali	Vogel: Portinaro 3 (1550): *Di Francesco Portinaro il primo libro di Madrigali a 5v.*

Francesco Viola madrigali	? No book of madrigals *a 5v.* by Francesco Viola is known to survive. Vogel: Viola 1 (1550): *Di Francesco Viola Il primo libro . . . a 4v.*, is not listed in Doni's catalogue of four-voice madrigals; this entry may simply be misplaced. It is curious that Doni did not list the two books of madrigals *a 4v.* by Alfonso della Viola (1539, 1540); perhaps the fact that they were printed in Ferrara put them outside his ken.
Giachet Berchem	Vogel: Berchem 1 (1546): *Madrigali a 5v. di Giachetto da Berchem . . . Libro primo.*
Giovanni Nasco	Vogel: Nasco 3 (1548): *Madrigali di Giovan Nasco a 5v.*
Iaches Buus	*Il primo libro di canzoni francese a 5v.*, 1550 (Scotto). See Eitner, *Quellen-Lexikon*, 2:255.
Lodovico Floriano	? The identity of this man is unknown to me. Eitner, *Quellen-Lexikon*, 4:3, lists a Mathias Floranus, a papal singer, d. 1547; Eitner, *Quellen-Lexikon*, 4:5, has a Cristoforo Floriani of Ancona, active in Vienna, known for two collections of sacred music published in 1620.
Nicolo Dorati	Vogel: Dorati 2 (1549): *D. Niccolo Dorati il primo libro di madrigali a 5v.*
Parabosco	Vogel: Parabosco (1546): *Madrigali a 5v. di Girolamo parabosco discipulo di M. Adriano.*
Perissone	Vogel: Perissone 1 (1545): *Madrigali a 5v. per l'ecc. musico M. Perissone Cambio . . .* Doni does not list Perissone's second book *a 5v.*, printed by Gardano in 1550 (the dedicatory letter is dated 3 March [1550]). But he does list two books for four voices (see above), of which only one is known today; the entries may be mixed up.
Verdeloth	Vogel: Verdelot 6 (*ca.* 1538), 6b (1541): *Di Verdelot le dotte et ecc. Compositioni de i Madrigali a 5v . . .* Note that Verdelot 6 is a reprint ("Novamente Ristampati & Ricorretti"); the date 1538 is probably much too early. Vogel: Verdelot 6b is a reprint of an edition of 1540 (6a); see above under

	"*Diversi duo libri.*" For Verdelot's 5-voice madrigals printed in two separate books see Vogel: Verdelot 4, 5, 5a.
[motets]	
Adriano	*Famosissimi Adriani Willaert Musica 5v . . . vulgo Motecta . . . Liber primus*, 1539, 1550 (Scotto).
Cipriano duoi libri	1) RISM 1544[6]: *Cipriani musici eccelentissimi . . . motectorum . . . liber primus quinque vocum* (Gardano); 2) *Cypriani Rore . . . Motetta*, 1545 (Gardano). Doni does not mention the third book of 1549 (Gardano).
Del Conte	*El Conte Bartholomei Comitis Gallici . . . Motetta 5v.*, 1547 (Gardano). See Eitner, *Quellen-Lexikon*, 1:355.[28]
Domenico da Nola	*Liber primus motectorum 5v.*, 1549 (Scotto).
Diversi duoi libri	1) RISM 1549[7]: *Primo libro de motetti a 5v. da diversi ecc. autori . . .* (Scotto). 2) ? Perhaps RISM 1549[6]: *Musica 5v. materna lingua moteta vocantur ab . . . varijs authoribus elaborata* (Gardano) [a reprint of Scotto's 1543?].
De la divinita	RISM 1543[3]: *Mutetarum divinitatis liber primus quae quinque absolutae vocibus . . .* (Milan: A. Castiglione).
D'Eliseo	[= Ghibel], *Motetta 5 voc. lib. 1*, 1546, 1548 (Scotto). See Eitner, *Quellen-Lexikon*, 4:225.
Francesco Portinaro	*Primi frutti de Motetti a 5v., lib. 1*, 1548 (Gardano). See Eitner, *Quellen-Lexikon*, 7:31.
Del frutto	RISM 1538[4]: *Primus liber cum 5v. Mottetti del frutto* (Gardano); cf. RISM 1549[4]: *Excell. autorum diverse modulationes que sub titulo Fructus . . .* (Scotto) *or:* RISM 1549[5] [same title and contents] (Gardano).
Gombert, duo libri	1) *Musica exc. N. Gomberth 5v. lib. 1*, 1539 (Scotto), *or:* RISM 1541[3]: *Nicolai Gomberti . . . harmonia, que 5v. Motetta vulgo nominantur . . . Liber primus* (Scotto) [repr., 1550]. 2) *N. Gomberti . . . Motectorum 5v . . . Liber secundus*, 1541 (Scotto) [repr.

	1550]. See Joseph Schmidt-Görg in *MGG*, 5:502.
Iachet	*Jachet . . . cardinalis Mantuae magistri motecta 5v., lib. 1*, 1539 (Scotto), 1540 (Gardano). See Anne Marie Bautier-Regnier in *MGG*, 6:1591; Eitner, *Quellen-Lexikon*, 5:259.
Iaches Buus	? No collection of motets *a 5v.* by Buus is known to exist. See Joseph Schmidt-Görg in *MGG*, 2:543; cf. H. Kraus, "Jacob Buus, Leben und Werke," *Tijdschrift der Vereeniging voor nederl. Muziekgeschiedenis* 11 (1927): 81–82.
Pionier	? A volume by Jean Pionnier is listed in Eitner, *Quellen-Lexikon*, 7:454: *Cantiones 5 voc. (quas mutetta) noviter impressas, lib. 1*, 1548 (Gardano). François Lesure, "Pionnier," *MGG*, 10:1287, does not mention this print; but the copy described by Eitner as being in the Biblioteca Canal in Crespano does survive, and is now owned by the Bibl. Marciana in Venice. I am grateful to the staff of the Marciana for supplying this information. Of collected motets by Pionnier Lesure says "Ein Buch 5st. Mot., *lib. primo*, Venedig 1561, ist in Gardanos Kat.[29] u. verschiedenen Bibliogr. verzeichnet, doch ist kein Exemplar erhalten."
Vincenzo Ruffo	*Il primo libro di Mot. a 5v. de l'egregio V. R. . . . 1542* (Milan, Castilliono). See Eitner, *Quellen-Lexikon*, 7: 353.
Motetti a sei, et Madrigali	
Adriano	RISM 1542[10]: *Adriani Willaert . . . musicorum sex vocum, que vulgo motecta dicuntur . . . Liber primus* (Gardano).
Del frutto	RISM 1539[3]: *Primus liber cum sex vocibus. Motetti del frutto a 6v.* (Gardano); *or* a reprint, RISM 1549[2]: *Exc. autorum diverse modulationes que sub titulo Fructus vagantur per orbem . . . Liber primus cum 6v.* (Gardano).
Gombert	? Five motets *a 6v.* are in RISM 1549[3]: *Il primo libro de motetti a 6v.* (Scotto); 12

	motets *a 6v.* are in RISM 1539[3] = 1549[2] (see entry just above).
Iaches canzone Francesi	[= Buus], *Il primo libro di canz. francesi a 6v.*, 1543 (Gardano). See Eitner, *Quellen-Lexikon*, 2:255.
Verdeloth, madrigali	RISM 1541[16], 1546[19] = Vogel: Verdelot 1 f. (1541, 1546): *La piu divina, et piu bella musica . . . delli presenti Madrigali a 6v. Composti per lo Ecc. Verdelot, et altri Musici . . .*
Terzi et Duo [trios]	
Archadelth	RISM 1542[18] = Vogel: Arcadelt 41 f. (1542, 1543): *Primo libro di madrigali d'Archadelt a 3v.*
Antonio Cimello, Villotte	Vogel: Cimello (1545): *Canzone villanesche al modo napolitano a 3v. di Thomaso Cimello da Napoli . . .*
Costanzo Festa	Vogel: Festa 1 (1543; a reprint, RISM 1547[15], not in Vogel: *Il vero libro di Madrigali a 3v. di Constantio Festa . . .* (Gardano); *or:* RISM 1541[13] = Vogel: Festa la: *Di C. Festa il primo libro . . . a 3v.*, the contents of which are chiefly madrigals by Gero.
Corona di Canzoni Francesi	RISM 1536[1]: *La Courone et fleur des chansons à troys* (Antico [A. dell'Abbate]).
Di Diversi	RISM 1549[13], 1549[14]: *Elettione de motetti a tre voci libro primo de diversi eccell. musici . . .* (Scotto); *Libro secondo . . . a tre voci* (Scotto). RISM 1537[7] = Vogel: 1537[3]: *Delli madrigali a tre voci* (O. Scotto) is a possibility, made slightly more plausible by the fact that Doni seems to be listing only one volume. A further possibility is that an earlier edition of RISM 1551[16] = Vogel: 1551[1]: *Madrigali a tre voci de diversi ecc. autori . . .* (Gardano) may have existed.
Domenico di Nola Villote	Vogel: Nola 6 f. (1541, 1545): *Canzoni villanesche de Don Ioan Dominico del Giovane de Nola. Libro primo et secondo* (Scotto). The 1545 reprint by Gardano is in two separate volumes.

Eliseo	? Vogel: Ghibel 3 (1552): *Di Heliseo Ghibeli il primo libro de madrigali a 3v . . . novamente . . . ristampato* (Gardano). Doni is citing an earlier print of this collection, now apparently lost.
Girolamo Scotto	Vogel: Scotto 2 f. (1541, 1549): *Di Girolamo Scotto i madrigali a 3v.*
Io. Mouton	? No collection *a 3v.* by Mouton is known. Individual pieces for 3v. by Mouton may be found in such collections as RISM 1536[1], 1541[6], and 1542[8].
Iachet Berdrem [sic]	? No collection *a 3v.* by Berchem is known to exist. The only surviving madrigal for 3v. by Berchem is part of a cyclic canzone, first printed in Doni's *Dialogo* of 1544.
Iachetto	RISM 1543[6] *Motetta trium vocum ab pluribus authoribus composita. Quorum nomina sunt Jachetus gallicus. Morales hispanus. Costantia Festa. Adrianus Wigliardus* (Gardano).
Io. Gero duo libri	? 1) Vogel Gero 3 (1553): *Quaranta madrigali a 3v. de . . . Ihan Gero Novamente . . . Ristampati & Corretti* (Gardano);
	2) Vogel: Gero 6 (1556): *Di Ihan Gero il secondo libro di madrigali a 3v. Novamente . . . Ristampati & corretti* (Gardano).
	Evidently these two volumes were first printed by 1550.
Rinaldo Burno napolitane	RISM 1546[18]. *Elletione de canzone alla napoletana a 3v. di Rinaldo Burno . . . Libro primo* (pr.?)
	This print is not listed in Vogel.
Tommaso Maio, Villotte	Vogel: Maio (1546): *Canzon vilanesche di Giovan Thomaso di Maio . . . Libro primo a 3v.*
Vincenzo Fontana Villotte	Vogel: Fontana (1545): *Canzone villanesche di Vicenzo Fontana a 3v . . . Libro primo.*
[duos]	
Anton Gardane	RISM 1539[01], 1544[14]. *Canzoni francese a 2v. di Ant. Gardane.*
Agostino Licino duo libri	1) Brown 1545[2]: *Primo Libro di Duo Cromatici di Agostino Licino . . .* (Gardano);

2) Brown 1546[12]: *Il Secondo Libro di Duo Cromatici di Agostino Licino . . .* (Gardano).

Bernardin Lupacchino

? Vogel: Lupachino 5 (1565): *Il primo libro . . . a 2v. composto per Bernardin Lupa-chino . . . di nuovo ristampati* (Scotto). Brown 1559[6] = RISM 1559[14] is an earlier edition, but this also is a reprint. Oscar Mis-chiati in *MGG* 1315, lists an edition of 1560 as well as that of 1559, and adds: *Er-stausg.unbekannt.* If Doni's entry is accu-rate the first edition was printed before or by 1550.

diversi autori

RISM 1543[19]: *Il primo libro a 2v. de diversi autori* (Gardano).

Girolamo Scotto

Vogel: Scotto 8 (1541): *Di Girolamo Scotto il primo libro de i madrigali a 2v.*

Gomberth

? No collection *a 2v.* known by Gombert. Indi-vidual pieces for 2v. are in collections such as RISM 1543[19] (see above).

Ioan Gero

Vogel: Gero 7 ff. (1541, 1543, 1545): *Ihan Gero. Il primo libro de madrigali italiani, et canzoni francese, a 2v.*

Passioni a due

? No Passion set entirely for 2v. is known to me. Two-voice sections may be found in the Passions of Nasco, Ruffo, and Jachet (see Arnold Schmitz, *Oberitalienische Figuralpassionen des 16. Jahrhunderts* [Mainz, 1955], and in those of Charles d'Argentil and Gaspar de Albertis (see Knud Jeppesen, "A Forgotten Master of the Early 16th Century: Gaspar de Albertis," *MQ* 44 [1958]: 319, 325). On the two-voice sections in Paolo Aretino's Passion see Kurt von Fischer, "Zur Geschichte der Passions-kompositionen des 16. Jhts. in Italien," *Archiv für Musik-wissenschaft* 3 (1954): 198: the sections *a 2v.* "werden . . . zu eigentlichen Bici-nien . . ."[30] The Passions of Asola have *locutio Christi* sections *a 3v.* published sep-arately (Gardano, 1583); see Schmitz, *Oberitalienische Figuralpassionen*, 10. The print is listed in Angelo Gardano's cat-

alogue of 1591; see Thibault, "Deux catalogues," *Revue de musicologie* 2 (1930):
10. It is conceivable that a separate print of
bicinia drawn from Passion settings could
have been made in a similar way.

Messe
Di Iosquino cinque libri

? What Doni means by this entry is not clear.
Petrucci's three books of Masses by Josquin were reprinted by Giunta in Rome in
1526. Other prints containing Mass compositions by Josquin could have been
included by Doni: of these RISM 1505[1],
Petrucci's *Fragmenta missarum*, seems
unlikely; RISM 1539[1], *Liber quindecim
missarum . . .* (Petreius), and RISM 1539[2].
Missa tredecim . . . (Grapheus), both
printed in Nuremberg, are more probable
in date, but Doni gives little evidence of
knowing the work of German printers.
RISM 1516[1], Antico's *Liber quindecim
missarum*, and RISM 1522: *Missarum . . .
decem . . .* (G. Giunta) are two other
possibilities.
  Yet another reading of Doni's entry is *Di
Iosquino cinque, Libri*; Petrucci's volumes
devoted to Josquin each contain five
Masses. This may seem far-fetched, but
Doni's cataloguing style is after all an
elliptical one.

Di Giachetto

RISM 1542[2]: *Sex missae cum 5v. quarum tres
sunt excell. musici Jacheti . . .* (Scotto). In
RISM 1547[3], a reprint by Gardano, it is
made clear that only one Mass is by Jachet
(of Mantua); the two other are by Jachet
Berchem.
  The Venetian editions devoted to Jachet's
Masses all seem to be later than 1550: *Il
primo libro a 5v.*, 1554 (Scotto); *Il
secondo libro a 5v.*, 1555 (Scotto); two
vols. of *Messe del Fiore a 5v.*, 1561
(Scotto). See Anne-Marie Bautier-
Regnier in *MGG*, 6:1591; and cf. entries
under Morales below.

Di Morale, a 4, 5, & 6

1) RISM 1540[4]: *Excell. musici Moralis his-*

pani, Gomberti, ac Jacheti cum 4v.
(Scotto);

2) RISM 1542³: *Missae cum 4v . . . Moralis
   hispani* (Scotto); this print contains a
   Mass by Jachet;

3) RISM 1544⁵: *Christophori Moralis hys-
   palensis missarum quinque cum 4v. secun-
   dus liber* (Gardano);

4) RISM 1540³, [1542]¹: *Quinque Missae
   Moralis hispani, ac Jacheti . . . liber primus, cum 5v.* (Scotto);

5) RISM 1543¹. *Quinque missarum harmonia diapente, id est quinque voces referens
   . . . Moralis hispani . . .* (Scotto). Cf. RISM
   1547⁴, an altered reprint by Gardano;

6) *Christ. Morales . . . Missarum Lib. 1,* 1544
   (Rome: Dorico); according to Robert Ste-
   venson in *MGG,* 9:557–558, there are two
   Masses *a 6v.* in this print, and also in
   Moderne's 1545 print of *Chr. Moralis . . .
   Missarum Lib. 1.*

di Gasparo Alberti	*Primo libro a 5v.,* 1549 (Scotto). See Eitner, *Quellen-Lexikon,* 1:84–85.
del Gardano a voce pari	RISM 1544³. *Liber quartus missarum cum 4v. paribus canendarum* (Gardano). Cf. RISM 1542³ (Scotto).
di Carlo Ostanno a otto voci	? *Ostanno* is a name unknown to me; the entry seems on the whole rather an improbable one. A Don Vincenzo Ostiano, composer of a book of *napoletane* printed by Angelo Gardano in 1579 (Vogel 2, 34), is the closest I have come to the name.
Messe familiari	? This entry refers to one (or more?) printed volumes of plainsong. The *Abecedarium* of Ferdinand Columbus lists a volume with this title (no. 9334; not in Chapman,): "Misse familiares n° 5 pᵃ b. marie et 5 de spū. s./in catu plano [Lyons]. 1525". A print of *Misse familiares* was issued by Moderne in Lyons; it is undated but may have been printed in 1557, the year a companion volume of *Misse Solennes* came out. It is possible that Moderne, whether or not his is the print of 1525

referred to by Columbus, had published a volume of *Misse familiares* well before 1557, perhaps about 1540. Francois Regnault issued a *Misse Familiares* in Paris in 1538. Perhaps similar volumes were brought out by Italian publishers.[31]

di diversi a 4 et a cinque parec-chi libri Magnificat & lamentationi

1) Magnificat. Among the possibilities are Ruffo, *Magn. a 5v.*, 1539 (now lost); RISM 1542[9]: *Magnificat Moralis ispani aliorum-que authorum . . . Liber primus* (Scotto); a volume of Magnificats by Genesium Dominicum de Villena, Milan, 1548 (Cicognera); another by Hoste da Reggio, ibid., 1550; and the Magnificats of Carpentras, printed by J. de Channey in Avignon, ca. 1535–1539—these last three perhaps less likely to have been seen by Doni. If Costanzo Festa's Magnificat settings, printed by Scotto in 1554, had an earlier edition now lost, these might also be included.[32]

2) Lamentations. RISM 1506[1] and 1506[2], Petrucci's two volumes of Lamentations, are possible although Doni in general does not refer to material this old. The cele-brated Lamentations of Carpentras, printed in Avignon in 1532 by J. de Chan-ney, might have been known to Doni. Less likely, despite its date of 1549, is the collec-tion of Lamentations published by Berg and Neuber in Nuremberg (RISM 1549[1]). RISM 1557[7]: *Piissimae . . . lamentationes Ieremiae Prophetae* (Paris: Le Roy & Bal-lard) could well, judging from much of its content, have been preceded by an Italian print of similar character. Of this period is a manuscript collection of Lamentations, Bologna, Civ. Mus. Bibl. Mus. Q 23: *Au-tori diversi. Pro hebdomada sancta (Lamentationes) plura div. auct . . . (a 4, 5, 6v.)*, no printed version of which survives. See Gaetano Gaspari, *Catalogo della Bibl. Musicale G. B. Martini di Bologna* (Bologna, 1892; reprint, 1961), 2, 169.

Ricercari
Intablature da organi, et da
  Leuto, d'Anton da Bologna,
  da Giulio da Modena, di
  Francesco da Milano, di
  Giaches Buus, piu di dieci vo-
  lume & la Contina [1557 ed.:
  la Continua; phrase omitted
  in 1580 ed.]

1) Brown 1523[1]: *Recerchari Motetti Canzoni Composti per Marcoantonio di Bologna* [= Cavazzoni]. *Libro Primo*. (B. Vercelensis.) Another possibility is Brown 1546[13]: *Intabolatura de Lauto di Marcantonio del Pifaro Bolognese* . . . (Gardano).

2) Brown 1540[3]: *Musica Nova accommodata per cantar et sonar sopra organi et altri strumenti* . . . [Arrivabene]. This collection, of which Moderne's *Musique de Joye*, Brown 154?[6] is an augmented reprint, contains eighteen pieces by Giulio Segni da Modena. See H. Colin Slim, ed., *Musica Nova*. MRM 1 (Chicago, 1964). Brown [1550][8] lists *Giulio Segni da Modena. Ricercari, intabulature da organi et da tocco*, after Francesco Caffi, *Storia della musica sacra nella già Cappella Ducale di S. Marco* . . . (Venice, 1854–55), 1. 105, with the added remark that a volume of Segni ricercares is mentioned by Doni. But it seems likely that what Doni was referring to was in fact the *Musica nova*.[33]

3) The following prints, too numerous for the giving of titles, are devoted to lute tablatures by Francesco da Milano: Brown 1536[3], 1546[6], 1546[7], 1546[8], 1547[2], 1548[3], 1548[4] (=RISM 1548[13], a print whose contents are equally divided between Francesco and Giulio da Modena). Compositions by Francesco appear in other printed tabulatures of the period also.

4) Brown 1547[1]: *Recercari di M. Jacques Buus* . . . *Libro Primo* (Gardano; partbooks); Brown 1549[4]: *Intabolatura d'Organo di Recercari di M. Giaches Buus* . . . *Libro Primo* (Gardano; keyboard score); Brown 1549[5]: *Il Secondo Libro di Recercari di M. Jacques Buus* . . . (Gardano; partbooks).

5) Brown 1549[2]: *Opera intitolata Contina*.

	Intabolatura di Lauto di Fantasie, Motetti, Canzona . . . composta per . . . Melchioro de Barberis Padoana . . . (Scotto).[34]
Libri diversi composti	
Pietro Aron, Toschanello di Musica	The *Toscanello* was printed in Venice in 1523 (Vitali), with reprints in 1529, 1531, and 1539 (Sessa). See Åke Davidsson, *Bibliographie der musiktheoretischen Drucke des 16. Jahrhunderts* (Baden-Baden, 1962), 11.
di Lucidario	Aaron, *Lucidario in Musica di alzune oppenioni antiche et moderne . . .* 1545 (Scotto). Davidsson, 11.
Stefano Vanneo, Ricanetto di Musica	*Recanetum de musica aurea . . . Vincentio Rosseto Veronensi interprete,* 1533 (Rome: Dorico). Davidsson, 78. According to Walther Dürr in *MGG,* 13:1226, Vanneo "seinem 1531 vollendeten Traktat . . . liess er sich von Vincenzo Rosetti ins Lateinische ubs." Since Doni lists almost all titles in Italian, it is not clear whether he might be referring to a printed edition of the Italian text.
Maria Lanfranco, Scintille di Musica	Lanfranco's *Scintille* was printed in Brescia in 1533 (L. Britannico). Davidsson, 48.
Regole di Musica	Bonaventura da Brescia, *Regula musice plane.* This popular treatise on the rudiments of music, written in a half-Latin, half-Italian jargon, was reprinted numerous times in Venice and Milan during the first half of the sixteenth century. See Davidsson, 17–18.
Ottomaro Lossinio, Musurgia Musices	O. Luscinius [= Nachtigall], *Musurgia seu praxis Musicae . . .* 1536, 1542 (Strasbourg: J. Schottus). On Luscinius see Klaus Niemöller, "O. Luscinius, Musiker und Humanist," *Archiv für Musikwissenschaft* 15 (1958): 42.
Cantorino de canto fermo	*Compendium musices confectum ad faciliorem instructionem cantum choralem . . . qui Cantorinus intitulatur.* Another popular musical primer, containing an introduction to the elements of music, followed by a *compendiolum* of plainchant, this work

Salvestro dal fontego diversi libri	was reprinted often in Venice between 1509 and 1550. See Davidsson, 20.
	1) Silvestri Ganassi dal Fontego, *Opera intitulata Fontegara*, 1535 (Ganassi);
	2) *Regole Rubertina . . .* 1542 (Ganassi);
	3) *Lettione seconda pur della prattica di sonare*, 1543 (Ganassi). See Davidsson, 40; Robert Donington and Hildemarie Peter in *MGG*, 4:1354.

Even if the reader charitably accepts all the identifications given above as correct, Doni's catalogue raises some questions. A glance at the queried entries in the list shows that Doni mentions editions of some prints earlier than any now known to survive: Berchem's first book of four-voice madrigals; Heliseo Ghibel's *Primo libro a 3v.*; Ihan Gero's first and second books for three voices; Lupacchino's duos (in this instance Doni suggests an edition a good ten years older than any now in existence). Further, the *Libraria* gives evidence of the existence of prints now completely lost, among them madrigal collections for four voices by Lamberto Courtoys and Tuduual; a book of four-voice motets by Vincenzo Ruffo; a collection *a 3v.* by Jachet Berchem; a volume of Passions *a 2*. Two otherwise unknown composers, Lodovico Floriano and Carlo Ostanno, appear in the catalogue; given the relative assurance with which most of Doni's entries in the *Prima Libraria* can be identified, one has to assume that he was speaking of men who actually existed, if perhaps not generally known by the names Doni gives them.

A longish list of omissions could be drawn up, for the *Libraria* is by no means a complete bibliography of Italian music prints current when the book was compiled; and it is noticeably less complete for prints of Masses and for theoretical treatises than for madrigals and motets. It is probably idle to try to guess why it was that Doni did not know this or that, but it is all the same disappointing to see, for instance, that he had not seen the now mysteriously rare *Primo Libro a 4v.* of Costanzo Festa, published in 1538, probably by O. Scotto.[35] And it seems strange that if the arguments for a now lost earlier edition of Willaert's *Musica nova* of 1559, first made by Armen Carapetyan, then convincingly elaborated by Edward Lowinsky,[36] are true, Doni did not know of a *Musica nova* or a *Peccorina* by the most famous of Venetian composers. (For a reference by Doni to a manuscript *Musica nuova*, not that of Willaert, see below.)

In spite of its omissions and of its generally casual, not to say haphazard character, Doni's *Prima Libraria* offers some valuable information to students of sixteenth-century music. Less informative about music, and by common consent less dependable in every way,[37] is the *Seconda Libraria* of 1551. The playful tone of this work is set in its preface, addressed to "those who do not read"; here Doni says that, having made a catalogue of printed books in the *Prima Libraria*, he will now speak of manuscript works by "gossipers" whose writings are unlikely to be printed. Should a reader want to know where to find one of these works, Doni will be glad to tell him, provided that the author has given his permission.[38]

Only three items in the *Seconda Libraria* are concerned with music. A "Vicenze Musico" is described as author of *Musica nuova.*[39] This cannot be Willaert's *Musica nova*, for Doni would not have mistaken "Vincenzo" for "Adriano." Nor does it seem very likely that he is referring to the madrigal collection of Vincenzo Ruffo printed in 1556 as *Opera nova di musica*;[40] there is no reason to think that this collection was circulated in manuscript years before its printing, and Doni is in all probability talking here about a book, not a volume of music. The only identification that strikes me as appropriate is that of "Vincenzo Musico" as the theorist Vicente Lusitano, whose surname was added merely to indicate his Portuguese nationality, and whose treatise *Introdutione facilissima et novissima* was published in 1553.[41] But this is only a guess.

A second entry dealing with music, three treatises by a "Vittorio Organista,"[42] called *Della facilità de tasti*, *De ricercari*, and *De Gruppi diminutioni, & tremoli della mano*, has a reasonable enough sound for the most part; but I can offer no identification of writer or works.

The only other entry concerned with music is a treatise called *Della proportione di tutti gl'istrumenti da sonare, dialogi due*, said to be the work of "Andrea Naccheri."[43] This book, described as being "nello studio mirabile del mag.co M. Lorenzo M.," is given a quite detailed list of contents, including portraits of and disquisitions on individual instruments by such famous musicians as Francesco da Milano [the lute], Anton da Lucca [the *cornetto*], and "Zoppino" [the organ]. A long list of instruments, the names of which Doni liked to string out,[44] is added. The passage has been reprinted more than once[45] and need not be given here. As for the work it describes, it is hard to say whether Doni is talking fact or fantasy. Fétis believed strongly enough in its reality to devote an entry to Naccheri in the *Biographie universelle* (from which a brief and rather cautious entry in Eitner's *Quellen-Lexikon* is taken). And Fétis discovered, in the correspondence of Marin Mersenne with Giovanni Battista Doni in the 1630s, what seems to be a request of Mersenne that G. B. Doni look for the book in Florence, with Doni's replies that it was nowhere to be found.[46] Nor has it turned up since. Luigi Parigi has devoted a good deal of effort to examining Doni's description of this work, concluding with regret that it is in all probability a figment of that fertile *novellatore's* imagination.[47] I can add nothing to Parigi's detailed exploration, can only suggest that his reason for undertaking it—the identification of the "mag.co M. Lorenzo M." with Lorenzo de' Medici—might be questioned; it is an identification like those given above for the items in the *Prima Libraria*; reasonable, or so one hopes, but not provable in any final way. Doni would hardly have said that Lorenzo the Magnificent, who died in 1492, would have owned a book about sixteenth-century musicians.[48] That it was in a room once Lorenzo's studio is possible but not very likely; and Doni does not say that it was in Florence at all. In fact he is much more likely to have been talking about things he had seen recently in Venice than about his native Florence, of which his memories were not on the whole happy. In this connection it might be remembered that another Lorenzo de' Medici, often called "Lorenzino," was living in Venice about the time the *Libraria* was compiled; he had settled in Venice after some wanderings begun when he assassinated his cousin Alessandro de' Medici in 1537. Lorenzino lived quietly but well in Venice, with the support and friendship of some well-placed men.[49] It is possible that Doni, himself an exile of a sort from Florence and on not particularly good terms with Cosimo de' Medici, may have known Lorenzino; he announced a project of writing a biography of the latter.[50] Lorenzino was, despite his status as fugitive, a *magnifico* if not history's *il magnifico*; whether he had a study or owned such a book as that Doni describes cannot now be known, but he was a man of letters at least to some extent.[51] His own death, a violent one, took place in Venice in 1548, so that he was dead when the *Libraria* was published; but the elder Lorenzo had been dead for almost 60 years when it came out.

At any rate the book, if it really existed, would surely have turned up by now, argues Parigi,[52] and he may be right. Or it may once have existed, is now lost; or it may yet turn up. Most likely to me is the supposition that something like it did exist, but was much embroidered by Doni's imaginative pen; whether we should recognize it if we found it is a real question. It is on this puzzling but highly characteristic note that we may take leave of Antonfrancesco Doni as bibliographer.

POSTSCRIPT

The antiquity of this bibliographical study is made clear by the fact that it was written before the appearance of *New Grove*, of the *Einzeldruck* series of RISM, of the *Nuovo Vogel*. In a sense I should have done the whole thing over again; but in looking through it I found only a few items to comment on and only one identification to change. I was perhaps luckier than I deserved; or I learned that new research tools make things easier but do not always supply new information.

Two excellent bibliographical articles dealing with the same general time period as Doni's work appeared subsequent to mine. H. Colin Slim, "The Music Library of the Augsburg Patrician, Hans Heinrich Herwart (1520–1583)," *Annales musicologiques* 7 (1964–77): 67–109, is a study of a great private library containing a number of the items listed by Doni; Herwart's library, acquired for the Bavarian ducal library in 1586, forms the basis of the splendid collection of sixteenth-century printed music in the Bayerische Staatsbibliothek of today. Lawrence F. Bernstein, "The Bibliography of Music in Conrad Gesner's Pandectae (1548)," *Acta Musicologica* 45 (1973): 119–63, provides an admirable account of Gesner's work, which overlaps Doni's to a considerable extent (there are thirty items in common between the two bibliographies). On two items, Gesner's 278 and 279, dealing with prints in which Mouton and Gombert figure, his description provides more detail than does Doni's (see pp. 114–15).

David Nutter, "Ippolito Tromboncino, cantore al liuto," *I Tatti Studies: Essays in the Renaissance* 3 (1989): 127–74, suggests plausibly (pp. 141–42) that the Tromboncino print referred to by Doni is not a frottola collection by Bartolomeo Tromboncino but rather a (now lost) madrigal volume by Ippolito Tromboncino.

One or two minor corrections should be noted. The Harding Collection, formerly in Chicago, is now in the Bodleian Library at Oxford. The phantom of an edition of Willaert's *Musica nova* prior to that of 1559 has now been laid to rest; see the remarks after chapter 12, above. Thus Doni is exonerated of guilt for not knowing about the print in 1550.

NOTES

1. See Salvatore Bongi, *Annali di Gabriel Giolito de' Ferrari da Trino di Monferrato, Stampatore in Venezia*, 2 vols. (Rome, 1890–95), 2:38: "Le due *Librarie* del Doni furono, come tutti sanno, i primi saggi di bibliografia italiana. . . . La prima *Libraria*, anche nella sua sostanza come catalogo bibliografico, è importante per esservi accennati la massima parte dei libri volgari che allor erano a stampa, pochissimi essendo veramente i dimenticati."

2. Information on the various editions of Doni's *Libraria* may be found in Cecilia Ricottini Marsili-Libelli, *Anton Francesco Doni, Scrittore e stampatore* (Florence, 1960), nos. 21, 22, 70. The *Prima Libraria* was printed twice in 1550; after Doni's death it was reissued by the Venetian press of Altobello Salicato.

3. It is possible that Doni's way of arranging his material, perhaps even the idea of compiling a bibliography, may have come from Conrad Gesner's *Pandectarum sive Partitionum universalium*, published in Zurich in 1548 as the second part of Gesner's monumental *Bibliotheca universalis*. The seventh book of the *Pandectarum* is devoted to music, with seven categories of entries ranging from classical citations on the nature of the art to printed music of current date. This catalogue deserves a special study.

4. See Marsili-Libelli, *Anton Francesco Doni*, nos. 32, 45, 67. Marcolini reprinted the *Seconda Libraria* in 1555. In 1577 a posthumous edition appeared in Venice; no printer's name is given, but since the bulk of the work is printed in the same type used by Marcolini for the earlier editions, this 1577 print must have made use of leftover pages from those earlier editions.

5. Marsili-Libelli, *Anton Francesco Doni*, nos. 48, 49. Giolito reprinted the volume in 1558. Doni may have contemplated another edition of the 1557 *Libraria*. See C. Arla, "Una ristampa della *Libraria* del Doni preparata ma non edita," *Rivista bibliografica italiana* 5 (1900), 250–54. Arla speaks of looking at a copy of the *Libraria* with annotations in Doni's own hand, which are transcribed in the article; there are none for the section devoted to music.

6. For one comment on Doni as bibliographer of music see Jean-Baptiste Weckerlin, *Bibliothèque du Conservatoire nationale de musique et de déclamation. Catalogue bibliographique* (Paris, 1885), 99: "Ce catalogue [the *Libraria*] donne des indications, précieuses sans doute à cause de leur date, mais bien incomplètes."

7. See Catherine W. Chapman, "Printed Collections of Polyphonic Music Owned by Ferdinand Columbus," *JAMS* 21 (1968): 34–84.

8. Cf. the lists published by Geneviève Thibault, "Deux catalogues de libraires musicaux: Vincenti et Gardane (Venice 1591)," *Revue de musicologie* 10 (1929): 177–83; 11 (1930): 7–18. And Doni's entries are better organized, less repetitious (also far less wide-ranging) than those in Gesner's *Pandectarum*.

9. For a modern edition of the *Dialogo* see Gian Francesco Malipiero, ed., *Antonfran-*

cesco Doni. Dialogo della musica (Vienna, 1965). See also Einstein, "The 'Dialogo della Musica' of Messer Antonio Francesco Doni," *ML* 15 (1934): 244–53, and chapter 12 above.

10. See chapter 13 above.

11. See Einstein, *Italian Madrigal*, 385, on Doni's inclusion of a motet by Cipriano de Rore in the second part of the *Dialogo*.

12. Doni suggests that he did own the music he lists. At the end of a letter to Iaches Buus, printed at the beginning of the section on music in the *Prima Libraria*, one finds the following remark (fol. 64v): "Hora in cambio di questo a viso V. S. mi fara un piacere scrivere a qualche musico in Francia, che ci mandi una lista di tutte l'opere di musica che sono stampate la, perche *nella mia libraria non ho altro che queste.*"

13. Doni's remarks to the reader in the *Libraria* are dated "Di Vinegia il primo di dell'anno MDL." The work must have been more or less finished some little time before this, for Giolito obtained a printing privilege for the book on 15 October 1549. See Bongi, *Annali*, 1:287. (This is pointed out by H. Colin Slim, "Francesco da Milano [1497–1543/ 44]: A Bio-Bibliographical Study," *MD* 18 [1964]: 77.) There are several entries of prints dated 1550 in the first edition of the *Libraria*, and it is unlikely that earlier editions of all these works existed. More probable is that Doni was still working on the contents of the *Libraria* after the printers had already set up the opening material. The printer Marcolini said of Doni that he sent manuscripts to press with the ink still wet, and that sometimes the printers had to stop because there was no more copy; see Gertrud Bing, "Nugae circa veritatem: Notes on Anton Francesco Doni," *Journal of the Warburg Institute* 1 (1937): 305.

14. Fol. 67: "Io mi credo, che s'io possuto mettere tutta la musica ch'io havrei fatto un libro piu alto che volume di canto che si trovi, pure a questa volta noi daremo termine a questo libretto."

15. See n. 12 above. Since a few items in the *Libraria* were printed outside Italy, Doni would seem not to have wished to limit the section on music to the output of Italian printers and nothing else.

16. See chapters 12 and 13 above.

17. See Bongi, *Annali*, 2:40–42.

18. In his preface to the edition of 1580, Altobello Salicato says "Il Doni . . . che a tempi nostri fu di vivacissimo ingegno . . . volle, mettando insieme una libraria, mostrar che le lettere, & i parti de gli huomini dotti, si debbono honorare, & tenere in pregio: onde scrisse il presente volume, il quale essendo quasi estinto fra tanta copia di libri: l'ho voluto rivificare: & di nuovo mandarlo fuori." Although the edition's title claims that "aggiuntivi tutti i libri volgari posti in luce da trenta anni in qua," no additions were made in the section on music. In fact, five entries present in the second edition of 1550, the *Villanesche* of Donato, the madrigals of Portinaro and of Francesco Viola (these three prints all dated 1550), the tablature of Barberiis called "Contina," and the *Lucidario* of Pietro Aaron, are missing; perhaps they were not in the first printing of 1550. (Giolito printed the *Libraria* twice in 1550; see n. 2 above. The copies I used in preparing this study, those owned by the Harvard College Library and the New York Public Library, are of the second printing.)

19. This is the title of Gardano's edition of 1539. According to Albert Seay, *Jacobi Arcadelt. Opera Omnia*, 3 (American Institute of Musicology, 1967), x, no other edition of the second book preceded this "vero libro"; but cf. Einstein, *Italian Madrigal*, Addenda and Corrigenda (1:163): "The spurious first edition of Arcadelt's *Secondo libro* has been brought to light . . . : the cantus part of it is in the library of W. N. H. Harding in Chicago. The date is 1539; no printer is given, but most probably Ottaviano Scotto commissioned by Andrea Antico da Montona. It contains twenty-five numbers of which only a few seem

actually to be Arcadelt's compositions." Thomas Bridges informs me that the altus part book of this print (unknown to Einstein) survives in the Bibliothèque Nationale in Paris (Rés. Vmd 25).

20. According to Einstein, *Italian Madrigal*, 380, there is an edition by Scotto of 1544, not recorded in Vogel or RISM.

21. Vogel, 1:172–73, lists a "Giovanthom. Cimello" and then a "Thomaso Cimello" (as a composer of a volume of canzone villanesche; see below); according to Einstein, *Italian Madrigal*, 382, these are one and the same person. How Doni arrived at "Antonio" I do not know, but he evidently means the same man. Fétis, *Biographie universelle*, 2:307, refers to him as "Jean-Antoine Cimello," but gives no documentation, and is corrected by Eitner, *Quellen-Lexikon*, 2:449.

22. Scotto's title page reads "Henricus Schaffen"; the composer in his dedicatory letter signs himself "Scaffen."

23. Vogel: Ciera 1 (1561), describes Ciera as "maestro di capella di San Giovanni et Paolo di Vnetia [sic]."

24. See Francesco Coradini, "Paolo Aretino (1508–1584)," *Note d'archivio* 3 (1926), where an entry of payment in Spoleto in 1573 was made for *lamentazioni a voci para dell'aretino*.

25. It is possible that by "Tutuual" Doni meant the composer listed by Vogel as "Menon, Tuttovale," whose *Madrigali d'Amore a 4 voci* were printed by Buglhat and Hucher in Ferrara in 1548, reprinted in Venice by Scotto in 1549.

26. A volume of Tromboncino intabulations is listed in the catalogue of Angelo Gardano of 1591; see Thibault in *Revue de musicologie* 11 (1930): 18.

27. For the contents of this volume see Robert Eitner in *Monatshefte für Musikgeschichte* 16 (1884): 113.

28. The contents of this print are given by Eitner in *Monatshefte für Musikgeschichte* 16 (1884): 115.

29. See Thibault in *Revue de musicologie* 11 (1930): 12.

30. For two-voice sections in other settings of the Passion see Otto Kade, *Die ältere Passionskompositionen bis zum Jahre 1631* (Gütersloh, 1893), 15, 22, 25, 29, 35.

31. The information about *Messe familiari* was kindly given me by Samuel F. Pogue before the recent publication of his *Jacques Moderne: Lyons Music Printer of the Sixteenth Century* (Geneva, 1969). See pages 211–12 of this work for Moderne's *Misse Familiares*.

32. On settings of the Magnificat see Winfried Kirsch, *Die Quellen der mehrstimmigen Magnificat- und Te Deum-Vertonungen bis zur Mitte des 16. Jahrhunderts* (Tutzing, 1966).

33. For argument that another, now lost, keyboard print by Giulio Segni may have existed, see H. Colin Slim, "The Keyboard Ricercar and Fantasia in Italy ca. 1500–1550 with Reference to Parallel Forms in European Lute Music of the Same Period" (Ph.D. diss., Harvard University, 1960), 140–41.

34. From the spelling "Continua" in the 1557 edition of the *Libraria* it would seem that Doni's publishers were not sure what he meant by this entry. The identification offered here was suggested by Howard Mayer Brown.

35. The cantus of this print is to be found in the library of W. N. H. Harding in Chicago. See Einstein, *Italian Madrigal*, Addenda and Corrigenda (1:260). What appears to be the altus of the same volume (unknown to Einstein) is in the Bibliothèque Nationale in Paris (Rés. Vmd 29).

36. See Armen Carapetyan, "The Musica Nova of Adriano Willaert," *MD* 1 (1946): 202–3; Edward E. Lowinsky, "A Treatise on Text Underlay by a German Disciple of Francisco de Salinas," *Festschrift Heinrich Besseler* (Leipzig, 1962), 245–49.

37. See Marsili-Libelli, *Anton Francesco Doni*, 132, for the judgment of a former owner of the *Seconda Libraria*: "Questo libro del Doni è sciocco, è una Perdigiornata, frivolo matto." This seems unduly harsh. A fairer estimate of the book is that of Eric Chiorboli, "Anton Francesco Doni," *Nuova Antologia* 63, fasc. 1347 (1938), 43–48, who says that Doni mixed "quel che era con quel che non era e si sarebbe goduto che fosse." Cf. Bongi, *Annali* 1:278: In the *Seconda Libro* Doni "dandovi pero tanta parte di fantasia che si resta in dubbio se sieno più le opere e gli autori inventati che quelle che avevano qualche fondamento di verità."

38. *Seconda Libraria*, 1555 ed., 10–11 (a preface "A coloro chi non leggono"): "Se qualche persona galante deside rasse sapere dove son queste opere, io son contento di dargliene aviso, con patto di non manifestare se non coloro, che dato mi hanno piena licenza di farlo."

39. *Seconda Libraria*, 1555 ed., 153.

40. On this set of madrigals see Alfred Einstein, "Vincenzo Ruffo's *Opera nova di musica*," *JAMS* 3 (1950): 233–35.

41. See Mario de Sempayo Ribeiro, "Lusitano," *MGG* 7:1328–30.

42. *Seconda Libraria*, 1555 ed., 153. A "Vittorio" and a "Vincenzo Trombone" are mentioned, in a list of Bolognese musicians active ca. 1550, by Innocentio Ringhieri, *Cento Giuochi Liberali, et d'ingegno* (Bologna, 1551), fol. 144r.

43. *Seconda Libraria*, 1555 ed., 27–28.

44. For shorter but similar lists of instruments see the *Lettere d'Antonfrancesco Doni* (Venice, 1544), fols. 117^v, 110 (the second of these, addressed to Ottavio Landi, is reprinted as the dedicatory letter to the bass partbook of Doni's *Dialogo della musica*).

45. See Fétis, *Biographie universelle*, 6:273; Luigi Parigi, *Laurentiana. Lorenzo dei Medici cultore della musica* (Florence, 1954), 71. For an English translation of the first part of Doni's description see Slim, "Francesco da Milano," 77.

46. See Slim, "Francesco da Milano," 82–83; Fétis, *Biographie universelle*, 6:273–74; *Correspondance de P. Marin Mersenne religieux minime*, ed. Cornélis de Waard (Paris, 1955), 4:391 (Doni to Mersenne); (Paris, 1959), 5:405 (Mersenne to Doni), 6:479 (Doni to Mersenne). In the first of these letters Doni, replying to a request from Mersenne (this first letter is apparently lost), says that he cannot find "ce livre qui traite de beaucoup de sortes d'instrumens de musique" in the "bibliotheque de S. Laurens de Florence." Mersenne then writes that Doni should have the "garderobbe" searched to see if "ce livre curieux de Florence des instrumentz sera dans la garderobbe, precieusement à raison des figures des instruments et de chasque musicien excellent de ce temps-là." (And Mersenne adds that while Doni is at it he should have a search made to see if a diamond "gros comme un oeuf de pigeon" is there, as he has heard it is.) Doni's last letter on the subject says the book is nowhere to be found.

47. Parigi, *Laurentiana*, 82–83.

48. Fétis noticed this discrepancy, although he like most others writing of this work associated it with Lorenzo the Magnificent.

49. See Adolfo Borgognoni, "Lorenzo di Pier Francesco de' Medici," *Nuova Antologia di Scienze, Lettere ed Arti*, 2d ser. (1876), 1:289–317; 1:491–521. Lorenzo, though an exile who was eventually hunted down and killed by orders of Cosimo de' Medici, was praised by many for killing his cousin Alessandro; he was acclaimed a second Brutus at the time of the murder. He lived in a rented *palazzo* in Venice, his expenses paid by the Florentine exile Piero Strozzi; and though he was in constant fear of death, he received guests, among them Benvenuto Cellini (see the *Vita*, ed. Orazio Bacci [Florence, 1934], 156), dined out with men such as Giovanni della Casa, even took part in carnival festivities in the city. For a detailed account of the last days of Lorenzo in Venice, see Cesare Cantù, "Spigolature negli archivij toscani," *Rivista contemporanea* 20 (1860): 321–58.

50. See Giusto Fontanini, *Biblioteca dell'eloquenza italiana, con le annotazioni del Sig. Apostolo Zeno*, 2 vols. (Venice, 1753), 1:373: "Quì tralascio altre cose, e dico solo, che il *Doni* promise di dar fuora *Vital di Lorenzino* [de' Medici] con la sua *medaglia*; ma questa non fu la prima cosa, da lui promessa, e poi non fatta" (*Libraria*, 1:30, 2nd ed.). On this subject Borgognoni, "Lorenzo," 299, says "Egli [Doni] promise di scrivere la vita di Lorenzino; e poi non la scrisse. Non fu questo un gran male, che chi sa quante bugie v'avrebbe messe!"

51. See Fontanini, *Biblioteca*, 1:363, on a comedy, *L'Aridioso*, by Lorenzino. The play was quite well known, and has been reprinted; see Anton Giulio Bragaglia, *Commedie giocose del Cinquecento* (s.l., 1946).

52. Parigi, *Laurentiana*, 82–83. As one further bit of evidence against the book's ever having been in Florence, I might point out that it is not mentioned among the "Libri di Musica in penna" in a list, dated 22 November 1553, of books belonging to the Medici in Florence. See Cosimo Conti, *La prima reggia di Cosimo I de' Medici nel palazzo già della Signoria di Firenze* (Florence, 1893), 239–40.

RENAISSANCE MUSIC IN NINETEENTH-CENTURY EYES

Berlioz and the "First Opera"

AT THE BEGINNING of *Les Soirées de l'orchestre* the musicians, eager to entertain one another since the evening's bill-of-fare is *"un opéra français moderne très-plat,"* are talking of Corsino, a composer and their first violinist, absent because he has been arrested for insulting—with provocation—the director of the opera. A violist, laying down his instrument, remarks that Corsino will, he hopes, find a way to revenge himself, as did that Italian who in the sixteenth century made the first attempt at writing musical drama. The Italian is identified as Alfonso della Viola, a contemporary of the famous artist Benvenuto Cellini; the violist has in his pocket a newly published story about the two of them, and he begins, *à demi-voix*, to read it to a select group while the rest of the orchestra goes on playing.

Thus Berlioz introduces the tale known as *Le Premier Opéra; Nouvelle du passé; 1555.* The story is in the form of an exchange of letters between Alfonso della Viola, writing from Florence, and Benvenuto Cellini, replying from Paris; it ends with a kind of coda, set in Florence, describing the composer's act of revenge on his fickle patron, Duke Cosimo I. A fantasy written in something of the spirit of E. T. A. Hoffmann's tales,[1] the story has nonetheless a certain basis in historical fact, as Berlioz notes on its earlier appearance in his *Voyage musical.*[2] It is interesting chiefly as evidence of how the composer's imagination was stimulated by his reading, in this instance reading of the autobiography of Cellini. But it also piques the curiosity of students of sixteenth-century music, if only because one would like to know how Berlioz got the notion that Alfonso della Viola, who had a successful if unspectacular career as composer of madrigals and as performer in the service of the Estense dukes of Ferrara, could be called the inventor of Florentine opera.

The tale being readily available,[3] a brief outline of its plot will suffice here. In the first letter (July 1555) Alfonso writes that he has been laboring for two years on a new kind of dramatic work, one in which accompanied song will replace speech. It will be expensive to produce but will succeed, whereas earlier attempts to blend drama with polyphonic music all failed. The chamberlain of Grand Duke Cosimo I, who admired Viola's setting of the Ugolino episode from the *Divine Comedy*, commissioned on his master's behalf a performance of the new work, the libretto of which was based on another episode from the *Inferno*—the story of Paolo and Francesca. The opera was to be performed, with no expense spared and with musicians imported from Rome and Milan, at a state wedding. In two months the work was written and put into rehearsal; then the duke "changed his mind" and canceled it, leaving the composer furious and vowing revenge.

Cellini's answer contains episodes from his life, illustrations of how he too had suffered from the dishonesty and fickleness of patrons. Now successful in spite of everything, he sends Viola a sum of money to enable the composer to mount the op-era—anywhere in Italy, Cellini directs, but Florence. A second letter from Cellini, dated two years later, contains an angry reproach: Viola, having succeeded with *Francesca* and three other *drames lyriques*, is now going to allow his newest work to be staged in Florence, in the Pitti Palace courtyard, with decorations by Michel-angelo. This to Cellini is no proper sort of vengeance.

Alfonso replies that he seems indeed to have given in. His *Francesca*, first per-formed in Ferrara, was successful there; only in Florence was it considered "de-void of meaning and sense." Despite this he promised his newest work to Florence, and he has become the man of the hour, so popular that the Grand Duchess herself has favored him by "singing a madrigal" with him. All is in readiness for the per-formance; and Cellini is invited to come to Florence the night of the premiere to see if the composer has after all been worthy of his friendship.

In the story's epilogue Cellini does appear in Florence, stopping to ponder his bronze Perseus and listening to the talk of people anxious to get to the performance by any means they can. In front of the Baptistry he meets Viola, who explains that everything is indeed ready, the crowd is assembled, the duke is there, the "huge or-chestra" (Cellini's letter of reproach had mentioned five hundred musicians en-gaged for the work) is in place. But he, the maestro, is absent, and with him is the score. He has "changed his mind," and the performance will not take place. Al-ready the outcry of the frustrated crowd can be heard. The tale ends thus:

> With clenched teeth and dilated nostrils, Cellini stared without a word at the terrible
> spectacle of the infuriated populace. His eyes, which shone with a sinister glow, his
> square forehead, furrowed with large drops of sweat, the almost imperceptible tremor
> of his limbs, sufficiently betrayed the savage intensity of his joy. At last, grasping Al-
> fonso's arm, he said:
>   "I leave for Naples this very minute; will you come?"
>   "To the end of the world, now."
>   "Kiss me then, and to horse! You are a hero."[4]

The story is written with great verve; its dashing character was noted even by Ambros, who clucked disapprovingly at its lack of historical accuracy.[5] Fact and fiction are here freely mixed; if only a love story were added, the tale could serve as the libretto for an *opéra-comique*. We shall see that *Le Premier Opéra* is in some respects rather like the libretto of *Benvenuto Cellini*, as if Berlioz wished to make use of materials the librettists of his opera had not touched.

Some of the "historical facts" Berlioz alludes to were drawn from the autobiog-raphy of Cellini, which he read in 1833–34 in the new French translation of D. D. Farjasse.[6] The idea of an opera on incidents in Cellini's life soon occurred to him, and by August of 1834 *Benvenuto Cellini* had been proposed to, and rejected by, the Opéra-Comique; it was reworked as a *drame lyrique* (or, as Berlioz once called it, an *opéra semi-seria*) for the Opéra, where it was first performed in September 1838.[7] The libretto makes use of some characters—notably Cellini's youthful as-sistant Ascanio—from the autobiography. The love story and the Roman carnival are more or less freely invented; and the libretto's central incident, the commissioning and dramatically successful casting of the bronze Perseus, is altered in place (from Florence to Rome), time (from about 1550 to the 1530s) and patron (from Cosimo I to Pope Clement VII).[8] It is understandable that the Perseus, the most imposing work of Cellini's maturity—its casting is described by the sculptor himself as well as by Berlioz's librettists in a highly melodramatic fashion—should here be depicted as the achievement of a romantically young hero. Librettos are not required to stick to the facts, and "fact" is itself a slippery item in Cellini's picaresque account of his life. One oddity in the libretto is its failure to make Cellini a musician as well as a sculptor; the artist often bragged in the *Vita* of his musical skills even though he cursed music for robbing him of time he wanted to spend on his chosen career.

Le Premier Opéra also contains episodes from Cellini's *Vita*, but the choice is for the most part different. The most important of these "facts" are as follows.[9] Viola's first letter refers to the death of Cellini's brother, Francesco. Cellini (first letter) talks of the stinginess of the bishop of Salamanca, and of his troubles with Clement VII over an ornamental clasp for the papal cape. He describes how he killed his former pupil Pompeo in a fight, an incident which also appears, altered in everything but the character's name, in the opera libretto. He tells about his imprisonment and sufferings at the hands of Pope Paul III. Even the casting of Perseus (now moved back to Florence and done at the behest of Cosimo de' Medici) is mentioned. His success at the brilliant court of Francis I is, he says, great, but even there he has enemies, chief among them the king's mistress, Madame d'Étampes.

Berlioz of course elaborates freely (thus, in Cellini's second letter, Viola's dramatic music is said to be all the rage at the French court) and alters at will. Dates are changed; in 1555–57 Benvenuto Cellini was actually back in Florence, had been there for ten years, and the design and casting of Perseus were done after, not before, his sojourn in France. He was imprisoned by Paul III but not, as Berlioz adds, by Clement VII as well. Francis I was dead, and Madame d'Étampes out of power, in 1555. The changes seem deliberate, not mere slips of memory, for at times Berlioz is very close to Cellini, not only in material but in language; the fight in which Cellini kills Pompeo is an example.[10] So sympathetic did Berlioz find the sixteenth-century Italian that he seems not so much to be copying from the *Vita* as to be writing an extension of it. Cellini's monologue on the miseries of the artist's life, delivered while he ponders his Perseus before going off to meet Viola, is not drawn from the *Vita*. At first reading it sounds like one of the periodic outbursts against fate that are found in that work; but the real Cellini always strikes a pietistic pose—something Berlioz would certainly not have imitated—in such passages. For Berlioz, Cellini is a contemporary, a soul-mate, almost an *alter ego*:

> "Why am I not a drover from Nettuno or Porto d'Anzio?" he mused. "Like the cattle in my care, I should lead a rough, monotonous life, but it would at least be free from the turmoil which since childhood has bedeviled my existence. Treacherous and jealous rivals—unjust or ungrateful princes—relentless critics—brainless flatterers—continual alternations of success and adversity, of splendor and of poverty—overwork

without end—never any respite, any comfort, any leisure—wearing out my body like a mercenary and feeling my soul forever chilled or aflame—can that be called living?"[11]

The composer's struggle to get his work performed and accepted reminded others, including Berlioz's friend Jules Janin, of Cellini's career.[12] And Liszt, in an atmospheric essay written from Florence where he too had meditated over the statue of Perseus, compares the two artists directly:

> Then in our days has come along another Cellini: a great artist, he too has taken the idea [of the classical Perseus myth] . . . and transformed it anew. Using sound as Cellini had used the sense of sight, he has clothed the idea with a new splendor, and made of Perseus a creation as grand, as complete, as finished as the others [classical sculpture, Cellini's statue]. . . . Combat, sorrow, and glory: the destiny of a genius. This was your destiny, Cellini; now it is also yours, Berlioz.[13]

Liszt goes so far as to say that if Berlioz were to write an account of the vicissitudes of his life they would resemble those of Cellini—a prophetic remark indeed. He must have had in mind, writing at the beginning of 1839, the failure of the opera *Benvenuto Cellini* at its first performances the preceding September. The apposite nature of such a comparison is lessened somewhat by the presence in the *Gazette musicale*, directly after Liszt's essay, of a brief but blandly favorable review of another performance of that work.[14]

Neither Berlioz nor his librettists made Cellini into a musician. But in *Le Premier Opéra* there is another romantically depicted artist, the composer Alfonso della Viola. The "historical facts" cited by Berlioz for Viola are simply that he was a contemporary of Cellini's and that he wrote an opera which was one of the first attempts at dramatic music in the sixteenth century (see above, n. 2). Where did Berlioz get this information? Not from Cellini's *Vita*, which has no mention of Viola.[15] The real Alfonso della Viola is known today chiefly as a competent madrigalist, whose work shows how quickly the Roman-Florentine art of the madrigal spread through Italy; his own compositions became a feature of musical life at the Ferrarese court in the 1530s.[16] He also composed music, over a twenty-five-year period from 1541 to 1567, to accompany performances of classicistic tragedies and pastoral plays done at Ferrara. One of these plays, Agostino Beccari's *Il Sacrifizio*, was performed in 1554 and published the next year, with the note that Alfonso della Viola had written the music.[17] Beccari's play is known to historians of literature as the earliest extant pastoral play.[18] Viola's musical contribution—he set choral responses, and also some monodic recitative—would thus in a way qualify him as the "first" composer of opera even though he did not set the whole of the play to music. But again, how would Berlioz have known this?

It is clear from other details in his story that Berlioz had read some account of the rise of opera. Festive performances in the courtyard of the Pitti Palace, held to celebrate Florentine dynastic marriages, suggest the *intermedi* of 1589 celebrating the wedding of Ferdinando de' Medici and especially the performances of *Dafne* in 1597 and of Peri's *Eurydice*, the traditionally revered "first opera," for Maria de' Medici's wedding in 1600. These and other landmarks in the early history of opera were cited by early nineteenth-century historiographers. Among these the most likely source for Berlioz is the *Dictionnaire historique* of Choron and Fayolle.[19] In the historical summary that opens this work is found the following statement: "It is claimed that in 1555 Alfonso della Viola set to music, for the court of Ferrara, *Il sagrifizio*, a pastoral play by Agostino Beccari."[20] Here is Berlioz's composer and the date of his tale; the name of the work he altered and its place of performance he changed to Florence, mentioned on the same page of Choron as the city of origin of *musique dramatique poprement dit*, composed at the end of the sixteenth century.

Other details mentioned by Berlioz could also have been taken from Choron and Fayolle. Among these are the failure of earlier attempts, including a performance of Poliziano's *Orfeo*, at musical drama; and the existence of a setting of Dante's *scène d'Ugolino*.[21] The *Dictionnaire historique*, citing G. B. Doni, gives the Ugolino setting to Vincenzo Galilei, its real composer, and says this about it:

> Vincenzo Galilei, father of the celebrated Galileo, . . . struck, like Bardi and the other Florentine amateurs, by the defects of the music—full of artificial display—of his own times, set himself to rediscover the musical declamation of the Greeks. Having thought up recitative, he applied it to the episode of Count Ugolino (from Dante).[22]

Berlioz suppressed Galilei and the whole Camerata in giving this achievement to Alfonso della Viola, who expresses his view of the music current in his time:

> Tell me honestly, do you really think that our madrigals dragging along in four parts constitute the highest perfection to which composition and performance can reach? Doesn't common sense suggest that in the matter of expression, as in that of musical form, these greatly vaunted works are but childish trifling?
>
> The words express love, anger, jealousy, or courage, but the music is always the same, and too much like the doleful chanting of the mendicant friars. Is this all that melody, harmony, and rhythm can do? Are there not a thousand applications of these elements of art still unknown to us? From an attentive examination of all that is, can we not foresee with certainty what shall be and ought to be? As for our instruments, have they been exploited to the full? What is one to think of our wretched accompaniments, too timid to leave the voice, and trailing after it continually in unisons or octaves? Is there such a thing as instrumental music taken by itself? And as regards vocal music, what prejudices, what routine habits! Why forever sing in four parts, even when the song is that of a character lamenting his loneliness?[23]

Whether all this could be embroidery of the *Dictionnaire's* version is hard to say; the "doleful chanting" (*triste psalmodie*) sounds, for instance, like an echo of Rousseau's condemnation of French music.[24]

If Berlioz did indeed get Alfonso della Viola out of the historical précis in the *Dictionnaire historique*, he could have been interested enough to turn to the entry for that composer. Here he could have read the following:

Viola (Alfonso Della), maestro di cappella of the Duke of Este at Ferrara ca. 1541, was born in that city. According to commonly held opinion he was the first to unite song and speech in the theater, *he would then have truly been the first composer of opera.*[25]

Berlioz is not likely to have bothered to question this "commonly held opinion," whether or not he knew something of the history of opera. He had missed, by the way, the first of the *concerts historiques* of Fétis—one devoted to the rise of opera and preceded by a disquisition on the subject by Fétis.[26] And there was not much else for him to read on the subject unless he should have turned to the sources on which Choron and Fayolle drew.[27] It would at any rate seem that he got from the *Dictionnaire historique* all the facts he needed.

This slender factual basis is of course altered almost beyond recognition. Alfonso della Viola has absorbed Vincenzo Galilei and by inference the ideas of the Camerata, a pastoral play with incidental music has become a Berliozian opera, with a "huge orchestra," on a tragically impassioned subject; Ferrara has become Florence (although Berlioz does have Viola say that his *Francesca* was first performed in Ferrara). Add to this the details that Cosimo I was not yet a Grand Duke in 1555, that the Pitti Palace was not used for musico-dramatic events until 1600, that the idea of Michelangelo doing the sets for a Medici spectacle is preposterous,[28] and it is no wonder that a serious music historian like Ambros was shocked by Berlioz's flippant attitude.

If the musical part of the tale is not factual recital, neither is it pure fiction; it is rather a kind of autobiographical fantasy. Clearly Berlioz identified himself not only with Benvenuto Cellini but also with the musician whose name he borrowed from history and whose personality he made very like his own. If as Cellini he could brood over the vicissitudes of his career, imagined as near its end, he could as Viola talk like the eager Berlioz of the 1830s:

> You know how doggedly I have worked for many years to augment the power and multiply the resources of music. Neither the ill will of the older masters, not the ignorant sneers of their pupils, nor the mistrust of the dilettanti who look upon me as a strange character, closer to madness than to genius, nor the material obstacles of every kind that come with poverty, have managed to stop me, as you know.[29]

In condemning the polyphonic madrigal for its lack of expressive power, Viola is simply Berlioz inveighing against what he saw as the bad music, especially the bad operatic music, of his day.[30] It should not be thought that he was ridiculing the music of the past; indeed, he always admired what he considered to be great music of the past. He may not have relished Fétis's "historical" performances, but in commenting on old music in general he took this view:

> It is we who get old, it is our sensibility that becomes blunted, it is our imagination that fails; but the strength and vital warmth of music does not diminish. On the contrary, it grows from day to day. Music as we know it is a very young art, just reaching its adolescence; its old age will not come for a very long time.[31]

This article deals mostly with Gluck, Berlioz's musical idol; but other music is cited, including Palestrina's madrigal "Alla riva del Tebro": "What could be fresher or more beautiful than this, in its calm majesty."[32] Tangible and intangible echoes of the past are a part of Berlioz's own music. The combination of audacious novelty with a certain archaistic severity of style that strikes modern admirers of Berlioz was noticed by a few people even in his own time.[33]

The dramatic music of *Viola* was thought to be completely lost. In fact one fragment of it survives, and by a curious irony it is music for *Il Sacrifizio*, the work published in Berlioz's chosen year of 1555. The fragment consists of a strophic recitative for solo voice with *lira* accompaniment, punctuated by four-voice choral responses in block-chord style; there is also a four-voice *Canzone finale*, in slightly more animated choral polyphony. Not the impassioned musical speech Berlioz-Viola dreamed of; and less interesting than the musical *intermedi* of the genuine Florentine court composers Francesco Corteccia and Alessandro Striggio. But a single character is given solo music, a dramatic chorus is given choral music; for that much verisimilitude Berlioz might have been grateful.

Under its pseudohistorical trappings, then, *Le Premier Opéra* may, like much of Berlioz's imaginative writing, have an autobiographical content. If this seems reasonable one ought to try to place this *nouvelle* in his career. Its date of composition, first of all: the *Soirées de l'orchestre* appeared in 1852, but a note at the beginning of *Le Premier Opéra* informs readers that the tale, along with some others, was being reprinted from the *Voyage musical en Allemagne et en Italie* of 1844, the author considering this latter *un livre détruit*, the materials of which could be salvaged. Berlioz added an introduction setting the telling of the tale in the pit of the *l'orchestre de x . . .* ; he deleted the note in the *Voyage* that stated the tale to be based on historical fact.

Le Premier Opéra first appeared in the *Revue et Gazette musicale* in October 1837.[34] Berlioz was fond of this tale; he thought it not only suitable for reuse, but good enough to serve as the opening of the *Soirées de l'orchestre*.[35] It serves well enough; but the occasion that prompted Berlioz to write it is in no way evident.

If the tale was written sometime in 1837, another source of inspiration if not of fact, emerges for it. A *nouvelle* by Stéphen de la Madelaine, a singer and one of the circle of Berlioz's youthful friends, called "Comment l'opéra fut introduit en France," appeared in the *Revue et Gazette musicale* in 1835.[36] This rather limp story of a French composer named Beaulieu (the historical figure Lambert de Beaulieu) who went to Florence, learned operatic style through study of the work of Orazio Vecchi, and returned home to write music for the *Balet comique de la Royne* of 1581, has some resemblance to Berlioz's tale in its easy mix of fact and fiction, and even in a detail; Beaulieu, when in Italy, learned of the new use of "recitative invented by Vincenzo Galilei" in place of the "overly monotonous forms of counterpoint."[37] One should not be too hard on the writers of these musical tales; serious historians of the time introduced fiction into their accounts as well, the only difference being—as Jane Austen's Catherine Morland complained—that their results were boring while the novelists' were full of interest. An example is G. W. Fink's contribution on opera to Schilling's *Encyclopädie*, in the historical section of which the *Orpheus* of Zarlino is said to be the first Italian opera produced in France.[38]

Berlioz made one or two casual references to *Le Premier Opéra* in his correspondence. A letter to his sister Adèle, dated 30 September [1843], speaks of the forthcoming *Voyage musical*, which is to contain among other things two *nouvelles* published "four years ago" in the *Gazette musicale*.[39] An undated letter to his friend Ernest Legouvé has a postscript begging Mme Legouvé to forgive the "brusqueness of certain expressions when she reads my *nouvelle* on Cellini. I was not in good humor when I wrote it."[40]

One would have assumed that Berlioz's bad humor was caused by the failure of *Benvenuto Cellini*, a work to which the tale is so closely related. The *nouvelle* was, however, written a full year before the premiere of the opera. In fact the event that provoked him, and that prompted him to write a story of revenge, is well enough known: in July 1837 his *Requiem*, already in rehearsal after the composer had worked feverishly to complete it, was canceled "for political reasons."[41] The successful performance of the *Requiem* in December of 1837 provided satisfaction but not precisely vengeance; the composer characteristically found his revenge in writing his tale, which must have been composed after the *Requiem*'s cancellation but published before the first performance of that work. Thus the motive for writing the tale had to do with a work already finished; its subject matter was drawn from *Benvenuto Cellini*, a work in the making.

Obviously *Benvenuto Cellini* was very much on the composer's mind when he wrote this story; the portions of Cellini's life included in the tale sound, as I have said, like materials Berlioz might have considered having put into the libretto of his first opera. The first opera of Viola is said, however, to be based on the story of Paolo and Francesca from Dante's *Inferno*. The three *drames lyriques* that followed it are mentioned in passing by Cellini, without any names being given. The great work with which Viola took his revenge is not named either. But in Viola's first letter there is a paragraph on the tragic love of Romeo and Juliet, mentioned as a true story that occurred "a few years ago" in Verona. Berlioz's love for *Romeo and Juliet*, and his dissatisfaction with Bellini's treatment of the subject, are well known.[42] And while it is clear that the details of a dramatic symphony on Shakespeare's play were being formed in the composer's mind as early as 1835—and perhaps even in 1827–28—nevertheless it may be the case that the *Paolo and Francesca* story may have been equally close to his heart.

Berlioz has Viola describe the episode and his reaction to it in fervid detail:

> I made a dash for my discarded libretto, which had lain yellowing in some corner or other for quite a while; I beheld once more Paolo, Francesca, Dante, Virgil, the shades, and the damned; I heard that exquisite love sighing and lamenting. Tender and graceful melodies, full of abandon, melancholy, and chaste passion, unfolded within me; I heard the outraged husband's awful cry of hatred; I saw the pair of corpses roll entwined at his feet. Next I saw forever united the souls of the two lovers, wandering

windborne across the depths of the abyss; their plaintive voices mingle with the dull and distant roar of the infernal streams, with the hissing of the fire, with the frenzied screams of the wretched beings it devours, and with all the frightful concert of eternal suffering. . . .

For three days, Cellini, I wandered about aimlessly in unremitting dizziness; for three nights I could not sleep. Not until this prolonged bout of fever had passed did I regain lucidity of mind and a sense of reality. It took me all that time of fierce, desperate struggling to tame my imagination and master my subject. I finally conquered.

In the huge framework of my plan each part of the picture gradually disclosed itself in a simple and logical order, clothed in somber or brilliant colors, in half-tints or strong contrasts. The human forms appeared, some full of life, others under the cold and pallid aspect of death. The poetical idea was always subordinate and never hampered the musical sense. I enlarged, embellished, and intensified the power of the one through the other.[43]

Berlioz had read, or had read in, Dante during his Italian sojourn of 1831–32;[44] on at least one occasion he quoted from the episode of Paolo and Francesca (*Inferno* 5. 73–142), characteristically mixing Dante, Shakespeare, and Virgil.[45] After seeing Bellini's *I Montecchi ed i Capuletti* in Florence in May 1831, Berlioz meditated on what a truly dramatic setting of the story of Romeo and Juliet should be like.[46] While in Italy he might possibly have seen, though he does not mention it, an opera based on the story of Paolo and Francesca.[47] Could the description in *Le Premier Opéra* be a similar kind of reaction? And could Berlioz have thought of writing an opera on *Francesca da Rimini*? He never said so explicitly; but if we accept the notion that Alfonso della Viola was Berlioz in transparent disguise, he may indeed have dreamed of a Dantesque opera—in the same way he was already dreaming of his great works to texts of Shakespeare and Virgil.

POSTSCRIPT

With this study I began what has been a continuing interest in the Romantic *conte musical* (see also chapter 16). Apart from the intrinsic charm of many of these tales, they can tell us much about their authors' interests in and attitudes toward the music of the past—whether or not intended as metaphor for present-day (1830s and 1840s) musical culture. Freedom from the need to tell the story "wie es eigentlich gewesen war" gives these historicizing fictions a color that seems to me quintessentially Romantic. They deserve fuller study. One step in this direction is Jacques Landrin, *Jules Janin, Conteur et Romancier* (Paris, 1978); see also Martha Fawbush, "The *Contes musicaux* of Jules Janin" (M.A. thesis, University of North Carolina, Chapel Hill, 1989).

D. Kern Holoman, an indefatigable Berlioz scholar, was the thoughtful and concerned editor who first saw this study into print; it is a bit disappointing to find that in his *Berlioz* (Cambridge, Mass., 1989), 184, *Le Premier Opéra* is described dismissively as "a thinly disguised essay on an unpaid commission."

On E. T. A. Hoffmann's influence in France see Elizabeth Teichmann, *La Fortune d'Hoffmann en France* (Paris, 1961). See also the articles of Hermann Hofer and Pierre Brunel in *E. T. A. Hoffmann et la musique. Actes du Colloque international de Clermont-Ferrand*, ed. Alain Montandon (Paris, 1987).

NOTES

1. Hoffmann's stories appeared in French translation from 1828, printed in, among other places, the *Revue et Gazette musicale*, a periodical to which Berlioz contributed regularly; for example, vol. 3, no. 1 (3 January 1836) contains the "Lettre du chat Murr." On Hoffmann in France see the bibliography given in Leo Schrade, *Beethoven in France: The Growth of an Idea* (New Haven, 1942), 253.

The musical *feuilleton* was a well-established literary genre in France by the 1830s, and was often though not always Hoffmannesque in character. One famous *nouvelle* on a musical theme, avowedly influenced by Hoffmann, is Balzac's *Gambara*, published in the *Revue et Gazette musicale* in 1837. See the introduction to Maurice Regard's edition of *Gambara* (Paris, 1964), 25–32.

2. *Voyage musical en Allemagne et en Italie*, 2 vols. (Paris, 1844), 2:229: "Cette correspondance fictive est baseé sur des faits historiques: Benvenuto Cellini, l'un des plus grands sculpteurs et ciseleurs de son temps, fut en effet contemporain d'Alfonso della Viola, auteur d'un opéra qui passe pour le second ou le troisième essai de musique dramatique fait au seizième siècle." The introduction given the tale in *Les Soirées de l'orchestre* (Paris, 1852), 5–6, is not in the *Voyage musical*.

3. There is a modern edition of the *Soirées*, ed. Léon Guichard (Paris, 1968). The work has been reprinted in facsimile (Farnborough, 1969; edition of 1853), as has the *Voyage musical* (Farnborough, 1970). There is an English translation of the story, by Jacques Barzun, in Hector Berlioz, *Evenings with the Orchestra* (New York, 1956), 10–26. Passages from the story cited here are given in Barzun's translation; all other translations are my own.

4. *Evenings with the Orchestra*, 26.

5. A. W. Ambros, *Geschichte der Musik*, vol. 3 (1868); 3d ed., ed. Otto Kade (Leipzig, 1893), 3:604n. Ambros writes "Eine Novelle ist freilich kein Lehrbuch der Geschichte, aber gegen solche heillose Willküre muss man doch ernstlich Einspruch erheben!"

6. The *Vita* of Cellini was written during the years 1558–66 but not published until 1728. For the Italian text see the edition of Bruno Maier (*Opere* [Milan, 1968]). The translation by Farjasse (1833) is cited by David Cairns, trans. and ed., *The Memoirs of Hector Berlioz* (London, 1969), 533. A good English translation is that of George Bull (Penguin Books, 1956).

7. By May 1834 Berlioz had decided to write an opera on episodes from the life of Cellini. He asked Léon de Wailly and Auguste Barbier to write the libretto, and after its rejection by the Opéra-Comique set about providing an altered version of the text (to which Alfred de Vigny contributed). This second version was accepted by the Opéra. The score was substantially finished by the end of 1836. For letters mentioning the progress of the work, see Hector Berlioz, *Correspondance générale* [hereafter *CG*] ed. Frédéric Robert (Paris, 1975), 2:184, 188, 196ff, 250f, 252f, 263, 281, 299f, 336f, 341, 413, 434. See also Jacques Barzun, *Berlioz and the Romantic Century* (Boston, 1950), 1:246, 257, 289; and Cairns, *Memoirs*, 242–45.

8. In performance Pope Clement VII became Cardinal Salviati. Berlioz explained this in

a letter to his sister Adèle, dated 12 July 1838: "La censure nous a ôté le Pape, il a fallu mettre à la place un Cardinal ministre. C'eût été curieux pourtant de voir Clément VII aux prises avec ce bandit-homme de génie de Cellini." See *CG* 2:444.

9. The episodes mentioned here may be found—not always quite the same as Berlioz has them—in Bull's translation of the *Autobiography of Benvenuto Cellini*, 47, 87ff, 96, 134ff, 188ff, 251ff, 272ff, 343ff.

10. The death-blow given Pompeo is described thus in the *Vita*: "Tiratogli per dare al viso, lo spavento che lui ebbe li fece volger la faccia, dove io lo punsi apunto sotto l'orecchio; e quivi raffermai dua colpi soli, che al sicondo me cadde morto di mano, qual non fu mai mia intenzione; ma, si come dice, li colpi non si danno a patti: (Maier ed., 230–31). I have not seen the French translation Berlioz used, but it would seem that he transcribed several passages, including this one, from that version (*CG*2:447n): "A mon premier mouvement pour le frapper au visage, la frayeur lui fit détourner la tête, et le coup de poignard porta précisement au-dessous de l'oreille. Je ne lui en donnai que deux, car au premier il tomba mort dans ma main. Mon intention n'avait pas été de le tuer, mais dans l'état où je me trouvais, est-on jamais sûr de ses coups?" (*Soirées*, facsimile ed., 16). At the end of the tale one of the orchestra members remarks, "J'aime aussi la modération de Benvenuto dans les coups de poignard: 'Je ne lui en donnai que deux, car au premier il tomba mort,' est touchant."

11. Barzun, *Evenings*, 24. If one compares this with the monologue and air of Cellini in Act 2 of the opera, the intensity of Berlioz's prose stands in strong contrast to the conventional language of his librettists. The opera has several religious moments (perhaps almost obligatory in the 1830s) for which Berlioz wrote beautiful music but which are of exceptional flatness of language.

12. Joseph-Marc Bailbé, "Berlioz, Janin et les 'Impressions d'Italie'," *Revue de littérature comparée* 45 (1971): 492: "Les luttes de Berlioz et sa farouche volonté évoqueront pour Janin les épreuves de Benvenuto Cellini, véritable héros du Romantisme, modèle d'indépendance et de l'amour du beau." In a letter to Adèle (30 September 1843) Berlioz remarks that "Janin . . . , malicieusement complimenteur, dit maintenant à qui veut l'entendre que j'étais né pour faire des feuilletons et non pour écrire de la musique." See *Hector Berlioz: Le musicien errant, 1842–1852*. Correspondance publiée par Julien Tiersot, 5th ed. (Paris, 1927), 58.

13. Franz Liszt, "Le Persée de Benvenuto Cellini [Extrait des lettres d'un bachelier ès musique]," *Revue et Gazette musicale* 6, no. 2 (13 January 1839), 14. On the strong probability that essays such as this were written with the help of, or even primarily by, Marie d'Agoult, see Serge Gut, *Franz Liszt; Les élémens du language* (Paris, 1975), 1.3, "Liszt écrivain," 29–42. Berlioz at any rate thought Liszt had written the essay in question; he wrote to thank him for it (*CG* 2:510–21).

14. *Revue et Gazette musicale* 6, no. 2, 15–16. The review is by Antoine Elwart of the Conservatoire, the man who justified Berlioz's worst fears by surviving him to give a speech at his funeral (see Barzun, *Berlioz*, 2:296–97).

15. Cellini's only remark that is in any way pertinent is that he found nothing good at Ferrara save for the presence of some "very talented musicians" (*Autobiography*, 250). On a supposed collaboration, unknown to Berlioz, between Cellini and the composer Francesco Viola, Alfonso's brother(?), see Claudio Sartori, "Viola," *MGG*, 13:1690.

16. See Einstein, *Italian Madrigal*, 300–306. Viola published two books of madrigals in Ferrara in 1539 and 1540; he is also represented in Venetian madrigal anthologies of the 1540s. See Vogel, *Bibliothek*, 2:322–23.

17. Einstein, *Italian Madrigal*, 301.

18. See the references (including a remark by Guarini) cited in Wolfgang Osthoff, *Thea-*

tergesang und darstellende Musik in der italienischen Renaissance (Tutzing, 1969), 1:312n.

19. Alexandre Choron and François Fayolle, *Dictionnaire historique des musiciens . . . précedé d'un sommaire de l'histoire de la musique*, 2 vols. (Paris, 1810–11; I consulted the second edition [Paris, 1817]). Berlioz seems to have known Choron, who had asked him to write an oratorio for solo voices with organ accompaniment as early as 1828 (*CG* 1:220); the composer alludes to Choron's *Dictionnaire* in a letter of 11 November 1836 (*CG* 2:313).

20. *Dictionnaire historique*, 1:liv.

21. Ibid., 1:liv–lv.

22. Ibid., 1:lv.

23. Barzun, *Evenings*, 12–13.

24. Jean-Jacques Rousseau, *Lettre sur la musique française* (Paris, 1753). See especially pages 640, 642f in the translation of Oliver Strunk, *Source Readings in Music History* (New York, 1950), where Rousseau calls French music a kind of plainsong and extols [Italian] unity and expressiveness of melody over learned counterpoint.

25. *Dictionnaire historique*, 2:409; italics mine.

26. This concert took place on 1 April 1832, before Berlioz's return to Paris from his Italian sojourn. For a description of this and the succeeding historical concerts, with samplings of critical reaction to Fétis's performances see Robert Wangermée, "Les premiers concerts historiques à Paris," *Mélanges Ernest Closson* (Brussels, 1948), 185–96. The program for the opera concert, which chose 1581 (the *Balet comique*) as its starting point, was printed in the *Revue musicale* 6, no. 9 (31 March 1832), 71—an issue which also contained Berlioz's "Lettre d'un enthousiaste sur l'état actuel de la musique en Italie."

27. Choron and Fayolle drew their entry for Alfonso della Viola from Ernst Ludwig Gerber, *Historisch-biografisches Lexikon der Tonkünstler* (Leipzig, 1790–92), 1:732–33. Gerber in turn used Jean-Benjamin de la Borde, *Essai sur la musique ancienne et moderne* (Paris, 1780), 3:243. Choron also used La Borde for general information about the history of opera (*Essai*, 1:49). La Borde frequently cites a *Traité du Mélodrame*, a work I have not searched for.

28. Cellini stood greatly in awe of Michelangelo, and at any rate knew that the latter would never consent to return to Florence, much less do stage designs for a Medici duke. Cosimo I had Cellini (he says) ask Michelangelo to return, but the artist was not interested (*Autobiography*, 350–52).

29. *Evenings*, 11.

30. See, for example, his opinion of Bellini's *I Montecchi ed i Capuletti*, expressed in a letter to his father of 2 March 1831: "ignoble, ridicule, impuissant, nul" (*CG* 1:418).

31. "Premier concert du conservatoire: quelques mots sur la musique ancienne," *Revue et Gazette musicale* 7, no. 5 (12 January 1840), 38.

32. *Revue et Gazette musicale* 7, no. 6 (19 January 1840), 45. In the fall of 1840 Berlioz directed a festival concert at the Opéra, using 450 "musiciens et choristes" to do a program including works by Gluck, Handel, "et un madrigal ['Alla riva del Tebro'] du vieux maître italien Palestrina" (letter of 2 November 1840; see *CG* 2:662). A review, which rather hurt Berlioz's feelings, complained that he had *écrasé* the work of Palestrina *sous la pompe des voix et des instruments*; he defended himself by pointing out that the performance had been unaccompanied (he did not say how many singers he used). See *CG* 2:668–69. But when he heard Palestrina performed in the Sistine Chapel in 1831, Berlioz took a negative view of Renaissance polyphony; see Cairns, *Memoirs*, 182–84; cf. *CG* 2:225.

33. See, for example, Joseph D'Ortigue, *Du Théâtre italien et de son influence sur le goût musical françois* (Paris, 1842), 119–20: "Nous avons cru trouver dans *Benvenuto Cellini* des inspirations de Gluck, de Grétry (le rôle de Balducci en est le preuve), de Spontini, des inspi-

rations même de Clari, de Handel et de Palestrina, jointes à toutes les combinaisons de l'art moderne symphonique."

34. Vol. 4, nos. 40–41. For a period in 1836–37 Berlioz took over the editorship of the *Revue et Gazette musicale* while Maurice Schlesinger was absent; see Jacques-Gabriel Prodhomme, "Bibliographie berliozienne," *Sammelbände der internationalen Musikgesellschaft* 5 (1903–4), 623. This would seem to have been the volume preceding the one in question here; cf. Barzun, *Berlioz*, 1:272n.

35. *Vincenza*, the tale following *Le Premier Opéra*, is an example of another story that Berlioz had used before; it was first printed in *Europe littéraire* (8 May 1833).

36. Vol. 2, no. 47 (22 November 1835), 377–81. On Madelaine see Barzun, *Berlioz*, 1:213; 2:296. A sketch of Madelaine's career is given in Fétis, *Biographie universelle; Supplement et complément*, ed. Arthur Pougin (Paris, 1888), 2:68–69. A hitherto unpublished letter from Berlioz to Madelaine is given by Ralph P. Locke, "New Letters of Berlioz," *19th Century Music* 1 (1977): 83.

Balzac's *Gambara* (see n. 1 above) appeared in the *Revue et Gazette musicale* in 1837 (23 July–20 August). Although Barzun (*Berlioz*, 1:262) sees the influence of Berlioz on Balzac in the composition of *Gambara*, there is nothing to suggest that this story in turn influenced the composer. Berlioz did not in fact think much of Balzac's efforts at musical criticism in this work (Barzun, 1:262n).

37. *Revue et Gazette musicale* 2, no. 47, 380. On Lambert de Beaulieu see Henry Prunières, *Le ballet de cour en France avant Benserade et Lully* (Paris, 1914), 87–88.

38. Gustave Schilling, *Encyclopädie der gesammten musikalischen Wissenschaften, oder Universal-Lexikon der Tonkunst* (Stuttgart, 1835–42), 5:239.

39. *Le musicien errant*, 58.

40. *CG* 2:366, where the letter is given the date *après le 8 octobre 1837*, the assumption being that the article was already in print.

41. *CG* 2:354–63, a series of letters to his father and to friends, dated 18 July through 2 August 1837. The *Requiem* was written in three or four months' time; see Barzun, *Berlioz*, 1:273ff. In *Le Premier Opéra* Viola says that he managed to complete *Francesca* in two months' furious work.

42. See Cairns, *Memoirs*, 160–61; Barzun, *Berlioz*, 1:323.

43. It is curious to see Berlioz dreaming of this kind of libretto while he was finishing the musical setting of *Benvenuto Cellini*, which as a literary work is almost totally lacking in Berliozian intensity. To the reader familiar with Berlioz's later career the description of *Francesca* has hints both of *Romeo and Juliet* and of *The Trojans*.

44. Barzun, *Berlioz*, 1:217, 228; Cairns, *Memoirs*, 173. On the vogue of Dante among French Romantics see the studies cited in Sharon Winklhofer, "Liszt, Marie d'Agoult, and the 'Dante' Sonata," *19th Century Music* 1 (1977): 20ff.

45. Cairns, *Memoirs*, 173.

46. Ibid., 160–61.

47. There were at least four operas called *Francesca da Rimini* premiered in Italy in 1829–32. See Clément and Larousse, *Dictionnaire des opéras*, 304; Franz Stieger, *Opernlexikon* (Tutzing, 1975), 481–82. One setting, by Giuseppe Staffa, had its premiere at the Teatro San Carlo in Naples on 12 March 1831. Berlioz was in Naples in September-October of that year, and went to the San Carlo (Cairns, *Memoirs*, 196); he does not say what he saw there, and I do not know if Staffa's *Francesca da Rimini* was repeated that autumn.

It might be noted that at the end of *Le Premier Opéra* Cellini and Viola are about to set off for Naples, as Berlioz and two of his friends from the French academy had done in 1831.

Music of the Renaissance
as Viewed by the Romantics

DURING THE FIRST HALF of the nineteenth century musical historiography made great strides. Assemblage of source materials, begun by Padre Martini and Gerbert, was continued but tended to focus on particular figures (Baini on Palestrina), places (Caffi on Venice), or periods (Winterfeld on sixteenth-century sacred music); straightforward chronicles, such as those of Hawkins and Burney, were succeeded by works including elements of historically grounded critical judgment, forming as in the case of Kiesewetter's study of the Franco-Netherlandish school the prototype for much later work on the period. Not long after Jacob Burckhardt's seminal volume on the Italian Renaissance came the first great modern synthesis of historical thought about music, A. W. Ambros's *Geschichte der Musik*.[1] The thoroughness with which Ambros treated the music of the fifteenth and sixteenth centuries, and the multiplicity of detail with which he illustrated his points, made his work a model for future scholars; Gustave Reese's *Music in the Renaissance* (1954) might be said to be the most distinguished but by no means the only twentieth-century continuation of Ambros's method. The work of Ambros, when compared with that of Burney, Hawkins, or Forkel, shows how much scholars had learned about the period in question between 1760 and 1860; in many of its essential outlines the musical history of the Renaissance had been rediscovered.

The accumulation of knowledge that made Ambros's work possible was of course gradual, if not always steady; but through much of the early nineteenth century there seems to have been no clear general picture of Renaissance music, and many individual aspects of the period were curiously, sometimes comically distorted. Much was corrected by Ambros and his contemporaries. Much but not all; some of the misapprehensions of the Romantics about Renaissance music lingered well into the twentieth century, and a few may not yet have been eradicated; for example, the importance, even uniqueness of stature given to Palestrina by the Romantics—as, to a lesser degree, by their predecessors—has only recently begun to be viewed critically, and we still do not perhaps have a truly balanced picture of this undoubtedly great but hardly unique figure.[2]

Ambros, like Burney and some other earlier historians, treats the history of music by national and regional schools as well as in chronological order. In another respect he also follows the precedent of eighteenth-century historians; the one-and-a-half volumes devoted to music of the fifteenth and sixteenth centuries are not subtitled "The Renaissance." In avoiding this classification Ambros escaped facing the problem of what "Renaissance" means in music. Some of us might be grateful for this, and even wish that later musicologists had followed him here; but the problem, once scholars began to see it as such, has remained with us and will not go away. Yet Ambros's work shows that the lead set by Burckhardt in conceptualizing the Renaissance as a period of cultural as well as political history was not immediately followed by music historians; when we blame historians of culture for being slow to include music in their work, we might remember that musicologists were themselves slow in approaching a definition of the Renaissance in music.

While Burckhardt was establishing his view of the Renaissance as a period sharply distinct from what preceded it—a view that was to become both familiar and generally accepted, though not to remain unchallenged,[3] historians of music were still regarding the art of the Renaissance as a continuation of medieval musical culture.[4] Thus Adrien de La Fage spoke in 1844 of "la seconde partie du moyen-âge ou la renaissance."[5] This view had fateful consequences. Josquin, even Palestrina were seen as belonging to a "Gothic" tradition in music, a tradition ended only by the rise of monody and opera. If one considered this a kind of Huizingesque antidote to a Burckhardtian view of music history, there might be a lot to be said for it; but such was not the case. Although the high polish and full sonority of Palestrina's polyphony was of course seen to differ from earlier music, Palestrina was thought to fit into the picture of medieval music as Romantic historians saw it, indeed to complete and round off the picture by being the perfect embodiment of Christian piety in music. Going along with a view of history that stressed the religious piety of the Middle Ages was the notion that the highest achievement of medieval music was the "wahre Kirchenmusik" of the sixteenth century, cultivated with almost unblemished seriousness by Palestrina.[6]

Admiration of Palestrina was not new; but the increasingly romanticized view of the Middle Ages was. Total seriousness and simplicity of religious faith characterized for the Romantics medieval man at his best.[7] The art of Palestrina and a few of his contemporaries was thought to capture this seriousness and simplicity perfectly.[8] Josquin, on the other hand, was seen—by means of a few anecdotes handed down by eighteenth-century historians who drew ultimately on Glareanus—as having a jesting, frivolous side that all but spoiled his art; this was Baini's view, and it is in strong and telling contrast to the unqualified admiration of Josquin seen in Burney's history.[9] The constructivist techniques of the "Netherlanders," Ockeghem and Josquin pre-eminent among them, were also thought to interfere with the purity of religious music; even Palestrina was criticized for his occasional use of such artifices as canonic technique or abstract cantus firmi.[10] Use of secular tunes as the basis for sacred compositions was of course frowned upon; scholars and dilettantes of the Romantic period, whether Catholic or Protestant, seem to have imposed on themselves a strict Counter-Reformation point of view when judging the music of the whole of the fifteenth and sixteenth centuries, and to have done so as a result of a one-sided and humorless view of medieval culture.

What did the sacred music of the sixteenth century sound like to the Romantics? For Abt Vogler the polyphony of Palestrina and his successors was simple, natural, unaffected, unadorned—a Rousseauesque vision.[11] To Anton Thibaut, the earnest champion of the frequent and precisely executed performance of old music, Josquin's *Stabat Mater* had greater moral strength than Pergolesi's, Senfl's *Sieben*

Worte Christi was stronger and purer than Haydn's setting; in Palestrina he heard mastery of the old modes and of music in "reinen Dreyklange."[12] To E. T. A. Hoffmann Palestrina was "simple, true, childlike, pious, strong and powerful—truly Christian in his works, like Pietro da Cortona and our own old Dürer in painting."[13] Alexandre Choron thought that proper performance of Palestrina's music would produce "un effet extraordinaire, qui a réellement quelque chose de surnaturel"; and indeed Victor Hugo, Alfred de Vigny, and Théophil Gautier were all much moved, or said they were, by Choron's renditions of Palestrina.[14] Joseph Mainzer, hearing the Sistine choir in the early 1830s, was not enamored of what he called the "brouillamini" of imitative polyphony, but he greatly admired a Victoria Passion, for the enjoyment of which he thought one's experience of modern music was but inadequate preparation; he loved the sublime simplicity of Palestrina's *Improperia* and of chant sung in *falsobordone* or in parallel tenths.[15] A few dissident opinions were heard from time to time. Anton Reicha thought Palestrina's music had little to say to nineteenth-century ears; Stéphen de la Madelaine, though he admired Renaissance counterpoint, admitted that its real existence was only in scholars' libraries, and he likened the historical concerts of Choron and Fétis to "séances archéologiques"; Berlioz, while admitting that Palestrina's music could induce in the listener a trancelike state that was not without charm, thought that the music was little more than chord progressions lacking in individuality or power.[16] But these are exceptions; perhaps many early nineteenth-century listeners were pleasantly bored by Renaissance music, but nearly everyone who described hearing it did so in terms of glowing if vague admiration.[17]

This music seemed appropriately religious to its authors, and in its tranquil beauty it suited their often rather sentimentalized—to one writer, "perfumed"—notions of an old and pure faith.[18] It also sounded picturesque; for example, Mainzer thought the "antique" sound of the music he heard in the Sistine Chapel was increased by the frequent flatting of the leading tone.[19] In the opinion of Carl Dahlhaus, the Romantics, even though they continued to use the Palestrina-Fux style for technical exercises, were unable to hear sixteenth-century music objectively; they considered the modes to be picturesque variants of major and minor tonality, and the music was for them a tonal reminder of a forgotten past, speaking to them with an unmistakable "Sehnsuchtston."[20] If this was true even for genuine admirers of old music, it was all the more so for the greater number of Romantic critics who used Renaissance polyphony as a stick with which to beat the "degenerate" church music of their own time. Palestrina was thus for many of the Romantics less a real musical figure than a symbol, representing a lost Golden Age that ought somehow to be recovered. The hyperbolic and usually, sometimes wildly, anachronistic comparisons—Palestrina was the Homer, even the Christ of music, but above all its Raphael—seem ridiculous when we consider the composer and his work as we understand it today.[21] Yet the pinnacle on which Palestrina was placed, and the religio-aesthetic trance his music induced in listeners, are significant as indications of Romantic sensibility, of a way of hearing music that, at least in the West, was new and was to affect composers as well as listeners during the course of the nineteenth century.[22]

In the early Romantic period there was not very much Renaissance music available for performance; historians such as Padre Martini and Burney transcribed and published a good deal for their own purposes, but others often relied on second-hand information or on what little music earlier scholars had transmitted.[23] During the first half of the nineteenth century a large amount of music was scored, and sometimes—though not always—published, by Choron in Paris, Ett in Munich, Thibaut in Heidelberg, Commer in Berlin, and Proske in Regensburg, to name but a few.[24] A thorough study of early nineteenth-century editions of Renaissance music sounds like something one would like to palm off onto a complacent robot; I have certainly not made such a study, but from what I have seen it would appear that most editions were simply scorings of the parts without editorial interference. Attitudes toward performance of this music were not, however, completely neutral. We have seen that an effect of the ineffably religious was aimed at. How was this realized? Choron's advice was as follows:

> As for the style of performance [of Palestrina's music], I will limit myself to saying that all this music must be sung in legato and sustained sound, very softly, with precision, in a moderate, even way, very simply but with much sweetness and tenderness.[25]

This of course sounds ineffably dull, and probably was; one thinks of Madelaine's remark about "archeological" concerts. Not everyone shared Choron's views; Kiesewetter, Gustav Billroth, and Otto Nicolai were all proponents of a more varied, less "Cecilian" style of performance for sixteenth-century music.[26]

There is some evidence of a more specific nature about one style of performance of Renaissance music by nineteenth-century enthusiasts. Franz Xavier Witt, a protegé and friend of Proske in Regensburg, left detailed sets of instructions for performance of certain works of Palestrina and Lasso. Witt's pupil Anton Walter printed two of these with admiring comments on Witt's prowess as a conductor of old music, adding that Witt's mode of performance was strongly in the Proske tradition; we may thus assume that these directions are descriptive of how Palestrina and Lasso were sung in the 1840s.[27] The two works chosen were Lasso's *Missa Qual donna attende* and Palestrina's *Missa Papae Marcelli*, the latter being described in greater detail. Witt was strongly critical of what he called a mechanical way of conducting this music, with tempi set for each movement by prearranged convention (Kyrie slow, Gloria a little faster etc.) rather than according to the character of the individual work.[28] His own method was hardly mechanical; in the *Missa Papae Marcelli* there are in Witt's version almost as many internal changes of tempo as in Artur Schnabel's edition of a Beethoven sonata. The tempi range from $\quarternote = 46$ for the Benedictus (though on consideration Witt decides that this was really too slow for the singers to manage) to $\quarternote = 132$ for the Amen of the Credo. Here is the Kyrie of the Pope Marcellus Mass in Witt's version:

> One should open the *Kyrie* not *forte* but sweetly, the first four measures <*mf*>; in the ninth bar a *forte* can be introduced, in some parts rising yet a degree higher in volume, in others subsiding to *mf*. If one begins with $\quarternote = 72$, the tempo should soon pick up, going to as fast as $\quarternote = 88$. By the third-to-last measure before the *Christe* in any event, one should be singing *ff*; the *ritardando* occurs only at the next-to-last bar.

The first section of the *Christe* comprises the first eight bars; these can be taken more quietly and tenderly, about ♩= 76. From bar nine on there is a gradual increase in tempo and rise in dynamic level. Bars 18–19 are the top of this rise. One can establish the following as a rule (the first exception occurs at the *Et incarnatus est*): all six-voice passages are to be sung in a louder, fierier, more accented way—and are so to be conducted—than the three- or four-voice passages; for the composer draws upon the full six voices in order to make a crescendo, to expand the importance the weight of tone and volume. Here the six-voice passages are bars 18–19 and 24–26. The *Christe* can be sung by half the chorus, or a double sextet. The choir director can let *Kyrie* II begin ♩= 92 and gradually and in certain places increase to ♩= 100.[29]

The other movements are treated similarly, with many *fortissimo* passages and much alteration of tempi. In the Agnus Dei individual figures are singled out; a frequently used cambiata figure is to be sung quietly and tenderly, while the motive for "qui tollis," full of skips, is to be done strongly and with a crescendo. In general, Witt concludes, this Mass can because of the breadth of its motives be taken much faster than most of Palestrina's later Masses.[30] Witt's use of the quarter note for metronome markings, and his admission that although Proske usually performed the Mass in C he transposed it to B♭, suggest that he was using a "performing" edition. Proske's own edition of the Mass, published in 1850, gives it in original note values, untransposed, and without tempo or dynamic markings.[31] An edition of the kind Witt was using does survive from this period, in Stephan Lück's *Sammlung* of 1859.[32] In this edition there are shortened note values, a transposition down a tone, and tempo, dynamic, and expression marks; they are not always identical with what Witt calls for, but the similarities are frequent and striking enough to suggest that this edition comes out of the same performing tradition.[33]

If faster than most other sacred pieces by Palestrina, the *Missa Papae Marcelli* in Witt's version is still rather slow by our standards, and the music is of course romanticized; it is an example of "wahre Kirchenmusik" as a general aesthetic type rather than an attempt at recapturing sixteenth-century musical style. This is how listeners, singers, conductors, even scholars thought of Renaissance polyphony; and composers wishing to create new works in *a cappella* style must have been strongly influenced by it, just as they were by contemporary modes of performing Bach's instrumental and concerted polyphony.[34]

We think of the study of historically accurate performance practice as a twentieth-century development, as indeed it is. But there is no reason why scholars in the early nineteenth century could not have begun such a study; no reason except that they felt no need for it. Just as they saw old church music as both a resuscitated ideal and a living reproach to the effete sacred music of their own time, so the Romantics were content to give it a "timeless" mode of performance, hence, paradoxically, one grounded specifically in the performance practice of their own time. The historicism of musicians in the nineteenth century was thus as eclectically conceived and motivated as that of painters or architects—perhaps more so.

Eclecticism in nineteenth-century culture is too well known a phenomenon to need emphasis here, but citation of a few parallel instances might be relevant. In

Vienna in the 1780s, at the height of the neoclassical movement in all the arts, Baron van Swieten's historical concerts of Baroque music, following the precedent set by Reichardt in Berlin, took place; during the same decade the "regothicizing" of Austrian churches was begun.[35] It is perhaps only natural then that Carl Maria von Weber, writing in 1821, should say that Bach built in his music a "wahrhaft gothischen Dom der Kunstkirche."[36] Classical, Gothic, Renaissance, even Romanesque building styles were mixed in the ambitious rebuilding of central Munich undertaken in the reign of Ludwig I (1825–68), just the years when Kaspar Ett was performing the works of Lasso along with those of Baroque polyphonists in that city.[37] The Paris of the historical concerts given by Choron, then by Fétis, themselves a mix of styles and periods, is summarized wittily by Alfred de Musset:

> Our century has no style of its own; we have not given the stamp of our own time to our houses, our gardens, or anything else. One sees in the streets men with beards trimmed in the style of Henri III, others clean-shaven, some with their hair arranged as in a portrait by Raphael, others as if these were the times when Christ was alive. And the houses of the wealthy are curio-cabinets: the antique, the gothic, the taste of the Renaissance, that of Louis XIII—all is mixed together. We have something out of every century but our own, a thing never seen before. Eclecticism is our taste; we take up everything we come upon—this for its beauty, that for its convenience; one thing for its antiquity, still another for its very ugliness—to the extent that we live as it were among debris, as if the end of the world were near.[38]

In this milieu it is no surprise that Louis Niedermeyer should proclaim, in the opening number of *La Maîtrise* (1853), "Pour le plain chant, nous disons Saint Grégoire; pour le musique sacrée, nous disons Palestrina; pour l'orgue, nous disons J.-S. Bach."[39] It is a well-known but nonetheless telling fact that renewed interest in Palestrina coincided with the beginnings of the Bach revival; the master of Counter-Reformation Catholic polyphony and the master of late Baroque Protestant church music were both viewed as "Gothic" musical saints and were both transplanted, like the historically costumed people of Musset's remark, into nineteenth-century surroundings.[40]

One indication of this growing eclecticism of culture is the choice of subjects for opera libretti. Although eighteenth-century operas were occasionally based on "medieval" chivalric topics descending from Ariosto and Tasso, serious opera at any rate continued to use classical myth and ancient history for its subject matter through the third quarter of the century. After this all kinds of exotic subjects were chosen, and in the early nineteenth century a strong preference for medieval and Renaissance subjects can be seen; the most popular source was of course the novels of Walter Scott. The pages of Loewenberg's *Annals* are full of such titles, and there must have been many more. An example of an opera on a Renaissance topic, one not reported by Loewenberg, is *François Ier à Chambord*, a two-act opera of unknown authorship premiered in Paris in 1830. The "historical" plot of this work is about Leonardo da Vinci's mistress, whose life is saved by Francis I at Marignano;

the king brings her to Chambord, but on her confession of love for Leonardo the king gives her to the artist and the lovers are united.[41] This libretto is of course not history but a *nouvelle* or *feuilleton* of the type that was beginning to appear in the Parisian press; and there were, as we shall see, *contes historiques* on topics in Renaissance musical history at this time.

It has been pointed out that nineteenth-century Italian libretti on historical subjects were concerned with character and situation, showing little respect for fidelity of historical detail.[42] Many French operas were similarly casual; but Scribe in his libretti paid much greater attention to the facts as they were known, and in productions of these operas there was real concern for historical accuracy in sets and costumes.[43] Not so with the music, of course, and this anomaly was occasionally remarked. In Fétis's *Revue musicale*, an account of a ball at the Opéra asks whether it is not a serious anachronism to see dancers representing the courtiers of Francis I or Charles IX perform to the music of Rossini and Meyerbeer.[44] To most people it evidently was not; and in fact this situation has lasted, with few exceptions, up to our own day in costume dramas on film or television. Opera composers certainly did not try to write in antique style, nor could they have; the only old music that was known to them by more than name was the sacred polyphony of the *stile antico*. An occasional prayer scene in pious chords or a ballad with some slight archaicism of detail might be used, but that was about all. Even Meyerbeer, nothing if not eclectic, seems not to have reached beyond the Lutheran chorale, harmonized in "neo-Gothic" style, in the direction of old music. It is of course possible that we might miss something heard as intentional historicism at the time. For example, Meyerbeer wrote a setting of a ballad of Marguerite of Valois, a poem said to have been published in 1540.[45] The song, a strophic setting in syllabic style, alternating in Schubertian manner between major and minor but with no archaicisms that I can see, was reviewed thus:

> The ballad of Marguerite de Valois, grandmother of Henri IV, was published in 1540; the melody to which she sang it has not, so far as I know, come down to us. But M. Meyerbeer has so beautifully grasped the color of medieval melodies, there is in his music such a flavor of old tales, that one would think himself hearing one of those epics that Blondel sang at the court of Richard Coeur-de-Lion. . . . The beginning, "Pour être un digne et bon chrétien," is especially remarkable for its gothic naiveté, further emphasized by the style of the accompaniment and by the mixing of major and minor modes.[46]

Note that Middle Ages and Renaissance are characteristically mixed together as "Gothic," that in 1540 one was assumed to have sung in the style of the late twelfth century. The reviewer was, by the way, Hector Berlioz, who knew how to use an occasional scent of "parfum antique" himself.[47]

From the eclectic use of historical novels and plays—themselves often not pedantically close to historical fact—for libretti, it is but a short step to the historical *nouvelle*, a genre popular in France and Germany in the early nineteenth century. Following the precedent of E. T. A. Hoffmann, a number of writers turned to musical subjects for historicist fiction, especially in France. The early years of the *Ga-*

zette musicale de Paris (1834–35) and its successor the *Revue et Gazette musicale* feature these stories quite regularly. Particularly interesting for us here are the stories contributed by Stéphen de la Madelaine during the years 1835–38, and the single but vivid contribution by Berlioz to the genre, a story on the creation of the first opera by Alfonso della Viola in the mid-sixteenth century, about which I have written elsewhere.[48]

Madelaine also wrote a story about opera in the sixteenth century, with the figure of Lambert de Beaulieu as hero and with a loose connection to what was then known about the *Balet comique de la Royne*.[49] In this tale Beaulieu goes to Florence, where he hears a new opera, *Endymion*, by "Horace Vecchi," who "laid the foundations of comic opera in 1595." The music to *Endymion* is lost, but Madelaine is able to say that

> it was written after the models provided by Emilio Cavalieri, Mei, and Caccini. In addition the composer made use in his work of the happy innovations with which Claude Goudimel had enriched harmony; and he substituted the *récitatif* invented by Vincenzo Galilei for the too-monotonous forms of counterpoint. Finally, choruses were introduced as finales for each act, just as Peri had provided examples of in his *Euridice*.
>
> All this music, though full of variety for the time, was excessively simple in form and mediocre in execution. But its style was pure, and its naive expression had a core of truth that our tormented melodies and our inflated instrumentation do not always achieve.[50]

A pretty full description of a lost score; and the historical bits read like a substandard student examination essay. Madelaine is here as elsewhere vague about chronology; as we shall see, he allowed the most glaring inconsistencies to pass, or perhaps he simply scribbled away, a journal deadline before him, and never looked back. He was certainly not writing history, and his stories must have been intended primarily as diversions. One of his main purposes, seen here at the end of the passage just cited, was to attack the present by extolling the past, something he did consistently in writing about sacred music. Still, he did know some facts, gathered from the survey provided by Choron and Fayolle, from other general histories available to him, and certainly from his association with Fétis, whom he appears to have known fairly well.[51] What is perhaps most interesting about his musical tales is that they show elements of knowledge, however casually handled, about the Renaissance filtering down from scholars to the reading public, which was clearly expected to find them picturesquely intriguing.

Stéphen de la Madelaine wrote two more pieces about early opera: "Francesca," a tale about a real musician, the gifted daughter of "Jules Caccini, l'un des pères de la musique dramatique," and "La Jeunesse de Bassini," a tale set in the 1630s about a personage Madelaine seems to have invented or compiled out of several real Bassanis.[52] His most extraordinary contribution to the genre of the musical *nouvelle* is, however, a series of three interrelated stories on Dufay, Josquin, and Mouton.[53] In the first of these tales, the aging and absent-minded Dufay roams the streets of Paris pondering the mysteries of musical science, after finishing a conversation with some respectful young students to whom he reveals his recent discoveries "sur l'harmonie tonale."[54] Entering the wrong house by mistake, Dufay meets by sheer accident the daughter of an old friend of his, now dead; he adopts the young woman and her illegitimate child, and makes them known to his favorite pupil Josquin, the son of his physician Grégoire Desprez. In an unfortunate household accident the infant dies; his mother Hélène is inconsolable and spends her time singing lullabies to an empty crib. Dufay, at the worst of moments always a musician, notes that the two lullabies sung by Hélène are somehow related; he and Josquin sing them together and in that happy moment—in the year 1465—"le contrepoint venait d'être découvert!" In the speedy dénouement Hélène recovers and ends by marrying the young Josquin, at this time maître of the chapel at Saint-Denis.

The second of these stories is set in the Paris of 1510, an ominous place full of spies and assassins. In a modest dwelling on the Left Bank the "savant Josquinus, le favori de messire Apollo," now maître of the Sainte-Chapelle, is literally burning the midnight oil while putting together his "combinations de la science." He is then seen playing "savantes modulations" on the organ while his wife Hélène (Dufay's adopted daughter) sings. Josquin is poor; he runs into debt by paying much of the expense for the brilliant wedding music for Louis XII and Anne de Bretagne—music consisting of "fragments de symphonies et même plusieurs morceaux à deux voix qui constituaient de véritables choeurs." The composer "qui instruisait l'Europe musicale" further ruins himself by keeping up a carriage; he is reduced to giving "leçons de plain-chant" to court ladies and to fulfilling their trivial commissions. At one point, sick of all this, Josquin sits down to write a piece for himself; the result is *Coeli enarrant gloriam Dei*, "en contrepoint et canon à quatre parties, savante composition," a work admired by Padre Martini and even by LeSueur, who in setting the same text was, says Madelaine, reluctant to compete with Josquin.[55] Josquin receives a benefice in Meulan; he suspects the donor, a certain "comte de Meulan," of designs on his wife, but is relieved when the count reveals himself to be Louis XII. Josquin lives to a ripe old age, dying in the early seventeenth century; among the "déplorations et contrepoint" written for him is one by "Jean Mantou," *maître de chapelle* of Francis I.

This wonderful mélange of fact and fiction, supremely indifferent to matters of chronology, is followed by the tale on Mouton (his name now spelled correctly). The young Mouton, an instrument maker, lodges in Paris with a woman whose favorite music is, prophetically it would seem, the *De Profundis* of Goudimel. At a religious celebration Mouton hears Josquin singing in one of his own Masses, and is so overcome that he falls into a fever, saying in his delirium "Josquinus ego sum, Josquinus musicorum princeps." He is cured by Josquin himself, who teaches Mouton the secrets of counterpoint. Mouton ends by becoming the first maître of the royal chapel, starting a tradition that ends only—by reason of the unfortunate political circumstances in nineteenth-century France—with LeSueur and Cherubini.

These stories were of course not meant as serious history;[56] still, their whimsicality and fast-and-loose treatment of fact make the fabled errors of Fétis pale into insignificance, Madelaine tired of or was discouraged from continuing in this vein; his name disappears from the masthead of the *Revue et Gazette* in 1839, and although he continued to write on music he did not, so far as I know, compose any more musico-historical *contes*.[57] Contributions of a historical nature in the pages of the *Revue et Gazette* from 1840 on are of a much more sober and technical nature, typified by the serious work of La Fage rather than the fantasy of Madelaine; this may well be a sign of changing attitudes, mid-nineteenth-century scholarship displacing Romantic tale-telling.

Chronological oddities were not peculiar to Madelaine; some of the most serious of his contemporaries fell, or leaped, into them. For example, Thibaut tells (or retells, from a source unknown to me) of a dream experienced by the painter Correggio (d. 1534) in which the artist died and on arrival in paradise met the awesome figure of Palestrina (b. ca. 1525).[58] The insistent coupling of Palestrina with Raphael, still met with in the pages of Ambros, is further evidence of the Romantics' attitude toward the Renaissance: the end of the Age of Faith was all one to them. This is a matter less of insouciance than of a dreamlike conceptualizing of the past as an *Engelkonzert* in which matters of chronological sequence were of no importance, or as an inconographic representation of aesthetic religious belief. To hear Bach fugues sounding in the background of such a picture was no anomaly. The errors were gradually weeded out; shortly before Madelaine wrote his account of Beaulieu hearing Vecchi's *Endymion*, Fétis presented a corrected account of the career and oeuvre of Vecchi.[59] And in the rising generation of scholars such as Robert Eitner and Emil Vogel there was great if not uniformly successful emphasis on factual accuracy; but by this time the Romantic glow had faded. Ambros deplored the inaccuracy of popular histories of the preceding generation, citing the enormities to be found in works such as Müller's survey, where Ockeghem is said to have been a papal singer in Rome and to have discovered his pupil Josquin while on a visit to Prato.[60] And as early as 1836, Bottée de Toulmon, librarian of the Conservatoire in Paris, lamented the inaccuracy of most histories of music, saying that not only was it difficult to uncover the facts but that since music was thought by most people to be "uniquement un art d'agrément" it was thought useless, even ridiculous, to study it in a scientific way.[61] But for as long as Romanticism held sway, it would seem that music of the past was either a monolithic reproach to the frivolous present—as for Madelaine[62]—or a thing too perfect to investigate in a detached way.

One further anomaly in the Romantic view of Renaissance music may be touched on here. We have seen that the music of Palestrina and of selected figures among his contemporaries, successors, and predecessors was looked upon as a thing of otherworldly purity and detachment, and the musicians themselves on the whole as figures of saintly remove from their surroundings—an analogy, deliberate or unwitting, to the notion of Romantic artistic alienation. Their work was consistently viewed as the sublimely tranquil culmination of the long centuries of the Age of Faith. This does not fit at all with the picture of the Renaissance drawn by historians such as Burckhardt; it is even more out of joint with the use made of the Renaissance in the literature of the late eighteenth and early nineteenth centuries.

For poets and dramatists of the *Sturm und Drang* period the Renaissance was a violent and godless period, with conspiracy and murder—sometimes but not always an idealistically motivated *Tyrannenmord*—its distinguishing characteristics. Florence under the Medici, from the Pazzi conspiracy of the 1470s through the end of the sixteenth century, was a favored location.[63] In general a "Gift und Dolchromantik" colored German Romantic treatment of the Renaissance in literature. Machiavellian intrigue and Cellinesque unbridled egoism and opportunism were prime subject material; in the case of Cellini the artist himself was a violent and irreligious type.[64]

Music (and doubtless religious painting as well) seemed to the Romantics to stand apart from all this. Opera libretti could stress violent aspects of the Renaissance, but it was as if sixteenth-century men, when they were in a secular mood, made music in nineteenth-century style. Occasionally one reads of the music that might accompany a scene of robbers (the *Räuberroman*, often set in the distant past, was a favorite early Romantic genre) or smugglers in action; but the music for such a scene, sounding like thunder or wind in the trees, would be a contemporary piece, not one by a Renaissance or Baroque composer.[65] The kind of vision that enabled Goethe to see both classical repose and tempestuous violence in Renaissance culture was denied to, or deliberated avoided by, musicians interested in the past.[66] They chose to isolate one aspect of Renaissance art, and in so doing they exaggerated and distorted its significance. Thus the study of music as an integral part of Renaissance culture was ignored, and it has taken a long time for the distorted image created by the Romantics to be corrected; indeed, we can hardly see the process of correction as completed today.

Thus in one way the straightforward chronicles of eighteenth-century historians such as Hawkins and Burney, despite their adherence to the aesthetic prejudices of their own time, are more direct ancestors of modern musical scholarship than the work of most of the Romantics, which in a way disrupted the forward march of scholarly inquiry. The Romantics, in looking at the Renaissance, often tell us more about themselves than about the subject they were writing about. This is of course a phenomenon interesting in itself. And further, Romantic enthusiasm provided an impetus for scholarly work, as the achievement of Ambros shows. The scholarly work which we, ever so cautiously and soberly, cultivate in the field of Renaissance music continues on occasion to reflect the glow cast upon the subject by the Romantics. It would be too bad to try to extinguish it altogether.

POSTSCRIPT

This study, in some ways an oblique contribution to the "authenticity" debates of the 1980s, is an abbreviated attempt to outline a subject I still hope to pursue at greater length. The Romantic birth of musical historicism and its nineteenth-century continuations has been of considerable interest to German musicologists, as the works cited in my notes show. A notable contribution has been made by Richard Boursy; see his "Historicism and Composition: Giuseppe Baini, the Sistine Chapel, and *Stile Antico* Music in the First Half of the Nineteenth Century"

(Ph.D. diss., Yale University, 1994), and also his "The Mystique of the Sistine Chapel Choir in the Romantic Era," *The Journal of Musicology* 11 (1993): 277–329.

Jessie Ann Owens pointed out to me that Ambros *does* use the word "Renaissance" in his great history. In the first edition of the *Geschichte der Musik* (Breslau, 1862–82), parts 3 and 4 are subtitled "Zeitalter der Renaissance." These subtitles are dropped in the third edition (vol. 3, ed. Otto Kade, appeared in 1893; vol. 4, ed. Hugo Leichtentritt, was published in 1909, both by the Leipzig firm that printed the first edition), the one I consulted when first preparing this article. For Owens's contribution to the subject see above, the remarks following chapter 3.

A further anomaly may now be added to Stephan de la Madelaine's Renaissance-musical *contes: Celi ennarrant gloriam Dei* has been persuasively denied as Josquin's work. See Patrick Macey, "*Celi ennarrant*: An Inauthentic Psalm Motet Attributed to Josquin," *Proceedings of the International Josquin Symposium, Utrecht 1986*, ed. Willem Elders (Utrecht, 1991), 25–44.

NOTES

1. Burckhardt's *Die Kultur der Renaissance in Italien* was published in 1860; the first volume of Ambros's *Geschichte der Musik* appeared in 1862 (the volume on the fifteenth and sixteenth centuries was published in 1868; the later sixteenth century in Italy is covered in vol. 4, which appeared posthumously in 1878).

For a survey of the character and influence of later eighteenth-century musical historiography see Elizabeth Hegar, *Die Anfänge der neueren Musikgeschichtsschreibung um 1770 bei Gerbert, Burney und Hawkins* (Strasbourg, 1932). The work of Kiesewetter is summarized in Herfrid Kier, *Raphael Georg Kiesewetter (1773–1850), Wegbereiter des musikalischen Historismus* (Regensburg, 1968).

2. On the growth of the Palestrina legend see Karl Gustav Fellerer, *Der Palestrinastil und seine Bedeutung in der vokalen Kirchenmusik der achtzehnten Jahrhundert* (Augsburg, 1929); Joseph Müller-Blattau, "Die Idee der 'wahren Kirchenmusik' in der Erneurungsbewegung der Goethezeit," *Musik und Kirche* 2 (1930): 155–60, 199–204; Otto Urspung, "Palestrina und Deutschland," *Festschrift Peter Wagner zum 60. Geburtstag*, ed. Karl Weinmann (Leipzig, 1926), 196–221. The publication of Giuseppe Baini's *Memorie storico-critiche della vita e delle opere di G. P. da Palestrina* (Rome, 1828) was an event of central importance in nineteenth-century growth of Palestrina worship. Baini's work was made known in Germany through Franz Sales Kandler's *Ueber des Leben und die Werke G. P. da Palestrina* [with a foreword by Kiesewetter] (Leipzig, 1834) and Carl von Winterfeld's *J. P. da Palestrina. Seine Werke und deren Bedeutung für die Geschichte der Tonkunst, mit Bezug auf Baini's neueste Forschungen* (Breslau, 1832).

3. See Wallace K. Ferguson, *The Renaissance in Historical Thought* (Boston, 1948), chapters 8–11, for the *Rezeptionsgeschichte* of Burckhardt's work.

4. For this view on the part of men such as Friedrich Rochlitz and Raphael Kiesewetter, see Tibor Kneif, "Die Erforschung mittelalterliche Musik in der Romantik und ihr geistesgeschichtliche Hintergrund," *Acta Musicologica* 36 (1964): 130–31.

5. *Histoire générale de la musique et de la danse*, 2 vols. (Paris, 1844), foreword, p. xiii, cited by Kneif, "Die Erforschung," 131. For La Fage, the period from the time of Guido [d'Arezzo] to the rise of opera was one epoch.

6. On the view that Palestrina's music stood, from the 1760s at least, for "wahre Kirchen-musik" to be admired, revived, and cultivated in Protestant as well as Catholic circles, see Müller-Blattau, "Die Idee der 'wahren Kirchenmusik'."

7. To what extent this was a real belief of the Romantics, as opposed to a standard set up for their own age to emulate, is hard to determine; but it may be thought of as primarily a historicist view rather than a genuinely historical one.

8. Nearly every writer of the Romantic period stressed these elements in Palestrina; see below, and n. 11. An eloquent statement to the point is that of E. T. A. Hoffmann in "Alte und neue Kirchenmusik," *Allgemeine musikalische Zeitung* 16 (1814): 577–84, 593–603, 611–19, esp. 581–83.

9. Baini, *Memorie*, 2:407–11. Baini recognizes "gradevoli melodie" in Josquin, and admits that he sometimes exclaims "bello" over a passage, but he concludes that "Jusquino era uomo nato non per cultivare la musica sagra, siccom' ei fece; ma per divertire le liete bri-gate con suoni scherzevoli." Traces of this attitude persist in Ambros even as he terms Jos-quin (*Geschichte*, 4:48) "dieses genialsten unter den Tonzetzern der Vor-Palestrinazeit."

On Burney as an enthusiastic admirer and thorough student of Josquin, see Don Hárrán, "Burney and Ambros as Editors of Josquin's Music," *Josquin des Prez*, ed. Edward E. Lo-winsky (London, 1976), 148–77.

10. See, for example, Baini's treatment of Palestrina's "artificial" style (*Memorie*, 423).

11. Fellerer, *Der Palestrinastil*, 328ff; cf. Müller-Blattau, "Die Idee der 'wahren Kir-chenmusik'," 200, where similar views on the part of Schubart (*Ideen zu einer Aesthetik der Tonkunst*, [Vienna, 1806]) are cited. An early French statement on the "naturalness" of Pa-lestrina's art is that of Jérome-Joseph de Momigny, *Cours complet d'harmonie et de compo-sition*, 3 vols. (Paris, 1803–6), vol. 1, "Discours préliminaire," 15. I am grateful to Ian Bent for referring me to Momigny's work.

Some writers of the time set up Palestrina's "naturalness" in opposition to what they saw as the affectedly and artificially dramatic style of the sacred music of their own day; this is true of Vogler and certainly of Hoffmann.

12. A. F. J. Thibaut, *Ueber Reinheit der Tonkunst* (1825), 3d ed. (Heidelberg, 1851), 53. On the strict criteria by which old music was judged and the severely serious atmosphere in which Thibaut's performances were conducted, see Wilhelm Ehrmann, "Der Thibaut-Behaghel Kreis. Ein Beitrag zur Geschichte der musikalischen Restauration im 19. Jahr-hundert," *Archiv für Musikforschung* 3 (1938), 428–83; 4 (1939), 21–67.

13. "Alte und neue Kirchenmusik," 583. This passage is cited in Lewis Lockwood, ed., *G. P. da Palestrina: Pope Marcellus Mass* (New York, 1975), 134–35.

14. See Willi Kahl, "Zur musikalischen Renaissancebewegung in Frankreich während der ersten Hälfte des 19. Jahrhunderts," *Festschrift Joseph Schmidt-Görg zum 60. Geburts-tag*, ed. Dagmar Weise (Bonn, 1957), 164–67.

15. [Joseph Mainzer], "La Chapelle Sixtine à Rome," *Gazette musicale de Paris* 1 (1834): 12f, 22f.

16. Hans Eckardt, *Die Musikanschauung der französischen Romantik* (Kassel, 1935), 37. For Madelaine's remark, made in passing in a historical tale, see *Revue et Gazette musicale* 4 (1837): 158. Reicha's views on music history, given in the introduction to his *Traité de haute composition musicale* (Paris, 1824–26; translated into German in Carl Czerny, *Vollstän-diges Lehrbuch*, 4 vols. [Vienna, 1832]), were attacked by Fétis and by Baini, who devotes several pages (2. 363ff) in his *Memorie* to bitter criticism of Reicha's unhistorical approach to counterpoint. Berlioz's views on Palestrina may be seen in David Cairns, trans., *The Memoirs of Hector Berlioz* (London, 1969), 182–84. Berlioz was here writing of the *Impro-peria* so much admired by Mainzer (presumably the "German" he mentions); but he ex-

tends his criticism to include all of Palestrina's works, which he thinks of as less striking than the harmonies made by an Aeolian harp in the wind, and "no one has ever thought of numbering the makers of aeolian harps among the great composers."

17. Only rarely does one find a balanced view such as that given by Edouard Fétis, "La Musique d'autrefois et la musique d'aujourd'hui," *Revue et Gazette musicale* 14 (1847), 22: "Roland de Lattre, Crequillon, Jean Mouton, Ciprien de Rore, Josquin-des-Près, avaient du génie; ils n'en avaient pas moins que Beethoven, que Rossini, et que Weber. Ils le manifestaient sous une autre forme, à l'aide de moyens que comportait l'art de leur temps, et dans la proportion des besoins de leurs contemporains; voilà toute la différence."

18. Eckardt, *Die Musikanschauung*, 35.

19. *Gazette musicale* 1 (1834), 13.

20. Carl Dahlhaus, "Traditionszerfall in 19. und 20. Jahrhundert," *Studien zur Tradition in der Musik: Kurt von Fischer zum 60. Geburtstag*, ed. Hans Heinrich Eggebrecht and Max Lütolf (Munich, 1973), 183. As early a work as Kiesewetter's *Die Verdienste der Niederländer um die Tonkunst* (1829) considered old folk music to be major-minor as opposed to the deliberately archaic use of modes of polyphony (p. 45).

21. See Thibaut, *Ueber Reinheit*, 55, where Palestrina is called the Homer of Music, a view echoed in Winterfeld, *Palestrina*, 34. According to Choron "Palestrina c'est le Racine, c'est le Raphael, c'est le Jésus-Christ de la musique," a remark cited in Monika Lichtenfeld, "Zur Geschichte, Idee und Aesthetik des historischen Konzerts," *Die Ausbreitung des Historismus über die Musik*, ed. Walter Wiora (Regensburg, 1969), 42. Lasso was thought to be receiving high praise when he was called the "Palestrina du Nord" (*Revue et Gazette musicale* 3 [1836], 329, in an article entitled "Souvenir de voyage. Munich").

Nearly everyone equated Palestrina with Raphael; perhaps little Counter-Reformation painting was known, but it is more likely that even for serious scholars aesthetic and religious affinities outweighed the chronological discrepancies.

22. For a telling example of this kind of reaction to Palestrina on the part of a later nineteenth-century composer, see the remarks of Wagner cited in Lockwood, *Pope Marcellus Mass*, 137.

23. In 1810, according to Choron, neither the Conservatoire nor the Bibliothèque impériale had any works by Palestrina; see Kahl, "Zur musikalischen Renaissancebewegung," 160.

24. The fullest bibliography of early publications of Renaissance music remains Robert Eitner's *Verzeichniss neuer Ausgaben alter Musikwerke aus der frühesten Zeit bis zum Jahre 1800* (Berlin, 1871). For a survey of early nineteenth-century collectors and collections of old music in Germany see Willi Kahl, "Offentliche und private Musiksammlungen in ihrer Bedeutung für die musikalische Renaissancebewegung des 19. Jahrhunderts in Deutschland," *Bericht über den internationalen musikwissenschaftlichen Kongress Bamberg 1953*, ed. Wilfred Brennecke et al. (Kassel, 1954), 289–94.

25. Cited in Eckardt, *Die Musikanschauung*, 29.

26. See Wiora, *Die Ausbreitung des Historismus*, 52, a contribution by Herfrid Kier to the article by Lichtenfeld, "Zur Geschichte . . . des historischen Konzerts," cited above, n. 21. La Fage also opposed the notion of a subdued style—what he termed "chanter en timbre obscur"—for performance of this music; see his "Avis sur l'exécution de la musique palestrinienne," *Miscellanées musicales par J. Adrien de la Fage* (Paris, 1844), 504.

27. Anton Walter, "Dr. Witts Zeugnis für Palestrina und Lasso," *Kirchenmusikalisches Jahrbuch* 9 (1894): 48–59; the remark about the Proske tradition is made on p. 53.

28. "Dr. Witts Zeugnis," 54.

29. Ibid., 53.

30. Ibid., 54.

31. Proske's edition, published in Mainz in 1850 (*Missa Papae Marcelli triplici concentu distincta . . . juxta editiones principes fidelissime in partitionem redegit . . . publicavit Carolus Proske*), includes the four-voice arrangement of the work by Anerio and the eight-voice version by Suriano. It preserves original clefs as well as note values.

For other early editions (from the 1840s and 1850s) see Eitner, *Verzeichniss*, 152. The Masses of Anerio and Suriano have been edited by Hermann J. Busch, *Two Settings of Palestrina's* Missa Papae Marcelli, RRMB, vol. 16 (Madison, Wisc., 1973).

32. Stephan Lück, *Sammlung ausgezeichneter Compositionen für die Kirche*, 2 vols. (Trier, 1859). I consulted the second edition (Leipzig, 1884), which is so far as I know an unaltered reprint of the music in the first edition. The Mass is printed in vol. 1, 149–99.

33. On Lück see Hugo Riemann, *Musik Lexikon*, 12th ed., ed. Willibald Gurlitt (Mainz, 1961), *Personenteil*, 2:107. La Fage's directions for performing Palestrina (*Miscellanées musicales*, 499–504) outline a less extreme but generally similar approach, with one exception: he advocates (p. 503) a constant *mezzoforte* for a chant cantus firmus "tandis que chacuns des autres parties nuancera convenablement."

34. On this point see Erich Doflein, "Historismus in der Musik," *Die Ausbreitung des Historismus*, 36–37.

35. Herfrid Kier, "Musikalischer Historismus im vormärzlichen Wien," *Die Ausbreitung des Historismus*, 58.

36. Doflein, "Historismus in der Musik," 12. The remark is in a biographical-critical notice on Bach, printed in C. M. von Weber, *Ausgewählte Schriften*, ed. Wilhelm Altmann (Regensburg, 1928), 294. On the preoccupation of the German Romantics with Gothic architecture (beginning with Goethe's essay on the Strasbourg Cathedral), see Brian Plimma, "Unity and Ensemble: Contrasting Ideals in Romantic Music," *19th Century Music* 6 (1982): 105f.

37. Doflein, "Historismus in der Musik," 13. On the career of Ett see Kahl, "Offentliche und private Musiksammlungen," 290.

38. *La confession d'un enfant du siècle* (1836), 89, in A. de Musset, *Oeuvres complètes en prose*, ed. Maurice Allem and Paul-Courant (Paris, 1960). Musset writes in the persona of a young man afflicted with *mal de siècle*; but his observation has the ring of truth about it. (The translation given here, like those elsewhere in this chapter, is my own.)

39. Cited in Eckardt, *Die Musikanschauung*, 43.

40. Sometimes there were attempts at a distinction between the nature of Bach's music and that of Palestrina. Thus Friedrich Rochlitz, "Ueber der zweckmässigen Gebrauch der Mittel der Tonkunst," *Allgemeine musikalische Zeitung* 8 (1805–6): 49, 56, 193, 199, using terminology common in the late eighteenth century, calls Palestrina's art an example of the "sublime" (Erhabene), while Bach's is that of the "great" (Grosse), differing from the earlier master in its greater complexity and more dramatic character. On the other hand Rochlitz does indulge in an unhistoric comparison of his own, calling Bach the "Albrecht Dürer der Musik" (col. 199).

41. A review of this work appears in the *Revue musicale* 7 (1830): 210ff.

42. Patrick Smith, *The Tenth Muse: A Historical Study of the Opera Libretto* (New York, 1970), 211–12.

43. Ibid., 212, 221.

44. *Revue musicale* 13 (1833), 403. The reviewer, probably the editor himself, takes the opportunity to praise the old dance music performed at Fétis's historical concerts.

45. The song was published in Giacomo Meyerbeer, *Quarante mélodies à une et à plusiers voix avec acc^t. de Piano* (Paris, n.d.).

46. *Gazette musicale* 2 (1835), 351.

47. See, for example, the "Roi de Thulé," subtitled "Chanson gothique," in the *Damnation de Faust*, as well as Berlioz's fanciful attribution of *L'Enfance du Christ* to one Pierre Ducré, "maître de chapelle of the Saint-Chapelle," said to have written the work in 1679. See Jacques Barzun, *Berlioz and the Romantic Century*, 3d ed. (New York, 1969), 1:486–87; 2:90.

48. See chapter 15 above. The story, "Le Premier Opéra: Nouvelle du passé, 1555," first appeared in the *Revue et Gazette musicale* 4 (1837). For Stéphen de la Madelaine, whose career was spent as a civil servant but whose avocation was music—he was a friend of Berlioz, a singer, an editor of the *Univers musical* and of musical *feuilletons* for the *Courrier français*, see Fétis, *Biographie universelle des musiciens et bibliographie générale de la musique, Supplement et complément publiés sous la direction de M. Arthur Pougin*, vol. 2 (Paris, 1880), 68–69.

49. "Comment l'opéra fut introduit en France," *Gazette musicale* 2 (1835): 377–84.

50. Ibid., 380.

51. Choron and Fayolle's *Dictionnaire historique des musiciens . . . précédé d'un sommaire de l'histoire de la musique*, 2 vols. (Paris, 1810–11), pp. 1, 65, has a good deal of the basic information used by Madelaine. The bit about Goudimel is Madelaine's own; one should remember, however, that at this time Goudimel was commonly thought to have been Palestrina's teacher. The first volumes of Fétis's *Biographie universelle* appeared in the mid-1830s, just before Madelaine wrote his *contes historiques*.

52. "Francesca," *Revue et Gazette musicale* 4 (1837): 37–44; "La Jeunesse de Bassini," ibid., 157–60, 166–69, 181–85.

53. "La Vieillesse de Guillaume Dufay," *Revue et Gazette musicale* 3 (1836): 453–60; "Les Psaumes de Josquin," ibid., 4 (1837): 109–13, 129–34; "Le Maître de Chapelle de François Iᵉʳ, Chronique du xvᵉ [*sic*] siècle," ibid., 5 (1838): 245–49, 253–57.

54. Compare the remarks of Fétis, *Traité de la théorie et de la pratique de l'harmonie* (Paris, 1844), on how he resolved musical problems and found the truth while walking "dans un chemin solitaire" (preface to the 3rd edition [Paris, 1849], xi).

55. *Coeli enarrant gloriam Dei* was published in Johann Nikolaus Forkel, *Allgemeine Geschichte der Musik*, vol. 2 (Leipzig, 1801), 580. I have not found Martini's reference to the work. The other pieces by Josquin mentioned in Madelaine's story are all cited by Choron and Fayolle, *Dictionnaire historique*, 2:357–58; their ultimate source is Glareanus.

LeSueur did indeed write a setting of *Coeli enarrant*, a clangorous C major setting for chorus and orchestra, published in *Deux Psaumes . . . composées par LeSueur* (Paris, n.d.). Whether LeSueur knew Josquin's piece would be hard to determine from his own composition.

56. They resemble Berlioz's tale of the "first opera" in making their protagonists typical nineteenth-century Frenchmen. It is possible that Madelaine was in these stories giving veiled portraits of contemporary musicians (Dufay = Fétis?), but one can only guess at who they might be.

57. In 1840 Madelaine published his *Physiologie du chant; Théories complètes du chant* followed in 1852, and *Etudes pratiques de style vocal* was issued in 1868. He also wrote a long series of novels of an educational Christian tone; see the entries of his work given in the *Catalogue générale des livres imprimés de la Bibliothèque Nationale*, vol. 103 (Paris, 1930), 179–82.

58. *Ueber Reinheit*, 67.

59. *Revue musicale* 3 (1828): 443f. This is followed, unfortunately, by a biography of Vicentino in which the latter is said to have had a talented pupil named Willaert.

60. Ambros, *Geschichte*, 3.3.477n., cites a work by Wilhelm Christian Müller, *Ueber-sicht einer Chronologie der Tonkunst mit Andeutungen allgemeiner Civilization und Cul-turentwickelung*. This is actually a kind of subtitle for Müller's *Aesthetisch-historische Ein-leitungen in die Wissenschaft der Tonkunst* (Leipzig, 1830); but Ambros reports the passage in question accurately enough. This book, intended as a textbook (Müller is described on the title page as "Lehrer an der Hauptschule in Bremen"), is a typical summary of what was known at the survey-text level about early music in the 1830s.

61. "Discours pronouncé par M. Bottée de Toulmon," *Revue et Gazette musicale* 3 (1836): 65–71, esp. 66. Bottée does pay some tribute to the seriousness of purpose of Fétis, in whose journal he was writing.

62. In a straightforwardly polemical essay, "De la musique réligieuse," *Revue et Gazette musicale* 3 (1836): 121–24, Madelaine calls for a revival, under government patronage, of church music of a serious and exalted nature.

63. Poets, novelists, and playwrights—among them Friedrich Maximilian Klinger, Jo-hann Christian Brandes, Wilhelm Heinse, and even the young Schiller—writing in the 1770s and 1780s were much preoccupied with this view of the Renaissance as a period of violent upheaval of every sort. See Walter Rehm, *Das Werden des Renaissancebildes in der deutschen Dichtung vom Rationalismus bis zum Realismus* (Munich, 1929), chapters 4 and 5.

64. The quoted phrase is from Rehm, *Das Werden*, 91. Goethe, who translated Cellini's memoirs, was fascinated by the latter's *terribiltà* (Rehm, 103, 110).

The libretto of Berlioz's *Benvenuto Cellini* in its final form was much toned down; for Berlioz's view of Cellini, his story of the artist, and his relationship to the musician, Viola, cited above n. 48, is much more revealing. Viola, an exceptionally vivid portrait of a Renais-sance musician, is of course Berlioz himself.

65. See the review by Carl Loewe of Beethoven's Sonata op. 27, no. 2, in the *Berliner All-gemeine musikalische Zeitung* 14, no. 4 (1827): 27, in which the third movement is com-pared to the creaking of an old storm-tossed tree or the sound of robbers in a mountain hide-out—all "Stoff zu einem Scherzo."

66. On Goethe's ambivalent attitude toward the Renaissance, whose violence appealed to him at the same time as its classicism and its relationship to antiquity, see Rehm, *Das Wer-den*, 103, 110, 117–18, 128.

ABOUT THE AUTHOR

JAMES HAAR is William Rand Kenan, Jr., Emeritus Professor of Music
at the University of North Carolina, Chapel Hill. Among his books are
Essays on Italian Poetry and Music in the Renaissance and, with Iain Fenlon,
The Italian Madrigal in the Early Sixteenth Century.